EMPIRE

The British Imperial Experience,
1765 to the Present

EMPIRE

The British
Imperial Experience,
from 1765 to the Present

DENIS JUDD

Basic Books
A Member of Perseus Books, L.L.C.

This book was first published in Great Britain in 1996 by HarperCollins Publishers.

Copyright © 1996 by Denis Judd.
Published by Basic Books, A Member of Perseus Books, L.L.C.

Library of Congress Cataloguing-in-Publication Data
Judd, Denis, 1938–
Empire : the British experience from 1765 to the present / Denis Judd. — 1st ed.
p. cm.
Originally published: London: HarperCollins, 1996.
Includes bibliographical references (p.) and index.
ISBN 0-465-01952-8 (cloth)
ISBN 0-465-01954-4 (paper)
1. Great Britain—Colonies—History—19th century. 2. Great Britain—Colonies—
History—20th century. 3. Great Britain—Colonies—History—18th century.
4. Imperialism—History.
I. Title.
DA16.J88   1997
941—dc21   97-12368

98 99 00 01 RRD 10 9 8 7 6 5 4 3 2 1

To the memory of
my late father, Denis, who supported
the British Empire,
and of my late father-in-law, Sam,
who did not.

CONTENTS

Contents

'Holding Operation'; Confrontations with Nationalist
Movements in Egypt, Cyprus, West and East Africa, the
Middle East and the Caribbean

ILLUSTRATIONS

Hostile American reaction to the imposition of the 1765 Stamp Act. (*The Mansell Collection*)

Patriotic American women sign a declaration to boycott British imports. (*Metropolitan Museum of Art, New York, Bequest of Charles Allen Munn, 1924*)

Sam Adams, a leader of American opposition to British colonial rule. (*Courtesy of the Museum of Fine Arts, Boston*)

Robert Clive receiving the *diwani* on behalf of the East India Company from Shah Alam, August 1765. (*By permission of the British Library [F29]*)

Governor Davey's 1816 pictorial proclamation to the Australian Aborigines. (*Fotomas Index/Barnaby's Picture Library*)

Emigrants set sail for Australia, 1869. (*Fotomas Index/Barnaby's Picture Library*)

Maori chiefs sign the Treaty of Waitangi in 1840. (*Barnaby's Picture Library*)

The Free Trader Richard Cobden forces the pace on a wary Robert Peel in the mid-1840s. (*The Mansell Collection*)

The construction of the *Great Eastern* in 1857. (*The Institution of Mechanical Engineers*)

An Englishwoman and her infants face a fate worse than death at the hands of murderous Sepoys. (*The Mansell Collection*)

Executed mutineers during the great Indian uprising of 1857–8. (*By permission of the British Library [B805]*)

Governor Eyre. (*The Mansell Collection*)

A contemporary depiction of the 1865 Jamaica crisis. (*Fotomas Index/Barnaby's Picture Library*)

Missionaries in West Africa in the 1860s. (*Church Missionary Society*)

Disraeli offers Queen Victoria the imperial crown of India. (*The Mansell Collection*)

Sir Evelyn Baring. (*Mary Evans Picture Library*)

The palatial offices of the Suez Canal Company at Port Said. (*Hulton Deutsch Collection Ltd*)

Indian indentured labourers building the Uganda railway. (*Foreign and Commonwealth Office Library Collection, London*)

The defeat of British troops by Zulu warriors at Isandlhwana in 1879. (*Hulton Deutsch Collection Ltd*)

After the British defeat at Majuba Hill in 1881, representatives of the Transvaalers talk terms with British officers. (*Foreign and Commonwealth Office Library Collection, London*)

Bismarck, the 'Irrepressible Tourist'. (*The Mansell Collection*)

A sturdy John Bull orders a disrespectful Frenchman to 'COME OFF THAT FLAG!!!' (*Mary Evans Picture Library*)

General Gordon. (*The Mansell Collection*)

Queen Victoria still has room in her heart for disaffected, potentially rebellious Ireland. (*The Mansell Collection*)

The Victorian postal service as a bond of Empire. (*By permission of the British Library/The Tapling Collection*)

Sir Frederick Lugard surrounded by Northern Nigerian chieftains on a visit to London Zoo in 1925. (*Hulton Deutsch Collection Ltd*)

Europeans amid warriors in late-nineteenth-century Borneo. (*Popperfoto*)

A reluctant John Bull decides to take yet another abandoned 'black baby', Uganda, into his care in 1894. (*The Mansell Collection*)

A 1910 reception in Zanzibar. (*By permission of the Syndics of Cambridge University Library*)

New South Wales Lancers celebrating Victoria's Diamond Jubilee in 1897. (*Hulton Deutsch Collection Ltd*)

General Kitchener. (*The Mansell Collection*)

A British engineer gives his orders to Chinese underlings at Wei-hai-Wei. (*Foreign and Commonwealth Office Library Collection, London*)

Cecil Rhodes dining with a young companion at his camp in the Matapos Hills. (*Rhodes Memorial Museum Trustees*)

Paul Kruger. (*Hulton Deutsch Collection Ltd*)

Sir Alfred Milner. (*Hulton Deutsh Collection Ltd*)

Dr Jameson sailing for Britain after the fiasco of the Jameson Raid. (*Hulton Deutsch Collection Ltd*)

Battle-weary men of the Hampshire Regiment cross the Valsch River Drift in the Orange Free State. (*Foreign and Commonwealth Office Library Collection, London*)

Londoners celebrate the relief of Ladysmith, 1900. (*Hulton Deutsch Collection Ltd*)

Lord and Lady Curzon in the 1903 Dunbar procession to mark Edward VII's accession as King-Emperor. (*By permission of the British Library [MSS EUR f111/270 No 35]*)

Illustrations

Rudyard Kipling. (*Hulton Deutsch Collection Ltd*)

Indian princes and British Army officers mingle in the Hyderabad Contingent's polo team. (*Hulton Deutsch Collection Ltd*)

The Colonial Conference of 1902. (*The Mansell Collection*)

The 1911 Imperial Conference. (*Hulton Deutsch Collection Ltd*)

The majestic buildings of New Delhi. (*By permission of the British Library [Photo 134/1(2)]*)

Indian Lancers answer the Empire's call. (*Hulton Deutsch Collection Ltd*)

Canadian troops in the trenches before Ypres in 1916. (*Imperial War Museum*)

Australian and New Zealand troops being landed at Anzac Cove in April 1915. (*Hulton Deutsch Collection Ltd*)

The shattered General Post Office in Dublin after the 1916 Easter Uprising. (*The Press Association*)

Arthur Griffiths and Eamon de Valera in Dublin, July 1921. (*Hulton Deutsch Collection Ltd*)

Brigadier-General Dyer. (*The Illustrated London News Picture Library*)

Mahatma Gandhi. (*The Mansell Collection*)

The great British Empire Exhibition, 1924. (*Cricklewood Library and Archive*)

A P&O poster puts the Empire at the centre of its advertising message. (*P&O Archives*)

Arab protestors confronting a British soldier in Jerusalem, 1937. (*Topham Picture Source*)

General Percival surrenders Singapore to the Japanese, 15 February 1942. (*Imperial War Museum*)

Australian machine-gunners during the Burma campaign, July 1945. (*Imperial War Museum*)

Arthur Creech Jones and Ernest Bevin at a conference on the problem of Palestine, January 1947. (*Popperfoto*)

Sir Stafford Cripps meets Mohammed Ali Jinnah during the ill-fated Cripps Mission of 1942. (*Hulton Deutsch Collection Ltd*)

The last Viceroy, Lord Mountbatten, at the meeting at which the partition of India was agreed, June 1947. (*Hulton Deutsch Collection Ltd*)

Muslim refugees packing a train taking them to their newly created homeland of Pakistan. (*Associated Press*)

President Makarios. (*Hulton Deutsch Collection Ltd*)

Colonel Grivas, the Leader of EOKA. (*Hulton Deutsch Collection Ltd*)

Eden and Nasser meet before the Suez crisis. (*Popperfoto*)

British tanks patrol the streets of Port Said, 8 November 1956. (*Associated Press/Topham Picture Source*)

Harold Macmillan in Lagos during his 'wind of change' tour of Africa in 1960. (*Associated Press/Topham Picture Source*)

Colonial Secretary Iain Macleod in conversation with Julius Nyerere. (*Camera Press*)

Hendrik Verwoerd leaves the 1961 Commonwealth Prime Ministers' Meeting after South Africa was denied readmittance to the Commonwealth due to its apartheid policies. (*Hulton Deutsch Collection Ltd*)

The Queen surrounded by leaders of the Commonwealth at the 1961 conference. (*Range/Bettmann/UPI*)

Julius Nyerere proclaims Tanganyika's independence in 1961. (*Hulton Deutsch Collection Ltd*)

Jomo Kenyatta greets rejoicing crowds after his release from detention in 1961. (*Hulton Deutsch Collection Ltd*)

Ian Smith signs his government's unilateral declaration of independence on 11 November 1965. (*Associated Press*)

Lord Soames congratulates Robert Mugabe on his election as Zimbabwe's first Prime Minister in 1980. (*Gubb/Gamma Press/Frank Spooner Pictures*)

Margaret Thatcher. (*Patrick Piel/Frank Spooner Pictures*)

Nelson Mandela. (*Rex Features, London*)

MAPS

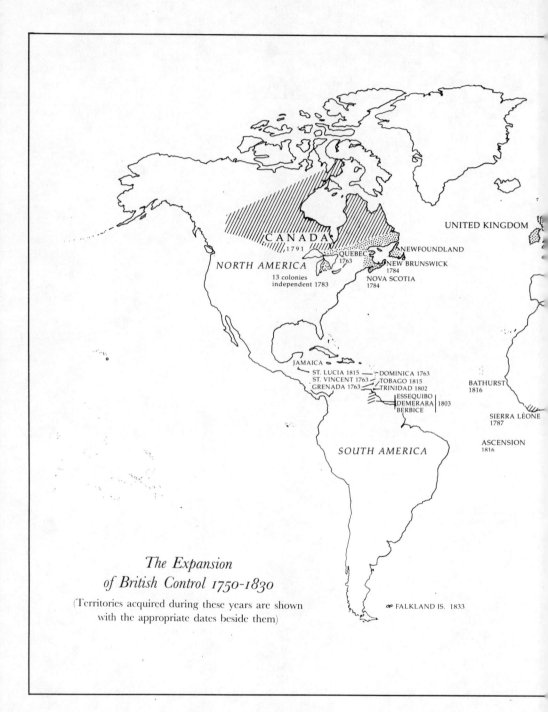

UNITED KINGDOM

CANADA
1791

NEWFOUNDLAND

NORTH AMERICA

QUEBEC
1763

NEW BRUNSWICK
1784

13 colonies
independent 1783

NOVA SCOTIA
1784

JAMAICA

ST. LUCIA 1815 ——— DOMINICA 1763
ST. VINCENT 1763 ——— TOBAGO 1815
GRENADA 1763 ——— TRINIDAD 1802

BATHURST
1816

ESSEQUIBO
DEMERARA 1803
BERBICE

SIERRA LEONE
1787

ASCENSION
1816

SOUTH AMERICA

*The Expansion
of British Control 1750-1830*

(Territories acquired during these years are shown
with the appropriate dates beside them)

⚓ FALKLAND IS. 1833

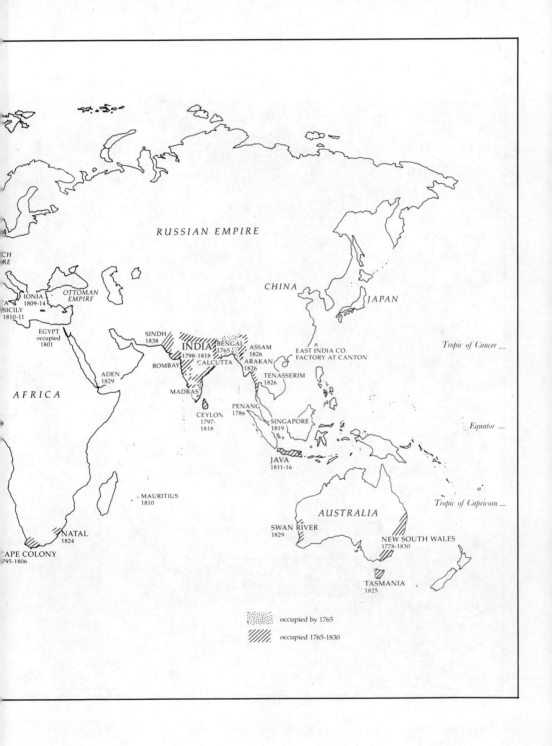

RUSSIAN EMPIRE

CH
RE

IONIA
1809-14
'A
SICILY
1810-11

OTTOMAN
EMPIRE

EGYPT
occupied
1801

CHINA

JAPAN

SINDH
1838

INDIA
1798-1818

BENGAL
1765

ASSAM
1826

EAST INDIA CO.
FACTORY AT CANTON

Tropic of Cancer

BOMBAY

CALCUTTA

ARAKAN
1826

ADEN
1829

MADRAS

TENASSERIM
1826

AFRICA

CEYLON
1797-
1818

PENANG
1786

SINGAPORE
1819

Equator

JAVA
1811-16

MAURITIUS
1810

AUSTRALIA

Tropic of Capricorn

NATAL
1824

SWAN RIVER
1829

APE COLONY
795-1806

NEW SOUTH WALES
1778-1830

TASMANIA
1825

occupied by 1765

occupied 1765-1830

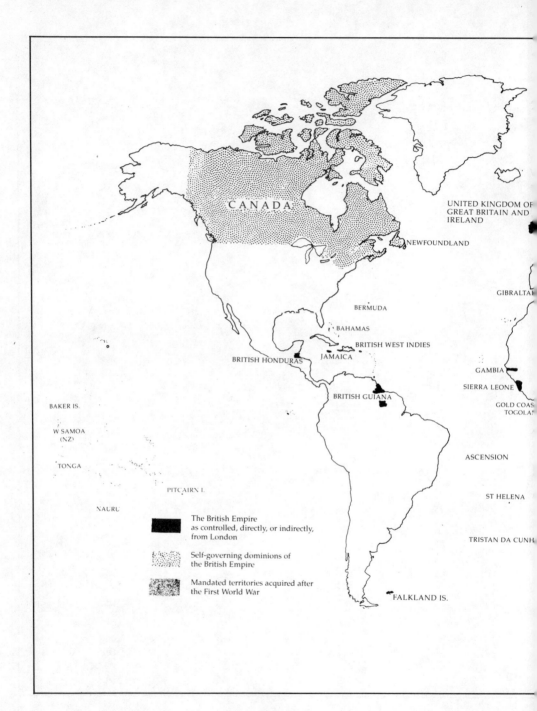

CANADA

UNITED KINGDOM OF
GREAT BRITAIN AND
IRELAND

NEWFOUNDLAND

GIBRALTAR

BERMUDA

BAHAMAS

BRITISH WEST INDIES

JAMAICA

BRITISH HONDURAS

GAMBIA

SIERRA LEONE

BRITISH GUIANA

GOLD COAST
TOGOLAN

BAKER IS.

ASCENSION

W SAMOA
(NZ)

TONGA

ST HELENA

PITCAIRN I.

NAURU

TRISTAN DA CUNH

The British Empire
as controlled, directly, or indirectly,
from London

Self-governing dominions of
the British Empire

Mandated territories acquired after
the First World War

FALKLAND IS.

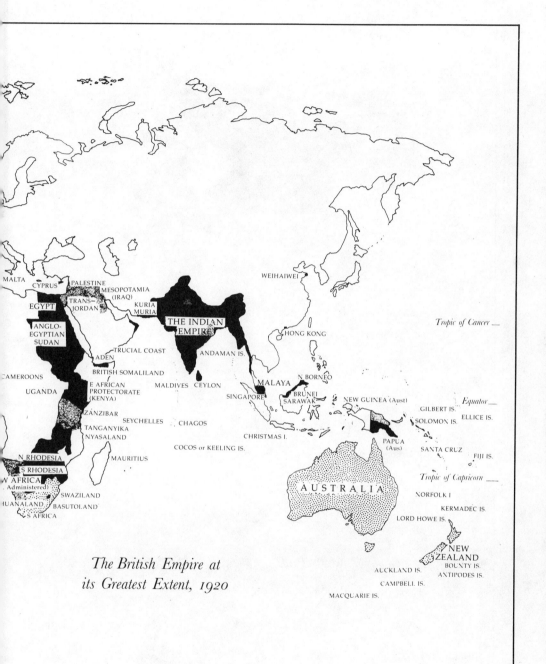

MALTA
CYPRUS
PALESTINE
EGYPT
TRANS-
JORDAN
MESOPOTAMIA
(IRAQ)
ANGLO-
EGYPTIAN
SUDAN
KURIA
MURIA
THE INDIAN
EMPIRE
WEIHAIWEI
Tropic of Cancer —
TRUCIAL COAST
ADEN
HONG KONG
CAMEROONS
BRITISH SOMALILAND
ANDAMAN IS.
UGANDA
E AFRICAN
PROTECTORATE
(KENYA)
MALDIVES CEYLON
MALAYA
N BORNEO
SINGAPORE
BRUNEI
SARAWAK
NEW GUINEA (Aust)
GILBERT IS.
Equator —
ELLICE IS.
ZANZIBAR
SEYCHELLES
CHAGOS
SOLOMON IS.
TANGANYIKA
NYASALAND
CHRISTMAS I.
SANTA CRUZ
FIJI IS.
COCOS or KEELING IS.
PAPUA
(Aus)
N RHODESIA
MAURITIUS
S RHODESIA
W AFRICA
. Administered)
Tropic of Capricorn —
A U S T R A L I A
NORFOLK I
SWAZILAND
HUANALAND BASUTOLAND
KERMADEC IS.
S AFRICA
LORD HOWE IS.

*The British Empire at
its Greatest Extent, 1920*

NEW
ZEALAND
AUCKLAND IS.
BOUNTY IS.
ANTIPODES IS.
CAMPBELL IS.
MACQUARIE IS.

CANADA

UNITED KINGDOM OF
BRITAIN AND
NORTHERN IRELAND

UNITED STATES
OF AMERICA

* GIBRALTA

• * BERMUDA

BAHAMAS
* TURKS & CAICOS IS.

* BRITISH VIRGIN IS.
* ANGUILLA
ANTIGUA AND BARBUDA
DOMINICA
ST LUCIA
BARBADOS
GRENADA
TRINIDAD & TOBAGO

* CAYMAN IS.
BELIZE
JAMAICA
ST CHRISTOPHER & NEVIS
* MONTSERRAT
ST VINCENT & THE GRENADINES

THE GAMBIA

SIERRA LEONE

GH

• * CHRISTMAS I. (Aus)

GUYANA

SOUTH AMERICA

* ASCENSION

• * COOK IS. (NZ)
* OENO I.   * HENDERSON I.
* PITCAIRN I.   * DUCIE I.

* ST HEL

*|TRISTAN DA CUNHA

The Commonwealth 1996

Territories not yet independent
are indicated thus *)

* FALKLAND IS.
* SOUTH GEORGIA

*|SOUTH ORKNEY IS   * SOUTH SANDWIC

* SOUTH SHETLAND IS.

*|BRITISH ANTARCTIC TERRITORY

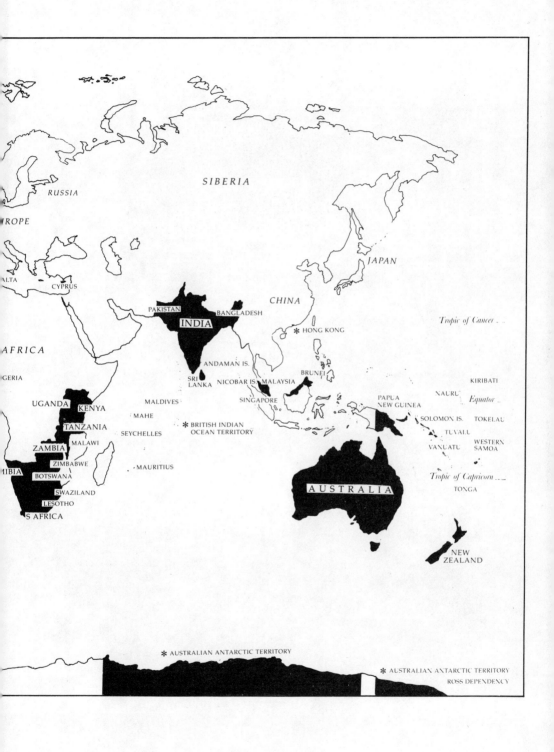

PREFACE

The invitation to write this book was both gratifying and somewhat unnerving. I was delighted at the opportunity to research and write upon a theme which has been central to my personal and academic interests at least since Oxford; indeed, I took 'The History of the British Empire' as an O-Level subject at school in the mid-1950s.

My pleasure at the commission was, however, tempered by the scale of the task I had taken on. I was also keenly aware of the huge range and high quality of so much of the writing that already existed on the subject of the British Empire and Commonwealth. In addition, where should I begin, and where should I end? What should I put in, and what should I leave out? I soon decided that I should approach the enterprise by limiting the chronology, starting in the mid-eighteenth century with the American Revolution and ending as near as I could to the present, in effect 1996. It also seemed to me that rather than attempting a vast narrative history I should select a number of imperial themes which could be examined and assessed in a manner that was both scholarly and accessible. In the process, I hoped that the reader might gain certain insights into the essential nature of the British imperial experience. Inevitably, some parts of the imperial story have been compressed, briefly summarised or even omitted. I hope, however, that the very substantial residue will be a useful aid to the understanding of one of the great historical phenomena of the modern age.

Among those I wish to thank for their encouragement and support from start to finish are Bruce Hunter of David Higham and Richard Johnson and Robert Lacey of HarperCollins. The University of North London awarded me sabbatical leave and research funding, thus enabling me to visit India, North America and South Africa. My colleagues Dr Dennis Dean and Professor John Tosh read the draft typescript and gave me valuable advice. Alina Wiewiorka helped to check the bibliography. Without the word-processing skills of Marcos and Michelle de Lima, progress would have been infinitely slower. Many colleagues and friends showed an interest and made useful suggestions. My parents, my wife Dorothy and our four children did their best to understand my enthusiasm for the undertaking and provided useful emotional support when it was needed.

The paperback edition of the book has given me the chance to make some minor amendments and corrections, and to add some extra material.

Denis Judd, London, 1996

1

ANATOMY OF AN EMPIRE

An Introduction

THIS BOOK DOES NOT seek to provide a complete and comprehensive narrative account of the British Empire from its early beginnings to its final collapse. Rather, it is predicated on the notion that far from the sum of the Empire being greater than its parts, generally the opposite was true. Few, surely, would attempt to convey the essential identity of a person by describing the whole – minutely detailing every internal and external physical and psychological characteristic of the individual in question. Each chapter of this book, therefore, will provide an assessment of the imperial experience by focusing on a particular episode or event and then interpreting its significance within the broad context of the history of the British Empire. In the process – to continue the anatomical metaphor – it is intended that all of the major organs, limbs and characteristics of the Empire will be subjected to a thorough and searching postmortem examination. In the course of the analysis it is inevitable that some parts of the imperial carcass will receive less attention than others.

The book begins, moreover, with an analysis of the events which led to the American Revolution, rather than taking the story back to John Cabot's discovery of Newfoundland in 1497. There is no intention in this choice of starting points to diminish or dismiss any aspect of imperial history that falls between these two events: the demands of commerce, the patterns of migration and settlement, the significance of the trans-Atlantic slave trade, the activities of great chartered companies such as the East India Company, the impact of colonisation and imperialism upon the lives and imaginations of British people are all significant and powerful themes. Rather the book begins in the late eighteenth century because this was when the British Empire became recognisably the greatest and most dynamic of European imperial structures, and when Britain, if not yet 'the workshop of the world', was well on the way to becoming the globe's greatest international trader and the chief carrier of the commerce of other nations. Above all, the aim of the book is to establish a clear and comprehensible identity of an empire whose history is both long and complex, riddled with paradox and contradiction, and which, at its height, encompassed a quarter of the human race and over a fifth of the world's land surface.

There will be a number of themes running through the book. One of the major preoccupations will be to examine and assess the Empire's impact upon the British identity. Briefly and simply put, what effect did the Empire have upon Britain and Britishness? What purpose did it serve in terms of consolidating the United Kingdom, in producing a national and imperial ethic, in promoting a national mythology that was not merely wrapped within the Union Jack but promoted – consciously and unconsciously – by an outpouring of imperial propaganda?

Immediately, of course, the issue of identification raises a host of difficulties and doubts. To start with, exactly who were the British? For a large part of its history the Empire was perceived to be the 'English' Empire; at least, that is how many foreign peoples saw it. A closer examination, however, reveals that for much of its existence, and especially at its apogee and during its decline, the Empire was manifestly British. The incorporation of Wales, Scotland and finally Ireland within the United Kingdom meant that the Celtic people of the British Isles were invited to participate in the imperial experience as partners of the English. Welsh farmers and missionaries, Scottish engineers and doctors, Irish soldiers and merchants all contributed profoundly to the imperial story. Indeed, in the case of Scotland, during the hundred years after the Act of Union, and especially in the period 1750 to 1800:

> Its economy expanded at a faster rate than ever before, in some respects at a faster rate than the English economy. Between 1750 and 1800, its overseas commerce grew by 300 per cent, England's by 200 per cent. In the same period the proportion of Scots living in towns doubled, whereas England's more substantial urban population increased by only some 25 per cent. And Scottish towns were now far more affluent places . . . made fat on imperial trade and graced with new, broad streets, elegant private houses and imposing public buildings . . . as both sides of the border came to recognise, there were senses in which Scotland was not England's peer but its superior.[1]

At various times, however, the Celtic partnership in the British imperial mission was ambivalent, not to say obstructive. After all, it was the English who claimed the hegemony of the British Isles, and who had in one way or another subdued and conquered the three Celtic peoples. Even in the case of Scotland, which was arguably the most independent and self-sufficient of the Celtic nations, the role was generally perceived as more that of junior partner than of equal, despite the apparent willingness with which the Scottish people entered the Union by negotiation in 1707, and despite the rapid growth of the Scottish economy and the self-confident deportment of the Scots within both the Union and the Empire. But the Welsh were far more clearly a dispossessed nation, driven from the lush and prosperous lowlands of England by the Anglo-Saxon invaders in the wake of the Roman retreat, and penned into a mountainous and frequently inhospitable terrain in their western principality. The Irish were even more palpably a conquered people, although here the equation was complicated by the passionate pro-Unionism of the Protestant settlers of the six northern counties.

Problems of identity arise, also, when considering the dominant populations of the white settler, self-governing colonies of the British Empire. Once more, foreigners tended to assume too easily that the ruling European populations of Australia, Canada, New Zealand and South Africa were simply extensions of the British, even the English, people overseas. This was, again, simply not the case. By the beginning of the twentieth century barely 12 per cent of the Empire's people were European, let alone British. French Canadians, Afrikaners, the descendants of Irish transportees and emigrants to Australia, even some of the predominantly Scottish communities settled in South Island, New Zealand, all demonstrated at the best ambivalence and at the worst downright hostility to British imperial rule, and to the concepts of 'Britishness' and 'Englishness'. There was therefore a multiplicity of identities both inside the United Kingdom and even among the European communities within the imperial system.

There is no question that the existence of the Empire brought profit and wealth to a substantial section of the British population. No one can doubt that the desire for profitable trade, plunder and enrichment was the primary force that led to the establishment of the imperial structure. But Empire served many other purposes. Some have seen it as a mainstay of the hitherto discredited Stuart monarchy, restored in 1660 after the relatively brief period of republican rule known as 'the Commonwealth and Protectorate':

3

After the defeat of the radicals in 1660, and the final elimination of the old regime in 1688, the rulers of England organised a highly successful commercial empire and a system of
class rule which proved to have unusual staying power. The
Protestant ethic dominated at least those thoughts and feelings which could be expressed in print.[2]

As well as acting as a stabilising influence in the post-revolutionary
Britain of the late seventeenth century, the Empire served many other
purposes. It provided a means of outdoor relief for substantial numbers
of the upper and middle classes. India was the main provider of employment, with young men of the 'propertyless leisured class' eagerly competing for employment as officers in the East India Company's armies
in the first half of the nineteenth century; later, India also provided
substantial employment outlets for a professional or 'service' middle
class. Outside of India, by the late nineteenth century other colonial
services employed a few thousand people, a total which had risen to
some 20,000 by the late 1950s.

The Empire also helped to maintain Britain as a military power on
an equal footing with the great Continental powers of France, Germany
and Russia. This was chiefly because the Indian Army could be shipped
all over the world to fight wars on Britain's behalf, and was also capable
of being rapidly expanded in a global emergency, as in 1914 and 1939.
This meant that for most of the history of British involvement and rule
in India, troops raised in the sub-continent and paid for largely by the
people of the sub-continent maintained Britain's global military status
and at the same time enabled British politicians to steer clear of the
potentially unpopular conscription of young British males.

By the late nineteenth century, and perhaps even earlier, the Empire
also served as a fig leaf to disguise the increasing nakedness of Britain's
claim to be a truly great power in economic, naval and military terms.
So successful was the camouflage that towards the end of the nineteenth
century newly unified nations like Italy and Germany hastened to
acquire colonies on the assumption that imperial possessions not merely
symbolised great-power status, but somehow guaranteed it.

The British Empire was perceived as underwriting the nation's
future in a variety of ways. British politicians of all parties were quick
to discern in the Empire a means of uniting the British people in a
common cause, as a means of inspiring a sense of international mission,
a device to blunt the edge of class warfare and egalitarian philosophies,

4

and above all as a way of looking to the future with more confidence than the realities intrinsically merited.

Rule over a host of indigenous peoples also provided untold numbers of British people with an easy psychological defence mechanism: a great and messy amount of personal and national rubbish could be dumped elsewhere – principally upon 'inferior' black and brown people throughout the imperial system, who thus became the repositories of much that was unwanted and disowned at home. As a consequence, the Empire helped to boost both the confidence of the individual and of the nation, and to keep fears of inadequacy, degeneration and decline at bay. It also provided manifold opportunities for personal, financial and sexual aggrandisement. It introduced strange and exotic foods, foreign flora and fauna, useful words, outlandish philosophies, new sports, other cultures, and a whole host of unfamiliar experiences into the British way of life.

There are inevitably many ways of interpreting all of this. It has been argued, on the one hand, that:

> The Empire penetrated the emotions of millions. It gave
> Britain its position among the nations and confirmed a
> national, not to say racial superiority. Taken together with
> Britain's insularity, the Empire marked out an 'island race'
> as a people set apart, with connections across the globe
> matched by no other state. 'British culture' had in these
> respects a psychological dimension shared by no other Euro-
> pean state, not even by France.[3]

Others have argued that the existence of the Empire was a matter of some indifference to most British people, who were scarcely aware of the imperial system's physical ramifications let alone of its significance. It has even been claimed that:

> The British Empire vanished quietly and almost impercep-
> tibly. Apart from those who had made their careers as col-
> onial or Indian civil servants, most people scarcely noticed
> the change. It had no particular economic effects, and stra-
> tegically was, if anything, a relief.[4]

There is, of course, a halfway house in all of this. There can be no doubt that the long-lasting experience of Empire affected the way in which people in Britain viewed both themselves and those whom they ruled. Perhaps, though, the Empire was more of a mirror in which

5

British identity and British needs and aspirations were reflected, than an historical phenomenon which single-handedly created some major features of modern Britain. It has recently been persuasively said of the Empire that, instead of seriously shaping or reshaping British society and British institutions:

> . . . it confirmed, it reinforced where it provided an additional outlet. Empire gave a people already generally antipathetic to foreigners and convinced of their own unique place in the world further grounds for such beliefs. Empire was consequence as well as cause of world-wide patterns of trade and the world-wide deployment of military and naval power. Subject to some delays in transmission, the mores of Empire were for the most part those current in Britain itself, at least until societies of British origin over a long period of time began to develop their own identity: for instance, many historians see colonial America becoming more rather than less 'Anglicised' in the eighteenth century . . .[5]

We are perhaps on safer ground when we consider the British and imperial impact upon the constituent countries of the Empire. Here it is easier to assess and weigh the consequences of military conquest and political control. The despoliation of local culture, often the consequence of British christianising and 'civilising' missions, the effect of various forms of emancipation – from the freeing of slaves to various social and political reforms, the necessity to accommodate and learn to live with both immigrants of British origin and rulers and officials exercising their power on behalf of the British state, are all well documented and comparatively self-evident. The opening up of colonial and imperial societies to British-based trade and European commercial entrepreneurism, the dislocation of local economies, the manipulation of indigenous markets and industries, all of this – although it varied from country to country and from continent to continent – can be reasonably well described and assessed.

So, too, can the introduction of a process of industrialisation based overwhelmingly upon the British model. British constitutional practices – notably the exaltation of the 'Westminster model', British concepts of law and order, British standards of public and private deportment, all of these, and much more besides, made their marks – some of them long-lasting. British habits of eating, living, playing sport, pursuing culture, expressing sexual needs, raising and educating children, impacted in a variety of ways upon those who were ruled under the British flag. After all, almost all of the countries within the Empire were incorporated, at least to some extent, into a European-based – but in the first instance British-controlled – world order.

Faced with the onward march of British imperialism and European civilisation, local peoples had to make a choice between acceptance and defiance, collaboration and resistance. It is small wonder that for the most part collaboration with the imperial authorities became the inevitable consequence of imperial expansion and control. Without the collaboration – or at any rate the acquiescence – of local elites, tribal and religious groupings, the different castes and sub-divisions of colonial society, the British would never have been able to carry out their stupendous task of conquering, ruling, dominating and controlling so large a proportion of the planet.

By the late eighteenth century, Britain had truly become a great imperial power, dominating huge swathes of territory and much trade from the New World to the Far East. But, simultaneously and paradoxically, the American Revolution seemed to menace this newly won global standing. Although the Caribbean and Canadian colonies remained loyal, thirteen mainland colonies rose in rebellion and threw off British control. Much national mythology needs to be addressed in this regard: the British, far from denying the Americans representation as they claimed, had already in principle offered it to them; a substantial number of the colonists were not even British, since there had been significant emigration from Germany and elsewhere; the majority of colonists were, at the outset, loyal; after the war, Anglo–American trade boomed as never before. In any case, Britain was turning increasingly to trade, and hence imperial relationships, with non-settlement territories: at the outbreak of the revolution there were already far more subjects of British rule in Bengal, which the East India Company had controlled since 1765, than in all of the Americas.

The next half-century saw a variety of responses to the dilemmas and opportunities of Empire. At first there was a tidying up: constitutional reform in Canada; a new administrative structure in India; an Act of Union with the perennially disaffected Irish, who were now invited, along with the Scottish and the Welsh, to collaborate in an expanding and enormously profitable world-wide enterprise. But there were countervailing pressures. The loss of the American colonies had pushed Britain into opening up the apparently unpromising Australian continent as a dumping ground for convicts. As free immigrants began to arrive, lured by the gold strikes and the chance of a fresh start, Australian voices were raised – often in Irish accents – demanding more colonial self-government. During the first year of Queen Victoria's reign, Canadians rose in rebellion in a similar cause.

The British authorities hastened to find a compromise, and offered the palliative of responsible, or full internal, self-government. Although there was a powerful movement in the Mother Country, backed by the increasingly influential capitalist lobby, to dump unprofitable colonies and to let the free market dominate all, the number of imperial possessions multiplied rather than contracted. There was now New Zealand and, taken from the Dutch during the Napoleonic Wars, the Cape of Good Hope, a vortex that was destined to suck Britain into a commitment of great complexity as well as profit. Elsewhere the rule of the East India Company continued to expand in the sub-continent and beyond, taking British influence into the Malay peninsula, Singapore, and as far as Hong Kong, China and the East Indies. In tropical Africa, although Britain's lucrative role in the slave trade was finished, imperial holdings continued to grow. The Empire was now manifestly, and apparently irrevocably, a global institution.

While the British public were benefiting from some of the wealth that filtered down from imperial trade, and becoming accustomed to cheap chocolate as well as cheap sugar and tea, a serious crisis was gathering for their rulers. It was put into dramatic form by the great Indian uprising of 1857, the 'Mutiny'. Gorged on the alleged atrocities of the treacherous sepoys, the mid-Victorian public found their preconceptions of the savagery and unreliability of the 'black' races amply confirmed.

No matter what humane attitudes might be preached by high-minded missionaries in 'Darkest Africa', the Maori Wars of the 1860s (with their embarrassing military reverses for white troops and settlers), the rejection of British rule by the Afrikaner trekkers of the Cape, and the Jamaica Rebellion of 1865 (the ingratitude of emancipated slaves was a further blow to contemporary self-esteem) fuelled national prejudices which already put French, Italians, Russians and Prussians, and indeed all non-Britons, beyond the pale. The imperial outlook henceforth comprised the certainty that the British were a superior people endowed by God and destiny to rule over an ever-increasing proportion of the world's surface for the good of its inhabitants. A form of imperial Darwinism was thus born.

Although governments tried to avoid further and unnecessary

imperial entanglements, however, the influence of 'the man on the spot' and the irresistible proliferation of capitalism led to a continuing expansion of the Empire. Improving technology, the superiority of British weaponry, the supremacy of the Royal Navy, all conspired to subdue a variety of foreign foes, from obscure African chieftains to the Emperor of China. Vague as most British people were as to the identity and whereabouts of colonial possessions, there seemed, in the end, no avoiding an imperial destiny that set Britain above the rest of the world and promised a fair and prosperous future.

With the monarchy, in the somewhat unlikely shape of Queen Victoria, now firmly, even passionately, attached to the titular leadership of the Empire, the various sub-sections of the social pyramid were far more likely to identify with imperialism as a matter of course. Despite its simplistic quality, the cry 'For Queen and Empire' had a potent appeal, not least to those struggling at the bottom of the social pile and to the aspiring, but chair-bound, clerical classes who could dream of adventure and derring-do on the High Veldt or in the Australian outback.

From the Indian Mutiny to the Boer War, the British Empire assumed a size and grandeur that surpassed that of all contemporary imperial systems. Britain's enthusiastic participation in the end-of-century frenzy of imperial rivalry and acquisitiveness had led to huge extensions of territory, particularly during the partition of Africa. But in South-East Asia and the South Pacific as well, British holdings were staked out. Expansionists, proconsuls and soldiers, like Cecil Rhodes, Alfred Milner, Lord Curzon, Field Marshals Kitchener and Roberts, were to become national heroes.

At home, the newly enfranchised masses were fed upon a rich diet of imperial propaganda which permeated much of society, from the school textbooks of the public and private educational sector to the columns of the rapidly expanding cheap, mass-circulation national newspapers; from brightly coloured biscuit tins to the robust patriotic ballads of the music halls; from great displays like Queen Victoria's Golden and Diamond Jubilees to the names given to new streets in the burgeoning suburbs.

In politics the Conservative Party now embraced imperial ideology more warmly than ever before: for one thing, Empire now produced profits rather than expenses; for another, there were votes to be had. It was Disraeli who bestowed the title of Empress of India upon a gratified Queen and who bought a vital stake in the Suez Canal

9

Company allegedly 'for her'. The Conservatives reaped a substantial reward for their efforts when the 'imperial' issue of Irish Home Rule split the Liberals and put them into almost permanent majority government between 1886 and 1905. Even the Liberals, despite the opposition of their left wing, bit the bullet and accommodated Empire, their right wing going so far as to call themselves 'Liberal Imperialists'.

But although Britain was in the process of stamping its mark upon the Empire, and enduring the traumas of Gordon's death at Khartoum and the early fiascos of the Boer War, the future was not quite as clear as many imperialists claimed. The bonds that held the Empire together were essentially fragile, even artificial. In important respects the British Empire was hardly British at all. Only a small proportion of its people were of British extraction, and Hinduism and Islam were its most commonly practised religions, not Christianity. Beneath the Union flag, British administration had hardly begun to penetrate and alter many indigenous societies. The self-governing colonies were asserting a growing sense of national identity, and for how long would India remain quiescent? Worse still, Britain's global pre-eminence was, for the first time, seriously under threat. Not merely was the nation's lead in the industrial race being steadily reduced, but Germany's determination to become a great naval power, as affirmed by the massive warship building programme begun in 1898, was a challenge of the most dangerous kind. How would the British fare in the twentieth century?

The Edwardian era demonstrated the glory and potency of the Empire, but also its potential for decay and dismemberment. The triumphalism of Elgar's 'Pomp and Circumstance' co-existed uneasily with the growth of the Indian National Congress as a serious political movement; Curzon's arrogance as the Viceroy of what some assumed was a 'Thousand-Year Raj' must be set against the increasing pressure from the self-governing colonies (called dominions from 1907) to be treated as separate nations; the final, protracted British victory in the Boer War (with its attendant horrors of concentration camps and farm-burning) against the establishment of the Union of South Africa under the political leadership of a clique of Afrikaner ex-generals; the continuing extension of British territory in Africa against the passing, though not the implementation, of the Irish Home Rule Bill; Joseph Chamberlain's charismatic campaign for tariff reform (or a system of imperial trade preferences) against the Liberal landslide of 1906; the apparent confidence and assurance of the Empire's rulers against hysterical flurries of national self-doubt, as illustrated by the celebrations on Mafeking Day in 1900 or by the great 'Naval Scare' of 1909.

Empire was increasingly celebrated in schoolroom, shop and factory, and from pulpit and political platform; there was Empire Day, a series of Colonial and Imperial Conferences, the imperial certainties expressed in the *Daily Mail* and other new, heavily subscribed dailies, the widely accepted concept of an 'empire upon which the sun never set'.

Yet there was also the spread of socialism, militant trade unionism and feminism at home; the Irish problem promised civil war, not a neat constitutional solution; Jewish immigrants were flooding into the East End of London and provoking ugly displays of chauvinism and prejudice; after 1910 the Liberal government depended for its survival upon the support of both the emerging Labour Party and the Irish Nationalists, neither of which was theoretically pro-imperialist; the German threat was only partly offset by the ententes (not true alliances, merely 'understandings') with France and Russia; Britain had even entered into a binding alliance with Japan in a bid to secure her holdings in India and the Far East, an odd, and to some dispiriting, display of dependence upon an Asiatic people's military prowess.

Far from being an age of genuine confidence and optimism, with a contented people basking under an imperial sun, the Edwardian era saw a nation wracked with insecurities and wary of the future. It was in a spirit of relief and exultation, as well as of anxiety, that many greeted the outbreak of war in August 1914. Now misgivings and contentious issues could be set aside, and the Empire's mettle tested in a struggle far more deadly than the imperial wars of the Victorian period. Few could have predicted, however, the impact of 'the war to end war'.

The British Empire emerged victorious from the war, its borders considerably extended by territory taken from Germany and Turkey. The acquisition of these new possessions, mostly in Africa and the Middle East, was in theory subject to the supervision of the newly formed League of Nations. In practice, Britain ruled Tanganyika, Palestine, Iraq and the rest as if they were *bona fide* colonies. Her intrusion into the Middle East on such a scale reflected her need to control sufficient oil-producing territory to lubricate the wheels of British industry and to provide fuel for the Royal Navy. In Palestine, however, Britain had taken on a problem of such complexity, with Jewish migration to the new homeland alienating the local Arab population beyond endurance, that an equitable solution was perpetually beyond reach. In many ways, the 'new' empire in the Middle East was to be more trouble than it was worth, and, since it had from 1914 formally included Egypt, was to lead to the final humiliation of the abortive Suez invasion of 1956.

The progress of the war had exposed the Empire's strengths and weaknesses as never before. On the positive side, the imperial system had survived intact. Men and money had been poured into the war effort on a prodigious scale. The dominions and India had joined Britain at the Imperial War Conferences of 1917–19 in planning both for war and peace; they had sat by Britain's side at the peace negotiations of 1919–20; they had taken their places as members of the League of Nations; they had become, with the exception of Canada, 'imperial powers' in their own right when they had acquired mandated territories of their own (South-West Africa, German New Guinea and so forth). India had provided a large volunteer army to fight in the Empire's cause.

But there was another, negative, side. The war had allowed malcontents to express their impatience with British rule. There had been a brief Afrikaner uprising in 1914; Irish Nationalists had staged the Easter Rebellion in 1916; French Canadians had rioted rather than accept conscription, and Australians had rejected it in two referenda; Indian Nationalists had demanded constitutional reform as the price of cooperation. Worse than this, although less evident and therefore less embarrassing, Britain had become massively in debt in order to finance the war. The dominions and India had given the Mother Country essential human and financial support. This was bound to alter, at the most fundamental level, the imperial relationship. The foundations of Britain's great-power status were now seriously and permanently undermined.

From 1918 to 1939 Britain strove to carry on imperial business as usual. Both George V and George VI cherished the Empire; even the ill-fated Edward VIII had been an indefatigable imperial tourist as Prince of Wales. Successive governments and a host of private and public organisations struggled to promote the imperial ethic. Thus a great Empire Exhibition was held in the unfashionable London suburb of Wembley in 1924 (though cynics said that its visitors were keener on the funfair than on the displays of imperial achievement). There was an Empire Marketing Board, the naming of Imperial Airways (eventually to become, by way of BOAC, British Airways), films showing the Empire at its best (*Lives of a Bengal Lancer*, *Sanders of the River*, *Kim* and many more), and the King's annual broadcast to his Empire over 'the wonderful wireless' on Christmas Day. In 1932 an apparently significant breakthrough had occurred with the introduction of a system of preferential trade within the Empire after the Imperial Economic Conference at Ottawa. The creation of the Sterling Area promised much. The passages of many migrants to the colonies were heavily subsidised.

Yet, to the perceptive, the days of the Empire were clearly numbered. Not only were the dominions acting as increasingly independent nations – and able to extract a surprisingly liberal definition of their new status from the 1926 Imperial Conference – but the Irish Free State had indicated its intention of quitting the Commonwealth at the first suitable opportunity. In India, Mahatma Gandhi had mobilised the masses into opposing the Raj through campaigns of civil disobedience, the potency of his appeal enormously enhanced by the horrors of the Amritsar massacre of 1919. Desperate to hold on to their greatest possession, the British made substantial constitutional concessions in the Government of India Acts of 1919 and 1935. But, ominously, it was no longer possible to recruit sufficient British candidates into the exalted and well-paid ranks of the Indian Civil Service. In the dependent Empire the first clear signs of disaffection were displayed in Africa, Ceylon and South-East Asia. Egyptian sovereignty, of a sort, had been restored through an agreement with Britain in 1922.

At home, the advent of Labour as a party of government, and the increased attractiveness of Marxism as a rallying point against fascism, seemed to bode ill for the imperial future. Moreover, in the final resort, the British public remained persistently and woefully ignorant of, and perhaps indifferent to, the Empire, as surveys carried out by Mass Observation illustrated. As war approached, the appeal of Empire as a symbol of national unity seemed more limited than ever before.

In 1945, for the second time in three decades, the Empire and Commonwealth emerged victorious from a bruising war with formidable foes. George VI was still King-Emperor and his Empire still intact. However, the surface success was shallow and illusory. India, now one of Britain's creditors, was in a state of barely repressed rebellion, and the granting of independence after the war was taken for granted. The swift, almost effortless early triumphs of Japanese arms in the East had inflicted further, and perhaps terminal, damage upon European pretensions to racial and industrial superiority. Britain's indebtedness to the Empire had increased, and she was irrevocably in hock to the now manifest global power of the United States. Not only was America a declared foe of British imperialism, but the victory of the Soviet Union over the Third Reich in Eastern Europe had entrenched another new power in a position from which it could subvert British influence as never before. In Africa, the Caribbean, South-East Asia, Burma and elsewhere challenges were being made to British hegemony.

Within Britain itself, a new mood was evident. In the election of July 1945 Churchill's bid for a peacetime mandate had been devastatingly rejected by the voters and a Labour government installed with a land-slide majority. It seemed to many that 'the Empire was on the way out, the welfare state was on the way in'.[6] Yet the Attlee administration was not composed of unreconstructed Bolsheviks. Several influential ministers, notably Ernest Bevin, Herbert Morrison and the Prime Minister himself, were in no mood to dismantle the British Empire, especially when Britain's position as one of the 'Big Three' seemed under threat, and when many trade unionists, however perversely, still equated imperialism with prosperity. It is worth noting that the new government actually toyed with the idea of incorporating part of Libya into the imperial defence system. But the process of decolonisation set in train so many years before was irreversible.

The Attlee government eventually honoured the earlier undertaking to grant independence to India. There was some prevarication, and a messy climax to this process. Muslim nationalism had to be assuaged by the creation of East and West Pakistan, itself a temporary accommodation as it turned out. Burma had already claimed its independence, opted for republican status and left the Commonwealth. The Irish Free State also became a republic and departed. In 1948 Ceylon was made a dominion, and Palestine was simply abandoned (partly due to American election-year pressure) and left to its own devices. Elsewhere, the Labour administration both rejected and sought to placate colonial nationalist movements. Economists noted, with satisfaction as well as some surprise, that as the Empire was being dismantled, the proportion of Britain's imperial trade rose to a level that would have delighted the Victorians and the Edwardians.

The return of the Conservatives to power in 1951, with Churchill as Prime Minister, resulted in a schizophrenic thirteen years. Up to 1957 the government, while allowing progress towards independence in the Gold Coast and the Sudan, set its face firmly against it in Cyprus and many other colonies. Another holding operation saw the establishment of a number of federations, in the West Indies, Malaysia and Central Africa, where local elites and big-business operators were offered the opportunity to construct a mixture of 'freedom' and capitalism in an often oppressive blend. The Suez fiasco of 1956, masterminded by the insecure and over-assertive Eden, exposed British imperial power for the sham it had for so long been.

Eden's successor, the urbane and surprisingly liberal Macmillan, took power with the United States' backing and pushed through a programme of decolonisation that at least equalled that of the Attlee government and in important respects surpassed it. As newly liberated colonies abounded, and the artificial federations were allowed to collapse, the British public were told that they had 'never had it so good'. Consumer spending and economic growth were the new gods, not Empire and crippling expenditure on forces 'east of Suez'.

The Macmillan era ended with the return of a Labour government under Harold Wilson in 1964. The 'swinging sixties' and the music of the Beatles seemed a far cry from the age of imperial supremacy and high-minded duty. But the Cabinet had at least one painful colonial dilemma – how to bring the 1965 rebellion of the Southern Rhodesian whites to a satisfactory end. Although other items of imperial business were carried through to a successful conclusion, Rhodesia was a chronic reminder of the impotence of a metropolitan power unwilling to use force to assert its will. Of the Wilson, Heath and Callaghan governments between 1964 and 1979, none was able to solve the Rhodesian riddle. It was left to the first Thatcher administration to negotiate the independence of Zimbabwe a little before the Prime Minister dramatically asserted her determination to reconquer the Falkland Islands in a short, sharp war reminiscent of so many colonial campaigns of the distant past.

Thereafter, the Conservative government reverted to its programme of retrenchment and the turning back of the frontiers of socialism and welfarism. Overseas it was compliant in the face of American intervention in the colony of Grenada, and was prepared to do a deal with Communist China over the future of Hong Kong. Post-imperial rhetoric was not translated into substantive action. Yet a sizeable, if fragmented and economically insignificant, Empire remained, though dwarfed by a Commonwealth that frequently berated Britain for its reactionary attitudes towards, for example, South Africa's apartheid regime.

The aftermath of Empire has been both constructive and destructive, though mostly the latter. There are innumerable historical connections between Britain and its former colonies, links which are mostly open to creative enterprise and initiative. The independent nations of the Commonwealth have displayed a generosity towards their former rulers of impressive, almost shaming, proportions. Business links, diplomatic cooperation, the provision of military bases, various forms of aid and mutual understanding are commonplace. So too, in great tracts of the Commonwealth, is a passion for cricket, and at least lip-service to parliamentary democracy. As John Strachey, a minister in the Attlee Cabinet, once said, 'To know a no ball from a googly and a point of order from a supplementary question is genuinely to have something in common.'

But there is a darker side. Centuries of supremacy have left many British people ensnared in a mesh of prejudice and shallow assertiveness. Imperialism rested on, indeed was sustained by, assumptions of superiority, where one white person was thought to be worth literally any number of blacks and browns. This deeply engrained tendency towards racial prejudice was lent greater strength by mass migration to the United Kingdom from the Caribbean, the Indian sub-continent and Africa (in 1980 there were officially 2 million New Commonwealth immigrants in the UK, and the forecast for the year 2000 is 3.5 million). There are few objections to immigrants from the 'white' Commonwealth, and certainly no backlash in the form of race riots. Citizens of the Irish Republic enjoyed full and free access to the United Kingdom. Even when people from Asia and the Caribbean are not objects of hatred, they can be ridiculed by stand-up comics, saloon-bar wits and the cartoonists of the gutter press. The continuation, in one form or another, of the Irish 'troubles' spawned a sub-industry of 'Irish jokes', a form of racial abuse which passes for humour and which has a transparent political imperative.

Empire also allowed British industry and various British institutions to shelter behind the privileges which imperial supremacy often involved. Thus, not only was modernisation put off, but Britain found herself stranded and effectively isolated in the post-imperial period. In compensation, much was made of the essentially shallow 'special relationship' with the United States, and the anti-European hysteria demonstrated in some quarters is yet another indication of displacement. What is Britain's role in the post-imperial age to be?

The story is not, of course, quite over yet. The Empire has not entirely evaporated. At the time of writing there are still a dozen colonies under various forms of British control: Hong Kong is easily the most heavily populated of these, and the rest include the Falkland Islands and its dependencies (South Georgia and the South Sandwich Islands),

Gibraltar, St Helena and its dependencies (Ascension and Tristan da Cunha), Montserrat, the Turks and Caicos Islands, the Cayman Islands, Anguilla, Bermuda, the Virgin Islands, British Indian Ocean Territory and British Antarctic Territory. There are still, therefore, responsibilities to carry out, difficult choices to be made. Will Antarctica eventually be the scene of a quasi-imperial scramble over mineral resources buried beneath the ice? Will the British people come to terms with their drastically reduced influence in the world, or will their country become the new 'sick man of Europe', snarling from the sidelines, and dreaming dreams of long ago and far away?

2

THE AMERICAN
REVOLUTION

The End of
the First British Empire?

ON 4 JULY 1776 the newly established American Congress issued a unanimous Declaration of Independence. At the heart of the declaration was an appeal to the enlightened propertied classes as well as to the dispossessed, the radical and the frankly envious:

> We hold these truths to be self-evident, that all men are created equal, that they are endowed by their Creator with certain inalienable rights, that among these are life, liberty and the pursuit of happiness. That to secure these rights, governments are instituted among men, deriving their just powers from the consent of the governed.[1]

Nearly two centuries later a cabal of white supremacist settlers in Rhodesia issued a Unilateral Declaration of Independence that mimicked the letter, although hardly the spirit, of the American Declaration, but which was apparently an equally reckless act of defiance towards a distant and unsympathetic imperial power.

In the 189 years that separated these two events, the British Empire rose to its magnificent, barely imaginable apogee before its decline into relative penury, dissolution and the Commonwealth of Nations.

For some time it was fashionable for academics and others to define a 'First' British Empire, a trade-driven and settler-based system, brought crashing down by the successful revolt of the thirteen American mainland colonies, and to discern a 'Second' British Empire, rising, almost miraculously, from the ruins of the old, powered by the irresistible expansion of Britain's industrialised economy, policed by the Royal

Navy and administered by the hard-headed, muscular Christians of the burgeoning public school system. Between the collapse of the 'First' Empire and the birth of the 'Second' lay, it seemed, the historical equivalent of a Black Hole.

Fortunately a number of historians have exposed this fallacy with graceful and powerful works of scholarship.[2] In so doing they have concentrated attention not merely upon the essential continuities of British imperial history, but also upon the potency of imagery and perception in the delineation of Empire. Ronald Hyam even goes so far as to claim in his brilliant survey of Britain's Empire during the nineteenth century:

> When you come to think of it, there was no such thing as Greater Britain, still less a British Empire – India perhaps apart. There was only a ragbag of territorial bits and pieces, some remaindered remnants, some pre-empted luxury items, some cheap samples. All that red on the map represented in truth at best only a dominion of opinion and a grand anomaly, and at worst a temptation to illusions of grandeur and a gross abuse . . . As the 15th Earl of Derby shrewdly remarked, 'Kings and aristocracies may govern empires, but one people cannot rule another.'[3]

This is not how it must have appeared to many of those who came, in one way or another, under British rule. Despite the tendency of the American rebels to dump the responsibility for the crisis on that arbitrary, confused figurehead, King George III, it was British rule, and taxes passed in the British Parliament, that was resented. To blame a distant landed and legislative oligarchy for many of the perceived wrongs visited upon American colonists was a tempting tactic, and potent propaganda, but it was the Britishness of the oppressors, their difference, that added the sharpest edge to the complaints. Although tens of thousands of American loyalists rejected the revolution, often suffering obloquy, the confiscation of their land and ejection from the new nation as a result, the War of Independence was in the end much more of a conflict between two nations, and two peoples, than a civil war.

The American crisis arose from the determination of an increasingly vocal and effective minority of colonial leaders and opinion-makers to resist the unexpected centralising and fiscal policies of the British government after the victorious conclusion of the Seven Years' War in

1763 had confirmed Britain as one of the great European imperial powers.

Hitherto the British colonial and imperial system had evolved piecemeal and largely as a result of different forms of private enterprise, despite the part played in its development by Britain's armed forces and by laws affecting trade and taxes passed by the Parliament at Westminster. The imperative of overseas trade, commerce and investment was one driving force. The migration of British-born settlers was another. These twin movements were what largely created the 'First' British Empire, not the secret deliberations or the elaborate public plans of ministers and Members of Parliament.

Apart from some peripheral holdings on the west coast of Africa and on the Malay peninsula, for almost all of the eighteenth century the British Empire was concentrated in two great spheres of influence and regulation: in North America and the Caribbean, and in the Indian sub-continent.

Of these two spheres, India was far and away the most straightforward with which to deal, despite the intricacies of maintaining appropriate relations with the Mughals, the princely states and the French. Quite simply, the British East India Company was there to make a profit from trade; there were no large communities of British settlers watchful of their interests and able to obstruct and oppose imperial legislation as in North America. Although the nabobs of the East India Company sought private profit, even personal aggrandisement, they did so within the framework of Company control, and within that system of control the British government became increasingly intrusive as the century progressed. Indeed as the Company's commercial profits dwindled and its territorial, and hence fiscal, responsibilities multiplied, the British administration carried out a programme of state intervention, or creeping nationalisation. There were few British administrators in India willing, or able, to resist this progress towards centralisation and parliamentary supremacy.

In North America, even in the Caribbean, the very opposite was the case. The system of local government that characterised the vast majority of the North American colonies had vested significant power in the local legislative assemblies. The selected oligarchies that held sway in colonies like Massachusetts, New York, Virginia and Jamaica were jealous of their privileges, and, for the most part, deeply involved in the commercial activities of their communities. To this well-established practice of protecting local interests must be added the dissenting

tradition that often derived from the founding imperatives of the leading colonial settlements, whether Puritan, Quaker or Catholic. It is
worth noting here that during the turmoil of the conflict between Parliament, Commonwealth and the House of Stuart in the early and mid-
seventeenth century, the American colonies had also provided a
relatively safe haven and power base for political and religious dissenters
and refugees – for example Sir Harry Vane, the younger, an emigrant
to the New World and a former Governor of the Massachusetts Bay
Colony, whose republicanism, rather than his regicidal tendencies,
caused the restored Stuart regime to exempt him from the Act of Obliv-
ion after the Restoration of 1660 and to secure his execution in 1662
on a trumped-up charge of 'treasonably levying war' against Charles
I.[4] The defiance of royal authority was thus part of a deep-rooted tradition in several of the major colonies.

Until the introduction of additional customs duties in 1764, and
particularly until the passing of the Stamp Act in 1765, however, local
oligarchies had overwhelmingly entered into cosy and mutual accommodation with the British authorities. In general, commercial interde-
pendence and shared cultural, political and legal practices accounted
for this. The settler communities also needed British protection and support in dealing with external, mostly foreign, trade rivals. They also
wanted access to inter-colonial trade, which was expanding rapidly, and
to the offices and land that were subject to Crown patronage. In return,
they cooperated, even collaborated, with the metropolitan authorities.

The crushing British victory over France and Spain in the Seven
Years' War in 1763 not only incorporated French North America and
Spanish Florida into the colonial system and stripped both powers of
coveted Caribbean territories, it also largely liberated the British colonists from the fear of the foreign military threat. Since the American
colonies had made a heavy contribution in men and money to the
victory, their sense of obligation to Britain was correspondingly diminished. In an early recognition of their manifest destiny, the American
colonists anticipated an era of expanding local and international commerce and the peopling of the newly acquired lands to the west of the
Appalachians.

The shift in British policy that was so dramatically indicated by
the passing of the Stamp Act of 1765 was therefore both unexpected
and bitterly resented. It destroyed forever the equilibrium, the political
and fiscal compromise, that had hitherto been the hallmark of relations
between Britain and the colonies.

What prompted this change of policy? Quite simply the British government did not share the colonists' optimism that the French threat, or indeed any other foreign threat, was at an end – a prudent and accurate assessment, in the light of the events of the next half-century. The case for maintaining a substantial military presence in North America to counter the foreign menace, or at least keep it under surveillance, and at the same time to deal with the potential frontier conflicts with American Indians that the western migration of settlers would inevitably precipitate, seemed unanswerable.

The crisis might have been diverted if the colonists had been able to offer Britain convincing guarantees that local troops or local militias would bear a substantial share of the burden of defence and frontier supervision. But none was forthcoming. The British authorities had also noted that even during the Seven Years' War the thirteen colonies had refused to accept any federal body to coordinate their military activities. Such cooperation was rendered even more unlikely by the apparently permanent defeat of France in North America. Nor would the colonists vote taxes through their local assemblies to defray the burden of defence.

Convinced that the task of defending the Empire in the western hemisphere was an inescapable metropolitan responsibility, the British government decided to impose a range of new taxes on the colonists. The additional customs duties of 1764 were part of an established, though unpopular, pattern, but the Stamp Act of the following year, which placed a tax on much legal paperwork as well as upon the publication of newspapers, broke new ground and, either through poor judgement or intransigence on Britain's part, bore down most heavily on some of the most influential, opinion-forming sections of colonial society, lawyers, newspaper owners, journalists, writers and the like.

Having thus enraged the eighteenth-century equivalent of the chattering classes, the British proceeded, in fits and starts, and not without bouts of indecision and even repentance, to impose additional taxes. They also tightened up their control over smuggling (a flourishing American undercover industry) and the issuing of paper currency, as well as pushing through legislation for the billeting of regular troops in colonial households.

By the time of the Declaration of Independence in 1776 most of the offensive taxes had been withdrawn and those that remained had ceased to excite controversy. Higher, or more innovatory, taxes, then, were not the direct cause of the revolutionary war.

Nor was the war due to Britain's denial of the colonists' demand for proper constitutional representation. The slogan 'No taxation without representation' was a plausible but essentially dishonest rallying cry. The colonists were, in any event, represented in the colonial assemblies – the rub was that they had refused to vote extra taxes through these bodies and had instead had them imposed from Westminster.

As for representation in the Parliament at Westminster, the colonists simply did not want it, even though during the 1754 discussions of the Albany plan – a proposal which to some degree anticipated the Commonwealth ideal that was established over a century later – the British had seemed to be willing, even eager, to offer it to them. Colonial reluctance to be represented in an imperial legislative assembly some 3,000 miles away from their constituents was perfectly understandable; quite apart from the problems of communication more than a hundred years before the invention of the telegraph, to be incorporated into an imperial parliament would threaten the determination of the colonists to remain as free as possible from central metropolitan control – indeed, a similar determination on the part of the self-governing colonies was later to wreck the proposals for imperial federation at the end of the nineteenth century.

What caused the final, even if erratic, descent to open confrontation and war was the erosion and breakdown of the old, relatively undemanding arrangement between the colonial elites and the British authorities. The more the British Crown and Parliament became associated with higher taxes and more restrictive and controlling legislation – the most resented described as the 'Intolerable Acts' – the more antagonised and obstructive the colonial oligarchies became.

The Quebec Act of 1774 seemed to many colonial citizens to be the final insult: not merely was a large area of unsettled land to the south and west of the Great Lakes – territory that American colonists legitimately perceived as open to their penetration and settlement – attached to Canada, but the Act allowed Catholics to hold office and also recognised the French Catholic Church in Canada. The purpose of the Quebec Act was plain: the government wanted to reconcile the large French-speaking population of the new colony to British rule, or at least to neutralise them, and thus to avoid a repetition of the Irish imbroglio, where a largely disaffected subject people might rise in revolt at an inconvenient time. To the overwhelming majority of American colonists, with their Protestant and Puritan faiths, and their traditions of dissent and anti-popery, the Quebec Act seemed an affront; soon New England pastors were warning their congregations that 'the Scarlet Whore [of Rome] would soon get mounted on Her Horned Beast in America, and, with the Cup of Abominations in her hand, ride triumphant over the heads of true Protestants'.

Into the political vacuums created by the widespread lapsing of the cooperation and collaboration between the colonial upper classes and their metropolitan rulers pushed American radicals like Samuel Adams. By leading the mob against both a distant British monarchy and an indigenous oligarchy, the radicals were able to bid for, and often seize, local political power.

In this great dislocation of the long-standing and self-interested arrangement between the colonial power-brokers and the British authorities may be witnessed one of the enduring themes of imperial history. From Ontario to the Punjab, from Northern Nigeria to Cape Colony, the wheels of the complex, often ill-designed machinery that enabled the Empire to function were oiled by the various forms of collaboration and accommodation between local elites and their British overlords.

In the 'old' thirteen mainland colonies war did not occur during the uproar over the 'unfair' taxes of the 1760s because the colonial professional, landed and middle classes, despite the misgivings that many of them felt, were still in control of local populations and not ready or willing for a final break with Britain. From the mid-1770s the political landscape had altered dramatically, and in many colonies power had passed to a new, often radical leadership that saw positive advantages in the overthrow of British authority.

Even within the changed climate only a minority of colonists actively pressed for an open revolt or demanded independence. If Britain had capitulated to colonial demands and withdrawn, or substantially modified, the 'Intolerable Acts' of 1774, the sporadic fighting in Massachusetts and the raising of a colonial army a year later might have been avoided. But rather like the pattern of events during the Irish Home Rule crisis of the mid-1880s, potential concessions by the British government were represented as an unacceptable capitulation by powerful interest groups. Thus the possible repeal of the 'Intolerable Acts' was denounced as an abject surrender of royal authority, just as the Irish Home Rule Bill of 1886 was condemned as an example of British folly and weakness that would lead, through the establishment of a dangerous, even subversive precedent, to the collapse of the Empire.

As a consequence, the moderate, non-revolutionary leaders in North American society were denied a plausible and solid platform from which to rally the largely silent majority of colonists. How great an opportunity was missed can be gauged by the extent to which internal and inter-colonial divisions threatened to wreck the revolutionary and nationalist cause. Up to 1776 the American Continental Congress was often a battleground between those who wanted a complete break with Britain and those who wanted further negotiations. Even the Declaration of Independence was the product of bitter debate and compromise.

The War of Independence drove many moderates into the revolutionary camp. It also provided Britain's worsted imperial rivals, France, Spain and the Netherlands, with a heaven-sent opportunity for a war of revenge and restitution. Despite the military and strategic ineptitude of British generals, despite supply lines that, in the last resort, were stretched over the 3,000 miles of the North Atlantic, despite the failure effectively to build upon the various enclaves of loyalist support, Britain lost the war not through the tenacity of the rebels, both politically and in the field, but finally through the intervention of revengeful European powers.

France's entry into the war in February 1778 was the turning point.[5] Within two years Spain and the Netherlands had also given their support to the embattled colonists. As a result, the Royal Navy's blockade of colonial ports was broken and Britain's supply routes disrupted for long enough to allow the Americans to regroup and win their decisive victory under George Washington at Yorktown in 1781.

The resignation of Lord North as Prime Minister in February 1782 removed from power a British leader associated with the hard line towards the American colonists, and opened the way to peace negotiations. At the final peace treaty signed at Versailles in September 1783, Britain recognised the independence of the sovereign United States of America.

There were many on both sides of the Atlantic who regretted the violent separation of two kindred people with apparently far more to keep them together than to set them at each other's throats. The Whig parliamentarian and political philosopher Edmund Burke had argued tellingly that 'A great empire and little minds go ill together,' and went on to assert that 'Magnanimity in politics is not seldom the truest wisdom'. Thomas Jefferson wrote somewhat ruefully in the first draft of the Declaration of Independence that 'We might have been a great and free people together.' Certainly the projected American Union, even proto-Commonwealth, envisaged in the abortive 1754 Albany Plan, drawn up by a committee that included Benjamin Franklin, might well have kept the rebellious colonies within the imperial fold for another fifty, perhaps even a hundred, years.

In Britain, the loss of the American colonies provoked prophecies of doom in some quarters. Lord Shelburne, shortly before becoming First Lord of the Treasury in July 1782, had argued that if the Americans won independence 'the sun of Great Britain is set, and we shall no longer be a powerful or respectable people'. The novelist Horace Walpole believed that England was destined to become little more than a province of France.[6] Joseph II of Austria thought that England was now 'a second-rank power like Sweden and Denmark'.[7] British merchants and statesmen feared a loss of trade, economic decline and depression.

None of this happened. The emergence of an independent United States and the rapid expansion of an American economy unencumbered by imperial trade restrictions, legislative oversight or demands for military support, meant that Anglo–American trade boomed as never before. The victorious ex colonists seemed almost to be competing with each other to see who could buy most British goods. The factories and workshops of Britain's fast-growing industrial base stepped up production to meet the increased demand from the United States market.

The truth is that Britain's commercial and industrial, and hence in important respects her imperial, needs were fundamentally shifting even before the American Revolution. The settlement colonies of the western Atlantic seaboard were becoming less important than British colonies, possessions and trading connections in India and the East. At home, the agricultural and industrial revolutions were reordering Britain's priorities in her external relations.[8] The old mercantilist theories, with their superstructure of controls and trade regulations – similar to those that had pushed the Americans towards revolt – were coming under increasing attack. At the end of the century the future Prime Minister, Lord Palmerston, was sent to Edinburgh University specifically to study Political Economy, and to imbibe the free-trading theories taught there by Professor Dugald Stewart, a friend of Adam Smith.[9]

Mercantilism, although it took an inordinately long time to die, was on the way out, and free trade was on the way in. This process both stimulated and was the result of the spread of what has been described as 'the imperialism of free trade'.[10] Formal political control, in many parts of the world, was deemed less important than the successful penetration of British exports and capital. Although, inevitably, political pressure was applied in varying degrees to client states and local rulers, from Argentina to China, these territories were not annexed to the British Empire.

This was just as well in view of what remained under British rule and of the steps that were taken to incorporate new territories into the Empire after the American Revolution. William Pitt, the younger, who became Prime Minister in the immediate aftermath of the American débâcle, set about reconstructing Britain's relations with her most important imperial holdings. Although the colonies in the Caribbean were left to get on with the management of their faltering slave- and sugar-dominated economies without any undue interference in their American-style colonial constitutions, within which the planter-controlled assemblies were the linchpins, the two most important remnants of British North America were not so fortunate.

In 1791 the Canada Act bestowed on the newly defined provinces of Upper and Lower Canada what was claimed to be a model of the English constitution. The claim was spurious. In neither Upper Canada (English-speaking Ontario) nor Lower Canada (French-speaking Quebec) was the executive branch of government responsible to the legislative assembly. Despite this the two Canadas were to survive until the Durham Report and the 1840 Act of Union.

Elsewhere in British North America the colonies of Newfoundland, Nova Scotia, Prince Edward Island and New Brunswick continued to develop, and by 1790 Spanish claims to the coast of what was to become British Columbia had been pushed aside. With the establishment of Vancouver, and the progress of colonists into the virgin lands to the east of the Great Lakes, the outlines of a new trans-continental North American empire had been drawn.

In India, too, Pitt asserted a significant measure of metropolitan oversight. The India Act of 1784 established the dual control of East India Company and British government in a partnership – admittedly an increasingly unequal one – that was to last until the great sepoy revolt of 1857. As compensation to the Company, 1784 also saw the passing of the Commutation Act that drastically reduced the duties on China tea from 120 to 12.5 per cent, thus boosting the East India Company's income by stimulating a huge increase in tea imports. British holdings in India were to expand dramatically, through conquest and treaty, over the next seventy years.

Further east, the great, sweeping voyages of Captain James Cook had opened up the Pacific Ocean, particularly in the south, to commercial, missionary and settler activity. In 1788 the First Fleet, its holds packed with convicted felons, had landed at Sydney Cove in what was to become the colony of New South Wales, and eventually, once the name had been generally accepted, Australia. The two islands of New Zealand had also been charted.

Less than a decade after the abject and humiliating ending of the war with the American colonies, Britain had thus reasserted its claim to a global commercial, naval and imperial supremacy. In this context, the loss of the United States to the British Empire seems at worst an awkward but largely irrelevant stumble, and at best a liberation of energies that could now be directed to more distant, less perplexing, and very possibly more profitable imperial and national goals.

This process was to be immeasurably enhanced by Britain's involvement in the wars against France and her allies between 1792 and 1815. It is clear that 'the French Wars saw the greatest expansion of British imperial dominion since the creation of the colonies of settlement in Ireland and America in the seventeenth century'.[11] What is more, the acquisitions and conquests of these years laid the foundations for the massive territorial expansion of the Empire during the Victorian era.

If it can be claimed that this imperial progress was to any degree precipitated by the American colonial revolt, the British Empire, and those who supported and managed it, were greatly in the revolutionaries' debt.

3

AUSTRALIA

The First Fleet of 1788, and the Subsequent
Settlements; Gold, Wool and Responsible Government

WITHOUT THE LOSS of the American colonies there would have been
no First Fleet sailing into Botany Bay in 1788. This was not simply an
act of imperial reparation and reconstruction, the replacing of one lost
possession by another. In any case, the empty and unpromising terrain
of New South Wales was hardly a satisfactory substitute for the
expanding markets, burgeoning population, increasing wealth and continental prospects of the new United States of America.

Quite simply, from 1783 the Old Thirteen, especially the colonies of
the deep south, were no longer available as the receptacles for Britain's
criminal transportees. But British jails and prison hulks remained full
of convicted felons, and enlightened opinion still regarded transportation, for life as it mostly turned out, to be a progressive way of ridding
the country of unwanted elements who might even flourish in their new
environment once they had served their sentences there. Although
critics of the system argued that it was ridiculously extravagant, and
that for less cost per man and woman the convicts could be clothed in
velvet and fed on beef and claret in London's Strand, the Prime Minister, William Pitt, assured the House of Commons in 1791 that 'No
cheaper mode of disposing of convicts could be found.'[1]

The first convicts who were landed on the wild shores of New South
Wales doubtless felt a mixture of dread, bewilderment and relief. Their
eight-month voyage, with all its hazards and – especially for the 180
female convicts aboard – abuse, was now mercifully at an end. On the
other hand, their exile to this uncharted colony on the other side of the
world seemed permanent, if not terminal. The future held nothing but
hard labour, vile rations and all the iniquities of an unremittingly brutal
penal system. The cat of nine tails, the chain gang and the unrestrained

29

sexual demands of their overseers and their stronger, more dominating fellow prisoners were scarcely enviable lots.

Transportation was to continue for over half a century, and convictism was to survive in Western Australia until 1867. During that time the Australian colonies were to receive hundreds of thousands of free immigrants, and to be the subject of daring, if not always successful, experiments in social engineering – as in the 'systematic colonising' plans of Edward Gibbon Wakefield, where attempts were made to plant model colonies with balanced social structures and land available at affordable prices. They were also to see some of the world's most hectic and dramatic gold rushes, and the establishment of a vast sheep-farming industry whose wool kept the mills of Bradford and Halifax turning.

Australia also became a multifaceted and potent symbol. It was where men and women of ambition and determination could go for a better life, and where moreover they could, with luck, make their fortunes. Nor did one have to be an upright citizen at home to succeed in the great southern continent. Both the feckless and barely honest Mr Micawber in Dickens's *David Copperfield* and the escaped, possibly cannibalistic, Magwitch in *Great Expectations* flourished in Australia. It was thus a land of hope and, even for the most wretched, a place that offered at least the prospect of redemption.

But Australia had a dark, ominous symbolism as well. In April 1790 a British officer complained that 'the country . . . is past all dispute a wretched one'. Early paintings of the landscape frequently showed a gloomy, darkling hinterland quite at variance with the sun-drenched country perceived by later observers. Peopled with the rejects and outcasts of Georgian Britain, the continent seemed an accursed place. The gods who dominated the culture and landscape of Europe were totally absent. In their place, the first British settlers discerned demons: the cockatoos were thought to squawk with the voices of devils; the bush was believed to exude miasma.[2]

Although Australia's indigenous inhabitants, the Aboriginal tribes – described as 'black fellows' – had their gods, they were inaccessible to the white colonists. Europeans, moreover, considered the Aboriginals to be the most uncivilised and miserable of beings; lacking the most basic inventive and organisational powers, filthy in their habits, barbarous in their superstitions, ludicrously backward in their treatment of illness, and virtually beyond redemption. Hunted as animals, poisoned like mad dogs, befuddled by the white man's alcohol, their women treated as universally available sexual objects, the 'black fellows' were soon consigned to the sidelines and slums of Australian history. Even the convicts could despise them. Indeed the vehemence with which they were condemned and ridiculed probably owed a great deal to the need of the transportees to find human beings worse off and lowlier than themselves.

The dark image of Australia also sprang from the 'unspeakable' sexual practices associated with chain gang and prison shed. Denied access to female company, the majority of convicts had to choose between celibacy and homosexual activity. This became one of the most closely guarded secrets of British colonial history.[3] Almost without exception, official accounts of the penal settlements, and of the frequent outbreaks of violence and revolt, fight shy of the subject of convict homosexual practice. In 1846 Gladstone, as the Secretary of State responsible, dismissed the Governor of Van Diemen's Land, which contained the notorious reformatory at Port Arthur, where 'all degrees and grades of juvenile vice grinned, in untameable wickedness', at least in part because he had been unable either to suppress the endemic homosexual activity or to keep it quiet.[4] When during 1846–47 a Parliamentary inquiry was eventually undertaken into homosexual activities in the Australian colonies not all of the evidence was published.[5]

The felons themselves, with some notable exceptions, chose not to advertise the commonplace practise of homosexuality. This owed much to the prevailing revulsion felt for 'unnatural vice', but was also a reflection of the brutal nature of many of the sexual encounters. Buggery was to convictism what money was to free society. It was associated with power and control, the prerogative of the overseer or of the entrenched old lags. Newly arrived prisoners, especially if youthful and unbroken, were routinely raped. Youths sold themselves for the protection of a stronger man, for tobacco or even for food. English transportees were more likely to be involved than Irish ones, thus adding another, intriguing dimension to the ancient confrontation. The homosexual experiences of so many of the prisoners left a further dark stain on the convict population of Australia, and made the acknowledgement of such origins even more difficult for later generations.

The early Australian colonies were viewed as a thankfully far-flung imperial dustheap for other reasons. Quite simply they were the places where, for over half a century, what was perceived as the rubbish and the excrement of society were unceremoniously dropped. If Georgian and early Victorian statesmen, many of them reformers, saw the great migrations of impoverished British citizens to the United States and the colonies as simply 'shovelling out the paupers', expelling convicted felons was an even more abrupt and dirty business.

In Australia, moreover, as one early observer put it, 'all nature seemed reversed'. The trees shed their leaves in the summer, or all the year round. The seasons ran on opposite, contrary timetables to those experienced in Britain. The wildlife was freakish and bizarre when compared with that of any other known continent: kangaroos, wombats and wallabies were marsupials, and the duckbilled platypus laid eggs but still suckled its young. When explorers began to push into the hinterland of the country they came across rivers that flowed, intriguingly and unnaturally, inland, away from the sea, not towards it.

It was little wonder, therefore, that the convicts, and indeed many free settlers, landed on the 'fatal shore' with much foreboding. The settlers' predictable and backbreaking labours to establish themselves were complicated by an environment in which few of the European certainties existed: the skies at night contained strange constellations, the trunks of trees were so hard that they broke axes, and European grain, cast onto the ground, often failed to grow or withered and died on the stem. The introduction of European livestock sometimes wrought havoc with the environment: sheep grubbed up the roots which had sustained the Aborigines for millennia; rabbits, rather like the settlers themselves, colonised the countryside, and ate their way up the east coast to such devastating effect that Queensland eventually fortified its frontier with a high wire fence.[6] Hunger was one of the early threats to the successful establishment of a British colonial society, and several settlements had to be rescued by emergency shipments of food from the more established parts of New South Wales.

The convicts were guaranteed their rations, but little else. As they trudged ashore in their leg-irons to join the chain gangs or to be swept up by settlers hungry for their labour, many of them must have despaired of ever seeing civilisation again, for their exile seemed hopeless and endless, and in a Georgian equivalent of outer space. To find their way home was a dream which many abandoned from the outset, although others entertained fantasies of escaping across the mountain ranges that fringed the coastal settlements, beyond which, so the rumours had it, lay China.

The transportation of convicts to New South Wales continued until the first years of the reign of Queen Victoria. In 1840 the system was ended in the colony, although it lasted another thirteen years in Van

Diemen's Land, and longer elsewhere. Transportation ceased chiefly due to the opposition of reforming critics in Britain, growing antagonism to the practice among Australian free settlers, and, more pragmatically, because a prison-building programme at home meant the United Kingdom could adequately house the convict population. In addition, the discovery of gold in the early 1850s dramatically boosted immigration to the southern continent, rendering convictism as a source of labour supply obsolete. As a contemporary laconically observed, why spend large sums of money sending felons to a land 'to which free men were clamouring to go of their own accord'?

By the time transportation to New South Wales ceased, however, it had left a dark smear upon Australian development. This shadow was not officially lifted until 1867, when convictism was ended in the last colony to practise it, Western Australia. In effect it lingered, like a bad odour, for many decades. As late as 1918 Mary Gilmore's poem reminding her readers of the fact that Australia had been built upon convict labour seemed a daring statement:

> *I was the convict*
> *Sent to hell,*
> *To make in the desert*
> *The living well.*
>
> *I split the rock.*
> *I felled the tree –*
> *The nation was*
> *Because of me.*[7]

Predictably, all manner of early colonial ills were laid at the door of the convict system. These complaints had more substance when the convicts were assigned to settlers as servants or labourers or, when on remission, were allowed to live in private lodgings. The squalor of the shanty towns that sprang up like fungus on the perimeters of fast-growing urban areas like Sydney, Melbourne and Perth, the all-too frequent recourse to hard liquor, the inevitable growth of prostitution, idleness and insubordination were all at various times blamed upon convicts and convictism.

It was also vehemently argued that free immigration was seriously inhibited by the transportation of felons. Not only did free labour find itself undercut, but a society so heavily dependent upon a large convict population (by 1840 there were over 56,000 transportees in New South

Wales and Van Diemen's Land alone) could not be considered a fit place for women and children.

It was undoubtedly the case that, at least up to 1840, the overwhelming majority of emigrants from Britain chose to cross the Atlantic rather than sail for the South Seas. But this trend reflected the pattern whereby migrants sought out those communities where success seemed more assured, and where familiar institutions had long been in place. Many of Britain's emigrants in the first decades of the nineteenth century came from famine-stricken Ireland, which was a further reason why the independent American republic was easily the more favoured destination.

Conscious of the deterrent to free emigration presented by convictism, various authorities did their best to lighten the problem. Reformers claimed that many convicts were spiritually saved even while on the high seas. The transport vessels were loaded with bibles, prayer books and tracts, and reading matter (for those convicts who could read, that is) included such uplifting and cautionary works as *Exercises Against Lying*, *Exhortations to Chastity* and *Dissuasions from Stealing*. It is unlikely that great inroads into the convicts' souls were made by such methods. But the Anglican Church and later the Catholic Church made staunch efforts to improve and edify. The Anglicans, moreover, as the established Church, were active in early educational endeavours. But the large numbers of Irish transported during the first half-century of Australian development gave the Catholic Church a role out of proportion to its contemporary standing in England or the United States. A Roman Catholic see was set up in Australia in 1835, and government assistance was extended to all religious bodies for church building, ecclesiastical salaries and so forth.

The great majority of convicts came from the impoverished and criminalised classes of both urban and rural Britain: pickpockets from Seven Dials as well as sheep muggers and cattle duffers from the West Country. Most of them, at least after 1815, had been transported for fairly serious crimes. But there were notable exceptions to this, particularly the political offenders like the Tolpuddle Martyrs of 1834, assorted Chartists, and rebels from the Canadian disturbances of 1837.

In addition, the continuing unrest and sporadic, violent political crises in Ireland resulted in a substantial amount of transportation from that country. The apparently savage sentences passed on Irishmen who had disobeyed curfew restrictions often reflected the establishment's need to make an example of potential rebels and the suspicion that such offenders were more than likely involved in clandestine and seditious political activities. In this way thousands of dragons' teeth were sown in the hot red soil of Australia, liable to spring up, fully armed, at inconvenient times in the future: during the conscription crisis of 1917, for example, or in the republican movement of the 1990s.

Serious thought was given to the need to promote adequate free migration. Several theorists of well-organised free settlement emerged. Among the more influential of these was the radical Edward Gibbon Wakefield, who advocated a system of 'systematic colonisation' for the Australasian continent. In his writing during the 1840s, Wakefield argued that a successful process of colonisation was dependent upon achieving a harmony between capital and labour and between the different classes of settler society. Thus unoccupied Crown land should be sold in order to finance the appropriate number, and class, of immigrant; once ashore, settlers should be prevented, by force if necessary, from occupying land at random; the administration should keep a firm control over the price of land.

Since private companies dominated the market in the face of government reluctance to get too deeply embroiled in the business of overseas migration, Wakefield's theories were finally given expression in the formation of the South Australia Company and the New Zealand Company. But it proved impossible at such a distance, and in an age so committed to *laissez faire*, effectively to control the process of settlement. Immigrants often asserted their own priorities and needs once they were disembarked, and the Crown was frequently wayward and inconsistent over the crucial matter of land prices. Wakefield despaired at the ensuing confusion, and resigned from the South Australia Company. The settlement, however, survived its early crises and eventually flourished. In New Zealand, the Wakefield initiative was more clearly successful, profoundly affecting the colonisation process in both North and South Islands.

During the early 1840s British emigration to the Australian colonies averaged 15,000 a year, achieving the exceptional total of 33,000 in 1841. This was still small-scale when compared with emigration from the United Kingdom to the United States, but sufficient, at least in the medium term, to guarantee that the great southern continent would remain coherently British in character. By 1842 the population of the parent colony of New South Wales numbered 160,000. By 1859 there were also strongly established settlements in the now independent daughter colonies of Victoria and Tasmania (as Van Diemen's Land had become). South and Western Australia had still to find their feet, and the Northern Territory was a distant and uncharted wilderness.

Two developments above all else secured Australia's future during these years. The first was the enormous success of sheep farming. The staple wool of most of Australia's flocks was ideal for the British woollen industry, and the mills of West Yorkshire and beyond were apparently insatiable. In 1821 the poundage of Australian wool sent to Britain was 175,000, but by 1850 over 39,000,000 pounds were exported 'home', about half of the nation's imports of wool.

The second important boost to the Australian economy was the discovery of gold. The early 1850s witnessed the great Australian gold rush. A gold strike near Bathurst in New South Wales in 1851 began a process that had already been established a couple of years earlier in California, and was to be repeated in other parts of the English-speaking world, most momentously in South Africa after 1886. The feverish excitement and speculation that accompanied the Australian gold strike of 1851 transformed the lives of thousands, although not always for the better. Men left loved ones, left their homes, abandoned jobs and a host of responsibilities to journey to Australia, where, beside some godforsaken creek, sluicing watery gravel through their pans, they might just be lucky enough to find some fragments of the precious metal.

Boatloads of fortune-hunters landed in Victoria, making for the now legendary gold towns of Ballarat and Bendigo. In September 1852 more than 19,000 people landed at Melbourne alone, and the colony's total of immigrants during that year reached 95,000, a sevenfold increase on the previous annual average. Although very few actually made their fortunes from prospecting for gold, a good number made a living, and some an exceptionally good living, out of the ancillary activities of the gold rush – land speculation, the provision of food, liquor, clothes, equipment and transport.

Wool and gold were potent stimulants to the Australian economy. The success of the wool industry from 1830 was the main reason why large-scale investments of private British capital began to be made in the Australian economy. The City of London also waxed enthusiastic, giving strong financial support to various emigration and land development schemes fostered by private companies and by government agencies. British banks sprang up in Australia, and for a time threatened to eliminate their local colonial competitors.

The discovery and export of gold from the early 1850s guaranteed the success of the Australian economy throughout the nineteenth century. Between 1850 and 1890, apart from some minor setbacks, the economy grew at the rate of 5 per cent each year, markedly higher than the British average. Britain, as late as 1912, took 40 per cent of Australia's exports and supplied half of her imports. The dependency of the Australian economy upon the British connection in particular, and upon the fluctuations of world trade in general, was, however, a fair-weather phenomenon. Global trade depressions, or a faltering in the levels of British industrial activity, could theoretically wreak havoc upon an economy so heavily reliant upon international commerce. As it happened, the Australian economy showed sufficient resilience during the nineteenth century to avoid such embarrassments. Capital and labour continued to flow strongly into the country.

The success of sheep farming and the great gold rush of the 1850s transformed Australia in ways other than purely economic. As the sheepmen ran their flocks upon land that the Crown claimed as its own, a bitter dispute arose over the price of such land. With the demand for wool soaring, many sheepmen simply defied the imperial authorities and appropriated the large tracts of land they needed for their sheep runs. Soon the 'squatters', as they were known, were lobbying the woollen textile industry in Britain and their bankers to bring the government to its senses. A substantial and sympathetic agitation at home soon produced a compromise. The squatters had rejected the authorities' demand for £1 per acre. Instead they were able to obtain leases for the land they required at a rent of £2.10s. for each thousand head of sheep. The land was theirs until somebody was able to offer the purchase price of £1 per acre, and even then they retained the right of pre-emption. The fence also made its appearance; constructed to delineate the white man's property, it was unknown to the Aboriginals, and often cut off, or at least obstructed, their access to their places of traditional worship. Another typically restrictive artefact of Anglo-Saxon civilisation and control was thus imposed.

The goldfields, too, had been the scene of a confrontation between colonists and the British authorities. Licences to dig cost thirty shillings a month, but the majority of miners managed to avoid payment. The local police, often brutal and corrupt, and significantly known as 'the traps', were charged with enforcing the payment of the licence fees. In December 1854 the dispute led to an armed confrontation at Ballarat between miners barricaded behind the Eureka stockade and the armed police and regular soldiers sent against them. In the fighting, twenty-two lives were lost, seventeen of which were miners'. The diggers, though, won the campaign. Monthly licences were scrapped and an annual fee of £1 introduced instead. The miners' leaders were acquitted of high treason, earnest efforts were initiated to moderate police heavy-handedness, and local courts were set up on the goldfields to dispense justice quickly and cheaply.

What did the triumph of squatter and digger mean in terms of Australian history? The squatters became the substantial land-owners of the colonial hinterland, and, at least in theory, conservative pillars of society. Their mansions were built, both metaphorically and sometimes literally, upon the foundations of their wooden huts. Contemporary commentators were soon defining a 'squattocracy', rather as others were delineating a 'plantocracy' in the British Caribbean. But there was not much in the comparison. Australian 'squattocracy' was not a crude mirroring of the English landed gentry, which was still overwhelmingly Anglican and Tory, nor did it depend upon the labour of black ex-slaves amid falling commodity demand as in the West Indies. The Australian melting pot already contained too many Catholics, Dissenters, Irish and radicals for the former comparison, and the local economy was expanding too quickly and exhilaratingly for any meaningful parallels to be drawn with the failing economies and disjointed societies of the British Caribbean.

Moreover, the protracted struggle between the squatters and the imperial government over land ensured that the wealthy would not automatically side with the authorities. An early Governor of New South Wales, Lachlan Macquarie, appointed to the post in 1810, was suf-ficiently liberal and sensitive to see that the freed convicts, the 'Emanci-pists', must be incorporated into Australian society as full and respected citizens in order for the colonies to thrive. He also insisted on personally addressing the prisoners of each convict transport ship as it docked in Sydney, assuring his audience that they had arrived in 'a fine fruiteful [sic] country', and explaining 'what he will do for them if there [sic] conduct merits it'.[8] Although Macquarie's liberalism earned him enough hatred in New South Wales and Britain to ruin his career, he had firmly set Australia upon a democratic path.

The bloodshed at the Eureka stockade had similar democratic implications. It was the bloodiest battle ever fought between whites on Australian soil, and one of the formative episodes in the nation's history. Yet although there were socialists and revolutionaries at Eureka, some of them doubtless imbued with the passions aroused by the 1848 disturb-ances in many parts of Europe, the confrontation was not part of a concerted attempt to set up an egalitarian Australian republic. Rather it was an important component in the long and successful history of Antipodean trade unionism, a movement which also owed much to the comradeship of the shearing sheds and to the tradition of 'sticking by your mates'.

All the same, a unique, fiercely independent and sometimes awkward colonial persona was evolving in this brave new world set in the southern seas. He and she were the product of a past which was both shameful and glorious. They were self-sufficient and self-reliant, yet heavily dependent upon their seaborne connections with Britain and Europe. They were both scornful of Old World snobbery and pretensions and at the same time linked by a complicated emotional network to the 'Old Country'. They were used to hardship and the privations of frontier life, but also eager for the luxuries and artefacts of European civilisation. They could survive, as the Aborigines had survived for thousands of years, in the bush, even prosper there, yet they hankered for the cities and towns of the coast with their orderly, straight colonial streets. If they tended to set aside and ignore the Aborigines, they were at the same time deeply committed to social equality and to the 'fair go' for themselves. An Australian nation was being created, perhaps in an image that was unthinkable, even unacceptable, to those who decided that the First Fleet should make its landfall in 1788, one year before the outbreak of the French Revolution.

4

IRELAND

The Union of 1800; the Agitation for Home Rule
and its Partial Resolution; Problems of Identity as Both
Imperial Partner and Subordinate Nation

THE 1800 ACT OF UNION between Britain and Ireland was part of
the process of imperial consolidation and rationalisation that had begun
in the aftermath of the American War of Independence, and was to
include legislation regulating the East India Company's activities in
the sub-continent as well as constitutional reform in Canada. Arguably,
the 1800 Act simply tidied up a constitutional anomaly, the existence
of a separate parliament in Dublin that could provide an awkward
counterpoint to the power of the Westminster Parliament.

More realistically, the Union was a strategic imperative. The war
against France had once more demonstrated Ireland's potential for
causing trouble in England's back yard. The 1798 uprising of the United
Irishmen had been supported by the landing of a small French force of
little more than a thousand troops under General Humbert in County
Mayo. The rebellion of 1798, in which both Catholic and Protestant
Irish participated, was crushed brutally and swiftly by British troops
and loyal Irishmen. The French invasion force lit up the scene brightly
and briefly, like a falling star. But the lesson for the British government
was plain; and as a result the Irish parliament was swept away and
Ireland was incorporated into the United Kingdom. Ireland's Protestants, too, whether members of the elite, nation-wide 'ascendancy' or
of the both fearful and assertive 'majority' settlers of Ulster, were now
driven to accept the logic and inevitability of union with England, Wales
and Scotland. A new English-dominated 'British Empire in Europe'
was thus constructed.[1]

The Act of Union came into effect on 1 January 1801. Henceforth
Ireland was to be represented by her MPs sitting in the House of

Commons at Westminster, not in Dublin. To emphasise the permanence of this reform, the elegant building that had housed the Irish Parliament in Dublin was sold to the Bank of Ireland for £400,000. The Act of Union can be seen as a belated climax to the seventeenth-century strategy of planting Protestant settlers in Ulster in order to safeguard the official state religion, and to help prevent Ireland being accessible to enemies like Spain or France through Irish treachery. It was also a move which seemed to guarantee the property and standing of the Protestant ascendancy throughout the country.

Ireland's incorporation into the United Kingdom was also a brilliant stroke of propaganda. It gave the impression to those not able or willing to probe too deeply that the whole of Ireland was now admitted to a partnership with England based on equality of opportunity, if not of function and political weight. Rather like the Scottish and the Welsh people, the Irish were now minor shareholders in Great Britain Ltd. As long as they did not seriously challenge the overwhelmingly English-dominated management, they were encouraged to participate in the expanding economy as equals and to share in the fruits of Empire as traders, administrators and soldiers. Among the other, more questionable, benefits of their new constitutional standing were English guarantees of 'good' government, the maintenance of law and order, and internal stability. They could also expect, on the Scottish and Welsh models, to be more fully opened up to a programme of Anglicisation which was often presented as a desirable process of liberation, emancipation and development. The future so clearly belonged to the Anglo-Saxon race, on this analysis, that to be incorporated into the United Kingdom was a consummation most devoutly to be wished.

The advantages that would accrue from economic integration also seemed self-evident. Not merely had the Irish population grown rapidly during the eighteenth century, from roughly two and a half million in 1753 to nearly four and a half million by 1791, but there had been a resulting expansion of internal economic activity and production. Exports of Irish linen and wool to England grew substantially in volume, and Ireland imported more of the new-fangled and increasingly desirable products of Britain's factories and workshops. The Irish economy was also trading more briskly with the North American colonies, up to and beyond the American Revolution, and with both British and French West Indian possessions. During the 1760s and 1770s, for instance, up to three-quarters of Irish exports of beef went either to Britain's trans-Atlantic colonies or to France for re-exporting to her colonies. When the American crisis disrupted this trade in beef, the English market, driven by the rapid population growth, eagerly bought up the surplus.

By the time of the Act of Union the integration of the Irish economy with that of Britain and the colonies was at an unprecedentedly high level. Ireland's agricultural products, which had been excluded from Britain from 1688, were once more flowing strongly across the Irish Sea. By 1800, indeed, more than 85 per cent of all Irish exports went to Britain, as compared with only 46 per cent in 1700. As a result of this successful and profitable augmentation in Anglo–Irish trade, considerable numbers of Irish merchants settled in London and other British centres of commerce, thus providing another example of the phenomenon of 'gentlemanly capitalism', with its social and demographic intertwining. By 1790, moreover, nearly two-thirds of Ireland's national debt was lodged with British creditors.[2]

Ireland's increasing involvement with Britain in economic and commercial matters was manifested in other areas of activity. Irishmen served in Britain's armies and navies both through necessity and choice. The army in particular took a disproportionate number of Irish Catholic recruits escaping from rural poverty, famine and the ravages of English absentee landlordism as well as ill-treatment by indigenous landowners. In this sense, the British army was as important a refuge for Irish migrants as the United States or Australia. Kipling's writing bears copious and generally positive witness to the contribution of the Irish to the imperial armed forces:

> *My name is O'Kelly, I've heard the Revelly*
> *From Birr to Bareilly, from Leeds to Lahore,*
> *Hong Kong and Peshawur,*
> *Lucknow and Etawah,*
> *And fifty-five more all endin' in 'pore.*[3]

At a more exalted level, a series of officers originating in the Anglo-Irish Protestant establishment, from the Duke of Wellington to Field Marshal Montgomery a century and a half later, rose to the highest positions in the army. At the end of the nineteenth century three such men dominated the military pantheon: Sir Garnett Wolseley, Commander-in-Chief of the British army; Field Marshal Lord Roberts of Kandahar; and Field Marshal Lord Kitchener of Khartoum. The fact that men like these were drawn overwhelmingly from the Protestant ascendancy has served to camouflage the huge recruitment of Irish Catholics into the other ranks.

The enormous contribution of the Irish to the armed forces, and their generally enthusiastic participation in the expansion of the imperial economy and in the administration of Empire, was one side of the deep split in Ireland's identity from 1800 to the establishment of the Irish Free State in 1922. This, together with Ireland's position as a fruitful Mother Country in her own right, illustrated the complexities of establishing a clear Irish national character. Even the leadership of the Irish nationalist movement was bedevilled by such apparent contradictions: both Parnell and his successor Redmond were from Protestant backgrounds.

Yet Ireland was also a thorn in Britain's side. The scale of Irish poverty and disadvantage was one of the constant and painful facts of British political life throughout the nineteenth century. Famine and rural discontent, as well as the race memories of Cromwellian and subsequent oppressions, were all irritants in the Irish sore. The miracle is that, apart from some ameliorative social legislation, Irish discontent did not force the problem centre-stage until the Home Rule crisis of the mid-1880s. This curious state of affairs arose partly from a British political consensus, to which the Protestants of Ulster made a shrill and threatening contribution, that Ireland was being adequately governed – in any case far better governed than if power was devolved to the Irish themselves – and partly from the continuing perception of the strategic necessity of keeping the country out of hostile hands.

It must also be said that for much of the nineteenth century Irish Nationalist MPs at Westminster were generally conservative in their social and political outlooks, and not prepared to rock the ship of state in which they had found themselves for the most part so comfortably berthed. The novels of Trollope portray a variety of well-heeled Irish MPs included as an integral part of the fabric of Victorian society. This was at odds with vicious caricatures of the Irish peasantry in English cartoons and lampoons, where they were presented as illiterate and confused louts at best, as sub-human, porcine creatures at worst. The British need to ridicule the Irish grew more pressing as the demands of Irish nationalism became more assertive and uncomfortable.

To those who chose to see, Ireland after the Union was not simply an increasingly well integrated part of the United Kingdom. It was also a colony, and an abominably treated one at that. Victorian liberals did not need to travel, like their modern equivalents, to India or Africa to witness abject poverty and degradation or to see examples of man's inhumanity to man. They merely had to cross the Irish Channel. The progressive sympathies of imperial administrators like Sir George Grey and Sir John Pope Hennessy were quickened by what they saw in Ireland, particularly in her western provinces. The irony was, however, that it was Maoris, blacks in the Cape, and Hong Kong Chinese who were the chief beneficiaries of such tender proconsular consciences, not the native Irish. The horrors of the Irish famine years of the mid-1840s, attended as they were by starvation, disease and mass emigration, did not bring about a fundamental rethink in British policy towards Ireland. The most charitable explanation of this inertia was that the disaster was on such a scale that mere mortals could wash their hands of any responsibility and pass it off as the will of God.

But there were other compelling reasons why the 'Irish problem' waited so long for a solution. Part of the difficulty lay in the prevailing tendency to discern an 'Irish problem', rather than to see it as an 'English problem' or as a 'British problem'. In other words, the Irish Catholic majority had brought their troubles on their own heads through their pig-ignorance and their refusal fully to recognise the benefits bestowed by Anglo-Saxon supremacy. Worse still, the influence and power of the Catholic Church in Ireland increased substantially as the nineteenth century progressed. This seemed like an affront to a British establishment based so firmly on the 'liberating' ideology of the Protestant Reformation and on the intermeshing of capitalism and the Puritan work ethic. Popery was still equated with obscurantism and the stifling of the initiative of the individual.

Despite the number of royal commissions and committees of inquiry that were set up to examine the 'Irish problem', most British politicians managed to keep Ireland low down on their list of priorities. One difficulty was that very few Victorian statesmen of the first rank actually visited Ireland to see it for themselves. Palmerston, with his Irish peerage and his estates in Connaught, was an exception, but Gladstone, the belated champion of Irish Home Rule, only went once, and Disraeli, the apostle of 'one nation' politics, never set foot there.

There are obvious reasons why the British Parliament was never sufficiently or consistently galvanised by Ireland's difficulties. For one thing, the British, especially the English, upper orders were deeply involved in Ireland as landowners and landlords. For another, the inequalities in Ireland went so deep that only unacceptably radical measures could bring about fundamental change. Land redistribution held the key, but to put such policies into practice proved highly controversial, if not impossible. The Land Act of 1870 was sabotaged in Cabinet, and the Land Act of 1881, which was an attempt to stabilise rents, to provide more secure tenure and to allow tenants the right of sale, was attacked as an example of socialist brigandry. The historian W.E.H. Lecky even described it as 'one of the most questionable, and indeed extreme, violations of the rights of property in the whole history of English legislation'.[4]

Why Gladstone took the decision to legislate for Irish Home Rule during his 1880–85 premiership is a fascinating question. It certainly appeared at odds with at least two early formulations of his government's imperial policy: the refusal to restore independence to the Transvaal, until compelled to do so by the humiliation of British arms during the fighting that culminated in the triumph of the Afrikaners at the Battle of Majuba Hill in 1881; and the invasion of Egypt in 1882, which reasserted the control of the Anglo–French Suez Canal Company over that strategically significant waterway, and effectively gave Britain oversight of Egyptian affairs for three-quarters of a century.

It would be a mistake, therefore, to assume that Gladstonian high-mindedness, despite the rhetoric, was the main reason why Irish Home Rule forced its way to the top of the legislative agenda. It is evident that Gladstone's 1880–85 administration was riven by conflict and lacked coherence over wide areas of policy. It contained the pushy, demagogic Radical Joseph Chamberlain, as well as Whig grandees like the Marquess of Hartington. But these handy labels did not necessarily survive immersion in the scalding water of political crisis: Chamberlain proved a more ruthless imperial interventionist than several Cabinet colleagues on the right wing of the Liberal Party. As is so often the case, pragmatism not principle dominated the government's decision-making.[5]

Gladstone took the decision to push for Home Rule for Ireland because he had concluded that it would be hard enough to push his legislative programme through a fractious Cabinet with the Irish question still unanswered. Some bold legislative surgery would cut out the Irish canker and thus enable the government to put its energies into other business. It has also been argued that the socially conservative, even snobbish, Gladstone was alarmed at the rising tide of class-based politics, and hoped by presenting Irish emancipation as a noble cause, above the sordid world of political class-warfare, to plant the flag of contemporary Liberalism upon the high moral ground of late-Victorian statesmanship. The hope of neutralising the potentially disruptive, spoiling tactics of the more militant members of the Irish Nationalist Party in the House of Commons must have been an additional incentive. It might also prove expedient, in the virtually inevitable event of the Conservatives eventually regaining some of the parliamentary seats they had lost in the general election of 1880, for the Liberals to have the goodwill and support of the Irish Nationalist MPs.

The Gladstone government was able to present a coherent and honourable package for the solution of Ireland's ills. The 1881 Land Act was designed to restructure the chronically unstable and confrontational relationship between landlord and tenant, and thus to make an important contribution to economic and social reform. The Home Rule Bill would partly be built upon these reforms and would, in Gladstone's words, lift from Britain 'the enormous weight of the Government of Ireland unaided by the people'. When the Home Rule Bill was finally put before the Commons in 1886 during Gladstone's third administration, the Prime Minister, apart from claiming that the Bill's passage would lift a costly administrative burden from the Treasury, also, quoting Sir Charles Duffy, drew a telling parallel with the Canadian constitutional reforms of the 1840s: 'Canada did not get Home Rule because she was loyal and friendly, but she has become loyal and friendly because she has got Home Rule.'[6]

By comparison with Canada's constitutional reforms, however, Gladstone's Irish initiative ended in a tempest of violent political controversy. This cataclysm not merely illustrated the deep and unyielding prejudices against the Irish held in Britain, but also split the Liberal Party so profoundly that, whereas in the mid-1880s they had seen themselves as the 'natural party of government', after the Home Rule crisis they were unable to form a majority administration for twenty years.

The opponents of the Gladstonian Home Rule proposals tried to have it both ways. On the one hand, Joseph Chamberlain apparently saw Ireland as such an important and integral part of the United Kingdom that even the very modest devolutionary powers contained in the 1886 Home Rule Bill were presented as a dagger plunged into the heart of the body politic, and the beginning of the end of the British Empire. On the other, the opposition to Home Rule, from the mid-1880s to the First World War, included the insistent assertion that the Irish were completely unfit to govern themselves. In this overcharged and hysterical atmosphere the old porcine and sub-human caricatures were once again colourfully and irresponsibly brandished. The Irish were described as 'naughty children', as being as 'unstable as water', and as 'voluble, ineffective – not trustworthy in business'. Ireland was dismissed as 'a backwater spawned over by obscene reptiles', and the great historian J.A. Froude only supported Home Rule because it would 'shut the Paddies out from Westminster'.[7]

Irish nationalism stank not merely in the nostrils of Ulster Unionists, it was also an offence to many of those who cherished the vision of a world increasingly subject to Anglo-Saxon domination and control. In this global order, the last thing that Anglo-Saxon supremacists wanted was an unseemly devolutionary concession to what many regarded as the politically immature, fey, 'backward' forces of Irish nationalism. If Britain admitted that Ireland merited a measure of Home Rule, why should not Indian nationalists, whose allegedly feckless and unreliable qualities were so akin to those attributed to the Irish, demand a similar concession? If India was so treated, which colonial possession would be the next to follow suit? The Chamberlainite nightmare would become a reality.

In these ways, the Irish Home Rule crisis was a dress rehearsal for later confrontations with a variety of colonial nationalist movements. At the root of the conservative, overwhelmingly British, response to such pressure were the routine doubts, often sorrowfully expressed, as to the fitness of applicants for the adult responsibilities of self-government. The nationalist case was almost always further diminished by the imperial power projecting a host of undesirable characteristics upon the colonial people, or by simply infantilising them. When colonial nationalists protested, or, better still, raged, at such condescension, this was treated as further evidence of political immaturity.

The Act of Union of 1800 thus turned out to be a snare and a delusion. It was the British, particularly the English, who made up the rules of the game. When the Irish seemed about to gain an important victory in the game, the Crown-in-Parliament changed the rules. This happened most dramatically and tragically in 1914 when, with the Home Rule Act on the statute books, having passed through Parliament and having received the royal assent, the outbreak of the First World War allowed Britain to put the implementation of the measure into cold storage for the duration of the conflict. It was small wonder that before the end of the nineteenth century, some Irish Nationalist MPs took it upon themselves to act as spokesmen for nationalists in India and other parts of the Empire denied a voice at Westminster.

There was, of course, a compelling reason why British statesmen of both main parties fought shy of any final settlement of the 'Irish problem'. This was the sheer intractability of the Protestant minority, especially in the north of the country, in the face of what they insisted on seeing as the Papist tyranny implicit in a quasi-independent united Ireland. As long as Ireland was a united country within the United Kingdom their fears were contained and their security assured. The prospect of Catholic majority rule, whatever that might mean in practice (for there was no guarantee, even likelihood, that Catholic voters would act as a solid block at election time), unleashed a flood of fearful fantasies. Rather than submit to these imagined horrors, the Protestant militants declared that they would take up arms.

The dilemma for British policy-makers was acute. In effect, Irish Home Rule meant the abandonment of what has been described as 'the loyal garrison of one million' Protestants. Britain was trapped, not for the first or the last time, by the strategy of propping up imperial power with the support of collaborationist groups. But in Ireland there were two such groups: the Ulster Protestants and those Irish Catholics who were doing well out of the Union in economic, commercial or career terms. As long as both groups could be kept content, the Union was safe. But by the 1880s, encouraged by Gladstone's thrust for Home Rule, sufficient numbers of the Catholic establishment and its opinion-makers opted for the nationalist cause and ruined the collaborationist strategy.

Another imperial juggling act was about to end in indecision, disarray and confusion. In the case of Ireland, however, the British government could not simply walk away from the scene of the disaster, immediate or potential (as they were later to do in India, Palestine, Nigeria and many other colonial possessions), showing the world a clean pair of hands. Ireland was too close a neighbour, geographically, economically and culturally for that. In addition, the Ulster Unionists had enough political clout, underpinned by the threat of armed resistance, to force their needs upon almost any British administration. Also, the presence in the United Kingdom of hundreds of thousands of Irish Catholic immigrants, many of whom were voters in British elections, gave that constituency a voice that could be inconveniently raised at difficult moments.

In the end, in 1922, partition, as was later to be the case in India and Palestine, was the outcome. The solution to the 'Irish problem' was indeed surgery, but of a very different kind to that implied by the Gladstonian initiative of the 1880s. Ireland's 'problem' was not so much the Irish (though a good case can be made for defining the Ulster

Protestants as the 'problem') as the British, chiefly the English, and their self-serving strategies of plantation and subordination begun in the seventeenth century.

5

CANADA

The Rebellions of 1837; the Durham Report;
Responsible Government; Settlement and Expansion;
Inter-Colonial Rivalries; the 1867 Confederation

1837, THE YEAR OF Queen Victoria's accession to the throne, saw both her English-speaking and French-speaking subjects in revolt, the former in Upper Canada, the latter in Lower Canada. Upper Canada approximated to the present-day province of Ontario, while Lower Canada incorporated the province of Quebec. This constitutional innovation had arisen in the aftermath of the American Revolution, when the British government had attempted to tidy up its remaining North American possessions and at the same time keep both its French and British citizens relatively content by passing the Constitutional Act in 1791.

The principle of trying to keep the French-Canadians sweet was already a well-tried stratagem of British colonial policy. It had been central to the settlement in the aftermath of the British conquest of French Canada in the mid-eighteenth century. Indeed, many English-speaking North Americans, including subjects of the Old Thirteen colonies, had subsequently felt that the French of Quebec and Montreal were a cosseted, obstreperous, and even worse, Catholic, minority: a blot on the fair face of English-speaking, largely Protestant North America. The wisdom of the British authorities' strategy, however, seemed justified by events: the French-Canadians had remained quiescent, even loyal, during the American Revolution, with its potential for fomenting disaffection, disruption and chaos throughout the whole continent.[1]

The post-revolutionary years, however, had brought new pressures to bear. Perhaps the most powerful of these was the continuing migration of British citizens to colonial North America. During and after the American rebellion several thousand Empire Loyalists, either through choice or displacement, had made their homes in Ontario and the Maritime Provinces. The presence of these ultra-patriotic citizens, with their experience of the freer colonial representative institutions of the rebellious Old Thirteen, had indeed been an important factor in the decision to introduce the reasonably liberal constitutions of the 1791 Act. The question was, would the reforms be enough?

Beyond this rather narrow consideration lay the larger fact that during the early decades of the nineteenth century, years of mass emigration from Britain, tens of thousands of new citizens were deposited in the colonies of British North America. By contrast Quebec received very few immigrants. The population balance was now swinging irrevocably towards the English-speakers. There was nothing surprising about this development. It seemed an inevitable part of the domination of the whole of North America by English-speaking settlers. What it did provoke, however, was an increased interest in the constitutional structures of the remaining colonies in British North America.

In the context of the 1830s such interest was no mere whimsy. The highly charged controversy in Britain over the great Reform Act of 1832, which significantly extended the number of male voters and abolished anomalies like 'pocket boroughs', was a matter of keen contemporary concern. In France there had been another violent uprising in 1830, resulting in a new constitution and an allegedly 'Citizen King', Louis Philippe. Many new immigrants arrived in British North America with an abiding hatred of a harsh Old World system that had driven them from their Highland crofts, Irish cottages and English towns. They thus wanted not merely economic opportunity but the political emancipation that seemed crucial to their fresh start and to their need to exercise significant control over their new environment.

If Britain chose to be unsympathetic to such aspirations, there was a very real chance that revolts and separation could ensue. Some Canadian reformers were also quick to point out that absorption by the rapidly expanding United States was a real possibility. Others drew attention to the recent and successful rebellions in Spain's South American empire. In Lower Canada the grievances of Quebec were given clear expression in the speeches of Louis-Joseph Papineau, the Speaker of Lower Canada's House of Assembly and leader of the separatist Patriotes during the 1837 uprising. In Upper Canada, English-speakers argued that the provisions of the 1791 constitution were inadequate. Conflict between new and old-established economic and social-interest groups also played its part in fomenting discontent.[2]

The rebellions of 1837 were small-scale, of little military significance, and in the last resort almost farcical. Nonetheless they served their political purpose. The British government, led by Lord Melbourne, saw that something must be done to pacify Canada, and dispatched a commission under Lord Durham to report on the discontent and to recommend a solution. There were good reasons for selecting Durham, nicknamed 'Radical Jack', to lead the inquiry. He was associated with a group of statesmen and theorists described as the 'Radical Imperialists', and thus presumably acceptable to political dissidents in Canada. He had considerable personal poise and charm, a rigorous mind and great energy. As an aristocrat, possessing enormous private wealth, he could not be bought. More prosaically, he had proved to be an awkward and independent member of the Cabinet, and both the easy-going Melbourne and the cautious Lord John Russell were glad to see the back of him.

Lord Durham took with him on his mission two of the most constructive and brilliant of contemporary colonial thinkers, Edward Gibbon Wakefield and Charles Buller. The three men made a formidable team. The confidence and sweep of the final report made it appear a Magna Carta of colonial constitutional development, commanding respect and admiration for over a hundred years. It is only in the recent historiography of the British Empire that the significance of the Durham Report has been scrutinised and its shortcomings analysed.[3] It is certainly true that Durham did not single-handedly invent the concept of 'responsible government' as a model for imperial constitutional evolution that linked the Canada of 1837 with the post-1945 period of decolonisation. It is also evident that the British government chose to act on only some of his recommendations and ignored others.

Despite these important reservations, the report, which was published in 1839, by which time Durham was dying, provided a perceived watershed in the relationship between Britain and her colonies of settlement. The centrepiece of the Durham report was the recommendation that 'responsible government' should be extended to Canada. Hitherto 'representative government' had been the most advanced form of British colonial constitution, with a governor and executive council balanced against a legislature that was partly nominated and partly elected. This form fell short of the 'responsible' model, as practised in Britain, where the executive, the Cabinet, was responsible to, that is accountable to, the legislature.

The Durham report dismissed the representative constitutional form with the words 'it may fairly be said that the natural state of government in all [our North American Provinces] is that of collision between the executive and representative body'. The proposal was that in future the elected members of the legislature should be trusted to form an administration, in which the governor would play a part very like that of the king in a constitutional monarchy. Government ministers would be ultimately *responsible* to the legislative body. The Crown's authority would be enshrined in the position of the governor, although Whitehall and Westminster were expected to steer clear of attempting to interfere through the agency of the governor in colonial domestic affairs. Matters of imperial concern, such as constitutional amendment, foreign and commercial policy and the disposal of public lands, should be reserved for the discretion of the British government.[4]

The report also recommended the constitutional union of Upper and Lower Canada. This seemed to fly in the face of Durham's avowed commitment to preserving French majority rule in Quebec, and accorded ill with the enthusiasm with which he had been greeted when he visited that province. What the recommendation indicated was Durham's conviction, shared by many English-speaking contemporaries, that the future of North America belonged unequivocally to the Anglo-Saxon people. To many observers, the French-speakers of Quebec seemed an anachronistic, conservative group, heavily dependent upon agriculture and still clinging to its heritage from the *ancien régime*. It was also reckoned that once the commercial, technological and political talents of English-speaking Canadians were given full rein, the awkward lump of Quebec would be broken down and digested in the great, prosperous body-politic of British North America.

The Melbourne government, as governments are wont to do, acted on those bits of the report that seemed expedient. The Union of the two Canadas was enacted in 1840. Responsible government, however, was not introduced in the Union until the end of the decade, a little after its introduction in Nova Scotia. The irony of this development did nothing to detract from the high reputation enjoyed by the Durham Report in the history of the British Empire. As with the Melbourne government, imperial theorists, politicians and constitutionalists concentrated upon those aspects and implications of the report that they most needed and admired.

Over the decades, the report was invoked like a magic potion to cure all manner of colonial ills. It was used, justifiably in most cases, to advertise the advantages of conceding self-rule to those communities which deserved it, thus keeping them tidily, and inexpensively, within the imperial system. It was dusted down as the Boer War came to an end in order to assure policy-makers, wrongly, that the Afrikaners (as the French-Canadians allegedly had been in 1840) could be absorbed, and then assimilated, within a dynamic, expanding, commercially vibrant Anglo-Saxon-dominated state.

In one respect the Durham Report was an unqualified success. Lord Durham believed that if the changes that were recommended took place, then the political separation between Britain and Canada that seemed inevitable would not occur. That the United States wanted to incorporate the rest of British North America within the union is beyond dispute. The seventh article of the original United States constitution provided for the admission of Canada on special, undemanding terms, and active American interest in acquiring Canada was to last for most of the nineteenth century.

Equally, British statesmen wanted to keep Canada within the Empire. The value of the country's ship-building timber trade had defence as well as commercial importance, Halifax was a significant base for the Royal Navy, and the British North American merchant marine was the third largest in the world. The Earl of Elgin, Governor General of Canada between 1847 and 1854, conjured up an unwholesome spectre when he wrote: 'Let the Yankees get possession of British North America with the prestige of superior generalship – who can say how soon they may dispute with you the Empire of India and of the Seas?'[5] Durham had himself provided the antidote to such a fearful prospect by arguing that 'it can only be done by raising up for the North American colonist some nationality of his own; by elevating these small and unimportant communities into a society having some objects of national importance; and by thus giving their inhabitants a country which they will be unwilling to see absorbed even into one more powerful.'

Although interaction between citizens of the United States and British North America was a part of everyday life, especially across the long frontier which so artificially divided the continent against the logic of geography and topography, diplomatic relations in the aftermath of the Durham Report were troubled. The New Brunswick–Maine border dispute was settled in 1842, but there was continuing bickering over the partition of Oregon in the west and rivalry for control of the proposed Panama Canal. The aggressive characteristics of the United States, as illustrated in the war begun in 1848 against Mexico, also aroused Canadian doubts over whether union with their great southern neighbour would be as comfortable and profitable as its advocates insisted.

The 1840s were years that established a pattern in British North America that was to lead within thirty years to the emergence of a confederated Canada. The responsible system of government recommended for the two Canadas in the Durham Report was first introduced in Nova Scotia in 1848. The Union of Canada soon followed suit. By 1855 all of the eastern colonies had become responsible self-governing colonies within the British Empire. A year later the western seaboard colonies of British Columbia and Vancouver Island were set on the same devolutionary path.

For a while it was unclear whether these constitutional developments, which were also taking place in Australia, New Zealand and the Cape, implied that the ripe colonial fruit was about to fall from the imperial tree. When Britain scrapped the Corn Laws in 1846 and followed this up with the repeal of the Navigation Acts in 1849 – thus ditching legislation that propped up and symbolised the old protectionist trading system – the whole structure of commercial and fiscal protection that had bound together the component parts of the Empire from its beginnings disintegrated.[6] On both sides of the Atlantic there were those who predicted, sometimes gleefully, the break-up, or at the very least the radical restructuring, of the British Empire.

The introduction of free trade and of free political institutions therefore overlapped, and at first appeared to threaten the integrity of the Empire. In 1845 the Canadian Union responded to the new opportunities of the free-trade era by signing a reciprocal commercial treaty with the United States, even though the ratification of this innovatory agreement required the approval of the British Parliament and the royal assent. More revolutionary still was the Canadian government's decision in 1859 to impose a tariff on steel imports, the vast bulk of which came from Britain. When the British government, embarrassingly caught in a trap of their own construction, demurred, the Canadian Finance Minister, Alexander Galt, called their bluff. The tariff, he argued, was designed to protect the development of Canadian industry; if the British authorities chose to block the measure they must be prepared to administer the colony against the wishes of its people.

This amounted to a threat of greater dependence, not of independence. The British government and the steel lobby withdrew their objections. An important precedent had been established. Canada was not forced into a revolutionary political act. The trade connection with Britain continued to be of great importance, and British steel exports continued to increase. The imperial connection was preserved.

Within a few years of this crisis, British North America was actively considering the desirability of federation. Paradoxically, the movement sprang from diversity and difference rather than from coherence and solidarity. Strung out like a necklace of beads, the colonies stretched from Newfoundland in the east to Vancouver in the west. There were three and a half thousand miles between St John's, Newfoundland, and British Columbia. Everywhere provincialism was strong, sometimes bitterly so. It was not merely that the French separatists of Quebec and the Tories of Ontario hated each other; even within the Maritime Provinces there could be a neighbourly suspicion and distrust between (say) the inhabitants of Prince Edward Island and New Brunswick. How best could the nearly empty prairie provinces be developed, and what was the future of the great northern tract of territory, from the Arctic wastelands to the Rocky Mountains, that was still ruled by the Hudson Bay Company? Above all, how could a sense of nationhood be developed, when so many of the obvious links in North America ran north to south, across the frontier with the United States, rather than east to west?

By the early 1860s, however, the idea of union with the United States lost more of its appeal. Growing American hostility to the reciprocal trade treaty aroused doubts over the potential advantages to Canadian commerce of a closer association. Armed Fenian raids across the border alarmed and antagonised loyalists. The ferocity and bitterness of the American Civil War of 1861–65, a conflict fought principally to preserve the Union, revealed a nation riven by profound regional, economic and political divisions, and thus made the prospect of Canadian absorption into a Greater United States far less attractive. Worse still, the triumph of the North over the South rendered the Union, especially after the assassination of Abraham Lincoln, even more triumphalist and expansionist than before.

In these circumstances, the notion of a closer British North American constitutional relationship became markedly more popular. Ontario Tories made common cause with Quebec politicians, Radicals with Conservatives, New Brunswickers with Prince Edward Islanders. It was the Maritime Provinces which first proposed that the discussions for their own union should be extended to the other colonies. A conference in 1865 in Quebec approved the principle of federation, no doubt encouraged by British offers of financial help for the proposed trans-continental railway so essential to both inter-colonial trade and inter-colonial unity.

In 1867 Westminster passed the British North America Act, providing for the federation of Upper and Lower Canada, New Brunswick and Nova Scotia. Prince Edward Island joined the federation in 1873, and the mid-continental and western colonies at appropriate stages in their development, though Newfoundland retained its separate status until 1949.[7]

Despite Newfoundland's claim to be the oldest dominion, federated Canada was the first true dominion; indeed, until the definition of the term in 1907, the only dominion to have been created. Its emergence established a number of significant guidelines for the evolution of the self-governing colonial system and eventually of the Commonwealth – a term used increasingly from the 1880s – as a whole. First, the British not the American constitutional model had prevailed. The governor general represented the absent British monarch in a constitution that included an upper and lower legislature and an independent judiciary. Second, provincial legislatures and administrations were maintained within the confederation, but with their powers carefully defined and enumerated. In areas not enumerated, the central government in the new capital at Ottawa was to have the final word. Third, the constitutional settlement, though approved by the British government and encouraged by them, had arisen primarily out of local not imperial need. Fourthly, any amendments to the constitution were the prerogative of the British Parliament.

The federation was, predictably, not destined to be free of constitutional problems. Provincial governments were to haggle a good deal over their rights in relation to Ottawa.[8] Despite this, Canada became something of a model for the other self-governing colonies, and frequently acted as spokesman on their account at colonial conferences, especially when constitutional matters were being discussed. It has also been argued that it was the continuing success of the Canadian economy – rather than that of the post-1886, gold-rich Transvaal – that prompted Joseph Chamberlain so forcibly to advocate closer imperial economic union at the turn of the nineteenth century. Finally, Britain, the Mother Country, could now treat Canada as the eldest daughter in a rapidly growing imperial family, a kindred nation with whom to confer when it seemed useful and expedient so to do.

6

THE REPEAL OF
THE CORN LAWS IN 1846

The Economics of Empire

IN 1846 THE LEGISLATION which had hitherto artificially protected the price of British-grown wheat and grain was repealed. At the most basic level the move opened up the domestic market to cheaper and plentiful grain from the American prairies, Russia and whoever else could produce it at the right price. One immediate aim was to provide abundant and reasonably inexpensive food for the rapidly expanding British population and to alleviate the destabilising and increasingly unacceptable effects of hunger and want. The Irish famine years and the impact of the 'hungry forties' upon other parts of the United Kingdom, especially Scotland, also helped to drive the government led by Sir Robert Peel to introduce the reform.

The response to the repeal of the Corn Laws was complex and dramatic. The benefits of cheap bread to the consumers, particularly working-class families, were palpable, and became imbued with such potent symbolism that six decades later, when Joseph Chamberlain's tariff reform campaign seemed to threaten the voter with higher food prices, rival candidates held up examples of the 'big' and the 'small' loaf at the hustings in order to make their campaign points.

The reform also became associated with the scrapping of economic protectionism and with the introduction of free trade. The repeal of the Corn Laws breached the protectionist dam, and within eight years the two most weighty remaining portions of the obstacle were swept away, the Navigation Laws in 1849 and the Sugar Acts in 1852. The last traces of the system of fiscal protection were removed in Gladstone's budget of 1860. The free-market economy, now liberated from its anti-quated shackles, was expected to deliver food at a low enough cost to keep Britain's toiling masses adequately fed. It was anticipated that two advantages were to flow from this. First, the expansion of Britain's fast-developing industrial economy would be boosted by the availability of cheap food and the labours of a relatively fit and healthy workforce. Second, plenty, in terms of food, wages and full employment, would maintain the social order and keep revolutionary politics at bay. Rather than rising in revolt, the proletarian army of the British industrial revolution would march contentedly on full stomachs.

In the short term, however, the great reform of 1846 drastically changed the political landscape. The Tory Party split. Many of the landed interest were affronted by the repeal of the Corn Laws, and cried impoverishment. Some Tories connected with finance, trade and manufacturing, on the other hand, saw the advantages of the new order and supported Peel. A new political grouping, the Peelites, of which Gladstone was arguably the most distinguished younger member, forsook Toryism, the majority eventually becoming a component part of the Liberal Party. Largely as a result of the Tory split, the Liberals held power for the vast bulk of the period 1846 to 1874.

The introduction of free trade was of enormous significance both at a symbolic and theoretical level and in practical, concrete terms. In Manchester the grateful cotton-rich oligarchy even raised an elegant, Renaissance-style building, the Free Trade Hall, completed in 1856 on the site of the Peterloo 'massacre', and one of Britain's very few public buildings to be dedicated to a principle rather than to a person or a place. The reforms were, of course, based on the perceived self-interest of the increasingly dominant manufacturing industry and of those who invested in, or who worked for, this new and powerful lobby. Crudely put, 'King Corn' was on the way out, 'King Cotton and King Steam Engine' were on the way in. As was so often the case, however, the fiscal reforms were given a brilliant theoretical, even ideological, gloss.

Politicians and opinion-makers jostled to present an alluring picture of the benefits that would inevitably flow from the ending of protection. Peel asserted that 'Advance' must be the imperial watchword, and that the nation, standing as 'the chief connecting link between the old world and the new', would flourish in the invigorating climate of free trade and competition.[1] Thomas Babington Macaulay dramatically asserted in 1842 that if the Corn Laws were scrapped the British 'might supply the whole world with manufactures and have almost a monopoly of the trade of the world' while being kept supplied with 'abundant provisions' raised 'on the banks of the Mississippi and the Vistula'.[2] What would today be called the 'trickle-down' benefits of Britain's continuing global economic supremacy were taken for granted, and in Parliament free-trade enthusiasts painted a picture of a post-protectionist Britain 'stretching her dominion over the wants of the universe'.[3]

Free trade was also associated with various forms of freedom. This was partly due, naturally enough, to the use of the word 'free' in the description of what quickly became the new economic orthodoxy. But there were other, seductive connotations. Free trade came to mean, in the imaginations and the memories of countless numbers of British and imperial citizens, freedom from hunger, freedom from long-term mass unemployment, freedom from a whole range of practical uncertainties. The implementation of the reforms also coincided with the extension of responsible forms of government to many of the colonies of European settlement. Free trade and free political institutions seemed to be linked in a benevolent pattern that connected commercial expansion and prosperity with the devolution of constitutional freedoms to colonial peoples.

To a large extent these perceptions were delusions, or at least half-truths. Free trade was introduced primarily to liberate British commerce and industry from the legislative restrictions of the old colonial system established under the early Stuarts and Cromwell. It was also a vital part of a bid to bind the rapidly growing economy of the United States, as well as the economies of Spain's ex-colonies in Latin America, to British interests. Until after the Civil War, the United States continued to form part of a trans-Atlantic co-prosperity sphere in which Britain remained the senior partner. Not only was Britain the United States' most important market at the time of the repeal of the Corn Laws, it also exported the bulk of the manufactured commodities needed by the republic, including textiles, iron and steel ware and other products. British investment in the United States remained high in the quasi-colonial and expanding areas of cattle ranching and railway building. It seems clear that one major benefit to Britain of the introduction of free trade was that the British economy could extend and strengthen its links with the go-ahead states of the north and west at the expense of its old, colonial-style trading connections with the agricultural, slave-owning states of the mid and deep south.

This strategy had limited success. The triumph of the Union over the Confederacy in the Civil War was followed by the opening-up of the American west to the financial houses and manufacturing-based industry of the Northern states. The United States government's growing determination to protect its developing industries from foreign, especially British, competition was an additional obstacle. When, towards the end of the nineteenth century, many of Europe's industrialised nations, led by imperial Germany, joined the United States in introducing protective fiscal measures, Britain's strategy virtually collapsed and an urgent restructuring of policy was deemed essential.

At the time of the introduction of free trade, the needs of Britain's colonies were more or less ignored. This was curious in the light of the profound dependency of the economies of the colonies of European settlement upon Britain's preferential treatment of their products. In the brave new world of the free market, however, it was sink or swim. Those colonies that survived would have merited their success. The main risk, however, was not the extinction of colonial settlements, but that they would take the abandonment of the system of fiscal protection as a licence to cut themselves free from their imperial constitutional connections. Free trade would thus be associated with a further, more controversial, freedom, the freedom to secede from the British Empire.

Despite some contemporary anxieties on this score, nothing came of it. Of all the settlement colonies Canada was the most critical of the repeal of the Corn Laws, and the Montreal Board of Trade went so far as to complain that the reforms were an assault on 'an entire system of government'. This was a pardonable exaggeration, and the precursor of a number of Canadian complaints, made with varying degrees of conviction, over the next hundred years, that Britain was too quick to sacrifice Canada's interests to her own economic and diplomatic needs. In fact, Canada took the opportunity to extend and consolidate her trading links with the United States, a process positively boosted by the 1849 repeal of the Navigation Acts which led to more commercial traffic between the two countries flowing along North America's inland waterways.

Despite Canadian protests, there was no serious move to make a constitutional break with Britain. Instead Canada assumed the role of senior self-governing colony, and after 1907 senior dominion, within the British Empire. This at least gave it the opportunity to voice, and sometimes to lead, opposition to British policy as it bore upon the Empire, something which a number of Canadian prime ministers did to great effect in the Colonial and Imperial conferences that became a regular part of the imperial system from 1887.

If Canada, secure in its North American stronghold, increasingly intermeshed with the United States in terms of trade and culture, and in the last resort protected rather than threatened by Washington's supremacy in the western hemisphere, chose to remain within the British Empire, the other, more dependent, colonies of European settlement had far less chance of making a break.

The colonies in Australia, New Zealand and southern Africa, as well as the remnants of the old colonial system in the Caribbean, were far more reliant upon Britain for their commercial well-being and their military protection. In particular, the Australasian colonies could be seen, depending on the viewpoint, as either stuck on the periphery of Asia or marooned in the south-west Pacific. In any event, they were thousands of miles adrift from the Mother Country, and as dependent upon her protection as the babes in the wood. The internal security of the New Zealand colonists was also, in the last resort, guaranteed by the metropolitan power, as the need for the intervention of British regular troops in the Maori Wars during the 1860s clearly demonstrated. The English-speaking settlements in South Africa, whether in the Cape or Natal, were similarly dependent upon the support of British forces to keep African tribes in check and to snuff out and deter Afrikaner hostility and aggression. The Caribbean colonies, their declining economies further depressed by the abolition of the Sugar Acts in the early 1850s, even lacked that potential for growth which formed such an important part of the identity of the colonial settlements in North America, Australasia and South Africa.

With the exception of Canada, these colonies were equally dependent upon Britain for their trade and commerce. The ending of imperial protection had no serious impact upon the intimate economic ties that bound Mother Country and colony together. These links were further strengthened by the web of credit, banking, bonding and currency interactions that so often proved more powerful factors than the more blatantly advertised pulls of a common imperial citizenship, a common allegiance to the Crown, the shared inheritance of a common language and culture, and shared legal and constitutional practice.

The dependence of colonial economies upon Britain during these years was never absolute, but it was overwhelming. Curiously perhaps, in most cases the introduction of free trade seems to have resulted in an augmentation of British–colonial trade rather than the reverse. One instructive illustration can be found in the wool trade with Australia. In 1824 virtually the whole of Britain's imports of wool came from Germany and Spain, with Australia supplying the minute quantity of 0.4 million pounds weight out of a total of 22.6 million pounds. Within four years of the repeal of the Corn Laws, Australia was exporting 39 million pounds to Britain out of a total of 74.3 million, and by 1886 the figure had risen to 401.4 million pounds out of 596.5 million, or over 60 per cent.[4] Similar increases in trade, sometimes to the point of an apparently abject colonial dependency on the United Kingdom, can be discerned with other colonies of European settlement.

In the case of those territories ruled either directly or indirectly by Britain, from India to Hong Kong, the economic relationship was one of straightforward metropolitan self-interest. For most of the nineteenth century there were few locally elected assemblies able to grumble, obstruct and protect colonial interests. British administrators and merchants naturally did their best to secure the cooperation of influential local elites, but beyond that the dependent empire was open to penetration and exploitation. In many cases British economic self-interest was ruthlessly pursued.

In the early years of the nineteenth century, for example, the export of cotton and woollen textiles was what really made Britain 'the workshop of the world'. In order to benefit the cotton merchants and the cotton spinners and weavers of Lancashire, India, in effect, had to be de-industrialised. The East India Company, already partly nationalised by the British government, supervised this assault on the local cotton industry, a process carried through with such vigour that the plains of India were soon described as 'white with the bones of Indian weavers'; as late as the 1890s 40 per cent of Britain's cotton exports went to India. Even when such socially destructive imperatives were absent, possessions like India provided a safe target for British investment and attracted capital accordingly. As if the security of British rule was insufficient, the British government for a while guaranteed a fixed annual return on money invested in the development of the Indian railway network, in a neat conjunction of military, financial and economic self-interest. Towards the end of the nineteenth century India took nearly 19 per cent of Britain's exports, and over 20 per cent of British investment overseas was lodged there.

When the broad view is taken of Britain's economic and commercial relationship with the Empire in the half-century following the repeal of the Corn Laws, free trade seems to have enhanced the trading relationship between Mother Country and colony rather than ruined it.

The truth is that patriotic and imperial sentiments were never sufficient in themselves to initiate and sustain patterns of trade. They could at times encourage and enhance commercial interaction, but if the price was wrong and the delivery date too unreliable, importers and exporters looked elsewhere. As the metropolitan consumer market became increasingly urbanised and proletarian during the nineteenth century, it became more concerned with value and availability, and even less preoccupied with whether the product originated in the Empire or outside it. If cane sugar from the British West Indies was cheaper than beet sugar from Europe the shoppers bought it, but not if it was more expensive. Few could afford to put loyalty to a nebulous imperial ideal before their own self-interest, and even those who could have done so generally did not.

This tendency is particularly marked if the overall balance and direction of Britain's commerce and investment during the nineteenth century are assessed. New portfolio British capital investment between 1865 and 1914 went in proportions of 40 per cent to the Empire and 60 per cent elsewhere.[5] This compares favourably, however, with the proportion of British exports to the Empire during roughly the same period. Between 1846 and 1850 the Empire took 27.3 per cent of Britain's exports, and the rest of the world 72.7 per cent; between 1871 and 1875 the respective figures are 26.8 per cent and 73.2 per cent; between 1881 and 1885 they are 35 per cent and 65 per cent; between 1896 and 1900, 34.1 per cent and 65.9 per cent; and between 1909 and 1913, 35 per cent and 65 per cent.[6]

At no time during the sixty to seventy years following the introduction of free trade, therefore, did the proportion of Britain's exports to the Empire exceed 35 per cent, and for nearly half that time it fell below 30 per cent. Nothing could more plainly illustrate the self-interest that fuelled the fiscal reforms of the 1840s and 1850s, nor the wisdom of maintaining and promoting the nation's trade with Europe, the United States of America and the countries of South America. Worse still for the cause of imperial consolidation and prioritising are the statistics of Britain's balance of trade relationship with the Empire between 1871 and 1900, when they averaged a deficit of £9,000,000 per year.[7] Finally, it is necessary to remember that for nearly every year of Queen Victoria's reign the British economy was actually in deficit in terms of the commodity balance of trade, and was only carried into surplus by the success of the 'invisible' exports like investment, banking, insurance and income from merchant shipping.

Weighed in the balance of Britain's place in the global market place, the Empire was both more significant than its detractors imagined and less important than its adherents claimed. The proportion of Britain's commodity trade with the imperial system remained disappointing for much of the nineteenth century and for the first forty years of the twentieth. When in the aftermath of the Second World War it shot up to over 40 per cent, the Empire was ironically on the point of its final collapse and disintegration.

It is evident that on almost every count, economic self-interest triumphed over imperial 'idealism' (whatever that was) or, towards the end of the nineteenth century, over calls for greater imperial unity. How it could ever have been otherwise is the puzzle, especially at a time when the disposable income of the vast majority of British families was next to nothing and the need to keep an eagle eye on the weekly food bill an imperative.

In these circumstances the decision of the Peel government to plump for free trade against protection was amply justified. In the folk memory of the Victorian people free trade was equated, if not with prosperity, at least with sufficiency and freedom from starvation. Protection came to be associated with high food prices and the narrow interests of a moribund landed elite. As with all collective perceptions, these were both misleading and inconvenient. One major problem arising from their widespread acceptance was the difficulty in shifting public opinion when economic circumstances changed, as the tariff reformers were so painfully to discover in the early years of the twentieth century.

The Empire, in the free market, *laissez-faire* aftermath of 1846, remained sufficiently buoyant in economic terms to encourage all but the most disenchanted and sceptical. It was, however, still as far as ever from providing the British economy with either fabulous enrichment or the rock-solid security amid the vagaries of international trade that so many of its supporters expected and assumed.

7

THE GREAT INDIAN UPRISING
OF 1857–58

The British in India

THE INDIAN REBELLION OF 1857 inflicted a deep wound upon the Victorian psyche. It was a challenge flung in the face of the comfortable British assumption that sound and efficient administration was enough to keep imperial subjects content, or at least uncomplaining. Because the uprising went beyond the army and involved considerable numbers of Indian civilians, it also provided an uncomfortable reminder that the disenfranchised masses at home might not be bought off in perpetuity by the already outdated constitutional reforms of the 1832 Act or by the wages and full employment apparently guaranteed as part of Britain's manufacturing supremacy. Perhaps they, too, might rise in revolt against property and privilege and the virtual monopoly of state power.

The rebellion had other, darker resonances. The assault of Indian rebels, particularly the mutinous sepoys of the Army of Bengal, upon sections of the European civil and military population included violence directed at British women and children. The Kanpur massacre of captive British females and their offspring confirmed some of the worst fantasies of the European imperial imagination. As in the uprisings of black slaves in the Caribbean and North America, the white, male response to the 'uppity nigger' of the Bengal Army was an explosive and lethal mixture of fear and loathing. At the heart of this uncompromising reaction was a horror of the sexual violation of white women by black men. The middle-class Victorian woman had not been placed on a pedestal in order to be flung onto the ground, raped, and then killed by brown heathens. The fact that the Indian rebels of 1857, overwhelmingly, it seems, did not rape their female captives did nothing to alter the conviction that an unspeakable violation had occurred.

The Victorian public was gorged on the horrors of the 1857 Indian uprising. Cartoons and drawings in newspapers and journals expressed a predictable sense of national outrage while at the same time titillating their readers' imaginations with lurid, and generally irresponsible, images of mayhem. Indian troops were shown tossing British babies on their bayonets for sport, and one print, entitled 'English Homes in India, 1857', depicted a pair of dishevelled and bloodstained mutineers about to lay their reeking hands upon the heads of defenceless infants and upon the bosom of a breast-feeding British mother.[1]

The 1857 revolt provoked other outraged responses on the part of the British. Perhaps the most telling of these, as well as the most unreasonable, was a sense of betrayal. The Indian troops who rose in rebellion, the civilians who abetted and sometimes joined them, the few local princes who lent support to the uprising were all denounced as ungrateful and treacherous wretches, unmindful of the benefits bestowed by Britain's civilising mission in the sub-continent.

This reaction had many causes. One of the most fundamental arose from the prevailing Victorian belief in progress. A nation that was not merely the world's leading industrial and commercial power, but was apparently extending to the Indian sub-continent the same sound and pragmatic reforms that were paving and lighting the streets of Britain's cities, had cause for self-congratulation. The Indian uprising was consequently interpreted as an unwarranted and destructive rejection of British reforming benevolence, and an assault on the very notion of progress.

Empire was increasingly a source of pride to British people, and the achievements of British rule were generally taken for granted. The conquest, control and reordering of indigenous societies in India and elsewhere at the least enabled the dispossessed of Victorian Britain to luxuriate in an unaccustomed feeling of superiority and virtue. Disgust at the rebels' delinquency included even those at the bottom of the domestic social structure, as illustrated in a cartoon of a begrimed dustman and sweep discussing 'this 'ere Hingia bisinis' and agreeing that 'It's just wot yer might expeck from sich a parcel o' dirty black hignorant scoundrels as them.'[2]

All of this helps to explain why the Victorians were so insistent that the uprising of 1857 was 'the Indian Mutiny'. By defining it in this fashion it was possible to contain the events within a military framework, and so to deny the wider, infinitely more threatening ramifications. The whole affair could be dismissed as the work of groups of malcontent Indian mercenaries, their benighted religious prejudices enflamed by the agitation of barrack-room lawyers, rather as the Chartists at home were caricatured as irresponsibly befuddling the minds of normally docile and Godfearing working men and women. It is also significant that Mangal Pande, the sepoy who was hanged for mutiny at Barrackpur in April 1857, was rumoured to have been under the influence of narcotics when he carried out his attack on his British officers. In these ways the 'unpleasantness' of 1857 could be written off as the results of over-indulgence in hashish or as the ill-informed responses of peasants in uniforms to unscrupulous agitation. So successful was this bid to rewrite the agenda for the rebellion of 1857 that it is only very recently that British historians and writers assessing the event have chosen words other than 'mutiny' to describe the uprising, or have acknowledged the part played by civilian rebels.

There is no doubt that the uprising of 1857 began as a mutiny in the Army of Bengal, and was subsequently sustained by the action of other regiments in that force. The outbreak occurred in Meerut, thirty-six miles north-east of Delhi, on 10 May. It was precipitated by the court-martial of men of the Third Native Light Cavalry for refusing to use a new greased cartridge that was being issued to units of the Bengal Army. Eighty-five of the mutinous sepoys were sentenced by a court, composed of Indian officers, to ten years' hard labour. The mutineers were subsequently humiliated by their divisional commander Major-General Hewitt, known as 'Bloody Bill', when on 9 May he had paraded them shackled with leg-irons before their comrades. That night the other sepoy regiments rose in rebellion, released the prisoners from jail, burnt down bungalows and offices, and killed any Europeans who fell into their hands. They then set off for Delhi.

What had pushed the sepoys at Meerut to the point of mutiny and rebellion? The controversy over the greased cartridges was undoubtedly the flashpoint. Between 1847 and 1857 the East India Company had decided to equip its sepoy regiments with the new Enfield rifle in place of the smooth-bored 'Brown Bess' musket. The rifled barrel of the new weapon necessitated a greasing of the cartridges in order to ram home easily the bullet that was placed in the base of each cartridge. The loading procedure for these new 'bored' rifles meant that the top of the cartridge had to be torn, or more probably, especially in the heat of action, bitten off, the gunpowder poured down the rifle barrel and finally the empty container with its bullet inside it rammed down the barrel.

As in many other aspects of interaction between the British and

India, the new Western military technology seemed to strike at the heart of Indian tradition and faith. To the Hindu the cow was a sacred animal; the Muslim believed that contact with the unclean pig would defile him. Rumours had been circulating since January 1857 that the great arsenal at Dum-Dum, near Calcutta, was coating the new-issue cartridges with cow and pig fat. Amazingly the suspicions of the sepoys seem to have been well-founded, and provided a clear indication of the insensitivity of the British authorities towards Indian religious sensibilities. Hostile reactions to the new cartridges had first occurred in February 1857 among Indian troops at Barrackpur, close to Calcutta, and had later spread to a number of Army of Bengal cantonments along the Ganges valley. Faced with mutinous regiments, some commanders took the sensible step of reassuring their troops that no attack on their religion was intended, while others tried by threats and bullying tactics to break the will of their sepoys. Some Indian regiments were disbanded, and on 21 April Mangal Pande was court-martialled and hanged. By early May there was widespread discontent amongst the regiments of the Army of Bengal.

Of itself the controversy over the new cartridge need not have led to a general uprising. But there were other reasons why Indian troops in the service of the East India Company were discontented. The fear that the Company was undermining their religion had precipitated earlier mutinies in 1806 and 1824, and as late as 1852 a regiment had refused service in Burma, since crossing the sea could have involved its Hindu troops in a loss of caste. By the mid-1850s the sepoys were being subjected to a process of military modernisation and adjustment. There were rumours that the army would be disbanded now that Britain had completed its process of sub-continental conquest and pacification. In 1856 the General Service Enlistment Act stipulated that all new recruits should in future swear that they would cross the sea for military service, though this would involve Hindu troops in ritual pollution and had to be undertaken for no extra pay.

In addition to this, the strains of barrack life and the demands of military routine and discipline could in themselves ferment a spirit of resentment, especially if British officers were unable to maintain close and cordial relationships with their men. There is, as it happens, a good deal of evidence to show that a wide gulf had opened up between officers and sepoys prior to the great uprising of 1857. An Indian officer in the Company's service, Subedar Sita Ram, who later published a book entitled *From Sepoy to Subedar*, recorded of the immediate pre-mutiny period: 'I always was good friends with the English soldiery and they formerly used to treat the sepoys with great kindness . . . these soldiers are of a different caste now – neither so fine nor so tall as they were; they seldom can speak one word of our language, except abuse.' A British observer, writing in the early months of the mutiny in the North-West Provinces, said of the British treatment of the sepoy: 'He is sworn at. He is treated roughly. He is spoken of as a "nigger" . . . The younger men seem to regard it as an excellent joke, and as evidence of spirit and as a praiseworthy sense of superiority over the sepoy to treat him as an inferior animal.'

The roots of the uprising went far deeper than mere military discontent and conflict. The territorial annexations and reforming tendencies of the East India Company had affronted many sections of Indian society in the half-century since the victorious conclusion of the Maratha Wars in 1818 had unquestionably established the British as the paramount power in the sub-continent. For the vast majority of the Indian people it was probably irrelevant whether the Mughal Emperor, the Maratha Confederacy or the East India Company ruled them; the perennial struggle for subsistence was the overwhelming preoccupation of peasant India, fatalistic and passive, and an unlikely recruiting ground for bloodstained revolutionaries.

Princes, landlords, religious leaders and members of the upper reaches of Hindu and Muslim society saw things differently. Through the agency of the East India Company, the British had toppled Indian rulers, dispossessed landlords, and seemed to encourage attacks on the indigenous religious and cultural order. The proselytising of evangelical Christian missionaries, and the reforming assault on local religious practices such as *sati* (the burning of Hindu widows), in conjunction with other social and economic reforms, had all seemed to be part of the Company's programme to subvert the Indian tradition.

The governor-generalship of Lord Dalhousie, between 1848 and 1856, intensified resentments that had been building up for many years. Dalhousie confidently asserted the paramouncy of the Company, thus also implying the superiority of British ways over Indian. His plans to improve road and rail communications were justified in terms of military security but seemed further, perturbing, examples of change to Indian traditionalists. Above all, Dalhousie's unbridled policy of territorial annexation was bound to alienate local rulers and their followers. As the climax to a series of annexations, Dalhousie brought the ancient province of Avadh under the Company's rule in 1856. The British justified the annexation on the grounds of endemic civil disorder and irresponsible government by its ruler. A far more compelling motive was the fact that Avadh, the last great independent province in northern India, lay between Bengal and the Punjab, straddling the Grand Trunk Road from Calcutta to Delhi as well as the Ganges and Jumna rivers and, of great significance, the newly completed railway link between Allahabad and Kanpur. The province had thus become an anachronistic obstacle to the Company's plans for territorial and military aggrandisement throughout the whole of the Gangetic plane.

The significance of the annexation of Avadh lay not merely in its strategic importance, but also in the fact that 40,000 sepoys, nearly a third of the total in the Army of Bengal, had been recruited from that province. Of the three armies maintained by the Company, those of Bengal, Madras and Bombay, by far the largest was the Army of Bengal, which comprised over 150,000 sepoys.

Unlike the rank-and-file soldiers of British armies recruited at home, substantial numbers of the Bengal Army were drawn from the more exalted sections of Indian society: from Brahmins and Rajputs if they were Hindus or from good class Muslim families if followers of Islam. On joining their regiments they did not become mere tools of Company policy; they maintained their religion, their caste, and their family connections. Their unbroken links with their families had a twofold significance: they were particularly sensitive to any fears or resentments that affected their families, and they had an important status to maintain in the eyes of their relatives. Any slight to their religion, any insult to their caste or standing, would have resulted in rejection by family and friends. The complicated interaction between sepoys drawn from the province of Avadh, their relations at home and the policies of the Company were central to the outbreak of the mutiny in 1857.

In addition to the turbulence surrounding the annexation of Avadh, the recent policy of the Company had broken one of the cardinal rules of the maintenance of British power in India, namely the policy of collaborating with powerful local elites. During his high-handed governor-generalship, Dalhousie had dispossessed local rulers, either by the application of the 'doctrine of lapse' (under which princes lacking a natural male heir could be stripped of their titles) or for alleged misdemeanours, and Company economies had caused a cutback in the pensions normally paid in compensation to displaced princes. Two of the foremost princely supporters of the mutiny, the Nana Sahib, the adopted son of the last of the Maratha rulers, in Avadh and the Rani of Jhansi, both felt ill-used in this regard.

The uprising that began at Meerut in May 1857 took eighteen months to put down completely. In some ways this was a remarkably long time. At the outbreak of the rising, however, there were only eleven British infantry regiments available for action, mainly because substantial numbers of troops were returning from the recent, triumphant war in Persia. British forces were simultaneously engaged in fighting the '*Arrow* War', the Second Opium War, against China. As a consequence several crucial strategic locations were without European troops, including the large arsenal in Allahabad, at the meeting-point of the Ganges and the Jumna, and Delhi, which was also an important military base as well as being the home of the last Mughal Emperor Bahadur Shah II. At the outset of the rebellion, therefore, the mutineers were able easily to take possession of strategic points and to seize a mass of arms and munitions.

The course of the uprising was erratic and full of contradictions. The armies of Bombay and Madras remained fundamentally loyal, and only a quarter of the sepoys in the Army of Bengal joined the revolt. With the exception of the Nana Sahib and the Rani of Jhansi, the Indian princes gave unswerving support to the British. Recently conquered territories like the Punjab remained quiet, and border states such as Afghanistan and Nepal offered no assistance to the rebels. Indeed, Sikhs from the Punjab and Gurkhas recruited in Nepal played a considerable part in suppressing the mutiny. No foreign power threatened to intervene, although after the reduction of French territory in India during the eighteenth century to a few coastal enclaves, it is difficult to see how any practical intervention could have taken place.

The mutineers themselves seemed to have lacked coherent leadership or any common plan. Some wished to restore the Mughal Emperor to his throne, but the old man refused to accommodate them. Others wanted to restore those bits of the past which they particularly cherished. Often bands of mutineers roamed the countryside looting, and as a consequence antagonising the peasantry to whom they might otherwise have looked for support. Those peasant groups that did join the rebellion, mostly from impoverished and declining areas, were soon cowed by the ferocity of the British and loyalist counterattack. Despite the avowed intention of most of the mutineers to overthrow British rule, many regiments progressed through the countryside with their bands playing British marching tunes and their regimental flags flying proudly above them.

Even though the Company's authority lapsed for a time in Delhi, Avadh, north central India and some of Bengal, two-thirds of the country remained absolutely passive. In real terms, British supremacy was not seriously threatened. By comparison to contemporary campaigns like the Crimean War, for example, or the American Civil War, the Indian Mutiny involved small numbers of men. The main problems for the British forces were those of distance and supply.

The uprising, particularly after the massacre of British women and children at Kanpur, unleashed a hurricane of retribution. British troops went to unpalatable lengths to revenge their nation and their people. Muslims were sewn into pigskins prior to hanging, a vile and terrible fate for any follower of Islam. On discovering the bloody evidence of the massacre at Kanpur, the British indulged in an orgy of vengeance, culminating in Brigadier-General Neill's order that Indian prisoners should be made to clean up a small portion of the bloodstains, forced by the lash if necessary, and that those who objected should be made to lick up part of it with their tongues. Neill and others were confident that the Almighty was glad to see so righteous and implacable a retribution.[3] Those mutineers who were blown into fragments of flesh and bone from the mouths of cannon, or summarily hanged, were among the fortunate ones.

Many bitter hatreds were left by the mutiny. Deep-seated prejudices which had already been much in evidence before 1857 were confirmed and strengthened. The gulf which had already opened between the two races widened to almost unbridgeable proportions. Distrust was heightened. How could the British officer, merchant, or even administrator, see Indians in the same light ever again? In a matter of moments, apparently steadfast soldiers and loyal servants had been transformed into murderous fiends. The almost universal approval in Britain of the steps taken to put down the uprising were part of a national mood of retribution and despair. As a result, among the many casualties of the rebellion were some of the more liberal assumptions concerning Indian progress and possible political developments.

In February 1858, as the uprising was coming to an end, the *Manchester Guardian* did something to set right the accounts of sepoy atrocities, including the rape of white women:

Treacherous and cruel as have certainly been the enemies who have started up from the ranks of our dependants, the error of imputing to them an excess of infamy from which they shall hereafter be proved to have been substantially free, must be held to reflect discredit on our national fairness as much as it has disturbed our policy and lacerated our feelings . . .

Belief in horrible stories of torture, mutilation and dishonour worse than death, inflicted on our countrymen and countrywomen in India, has been universal . . .

Cause for misgiving was furnished some months ago by the authoritative denial given by the *Lahore Chronicle* to the story that Miss Jennings and Miss Clifford were outraged previous to their murder in Delhi . . . a correspondent of *The Times* . . . declares his total dissent from the belief that the incensed Indian soldiery, besides murdering their English victims, inflicted upon them torture and disgrace.[4]

Such liberal doubts were too late to have any impact upon the course of British retribution, much of which had been casual and routine. As an ordinary British soldier was later to recount, killing on the flimsiest evidence was commonplace:

I seed two Moors [Indians] talking in a cart. Presently I heard one of 'em say 'Cawnpore'. I knowed what that meant. So I fetched Tom Walker, and he heard 'em say 'Cawnpore', and he knowed what that meant. So we polished 'em both off.[5]

The rebellion of 1857 was a watershed in the history of Britain's relationship with India. Ironically, although perhaps inevitably, the East India Company was the main casualty of the uprising. The 1858 Government of India Act swept away the power of the Company, which was assumed by the Crown. For all practical purposes the British government had been the masters of India since 1813. Now, however, theory had been brought into line with practice. The Company continued as a trading concern, but its great days were over. The governor-general was given the title of viceroy by royal proclamation, but carried out the same duties. The British government, in order to sharpen its authority in London, established a Secretary of State for India and a council of fifteen to advise him.

The existence of a Secretary of State for India, responsible to Parlia-

74

ment and advised by the India Council, was not without its problems. At the outset, the India Council consisted of ex-servants of the Company and thus tended to be conservative in its policies. The secretary of state could, if he wished, ignore its recommendations and base his authority on Parliament. Here, too, parliamentary supervision could only be effective if members made it so. Since Indian affairs were remote from the interest of most Members of Parliament, and, notoriously, the annual debate on the Indian budget sent MPs packing, the secretary of state could often operate as he and the Cabinet thought fit. But even given a masterful secretary of state and a compliant Parliament, there was still the matter of supervising, and if necessary controlling, the viceroy. Not until the introduction of the telegraph in the 1880s could this be anything but a lengthy and hazardous process of communication.

Within India there were some attempts to broaden the framework of government. The Central Legislative Council was expanded in 1861 by the addition of several non-official members, of whom two were Indians. This was the first time that any members who were not European had been admitted to this body, although there had been an unsuccessful proposal in 1853 to appoint some Indians to the Governor-General's Council. This was, however, an almost worthless reform. The Legislative Council had hardly any legislative functions, and no power at all over the Viceroy's Executive Council, which acted as British India's Cabinet. The two Indian non-officials on the Central Legislative Council were safe loyalists, not revolutionary and seditious politicians. The Viceroy's Council, moreover, was untrammelled by any restraining democratic forms, and it was the Viceroy's Council that ruled India.

One other administrative development is worthy of note. This was the restoration of legislative functions to the overwhelmingly white councils of Bombay and Madras, and the establishment of legislative councils for Bengal, the Punjab and the North-West Provinces. Here again, the power was more illusory than real, though the councils could conceivably be, and indeed later were, utilised as vehicles for democratic experiment.

The army, naturally, was reconstructed after the mutiny. All of its troops were placed under the Crown. There was a determined attempt to increase the proportion of British soldiers, and initially a refusal to let Indian troops handle artillery. Since, however, Indian soldiers continued to outnumber British troops by two to one, an attempt was made to recruit reliable men. Subsequently the Indian army came to rely heavily on Sikhs, Gurkhas and the frontier tribes of the north-west.

One unexpected result of the crushing of the mutiny was the strengthening of conservatism within the sub-continent. Orthodox Hinduism was revived. Before 1857 reformist elements had been in the ascendant, but subsequent reaction tended to exalt the more obscure and traditionalist qualities of Hinduism as a protection against the inroads of British ideas and influence.

Another bastion of conservatism was reinforced by the uprising. The Indian princes had displayed almost unanimous loyalty during the rebellion, and they now reaped their reward. The British administration clearly regarded them as stalwart supporters of the regime. As a consequence, the princely states were now safe from encroachment as long as they accepted British overlordship and advice. Another bonus for the princes was the new caution exercised by Britain over the process of reform. Fearful to set in motion an Indian reaction similar to the one that had precipitated the great uprising of 1857, the government avoided drastic political and social change. Missionary activity was curbed.

As a result of these reforms and reactions, by the 1870s British India stood pacified and, to some extent, reformed. Economic progress was made, and there were some improvements in the areas of communication, education and agriculture. Overall, therefore, India became more British as a result of the mutiny, not less so. The numbers of British officials and non-officials increased markedly, and many more memsahibs arrived to bring up their families at their husband's side. As a result, Anglo-Indian high society became more self-contained and self-confident. There was even an attempt to attract European settlers, though not much came of it.

The self-assurance of the British community was, however, often near to arrogance. This arose partly from the sheer scale of Britain's Indian enterprise: 'mastery of the enormous territory conferred on British character a sense of inflated imperial pride and it also engineered a set of prejudices.'[6] British supremacy in India also tended to confirm some of the less pleasing characteristics of the rulers: in E.M. Forster's *A Passage to India* Adela thinks of Ronny that 'India had developed sides of his character that she had never admired. His self-complacency, his censoriousness, his lack of subtlety.'[7]

While it was convenient, almost obligatory, to despise Indians, there was also the uncomfortable feeling that one day they might entertain inconvenient political and social ambitions. Few British doubted that some Indians could be clever, indeed could be trained in any number of skills. But could they act like responsible gentlemen, and bear, without much reward, the unquestioned burdens of imperial responsibility? There was the rub. The bitter aftermath of the mutiny, with a distinct hardening of racial attitudes and a tendency for crude stereotyping, meant that a genuine dialogue between the two races was, for the foreseeable future, out of the question. By the mid-Victorian age, 'the white man's burden' in India had become, at least in part, the colour of his skin. In the eyes of many of the British in India, however, the brown skin of the indigenous man and woman was perceived to be an even greater burden, serving as a badge of inferiority and a bar to progress towards European political rights and freedoms.

That the British wished to maintain control of India against almost any odds was based on one simple calculation. Britain could simply not afford to lose her greatest dependency. The extent of the total British investment in India, and the capacity of the Indian market to take up to 20 per cent of British exports by the 1880s, meant that Britain would not willingly abandon her rule in the sub-continent. Anglo–Indian trade was greatly stimulated by the opening of the Suez Canal in 1869, and by the cheaper freight costs of the Suez route as compared with the traditional, much longer sea passage round the Cape of Good Hope. Trade with India took on a new significance for Britain. The value of exports to India had totalled only £23 million in 1855, but by 1910 they were worth £137 million. During the same period the value of imports from India rose from £13.5 million to £86 million, leaving Britain a favourable net balance of trade of some £51 million. By 1900 nearly all of that British staple drink, tea, came from India, whereas a century before it had been produced in China. If the taxes and revenues raised by the British Raj in India are also taken into account – the country was paying £10 million per year in interest to Britain by 1900, as well as bearing the cost of the salaries and pensions of the administration – India was an enormously profitable, self-financing enterprise, approximating very closely to the Victorian capitalist and imperial ideal.

In addition, the Indian Army was a readily available source of manpower which did not cost the British taxpayer one penny. By the end of the nineteenth century 40 per cent of Indian revenue was being spent on the military. It was in effect the Indian Army, with its huge reserve force, that enabled Britain to function as a great military power, able in theory to square up to the large conscript armies of Continental states like Germany, France and Russia. Throughout the nineteenth century, the Indian Army was sent on numerous occasions to fight for British interests in campaigns outside the sub-continent: in China, for instance, in 1839, 1856 and 1859; in Persia in 1856; in Abyssinia in 1867; in Egypt in 1882; in Nyasaland in 1893; in the Sudan from 1896 to 1898, and so forth. If the vital contribution of the Indian armed forces during both world wars is taken into account it is clear why India was so persistently and predictably described by British imperialists as 'the jewel in the crown'. It was India's capacity to transform Britain's world standing, in this and other ways, that prompted the Viceroy, Lord Curzon, to announce in 1901: 'As long as we rule India, we are the greatest power in the world. If we lose it we shall drop straightway to a third rate power.'[8]

The Raj was a source of inestimable pride to so many Britons for another reason. It was, in their eyes, an almost philanthropic venture, though conveniently based on sound money. Good and fair government, an expanding economy, and a whole range of improvements from famine relief to irrigation schemes, from the medical assault on cholera to the establishment of a Europeanised educational system, all bore witness to the high-minded agenda of British rule. Few in Britain imagined that the handing over of power to Indians would be anything but a catastrophe, bringing corruption, maladministration and chaos in its train. Moreover, despite the magnificent pomp of the Raj at its most ceremonial, there were, so it was asserted, a host of Britons modestly doing their duty, quietly, efficiently, patriotically and judiciously:

> Now here is Tom, in his thirty-first year, in charge of a population as numerous as that of England in the reign of Elizabeth . . . he rises at daybreak, and goes straight from his bed to the saddle. Then off he gallops across fields bright with dew to visit the scene of the late robbery; or to see with his own eyes whether the crops of the *zemindar* [landlord and tax collector] who is so unpunctual with his assessment have really failed; or to watch with fond parental care the progress of his pet embankment.[9]

The whole administration of the Raj, benevolent or otherwise, was financed by taxes levied on the Indian people. Although it was possible for the British to boast that India had never been so well governed, the fact was that Indians not only paid for their own government, but had no say in its structure.

In some ways the Raj was a bluff. By the end of Queen Victoria's reign, some 300 million Indians were ruled by barely 1500 administrators of the Indian Civil Service. There were perhaps 3000 British officers in the Indian Army. Leaving aside the British regiments serving in India, the total number of Britons in the sub-continent at the end of Victoria's reign was something like 20,000. If the Indian people had chosen to throw off their overlords in a fashion more consistent and concerted than that of 1857, there would have been little to prevent them. The regiments of infantry tramping down the Grand Trunk Road, the double firsts from Oxford and Cambridge who served in the Indian Civil Service, the social exclusiveness of the British clubs, the justice apparently handed out so even-handedly, would have been of no avail. The divisions within Indian society, however, meant that such concerted action was very unlikely to occur. The British continued to maintain their authority, and the power and strength of the Raj, through the exploitation of the differences and divisions within the sub-continent.

There were times when the possession of the Indian empire seemed more trouble than it was worth. This was not due, overall, to serious internal unrest or disaffection, although it is now clear that the image of a tranquil sub-continent contentedly luxuriating in British rule was a self-serving piece of propaganda, and that each year brought its quota of local difficulties and confrontations somewhere or other in India. It was chiefly to do with the size of the country and its complexity. By the end of the nineteenth century, India's huge population – approximately 80 per cent of all the subjects living within the British Empire – was a staggering total to imagine, let alone control and administer. As if this was not enough, each town and village was thronged with people: people buying, selling, walking, talking, pushing, watching, waiting, fixing, mending, carrying, lifting, calling, arguing, travelling, arriving. No wonder the British kept themselves apart, spending much of their working lives and the vast bulk of their leisure isolated from the Indian masses. The business of confronting and disciplining the Indian population were tasks overwhelmingly carried out by other Indians, especially those who served the Raj in the army, the police or the lower grades of the civil service.

There was also the problem of guarding the frontiers of India both against the incursions of border peoples like Afghans and Tibetans, and, more seriously, against the threat of the potentially hostile and expanding power of Russia. A good deal of energy and money was spent on discerning and then countering Russian influence on the borders of India. Afghanistan was invaded twice by British and Indian forces during the nineteenth century, and Tibet in 1903, each time for the purpose of eliminating Russian influence. The only trouble was that the Russians were never in evidence; rather, it was the Russians who should have been resentful of British aggression across the Indian frontier. Even when the great European powers like Germany, France or Austria-Hungary seemed to pose no threat to the integrity of the Indian empire, the British possession of India was sometimes an irritant and a cause of envy.

There was one final disadvantage to the business of ruling India. This was the sheer discomfort of the whole affair. The vast majority of the British in India lived in a luxury beyond the imagination of the masses. There were the bungalows and the clubs with their punkahs and cool drinks. Servants were in plentiful supply, from ayahs to look after the children to cooks, gardeners, grooms and sweepers. These servants were not always well treated by the sahibs and memsahibs, and were:

> often visited with blows and such abuse as no respectable man will bear; very often too for no other fault than that of not understanding what the master has said, who has given his directions in some unintelligible stuff from ignorance of the language.[10]

Despite the undoubted cosseting of the British in India, however, death and disease were never far away. It has been estimated that from first to last about two million Britons died in India. There were the deadly onslaughts of plague, smallpox, typhoid fever and cholera. Even if these killers were avoided there was always the prickly heat:

> . . . a sort of rash which breaks out on you, and . . . is prickly in its nature. I can only compare it to lying in a state of nudity on a horse hair sofa, rather worn, and with the prickles of the horse hair very much exposed, and with other horse hair sofas above you, and all around, and tucking you in. Sitting on thorns would be agreeable by comparison . . .[11]

Service in India often disrupted family life, leaving wives alone with their servants for lengthy stretches while their husbands were fulfilling their duties, or separating parents from children when the latter were sent back to Britain to go to boarding school. The pain and damage that India could inflict on children separated from parents, or on children whose parents died, were reflected in a number of contemporary books for young people. Among the most powerful of these is Frances Hodgson Burnett's *The Secret Garden*, published in 1911, with its lonely, sickly, rejected boy. Not even the high salaries and the handsome pensions of the majority of the British civilians serving in India could compensate for such privation and suffering.

Despite all of this, few questioned the need to maintain the Raj. Britain's determination to stay in control of the sub-continent's destinies was given the most potent expression in 1876 when Queen Victoria was proclaimed Empress of India. This was another of Disraeli's propaganda coups and was designed to bind the Indian princes, who ruled a third of India, even more closely to the ceremonial centre of British power, as well as to gratify the Queen. A spectacular proclamation ceremony involved the Indian princes in the new dispensation from the start, and the alteration to the royal style and title was to last until the reign of Victoria's great-grandson, King George VI.

For herself, the Queen-Empress never deigned to visit her Indian empire. India remained an empire all the same.

8

THE JAMAICA REBELLION
OF 1865

British Interests in the Caribbean and
the 'Nigger Question'

IN OCTOBER 1865, at Morant Bay in Jamaica, a crowd of some four hundred African Caribbeans attacked the local courthouse. They were protesting against the decisions of the local magistrate, which they felt conflicted with their interests. Several of them were armed, and they eventually broke into the courthouse and rescued one of their fellows on trial there. They subsequently resisted arrest, in the process killing a handful of local white volunteers sent against them. In the confused aftermath of the affray, some 2,000 blacks disappeared into the countryside and over the next few days sporadic outbreaks of violence occurred in two or three locations. Eventually just under twenty men, of whom half were white, were killed by the malcontents and thirty-five people wounded.

This was hardly a rebellion on the scale of the recently crushed Indian uprising of 1857–58. Even when viewed within the context of British nineteenth-century imperial history, the affray at Morant Bay was, in terms of its military significance, merely an irritating pimple upon the body politic.

With cool handling, the whole affair might have been easily contained. But the Governor of Jamaica, Edward John Eyre, his judgement clouded by the persistent lobbying of the white settler minority, and his imagination fed on the lurid prospects of black revolution, acted with intemperance and ferocity. All local volunteer forces were mobilised, reinforcements summoned from as far away as Canada and the Bahamas, and martial law proclaimed.

One of the most shameful chapters in British colonial history ensued. Government forces, within which the local white militia pre-dominated, shot, hanged and flogged on the slightest provocation. The summary executions of captured blacks were frequent and predictable, house-burning commonplace. The Royal Commission which later heard evidence relating to the rebellion and its repression revealed horrifying details:

> Having flogged nine men and burnt three negro houses, we then had a court-martial on the prisoners . . . Several were flogged without court-martial on a simple examination. One man . . . got fifty lashes; one man got one hundred . . . shot nine and hung three; made rebels hang each other; effect on the living terrific.[1]

In the bloody, almost hysterical, repression of the uprising 439 blacks were killed, of whom 354 were executed after courts-martial. At least 600 more were flogged barbarously, and over a thousand houses were burnt down. The hangings continued for five weeks after the upris-ing. Men who were flogged received up to a hundred lashes each, and women thirty. Some women were flogged on a simple charge of stealing, wire being twisted around the cords of the cat-o-nine-tails in order to make their punishment more agonising. The fact that some of the regu-lar troops drafted in to restore order had seen service during the Indian Mutiny may to a certain extent explain the ferocity of the white reaction.

Although the uprising was started by Paul Bogle, a black agitator, Governor Eyre identified G.W. Gordon as the man responsible for the rebellion. Gordon was the son of a wealthy white planter and a black mother, a member of the Jamaica House of Assembly, a magistrate and a self-ordained Baptist minister. He had emerged during Eyre's governorship as an eloquent and unrestrained spokesman for the griev-ances of the black peasantry. Despite his unimpeachable record as a magistrate and his support for orderly constitutional reform, the Jamaica plantocracy accused him of advocating the elimination of white rule and the establishment of a 'New West India Republic'.[2]

Gordon was arrested in Kingston, but as martial law did not extend beyond Morant Bay, Eyre had him moved to the area of the uprising so that he could be court-martialled. Brought before a flimsily constituted court-martial, and with insubstantial evidence against him, Gordon became a scapegoat to the European settlers' thirst for revenge and to Eyre's desire to be rid of him. The court-martial refused to impose the death penalty, and Eyre proceeded to order it himself. Gordon was hanged within a few hours of his trial. The Governor was later to justify his action on the grounds that he could not simply punish the ignorant participants in the uprising but must properly punish the educated, and implicitly more dangerous, leader.

The controversy surrounding these events prompted the British government to a speedy response. Eyre was suspended from office, and a Royal Commission appointed to investigate the affair. The Commission praised Eyre for his prompt action, but condemned the excesses perpetrated under martial law. It also denied that the martyred Gordon was involved in any conspiracy to cause an uprising or to overthrow the state. Eyre was recalled in disgrace, although he remained a totemic hero to various supporters and partial observers. When he was eventually brought to trial in England, the dismissed Governor's supporters launched an Eyre Defence Aid fund. Their opponents organised the Jamaica Committee. Eyre was, however, finally acquitted of any crimes or misdemeanours, and lived to receive a state pension from Disraeli's Conservative government in 1874.

Why was the so-called Jamaica Rebellion of 1865 so emotive and contentious an issue? One explanation can surely be found in the process of economic decline and stagnation that had beset the British West Indies since the late eighteenth century. In the early nineteenth century cut-throat competition from beet-sugar-producing nations in Europe, as well as from the cane sugar-dominated economies of the Caribbean colonies of France and Spain, had produced a glut in world sugar. By 1800 world production stood at 250,000 tons, eighty years later it was 3.8 million tons, and by 1914, 16 million tons.[3]

The white oligarchy of the British West Indies, planters, merchants, and a variety of middle men, were not merely faced with the plummeting value of their land and investments as the bottom was knocked out of the cane sugar market. In response to humanitarian and evangelical pressures, as well as the harsh facts of economic decline, but also with an eye to political and strategic expediency, the British government prohibited the slave trade in 1807.

In 1833 an Act abolishing slavery throughout the British Empire was carried through Parliament. Despite the nearly £20 million that was paid to the former slave owners of the British Caribbean territories, the planters remained aggrieved. This was partly due to the fact that much of the compensation went straight into the pockets of their creditors, but also because, despite the system of apprenticeship tried in lieu of slavery, it proved almost impossible to keep emancipated slaves at work on the sugar estates in anything like their pre-1833 numbers. The planters felt beset by chronic labour shortages, as well as by problems of inadequate capital and the fierce competition from foreign sugar. In the early 1850s their aspirations were dealt a further shattering blow by Britain's abandonment of the legislation protecting sugar as part of the move to free trade.

Within the British West Indies, no colony was harder hit than Jamaica, where there were 859 sugar estates in 1804, but only 330 by 1854. In approximately the same time, sugar production fell by over half, and between 1828 and 1850 Jamaica's share of the world total sugar production plunged from 15 per cent to 2.5 per cent. Planters desperately scoured the globe for fresh sources of labour. Workers were imported from Britain, Germany, even the United States. More satisfactory and long-term replacements were found in the form of Indian and Chinese coolie labourers, many thousands of whom were brought to the Caribbean and indentured to work in the sugar plantations, thus changing forever, especially in British Guiana and Trinidad, the ethnic balance of the population.

The West Indian plantocracy took the easy course of blaming the British government for their plight. To this easy option was added another. The perhaps understandable paranoia of the white oligarchy of the British Caribbean focused on the ex-slaves. The alleged improvidence and idleness of the black population of Jamaica, which had over half of the emancipated slaves of the British West Indies, was irrationally blamed for the current economic depression and various forms of social dislocation. Rather like the convicts in Australia, or the mutinous sepoys in India, the emancipated blacks of Jamaica became the receptacles for all manner of grievances, hatreds and fears which more properly belonged to the indigenous whites.

The dislike and contempt generally felt for the black population by the white oligarchy of the British Caribbean were not conveniently isolated in the sugar islands. Despite the activities and successes of the anti-slavery movement and the high-minded deliberations of the House of Commons' Aborigines Committee, there were plenty of propagandists in Britain willing to see things very much as the white planters did. As was so often the case in British imperial history, liberal attitudes on racial matters were more readily and easily expressed while black people were obedient and quiescent or, better still, conveniently out of sight. During the first half of the nineteenth century there was no black population worth speaking of in Britain itself. Until the emancipation of slaves throughout the Empire, moreover, the pattern of relationships between the British and people with brown or black skins had been overwhelmingly that of master and slave or servant, of officer and sepoy, merchant and eager supplier or middle man.

Between 1840 and the Jamaica Rebellion of 1865, however, there was a significant shift in perception. Or, at least, racist views gained currency and popularity. One of the main reasons for this was that, in various ways, indigenous people as well as emancipated slaves were causing trouble. In New Zealand the Treaty of Waitangi of 1840 had predictably not established a lasting peace between the Maoris and land-hungry British settlers, and in 1860 a decade of serious conflict, known by contemporaries as the Maori Wars, had begun; there had been a lengthy sequence of violent frontier clashes over territory and cattle in Cape Colony, conveniently dismissed as 'the Kaffir Wars'; finally, there had been the bloody and embarrassing Indian uprising of 1857 to 1858. Each of these confrontations had thrown down a threatening challenge to white supremacy and had, in the process, given full rein to destructive European fantasies.

Within a few decades, the comfortable and homely image of dependable, hard-working 'black Sambo', and of the highly disciplined, self-sacrificing Indian sepoy, was unceremoniously ditched. The career of Governor Eyre provides a neat illustration of this hardening of racial attitudes, especially at moments of crisis. Eyre had come to his appointment in Jamaica after a career in colonial administration which, at least on the surface, included an apparently worthy record in the notoriously tricky area of race relations. In Australia he had been appointed a district protector of the Aborigines, a generally thankless task, and later in Trinidad he had briefly held the post of Protector of indentured Indian immigrant labourers. In practice, however, British protectors such as Eyre were frequently subordinated to the demands and blandishments of white plantation-owners and settlers, determined to obtain the protection of their own economic needs rather than to accede to the just treatment of their workers, or of the local indigenous population.

Faced with what he interpreted as a concerted and widespread rebellion in Jamaica in 1865, and having come under the influence of a vociferous section of the planter-dominated oligarchy, Eyre had no hesitation in moving to crush the uprising swiftly and crudely. He was in essence obdurate, reactionary and not particularly intelligent. Moreover, his earlier protectorships of indigenous people had led him to a low opinion of his subjects.

Opinion-makers in Britain had also recently fanned the flames of racial prejudice and intolerance. The emancipation, in a variety of forms, of the black populations of a number of Caribbean territories only exacerbated these anxieties. The creation of what became the black-ruled Republic of Haiti during the French Revolutionary and Napoleonic Wars provided abundant evidence for white reactionaries and conservatives. Lord Elgin described the Republic of Haiti thus during the 1840s:

> As respect moral and intellectual culture, stagnation: in all
> that concerns material development, a fatal retrogression . . .
> a miserable parody of European and American institutions,
> without the spirit that animates either: the tinsel of French
> sentiment on the ground of negro ignorance.[4]

The British writer and historian Thomas Carlyle, in his vituperative essay 'Discourse on the Nigger Question', published in 1849, addressed the issue of slave emancipation in crude and vivid prose: 'Our beautiful black darlings are at last happy; with little labour except to the teeth, which surely, in those excellent horse-jaws of theirs, will not fail!' Sensitive to accusations of prejudice, Carlyle went on to deny his hostility: 'Do I, then, hate the negro? No; except when the soul is killed out of him, I decidedly like poor Quashee; and find him a pretty kind of man. With a penny worth of oil, you can make a handsome glossy thing of Quashee.'[5]

There is perhaps a further reason why British attitudes towards indigenous people and emancipated slaves were hardening. During the mid-Victorian period both the British state at home, and British influence and standing overseas, were facing formidable challenges. At home, the growth of Chartism, socialism and trade unionism all seemed to put property and the prevailing social order at serious risk. Overseas, indigenous societies were proving resistant to British cultural, religious and even commercial aggrandisement in a variety of ways.

During the 1850s and 1860s the edge of British commercial enterprise was being blunted on a number of fronts. The Chinese market, of which a great deal had been hoped, was proving surprisingly resistant to Western commercial penetration. Latin America, which leading statesmen like Castlereagh and Canning had confidently expected to provide British exporters with an eager and profitable market, was proving to be a disappointment. The abolition of the slave trade by Britain had left her with an emaciated and uncertain legitimate commerce in West Africa. A blight eliminated the production of coffee in Ceylon at a stroke.

Nor were Britain's missionary endeavours doing much better. Despite their high domestic profiles, the funds at their disposal and the self-confidence of their evangelical convictions, Britain's missionary societies were in fact making comparatively little headway with a host of indigenous people. From Basutoland to Nigeria, from New Zealand to China, Christian missions were achieving surprisingly few conversions, and even those converts that existed were apt to lapse under pressure from local communities and established traditions. Not only did missionaries bring with them a variety of diseases, some of them no doubt transmitted during demonstrations of the 'missionary position', but local hierarchical, traditional elites frequently saw Christianity as an egalitarian ideology and hence politically subversive and destabilising. Some missionaries, of course, hardly bothered with the tiresome job of conversion. David Livingstone, arguably the most famous of them all, was far more effective as a *de facto* agent of the Royal Geographical Society, and hence of imperial expansion, than as a saver of African souls.

Europeans frequently had as low an opinion of Africans living in the 'Dark Continent' as of the ex-slaves of the Caribbean. In 1863 the explorer Sir Samuel Baker, writing in his journal of the indigenous inhabitants of the Nile Basin and Lake Albert, wished that:

> the black sympathisers in England could see Africa's inmost heart as I do; much of their sympathy would subside. Human nature when viewed in its crude state as pictured amongst African savages is quite on a level with that of the brute, and not to be compared with the noble character of the dog.[6]

Sir Richard Burton was equally scathing, comparing Africans with animals, and believing that they were virtually incapable of self-improvement since their brains were soon addled by 'a very little learning'. During his great explorations of the Congo basin, Henry Morton Stanley, the 'finder' of David Livingstone (who was not lost, anyway), was accused by contemporaries of shooting Africans 'as if they were monkeys'.

Crude misinterpretations of the revolutionary and bitterly controversial theories of Charles Darwin also played their part in the tendency to dismiss Africans, in common with other indigenous peoples, as inherently inferior to Europeans and doomed to be the hewers of wood and the carriers of water. Everywhere, even in liberal and intellectual circles, there was a backing away from, and often a virulent repudiation of, the notion of a basic human equality. By 1866 the writer Charles Kingsley was asserting that he had changed his mind on the issue, and that his experiences over a quarter of a century 'have taught me that there are congenital differences and hereditary tendencies that defy all education from circumstances, whether good or evil'.[7]

Before the end of the century, the pendulum, inevitably, had begun to swing back. Interestingly, one of the reactions to the simplicities of social Darwinism, with its theme of 'the struggle for existence', was the growth of the cooperative movement, both in retailing and in party politics. On this analysis, it was cooperation 'which actually secures to the species the best conditions of survival'.[8]

All of this helps to explain the ferocity and intemperance of the white reaction to the so-called Jamaica Rebellion of 1865. But there is one further factor to be explained. From the years when the trans-Atlantic slave trade began to deposit millions of African slaves in the New World, the white settler populations of those communities developed a powerful and abiding fear of black insurrection. Control by violent means was the linchpin of the relationship between master and slave. But the floggings, chains and coercion of life on the plantations were as nothing compared to the private and public response to slave rebellion. In the British West Indies rebellious slaves throughout the eighteenth century were indiscriminately killed, had confessions tortured out of them and were often finally publicly executed by 'progressive mutilation, slow burnings, breaking on the wheel, or starvation in cages'.[9]

Jamaica had witnessed a sequence of gruesome judicial revenge following slave rebellions. In 1760 the uprising known as 'Tacky's revolt' resulted in one rebel's death by slow burning: 'his body being chained to an iron stake, the fire was applied to his feet. He uttered not a groan, and saw his legs reduced to ashes with the utmost firmness and composure';[10] and two others were starved to death on the gibbet in Kingston's main public square. The Jamaican revolt of 1831 to 1832, known as the Baptist War, produced a violent and bloody reaction that left nearly five hundred slaves dead.

Some of the recollections of the horrors of the Baptist War were being revived in the half-decade before the Morant Bay rebellion. Beginning in 1860, Jamaica experienced the 'Great Revival', a religious movement centred on local Baptist and, to some extent, Methodist churches.

A recent study has emphasised the ways in which religious revivalism and political discontent intertwined:

> ... the influence of the Baptists provided a particular political agenda that emphasised the plight of the black in post-emancipationist society ... the native churches, and especially the Native Baptists, provided a structure around which resistance could develop.[11]

Although hitherto white nonconformist missionaries and pastors in Jamaica had generally supported their black congregations in their struggle for greater freedoms, the political menace behind some of the manifestations of the Great Revival gave them pause: 'missionaries increasingly reported the triumph of "fanaticism, disorder and delusion" and that in some cases those attending chapel made a mockery of the church'.[12]

In many ways, therefore, the Jamaica Rebellion of 1865 was the fulfilment of the most horrifying, terrible and, in a strange way, predictable of white fantasies. It was also merely the latest in a sequence of slave revolts, and the methods used to crush it formed part of an almost respectable tradition of panicky European reaction followed by the violent reassertion of white control.

At the very least, the Morant Bay uprising precipitated a serious debate within British society over the relationship between black and white within the imperial system. The British Liberal statesman and Quaker John Bright believed that 'the fame of England has never received a deeper wound or darker stain' than from the judicial murder of Gordon. The scientist Thomas Huxley described it as the worst case of political murder since Judge Jeffreys' 'Bloody Assizes' after Monmouth's rebellion of the late seventeenth century. John Stuart Mill wrote that 'There was much more at stake than only justice to the negroes, imperative as was that consideration. The question was, whether the British dependencies, and eventually, perhaps, Great Britain itself, were to be under the government of law or of military licence.'[13]

Those who defended Eyre, on the other hand, included Charles Kingsley, Ruskin, Carlyle, Tennyson, Dickens and many leading members of the Anglican clergy. It is perhaps worth noting that of those leading members of the Eyre Defence Committee both Ruskin and Carlyle suffered from sexual impotence, a factor which may have lent an edge to their bitter denunciations of feckless, uninhibited blacks.

Steering a judicious middle way between these inflamed factions, *The Times* judged that Eyre was neither a hero nor a murderer, but rather a man who had acted rationally and precipitously under enormous pressure. It went on to pronounce:

> Though a flea-bite compared with the Indian Mutiny, it touches our pride more and is more in the nature of a disappointment . . . Jamaica is our pet institution and its inhabitants are our spoilt children . . . It seemed to be proved in Jamaica that the Negro could become fit for self-government . . . Alas for the grand triumphs of humanity, and the improvement of races, and the removal of primeval curses, and the expenditure of 20 million sterling, Jamaica herself gainsays the fact and belies herself . . . It is that which affects us much more than even the Sepoy revolt.[14]

The Jamaica Rebellion produced an important shift in British colonial policy. It provided the government with the excuse to move against, and sweep away, the anachronistic colonial constitutions in the West Indies. The old Colonial Assemblies that had been established on the same model as those of the North American colonies before the revolution of 1776 had become overwhelmingly the vehicles of a grotesquely inflated white settler power. In Jamaica, and many smaller islands, Crown Colony rule was now established. Although Barbados, Bermuda, the Bahamas and British Guiana kept their ancient institutions, these were now the exception in the Caribbean. In its early stages Crown Colony rule was fundamentally autocratic, and a form of direct rule from Britain. But at least it placed power in the hands of a supposedly impartial Colonial Office. At the same time it denied overlordship to an insular white minority, while not handing over government to an uninstructed black majority.

At its best, however, it provided the basis from which to begin the long haul, via representative government, to responsible government. Perhaps in that regard the trauma, bloodshed and soul-searching that accompanied the Jamaica uprising were prices worth paying. The road of constitutional reform, however, was to prove a long and wearying one, and it was not until 1962 that Jamaica obtained its full independence. In the meantime, the subjects of British rule in the Caribbean were, in overwhelming numbers, obliged to continue their perennial struggle to retain their dignity and to make ends meet amid the continuing economic decay of King Sugar's once prosperous realm.

9

THE OPENING
OF THE SUEZ CANAL IN 1869

Britain in Egypt and the Sudan; Gordon at Khartoum, and
Kitchener's Reconquest of the Sudan

IN DECEMBER 1869 the Suez Canal was completed and formally
opened. Lavish ceremonial and expensive junketing, attended by the
representatives of many nations, inaugurated a new age of maritime
communication. There were some impressive statistics for the guests to
digest together with the *Poisson à la Reunion des Deux Mers* and the *Crevettes
de Suez au Cresson*: the canal was a hundred miles long, three hundred
feet wide at its surface, and seventy-five million cubic meters of earth
had been shifted to build it. Verdi was commissioned to write a new
opera, *Aida*, for the event, but the costumes were not ready in time,
and on the opening night at Cairo's new opera house *Rigoletto* had to
be performed instead. Behind the tumult of acrobats, the gyrations
of the belly-dancers and the explosions and glitter of the celebratory
fireworks, however, were some harsher political, economic and strategic
realities.[1]

No nation stood to benefit more from the opening of the Suez Canal
than Britain. A waterway connecting the Mediterranean with the Red
Sea at a stroke shortened the sea route to India, the Far East and
Australasia substantially, thus enabling freight to be transported more
quickly and at a lower cost, and also providing for the more rapid
movement of British warships and troops to trouble-spots and points
of tension east of Suez.

The opening of the canal forced Britain to make a number of significant policy adjustments. Not only were British governments to
become progressively entangled in the internal affairs of Egypt, an intimate involvement that caused the military intervention of 1882 and

thence ran right through to the Suez invasion of 1956, but countries on the Egyptian periphery were also drawn into Britain's sphere of influence. Britain thus became progressively involved in the internal affairs of Sudan, Aden, Bahrain, Muscat and Oman, and other states in the Persian Gulf. It is also evident that the strategic ramifications of the opening of the Suez route played a significant, though often hotly disputed, part in the process of European imperial aggrandisement that is sometimes described as 'the scramble for Africa'.

For three-quarters of a century before the opening of the Suez Canal, British statesmen had striven to prevent either France or Russia becoming dominant in the eastern Mediterranean in general and over the Suez isthmus in particular. They were right to be anxious. Napoleon Bonaparte's invasion of Egypt in 1798 brought the swift response of a Royal Navy expedition led by Nelson. The Battle of the Nile effectively marooned the French forces in Egypt, but not before Bonaparte's engineers had got as far as surveying possible routes for a canal through the isthmus. Ambitions for the construction of such a canal had been cherished by France as far back as the reign of Louis XIV, when the project was seen as a bid both to restore the old Mediterranean prosperities and to damage the newly risen Atlantic powers of England and the Netherlands.[2]

The early years of the nineteenth century saw considerable interest in Britain and other European states in the establishment of quicker communications between the Mediterranean and the Indian Ocean. The development of the railway and the steam engine, however, created a new technological climate which apparently rendered the older technology of the canal out of date. The developers' interests, therefore, were principally concentrated upon methods of creating speedier overland routes. In 1840 the British engineer R.M. Stephenson announced his plan 'to girdle the world with an iron chain, to connect Europe and Asia from their furthest extremities by one colossal railway'.[3] But the invention of the steamship as well as the steam engine had brought Europe dramatically closer to Asia, and from 1835 Thomas Waghorn's Overland Mail system was able to provide a quick connection between the steam packets with which it could link up in both the Mediterranean and the Red Sea. Waghorn's Overland Mail was officially recognised and used by the East India Company in 1837, and indisputably brought Calcutta nearer to London.[4] Heavy loads of freight, however, could not so easily be moved that way, and even the cost of a letter between India and Britain was exorbitantly high at 5 shillings and 5 pence.

93

The initiative to cut a canal through the Suez isthmus was dramatically seized in 1854 by the French engineer Ferdinand de Lesseps when he obtained a concession from the Khedive of Egypt to begin construction.[5] The formal launching of de Lesseps' Suez Canal Company in 1858, in which the Khedive held a 40 per cent minority holding of shares, with most of the rest owned by the French government and French commercial interests, once more faced the British Cabinet with the nightmare of French control of the short route to India and the Far East. Many British businessmen and exporters, however, saw things differently and enthusiastically supported de Lesseps' venture.

British foreign policy-makers, dominated by the forthright and dogmatic Lord Palmerston, threw their considerable weight against the Suez Canal project. One of the main planks of British foreign policy in the eastern Mediterranean was the determination to prop up the Ottoman Empire – ramshackle, inefficient and an inordinately long time a-dying – as a bulwark against Russian, and to a lesser extent French, ambition. In the Crimean War of 1854 to 1856, Britain had fought as an ally of France and Turkey in order to limit Russian expansion. Since the Khedive Ismail, the ruler of Egypt, was technically under the suzerainty of the Ottomans, Britain quickly cashed in some of her credit at Istanbul by obstructing the work of the Suez Canal Company.

In 1863, with the canal half-built, the British ambassador in Istanbul persuaded the Turkish Sultan to order a halt in the construction work on the grounds that de Lesseps' company had so far used over 60,000 forced labourers from among the Egyptian *fellahin*. So successful were Britain's obstructive tactics, and so powerful was British influence, that work on the canal did not restart properly until 1866.[6] The irony, however, of Britain's diplomatic success was that the French government finally and officially backed the canal project and promised financial support to the company. De Lesseps could now press ahead with the completion of the canal.

The opening of the canal did not immediately transform the patterns of British overseas trade. Many British merchant shipping companies were reluctant to reroute their vessels and abandon the longer but familiar voyage round the Cape. During the 1870s much more commercial use was made of the Cape route than of the Suez Canal. This proved to be a temporary phenomenon. The overland routes withered away, and the Suez Canal Company was able to reward its shareholders suitably and to repay outstanding interest on loans. British trade with India in particular was stimulated by the short route, and expanded substantially during the remaining years of the nineteenth century.

Although the British government appeared to have lost its battle to keep France from a dominating role in Egypt, it was soon to recoup the position. Britain's economic and strategic imperatives were the driving forces behind this counter-offensive, but the path was cleared by the internal problems of Egypt. In a pattern that was to be repeated manifold in the post-imperial years of the late twentieth century, the government of the Egyptian Khedive became increasingly indebted to European creditors. Ironically this was due to Ismail's enlightened attempts to 'Europeanise' his country. But schemes to develop Egypt's irrigation system, agricultural methods and communications, although they commended the Khedive to European opinion, simply plunged his government deep into debt. Unable, or unwilling, to purge his own administration of corruption, the Khedive reeled from one financial crisis to another, gradually exhausting his credit in London and Paris.

By the mid-1870s Egypt's financial misfortunes had enabled Disraeli's Conservative government to purchase a large quantity of the bankrupt Ismail's shares in the Suez Canal Company, and thus to buy Britain parity with France in it. In 1876 the Khedive, unable to maintain the repayments of interest, had to accept the setting-up of an international committee, *La Caisse de la Dette Publique*, to handle these revenues and to ensure that the appropriate repayments to foreign bankers were made. This was followed by the establishment of a British and a French controller to manage the finance departments of the Egyptian government. By 1878 Britain and France had forced the Khedive to appoint a responsible ministry which included one French and one British minister.[7] Simultaneously the number of resident Europeans in Egypt increased dramatically by tens of thousands.

The system of Anglo–French Dual Control was primarily aimed at rendering Egypt once more solvent and at strengthening the Khedivate. It amounted to Britain's acceptance that it should share the problems of managing Egypt in an equal partnership with France. This strategy was ruined, however, by a revolt in Egypt. Originating in the army, and led by an Egyptian colonel, Urabi Pasha, the revolutionary movement was designed to eliminate, or at least substantially diminish, European control of Egyptian affairs. The Egyptian Army revolt coincided with a change of government in France. Although it could not have been predicted at the time, these two events were to hand Britain the dominion of Egypt.

Supported by many elements within Egyptian society, from constitutional liberals to landlords, and including Muslim traditionalists and the long-suffering peasantry, Urabi Pasha and his junta of colonels continued to wring a series of constitutional concessions from the newly appointed Anglo-French puppet Khedive, Taufiq. When, in 1882, Urabi became Minister for War, and one of his supporters Prime Minister, Anglo-French interests were faced with a thorny choice.

The recently elected Liberal administration in Britain, led by Gladstone, vacillated as to the best response. The Prime Minister himself was genuinely ambivalent in his attitude. On the one hand, he recognised the strength of Egyptian nationalist sentiment; on the other, he felt bound to uphold British interests in the Suez route. It is, however, worth noting that Gladstone, like many in his party – the prominent Radical M.P. Henry Labouchere, for instance – had a private financial interest to consider as well as the well-advertised public ones. Some 37 per cent of the Prime Minister's investment portfolio was sunk in Egyptian shares.[8] Although initially his Cabinet seemed dangerously divided on the issue, it is therefore perhaps not surprising that the interventionists, strongly and perhaps unexpectedly supported by the extreme Radical Joseph Chamberlain, soon gained the upper hand.

When Anglo-French diplomatic pressure and a naval demonstration off Alexandria failed to overawe the Urabi government, the propaganda machines of both countries began to paint a lurid and misleading picture of what they perceived as the 'Egyptian crisis'. It was asserted, despite the lack of concrete evidence, that the Suez Canal was unsafe in Egyptian hands. When rioting in Alexandria in June 1882 resulted in the death of some forty Europeans, British and French newspaper reports produced horrendous and largely fictitious accounts of violent disorders that had allegedly left up to three hundred Europeans dead.

Its collective mind now made up by reports of the Alexandria riots and by the pressure and clamour of alarmed British investors and Suez Canal Company shareholders, the Gladstone Cabinet decided on military intervention. A weak and divided French government opted out. In the autumn of 1882 a British expeditionary force, led by Sir Garnet Wolseley, routed the Egyptian forces at the battle of Tel-el Kebir. Urabi was imprisoned, and the forces of Egyptian nationalism scattered.[9] Perhaps genuinely, the British drew up a timetable for withdrawal once the internal affairs of Egypt had been stabilised to their satisfaction. But the truth was, as Gladstone asserted, 'We have done our

Egyptian business, and we are the Egyptian government.'

Amid the ruins of the principle of Dual Control, Lord Cromer, a member of the distinguished banking family of Baring, was sent out as British government agent and consul-general; in effect, he became the real ruler of Egypt. Cromer thought little of the Egyptians, including the Khedive, who was once observed to turn pale at the approach of the consul-general's carriage, anxiously wondering what he was now going to be told to do. As for the Egyptian masses, Cromer's views were expressed in a forthright essay entitled 'The Government of the Subject Races':

> We need not always enquire too closely what these people, who are all, nationally speaking, more or less in statu pupillari, themselves think is in their own interests . . . it is essential that each special issue should be decided mainly with reference to what, by the light of Western knowledge and experience . . . we conscientiously think is best for the subject race.[10]

While professing its intention of withdrawing from Egypt when conditions permitted, the British government in fact hastened to consolidate its hold. Although Cromer succeeded in balancing the Egyptian budget by 1888, British engineers, civil servants and businessmen continued to infiltrate and dominate many of the country's institutions and services. Heavy loans were raised. Some of the money was pumped into the Department of Public Works, which was the chief instrument of a number of agricultural reforms that included improvements in the irrigation system, thus, ironically, building on the achievements of the ex-Khedive Ismail. The heavy hand of British military control was made manifest in the permanent military garrisons stationed in the major cities and along the canal. Despite retaining his throne, the Khedive Taufiq was overwhelmingly obliged to do Cromer's, and Britain's, bidding.

The British presence in Egypt, which was to last for over seventy years, was at the outset both confused and effective. The confusion lay in Egypt's status, which was theoretically that of an independent country owing allegiance to the Turkish Sultan. In reality, it was the British who ruled Egypt, while pretending not to do so. At least this ludicrous situation was rationalised at the outbreak of the First World War when Egypt was simply declared a British protectorate.

In Cairo and other centres of power, British influence was

undisguised and apparently permanent. A sumptuous hotel, Shepheard's, provided British and European visitors with tea and cakes and a refuge from the flies. European residents were given special, protected legal status, and there was a British residential area in Cairo where British social routine flourished undisturbed. Three-quarters of Alexandria's trade was carried in British shipping, and British tourists proceeded up the Nile in spotless paddle-steamers. To some extent, the fortunes of Thomas Cook and Company were made on the back of the British intervention in Egypt, since the enterprising travel agents were able to cash in on the keen interest in the culture of Ancient Egypt felt by the European intelligentsia and the well-to-do. It is worth noting that Thomas Cook and Company were also sometimes active agents of British imperialist policy, as in the autumn of 1884 when they supplied coal, food and steamships to the expedition proceeding up the Nile with the intention of rescuing the besieged General Gordon at Khartoum.

Britain made convincing enough claims that Egypt was benefiting greatly from the introduction of British standards of administration and financial probity. But despite the undoubted improvements in the administrative efficiency of the country, the British experience in Egypt was in itself corrupting. Regimes were manipulated so shamelessly, Kedhives overawed so easily, common Egyptians pushed out of the way so carelessly, that in the end there was nothing for the British to respect in contemporary, native Egypt. Archaeologists might stand in rapture before the well-preserved magnificence of the Pharaohs, but to most observers there seemed very little in common between Rameses II and a Khedive who combined an Oriental taste for luxury with indebtedness to European bankers.

Over seventy years of occupation also helped confirm, as well as create, British prejudices against the 'Orient'. During this period the hundreds of thousands of British troops who served in the canal zone and the garrisons at Cairo and Alexandria often brought back a contemptuous and ribald assessment of the Egyptians. Unlikely to have experience of the progressive intellectuals of Alexandria, or Cairo's fastidious and Europeanised aristocrats, they would have judged Egyptian society by other measures. Their encounters with the impoverished and subdued peasantry, the cringing and persistent beggars, the purveyors of dubious pleasures and the sellers of the legendary 'dirty postcard' tended to stick in the mind and thus served to inflate and consolidate their feelings of superiority. Although 'Egyptian jokes' were never manufactured on the same vast scale as those directed at the Irish, some contemptuous and crippling stereotypes of the 'typical Egyptian' were soon embedded in the national subconscious. It became possible to reduce members of theatre, and later film or television, audiences to hysterics simply by enacting, to the accompaniment of Arabic music, a sinuous dance between men clad in fezzes and long, striped, ankle-length gowns.

If the Egyptians could not be treated seriously as a race, then the aspirations of their nationalist politicians could be equally abruptly dismissed. It was therefore one of the exquisite humiliations of British imperial history that in the mid-1950s a revolutionary Egyptian government led by army colonels, very like Urabi's movement three-quarters of a century before, abruptly ended Britain's control over the canal and provoked an international crisis which revealed Britain's, and indeed France's, reduced powers in their proper light.

Having become in 1882 'the Egyptian government', the British authorities also assumed the responsibility for Egypt's external relations. Principally this involved the administration of the Sudan, an enormous territory that the Egyptians had conquered piecemeal from the beginning of the nineteenth century, and which was ruled from Cairo through provincial governors. The Egyptian crisis of 1881 to 1882, and the consequent assertion of British overlordship, assisted the rise of the Mahdi, an inspirational religious leader, in the Sudan. Preaching a holy war that would culminate in his elevation to the throne of the Turkish sultans as the fountainhead of a purified Islam, the Mahdi rallied around him the pious tribesmen of the Sudan and threatened Egyptian suzerainty. Province after province fell to the Mahdist forces.

Only in 1883 did the Egyptian government arouse itself sufficiently to dispatch a raggle-taggle expeditionary force under the joint command of Colonel William Hicks, a retired Indian Army officer known as Hicks 'Pasha', and a decrepit Egyptian general. The expedition was doomed from the outset. Not only was it grudgingly financed, but the purge of the army following the defeat of Urabi Pasha's revolutionary movement had left it weakened and irresolute. In November 1883 Hicks Pasha and his troops were overwhelmed and slaughtered by the dervishes of the Mahdist movement.[11]

Gladstone's Liberal government decided to abandon the Sudan and evacuate the remaining Egyptian garrisons there. To this purpose, and against his better judgement, the Prime Minister chose Major-General Charles Gordon to go to Khartoum and effect the evacuation.[12] Gordon was one of those colourful, eccentric, evangelical, unorthodox and essentially unreliable personalities with which Victorian history is littered. Every bit as convinced of his own righteousness as was the Mahdi, he was no sooner in Khartoum than he decided to stay put. Solitary, visionary and obstinate, Gordon, with equally strong tastes for brandy and independent action, was a difficult man to winkle out. His appeal to the Victorian public emanated from a charismatic career which had fixed him in the public imagination as the no-nonsense sword-bearer of evangelical Christianity. Though some eyebrows were raised at his taste for the company of small boys and his devotion to Boys' Homes, such propensities were generally accepted as part and parcel of his religious zeal.

As the Mahdist forces closed in on Khartoum, the British government prevaricated over the best course of action. Eventually, although just too late as it turned out, a relief expedition under General Sir Garnet Wolseley began a slow progress up the Nile. Two days before the paddle-steamers sighted Khartoum, however, the city had fallen and its garrison, including Gordon, had been massacred by the dervishes. Despite a self-indulgent and hysterical public reaction in Britain, and the unbridled criticism of an incensed Queen Victoria, Gladstone's government survived the crisis and went on comfortably to win the general election in the autumn of 1885. Even when a Conservative administration was formed under Lord Salisbury in June 1886, in the aftermath of the Irish Home Rule crisis, there was little option but to abandon the Sudan to Mahdism. For a decade, successive British governments steered clear of intervention.

Only in 1896 did events in East Africa force the government's hand. The reassessment of British policy towards the Sudan began in the aftermath of the humiliating defeat of Italian forces attempting to annex Abyssinia at a great battle at Adowa. British statesmen noted with alarm that the Abyssinian army had been assisted in its triumph by French and Russian military advice and assistance. In addition, the victorious King Menelek of Abyssinia seemed about to enter into an alliance with the dervishes of the Sudan. The British government, and their Egyptian subsidiaries, were thus faced with the unwelcome threat of Russian and French intrusion in East Africa and an inconvenient alliance between two independent African countries. A little over a week after the Battle of Adowa, Salisbury announced the invasion of the Sudan.

The Sudan campaign culminated in the Battle of Omdurman, on 2 September 1898. The confrontation between the Anglo-Egyptian army, led by General Kitchener, and the dervish host, badly led and armed with primitive weapons, resulted in the predictable triumph of Western technology. Thousands of dervishes led by the Khalifa, the Mahdi's successor, obligingly and heroically ran full-tilt at the well-served rifles and maxim guns of their opponents. When the last shots were fired, the Anglo-Egyptian army had lost forty-eight men, but over 11,000 of the enemy were left dead upon the battlefield.[13] There could have been no more graphic inspiration of Hilaire Belloc's famous couplet, published in the same year in *The Modern Traveller*:

> *Whatever happens, we have got*
> *The Maxim Gun, and they have not.*

Kitchener, rigid and single-minded, obsessed with detail and coldly reserved even under the blazing desert sun, had won a great triumph for the imperial cause. The complexities of his personality were illustrated in the immediate aftermath of his triumphal entry into Khartoum, when he wept publicly for the memory of the martyred Gordon, but a little later ordered the desecration of the Mahdi's tomb and gave serious thought to using the dead leader's skull as an inkstand. British liberal opinion reacted with horror, and Kitchener made haste to reassure an anxious Queen Victoria and disarm his critics.

The conquest of the Sudan pitched Britain into one of those face-to-face confrontations with a rival imperial power that were so rare in the history of the European partition of Africa. As the victorious Anglo-Egyptian army proceeded up the Nile they came across a small detachment of French troops, led by Captain Marchand, at Fashoda. Unlikely as it may seem, Marchand's orders were to find the site for the building of a dam to divert the waters of the Nile, thus holding the British, the acknowledged masters of Egypt, to ransom.

In the highly charged atmosphere of Anglo–French relations, the fact that the scheme for building such a dam was quite impractical was soon forgotten. It was the symbolism of the French presence at Fashoda that was far more significant. From the British point of view, Marchand seemed to be attempting to exact a retrospective strategic revenge for Britain's decision to go it alone in 1882. The French government gave no indication that they were prepared to back down, and for good measure rattled some sabres. A diplomatic incident of enormous and essentially ludicrous proportions ensued. In both countries public opinion, inflamed by the lurid editorials in the recently established popular press, became more bellicose. For a while, although it was essentially an illusion, Britain and France seemed on the brink of war.

If the Fashoda Incident had resulted in a military conflict, it would have been a rare exception to the rule which had prevailed throughout the latter part of the nineteenth century when European powers had expressed rival claims to African territory. The so-called 'scramble for Africa' had been characterised by sensible negotiations and accommodation, not by the heavyweight bruisers of European imperialism slugging it out in the field. The fact that by the end of the nineteenth century nearly 40 per cent of Africa's frontiers were made up of straight lines provides the clearest possible evidence that the partition of the Dark Continent was the result of diplomatic compromise rather than bloody and unrestrained conflict.

In the end, the Fashoda Incident proved to be no exception. Kitchener dealt pragmatically with the crisis on the spot, invited Marchand aboard his paddle-steamer, treated him with unusual forbearance, and proposed that, as two military men of honour, they should let 'those swines of politicians' sort out the problem.

In truth, France had little option but to surrender. Britain, with Kitchener's victorious army poised to proceed up the Nile, held all the trump cards. The confrontation at Fashoda at least had the merit of leading to both great imperial powers agreeing on a border between Sudanese and French territory to the south-west.[14]

The Fashoda Incident satisfactorily resolved, Kitchener spent the rest of the year after the Battle of Omdurman mopping up dervish resistance and relishing his autocratic powers as Governor-General of the Sudan. From Britain's point of view, the mess in the Sudan was neatly tidied up. The Khalifa and his surviving emirs were hunted down by Anglo-Egyptian forces and shot. The civil administration of the country was thoroughly reorganised and high-flying British civil servants, described with some exaggeration as 'the heaven-born', recruited to run it. In 1899 the Sudan was made a condominium, with Britain and Egypt being declared jointly responsible for its government.[15] As in the case of the Suez Canal Convention of 1888, which had apparently guaranteed all nations freedom of passage through the waterway in time of peace and war, the establishment of the condominium was a farce. The British got all that they wanted. They continued to control the Suez Canal, and since they were the effective rulers of Egypt, they also administered the Sudan. During its half-century of condominium status, the Sudan never had an Egyptian governor-general, and the civil service was dominated by British administrators.

Once more Britain had triumphed in a struggle to assert its imperial and commercial interests. It had also managed to do so by pretending quite otherwise. It was small wonder that French patriots denounced perfidious Albion, and that in international circles British, especially English, hypocrisy became a byword.

10

THE BATTLE OF
MAJUBA HILL, 1881

Bantu, Briton and Boer in South Africa;
from the British Annexation of the Cape
to the Convention of London 1884

IN FEBRUARY 1881, a small British army commanded by General
Sir George Pomeroy Colley was humiliatingly defeated by Afrikaner
forces at the Battle of Majuba Hill on the border between Natal and
the Transvaal. Colley himself was shot through the head at close range
as his men were driven off the summit of Majuba. British losses were
ninety-three killed, 133 wounded and fifty-eight taken prisoner. Boer
losses were absurdly small – one man killed, and five wounded, of whom
one subsequently died.

Compared with many other battles fought by Britain during the
nineteenth century to extend or preserve its imperial hegemony, the
Battle of Majuba Hill seems a trifling affair. Britain's military humiliation, however, produced a reaction out of all proportion to the size of
the defeat. At home, the Gladstone government and the British public
were embarrassed and shocked at the disaster. For a while British prestige throughout southern Africa was shattered. The Afrikaners of the
Transvaal, whose rebellion against the British annexation of their
republic in 1877 had culminated in the Battle of Majuba, took heart
from this display of imperial military incompetence. General Colley had
been regarded as one of the rising stars of the British Army, and had
graduated from Staff College with 4,274 marks, the biggest total on
record and more than five hundred ahead of his nearest rival. Despite
his academic brilliance, however, he had only trifling front-line experience of military action, and at Majuba he led his troops into such a
vulnerable position on the mountain summit that the Transvaal marks-

men opposing him had been offered a large number of inviting targets. The Boer triumph at Majuba, moreover, was not an isolated embarrassment for British arms. During the Transvaal War of 1880 to 1881, Afrikaner forces, organised in commandos manned by armed civilians, had already inflicted three sharp, if minor, defeats upon the British army.

The Battle of Majuba became a byword for British incompetence and Boer military accomplishment. It rewrote a chapter of South African history, forcing the Gladstone government reluctantly to restore independence to the Transvaal. It also convinced Afrikaans-speaking people throughout South Africa that, in the last resort, the vastly superior resources of the British military machine could be scorned, defied, and ultimately defeated.

'Majuba' became a watchword for both sides: the Transvaalers celebrated 'Majuba Day', patriots in Britain urged everyone to 'Remember Majuba'. When the South African War broke out in October 1899, and the British Commander-in-Chief, General Buller, and his staff boarded ship at Southampton for the Cape, a big, red-faced onlooker repeatedly shouted at them 'Remember Majuba!' As a member of Buller's staff was later ironically to recall, 'He need not have worried, we soon had plenty of Majubas of our own.'[1]

The mess in which the British found themselves in the Transvaal, and indeed throughout the whole of South Africa, in the aftermath of Majuba Hill, was a striking illustration of the complexities and perils that very rapidly seemed an intrinsic part of Britain's involvement in the region following the formal annexation of the Cape of Good Hope in 1815. The original reason why Britain had retained control of the Cape, which it had taken from the Dutch during the French Revolutionary and Napoleonic Wars, was quite simple. Before the opening of the Suez Canal, the only practical sea route to India and the Far East was round the Cape. Having acquired the maritime facilities of Cape Town, and with Simonstown as an increasingly important Royal Navy base, many British policy-makers would ideally have wished to avoid involvement with the Cape's hinterland. Instead, a number of factors and processes dragged Britain into an increasingly complicated, and for a considerable time unrewarding and unprofitable, involvement with the whole of South Africa.

This was partly due to the inexorable and predatory demands of the imperial frontier. The new rulers of the Cape had been obliged to take on the responsibility for governing, or at the very least controlling, the 'Cape Dutch', the Afrikaans-speaking European settlers, numbering some 40,000 in 1815. The British imperial authorities were also brought, whether they liked it or not, into face-to-face confrontation with the different African tribespeople of southern Africa as well as becoming responsible for the Cape Coloured population – the result of two centuries of sexual activity between the dominant white settlers and black women.

British rule in the Cape would undoubtedly have been easier and more tranquil in an age of fixed local populations and stable patterns of commerce and trade. South Africa, however, was in the last resort frontier territory, an equivalent to the American Wild West at the southern tip of Africa. Groups of white settlers tended to push, according to their needs, to the north, while various Bantu tribes were also on the move. For many years the Afrikaner political imperative asserted that as white settlers moved north, black tribespeople moving south met them head-on. This was a partial truth. Overall, population movements throughout the region were not a simple matter of groups of people from the north colliding with groups migrating from the south. In response to their subsistence, economic, political and military needs, a variety of people within South Africa moved north, south, east and west to wherever there was better grazing, free, available land, and the chance to shake off a variety of persecutors, including tyrannical rulers or overbearing rival tribes.

In this sense, the Afrikaner people of the Cape were simply another tribe, although a white one. They were also sustained by a coherent and fundamentally inflexible ideology. Composed of different nationalities, Dutch, Flemish and German, and with a strong contingent of exiled French Huguenots, the Afrikaners shared an adherence to Calvinist principles and an intense dislike of overriding government authority. Seeing themselves as a racially pure elect in a black continent, and accustomed to decades of neglect by the Netherlands government, they considered themselves to be in charge of their own destiny. For their part, the British administrators of the Cape, coming, like British missionaries and settlers, from a social and cultural environment strikingly at odds with the rough and isolated life of the hinterland, saw no reason to wash their hands of the Afrikaner settlers.

Within two decades of the final establishment of British control over the Cape, relations between the Afrikaners and the imperial authorities had been stretched to breaking point. At the root of this disaffection lay the Afrikaner conviction that the British were mounting both an overt and a covert assault on their privileges and position. British administrators, and certainly the British settlers, had no immediate ambitions to overthrow the Afrikaner people and to promote the black African tribes in their place. On the other hand, the humanitarian standards of the imperial administration, and the liberal impulses of the British evangelical missions, seemed a double threat to a set of convictions of nearly two centuries' standing.

Neither British administrators nor British missionaries had a separate political agenda for South Africa. The British colonial empire was governed according to certain common policies, and these could not be waived simply to placate a few thousand Afrikaner farmers. It was also true that British missionaries often subscribed to a less dogmatic analysis of racial differences than the Calvinist, Dutch Reformed Church of the Afrikaners. Afrikaner fears for their position at the apex of Cape society resulted in a distressingly predictable cycle of paranoia, attended by exaggerated fears and wild misconceptions. British rule seemed, on this analysis, to be wilfully and deliberately out of touch with Afrikaner sensibilities and, worse still, to be irredeemably biased towards the blacks.

On top of this, Britain seemed determined to limit Afrikaner expansion to the north. There were clear enough reasons for this. If the Afrikaners could be contained, then it was easier to tax and administer them. If they were allowed to shake off imperial control, their expansion to the north and east would inevitably bring clashes with the Bantu and so disturb, perhaps for an impossibly long time, the peace and stability that the British so craved for Cape Colony.

The Afrikaner people saw things quite differently. They argued that the scourges of drought and cattle disease made the continual acquisition of new grazing lands essential. They pointed to the almost continual frontier clashes with Bantu tribespeople, conflicts that centred primarily on the possession of land and cattle. The Kaffir War of 1834 to 1835, though merely one of a sequence, was attended by more than the usual measure of bloodshed, farm burning and cattle slaughter, thus stimulating white settler movement into more peaceful regions.

The abolition of slavery throughout the British Empire in 1833 was an even more fundamental blow to Afrikaner susceptibilities. As it happened, comparatively few Afrikaner farmers owned slaves. Their way of life, however, did depend heavily upon the dirt cheap labour of farm hands and domestic servants. The abolition of slavery seemed to provide the clearest indication that the British were bent on the subversion of the Afrikaner order of things in the Cape. To these anxieties was added the insult of inadequate compensation both for freed slaves and for losses incurred during the 1834–35 Kaffir War.

As so often proved to be the case among European communities far from home, especially those facing unpalatable changes, feverish Afrikaner imaginations were soon feasting on fantasies of the British administration handing over vast tracts of available land to blacks, sponsoring mixed-race marriages and even forcibly imposing Roman Catholicism on the devoutly Calvinist Boer population. Much of this was perceived as merely the worst excesses of a deliberate programme of Anglicisation which had made English the official language in 1827, brought about the scrapping of the Dutch military system and introduced the British legal structure.

Beginning in the mid-1830s, one of the climactic events of Afrikaner history took place. Known in Afrikaner folklore and mythology as the Great Trek, the migration of some 14,000 Boers across the Orange River to lands to the east and the north changed the course of South African history. It was essentially an act of civil rebellion, the rejection of a government whose policies seemed at variance with the self-interest of the trekkers. In their covered ox-wagons, attended for the most part by their black servants and labourers, Afrikaner families struck off into the wilderness hoping for better days, better land and, above all, freedom from British rule, or indeed from any other rule.

The depths of Afrikaner feeling against the perceived drift towards racial equality can be seen in the words of Ana Stenkamp, a sister of the Voortrekker leader Piet Retief, when she asserted that the Afrikaners trekked because of 'the shameful and unjust proceedings with reference to the freedom of our slaves – and yet it is not their freedom that drove us to such lengths, as their being placed on an equal footing with Christians, contrary to the laws of God . . . wherefore we rather withdrew in order to preserve our doctrines in purity'.[2] Jacobus Boshof, a Voortrekker and a future President of the Orange Free State, also complained of what he saw as the oppression of European citizens 'as every new law or ordinance in which the black population was concerned betrayed the most tender and paternal care for them, and a disregard of the interests of the whites'.[3]

The Great Trek was the equivalent of the seventeenth-century migration of political and religious dissenters across the Atlantic, or perhaps of the discontented, destitute and ambitious to Australasia during the nineteenth century. By no means all of the Afrikaner population of the Cape left, and despite the British government-sponsored landing of some 5,000 English-speaking settlers at Albany on the Cape in 1820, the Afrikaans-speaking section of the European population there continued to comprise at least two-thirds of the whole white community well into the second half of the twentieth century.

For their part, the British did their best to tidy up in the aftermath of the Great Trek. They were not content to see an Afrikaner republic established on the Natal coast, and in 1843 annexed that province, as a consequence driving the majority of Boer settlers inland, where many of them ended up in what became known as the Transvaal. Having denied the Voortrekkers access to the coast bordering on the Indian Ocean, the British authorities now had to decide what policies to adopt towards the various Afrikaner settlements in what became known as the Orange Free State and the Transvaal.

Essentially, Britain decided to let the trekkers get on with it. It is important to understand that at this time, and arguably for at least another half-century, the Afrikaners were no homogeneous, united people. There were, for example, several petty Boer republics established across the Vaal River as a consequence of the Great Trek and subsequent migrations, including Vryheid, Zoutspansberg and Lydenburg. The separate republics were quite often at odds with each other, even to the point of military conflict. Indeed, early in 1857, forces from the Transvaal, led by Andries Pretorius, actually invaded the Orange Free State in an unsuccessful attempt to bring about a forcible union between the Afrikaner republics.

It is easy to see why the imperial government, in the years following the Great Trek and its subsidiary migrations, was content not to assert control over the newly settled territories. They judged, quite simply, that the various ramshackle structures would simply fall apart, destroyed by the aggression of Bantu tribespeople and by their own obscurantist ideologies, backward pastoral economic practices and chronic bankruptcy.

In order to set the record straight, so to speak, the British government negotiated separate agreements with the two main Afrikaner republics. In 1852 the Sand River Convention recognised the independence of the 15,000 Transvaalers. Two years later, the Bloemfontein Convention acknowledged the sovereignty of the Orange Free State. Both treaties addressed one of the chief causes of British anxiety at the great Afrikaner migration when they laid down guarantees for the

security and integrity of the northern frontiers of the two Boer republics. In exchange for the undertaking not to push further north, the
Afrikaner people of the Transvaal and the Orange Free State were
allowed a free hand in their internal affairs. In particular they now had
complete control over the black tribespeople within their borders.

The constitutional settlement of the early 1850s was primarily an
exercise in co-existence. From Britain's point of view, it was also
a comparatively low-risk, low-cost policy. Until 1870 South Africa
seemed, in comparison to other areas of European settlement, an
unprofitable and unduly troublesome region. Neither capital nor immigrants were attracted there in any substantial quantity. To the severe
droughts which rendered the climate so unreliable was added a generally impoverished soil and the disruptions caused by plagues of locusts
and cattle disease. The great staple products and crops so central to the
expanding colonial economies of Canada, Australia and New Zealand,
timber, wheat, wool, coffee, sugar and tobacco, all failed to establish
themselves adequately in South Africa. Of these, wool was the most
successful, and by 1862 25 million pounds was being exported. The
quality of South African wool, however, particularly that raised in the
Transvaal, was among the lowest in the British market.

Even the docking and maritime facilities of Cape Town were underdeveloped until the 1860s, thus limiting the opportunities for employment and labour for British immigrants. English-speaking migration to
South Africa remained disappointingly low until the 1870s, even compared with Australia and New Zealand, which were in turn less attractive to British emigrants than the United States. To compound all
these difficulties there was also the intractable nature of much of the
Afrikaans-speaking population and the chronic prospect of armed conflict with various African tribespeople over land-grazing rights, water
supplies and cattle.

Nonetheless, in those territories ruled directly by Britain, the Cape
and, after 1843, Natal, the constitutional developments that characterised other parts of the British colonial system also occurred in South
Africa. In 1854 a new parliament met in Cape Town, in which both
houses were elective and thus in advance of either Australian or Canadian practice. Of even more significance was the fact that the Cape
franchise was open to those of all races, although the financial qualification for voting rights was sufficiently high to disenfranchise the vast
majority of Cape Coloureds and the overwhelming majority of Bantu.
Although it was technically possible for a non-European to sit as a

member of the Cape legislature, the plain fact was that during the entire life of the Cape Parliament, from 1854 to 1910, none actually did so.

Constitutional developments in Natal, which lagged several decades behind those of the Cape, nevertheless followed the Cape pattern. As in the Cape, the Natal constitution, although theoretically 'colour-blind', set the financial qualification for voting so high that very few non-Europeans managed to register. At least the franchise arrangements in both the Cape and Natal allowed for the possibility that black or coloured people could become voters. In the Afrikaner republics to the north, there was no such pussy-footing liberalism. Voting in the Transvaal and the Orange Free State was strictly reserved for whites.

Despite the relative lack of promise of the South African economy, despite the obduracy of the Afrikaner people, particularly those in the newly established republics, some British statesmen still cherished the hope of bringing about a federal solution to the awkward interaction of the various groups in the region. During his governor-generalship from 1854 to 1861, Sir George Grey, fresh from his outstandingly successful administration in New Zealand, tried hard to bring about a federation of the different European-dominated provinces; he also advocated the annexation of troublesome tribal areas. The British government, how-ever, shied away from the possible expense and almost certain diffi-culties involved in the enterprise. By the time Grey's governorship ended, the federation issue was apparently dead and buried.

For the European settler communities of South Africa, life was a strange and unpredictable mixture of solid certainty and high risk. The beautiful, whitewashed Dutch architectural-style farms of the Cape were symbols of prosperity and social standing. Often with three or four wings, these cool, self-sufficient buildings, with their outhouses and servants' quarters, had a good deal in common with the planters' man-sions of the American Deep South. They also had much in common as the focal points of an agricultural system employing large numbers of blacks and, by implication, serving as fortresses of white supremacy.

The humbler farms of the Free State or the Transvaal were equally sturdy outposts of European colonisation. Hospitality for fellow-Europeans was as a rule generous, and the sheltering of travellers the hallmark of a pioneer society. The bonds of family were especially strong, and neighbours generally cherished. In these ways, the authority of scattered, sparsely populated white settlements was maintained. The Afrikaner family relied heavily upon the authority of the Bible and of the Dutch Reformed Church and its pastor. Frontier medicine was primitive and generally based on ignorance and superstition. Homeopathy and sometimes ludicrously 'unscientific' remedies learned from the tribespeople were often the only available medicines. The Afrikaners of the still overwhelmingly rural Transvaal were frequently written off by British commentators:

> These Boers lead a lazy pastoral existence. They appear to have very little tincture of civilisation left, are stolidly unenterprising and occupy a magnificent country without attempting to develop in any way its resources. Towards the natives they have been brutal and domineering, dispossessing them of their lands and reducing many of them to slavery.[4]

In the towns, especially those of the Cape, but also gradually in settlements like Durban, Bloemfontein and Pretoria, there was at least a veneer of European civilisation. Theatres, music halls and libraries were established. Organised sport developed, and if the Afrikaners vehemently rejected what they perceived – often, in practice, mistakenly – as British theories of racial equality, they eagerly embraced the British sports of rugby football and, eventually, cricket.

By 1870 the European settler minorities in southern Africa were firmly rooted, if divided among themselves. The British control of the Cape seemed permanently established. There were some, indeed, who saw Cape Town as holding a pivotal position in the emerging British world order as 'the true centre of the Empire . . . clear of the Suez complications, almost equally distant from Australia, China, India, Gibraltar, the West Indies and the Falklands'.[5]

There was also the sheer bulk of British trade to, or passing around, the Cape. In 1878 this totalled £91,352,000, compared to £65,660,000 passing through the Suez Canal.

The British calculation was that within South Africa itself, growing commercial and economic interchange between the different communities would soften the hard edges of political separatism, and a voluntary federation would ensue. On the most optimistic assessment, this meant that a natural evolutionary process would bring about the gradual and inevitable unification of South Africa, in which the richer, more populous and British-controlled Cape Colony would dominate.

There were, however, two potential obstacles to this gradualist and fair-weather philosophy. One was predictable, and, given the circumstances of white control, inevitable: that is, serious trouble with the Bantu people. The second obstacle in the path of the gradual, peaceful and inevitable assertion of British supremacy was, as it turned out, much more difficult to envisage. This was the discovery, beginning in 1867, of such substantial deposits of diamonds, and later of gold, that, in the words of the Afrikaner historian F.S. Malan, in the end catastrophe overtook the two Boer republics 'in the form of fabulous riches'.[6]

The discovery of diamonds at Kimberley in 1869 injected a further and telling element of conflict into southern Africa. Kimberley was situated in Griqualand West, which was disputed territory between Britain and the Orange Free State. This immediate crisis was only resolved in 1876 when the British government bought out the Free State's claims for £90,000. The diamond fields, centred on the 'Big Hole' at Kimberley, boomed, enabling a few individuals to make their personal fortunes, among them a sickly and querulous young man called Cecil Rhodes. With Kimberley incorporated into the Cape Colony, and the principal mines under British control, a new optimism characterised British attitudes towards South Africa.

Cape Colony enjoyed some immediate benefits. The revenue generated by diamond mining freed the Cape from its reliance upon the funding of a parsimonious British government at Westminster. Full responsible government, so often the reward for economic self-sufficiency as well as political maturity, was granted in 1872.[7]

The rapid development of the diamond-mining industry came at a bleak time in the economic fortunes of the Cape. Various agricultural exports had suffered as a result of their exposure to the market forces of free trade, and the farmers' problems were exacerbated by a series of natural disasters, including the drought and rinderpest which affected much of southern Africa after 1869. Cheap loans were more difficult to get via the cautiously orthodox finance houses of Britain. This in turn generated a demand amongst both English-speaking and Afrikaans-speaking settlers for the establishment of 'country banks', which were perceived as being more in tune with local needs.[8] The comparatively high wages paid to workers in diamond mining also further depressed the labour market on farms and estates.

British policy-makers paid less attention to the problems of South African agriculture than to the immediate and profitable consequences of the diamond discoveries. Perhaps other valuable mineral deposits would soon be unearthed. Imperial policy towards South Africa was dramatically transformed, and the old game of waiting for the Boer republics to fall like ripe plums into Britannia's lap was abandoned. During the 1870s there were four attempts to achieve a confederation of the South African colonies, an initiative which included a determined wooing of the Afrikaner republics as well.

The federal idea failed for a number of reasons. Firstly local white settler opinion, even in the two British colonies, could not be won over in sufficient quantity. Even the most persuasive and persistent of British confederators, Lord Carnarvon, Colonial Secretary in the mid-1870s, failed to convince enough doubters. (Perhaps this, as well as his fussy manner, had something to do with Disraeli's mocking nickname for him – 'Twitters'.) The European colonists wanted better communications and more unified and coherent policies towards land and labour, but not at the price of surrendering local autonomy. Many Cape Colonists argued that their relatively prosperous economy would simply have to bear the financial burdens of their impoverished neighbours. The Cape Dutch, moreover, feared federation as a reassertion of imperial control through other means.

Carnarvon's determination and drive did, however, lead to the unexpectedly easy annexation of the Transvaal in 1877. The medium-term calculation was that the Orange Free State, with its far more intimate economic and commercial relationship with the Cape, would be obliged to join a federation in due course. The problem was the Transvaal, the flagship of Afrikaner separatism, the homeland of all those Boers who had trekked as far as they could to escape British imperial control.

The rural economy of the Transvaal was, however, in desperate straits in 1877. When Carnarvon's agent, Theophilus Shepstone, arrived in Pretoria he found the treasury almost empty and the government, under President Burgers, surprisingly prepared to consider the advantages of annexation. In April 1877 the Transvaal was annexed to the British Crown. It was a prodigious advance for British policy, and appeared to run smack in the face of seventy years of Anglo–Afrikaner antipathy and disengagement.

The deal that Britain offered to the Transvaalers was essentially straightforward. The administration would be put upon a sound financial footing, steps to increase revenue and implement a substantial degree of local autonomy would be speedily taken, and, of great immediate concern, the imperial armies would rid the northern and eastern regions of South Africa of the Zulu menace, for good – thus hastening, in the view of the newly arrived Governor of the Cape, Sir Bartle Frere, the federation of South Africa under British control.

Accordingly, in 1879 Frere engineered the outbreak of the Zulu

War with the issuing of a pugnacious and uncompromising ultimatum to the Zulu King, Cetewayo. The Zulu War provided Afrikaners, not merely in the Transvaal but throughout southern Africa, with two comforting spectacles. One was the early, brusque and humiliating defeat of British troops by the Zulu impis at the Battle of Isandhlwana. The other, paradoxically, was the eventual triumph of British arms at the Battle of Ulundi, which appeared to break Zulu power forever. The victory at Ulundi, however, also removed at a stroke the most cogent justification for Britain's annexation of the Transvaal – the protection of its European citizens from black aggression.

The annexation of the Transvaal and the Zulu War had occurred during the premiership of Benjamin Disraeli, from 1874 to 1880. By the mid-1870s, Disraeli, hoping to restore the political fortunes of the Conservative Party in the face of the long post-free-trade ascendancy of the Liberals, and believing that a close association with imperialism would serve that purpose, had pursued a policy of imperial aggrandisement. The package included the acquisition of the Khedive of Egypt's Suez Canal Company shares, the annexation of the Transvaal, the precipitation of the Zulu War and the invasion of Afghanistan. Lord Carnarvon's drive, as Colonial Secretary, and the enthusiastic cooperation of various imperial 'men on the spot', had given the package its cutting edge.

In the general election of 1880, however, Gladstone and the Liberals were returned with a substantial majority. Gladstone, moreover, had campaigned, at least partly, on the issue of the immorality and selfish nationalism which he perceived as part and parcel of Disraeli's foreign and imperial policies. Once in power, though, Gladstone's political choices were seriously limited by what was practically achievable, and also by the need to keep his divided and quarrelsome Cabinet as united as possible.

It is also clear that, particularly in regard to South Africa, both Conservative and Liberal administrations in practice followed a policy of bipartisanship. In June 1880, within a few weeks of winning the general election, the new Prime Minister met a Transvaal delegation headed by the subtle and intransigent Paul Kruger, ex-Vice-President of the fallen republic and a leading spokesman of the growing faction that opposed British rule. Soon Gladstone, in an astonishing *volte face*, announced: 'Our judgement is that the Queen cannot be advised to relinquish her sovereignty over the Transvaal.'[9]

In the eyes of most Transvaalers, this act of Gladstonian treachery and hypocrisy was the breaking point. On 15 December 1880 the first shots were fired in the Transvaal's uprising against British rule. The defeat at Majuba Hill destroyed the possibility that, somehow, Britain could retain control of the province. At the Pretoria Convention, in the immediate aftermath of Majuba, the Transvaal regained its independence. This agreement was partly renegotiated and finalised at the Convention of London in 1884. The settlement was, however, blurred and confused in one significant aspect. The Convention of 1881 had contained a clear reference to 'the suzerainty of Her Majesty', yet this phrase was deleted in the agreement of 1884. Although it was accepted that Britain should have oversight of future treaties between the Transvaal and any other nation (except the Orange Free State), and with African tribes to the east and the west, the wider issue of suzerainty remained obscure. At all events, the Transvaal, led after 1883 by Paul Kruger, denied that suzerainty existed, while the British government would not admit to this. The issue of Anglo–Transvaal relations was to be revived in dramatic circumstances in 1886.

11

CECIL RHODES' LEGACY

Fantasy, Power and the Partition of Africa

IN 1877 CECIL RHODES, already a multi-millionaire at the age of twenty-four, made his first proper will and testament. This extraordinary document was written in the same year as the Transvaal was annexed by the British Crown. Rhodes named two executors: the Colonial Secretary, Lord Carnarvon, and the Attorney-General for Griqualand West, Sidney Shippard. These two unsuspecting men were given the responsibility for establishing a secret society, the aim of which was to be the extension of British rule throughout the world. This secret brotherhood was to bring the entire continent of Africa under British rule, to populate South America, the Holy Land, the seaboards of China and Japan, the Malay Archipelago, the islands of Cyprus and Candia, and any islands in the Pacific not already possessed by Britain, with British settlers. As if this was an insufficient task, they were also instructed to recover the United States for the British Empire, work to consolidate the Empire as a whole, and to introduce a system of colonial representation in the British Parliament to bring about the establishment of 'so great a power as to hereafter render wars impossible and promote the best interests of humanity'.[1]

At first sight, this document seems to be the product of a deranged mind. Yet in terms of his career hitherto, Rhodes had more solid, practical achievements than almost any of his contemporaries. The son of a controlling, puritanical and emotionally cold Hertfordshire vicar and a pitifully overworked mother, Rhodes was a repressed, awkward and sickly child. As he reached manhood, his personality was fractured, and in some respects conspicuously immature. Squeaky-voiced, never physically robust, obsessed with considerations of hygiene, and abnormally fearful of women, there was little in the youthful Rhodes that suggested he was to be one of the most masterful and successful of British Empire-builders.

But for his chronic ill-health, Rhodes might have ended his life as a moderately successful lawyer or clergyman in the United Kingdom. He may have become a minor English eccentric, solitary, tetchy, ill-at-ease in society, and a confirmed bachelor. But the fact that he was diagnosed as suffering from tuberculosis when he was sixteen years old and had recently left school changed his life forever. His brother Herbert had recently emigrated to South Africa and was sending home enthusiastic letters describing his success as a cotton grower in Natal. The family decided that Cecil should join him there, chiefly for his health, but also to provide him with a career. It was an English version of the American urge to push west, although in this case the young man was exhorted to 'go south'. Rhodes set sail for South Africa at the end of June 1870, on a voyage that was to transform both his life and the continent of Africa.

Within a decade, demonstrating an unsuspected business acumen, Rhodes had made himself a diamond millionaire at Kimberley, and was soon to graduate with a pass degree from Oxford University. His determination to study at Oxford led him into a curious double life for eight years. In South Africa he was the budding diamond magnate who, for the outlay of a prodigious sum in steamship fares, was also able to study at one of England's two ancient universities, where he was liable to cast down a fistful of diamonds to impress his fellow students and to show them what could be achieved far from the dreaming spires. In the Cape and in the diamond fields, Rhodes, though often perceived as awkward in the company of other diggers, was acknowledged as a shrewd man of business.

Despite his hard, personal physical labours in the diamond mines, his fortune was really made, somewhat ironically, as a result of the first great slump at Kimberley in 1875. The yellow ground which had already yielded considerable quantities of diamonds suddenly gave out, and the diggers struck a layer of blue clay soil. Fears that the blue soil would prove worthless coincided with a worldwide trade depression and a sharp fall in the price of diamonds. Many diggers gave up, and Rhodes and his partner Rudd took the risk of buying up many of the abandoned claims. Soon the blue ground proved rich beyond the most optimistic expectations, and by March 1881, nine months before Rhodes took his degree, he and Rudd amalgamated their interests with that of a rival company and consolidated the De Beers Mining Company

Limited. This company was launched with a capital of £200,000 and was to provide the means by which Rhodes confirmed his overwhelming control of the diamond industry, and went on to take a major share in the gold industry following the gold strike on the Rand in the Transvaal in 1886.

By the early 1890s, Rhodes' achievements, both in the field of commerce and in the redrawing of the map of southern Africa, were so successful as to beggar belief. His nickname 'the Colossus' seemed entirely apt. The enormous wealth generated by his great diamond and gold companies, De Beers and Consolidated Goldfields Limited, gave him the means to change history. Desperate to bypass the Afrikaner republics and to continue the drive of British power to the north (which was meant to culminate in a line of imperial possessions from the Cape to Cairo), Rhodes had already agitated for the annexation of Bechuanaland in 1884. In 1889 the troops of Rhodes' British South Africa Company, armed with rifles and a Royal Charter, had crossed the Limpopo River and opened up Rhodesia – the counterpoise in the north to the Boer republics further south. By 1890 he had allied the English-speaking Progressive Party in Cape Colony with the Afrikaner moderates led by Jan Hofmeyer. This achievement in moderation and compromise had brought him the premiership of the self-governing Cape, and was consistent with his desire to woo the Afrikaners into federation.

By the time of his death in 1902, Rhodes had made an even more profound impact upon the history of South Africa and the British Empire. British possessions in southern Africa now stretched from the Cape to the borders of German East Africa and the Congo Free State in the north. Rhodes had in effect a private empire in Southern and Northern Rhodesia, countries named after him and comprising far more territory than the ex-Boer republics and almost as much as the future Union of South Africa. More than this, he had been the power behind the over-ambitious and ultimately disastrous Jameson Raid of 1895, a coup aimed at overthrowing Kruger's republic by violent means. He had also persistently advocated the use of force by the imperial government to cow the Boer republics and to bring about the desired unification of South Africa.

Why did Cecil Rhodes undertake such labours, and how did he achieve so much? First, it must be said that he was not an isolated example. Late-nineteenth-century British governments were generally reluctant to commit themselves either financially or in terms of time and energy to a wholesale, virtually non-stop, process of colonial expansion.

They were, on the other hand, content to let capitalist entrepreneurs undertake the dirty work of conquest and penetration on their behalf. Rhodes, with his great international trading companies, his private army in the form of the British South Africa Police Force, and his steamships on the Zambezi River functioning as a small private navy, was merely the most successful and ruthless of these entrepreneurial personalities. The intricate and complex links that bound Rhodes' South African-based companies to the City of London and other European financial centres were replicated in other enterprises. Sir George Goldie's Royal Niger Company, and Sir William Mackinnon's Imperial British East Africa Company, were both agents for British imperial expansion and consolidation in other parts of Africa.[2]

In Britain, Liberal and Conservative administrations alike had few practical objections to the activities of these great chartered companies. So long as company rule was not marked by excessive brutality or unacceptable atrocities in its dealings with indigenous people, Westminster and Whitehall were content to let well alone. This was imperialism on the cheap, and therefore of real benefit to both administration and taxpayer. Essentially Rhodes' British South Africa Company was a front for the conquest and control of the Rhodesias, and especially for the subjugation of the Shona (Mashona) and Ndebele (Matabele) of Southern Rhodesia. No great mineral deposits were found in these territories to rival the diamond and gold discoveries of South Africa, and during its lifetime the British South Africa Company failed to pay shareholders a single dividend.

What drove Cecil Rhodes to his undoubted, although often tarnished and unscrupulous, achievements? One answer is that he was inspired by, and found it easy to identify with, the fashionable theories of Anglo-Saxon racial superiority. He also strongly, even fanatically, subscribed to the increasingly persuasive political imperative that saw Empire as the only true means of salvation for Britain's declining world status. As British industry faced the rising and eventually irresistible challenges of German and United States industry, as American and later German navy-building programmes threatened the long-established global supremacy of the Royal Navy, the expansion and consolidation of the British Empire seemed an obvious antidote to any number of ills.

The intellectual influences which Rhodes absorbed during his lengthy and disjointed period of study at Oxford University gave him a coherent framework for his political convictions. He was later to con-fide to the journalist and editor W.T. Stead that at Oxford he had been deeply impressed by Aristotle's statement that it was supremely important to have an aim in life sufficiently lofty to justify spending one's entire career in endeavouring to reach it. He also told Stead that he 'had no hesitation in arriving at the conclusion that the English race – the English-speaking man, whether British, American, Australian or South African – is a type of race which does now, and is likely to continue to do in the future, the most practical, effective work to establish justice, to promote liberty, and to ensure peace over the widest possible area of the planet'.[3] Rhodes was also deeply affected by John Ruskin's famous inaugural lecture at Oxford in 1870. In ringing words, Ruskin, the great art critic, writer and somewhat unorthodox socialist, declared:

> There is a destiny now possible to us, the highest ever set before a nation to be accepted or refused. Will you youths of England make your country again a royal throne of kings, a sceptred isle, for all the world a source of light, a centre of peace; mistress of learning and of the Arts, faithful guardian of time-honoured principles? This is what England must do or perish: she must found colonies as fast and as far as she is able, formed of her most energetic and worthiest men; seizing every piece of fruitful waste ground she can set her feet on, and there teaching these her colonists that their chief virtue is to be fidelity to their country, and their first aim is to advance the power of England by land and sea.[4]

Rhodes' early triumphs in the diamond fields of South Africa, and his years at Oxford, also coincided with Disraeli's 1874–80 Conservative government. Disraeli's bid to make Empire the ideological, emotional and political property of the Conservative Party was given its theoretical framework in his great Crystal Palace speech of 1872, when he told his audience that the nation's choice was between being 'a comfortable England, modelled and moulded upon Continental principles and meeting in due course an inevitable fate', or 'a great country, an imperial country, a country where your sons, when they rise, rise to paramount positions, and obtain not merely the esteem of their countrymen, but command the respect of the world'.

Disraeli's determined and colourful marketing of the Empire, together with the formidable number of imperial achievements and adventures of his premiership, from the buying of shares in the Suez

Canal to the Zulu War, from the annexation of the Transvaal to the proclamation of Queen Victoria as Empress of India, had helped to fix the concept of imperialism as a common good, and, moreover, as the key to Britain's continuing prosperity and world power, firmly in the minds of people as impressionable as the young Cecil Rhodes.

There is, however, a further way of understanding Rhodes' relentless, almost obsessional pursuit of power, and the grandiose imperial fantasies in which he indulged. Rhodes never married, and he remained ill-at-ease with women throughout his life, being reduced to panic and flight when the Polish adventuress Princess Radziwill set her cap at him. The Princess relentlessly pursued Rhodes from London to Cape Town, where she forced herself on him so persistently that her quarry posted lookouts to enable him to mount his horse and thus to escape whenever she approached his residence.[5] To his contemporaries Rhodes was known as a 'confirmed bachelor' or a 'misogynist'. Once, on meeting Queen Victoria, the monarch asked him directly whether it was true that he was a woman-hater. With great presence of mind, Rhodes replied that he could never hate a sex to which Her Majesty belonged.

It seems evident that Rhodes' emotional and sexual needs were unconventional, and in any event fulfilled by both his imperial achievements and the company of a succession of young men. Lacking the sexual orientation and drive that would have made him a husband and a father, he proved his potency through the pursuit and conquest not of women but of territory and, at an even more exalted level, of an ideal. On this analysis, if the two territories of Northern and Southern Rhodesia were two homely and relatively obedient wives, the extravagant commitment to British global supremacy as set out in his will of 1877 represented love on an ethereal and sublime plane far removed from the sordid lusts of the flesh.

To minister to his earthly comforts, however, Rhodes had a number of intense emotional relationships with a series of young men in South Africa and Rhodesia, many of whom served as his private secretaries. Of these, Neville Pickering was the most important and the most dearly loved, although, after Pickering's premature death, young men like Harry Currey and Johnny Grimmer provided important emotional support and gratification. It is worth noting, incidentally, that even after his death Rhodes continued to patronise young men of promise and ability through the funding of the Rhodes scholarships to Oxford.

Pickering was the type of young man whom Rhodes was to admire throughout his life. He was an alert and fresh-faced youth, blue-eyed, clean-cut and open. He was no intellectual, but down-to-earth and, in a contemporary description, the archetype of a 'frank, sunny-tempered young Englishman'. For almost five years Rhodes and Pickering lived together as a couple in a cottage facing the Kimberley Cricket Ground. Few people visited them there. In 1882 Rhodes made his third will in which, 'being of sound mind', he left all of his very substantial worldly wealth to Pickering.

In 1886 Pickering, who had two years earlier suffered a riding accident which had permanently damaged his health, became mortally ill. For almost two months, Rhodes hardly left his sick bed. Pickering, although attended by the well regarded Doctor Jameson – who became another close friend of Rhodes as a result, and was later to lead the doomed raid that bears his name into the Transvaal in 1895 – died in October 1886, held in Rhodes' arms. At Pickering's funeral, Rhodes showed hysterical grief. He was never again to live in the house he had shared with Neville Pickering.

The urgency and zeal of Rhodes' bid to bring the whole of southern Africa under British dominion, and to extend Anglo-Saxon, and particularly British, influence and authority throughout the globe, were the individual manifestations of a far more widely-based impulse. By the end of the Victorian era very few territories in Asia, Africa, or the Pacific had escaped European annexation or domination. In Africa, only Abyssinia, having defeated Italy's attempt to conquer it, remained truly independent; on the west coast, Liberia, a freed-slave foundation, was fundamentally in hock to the United States of America. In Asia, Thailand was allowed to maintain its independence primarily as a buffer zone between competing British and French colonial interests on either side; Afghanistan also clung to its autonomy despite sporadic bullying and assaults by the British Raj; China, its coast pockmarked by the naval and military bases of various European imperial powers, its economy increasingly manipulated by Western, including United States, commercial policies, could not be considered as a truly independent nation. Nor, for that matter, could Persia. Only Japan, on the edge of the Asian land-mass, possessed such strength and vitality that the great imperial powers either eyed it warily or courted it diplomatically. But Japan, with its growing and predatory involvement in China and Manchuria, was an almost absurdly successful exception to a worldwide pattern of European domination and control.

In South-East Asia, most of Malaya had, by the end of the nineteenth century, been brought either directly or indirectly under British control. Although the Crown Colonies of Singapore and Penang stayed outside of the Federation of Malay States created in 1896, they were even more directly ruled by Britain. To the east of the Malay Peninsula, the British Empire controlled, in contrasting ways, three more territories, Brunei, North Borneo and Sarawak. The Sultan of Brunei was under the protection of the British government; in Sarawak the sultan was British, and known as Rajah Brooke; North Borneo was ruled by another of the chartered companies that had burgeoned in the later years of the nineteenth century. These South-East Asian possessions provided rubber and eventually oil for the British economy. In addition, the Malay states, as well as producing rubber, also provided tin. Singapore was to South-East Asia what Hong Kong was to the China Sea, a gigantic entrepôt for British commerce.

In the Pacific, Britain had extended her influence and her rule over a number of territories including south-eastern New Guinea, Fiji, Tonga, the Cook Islands and a number of other smaller island groups. The demands of commerce, and the influence of humanitarian and religious pressure groups, had played important parts in this extension of British influence and power. So had the anxieties of the Australian and New Zealand self-governing colonies, alarmed by the incursions into the area of imperial Germany, and perpetually conscious of their isolation on the fringes of Asia and of their vulnerability to one of the great potential, but in reality insubstantial, threats of the age – the Yellow Peril.

These considerable acquisitions of territory, however, failed to capture the public imagination as powerfully as Britain's role in the partition of Africa during the last two decades of the nineteenth century. Described by some contemporaries as the 'scramble for Africa', the process by which European rule was extended over almost the whole of the African continent is one of the most remarkable, and at one level puzzling, phenomena of imperial history.

The essential question to be answered is: was Britain's involvement in the partition based on real needs, or was it primarily the manifestation of growing national insecurity at a time of apparently inexorable economic and military decline in the face of intense competition from other powers? Was it largely undertaken in order to reassure an increasingly nervous and volatile electorate at home? Was it simply a fig leaf behind which Britain could hide its nakedness from the scrutiny of the international community? Was it, in essence, part of a process of camouflaging British decline with a gaudy and triumphal policy of imperial acquisition and expansion, as a result of which foreign powers would remain convinced that they should treat Britain with respect – as Kipling put it so plainly in his poem 'The Widow at Windsor':

> *Walk wide o' the Widow at Windsor,*
> *For 'alf o' Creation she owns:*
> *We 'ave bought 'er the same with the sword an' the flame,*
> *An' we've salted it down with our bones.*
> *(Poor beggars! – it's blue with our bones!)*
> *Hands off o' the sons o' the Widow,*
> *Hands off o' the goods in 'er shop,*
> *For the Kings must come down an' the Emperors frown*
> *When the Widow at Windsor says 'Stop!'*[6]

Certainly Africa was the continent upon which most European commercial, diplomatic and military energies were unleashed towards the end of the nineteenth century. In some ways, the contemporary description of the 'scramble for Africa' was woefully inaccurate, but symptomatic of the hysteria that galvanised foreign ministries, newspaper editors, the great banking and financial houses, and certain sections of the public. British policy-makers displayed an almost leisurely approach to the partition of Africa, particularly when contrasted with the strident and urgent ambitions of *parvenu* colonial powers like Germany or Italy. The dialogue of the boundary commission, not the clash of arms, was the preferred means of the extension of British power in Africa.

Despite this, the list of British acquisitions in Africa between 1880 and 1902 was full and impressive: Egypt (not formally annexed until 1914), the Sudan, British Somaliland, Uganda, Kenya, Zanzibar, Northern and Southern Rhodesia, Nyasaland, Bechuanaland, much of Nigeria, the hinterland of the Gold Coast, and finally the Orange Free State and the Transvaal.

Many contemporaries were convinced that the African 'scramble' was the result of heightened European rivalries – Britain jumping in ahead of Germany, France forestalling Italy, and so forth. Although this theory seems at first sight convincing and attractive, it tends to ignore clashes and confrontations between European and African nationalisms, which were often more significant locally than inter-European rivalries. For example, Britain was arguably drawn into its two most spectacular and perilous African commitments chiefly by the need to control Egyptian and Afrikaner nationalism. On a less dramatic scale, the resistance and, often, the counter-offensives of black nationalism, or at least tribalism, were frequently the crucial factors requiring military intervention. In any event, the thesis of an irresistible intrusion of newly ambitious European powers like Germany, Italy and Belgium into Africa is largely incompatible with the prevailing facts of military life. With the overwhelming superiority of the Royal Navy at its disposal, Britain could simply have snuffed out the imperial ambitions of such nations by obstructing their access to the 'dark continent'. That Britain did not even seriously attempt this is an indication either that it had no stomach for the fight or, much more likely, that it felt there was enough territory to satisfy a number of European imperial appetites, including – most significantly – its own.

Another explanation of the African partition is that pressing economic incentives, in the form of new markets and the need to control the sources of raw materials, were instrumental in precipitating European colonisation. At the time, both the radical British theorist J.A. Hobson and the Russian revolutionary Lenin convinced many with their fundamentally similar argument that the advanced societies of the West needed to acquire new territory in order to export surplus capital there and to boost exports. It is undoubtedly true that Britain's faltering lead in terms of manufacturing and industrial output during the second half of the nineteenth century seemed to prove the case for the incorporation of new African territories within the Empire.

The trade statistics from the time, however, are not particularly conclusive. Although between 1865 and 1894 British trade with tropical Africa doubled, it also doubled with South America and Australia, and with the expanding economy of South Africa it trebled. In addition, the proportion of British trade with tropical Africa actually declined during the 1890s. Between 1865 and 1890 this proportion of the whole of Britain's trade was a mere 0.80 per cent; but between 1890 and 1894 it shrank to 0.77 per cent.[7] It was therefore clear that 'Despite its vast size, this region accounted for only a minute share of Britain's overseas trade.'[8] In Nigeria and the Gold Coast, however, there was a significant trade to be sustained: British manufactures being exported to the region in exchange for gold, palm oil, cocoa and other primary products.

There was, of course, the potential of the market for African products elsewhere: for example, cloves and ivory from Zanzibar and coffee and rubber from Uganda. It was this as much as anything that caused powerful economic lobbies and persuasive capitalist propagandists within Britain to urge the government to seize new territories in Africa. How much notice prime ministers like the aristocratic Conservative

Lord Salisbury, or the apparently high-minded Liberal William Gladstone took of these advocacies is open to question. British socialists and many on the left wing of the Liberal Party undoubtedly suspected the great gold-mining companies and the Rand millionaires of forcing the Boer War on the nation. Others were scornful of the usefulness of newly acquired African territory, and the future Liberal Prime Minister Sir Henry Campbell-Bannerman said in 1899: 'The danger of a good deal of this expansiveness . . . is that it withdraws the energies and enterprises of our countrymen from markets which they used to control . . . in the vain pursuit of what is little more than a will-o'-the-wisp . . . of a market which does not exist.'[9]

More persuasive than the economic argument, perhaps, is the thesis that Britain's part in the African scramble was driven by the overwhelming need to preserve the Suez route to the old Empire in India and Australasia. This does not, naturally, explain why large sections of West Africa were added to the British Empire during this time, but it does explain British acquisitions in East Africa and in areas significant to the short route to the East. There is no doubt that many British statesmen and military leaders became almost obsessed with the need to protect the Indian Empire from the imagined foreign threat, and thus by the need to secure the Suez Canal during the last two decades of the nineteenth century. As a consequence, territories bordering Egypt were jealously guarded and, if necessary, annexed. In this sense, imperial expansion in much of north-east Africa was essentially defensive, and a new empire was brought into being to protect the old.

If economic necessity, and the lust to exploit a vast new African empire in the tropics, had appeared to be of overwhelming importance during the African partition, Britain's response to her success seems to prove otherwise. Uncertainty, even a lack of enthusiasm, often characterised Britain's response to the economic development of her newly acquired African territories. Soon after becoming Colonial Secretary in 1895, Joseph Chamberlain, one of the few members of Lord Salisbury's Unionist government to have any practical experience of industry and commerce, was arguing that the tropical Crown Colonies in Africa, the West Indies and South-East Asia were like 'the underdeveloped estates' of some great landowner.

But even the forceful and persuasive Chamberlain was unable to bring about any effective switch of British capital and investment from profitable markets outside the Empire to the newly acquired 'underdeveloped estates of the realm'. He did, however, persuade the government to put up public funds, in the form of grants and loans totalling nearly £600,000, to support the declining economies of the West Indies after the Report of the Norman Commission in 1897 had painted a bleak picture of economic decay and potential social disruption in many parts of the British Caribbean. But this remarkable breakthrough did not herald an era of state intervention in the field of colonial development. Indeed, within a few years government aid to the West Indies dried up.

Not many white settlers were attracted to the new tropical African colonies, with the exception of the few thousand who went to settle the Kenyan Highlands. Until their economies proved attractive enough, Britain's African colonies continued to languish near the bottom of the imperial pyramid. In 1903 the Colonial Office even made a serious offer of Uganda to the Zionist movement as a possible Jewish homeland.

How far, then, did Britain exploit her dependent colonies, in Africa and elsewhere? It was for much too long easy to assume that a gross manipulation of colonial economies was the hallmark of all European imperial powers. The facts, however, do not seem entirely to bear out this analysis. Of course, just as the Indian cotton industry was badly damaged in the nineteenth century in the face of privileged competition from Lancashire, the demands of British commerce also disrupted local economies in Africa, in particular by forcing specific cash crops upon local communities and sometimes ruining agricultural harmony and local self-sufficiency as a result. Some private trading companies were able to pay very large dividends on their African investments and commerce. Few of the profits of trade were ploughed back into colonial economies. Most tribal societies saw no dramatic rise in their standard of living.

It would be a mistake, however, to imagine British capitalists wantonly and routinely plundering dependent lands. They certainly sought profits, but these were often no greater than profits from industries established in non-colonial territories. Dividends from capital investment could be higher from Argentine railways than from Ugandan rubber. The Chinese economy was hardly treated with greater respect than that of the Gold Coast. In any event, Britain's adherence to the principles of free trade in theory gave her no greater commercial advantage in her own colonies than any other nation. Looking back at the dependent Empire during the Victorian period and even beyond, one is struck by the low level of investment, the absence of systematic economic development.

More damaging than economic dislocation and the breaking of old patterns of agriculture was the widespread assumption in Britain that all Africans were savages and unfitted for self-government. There were, it is true, some contradictions to swallow. In Northern Nigeria and elsewhere, particularly in West Africa, the establishment of a system of 'indirect rule' based on the work of the highly influential administrator Frederick Lugard, one of the most creative and thoughtful of British colonial theoreticians, seemed to accord respect to local societies, or at least to local elites. Africans were permitted to sit, admittedly in very small numbers, upon the legislative councils of certain African colonies during the latter years of the nineteenth century. In general, however, British administrators in Africa, and even more so the British public at home, chose to ignore the fact that before the advent of Europeans, Africans had governed themselves quite adequately. Indigenous African government had not, it is true, been on the Westminster model, but, barbarous as some of the manifestations of African self-rule had unquestionably been to Western eyes, it had worked.

Britain's late-nineteenth-century imperial mission, however, could not accommodate such niceties. Missionaries, colonial administrators, settlers, traders, observers of all sorts undoubtedly exaggerated the defects of African self-rule in order to justify their own activities. The massive ancient ruins of Zimbabwe were thought to be beyond the capacities of local Africans, and eventually it was speculated that visitors from outer space were responsible for them. The substantial achievements of West African civilisation also tended to be written off and ignored.

At the outset of the twentieth century, Britain had acquired huge fresh territorial responsibilities, mainly in Africa, but had not yet fully adjusted to the fact. It was ironical that by the time a measure of administrative uniformity had been impressed upon these colonies, the reasons for their original annexation had frequently become less relevant. British national interests had changed, and the pretext of African domination suffered accordingly. Partly as a result of the frenzied empire-building of Cecil Rhodes and many others, the late Victorians had acquired a colonial empire of vast proportions that their descendants were to neglect for half a century and then abandon within a few years.

QUEEN VICTORIA'S
DIAMOND JUBILEE, 1897

The Uses and the Misuses of Empire;
an Imperial Triumph, or Whistling in the Dark? *Fin de Siècle*
and the Problems and Opportunities of Empire

BETWEEN 19 AND 24 JUNE 1897, Britain and the British Empire celebrated the sixtieth anniversary of Queen Victoria's accession to the throne. During these days the public was able to gorge on a rich diet of ceremonial and display, speech-making and official processions. Among the events held to mark the Jubilee were a military tattoo at Windsor, a special service at St George's Chapel, Windsor, at which Madam Albani sang Mendelssohn's 'Hymn of Praise', the Countess of Jersey's garden party at Osterley Park, the great royal procession to St Paul's Cathedral for the Thanksgiving Service on 22 June, and countless street parties, speeches, receptions, balls and shows.

Tribute, much of it material, was paid to the monarch. Among the presents sent to the Queen-Empress was a diamond, valued at £300,000, from the Nizam of Hyderabad, which was unfortunately stolen before it reached its destination. Throughout Britain and the Empire statues were unveiled, free food distributed to impoverished families, prayers and incantations raised, Royal Navy warships dressed overall, toasts drunk and vast quantities of food consumed. The Princess of Wales' Jubilee Feast for the Outcast Poor, aimed at feeding 400,000 people throughout London, needed 700 tons of food, nearly 10,000 waiters, and the support of the retail millionaire Sir Thomas Lipton, who sent a sensibly priced menu and a cheque for £25,000.[1]

Reactions from many other nations, especially those which had cause to feel jealous of Britain's imperial supremacy, were generally charitable, as if hostilities had been temporarily suspended. The French newspaper *Le Figaro* pronounced that Rome itself had been 'equalled, if not surpassed, by the Power which in Canada, Australia, India, in the China Seas, in Egypt, Central and Southern Africa, in the Atlantic and in the Mediterranean rules the peoples and governs their interests'. The *New York Times* even went so far as to assert: 'We are a part, and a great part, of the Greater Britain which seems so plainly destined to dominate this planet.' The Berlin *Kreuz Zeitung*, perhaps a shade wistfully, described the Empire as 'practically unassailable', and in Vienna the Emperor Franz Josef called at the British Embassy wearing the uniform of his British regiment and the insignia of the Garter.[2]

For the populace as a whole, both rich and poor, the climax of the Jubilee celebrations was the great royal procession to and from St Paul's Cathedral on 22 June. Before she left Buckingham Palace at 11.15 a.m., Queen Victoria pressed a button sending by telegraph her personal message to every corner of the Empire: 'From my heart I thank my beloved people. May God bless them.' Within two minutes this bland and predictable greeting had passed through Teheran and was speeding on its way to India and all the Eastern possessions of the Crown. Then, with the national hero Field Marshal Lord Roberts, V.C. – known affectionately as 'Bobs' – at its head, the whole procession set off. Over 50,000 troops in wave after glittering wave made up the procession: Hussars from Canada, the Royal Nigerian Constabulary, the Cape Mounted Rifles, the Trinidad Light Horse, Zaptiehs from Cyprus (whose fezzes caused some in the crowd to hiss them as Turkish interlopers), headhunters from the dyak police of Borneo, 'upstanding Sikhs, tiny little Malays, Chinese with the white basin turned upside down on their heads', Hausas from northern Nigeria, Jamaicans in white gaiters, and turbaned and bearded Lancers of the Indian Empire 'terrible and beautiful to behold'.[3]

As the American writer Mark Twain so shrewdly observed, however, the Queen herself was the real procession, and 'all the rest was embroidery'. Wearing a bonnet with ostrich feathers and sheltering beneath a white silk parasol, Queen Victoria gravely acknowledged the tumultuous acclamation of her people.

The Diamond Jubilee celebrations were at one level a self-indulgent affirmation of the achievements of the British people and of the glory of the British Empire. They were marked by over-wrought sentiment, financial extravagance, brash and patriotic tunes thumped out by brass bands, and by flags and bunting and glittering illumination. The *Daily Mail*'s brilliant young correspondent G.W. Steevens wrote that it was 'a pageant which for splendour of appearance and especially for splendour of suggestion has never been paralleled in the history of the world'. *The Times* believed that 'History may be searched, and searched in vain, to discover so wonderful an exhibition of allegiance and brotherhood among so many myriads of men . . . The mightiest and most beneficial Empire ever known in the annals of mankind.'[4] The 'Jubilee Hymn', composed by Sir Arthur Sullivan, was to be played in all churches and chapels on Sunday 20 June. The Poet Laureate Alfred Austin composed a celebratory poem, which provoked some sharp contemporary criticism, and included the verse:

> *From steel-capped promontories stern and strong,*
> *And lone islands mounting guard upon the main,*
> *Hither her subjects wend to hail her long*
> *Resplendent Reign.*

When the celebrations were over, the *Daily Graphic* delivered a self-contented summing-up:

> To us the survey of the Sixty Years Reign and of the micro-cosm of Empire with which we have filled our streets has been a source of subjective complacency. It has told us nothing we did not know before; it has been prized for no ulterior purpose. To the foreigner, however, it has been a revelation. He has been enabled to realise for the first time the stability of English institutions, the immensity of the British Empire, and, finally, the strength of the bonds by which the family of nations owing allegiance to the British Crown is united . . . He now finds that England has sources of strength in her internal social peace and in the enthusiastic loyalty of her Colonies by the side of which the alliances of a Continental Power, or even of a group of Continental Powers, is of small consequence. In a word he has realised that Splendid Isolation is not an empty British boast.[5]

The Diamond Jubilee was staged for a variety of reasons, some idealistic, some cynical, some confused, even contradictory. It was not, of course, the first such celebration during Queen Victoria's reign. The Golden Jubilee of 1887 had both provided a dress rehearsal for the larger-scale event in 1897 and indicated the potential benefits that could accrue from such a national and imperial extravaganza.

It was no coincidence that Joseph Chamberlain, appointed Colonial

Secretary in 1895 and profoundly committed to the expansion and consolidation of the Empire, was one of the chief instigators of the celebrations. Chamberlain was the foremost example of a new breed of
politicians who were skilled in public relations. Of relatively humble
social origin, and with considerable personal experience of industry and
commerce, he was a brilliantly effective communicator able to utilise the
press, particularly the newly established popular press, to outstanding
propaganda effect.

In the hands of such astute organisers, the Diamond Jubilee was
meant to make the vast majority of British citizens feel proud of their
country and Empire, and as a consequence to be content with their lot.
It was a British version of the ancient Roman formula of 'bread and
circuses'. During the hectic few days of the Jubilee celebrations, there
is no doubt that the mass of the population were sufficiently intoxicated,
often quite literally, to participate with gusto. The historian G.M.
Young believed that the Jubilee represented 'the concentrated emotion
of a generation', and the future Fabian and socialist luminary Beatrice
Webb recorded in her diary: 'imperialism in the air, all classes drunk
with the sightseeing and hysterical loyalty'.

On this analysis, therefore, the monarchy, the political establishment, the aristocracy and gentry, the wealthy manufacturing classes,
the established Church, most of the 'haves' and even a vast majority
of the 'have-nots' could share in both the immediate splendour and the
warm afterglow of the Jubilee, and as a consequence feel, at least for a
time, strengthened and fulfilled by it.

Imperial propagandists hastened to cash in on the imagery and
symbolism of the Diamond Jubilee. Even the use of the description
'Diamond' was unusual, part of the invention of imperial tradition, and
also a reminder that the Empire contained the diamond fields of South
Africa and, as a result, had put the wearing of such jewellery within
the grasp of millions of British females, including newly-engaged young
women from relatively humble backgrounds. Imperialists also took pleasure in the representation of so many subjects of the Empire in the
spectacular procession of 22 June. A great deal of irrational pride was
taken in the physical size of many of the participants, and Captain
Ames, at six feet eight inches the tallest man in the British Army, was
put at the front of the Jubilee Day procession, proof positive that British
was not only best, but biggest. One image that was processed and
reprocessed, in numerous speeches, but more especially through the
columns of a variety of newspapers, was the concept of the Empire as

a great international organisation, essentially a family firm, in which the British and their white colonial cousins were the natural leaders, instructors and bringers of civilisation. No journalist encapsulated these sentiments more vividly or more movingly than G.W. Steevens:

> Up they came, more and more, new types, new realms at every couple of yards, an anthropological museum – a living gazetteer of the British Empire. With them came their English officers, whom they obey and follow like children. And you began to understand, as never before, what the Empire amounts to. Not only that we possess all these remote outlandish places . . . but also that all these people are working, not simply under us, but with us – that we send out a boy here and a boy there, and a boy takes hold of the savages of the part he comes to, and teaches them to march and shoot as he tells them, to obey him and believe in him and die for him and the Queen . . . A plain, stupid, uninspired people, they call us, and yet we are doing this with every kind of savage man there is. And each one of us – you and I, and that man in his shirt-sleeves at the corner – is a working part of this world-shaping force. How small you must feel in face of this stupendous whole, and yet how great to be a unit in it![6]

There were, however, some dissenting voices. The Labour politician Keir Hardie wrote a trenchant piece several days before the beginning of the Jubilee:

> From the uttermost ends of the earth statesmen and soldiers will ride in princely procession in the train of Queen Victoria, the titular head of the British Empire. East, West, North and South will be lost to view for the moment – absorbed in the world-embracing Empire . . . To the visitor from Mars, two things might seem incontrovertible – first, that the world was at peace; second, that the thrones of the world were firmly embedded in the hearts of a loyal and grateful people.
>
> And yet the Martian visitor would be totally mistaken. The cheering millions would be there and cheer just as lustily if the occasion were the installation of the first President of the British Republic; the soldiers are there because they are paid for coming, and nine out of every ten of them will heartily curse the whole affair as a disagreeable and irksome

Above Hostile American reaction to the imposition of the 1765 Stamp Act.

Left Patriotic American women in North Carolina neglect their household duties in order to sign a declaration to boycott British imports, including tea, in 1775.

Sam Adams, a leader of American opposition to British colonial rule.

Robert Clive receiving the *diwani* (the licence to tax Bengal, Bihar and Orissa) on behalf of the East India Company, from Shah Alam, August 1765. The Company thus became a major administrative force in the sub-continent.

Above Leaving old England. Emigrants set sail for Australia, 1869.

Left Governor Davey's 1816 pictorial proclamation to the Australian Aborigines promising them justice in their dealings with British settlers and authorities. In practice, the needs of whites almost always prevailed.

Left Maori chiefs sign the Treaty of Waitangi in 1840. Although the property rights of the Maori people were recognised in the treaty, conflicts over land were to remain bitter and commonplace for several decades.

PAPA COBDEN TAKING MASTER ROBERT A FREE TRADE WALK.

Below The industrial power of Britain is demonstrated by the construction of Brunel's ship the *Great Eastern* in the dockyards at Millwall in 1857.

The Free Trader Richard Cobden forces the pace on a wary Robert Peel in the mid-1840s.

An Englishwoman and her infants face a fate worse than death at the hands of murderous Sepoys in a print entitled 'English Homes in India 1857'.

Executed mutineers during the great Indian uprising of 1857–8. Some rebellious Sepoys were hanged in pig skins – if Muslim – or blown to fragments from the mouths of cannon.

Left Governor Eyre, whose bloody repression of the 1865 Jamaica Rebellion split Victorian opinion and hastened the extension of crown colony rule to the British West Indies.

Below A contemporary depiction of the 1865 Jamaica crisis: 'Volunteers fire on the mob'.

A sombre group of missionaries in West Africa in the 1860s.

Sir Evelyn Baring, the banker and administrator, who effectively ruled Egypt from 1883 to 1907 after the British invasion of 1882. Known as 'over-Baring', Sir Evelyn did much to reconstruct Egyptian public finances and government under British oversight.

'New crowns for old.' The Eastern salesman, Disraeli, offers Queen Victoria the imperial crown of India. Victoria assumed the title Queen-Empress in 1876.

The palatial offices of the Suez Canal Company at Port Said on the banks of the canal.

Above Indian indentured labourers building the Uganda railway. Considerable numbers of Indians were shipped to East Africa as indentured 'coolies' in the latter part of the nineteenth century.

Left The comprehensive and unexpected defeat of British troops by Zulu warriors at Isandlhwana in 1879.

Below After the British defeat at Majuba Hill in 1881, representatives of the victorious Transvaalers talk terms with British officers at a nearby farmhouse. Paul Kruger is left of centre, raising his hat. Right of centre Sir Evelyn Wood holds a swagger stick and his pith helmet.

THE "IRREPRESSIBLE" TOURIST.

B-sm-rck. "H'M!—HA!—WHERE SHALL I GO NEXT?"

Plain English!

JOHN BULL. "Look here, my little Friend, I don't want to hurt your little feelings—but, COME OFF THAT FLAG!!!"

84

Two views of the 'scramble for Africa' from *Punch* during the mid-1880s.

Above left Bismarck, the 'Irrepressible Tourist', represents the newly-formulated and often troubled imperial ambitions of a united Germany.

Above right A sturdy John Bull orders a disrespectful Frenchman to 'COME OFF THAT FLAG!!!'

General Gordon, soldier, evangelical and awkward customer. After his death at the fall of Khartoum in 1885, he assumed a martyr's status in the eyes of many in Britain.

Above Queen Victoria, surrounded and comforted by her imperial subjects, still has room in her heart for disaffected, potentially rebellious Ireland, declaring, 'With all thy faults I love thee still.'

Left The Victorian postal service as a bond of Empire. The stamps for Barbados, the Cape, New South Wales, New Zealand and India were issued during the 1850s. The Newfoundland stamp pictures Victoria in old age.

additional duty; the statesmen are there because Empire means trade, and trade means profit, and profit means power over the common people . . . Every such show as the present hastens the end. Millions will go out on Tuesday next to see the Queen. What they will see will be an old lady of very commonplace aspect. That of itself will set some a-thinking. Royalty to be a success should keep off the streets . . . The consolidation of the Empire is a good thing in itself. It is bringing nearer the reign of democracy and breaking down the barriers which keep nations apart. But this has no connection with royalty. The workers can have but one feeling in the matter – contempt for thrones and for all who bolster them up, but nonetheless a genuine desire to bring the nations of the earth closer together in unity – not on the basis of a royal alliance nor on a commercial union, but on that of a desire to live in concord. King and diplomat and trader are each, all unwittingly, preparing the way for this consummation so devoutly to be desired.[7]

Even Rudyard Kipling, unashamed patriot and poet of the Empire, sounded a cautionary note in his poem 'Recessional', published to mark the Diamond Jubilee:

> *God of our fathers, known of old,*
> *Lord of our far-flung battle-line,*
> *Beneath whose awful Hand we hold*
> *Dominion over palm and pine –*
> *Lord God of Hosts, be with us yet,*
> *Lest we forget – lest we forget!*
>
> *The tumult and the shouting die;*
> *The Captains and the Kings depart;*
> *Still stands thine ancient sacrifice,*
> *An humble and a contrite heart.*
> *Lord God of Hosts, be with us yet,*
> *Lest we forget – lest we forget!*
>
> *Far-called, our navies melt away;*
> *On dune and headland sinks the fire:*
> *Lo, all our pomp of yesterday*
> *Is one with Nineveh and Tyre!*

Judge of the Nations, spare us yet,
Lest we forget – lest we forget!

If, drunk with the sight of power, we loose
Wild tongues that have not Thee in awe,
Such boastings as the Gentiles use,
Or lesser breeds without the Law –
Lord God of Hosts, be with us yet,
Lest we forget – lest we forget![8]

Kipling's stirring yet disturbing verses were at odds with the over-enthusiastic contemporary reaction to the Diamond Jubilee. Not merely did they contain a sober warning against patriotic and imperial excesses, but they also clearly identified one of the deep, but barely acknowledged, explanations of the Jubilee extravaganza. Tennyson, also a confirmed although less obtrusive imperialist, had earlier raised similar anxieties:

Are there thunders moaning in the distance?
Are there spectres moving in the shadows?

Quite simply, pessimism, not joyous triumphalism, was the prevailing mood among Britain's leaders and opinion-makers as the century drew to its close. The re-emergence of France as a heavyweight and expansionist European imperial rival, and the inconvenient arrival on the scene of recently united, colonising nations like Germany and Italy, disturbed the old order and put Britain under unwelcome new pressure. The falling order books of British exporters, the uncomfortable fact that only 'invisible' exports took the balance of trade into profit, and the obvious threat posed to British manufacturing and commercial supremacy by the rapidly expanding capacities of both Germany and the United States, were further, unsettling challenges.

Many late Victorians were also increasingly worried over what they perceived as a number of serious challenges from within British society: from the 'new', more militant, mass trade unionism; from the 'new' man as well as from the 'new' woman; from the adulteration and processing of foodstuffs and the dilution of beer; from the persistence of Irish nationalism; and from the perils apparently posed by the growth of domestic socialism – even anarchism. There was a generalised and growing anxiety, especially after the conviction of Oscar Wilde in 1895 for homosexual activities, that the nation, the 'race', was on the slippery, downward slope of decadence and decline.

136

Even Britain's global naval supremacy was under threat. 'Far-called, our navies melt away', Kipling had written in 'Recessional'. The rise of the United States as a great naval power, and Germany's intention, finally made explicit in the 1898 Navy Law, of building a modern fleet, gave substance to this nightmare – a nightmare soon given menacing fictional form in Erskine Childers' best-selling novel *The Riddle of the Sands*, published in 1903. The world, it seemed to many, was being rapidly divided up among a few vigorous and single-minded nations. It was this fear of losing out in the division of the spoils that prompted Britain to take so active a part in the 'scramble for Africa'. Suddenly it seemed, to Western eyes at least, that the world was running out of space. Time did not appear to be on Britain's side.

As the end of the century approached, the impression of running out of time was heightened. The nineteenth century, which many British people associated with imperial expansion, naval supremacy, commercial and industrial success, rising living standards and a host of comforting manifestations of international supremacy and domestic triumph, was dying. It was also evident that three of the leading totemic national figureheads were nearing the ends of their lives. For as long as most people could remember Queen Victoria had reigned over them; since 1880 – save for the two years of Lord Rosebery's premiership in 1894–95 – two major statesmen had alternated as Prime Minister, W.E. Gladstone for the Liberals and Lord Salisbury for the Conservatives. In 1897 Gladstone was stricken with cancer of the throat, and neither the Queen nor Salisbury could expect to live much longer. In the event, Gladstone died in 1898, the Queen three years later and Salisbury two years after that.

It is worth considering, at this point, the impact that Queen Victoria's death in January 1901 had upon the nation's and the Empire's sensibilities. Victoria had hardly been a beacon of intellectual and cultural excellence. She had become increasingly self-absorbed – especially after Prince Albert's premature death in 1861 – retreating into a heavily defended, inward-looking world, characterised by her political partiality and by her narrow-mindedness and bigotry. She had been as fertile as almost any of her female subjects, producing nine children; but she does not seem to have been a particularly warm or accessible mother, and often terrified her grandchildren when they were brought before her.

In the Empire she was hailed as the 'Great White Queen over the Water', the mother of her subjects, but although she fretted over imperial reverses, as most famously at the death of General Gordon at Khartoum in 1885, she resolutely chose not to visit her far-flung peoples. The Empress of India never set foot on Indian soil; but then, nor did she go to Australia, the Cape, Canada, Nigeria or Singapore. Trips to Balmoral, Sandringham and Osborne on the Isle of Wight seem to have suited her best. She did, it is true, pay a visit in 1900 to Ireland, which prompted some celebratory verse:

> Come back to Erin, Victoria Regina,
> Come back to Erin, our dear Empress-Queen;
> Come back in the springtime, Victoria mavourneen,
> Come back when our meadows with shamrocks are green.[9]

These somewhat cloying sentiments were reinterpreted and recycled in 'Monto', a pastiche of Victorian Dublin which included the lines:

> The Queen she came to call on us.
> She wanted to see all of us.
> I'm glad she didn't fall on us.
> She's eighteen stone.[10]

Was Queen Victoria a woman of substance in other ways? Was Kipling justified in ascribing such potency to 'The Widow at Windsor'? To judge by two editorials printed in *The Times* on either side of her death, Victoria had the capacity to symbolise greatness and to encapsulate and encourage feelings of security. On 1 January 1901, while the Queen was still alive, the editorial was a frankly self-congratulatory piece of smug, patriotic journalism, pronouncing that 'with a people prosperous, contented, manly, intelligent and self-reliant, we may look forward with great hope'. Three weeks later, however, the Queen had died, and it is as if the heavens had fallen in. The future is somewhat bleak, and the nation's prospects unsure: 'The command of natural forces that made us great and rich has been superseded by newer discoveries and methods, and we may have to open what may be called a new chapter.'[11]

This is what the deaths of national totems and the ending of centuries and millennia tend to do to human beings, irrespective of their educational attainments, their capacity for rational thought or their psychological well-being – they cause them to take stock, and may also destabilise them.

There was, admittedly, enough to destabilise the most resilient of British observers at the end of the nineteenth century. The external challenge, and the crowding in of a host of internal problems and anxieties, provoked sufficient clamour and strident sentiment to convince both critics and supporters of Empire that unprecedented forces were in operation. The term 'New Imperialism' was coined to describe the phenomenon. Although British imperial expansion continued at much the same rate as at previous periods in her history, the perception of a 'New Imperialism' lent a fresh and vivid urgency to the proceedings.

The jingoism of the music halls, and the literary and journalistic excesses of imperial devotees, became more assertive and apparently self-confident as a number of confrontations with European imperial rivals, as well as successful military campaigns fought against generally backward and 'uncivilised' indigenous peoples, seemed to confirm British supremacy. The competition for colonies in Africa and the deepening crisis in the Transvaal lent an untypical excitement to routine diplomatic and political manoeuvring. It was now easier than ever before to put vivid and accessible accounts of these great affairs before the late-Victorian public.

The *Daily Mail* had been launched in 1896, an event which, despite the Prime Minister Lord Salisbury's contemptuous dismissal of the paper as being 'written by office boys for office boys', led to the rapid development of a cheap popular press that could present great events for the digestion and titillation of a barely literate readership, and fed countless starved imaginations – after all, the office boys needed information and entertainment as much as aristocrats. Moreover, many of them now had votes, while the peers did not. Industrialisation had herded Victorian working men and women into factories and workshops, and subjected them to industrial regulation and control, while at the same time the constitution had denied them full political freedom: until 1918 women could not vote, nor could approximately 40 per cent of adult males. It was thus understandable that many took a personal pleasure at the far-flung victories of the British Army or the Royal Navy. A sense of national pride became commingled with the revived imperialist sentiment.

Feelings of national insecurity, however, were at least partly at the root of much jingoistic exaltation and triumphalism. For all Britain's imperial pomp and splendour, the country was, during the 1890s, without allies and openly – indeed passionately – disliked by many in Europe and the United States. 'Splendid Isolation', so accurately and pessimistically diagnosed by Lord Salisbury, was in truth uncomfortable and increasingly costly, a rationalisation of a predicament, not a calculated and self-confident policy. The over-reaction of the public to military triumphs such as the slaughter of the dervishes by Western military technology at the Battle of Omdurman in 1898, or to the over-due relief of the besieged town of Mafeking during the Boer War two years later, can be interpreted as the responses of an insecure and uncertain people.

In this sense, the Diamond Jubilee celebrations of 1897 were a fundamental part of the process of 'inventing tradition': of using the purely fortuitous longevity of Queen Victoria, and the nearing of the end of the century, as a means of focusing unprecedented attention upon the British imperial achievement and, in the process, preaching a revamped, more coherent, version of the gospel of Britain's imperial mission. At the same time, the faltering sense of national purpose could be refurbished and revitalised for the undoubted challenges of the imminent new century.

On this analysis, the celebration of Empire was both a means of highlighting British achievements and of boosting flagging national morale. It was a further manifestation of the imperative to use Empire as a means of diverting attention from fundamental failures and chronic uncertainty. The Jubilee provided a gaudy and brightly-lit shop front while, inside, the shop's owners faced bankruptcy and ruin amid their increasingly outmoded stock. Britain's faltering great power status could thus be underwritten by magnificent displays like the Diamond Jubilee, and her position of global supremacy therefore preserved. In short, it amounted to a gigantic confidence trick.

The potency of the Empire's appeal as the key to future security and success, as providing a remedy to an unspecified number of national ills, was reflected in the increasingly bipartisan approach to imperial affairs during the latter part of the nineteenth century. Disraeli's bid, during the 1870s, permanently to identify Empire with the fortunes of the Conservative Party had been essentially a sham, although a seductive one. The imperial aggrandisement of the Gladstone administration of 1880 to 1885 had conclusively demonstrated that imperial interests were at least as safe in Liberal hands. Nevertheless, Gladstone's retirement from the premiership in 1894 had, at a stroke, removed from the scene the most senior Liberal statesman associated, however wilfully and misleadingly, with anti-imperialist policies.

With Lord Rosebery briefly installed as Prime Minister between 1894 and 1895, the forces of Liberal Imperialism were able to come out of the closet. Although there were still many Gladstonian Liberals,

Radicals and, for good measure, Labour men who expressed distaste for the politics of imperialism, the Liberal Imperialists, led by such promising younger politicians as Rosebery, Asquith, Grey and Haldane, seemed likely to inherit the party's future. With the Conservatives, even under the leadership of the intellectual and fastidious Salisbury, firmly identified by the public as the party of Empire, imperialism now became a respectable political philosophy and one which, moreover, seemed to unite the two main parties at least as much as dividing them.

A further difficulty that faced all of those who hoped to promote and consolidate the British Empire was the sheer complexity of the organisation. In many ways, it was characterised more by variety than by order, more by disunity than by unity. It was possible for some imperial theorists to draw comforting equations between diversity and strength, even between diversity and democracy, but others strove to impose an acceptable pattern on the components of the Empire. In the event, the Empire could not be knocked into a uniform shape, although it proved possible, after great difficulty, to smooth out some of its worst irregularities.

It was easier, of course, clearly and rationally to describe the different groupings within the imperial system. First there were the self-governing colonies, acknowledging the British monarch as sovereign, and still theoretically restricted in a few trivial constitutional fields by the oversight of the Parliament at Westminster. But in practical terms, these colonies really were internally self-governing. Their external defence and foreign policies, however, were in Britain's hands, and it was in these areas that the efforts of imperial unifiers could most profitably be concentrated.

Next there was the great dependency of India. This offered at least a geographical and administrative coherence of some sort. But even here, there was the dichotomy between British India, two-thirds of the whole, and the India of the princes, as well as striking contrasts between different provinces. Nonetheless India, overall, could be treated as a unit. The Viceroy, the provincial governors, the Indian Civil Service were all weighty parts of the complicated but functioning machinery of the British Raj.

By the end of the nineteenth century, the dependent Empire was a jumble of possessions. There were crown colonies, like Ceylon, Jamaica or Trinidad, ruled by the Colonial Office through a governor, who was sometimes assisted by executive and legislative councils. There were also protectorates, such as Uganda, Nyasaland or Aden, mostly ruled by the Foreign Office, and frequently maintaining local institutions. Protected states within the Empire were one stage removed from protectorates, in that indigenous rulers remained in office but were subject to the advice of powerful British residents. This meant that the protected states, from friendly Tonga to strategically vital Egypt, were also a Foreign Office responsibility. There were, in addition, the chartered territories, like the Rhodesias and North Borneo, which were governed by chartered companies allowed virtually a free hand by Westminster. The Empire also contained two condominiums, the Sudan and the New Hebrides, which were ruled jointly with Egypt and France respectively.

The quest to find and to consolidate links binding together this global, and potentially ramshackle, imperial structure was lent a new urgency by the fresh challenges that Britain faced at the end of the nineteenth century. One central link was, of course, the British Crown. The monarch was Queen not only of the United Kingdom, but also of all the self-governing colonies. She was Empress of India, and elsewhere a focal point of allegiance and respect, if not always of love. At the time of the Diamond Jubilee, it was discovered that even very large numbers of British citizens were surprisingly ignorant about the Empire whose scope and splendour so many of them were passionately celebrating. It should not be supposed, therefore, that a dyak in Borneo or a Hausa in northern Nigeria had an especially clear picture of the distant British monarch. Citizens of Vancouver or Adelaide were undoubtedly better informed, but even in their case, the British royal family was very far removed from their daily experiences, and impacted very marginally upon their everyday lives. All the same, the authority bestowed by the Crown was evident throughout the Empire in the deportment of its representatives, from the Viceroy of India to the most isolated district officer.

Another bond of Empire was the British Parliament. But here the link was legalistic and sometimes slipshod. A majority at Westminster could overthrow a governor-general, vote money for a punitive expedition, or even alter the constitution of a self-governing colony, but in many ways power continued to be held by the administrators of Empire, the 'men on the spot'. Partly because it was aware of the realities of the situation, and partly because imperial issues were generally low on most MPs' list of priorities, Parliament tended to hold the reins of Empire lightly. So lightly, in fact, that relatively few tended to notice when dextrous executive or proconsular hands whisked the reins away.

English law was another link binding the component parts of the Empire. In theory, each one of the Queen's subjects could avail himself of the apparatus of civil justice. Equality before the law theoretically existed. In practice, it was extremely difficult, if not impossible, for most of the Queen's humbler and less well educated subjects to take advantage of this right. Even those many local laws which were retained to operate within the overarching framework of English Common Law were often inaccessible. Very few colonial subjects indeed availed themselves of the final court of appeal for the whole Empire, the Judicial Committee of the Privy Council.

The civil servants of the Empire lent a degree of uniformity to widely scattered administrations. In the first rank stood the god-like members of the Indian Civil Service and of the Sudan Civil Service, with their high level of academic attainment and their compulsory knowledge of local languages, history and law. Although recruits to the administrations of the crown colonies and other possessions were not so high-powered, they did share similar social backgrounds and had undergone similar educational experiences.

The old school tie therefore provided one of the few genuine bonds of Empire – an apt reminder of the enduring contribution to the administration and control of the Empire of the public-school ethic, an ideology fostered so assiduously from the days of the renowned Dr Arnold of Rugby School. Many Victorian public schools became exclusive and intensely hierarchical institutions where the sons – and, rather later in the day, some of the daughters – of Britain's ruling elite were sent to be subjected to a regime of discipline, high thinking and low living, compulsory sport, and sometimes inspired teaching. There was the risk of bullying and other forms of sadistic torment. 'Unnatural' sexual practices might also be part of the public schoolboy's educational experience. Having survived all of this, the average young man who rolled off the public-school production line was considered to be ideally equipped to carry the doctrines of 'muscular Christianity', 'fair play' and 'decent behaviour' into any nook or cranny of the Empire. For their part, 'the natives' were expected to respond with gratitude and respect, and to obey the orders of their 'sweet, just, boyish masters'.

Apart from the monarchy, the only realistic and historically validated imperial link was the experience of British rule. The dependent territories were controlled, either directly or indirectly, by Britain. The self-governing colonies, however, were free of such subordination. In general, they need only cooperate with the mother country when, and how, they saw fit. They could not be browbeaten into obedience, although they might, on the other hand, be wooed. It was inevitable, therefore, that talk of imperial unity concentrated almost exclusively upon the relationship between Britain and the self-governing colonies. These were not only the most advanced components of the Empire, in terms of their economies and their political institutions, but they were also the territories which displayed the most independence.

While the 1897 celebration of Empire was an attempt to gloss over the disunity and confusion within the imperial system, a wide range of political and academic propagandists had, for some time, recognised the problems. Earlier, Sir John Seeley's *Expansion of England*, J.A. Froude's *Oceana* and Charles Dilke's *Greater Britain* had powerfully put the case for greater imperial unity, and were read by tens of thousands of people in many editions. In 1884 the Imperial Federation League had been founded to propagate the theme of imperial cooperation through constitutional reform. The English-Speaking Union was another body dedicated to the cause of Anglo-Saxon global solidarity. By the end of the century the Round Table group had also emerged as eloquent advocates of imperial consolidation, preaching their message chiefly through the regular publication of a journal of that name. In 1895 the cause of Empire had received a dramatic political boost when the most dynamic and persuasive advocate of greater imperial unity, Joseph Chamberlain, became Colonial Secretary. He held the office for eight years, ostentatiously playing the part of an imperial knight errant in relentless pursuit of the elusive grail of imperial cooperation.

What remedies lay at hand for those who wished to consolidate and unify the Empire, and at the same time to protect Britain from the unwelcome impact of increasing international competition? The attempt to hoist imperial issues to the top of the national political agenda was essentially a failure. The public's attention could occasionally be concentrated, and then only by an effort, upon matters of great imperial portent, such as the African partition, the Boer War, or the need to replace free trade with imperial preference. For the most part, however, the late-Victorian population stuck to what they perceived as bread-and-butter-issues, literally in the case of food prices, but also conditions of housing, the threat of unemployment, the reform of education and so forth.

Exasperated by this domestic taste for navel-gazing, imperial reformers and expansionists pressed on with their programme of regeneration and revivalism. One means of attracting the public's attention was to advertise the virtues of the English-speaking people. With

Chamberlain as its chief apostle, but strongly supported by men like Cecil Rhodes and Alfred Milner, and by a number of newly-founded organisations, the movement to glorify and to promote the Anglo-Saxon race did not pull its punches. As well as attempting to foster closer relations with the English-speaking populations of the self-governing colonies, the activities of pan-Anglo-Saxonists concentrated on improving relationships between the United States and Britain.

Facing up to the prospects of its own inevitable decline, Britain made a calculated attempt to encourage the New World to come to the rescue of the Old. This was made possible for a number of reasons. One was that, in general, Britain's global interests were not seriously in conflict with those of the United States. Where clashes did occur, over the Venezuelan boundary with British Guiana, over the Hay–Pauncefote Panama Canal Treaty, and over the Alaskan border with Canada, Britain sold out on each occasion to the demands of the United States. This was appeasement on a scale that few contemporaries were able, or prepared, to recognise. Another factor was the substantial level of social interaction between leading British and American families. This manifested itself most strikingly in marriages between British statesmen and American women, most of them of considerable financial means. Among those Britons who married American women were Rudyard Kipling, the Liberal statesman Lewis Harcourt (Colonial Secretary in the years prior to the First World War), the Duke of Manchester, Lord Randolph Churchill, Lord Curzon and Joseph Chamberlain. During the 1880s and 1890s, it was commonplace to find British statesmen and opinion-makers emphasising Anglo–American links rather than differences. As well as the interconnections of banking, insurance and trade, a shared linguistic, cultural, political and legal inheritance also played its part in smoothing the way towards *rapprochement*.

On this analysis, the Americans stood shoulder-to-shoulder with the British people as upholders of Anglo-Saxon civilisation. Speaking in 1887, Chamberlain said: 'I refuse to think or to speak of the USA as a foreign nation. We are all of the same race and blood. I refuse to make any distinction between the interests of Englishmen in England, in Canada and in the United States . . . Our past is theirs – their future is ours . . . I urge upon you our common origin, our relationship . . . We are branches of one family.'[12] He was to return often to this theme, announcing, for example, 'I have been called the apostle of the Anglo-Saxon race, and I am proud of that title . . . I think the Anglo-Saxon race is as fine as any on earth.' Kipling's much-quoted poem 'Take up the White Man's Burden' was an exhortation addressed not, as is commonly supposed, to British imperialists, but to the United States during its war with Spain in 1898.[13] In a host of histories, novels and, perhaps most insidiously, school textbooks, Anglo-Saxon racial superiority was not merely taken for granted, but vehemently asserted.

Britain's resolve to use the United States as a means of lightening the burdens which it bore, 'staggering,' as Chamberlain claimed, 'like a mighty Titan beneath the too vast orb of its fate', was carried into the early years of the twentieth century. The Fisher naval reforms of the Edwardian era depended at least partly for their success upon withdrawing Royal Navy warships from Caribbean and North American waters and, as a consequence, handing over the protection of British and imperial interests to the United States. The myth of the 'Special Relationship' between Britain and the United States, which was to last for nearly a century, was at least partly the rationalisation of this necessary accommodation.

In its search for new allies, Britain went even further afield, and in the treaties of 1902 and 1905 formally enlisted the rising imperial and naval power of Japan in support of British interests in India and the Far East. It is possible to say, without exaggeration, that after 1902 the defence of British interests in India, China and South-East Asia rested as much upon the goodwill of Japan as upon British military and naval provision. The conclusive Japanese victory in the 1904–5 war with Russia – although an embarrassing defeat of a European imperial power at the hands of an Asian nation – seemed to show what a prudent choice Britain had made in its foray into twentieth-century treaty-making. The 1904 entente with France was simply an extension of the new enthusiasm for constructing a system of alliances and military and diplomatic understandings with powerful foreign states.

There were also attempts to achieve imperial reforms from within. These concentrated on three areas: schemes for greater constitutional unity, including federation; the encouragement of greater cooperation in matters of imperial defence; and the restructuring of trade relations.

Imperial defence seemed to offer one of the most promising areas for promoting greater unity and cooperation within the Empire. The defence of Britain and her colonies was not a matter to be taken lightly, and some of the issues involved could be presented as matters for practical and urgent decision. To a large extent, the diversity and confusion which the British government faced in the late 1890s in the field of imperial defence was the result of earlier administrations' determination to pass over as much of the cost as they could to component parts of the Empire. India not only paid for its own defence, but also maintained an army which was often used to support the activities of British forces in a variety of world trouble-spots. As internal self-governing status had been bestowed upon the majority of the colonies of European settlement from mid-century onwards, the burden of shouldering local defence costs had also been devolved upon these emergent communities. By the early 1870s local military defence was clearly the responsibility of the self-governing colonies. During exceptional emergencies like the Second Maori War or the conflict with the Boers in South Africa, however, the intervention of British regular troops was considered to be essential. These divided responsibilities underlined the case for a more efficient approach to inter-imperial defence planning and cooperation, particularly as regards the land forces of the Empire.

Naval defence, however, was still overwhelmingly the responsibility of the British government. Although by the beginning of the twentieth century self-governing colonies of some standing like Canada, or the newly federated Commonwealth of Australia, were seriously addressing the task of building up their own naval forces, it seemed impossible to contemplate an era when the Royal Navy would not provide the whole imperial system with its main bulwark of defence against foreign aggression and interference.

It might have been innocently imagined that the issue of imperial defence would have been of such importance as to have miraculously concentrated the minds of statesmen and of military and naval leaders. This would be, however, to misunderstand the competing and often contradictory factors at work. The self-governing colonies, constantly treading the devolutionary path, and confident that in an emergency the British Army would come to their defence, were in general extremely reluctant to commit themselves to any military arrangement that might prove embarrassing and inappropriate. Within Britain, those politicians, like Arthur James Balfour, who were beginning in the latter years of the nineteenth century to coordinate the activities and responsibilities of Britain's army and navy, were encountering serious obstacles.

The main obstacle was that the British Army and the Royal Navy were not necessarily willing or cooperative partners in the matter of defence planning. Both services had to compete ferociously for the relatively scarce resources which went towards the annual defence estimates passed through the House of Commons, and as a result tended to see themselves as competitors rather than allies. A surprisingly large

number of senior staff in both services were inclined to view their opposite numbers with suspicion, even occasionally with hostility and contempt. Before the end of the nineteenth century, neither service was
anxious to let the other know details of its strategic planning.

At the time of Queen Victoria's Diamond Jubilee, progress towards
a greater degree of inter-imperial defence planning seemed to have been
made in only one area. The breakthrough had come as a result of
discussions between the British government and colonial prime ministers who had assembled in London for the Golden Jubilee celebrations
ten years earlier. At this time, the Australian colonies and New Zealand
had accepted the British case that the maintenance of squadrons of the
Royal Navy in Australasian waters was a costly business. From 1887,
therefore, the Australian colonies and New Zealand agreed to make
annual payments for the upkeep of the Royal Navy. In the first year,
£850,000 was appropriated, a substantial amount in contemporary
terms.

It was possible to see this apparent breakthrough, however, in terms
of self-interest rather than of imperial patriotism. The Australasian
colonies were sparsely populated European settlements on the fringe of
the Asian land-mass, and were conscious of their isolation. The rising
power of Japan, and the threatening, if demonstrably inefficient, presence of Russia in the Far East, heightened the sense of isolation and
insecurity. There is no doubt that the colonies were buying a measure
of security with their annual payments to the Royal Navy's upkeep. At
the Diamond Jubilee of 1897, which once more provided the opportunity
for the British government to enter into formal conference with the
leaders of the self-governing colonies, the Cape also agreed to contribute
to the navy's upkeep. The gesture was timely in view of the growing
crisis in South Africa. By the time the next Colonial Conference met in
1902, Natal had joined the list of subscribers, although this decision
could be seen primarily as a vote of thanks to Britain for her role in
recently subduing the Boer republics.

One way of properly evaluating the significance of the self-governing
colonies' growing willingness to make annual contributions to the
upkeep of the Royal Navy is to consider the case of Canada. The Canadian government, secure under the mighty wing of the United States,
and only 3,000 miles away by sea from the Mother Country, chose not
to pay out one penny to the Royal Navy, and showed a strengthening
determination to establish a navy of its own.

Other attempts to improve imperial defence cooperation bore little fruit until the early years of the twentieth century. Up to 1878 the final responsibility for the defence planning for the Empire was borne by the Cabinet, which was frequently ill-equipped to give sufficient time or consideration to such problems. The creation of a Colonial Defence Committee in 1878 was largely an *ad hoc* response to the Russian war scare of that year. It was, however, a feeble body and expired within a year. The incoming Salisbury government of 1885 revived it, and it continued to collect and circulate information in a rather lackadaisical fashion. In 1890 a Joint Naval and Military Defence Committee was established, but it was bedevilled by inter-service disputes, and its work generally lacked clarity or distinction.

The Conservative and Unionist general election victory in 1895 led to the establishment of the Cabinet Defence Committee. The self-evident growth of the external threat to Britain's military and naval integrity was a powerful boost to the establishment of this committee, as was the development of an influential and articulate services lobby in the House of Commons, and the skilful and persistent advocacy of Arthur Balfour, Lord Salisbury's nephew and ultimate successor as Prime Minister. The Cabinet Defence Committee, however, was not particularly successful. It lacked real authority, and the Prime Minister of the day, as well as the Foreign and Colonial Secretaries, and even the professional heads of the armed services, did not attend its deliberations. No minutes were kept of its meetings, and its work was fundamentally ill-defined and ineffective.

The accession of Balfour to the premiership in 1902, coming hard on the heels of the embarrassing military fiascos of the Boer War, paved the way for a more effective initiative. By 1904 the Cabinet Defence Committee had been reconstituted as the Committee of Imperial Defence. It had a permanent secretariat, in itself a revolutionary step, was chaired by the Prime Minister, and included the Secretary for War, the First Lord of the Admiralty, the First Sea Lord, the Commander-in-Chief and the heads of Naval and Military Intelligence. It was also able to invite any minister, service expert or colonial statesman to its meetings. Although essentially an advisory body, it was a powerful one because of its membership. At least now an appropriate mechanism had been established for better cooperation between Britain and the self-governing colonies in matters of defence. Not all of Balfour's aspirations for the Committee of Imperial Defence were fulfilled, but at least a precedent had been established, and it was capable of healthy and sustained growth.

Imperial trade seemed to offer another promising area for improved cooperation. By the end of the nineteenth century the proportion of Britain's trade with the Empire was a little less than 30 per cent of the whole, and actually declined from 28.5 per cent during the 1880s to 27.5 per cent by 1900. The European and United States markets were still vitally important to Britain, but here the British balance of trade was ominously and regularly running into deficit. Nor was Britain able to keep as far ahead of her main trading rivals as hitherto; the gap was steadily closing. Although in absolute terms British foreign trade increased by a healthy 25 per cent between 1880 and 1900, in relative terms it was falling as compared with some of its chief competitors – Germany's foreign trade, for instance, grew by 80 per cent during the same period.

Since the principles of free trade still dominated British economic theory, and commanded bipartisan support in Parliament, the opportunities for restructuring imperial trading relationships on the model, say, of imperial Germany's *zollverein* (or customs union) were severely limited. In the case of the British Empire, imperial loyalties, such as they were, were less significant than commercial realities.

From the 1870s, however, the mid-Victorian economic boom began to fade, chiefly due to the competition from other manufacturing and industrial countries. Throughout the 1890s there were a number of economic depressions, culminating in the great depression of 1896 – a troubling indicator of decline and a further justification for the morale-boosting Jubilee of 1897. During these years British exports suffered alarming fluctuations, and there were severe bouts of commercial dislocation and unemployment. Not only were other nations, notably Germany and the United States, expanding their industrial activities on a scale which threatened eventually to overtake Britain's early lead, but by the 1890s most of the major manufacturing countries had adopted some measure of fiscal protection. Britain alone clung to free trade. As a result of this, the 1880s and 1890s saw the rise of a protectionist lobby in Britain, its views most clearly articulated by the Fair Trade League.

In 1895 the accession to the Colonial Office of Joseph Chamberlain, with his political power-base in the industrial West Midlands, his experience of Birmingham manufacturing, and his self-declared mission to promote a greater degree of imperial unity, put a potentially deadly enemy of free trade in a position of considerable influence. By 1902, Chamberlain, frustrated in his plans for imperial councils and for precise schemes of imperial defence, sought to amalgamate economic self-interest with the cause of imperial unity in a crusade for tariff reform, expressed through a system of imperial trade preferences.

There were some promising developments for people of Chamberlain's persuasion. Beginning in 1897, the Canadian government offered a series of trading preferences to Britain, which by 1900 amounted to a 33.3 per cent discount on British manufactures entering Canada. Still bound by the prevailing fiscal orthodoxy of free trade, however, the British government was unable to make any practical response. Other self-governing colonies were simultaneously showing an interest in some form of inter-imperial preferential tariffs.

An imperial common market, however, was still way beyond reach. Self-interest, not imperial idealism, dominated colonial economic policies. Colonial statesmen still wanted to protect their infant industries, and British politicians feared the electoral consequences of importing food made dearer by the imposition of protective tariffs. In the end the best that could reasonably be achieved was the construction of a system of tariff barriers, both in Britain and in the self-governing colonies, which would in effect impose taxes on foreign goods entering those countries. Imperial preference could then be introduced by the lowering of these tariff barriers against goods produced in the Empire. At the time of Victoria's Diamond Jubilee, this potential programme of fiscal reform was fundamentally unpopular within both major political parties, and needed passionate and inspired advocacy to sell it to a confused, unconvinced and generally uninterested public.

If the push for imperial preference, or tariff reform, had not yet properly developed, plans for imperial federation also remained unfulfilled. Although there were enthusiastic exponents of federation in Britain and the self-governing colonies, including the Imperial Federation League, the practical difficulties facing such a proposal were enormous. Any rational plan for imperial federation begged the question of the composition and power of a centrally situated Imperial Assembly. What subjects were to be reserved for this legislative body? How would it be possible to avoid clashes and a chronic collision of interests over sovereignty between any central assembly and the parliaments of the self-governing colonies? Who would sit in any prospective Imperial Federal Parliament? If delegates were to be elected on the basis of proportional representation, then the British members would swamp those from the self-governing colonies, with their much smaller populations.

Although proposals for imperial federation were not finally to be disposed of until just before the First World War, the surface show of unity and cohesion which marked the Diamond Jubilee encouraged federationists to believe that their hour had come. Such perceptions, however, were illusory. Political expediency, and the already well-established realities of colonial devolution, proved insuperable obstacles. The upshot, as was so often the case, was a typically pragmatic British compromise – uncontroversial, reasonable, economical and, by choice rather than by accident, not particularly efficient. Since it was impossible to agree on the form and structure of an Imperial Federal Parliament, the Empire determined to make the best use it could of the Colonial Conference system. The first Colonial Conference had met at the time of Victoria's Golden Jubilee celebrations in 1887, and the event was repeated at the Queen's Diamond Jubilee in 1897. The establishment of this precedent probably constitutes Victoria's most valuable contribution to the evolution of her Empire. It was an achievement that owed nearly everything to her longevity rather than to her innate abilities. By attaining a ripe old age, Queen Victoria provided a substantial measure of practical assistance to the better organisation of the imperial family.

At the Jubilee of 1897 it was agreed to hold Colonial Conferences at five-yearly intervals. The system thus established, with suitable adaptations, led directly to today's regular meetings of the heads of Commonwealth governments. The conferences that met in the late nineteenth and early twentieth centuries were never occasions for dynamic and fateful decision-making. Hefty agendas were presented to the delegates, who ranged freely over many topics of common interest, but any policies agreed at the conference had then to be vetted by the local colonial legislatures. The principle of colonial autonomy was thus retained intact. In a word, the Colonial Conferences could only be as useful as the delegates wanted them to be. They did, of course, have some symbolic significance, and their participants frequently felt that the free exchange of opinions helped to clear the diplomatic air.

In the final analysis, the Diamond Jubilee of 1897 achieved very little of any practical significance. It allowed an outpouring of emotion from those who wished thus to liberate themselves, but it did not change the imperial structure to any significant degree. As the captains and the kings departed – or, more accurately, as the colonial statesmen and the huge crowds of metropolitan onlookers departed – long-standing political imperatives silently reasserted themselves, and the vast bulk of active celebrants among the public returned to the mundanities of daily living.

A realistic assessment of imperial weaknesses and strengths ultimately prevailed. It was generally accepted, despite some further Chamberlainite initiatives, that the most realistic course of action was to fasten onto those links that already existed between the component countries of the Empire, rather than to forge new and potentially troublesome ones. The existing bonds of Empire, though unrestrictive, were not without intrinsic strengths of their own. These included the monarchy, a shared history, a common law and civil institutions, and, at least for the great majority of white citizens, a sense of cultural identity. These, if anything, were the bones that held the imperial body together. Imperfect though any of these links and bonds undeniably were, they were essentially organic growths rather than the result of hasty grafting and abrupt surgery. Loyalty to the Mother Country, no matter how vaguely and fitfully expressed, was better than a formal alliance; a set of common interests was more reliable than a formal set of bilateral treaties. Thus constructed, and acknowledged, the relationship between Britain and the self-governing colonies that dominated the British Empire at the end of the nineteenth century was to prove capable of the most remarkable endurance.

Essentially the Diamond Jubilee had been a brilliantly stage-managed act of defiance, a truculent assertion of national and imperial greatness in the face of a clutch of uncomfortable realities. Perhaps this was enough. Tennyson had written:

> *A song which serves a nation's heart*
> *Is, in itself, a deed.*

In the summer of 1897 the deed was done. In answer to Tennyson's other unsettling questions, there was indeed 'thunder moaning in the distance' and 'spectres moving in the shadows', as the years between 1897 and 1914 were so terrifyingly to demonstrate.

13

THE BATTLE OF SPION KOP, 1900

Crisis, War and Union in South Africa

ON 24 JANUARY 1900 a force of 30,000 British troops, led by the Commander-in-Chief in South Africa, General Buller, suffered a major defeat at the Battle of Spion Kop in northern Natal. In an operation which was meant to relieve the siege of Ladysmith, Buller instead stumbled to one of the most humiliating defeats of the 1899–1902 Boer War. The disaster at Spion Kop was eerily reminiscent of the catastrophe at Majuba Hill two decades earlier. As at Majuba, British forces had been commanded by a general whose inadequacies in the field belied his high reputation; had apparently gained a significant strategic advantage by occupying a commanding summit, Spion Kop; and had then discovered, when the darkness and mist lifted, that they were in a pitifully exposed position, enfiladed on all sides and at the mercy of extremely accurate enemy fire. In 1900, however, British losses were seven times higher than at Majuba Hill. When the humiliated General Buller withdrew across the Tugela River, he left behind 1750 men killed, wounded and captured; the Afrikaners had lost a mere 300. Ladysmith, of course, had not been relieved.

The news of the disaster at Spion Kop was hardly the New Year's gift that Britain wanted at the turn of the century, and seemed to confirm some in their gloomy prognostication of imperial decline and disintegration. The Colonial Secretary, Joseph Chamberlain, described it as 'a stunning fiasco', and Arthur Balfour, writing to his brother-in-law on the day of the battle, confided, 'I not only think blunders have been committed, but I think they have been of the most serious kind, imperilling the whole progress of the war . . . The chief blunders had been made, in my private opinion, by our generals in the field.'[1] In the besieged town of Ladysmith, Doctor Alec Kay, the civil surgeon at the Stationary Hospital, wrote: 'We all expected bad news and now we have it with a vengeance. Everyone is very down and depressed.'[2] In Britain, accusations of muddle and incompetence multiplied. The 'Pro-Boers', whose most eloquent and effective spokesman was the increasingly influential Liberal David Lloyd George, were encouraged in their criticisms of the war. British football supporters marked the event (and perhaps rendered it less painful) by naming the high terracing in some Association Football grounds, like those of Liverpool and Northampton Town, 'the Kop' or 'Spion Kop'. Throughout much of Europe, and indeed among many people outside Europe, further delight was taken in British discomfort.

The South African War of 1899–1902, popularly known as the Boer War, was invested with an enormous amount of contemporary symbolism and meaning. The British government, and the majority of the citizens of the self-governing colonies, as well as countless others throughout the dependent Empire, supported the war, which was presented by patriotic propaganda as almost a crusade to rescue the underprivileged and ill-used English-speaking population of the Transvaal. In South Africa, the budding apostle of non-violence, Mahondas Karamchand Gandhi, even organised an ambulance team to assist the imperial armies. As Kipling wrote at the outset of the war, in a successful attempt to whip up popular support for the British cause:

When you've shouted 'Rule Britannia,' when you've sung 'God Save the
> *Queen',*
When you're finished killing Kruger with your mouth,
Will you kindly drop a shilling in my little tambourine
For a gentleman in Khaki ordered South?
He's an absent-minded beggar, and his weaknesses are great –
But we and Paul must take him as we find him –
He's out on active service, wiping something off a slate –
And he's left a lot of little things behind him![3]

For those who opposed the war, or merely criticised the methods employed in it, the conflict seemed to represent all that was reprehensible in British imperialism. Britain, the 'mother of democracy', had on this analysis brought about a war with two puny but independent states, the Transvaal and the Orange Free State, for the sole purpose of laying its bloodstained hands upon the gold mines of the Rand, whose development since the 1886 had transformed the region's economy.

Some British radicals insisted from the outset that the war was being fought on behalf of Cecil Rhodes, international capitalism and the faceless and sinister financiers of 'Jewberg'. As the conflict became more protracted, and the British forces proved inept at finishing off Afrikaner resistance during the period of the guerrilla war from 1900 to 1902, as farm-burning increased and the newly-established concentration camps filled up with Boer civilians, the outcry against the conflict reached new heights. Sir Henry Campbell-Bannerman, leader of the Liberal Party from 1898, asked the potentially lethal question: 'When is a war not war? When it is carried on by methods of barbarism in South Africa.'[4]

It was claimed at the time, and has been asserted subsequently, that the Boer War was a highly significant watershed in the history and evolution of the British Empire; that its context, agenda and prosecution marked it out from other imperial conflicts, and imbued it with portent and substance. The campaign, it was argued, proved conclusively that imperial expansion could not always be had on the cheap; moreover, there was no guarantee that the process of imperial conquest would provide a glorious or edifying spectacle. It was also asserted that, coming after the crude excesses of late-nineteenth-century jingoistic imperialism, the fiascos of the Boer War obliged the British people to return, with a proper sense of puritanical guilt, to nobler and more restrained and traditional imperial pursuits.

Perhaps the war in South Africa made such an impact upon contemporary opinion, and has excited such interest ever since, for altogether more straightforward reasons. For one thing, it was a far bigger, costlier – both in terms of men and money – and more protracted affair than had been anticipated at its outset. The scale of its embarrassments and traumas was not merely shocking in itself, and likely further to undermine national self-esteem, but was also subject to the intense scrutiny and vivid journalism of the newly-established, increasingly sensationalist popular press. It was, moreover, the only war of any duration that Britain fought against opponents of European origin, except for the 1854–56 Crimean War, during the hundred years from 1815 to 1914, and it was as a consequence seen as a truer test of the nation's mettle than victories over poorly armed indigenous people.

The final reason for the perceived significance of the war probably owed more to the calendar than to more complex and deep-seated causes. The war began less than three months before the end of 1899, at a time when popular speculation as to what the next century would hold for Britain and the Empire had been widespread. When the 1900s opened with further demonstrations of British military incompetence, culminating in the catastrophe of Spion Kop, the worst fears of the pessimists were realised and the hopes of optimists dashed. Crudely put, the answer to the question of what the future held for Britain was disaster and humiliation.

The South African War became unavoidable during the years 1894 and 1895. Before then it was still possible to believe in the long-term strategy of waiting for the Transvaal, and the less prosperous Orange Free State, to be drawn into a unified South Africa dominated by British business interests and British political practice. At first the discovery of substantial gold deposits on the Witwatersrand reef in 1886 seemed to confirm this analysis, or at least to encourage those who believed in the eventual absorption of the Transvaal into a British-dominated South Africa. Tens of thousands of fortune-hunting foreigners, most of whom claimed British citizenship, flocked to the gold mines of the Transvaal. Within ten years these predominantly English-speaking immigrants, backed and empowered by their technological skills and the investment of capital from overseas, as well as from within South Africa, had established a thriving industrial economy centred on the rapidly developing city of Johannesburg.

It was soon reckoned (wrongly as it transpired) that the foreign migrants, described by the Afrikaners as 'Uitlanders' – outsiders or foreigners – outnumbered the Afrikaners of the Transvaal. On this analysis, the influx of Uitlanders promised to hand British imperial policy a bloodless victory through the transformation of the Transvaal into a community dominated by its English-speaking citizens. Although the Transvaal government, led by Paul Kruger, was determined to avoid this fate, and persistently refused to admit the Uitlanders *en masse* to full citizenship, it did not seem likely that these delaying tactics would be effective for long.

By 1894, however, optimistic assessments that the South African Republic would somehow implode and collapse internally, or simply wither away as the result of inexorable demographic change, were dashed. To begin with, the gold deposits on the Rand were shown to be the largest in the world, and capable of profitable production for at least another hundred years. As deep-level mining became the predominant method by which the gold ore was extracted, both the technological and labour costs increased sharply. Since, however, the price of gold was fixed on the world market, it was not possible to meet increased costs simply by hiking up the price of gold. The great deep-level gold-mining companies of the Rand therefore needed a government in the

Transvaal that was sensitive to the needs of the industry and willing fully to cooperate in its development. Rhodes, backed by other deep-level mining companies such as Wernher and Beit, claimed that, with the support of a sympathetic regime, mining costs could be cut by at least six shillings on every ton of earth dug up, saving the industry over £2,500,000 a year. He also wanted the government to allow a large increase in the recruitment of black labour; this, together with a ruthless policy of wage-cutting, would improve productivity.

Unfortunately the Kruger government, obscurantist and fundamentally fearful and resentful of the changes being brought about in the Transvaal through immigration and industrialisation, was only minimally cooperative. Kruger was perhaps encouraged in his resistance to the demands of Rhodes and his supporters by the fact that five of the ten leading mining companies, including Lewis and Marks, and Joseph Robinson, tended to back him in the confrontation. This split in the mining hierarchy was chiefly, although not entirely, the product of different economic and hence political needs; deep-level mining companies opposed the Kruger government, while those still substantially committed to shallow-level methods were more supportive. The division not only bore out Rhodes' assertion that it was the economics of deep-level mining that made the overthrow of Kruger's republic essential, but also goes some way to explain the half-hearted Uitlander response to the Jameson Raid at the end of 1895. In any event, the Kruger administration continued to levy heavy taxes on Transvaal industry, and to extract all that it could from monopolies like that imposed on the sale of dynamite.

Statesmen and industrialists, both in South Africa and in Britain, began to despair of a peaceful and, on their terms, 'sensible' resolution of the growing conflict of interests between the Kruger government and outside pressure groups. Not merely was the anticipated process of attrition from within thwarted by the Transvaal government's refusal to extend full citizenship and voting rights to the Uitlanders, but imperial Germany seemed determined to involve itself in Transvaal affairs and to act as a champion of the Krugerite regime. By 1895 over 5,000 Germans were living in the Transvaal, and formed a substantial, well-to-do, and generally pro-Krugerite community. German mining enterprises were being established, and German investment was soon in excess of 300,000,000 marks.

The earlier British Colonial Office assumption that a 'peaceful commercial annexation of the country' would result from the impact of

British enterprise, technology and migration seemed increasingly ill-founded.[5] The balance of power in South Africa appeared to be shifting inexorably and permanently away from the Cape to the Transvaal. Suddenly the South African future seemed destined to be dominated by a revitalised Afrikanerdom, sustained by the continuing exploitation and development of the Rand. Few British statesmen put the position more plainly than Lord Selborne, Under-Secretary of State at the Colonial Office in Salisbury's Unionist government of 1895 to 1900, when he wrote:

> In a generation the South African Republic [the Transvaal] will by its wealth and population dominate S. Africa. S. African politics must revolve around the Transvaal, which will be the only possible market for the agricultural produce or the manufacture of Cape Colony and Natal. The commercial attraction of the Transvaal will be so great that a Union of the African states with it will be absolutely necessary for their prosperous existence.[6]

Selborne's pessimism, expressed in the autumn of 1896, had been partly provoked by two recent developments. The first of these was the realisation that Cecil Rhodes' 'drive to the north', which had resulted in the opening up of the Rhodesias, was not going to redress the geopolitical balance in South Africa. There were no great mineral deposits in the Rhodesias, and Rhodes' assertion that 'the gist of the South African question lies in the extension of the Cape to the Zambezi' had been proved wrong. The 1896 Ndebele and Shona rebellions against white rule seemed further confirmation that the Rhodesian future was at best uncertain, and at worst bleak, compared with that of the Transvaal.

The second development of the mid-1890s which seemed, once and for all, to wreck every hope of a peaceful resolution of the 'Transvaal problem' was the Jameson Raid. Cecil Rhodes was the inspiration behind this episode. By 1895, he had become convinced that, for British interests to thrive throughout the whole of South Africa, Kruger's republic must be overthrown by force. As it happened, this was a perfectly rational assessment, and Rhodes was not alone in making it. What is significant is the fact that he felt compelled to do something practical about it. His determination to topple the Kruger regime through armed intervention also arose from his unbridled ambition and from his remarkable success hitherto. Rhodes' wealth had enabled him to put flesh upon the bones of his imperial and expansionist fantasies. The multi-millionaire and conqueror of the Rhodesias – the 'Colossus' of southern Africa – had no need to balk at mounting a coup aimed at the destruction of an apparently moribund and obstructive Transvaal government.

Rhodes' plans for the subordination of the Transvaal were well laid and not unrealistic. From the Rand, sufficient Uitlanders gave assurances that they would arm and organise themselves and, at the appropriate time, rise in rebellion. The uprising would be supported by an armed expedition into the Transvaal, composed of detachments of Rhodes' British South African Police Force. International indignation and protest would be unable to prevent the coup. Rhodes was Prime Minister of the Cape, and in alliance with the moderate Afrikaner Bond led by Hofmeyr. Natal, dominated by its English-speaking settler population, would support the enterprise. It would, moreover, be possible to present the intervention in quasi-humanitarian terms, claiming that it was necessary in order to guarantee the Uitlanders their birthright of free and equal citizenship.

Rhodes also felt confident that the British government would support him in his attempt to overthrow Kruger's republic. He had made discreet overtures to the Liberal government led by the Liberal Imperialist Lord Rosebery, before it fell from power in the summer of 1895, and had not been discouraged in his plans. The formation of Lord Salisbury's Unionist government, a coalition of Conservatives and Liberal Unionists, in July 1895 seemed even more propitious. The new Colonial Secretary, Joseph Chamberlain, shared Rhodes' desire to be rid of the Kruger regime, although he was obliged to act more circumspectly. There is no doubt whatever that Chamberlain connived at Rhodes' plan for an invasion of the Transvaal, knew about the planned Uitlander uprising, and went out of his way to promote the venture by ceding the Pitsani strip, part of the Bechuanaland Protectorate, to the British South Africa Company as a convenient base from which to launch the attack.

On 31 December 1895 the invasion of the Transvaal was undertaken by troopers of the British South African Police Force, led by Rhodes' confidant Dr Leander Starr Jameson. Jameson had enjoyed Rhodes' affection and trust ever since he had attended Neville Pickering, the 'Colossus's' greatly loved companion, on his deathbed. Whether Jameson was the right man for the job of leading the raid is doubtful. In some ways as impetuous as Rhodes himself, 'Dr Jim' seems to have jumped the gun and to have decided to make an end of waiting with a brusque and premature intervention.

The Jameson Raid was a disaster. The Uitlanders of Johannesburg and the Rand were meant to rise in rebellion and link up with Jameson's invading troopers. The British High Commissioner for South Africa and Governor of the Cape, Sir Hercules Robinson (who was incidentally a shareholder in Rhodes' British South Africa Company), set out for the Transvaal, planning to step into the confusion that would have resulted from the overthrow of the Kruger government as a mediator, although, in the circumstances, a decidedly partial one. It was expected that the speed and success of the coup would leave the international community breathless, and nullify their hostility. In any event, it was difficult to see what any foreign power that wished to support the Transvaal government, even imperial Germany, could do about it in practice. None of this worked out as Rhodes and his supporters had planned. The Uitlander uprising was a half-cocked affair, seeming to confirm the views of a number of British statesmen on both sides of the political divide that Mammon, not Queen Victoria, was the true idol of Johannesburg. Dr Jameson's invasion force was routed, speedily rounded up by Afrikaner commandos, and handed over to the British authorities for trial.

The raid, and especially its failure, was a prodigious reverse for Rhodes' 'forward' policy in South Africa. He was forced to resign as Prime Minister of the Cape, his alliance with Hofmeyr's Afrikaner Bond in ruins. Afrikaner opinion throughout South Africa rallied to Kruger and his beleaguered government. Within the Transvaal, moderate, anti-Krugerite factions which had hitherto been optimistic of winning the imminent presidential election were temporarily silenced. The Orange Free State was drawn closer to its northern sister republic. In the Cape, the Afrikaans-speaking people, who accounted for two-thirds of the white population, were encouraged to feel more strongly than ever their ties of kinship with the Afrikaners of the two republics. The German Kaiser, Wilhelm II, sent Kruger a telegram of unabashed and provocative congratulation.

In Britain, liberal opinion was horrified at the aggression, and an inquiry was called for. At the Select Committee of the House of Commons which handled – or, as some thought, mishandled – the inquiry into the Jameson Raid the British establishment closed ranks. Liberal members of the Committee pulled their punches, anxious not to reveal their complicity in the early planning stages of the raid. An unrepentant

Rhodes treated the inquiry with breathtaking insolence, even remarking to the Liberal Leader of the Opposition, Lewis Harcourt, 'Nobody is going to name a country after you.' Chamberlain, widely suspected of plotting with Rhodes, was confident that the inquiry would not 'do any harm'.[7] He was right to be so confident. The Colonial Secretary denied all knowledge of the raid, although admitting that he knew of the potential Uitlander uprising. Neither Rhodes nor Chamberlain was obliged to produced the 'missing telegrams' that allegedly implicated both of them in the plot.

The Committee of Inquiry was a whitewash, and was soon being written off as the 'lying-in-state at Westminster'. Realistically, it is easy to see why neither Rhodes nor Chamberlain was brought to book over the Jameson Raid. Each could so seriously harm the career and reputation of the other that both were as a consequence entirely safe: Rhodes could reveal the evidence of Chamberlain's complicity; for his part, the Colonial Secretary could seriously undermine Rhodes' imperial mission by stripping his British South Africa Company of its Royal Charter, the effective authorisation for its continuing rule of the Rhodesias.

Unbowed by the attacks on his integrity and by the embarrassment of the official inquiry, Chamberlain, with the support of his ministerial colleagues, set about restructuring British policy in South Africa. Within a year of the inquiry he had appointed Alfred Milner, an avowed 'race-patriot', as Governor of the Cape and High Commissioner. Milner's task was to regain the diplomatic and political initiative against Kruger's republic and to isolate and denigrate the Transvaal government.

In a brilliant and unexpected diplomatic coup, the Transvaal was cut off from its most likely form of outside assistance. In 1898 the Anglo–German agreement over the possible future disposal of Portugal's southern African colonies was signed. The Anglo–Portuguese Convention, concluded in 1891, had given Britain the right of pre-emption over all Portuguese possessions south of the Zambezi. By 1898 the Portuguese government was bankrupt and near to collapse. If it should be forced as a result to sell some of its colonies, it was agreed that Britain was to have Mozambique and Germany was to have Angola. In September 1898, Arthur Balfour was able to tell the Cabinet that Germany had resigned 'all concern in Transvaal matters'. This judgement was made barely two years after the Kaiser's enthusiastic telegram in support of Kruger after the Jameson Raid. When, in the autumn of 1899, large British forces were transferred to South Africa to fight the

Boer republics, Kaiser Wilhelm II, far from protesting, went out of his way to compliment the British War Office on the efficiency of its organisation. With Germany out of the way, there was no other nation that was likely, or indeed able, to assist the Transvaal in a military confrontation with Britain.

Chamberlain, although perceived by many as being morally impoverished by the Jameson Raid, shrugged off his critics and, with Milner's skilful assistance, gradually re-established the propaganda campaign on behalf of the Uitlanders and, as a result, of Britain's legitimate interests in the internal affairs of the Transvaal. Slowly, carefully, the Uitlanders were re-represented as a community deprived of civil rights and ill-treated by the Krugerite regime. Although the Transvaal government became increasingly prepared to make some retrospective concessions over the Uitlander franchise, British propaganda was always able to present such offers as insufficient and too late. Chamberlain and Milner's unashamed propaganda campaign even left some members of the Unionist government uneasy, and Balfour argued, with commendable honesty, in a paper put to the Cabinet that 'were I a Boer . . . nothing but necessity would induce me to adopt a constitution which would turn my country into an English Republic, or a system of education that would reduce my language to the "patois" of a small and helpless minority'.[8]

By 1899, however, the crisis in South Africa was moving towards a final resolution. Milner argued that what was really going on was a 'great game between ourselves and the Transvaal for the mastery of South Africa', with the object of 'uniting South Africa as a British State'. Chamberlain asserted, with characteristic clarity and hyperbole, that 'Our supremacy in South Africa, and our existence as a great power in the world are involved.'[9] The deep-level mining magnates, the 'Park Lane millionaires' of British liberal demonology, had been suspected of putting up money for the Jameson Raid. There is no doubt that, with Rhodes and Alfred Beit at the forefront, they offered crucial financial support and thus, in effect, indemnity to the British government in the event of a full-scale war to destroy the South African Republic of the Transvaal. The City of London was generally enthusiastic at the prospect of the overthrow of the Kruger regime; in 1899 investment in the gold-mining industry totalled some £74,000,000 of which the British share was about 70 per cent.[10]

In May 1899 the British adroitly played the diplomatic card by arranging a conference at Bloemfontein, in the Orange Free State, to attempt to resolve the differences between the Transvaal and Britain. The Bloemfontein conference turned into a face-to-face confrontation between Kruger and Milner. The meeting predictably failed to resolve any of their differences, and left the Transvaal President convinced that 'It's our country that you want.' Within a month, Chamberlain and Milner were discussing both the form of an ultimatum to the Transvaal and the matter of military reinforcements and troop movements. In July, Kruger made the substantial concession of offering the Uitlanders a retrospective franchise dating back seven years, and five new seats in the Volkrsraad, the Transvaal's parliament. His offer was rebuffed.

By August, both the Colonial and War Offices, and the British imperial authorities in South Africa, were actively preparing for war. The Sudan campaign was conveniently over, and the British public, still basking in the afterglow of Kitchener's defeat of the dervishes, could now focus its attention upon affairs in the Transvaal. Several weeks before the outbreak of hostilities in October, nearly 70,000 British and imperial troops were either stationed in South Africa or were bound there on the high seas.

In October 1899 the British diplomatic offensive was neatly concluded when the movement of imperial troops forced both the Transvaal and the Orange Free State to present an ultimatum calling for the withdrawal of these forces from the Transvaal's frontiers, and for the recall of all reinforcements dispatched since June. Britain, having provoked the ultimatum, naturally ignored it. Those in the Cabinet who doubted the wisdom of military intervention now swallowed their qualms and admitted the necessity for a military showdown in South Africa.

Essentially, of course, the brinkmanship of Chamberlain and Milner's diplomatic offensive had failed to deliver the goods – or a bloodless surrender by the Transvaal at any rate. The concessions which had been demanded of the Kruger government were simply too great to be practical politics. At least Britain could protest its good intentions, point to its diplomatic initiatives, and officially regret the fact that a military confrontation now seemed unavoidable. For its part, the Transvaal, strongly supported by the Orange Free State, and with offers of help flooding in from thousands of Cape Afrikaners, decided that it had nothing to lose by standing firm. No doubt memories of Britain's brisk humiliations during the Transvaal war of 1880–81 influenced this determination. It was, moreover, October, and the spring grass was up, essential fodder for the horses so central to the successful deployment of Boer commandos. The Boer War, which had been so long anticipated, dreaded and desired, at last began.

At the outset, the war which broke out in October 1899 provided, at least superficially, a repeat performance of the one-act tragedy, or farce, enacted in 1880 and 1881 in the Transvaal. The British Empire was pitted once more against the determined Transvaalers, who were again struggling for their independence; yet again the British Army found itself outmanoeuvred, outfought and outwitted; even the leaders of the Transvaal were the same, since Paul Kruger was President and Piet Joubert Commandant-General.

The similarities, however, end there. The earlier Transvaal War saw less than 8,000 Afrikaners defeat little more than 1,000 active British troops; during the second conflict, nearly 450,000 men from Britain, her self-governing colonies and India slowly and relentlessly wore down their 45,000 Afrikaner opponents. The campaign of 1880–81 was over in nine weeks; the war that began in October 1899 lasted for over two and a half years. In 1880 the Transvaal stood alone; in 1899 the Orange Free State also fought for independence, and nearly 10,000 Cape Dutch from Cape Colony rallied to the colours of the two republics. In 1881 the Transvaal regained its republican status; in 1902 the two Boer republics were annexed to the British Crown. In the first war, one inexperienced general, Sir George Colley, led the British forces; in the second war, many of the greatest military commanders of the Empire were dispatched to South Africa, among them Sir Redvers Buller, Field Marshal Lord Roberts of Kandahar, Lord Kitchener of Khartoum, General Sir George White, Lord Methuen and General Sir John French.

Although there was some overlap between Britain's political and diplomatic aims in both conflicts, the two wars broke out in very different fashions. In 1880 the British government had hoped to avoid conflict, and was caught by surprise when the Transvaalers rebelled; in 1899 the British Cabinet, led by the nose by Joseph Chamberlain and Alfred Milner, had eventually decided to push Kruger to the brink of war, and, if necessary, over the brink. In 1880 the Transvaalers had argued, in righteous and outraged terms, that they merely wanted self-government; in 1899 it was the British government that touted what passed for a moral justification for the war, arguing that the plight of the Uitlanders in the Transvaal demanded intervention.

The Boer War was divided into several distinct movements, rather like some great symphony. The opening movement was *con brio*; it was followed by a depressed, muted movement that culminated in 'Black

Week'; then there was the apparently triumphant *andante* of Roberts' and Kitchener's counter-offensives, leading to the victory at Paardeberg in February 1900, followed by the slow and frustrating movement of the guerrilla war; the performance was rounded off by an exultant climax at the Boers' final, exhausted surrender in May 1902.

For a war which, like so many others, was 'going to be over by Christmas', the opening months of the campaign provided crushing disappointment for Britain. The strategically significant towns of Kimberley, Mafeking and Ladysmith were surrounded and besieged, and the three defeats of 'Black Week', at Stormberg, Magersfontein, and Colenso, shattered any hopes of an early British imperial victory. These disasters were brought about by a combination of British ineptitude and the brilliantly unorthodox and determined tactics of the Afrikaners. Not merely was the sweep and daring of the mostly mounted Boer commandos far ahead of the fumbling and predictable tactics of the British regular army, but the Afrikaners had prudently equipped themselves with excellent rifles and field pieces, mostly made in Germany and, ironically, nearly all purchased out of the taxes levied by Kruger on the Uitlanders.

The next stage of the war was a contrapuntal episode. British and imperial forces, marshalled by Roberts and Kitchener, and led in the field by dashing commanders like Sir John French, swept into the Transvaal and the Free State. Pretoria fell, Johannesburg and the Rand were 'liberated', and the remnants of Kruger's government sped down the railway line to Delagoa Bay.

By December 1900, the war seemed as good as over. The Boers had been formally defeated at Paardeberg. Kimberley, Ladysmith and Mafeking had been relieved, the latter to the accompaniment of hysterical rejoicing in London. Despite the rebellion of a substantial minority of Cape Dutch, the colony had not been torn by the civil war that some had anticipated. The hostility of European powers critical of what they saw as Britain's war of aggression had been of no practical use to the two Boer republics. The self-governing colonies had, by choice, stood firmly behind the British cause, and had even sent 55,000 men to support it. The rest of the Empire, most notably India, though lacking a choice, had also appeared solidly to support the British war effort.

Towards the end of 1900, when it had seemed that the war would be over very soon, Lord Roberts returned to Britain, leaving Kitchener in command. Victory parades were held in London and other cities. In October the Unionists fought the 'Khaki' election, hoping to cash in on the apparent triumph in South Africa. Although the election campaign was marked by bitter exchanges over the war, and by virulent attacks on Chamberlain as the architect of the conflict, the electorate returned the Unionists with a slightly increased, and very comfortable, majority.

The war now entered its final, longest and ugliest stage. The British government claimed that it had a mandate for pushing on to the bitter end. The main problem was the continuing resistance of some 15,000 Boer commandos who refused to surrender. Led by such gifted generals as Louis Botha, Jan Smuts, J.B. Hertzog, Christiaan de Wet and Koos de la Rey, the commandos made expert use of the terrain and were supplied by a friendly local white populace.

Unable to run the commandos down, the huge British army, strung out over hundreds of miles of veldt, and commanded by the ruthless Kitchener, now applied controversial counter-measures. A massive programme of farm-burning was carried out. Between June and November 1900 over six hundred farms were burnt in the Orange Free State alone. This scorched-earth policy made thousands of Afrikaner civilians homeless. Partly to cope with the flood of refugees, partly to keep them under supervision, and partly as a form of punishment, the British authorities herded them into the world's first concentration camps. The camps, it must be said, were not blueprints for Auschwitz and Dachau, but they soon acquired an evil reputation. Poor and careless organisation, and early deficiencies in diet and sanitation arrangements, led to heavy mortality among the inmates. By June 1902 over 20,000 Afrikaner civilians had died in the camps, most of them women and children. A public outcry in Britain, led by Emily Hobhouse, the secretary of the women's branch of the South African Conciliation Committee – 'that bloody woman', as Kitchener called her – caused a reasonably prompt improvement in conditions, but deep disquiet and resentment remained. To the vast majority of Afrikaners it seemed as if the British were trying to exterminate them; British liberal opinion was outraged, and Campbell-Bannerman gave voice to this disgust when he denounced 'methods of barbarism'.

In May 1902 the Boer guerrilla leaders, after lengthy negotiations with Kitchener and the British authorities, surrendered. They were not, however, a beaten army. They had kept at bay a force vastly superior in numbers and equipment. The peace settlement signed at Vereeniging was a negotiated one which, although it incorporated the fallen republics within the Empire, also contained important concessions: generous financial assistance was granted in the form of £500,000 to restore families to their homes and work, and interest-free loans were made available for two years; more significant, especially to the long-term development of South Africa, was the shelving of any proposals to enfranchise non-Europeans until the Transvaal and Orange Free State were once more self-governing. In effect, this guaranteed that in these two provinces blacks, Indians and coloureds would remain voteless and underprivileged.

Despite its triumphalist passages, and its victorious conclusion, the war had exposed a daunting number of British weaknesses. As Kipling ruefully admitted in a celebrated verse:

> Let us admit it fairly, as a business people should.
> We have had no end of a lesson: it will do us no end of good.[11]

Among the lessons learnt was that the leadership and exercise of British arms was barely adequate. The generalship of commanders like the hapless Buller, and others, had been exposed as outmoded, indecisive and over-cautious. There had been other scandals, perhaps less likely to catch the headlines, but equally symptomatic of low morale, disorderliness and a cynicism not generally associated with the high idealism of Empire promoted by the *Daily Mail* and much of the Tory press. It emerged during the trial of 'Breaker' Morant and several other Australian officers that Boer prisoners-of-war had been shot in quite substantial numbers simply to dispose of them so they would not hinder the movements of their captors. After the Boer surrender, as the Butler Committee of Inquiry revealed in 1905, enormous quantities of military supplies no longer needed by the army had been sold off in South Africa, and it became clear that certain British officers had defrauded the government and pocketed the proceeds. The Liberal opposition claimed that as a result the government had been robbed of something like £7 million.[12] Joseph Chamberlain was also publicly accused of profiting from the war by not severing his connections with Kynochs, a West Midlands arms-manufacturing firm in which he had previously held shares.[13] All of this compounded incompetence and a dubious *casus belli* with sleaze and more than a whiff of corruption.

The revealed inadequacies of British arms at least prompted an avalanche of reform. The Committee of Imperial Defence was established in the aftermath of the war. The Elgin Commission, and the War Office (Reconstruction) Committee, recommended sweeping military and organisational reforms. Conscious of her isolated diplomatic position during the conflict, Britain took immediate steps to restructure her foreign policy. Between 1902 and 1904 she concluded an alliance with Japan and an entente with France. In these ways, at least on paper, Britain emerged from the humiliations of the Boer War in a stronger position than after many of her previous victories.

Within South Africa itself, the aftermath of war was less encouraging and productive. The victorious Milner was able to persuade the four British-dominated colonies and Rhodesia to join a customs union in 1903; but he had not achieved the federation of South Africa by the time he resigned as Governor of the Cape and High Commissioner in 1905, despite his cynical recipe for success: 'You only have to sacrifice "the nigger" and the game is easy.' More significantly, the overall aims of 'Milnerism' failed. Permanent British supremacy was not established in South Africa. The wider use of English did not relegate Afrikaans to the status of a second-class language. Afrikaner nationalism was not swamped by the rising tide of Anglo-Saxon cultural influence, constitutional practice and business dominance. Indeed it is arguable that the war refined and subtly strengthened Afrikaner nationalism, which, embittered by defeat and the experience of the concentration camps, became much more difficult to browbeat and subvert. It is significant that every Prime Minister of the Union of South Africa from 1910 to 1961, and every Prime Minister and State President from the establishment of the Republic of South Africa to the election of Nelson Mandela in 1994, was an Afrikaner.

British control of the Rand's industries was now, however, guaranteed. In the Transvaal the English-speaking Uitlanders became full citizens, thus fulfilling one of the chief justifications for the war. The regulations applying to African workers, especially mine workers, were improved and liberalised, although their conditions of work remained shameful by European standards. A somewhat more humanitarian approach characterised the official attitude towards indigenous people. The Simonstown naval base could expect decades of security. These were all substantial achievements for the British government.

A further achievement, though not one which the outgoing Unionist government welcomed, was the restoration of the Transvaal and the Orange Free State's autonomy by Campbell-Bannerman's Liberal government in 1906. By 1907 elections to install the first responsible governments of the Transvaal and the Free State had resulted in a dramatic come-back for the defeated Afrikaners. The whites of the Free State returned a solid Afrikaner majority. Even in the Transvaal, with its large English-speaking population, Afrikaner solidarity triumphed with the election of the Het Volk party, led by the ex-generals Botha and Smuts, over the divided political allegiances of the English-speaking Transvaalers. Some contemporaries ruefully noticed that the Uitlanders were apparently as unreliable in victory as they had previously been in adversity.

The election of Het Volk in the Transvaal in practice brought Britain substantial benefits. Botha and Smuts were Afrikaner leaders of broader vision and more urbane sympathies than the departed Krugerite hierarchy. The old alliance between Afrikaner moderates and English-speaking South Africans, which had served Cecil Rhodes so well but so briefly in the Cape, was revived within a wider political framework. This alliance dominated the first years of the Union of South Africa after 1910, and in 1914 Botha and Smuts led their people, despite the protests of a dissident minority, into the First World War at Britain's side. By 1914 it appeared, therefore, that all of the old goals of British policy had been achieved: federation, a suitable political and economic climate within which local and international businesses could thrive, the incorporation of the Boer republics into the Empire and, at the same time, a working accommodation with the Afrikaner people. The greater South Africa, for which so many had yearned in the years before 1899, had apparently arrived.

THE SUICIDE OF
SIR HECTOR MACDONALD, 1903

Sex and the British Empire

IN THE SPRING OF 1903, Sir Hector MacDonald, the Commander-in-Chief of British forces in Ceylon, shot himself in Paris where he had broken his return journey to his military command after being summoned to Britain. The immediate cause of MacDonald's suicide was the news, published in the European edition of the *New York Herald*, that serious charges were to be pressed against him on his arrival in Ceylon. The essence of the accusations which had led MacDonald to the brink of a court-martial was that he was a pederast. His ruin had begun some months earlier when a British tea-planter had discovered him engaged in some sort of sexual activity with four Sinhalese boys in a compartment of a railway carriage at Kandy.

MacDonald's behaviour in Ceylon had already aroused scandalous gossip. It had been noted that he belonged to a club of doubtful reputation where British and Sinhalese youths mixed with older men. He had moreover become extremely friendly with the two sons of a Burgher, that is mixed-race, family called de Saran. MacDonald's relationship with the two de Saran boys had confirmed the impression of many British planters that he preferred the society of local waiters and dancing boys to their own. Having caught the Ceylon Commander-in-Chief, quite literally, with his trousers down, the tea-planter who had stumbled into the curtained railway compartment proceeded to stir up expatriate opinion against him.

A number of damning charges were laid before the Governor, Sir Joseph West Ridgeway, in the middle of February 1903. Ridgeway became convinced that MacDonald had taken advantage of the relatively relaxed Sinhalese attitude towards homosexual activity to become

systematically involved with, possibly, scores of local boys. Some of
these, Ridgeway ruefully noted, 'are the sons of the best known men in
the colony, English and Native'. It was, incidentally, widely believed
that Ridgeway's own son had been seduced by the Commander-
in-Chief.

MacDonald's abrupt fall from grace, and his decision to take his
own life, is worth analysing for a number of reasons. First, 'Fighting
Mac' had become a national hero as a result of his military activities
during the Sudan campaign and the Boer War. It is surprising that his
fame proved insufficient to protect him from the threats of exposure,
humiliation and court-martial which led to his suicide. After all, other
contemporary national military idols had shared his taste for the company of boys or young men, including General Gordon and Kitchener
of Khartoum. Secondly, the British military and political establishment
seems to have turned savagely on MacDonald: Field Marshal Lord
Roberts had told him in London, when he arrived to respond to the
initial charges made against him, that he must either clear his name or
leave the army, and in any event must return to Ceylon to face a
court-martial. While in the United Kingdom, MacDonald was also
called to a meeting with King Edward VII. Although it is not clear
what passed between monarch and general, there has been speculation
that the King may have told him that, in the circumstances, he should
do the honourable thing and end his own life. If this was indeed the
case, it was an astounding piece of effrontery from a monarch whose
insatiable taste for adulterous, though heterosexual, liaisons surpassed
even his grotesque gluttony. Finally, perhaps MacDonald was dealt
with so unsympathetically by the establishment not simply because his
sexual tastes were homosexual and his pursuit of them a public scandal,
but because of his humble origins; he was, after all, a Scottish crofter's
son, not the scion of some noble, blue-blooded aristocratic family.

The tragic and sordid downfall of 'Fighting Mac' provides a more
than usually clear illustration of both the opportunities and the pitfalls
that were so widespread and intimate a part of the history of the British
Empire. Just as explorers, missionaries, traders, administrators, soldiers
and settlers could make their fortunes, enhance their reputations or,
indeed, fail miserably, as a result of their activities within the Empire, so
they could follow, indulge, or even discover their sexual needs. Empire
provided countless men, and even some women, with the opportunity
to express their sexuality in ways which would have been difficult, if
not downright impossible, at home. In a variety of ways, the British

Empire acted as a liberating agent, allowing British libidos unrestrained fulfilment overseas.

There were several obvious reasons why this should have been the case. To begin with, over the decades, millions of British men either served in the armed forces which conquered and controlled the Empire, pushed forward the frontiers of settlement or became administrators and traders within the imperial system. Far more often than not, they were not accompanied, at least initially, by British women. As a result, sexual release and satisfaction could only be found in the arms of prostitutes or the women of indigenous cultures. A substantial number of British men, of whom Hector MacDonald was simply one of the most prominent and the most unfortunate, also pursued their taste for sexual intercourse with men or boys.

Within the Empire there were manifold opportunities to act out heterosexual inclinations in contact with indigenous societies whose attitude towards a wide range of sexual needs and tastes was far more relaxed and compliant than those officially upheld with such puritanical rigour at home. In addition, the vast majority of British men living or serving within the British Empire held positions of power and authority, whether based on their official status, their wealth, or their positions as landowners, merchants, explorers, missionaries and the like. It has often been remarked that political power is one of the most potent of aphrodisiacs. So, too, was the power – official, personal and financial – wielded by plantation overseer, chain-gang leader, prosperous trader, the wearer of a military uniform, or even the possessor of a white skin.

There is no question that sexual relations between individuals or groups of people are frequently based on, or largely manifest themselves in, struggles for power or financial reward. Within the Empire there was, for the most part, no doubt where power lay. This is not to say that sexual relationships between rulers and ruled were invariably exercises in power and control. The history of the British Empire is littered with examples of loving and tender contact and of fond, long-term relationships between the British and their subject peoples, as well as between countless individuals of different colour, ethnicity and national identity. Although there is considerable evidence that the British abused their power in a variety of ways within the Empire, and mostly at the expense of local women, who were raped, abducted, forced into unwelcome liaisons or simply seduced, there were also many examples of permanent or semi-permanent relationships; these included marriage or long-term concubinage (as it was rather quaintly called by contemporaries), in the negotiating of which local forms and customs were often followed scrupulously. Lonely British administrators in the African bush, or in the rainforests of South-East Asia, quite frequently went through the formalities of paying the 'bride-price' for the women with whom they formed partnerships and liaisons.

Nor is there a great deal to choose between the undoubted power exercised by British men over the women of indigenous cultures and the way in which such females were subjected to the authority and control of their own menfolk. In a material sense, and perhaps also in terms of the respect and attention paid to her, a 'native' woman might well be better treated by a European male than by a husband or partner from her own tribe or race. The wholesale subordination of women, and indeed children of both sexes, to the needs and desires of indigenous males was unmistakable throughout the history of the British Empire, and is plainly discernible today throughout much of the world. This fact does not, of course, excuse or modify the British imperial male's exploitation of power and position in regard to sexual satisfaction, but it does at least put it into some sort of perspective.

It has often been argued that within the great sweep of territories that comprised the British Empire, men – and they are overwhelmingly men, not women – were also able to find sublimation or release in a variety of activities, from the demands of military campaigning to exploration, from administrative triumphs to the founding of new colonies. On this analysis, the 'asexual' male was able to 'sublimate' his sexual feelings in the undertaking of satisfying and constructive work, or in the completion of noble, or indeed ignoble, missions. Thus men described by their contemporaries as 'misogynists' or 'women-haters', like Rhodes, Gordon, Kitchener or Baden-Powell, found fulfilment and, often obliquely, the satisfaction of their erotic needs in deeds of Empire.

The trouble with this theory is that it does not fully explain either the causes or, indeed, the consequences of the apparent asexuality allegedly sublimated in imperial activity and success. For one thing, it seems highly likely that the disinclination and distaste for sexual activity, or even the fear of sex, expressed by a considerable number of men who fall into this group, arose directly from an earlier and overwhelmingly unhappy and traumatic sexual experience. General Gordon confessed that he had often 'wished I was a eunuch at fourteen . . . I never had a sorrow like it in my life, therefore I love children so very much'.[3] Benjamin Jowett, sometime Master of Balliol College, admitted that his 'deeply laid antipathy to the very idea of carnal knowledge' arose from an unhappy youthful sexual encounter.[4]

If it is probable that the origins of most of these cases of alleged asexuality sprang from earlier and painful sexual encounters, it would be mistaken to suppose that the resolution of such problems could be straightforwardly achieved through lives of chastity and abstinence. It may be technically true that very few of these British asexuals ever enjoyed full penetrative sexual intercourse with females, but that does not mean that they did not lead sexual lives of some sort. General Gordon derived considerable pleasure from scrubbing down dirty urchins in bathtubs; Baden-Powell enjoyed seeing youthful naked bodies; Kitchener and Rhodes had a number of intense and passionate relationships with young, good-looking men. Even if the sexual interests of these, and numerous other, asexual British males did not involve some form of physical contact with members of either sex, it is almost inevitable that relief was found in masturbation. It is obvious that the historian will never know whether most of these self-proclaimed celibates, misogynists or asexuals masturbated or not, but it is beyond belief that none of them engaged in the classical 'solitary vice' that so perturbed the moralists and puritans of the nineteenth and twentieth centuries. Indeed, the intensity and passion with which men like Baden-Powell sought to discourage and stamp out the 'sin' of masturbation is in itself worthy of comment, and may well be evidence of the disgust and self-loathing felt by the moralist himself for his own masturbatory activities and fantasies.

So, perhaps, there was, and is, no such thing as an asexual person. Rather, men and women are obliged to express their sexuality according to patterns and habits established early in their lives, and arising out of their varied experiences while growing up, and they do so in a bewildering variety of forms, employing a multitude of techniques. What the Empire provided for those British citizens who emigrated to it, served in it, or ruled it, was a wider, more complex, more varied, and often more compliant environment in which to fulfil their sexual needs than at home. It was often waggishly remarked during the heyday of British imperialism that 'the sun never set upon the Empire' because the Almighty was unable to trust what the British would get up to in the dark. It is now clear that at least some of what the British got up to in the dark was sexual and erotic in nature.

Even when this was not the case, a variety of perverse tastes could more easily be satisfied in the Empire's service. It was, for example, almost inevitable that service overseas involved British officials and officers in the handing out of punishment to both indigenous people and British subjects in the colonies. To those with a love of blood-letting, or simply with the desire to terrify and dominate their victims, the Empire was rich in opportunity.

This temptation to indulge sadistic inclinations could be found at the highest level. The activities of Lord Curzon, Viceroy of India between 1898 and 1905, are instructive in this respect. It is evident that Curzon was easily hurt, and also enjoyed hurting others. He was cruel to his exotic mistress, Elinor Glyn – of 'tiger skin' fame; he bullied his subordinates so constantly that when he left India it was said that there was not a single administrator of any standing whom he had not personally insulted; he routinely humiliated Indians, even the princes he affected to admire; he dismissed whole nations out of hand – Greeks, Bengalis, Egyptians and Turks.

But Curzon was not just a sadistic tormentor – a trait which perhaps sprang from what he claimed was a tyrannical fathering, and perhaps from homosexual harassment at Eton – he was also a masochist. He suffered for most of his life from the agonies – as he described it – of a permanently injured back. He reacted to political and administrative frustration with self-pitying disbelief. As Balfour shrewdly told him: 'You seem to think you are injured whenever you do not get exactly your own way!'[5] His bitter quarrel with Kitchener over whether the latter – as Commander-in Chief of the Indian Army – or the Military Member of the Viceroy's Council should have control of military policy and spending left him so broken and humiliated that he resigned his office in a tantrum. Almost his last great reform in India was the highly controversial partition of Bengal; this can be seen as both an act of cruel viceregal butchery and a Samson-like display of self-destruction, in that it ruined at a stroke his proclaimed strategy of convincing the Indian people that British rule was benevolent and superior to the rule of their own leaders.[6]

It should not be supposed, however, that nineteenth- or early-twentieth-century Britain was a bastion of morality, peopled either by a race of rigidly controlled puritans or by individuals with uncomplicated, unwavering heterosexual tastes. The caricature of Victorian society as one of almost universal sexual repression and restraint is exactly that – a caricature. Despite the fact that the age of marriage among men was unusually high compared with that throughout much of the African and Asian countries of the Empire – averaging twenty-nine for males at the middle of the nineteenth century; despite the fact that upper- and middle-class opinion-makers and moralists insisted that children had no interest in sex and that 'respectable' women found little or no pleasure in sexual intercourse; despite the conspiracy of silence over sexual matters that descended all too often upon the home and almost completely upon the school classroom; despite the tendency to deny – or vehemently condemn – illegitimacy, prostitution and 'fornication', the Victorians were at least as sexually active within the United Kingdom as the generations that came before and after them.

For males from the upper and middle classes, heterosexual opportunities were almost limitless. By the 1880s the servant population, which was overwhelmingly female, numbered nearly 1,500,000, many of whom 'lived in'. Chambermaids and assistant cooks often carried out the 'off-duty' work of initiating young male members of the household into sexual knowledge and techniques. Nor did exile to boarding school mean the end of sexual experience. The public school system not merely taught Greek and Latin, the games ethic and various forms of muscular Christianity to its pupils, but also provided a flourishing venue for extra-curricular activities such as buggery and bullying.[7]

For those older public school boys who preferred it, heterosexual sex was readily and cheaply available, often only a short walk from their seats of learning. Prostitution was one of the major industries of Victorian Britain. Although, unfortunately, it could do nothing to reduce the annual deficit in commodity trading, Victorian prostitution was an established fact of life throughout the country. Naturally enough, prostitutes worked mostly in the cities and towns of Britain: by the mid-nineteenth century it has been estimated that some 80,000 operated in London, with proportional amounts scattered throughout other cities and towns. The widespread use of prostitutes – particularly by men from the middle and upper classes – at least kept the ideals of the virgin bride and the chaste wife intact. A considerable number of female prostitutes were juveniles, perhaps not surprisingly in an age when so many families lived in poverty and when the age of consent for girls remained at twelve until 1875, when it was raised to thirteen.

The age of consent did not apply to boys at all, which may well have accounted for the considerable number of youthful male prostitutes who not merely worked in brothels but also hung around the London parks and railway stations, and were to be found in other major urban areas.

To all of this must be added the widespread accessibility and prevalence of pornography. The British Vice Society confiscated over 250,000 pornographic photographs between 1868 and 1880, and London was recognised towards the end of the century as the capital, not only of the British Empire, but of a booming international trade in erotic pictures and pornographic writing.

The poverty, and the overcrowded and brutal living conditions, which far too often characterised the life of the urban poor were doubtless important contributory factors to what Victorian moralists denounced as 'vice'. A considerable number of working-class marriages – perhaps as many as a third – took place with the woman already pregnant. As if all of this was not bad enough for the moralists, the level of venereal disease, and the difficulty in curing it, gave rise to widespread concern. The embarrassing discovery at the outset of the Boer War in 1899 that a very substantial number of working-class volunteers were unfit for military service merely confirmed in a dramatic fashion the various forms of ill-health that were endemic among an alarming proportion of the population.

All of this accorded ill with the late-Victorian and Edwardian need to see Britain as a nation fit to triumph in the struggle between rival imperial systems and economies. It also coincided with, and partly provoked, the increasingly widely expressed anxieties over national degeneracy and decline, anxieties that became linked in the minds of many individuals and groups with the perils of masturbation and licentious living. Lord Rosebery asserted in 1900 that 'An Empire such as ours requires as its first condition an Imperial race – a race vigorous and industrious and intrepid. Health of mind and body exalt a nation in the competition of the universe. The survival of the fittest is an absolute truth in the conditions of the modern world.'[8]

This rising tide of anxiety and self-criticism not merely encouraged the social reforms of the Edwardian era, but had already helped to launch a vigorous and frequently intolerant 'Purity Campaign' towards the end of the nineteenth century. Although it is difficult to estimate the impact of the Purity Campaign upon sexual activities of all kinds, there is no doubt that it led many leading figures in British society to pursue their sexual inclinations with far more prudence than before. It was in juxtaposition to this trend that the trial and prosecution of Oscar Wilde in 1895 became such a *cause célèbre*, not least because Wilde was perceived as hurling an obscene challenge at the purity campaigners through the ostentation with which he flaunted his homosexuality.

As a result of all this, by the turn of the century it had become virtually impossible to discuss sexual matters in public, and almost as difficult to speak of them in private. Rather than face condemnation, disgrace and ridicule, the overwhelming majority of British people, especially those from the upper and middle classes, refrained from mentioning sexual matters and as a consequence failed to address, either in public or in private, sexual problems and difficulties.

Within the British Empire, however, it was far easier to lead relatively uninhibited sexual lives. There is overwhelming evidence that throughout the imperial system white men continued to liaise with, abuse and exploit the women of indigenous societies wherever the British flag was raised. Sexual contact with 'native' women became a perk of the imperial system, something to be anticipated and enjoyed rather than avoided and disguised. Indeed, many Victorian men glorified in the sexual opportunities thus vouchsafed them, and recorded their pleasures unashamedly:

> [Native women] understand in perfection all the arts and wiles of love, are capable of gratifying any tastes, and in face and figure they are unsurpassed by any women in the world . . . It is impossible to describe the enjoyment I experience in the arms of such syrens.[9]

The dancing girls of South India, the Chinese women of Malaya, girls from Nigeria, the exotic maidens of the South Seas, and the mixed-race females of the West Indies were all praised for their sexual skills and their passion, as well as for their availability.

The sexual services of local boys and men were also widely available throughout the Empire, nearly always on the basis of payment, or at least material reward. Despite the moral indignation that evidence of such 'free-market' sodomy provoked among the purity campaigners and many others, the economic imperatives of Empire, particularly manifested in the shipping of tens of thousands of indentured labourers to man plantations, build railways or work the mines, made homosexual activity in the workers' compounds an inevitable part of the process. The moral outcry that accompanied the campaign in Britain against the system of 'Chinese slavery' in the gold mines of the Transvaal after the Boer War owed at least part of its intensity to the belief that homosexual activity was commonplace within the mining compounds.

Indentured labourers and miners locked up in their dormitories at night could at least protest that they were being denied access to women. For their part, many British men who engaged in sexual relationships with 'native females' also tended to claim that they acted as they did chiefly because they were unable to find enough European women to meet their needs. For much of the history of the British Empire, service overseas often did indeed mean a solitary lifestyle or living within an all-male environment. Despite the disapproval of purity campaigners, it was generally recognised that sexual activity brought emotional release and some degree of private satisfaction to individual lives.

It was thus possible to construct a plausible argument that sexual relationships with African and Asian women, and, at a pinch, with local males, fulfilled an important imperial function. If the energies and activities of traders, military personnel, administrators and emigrants – among others – made the wheels of Empire turn, the complex machinery was at least partially lubricated by the sexual activities of the British overseas.

In India during the eighteenth century, British servants of the East India Company had been positively encouraged to enter into liaisons with, or even to marry, Indian females. No doubt such contacts helped to improve and consolidate the commercial and political relationships between Europeans and the indigenous people. By the end of the eighteenth century, however, official policy stamped out the hitherto cosmopolitan and inter-racial character of the British presence in the sub-continent. Not merely were Indians prohibited from holding military and civil office under the East India Company, but Anglo-Indians – the products of inter-racial marriage and intercourse – were denied office and barred from official functions. By the beginning of the nineteenth century intermarriage between British and Indians had virtually ceased.

Later, by the mid-Victorian period, the improved and speedier communications between Britain and India, as well as the need to stabilise and consolidate British control in the post-Mutiny period, had led to the arrival of large numbers of British women in the sub-continent. As the memsahibs grew in number, social contacts between British males and Indians, whether male or female, dwindled. The presence of the memsahibs also made British men more sensitive to the perceived dangers of Indian men finding British females sexually attractive. The end-product of all of this was a deepening of distrust and an increase in intolerance.

There was another price to pay for British imperial expansion. This was, quite simply, a substantial increase in overseas prostitution, and the concomitant increase in venereal disease amongst British men serving in the Empire. In order to keep some control of the situation, the British authorities in India sanctioned the introduction of regulated prostitution. During the post-Mutiny period, until the late 1880s, seventy-five cantonments were designated as centres of regulated prostitution, complete with medical examination, systematic registration, and the hospital facilities to treat prostitutes suffering from venereal disease. The introduction of the system had more to do with maintaining the good health of the troops and, as a consequence, military efficiency, than with demonstrating liberal enlightenment.

It was, nonetheless, an effective arrangement. Between 1880 and 1888, when these practical arrangements were officially suspended as a result of the objections of the moral purity campaigners, the incidence of syphilis in the army in India was running at a rate below that recorded among soldiers serving in the British Army at home. But after 1888 there was a dramatic increase in the occurrence of syphilis in the Indian Army, peaking at over 250 per thousand troops in 1895. So bad had the situation become that by 1897 new regulations were introduced which had the effect once more of dramatically reducing the incidence of syphilis in the Indian Army, which had fallen to a new low by 1908.[10]

During the twentieth century, and particularly after the First World War, the elaborate prostitution networks which had characterised the latter part of the nineteenth century, as well as the incidence of venereal disease among British men serving overseas, diminished. Among the factors that contributed to this were the improvement in the employment prospects of women, particularly in Europe, the greater availability of the condom for the male, improved standards of personal hygiene and somewhat more open attitudes towards sexual identity and sexual problems.

In 1909 members of the British Colonial Service were issued with a directive which attempted to discourage sexual relations with native women and threatened serious penalties to those who disobeyed. The circular issued by the Colonial Secretary, Lord Crewe, asserted that:

> Gravely improper conduct of this nature has at times been the cause of serious trouble among the native populations and must be strenuously condemned on that account; but an objection even more serious from the standpoint of the Government lies in the fact that it is not possible for any member of the administration to countenance such practices without lowering himself in the eyes of the natives, and

diminishing his authority to an extent which will seriously impair his capacity for useful work in the Service in which it is his duty to set an honourable example to all with whom he comes into contact.'[11]

Although the custom of concubinage by no means disappeared in the Colonial Service as a result of the Crewe circular, it certainly became less commonly practised. The circular seems to have been particularly effective in British colonies in Africa, but it may also have coincided with the greater availability of European women, and perhaps with an increasing disinclination to enter into intimate relationships of any kind with Africans. In more far-flung parts of the Empire concubinage flourished unabated – in Sarawak, for instance, until after the Second World War.

Even in Africa, however, it would be naive to imagine that sexual contact between white men and indigenous women did not remain fairly common in the inter-war period and beyond. To give one example, the recently published testimony of Terence Gavaghan, who attended a Jesuit school in the early 1950s and was posted to Kenya in the Colonial Service in his early twenties, shows how easily – casually, perhaps – sexual contacts were made:

> I remember one particular girl with great pleasure – she was half Arab and half Nandi. We enjoyed a happy association which lasted a number of years; but she lived in her own village with her family and I lived in my house alone . . . It was an unspoken thing that she wouldn't call on me openly, and wouldn't come to the house if I had a dinner party, for example.[12]

And again:

> I remember there was one young woman who was tall, very dark, dressed in long, very concealing clothing, with a silk shawl over her head. She used to come around selling baskets. I was very struck with her, and it appeared to be reciprocated. We didn't exchange money and she used to come and visit me . . . as often as it could be arranged . . . I remember practising my romantic Swahili on her . . . I remember her laughter, her conversation, gossip, chat, intimacy. Her gossamer hair, her delicate physique. I remember one overlapping front tooth, as if it were yesterday.[13]

Nor did white men always want conventional sex. Marion Nasoor, who worked for various white families in Kenya from the mid-1930s, recalls:

> The really important thing, the one thing they couldn't get
> – and please be discreet here – was that if you agreed that
> he could do it to you from behind he would even give you a
> ring – he would promise you the earth, and he would never
> let you go. That was the thing. To go in from the back.[14]

Beyond the bounds of officialdom, but often acting as the advanced guards of European civilisation, British missionaries also played an important part in both criticising the sexual and social activities of local populations and encouraging restraint on the part of Europeans living amongst indigenous people. There was certainly enough for missionaries and their supporters to criticise. Particularly in Africa, many indigenous people could be denounced for practices such as nudity, polygamy, the buying and selling of brides, initiation ceremonies – including particularly female circumcision – various courtship rituals, displays of 'lascivious' public dancing, anal heterosexual intercourse, group sexual activity and a great deal more besides. In some instances, missionary objections to local practices, backed up by the colonial authorities, precipitated serious political crises, and in one case – that of Kenya – may well have altered the course of local colonial history.

One of the most dramatic and disturbing confrontations between Christian missionaries and colonial people occurred in Buganda, a province of Uganda, between 1885 and 1887. The conflict centred on the sexual practices at the court of the Kabaka, the hereditary ruler of Buganda. The Kabaka, Mwanga, as well as many of his court officials, was addicted to and vigorously practised sodomy. Although a harem of women was available, Mwanga strongly preferred the boy pages of his court. The Church Missionary Society in Buganda converted a number of the pages to Christianity, and encouraged them to refuse to grant sexual favours to the Kabaka and like-minded members of his court. Quite apart from denying Mwanga and others the sexual gratification that they preferred, the campaign against sodomy could also be interpreted as the assault of puritanical Christians upon the older, more tolerant Muslim customs of the court.

In an act of terrible revenge, the Kabaka persecuted scores of youths who now denied him their sexual favours. Perhaps a hundred of them died – many of them being burned alive – and a considerable number were castrated. Mwanga was eventually removed from power and died in exile in the Seychelles in 1903, having belatedly converted to Christianity. In the wake of these terrible events, the Christian missions in Buganda were able to establish themselves as the dominant religion in the country. The price for the Christianising of the country had been a very high one.[15]

A second confrontation between Christian missionaries, the colonial authorities and indigenous people occurred in Kenya during the 1920s and 1930s, and was a direct contributory factor to the alienation of the Kikuyu people and, eventually, to the rise of Mau Mau. Female circumcision, or more accurately clitoridectomy, had first been systematically criticised by missionaries in Kenya in 1906. In 1929 the Church of Scotland Mission precipitated a crisis by asking school teachers in their service to sign a declaration renouncing 'the sexual mutilation of women'. They were also asked not to belong to the Kikuyu Central Association until that organisation dropped its opposition to the CSM on the issue of clitoridectomy. Some members of the Colonial Service in Kenya urged restraint on the reformers and zealots of the Church of Scotland mission, arguing that African society was different from European, and, moreover, was evolving more slowly and in different ways.

The Kikuyu Central Association seized on the issue as a way of winning over older and more conservative elements within the tribe, and of asserting themselves as the champions of local tradition and practice. Moreover, it was almost impossible to stamp out the practice of female circumcision, since the operation involved only a few brisk movements of a sharp instrument. The crisis over female circumcision came to a head between 1929 and 1930, and led to such bitter feelings that in January 1930 a seventy-year-old missionary, Miss Hulda Stumpf, died after allegedly being raped and then 'viciously circumcised' – although the assault seems to have been the work of men from the Mkamba tribe rather than of the Kikuyu.[16] In any event, the confrontation resulted in the foundation of the Kikuyu independent schools movement as well as in the formation of breakaway separatist Kikuyu churches.

There is no evidence at all that clitoridectomy decreased as a result of the confrontation, rather the opposite. It has been estimated that by the 1960s 90 per cent of women in the villages of Kenya had been circumcised. It was not until 1982 that the government of independent Kenya officially banned the practice, as the result of a scandal in which fourteen girls died following the operation. It is also highly likely that one of the results of the widespread practice of female circumcision throughout Africa, with its attendant lessening of vaginal sensitivity, has been the tendency to resort more frequently to heterosexual anal intercourse. This may, at least in part, explain the rapid spread of AIDS among heterosexual women in societies that have practised clitoridectomy.

It would be a pointless exercise to attempt to evaluate what nearly four centuries of contact between the British and the indigenous people of their colonies amounted to. It has been argued that, on balance, 'Sexual interaction between the British and non-Europeans probably did more long-term good than harm to race relations.'[17] Whether anybody can arrive at a more concrete and confident judgement is extremely doubtful.

As in the lives of individuals and communities throughout the world, sexual contacts within the British Empire were characterised by joyful discovery, mutual esteem, exploitation, abuse, violence, compromise and accommodation. Although whites were overwhelmingly in control of the interaction, they were not universally so, and some at least, like the suicidal Hector MacDonald, paid a terrible price.

In one area, moreover, the potential for sexual interaction between the races was almost always damaging and destructive. This was when black or brown men made advances to, were perceived to desire, or even had sexual relationships with, white females. On these rare occasions, the cause of race relations was certainly not advanced, and violent and deep-seated hatreds of black or brown men, who were perceived – consciously or unconsciously – as representing the primitive, atavistic 'other', became common currency.

Finally it must be remembered that very large numbers of British men overseas refrained, for a whole variety of reasons, from sexual relationships with indigenous females. Although Empire was almost always about economic profitability and political power, it would be wrong to assume that the ruthless and unbridled sexual exploitation of the black and brown subjects of imperial rule was an inevitable part of the power structure – a perk of office like a handsome pension or a solar topee.

At the same time, it is perhaps too much to claim that 'There are, at least in the pre-AIDS era, worse sins in running an empire, as in life, than the sexual ones.'[18] The use of one individual by another solely for the purpose of self-gratification, however, is rarely an edifying spectacle, as even the briefest assessment of late-twentieth-century prostitution, particularly of the growth of 'sexual tourism' to economically needy states like Thailand or the Philippines, will reveal. In this regard the British Empire can claim no special dispensation. The imagery of imperial control reeked of sexuality: continents were 'penetrated', tribes 'subdued', districts 'ravished', territories 'mastered', local potentates 'seduced', countries 'raped'. It was small wonder that uncountable numbers of indigenous people suffered similar fates.[19]

15

JOSEPH CHAMBERLAIN AND THE CABINET SPLIT OF 1903

Tariff Reform, Economic Decline and Imperial Preference

ON 14 SEPTEMBER 1903, Balfour's Unionist Cabinet was torn from top to bottom by one of the great splits of modern British political history. Although the full extent of the disaster was not known until 1 October, when the solid and respectable Duke of Devonshire eventually announced his resignation from the government, five Cabinet ministers either resigned or were sacked by the Prime Minister. Among those who resigned was Joseph Chamberlain, widely regarded as the most charismatic and effective minister, but also as so dynamic and single-minded that he was always likely to upset the apple-cart. C.T. Ritchie, the Chancellor of the Exchequer, and Lord Balfour of Burleigh were virtually drummed out of the Cabinet at the meeting on 14 September. Lord George Hamilton, the Secretary of State for India, resigned the next day.

What had led to so much spilling of ministerial blood? The immediate cause lay in the political controversy precipitated by Chamberlain in May 1903, when, from his political power-base in Birmingham, he had delivered a powerful and eloquent speech in which he argued that the British people faced an entirely new and perilous economic situation. The choice before the country and the Empire, Chamberlain asserted, was between a strict adherence to the principles of free trade, which appeared to be failing the nation, and the introduction of a programme of tariff reform that would both boost the British economy and also stimulate inter-imperial trade through introducing a system of preferential tariff agreements between different countries within the Empire. Was it, Chamberlain asked, 'better to cultivate the trade with your own people or to let that go in order that you may keep the trade of those who . . . are your competitors?'[1]

Chamberlain's speech at Birmingham began a crisis which was to change the political landscape, split the Cabinet and the Unionist Party, play a crucial part in the landslide Liberal general election victory of January 1906, and make tariff reform one of the hottest political issues of the Edwardian age. Tariff reformers and protectionists were delighted by the speech, and Leopold Amery, who had recently served with Milner in South Africa and who was to become one of Chamberlain's most ardent supporters, called it 'a challenge to free thought as direct and provocative as the theses which Luther nailed to the church door at Wittenberg'.[2] The Liberals were equally delighted, although for different reasons; the sacred cause of free trade would not merely reunite their divided party, but would also deal the Unionists a potentially fatal blow. Herbert Asquith thought Chamberlain's speech 'wonderful news . . . it is only a question of time when we shall sweep this country'.[3]

Why did Chamberlain resign from a ministerial position that had put him at the centre of the political stage and enabled him to concentrate the nation's attention upon the most consistent theme that he addressed throughout his political career?

Increasingly perturbed by the immediate manifestations and long-term implications of Britain's economic decline, Chamberlain had become convinced by 1902 that not merely would the prompt and efficient development of the Empire's resources provide the antidote to that decline, but that the immediate introduction of a system of reciprocal imperial preferential tariffs was the essential first step in the process. Forced to realise, after serving seven years as Colonial Secretary, that the goal of imperial unity could not be achieved through constitutional reforms or by the overhaul of defence organisation, Chamberlain now believed that an appeal to economic self-interest was the most promising means of achieving his objectives.

Before he had undertaken his triumphal tour of South Africa in November 1902, Chamberlain had apparently won the Cabinet's agreement to introduce a remission on the tax levied on foreign corn and wheat in favour of the self-governing colonies in the next budget. A corn registration tax had been announced in the budget of April 1902, chiefly to raise revenue to pay for the Boer War. This had now opened the way to make a belated response to the raising of Canadian tariffs against foreign manufactures in 1897 and 1900, and the subsequent offer of a 33.3 per cent discount to British manufactures entering Canada.

When Chamberlain arrived back from South Africa in the spring of 1903, however, he discovered that a fortnight before his return the new Chancellor of the Exchequer, C.T. Ritchie, had threatened Balfour with resignation unless the corn tax proposals were abandoned. Balfour had surrendered, free trade orthodoxy seemed to have triumphed, and Chamberlain had every reason to feel betrayed. Towards the end of his life Balfour admitted, perhaps a little too ingenuously, that:

> Joe was ill-used by the Cabinet. We had discussed the prin-
> ciple of taxing food-stuffs before he left the country, and he
> certainly had a right to suppose that the bulk of the Cabinet
> were in favour of a shilling duty on corn, or some analogous
> small tax. That was my impression, and I was perfectly horri-
> fied at what happened.[4]

There was, therefore, a powerful personal reason why Chamberlain chose, in effect, to open the campaign for tariff reform within a few weeks of this shoddy piece of political manoeuvring. On the other hand, since he was one of the most robust politicians of his age, and had received as many hard knocks as he had given, why did the 'corn tax betrayal' of April 1903 prove such a turning point? He had perhaps relied too much on the friendship and support of Balfour, a passionless Tory aristocrat of the sort Chamberlain had savaged in his earlier career as a Radical Liberal. He was to become progressively disillusioned with the Prime Minister as the Unionist Party floundered in the quagmires of the tariff reform controversy.

The humiliating failure of Chamberlain's corn tax initiative also served to emphasise his perilous and uncertain political status early in 1903, and provides another explanation of his decision to plump for tariff reform. The 1902 Education Act, with its central proposal to put Church of England schools 'on the rates', had outraged Nonconformist opinion and, as a consequence, seriously undermined support in Chamberlain's Liberal Unionist political stronghold in Birmingham and the West Midlands. The spectre of Irish Home Rule seemed, at least temporarily, to have been exorcised, thus diluting the historical justification of the Conservative and Liberal Unionist alliance. Balfour was proving to be a shifting and unreliable colleague in comparison to the recently departed Prime Minister, Lord Salisbury. Chamberlain had no real allies among senior Cabinet ministers. The Boer War had stirred up as many problems as it had solved. His grandiose schemes for promoting imperial unity had been smashed upon the rocks of colonial self-interest and indifference.

Chamberlain had also failed to induce the government to introduce the social reforms that he believed would permanently bind enough of the working classes to Unionism to guarantee its future. The government's record in the field of social reform since 1895 was virtually non-existent. Even old-age pensions, one of Chamberlain's most cherished causes, seemed as far out of reach as ever. The unexpectedly high cost of the Boer War had placed so heavy a burden on the Exchequer that even if the government had possessed the will to introduce old-age pensions, the money quite simply was not there. Chamberlain was thus caught in a trap of his own devising. 'Chamberlain's War' had proved a major stumbling-block in the way of Chamberlainite social reform. Indeed, revenue for all government spending was in short supply. Extra revenue could of course be raised through a hike in the level of income tax. But direct taxation of this sort was not acceptable either to Chamberlain, with his increasing distaste for 'socialistic' fiscal measures, or to the vast bulk of the Unionist Party. Tariff reform, however, amounted to an indirect tax, and therefore stood a chance of being accepted by a substantial section of the party.

As a consequence, tariff reform had become the key with which Chamberlain might open many doors: he could promote an old-age pension scheme; he could confirm his mastery over the voters of the industrial West Midlands; through the promotion of a constituency-based tariff reform movement, he could hope to build up a new power-base throughout the country; if the push for tariff reform succeeded, he would become the obvious man to lead a government committed to the revision of free trade. Quite simply, tariff reform became the obsession of the last years of 'Radical Joe's' public life; an aim to be pursued with all his energy and power, and with ruthless consistency. In the process, old-age pensions virtually ceased to be a Chamberlainite preoccupation. The means became more important than the ends, and were in due course transformed into the ends themselves.

The weight which Chamberlain gave to the issue of tariff reform is illustrated by his remarks in April 1902, having been invited, as a distinguished guest, to dine with a small Parliamentary society nick-named 'The Hughligans'. The young Winston Churchill was present, and he later wrote:

As [Chamberlain] rose to leave he paused at the door, and turning said with much deliberation, 'You young gentlemen have entertained me royally, and in return I will give a priceless secret. Tariffs! They are the politics of the future, and of the near future. Study them closely and make yourself masters of them, and you will not regret your hospitality to me.'[5]

The great controversy over tariff reform that Chamberlain unleashed in May 1903 set members of the Unionist coalition at each other's throats. In general, Liberal Unionists who had deserted their former party over the issue of Irish Home Rule in 1886 were committed free traders. But so was a large section of the Conservative Party, including some of its more aristocratic members such as Lords Hugh and Robert Cecil. In July 1903 fifty-four Unionist MPs inaugurated the Free Food League, a pressure-group and a first line of defence against tariff reform. Three weeks later the Tariff Reform League held its first meeting.

The contrast between the Free Food League and the Tariff Reform League was striking. The Free Fooders were a committed but poorly organised and financed group. The Tariff Reform League, however, soon had its ranks swelled by captains of industry, aristocratic Tory landlords, the bulk of the Unionist MPs, survivors of the protectionist National Fair Trade League, and assorted manufacturing and industrial magnates. In Fleet Street, the League's cause was supported by the *Daily Express*, the *Daily Mail* and the *Standard*, and had prominent sympathisers in *The Times* and the *Daily Telegraph*. In 1905 the newspaper magnate Alfred Harmsworth bought the *Observer* to promote the cause, and the *Spectator* was left as the only leading Unionist free trade journal.

The Tariff Reform League soon had the funds to launch a lavish propaganda campaign. It aimed to convert significant interest groups such as trade union leaders and industrial workers to the cause, and to spread its message to the public at large through intensive and expensive campaigning, including doorstep leafleting and the playing of recorded speeches by Chamberlain and others in countless town and village halls.

The Prime Minister, Balfour, was immediately pitched into deep and perilous waters. His party was in the process of splitting into two warring factions, a division that would almost inevitably result in catastrophe at the polls. Unwilling to become the Sir Robert Peel of his day, presiding over a Tory split over economic policy that would leave the party in the political wilderness for decades, Balfour sought for compromise. He had no personal disinclination to review the nation's fiscal policy, and he professed a refined agnosticism on the issue of tariff reform. He also shared the fears of the free traders that the dearer food prices implied by tariff reform would lead to electoral disaster. On the other hand, he was aware that the tariff reform initiative might appeal to a wide public and revitalise the flagging cause of Unionism. He therefore led a third grouping within the party: a small and ultimately ineffectual band, which undertook to keep an open mind on the tariff issue until all the options had been thoroughly discussed.

Balfour's bid for the middle ground was one of the chief causes of the Cabinet split of October 1903. With Chamberlain's letter of resignation in his pocket, the Prime Minister had engineered the departure from the Cabinet of four of the most committed free trade ministers, and had subsequently announced the Colonial Secretary's resignation. While the free trade Cabinet ministers expressed their bitterness at Balfour's sleight of hand, Chamberlain had every cause to feel content.

The truth was that Balfour and Chamberlain had done a deal before the fateful Cabinet meeting of 14 September 1903. 'Radical Joe' would resign from the government to lead a grassroots tariff reform crusade to convert the country to his new cause. If all went well with the campaign, Balfour could then lead the loyalist bulk of the Unionist Party along the pathway that Chamberlain had blazed. This meant that Balfour would keep control of the party, and Chamberlain would be free to campaign outside the Cabinet in an attempt to convince the country that tariff reform offered economic salvation and regeneration.

Perhaps most significant of all, Chamberlain's elder son, Austen, was promoted to the key post of Chancellor of the Exchequer in Balfour's reconstructed Cabinet. The free trader Ritchie was thus replaced by the tariff reformer Austen Chamberlain. Nothing could more clearly illustrate the continuing influence of Joseph Chamberlain, nor Balfour's eye for the main chance.

What were the deep-seated pressures which had plunged a government with a majority of a hundred parliamentary seats into so profound a crisis, and which were to stir up so much passion in public debate? After all, Chamberlain, Balfour, Asquith and other political leaders were simply articulating fears, hopes and aspirations that arose from a variety of tensions and challenges which had been building up over the last few decades.

One inescapable problem was that the cost of the Boer War, coming on top of a steady increase in naval and military spending in response to the varying threats of French, Russian and finally German expansionist policies, had resulted in a financial crisis. The rising bills for defence, and the need to respond to the growing demand for more expenditure on welfare, demanded action. The Liberals, with their commitment to free trade, saw direct taxation as a legitimate, prime means of raising extra revenue. The Unionist coalition, within which the Conservatives were easily the more senior and numerous partners, disliked direct taxation, and were far more attracted by the notion of introducing indirect taxes.

In this respect, it is odd that Chamberlain's tariff reform initiative did not win far wider support within the Unionist Party than it did. It was not even as if the idea of introducing tariff reform was a bolt from the blue. In his famous Crystal Palace speech in 1872, Disraeli had argued that the extension of self-government to the colonies of European settlement should have been associated with 'a great policy of Imperial consolidation, it ought to have been accompanied by an Imperial tariff'.[6]

Subsequently, however, both Disraeli and Salisbury, the only Conservative Prime Ministers of the last quarter of the nineteenth century, had played down the tariff issue. One reason for this was the electoral unpopularity that would be risked by adopting such a policy. Another was that towards the end of the century the Conservatives had ceased to be so dependent upon landed or protectionist interests as hitherto.

It is still, nevertheless, surprising that the Conservatives and their Liberal Unionist allies were unable to unite behind Chamberlain, especially when he offered them the means to challenge the rise of the New Liberalism, as well as socialism, with their interventionist and statist ideologies. Perhaps there was also a reluctance to back a man who had spent the earlier part of his political career ridiculing the aristocratic and inert qualities of Conservatism. Chamberlain had also behaved indiscreetly by dragging the skeleton of tariff reform out of the cupboard and thrusting it before the public for their perusal and analysis. Finally, it is very likely that 'what made Chamberlain's initiative so devastating to the Conservatives was that it could easily be construed as an attack on the complex of gentlemanly economic forces which were in control of the party by the turn of the century'.[7]

How accurate was the Tariff Reform League's diagnosis of Britain's economic decline? More particularly, was Chamberlain, like the Fat Boy in Dickens' *Pickwick Papers*, trying to make the nation's 'flesh creep', by mounting an irresponsible and scaremongering campaign whose main objectives were political and personal, not economic?

Few disputed that the British economy had begun a steady decline, although there was substantial disagreement over the extent and significance of this process. Increasingly effective foreign competition, the growth of protectionism among Britain's main trade rivals, and the failure of much of British industry adequately to reinvest or to modernise, all put immense pressures upon the national economy. Despite the fact that Britain's balance of commodity trading with the rest of the world had been in deficit for almost all of the nineteenth century, her considerable surplus on 'invisibles' with nearly all her commercial partners had ensured that at the final settlement she was in profit.

After 1870, however, Britain's balance-of-trade deficit with industrialised Europe and the United States grew very rapidly indeed: from £32,000,000 between 1871 and 1875, to £157,000,000 in 1913. The commodity deficit on Britain's total world trade also grew from £63,000,000 between 1871 and 1875, to £134,000,000 in 1913. Vast increases in imported food and manufactures from these industrial and developed countries accounted for the sharp rise in the deficit, as did fluctuation in the nation's exports due to increasing uncompetitiveness and the protectionism of her rivals. As a consequence, Britain's reliance upon her invisible exports to bridge the trading deficit became more acute. Confidence in sterling also showed some decline by 1914, and a few sharp-eyed observers also discerned the worrying, although still small-scale, trend from manufacturing to services.

Chamberlain, with his customary intelligence, as well as his taste for publicity and controversy, concentrated the electorate's attention upon these uncomfortable facts during the tariff reform campaign of 1903 to 1906. Huge crowds gathered to hear his speeches, which were delivered in the lucid, combative style that had become Chamberlain's hallmark. He appealed to the self-interest of both workers and employers, 'bribing each class of the community in turn' (as the free-trader Lord Robert Cecil described it); he attacked the supine policy of allowing unrestricted free foreign imports into the country; he argued that tariff reform would lead to full employment. He also ridiculed the notion that workers thrown out of jobs by foreign competition could easily find alternative means of employment even if in new or service industries:

I believe that all this is part of the old fallacy about the transfer of employment . . . It is your fault if you do not leave the industry which is falling and join the industry which is rising. Well – sir, it is an admirable theory; it satisfies everything but an empty stomach. Look how easy it is. Your once great trade in sugar refining is gone; all right, try jam. Your iron trade is going; never mind, you can make mouse traps. The cotton trade is threatened; well, what does that matter to you? Suppose you tried dolls' eyes . . . But how long is this to go on? Why on earth are you to suppose that the same process which ruined the sugar refining will not in the course of time be applied to jam? And when jam is gone? Then you have to find something else. And believe me, that although the industries of this country are very various, you cannot go on forever. You cannot go on watching with indifference the disappearance of your principal industries.[8]

Chamberlain also played the dirty card of anti-foreigner prejudice. Aware that the tariff reform campaign would inevitably raise anxieties among working-class voters over potential rises in the price of food, he and other tariff reformers struck unashamedly chauvinistic postures. Tariff Reform League propaganda, both official and unofficial, painted a picture of foreigners infiltrating British society hard on the heels of foreign manufactured goods. The man on the Clapham omnibus was shown the gruesome prospect of Clapham High Street not only selling overwhelmingly foreign produce, but being taken over by foreign shop-keepers as well.

The growing insecurities of late-nineteenth- and early-twentieth-century Britain were thus part and parcel of the tariff reform campaign. The siege mentality which characterised so many Britons' perception of the world perhaps partly explains the nation's passionate involvement in the actual sieges of Mafeking and Ladysmith during the Boer War. It also encouraged patriots and chauvinists to seek for an enemy within the state, as well as discerning and identifying the enemy without.

Chamberlain and some of his supporters were able to compound these anxieties with an attack on Jewish immigration. The Edwardian era had seen substantial migrations of mainly East European and Russian Jews, fleeing at worst pogroms, at best persecution. Since London was one of the shipping centres of the world, where cheap tickets could be bought for the United States, South Africa, Argentina and elsewhere, many Jewish emigrants had made the city their first port of call. Although large numbers of them had moved on, very many decided to settle, overwhelmingly in the East End of London. Speaking at Limehouse, in London's East End, in December 1904, Chamberlain tried to convince his largely working-class audience of the emotive equation between foreign imports, foreign immigrants, and British unemployment:

> You are suffering from the unrestricted imports of cheaper goods. You are suffering from the unrestricted immigration of the people who make these goods. [loud and prolonged cheers] ... The evils of this immigration have increased during recent years. And behind those people who have already reached these shores, remember there are millions of the same kind who ... might follow in their track, and might invade this country in a way and to an extent of which few people have at present any conception ... If sweated goods are to be allowed into this country without restriction, why not the people who make them? Where is the difference? ... It all comes to the same thing – less labour for the British working man. [cheers][9]

Although it is possible to understand this crude appeal to prejudice in the light of the Tariff Reform League's need to attract working-class support, and on account of the sizeable number of vulnerable Unionist seats in the East End of London, there are other dimensions to consider. It was wholly consistent with Chamberlain's identity as 'the apostle of Anglo-Saxon unity' for him personally to entertain a low opinion of Jewish people. He is on record as telling *The Times* correspondent H. Wickham Steed, 'There is, in fact, only one race that I despise – the Jews, sir. They are physical cowards.'[10] It is also possible to interpret Chamberlain's offer of Uganda as a Jewish homeland in 1903 as an expression not of tolerance and understanding, but of dislike and a desire to rid Britain of some of its Jewish citizens.

The campaigning of Chamberlain and the Tariff Reform League was not, however, simply based upon such negative world views, nor upon heaping the blame for economic difficulties upon the foreigner. The resources of the Empire, it was argued, adequately developed and exploited, could save the situation. In fact most of Britain's economic ills could be cured by the introduction of a system of imperial preference. Chamberlain even claimed that dearer food would be caused not by

any tax that he had ever proposed, but by the continuing short supply
of wheat and corn:

> There is only one remedy for short supply. It is to increase
> your supply. You must call in the new world, the
> Colonies, to address the balance of the old. Call in the
> Colonies, and they will answer to your call with very little
> stimulus and encouragement. They will give you a supply
> which will be never-failing and all-sufficient.[11]

Chamberlain and his supporters claimed that the Empire 'if we
chose . . . might be self-sustaining'. It was extremely doubtful, however,
at the turn of the century, whether an imperial free trade area was
within the realm of practical politics. Within the market of the Empire,
British trade was actually losing ground. Between 1881 and 1900 British
possessions had increased their overall purchases by 17 per cent, but
the volume of British exports to these territories had decreased by 1
per cent. By 1901, moreover, another worrying trend was apparent:
foreign imports into the self-governing colonies were worth nearly
£50,000,000, and were steadily increasing. In India, Canada, Australia
and British South Africa, on the other hand, the proportion of imports
from the United Kingdom to total imports had fallen substantially
between 1881 and 1900. In 1901 Britain's trade with foreign countries
amounted to some £592,000,000, while only £210,000,000 was carried
on with British possessions.

Chamberlain was to argue, at the outset of the tariff reform campaign, that there was one favourable offsetting trend: over the previous
thirty years the United Kingdom's trade with British possessions had
greatly increased. This assertion was fundamentally inaccurate, and
was flatly disputed by Sir Robert Giffen, who had been the permanent
official at the Board of Trade during Chamberlain's tenure of the presidency of that department from 1880 to 1885. Giffen challenged Chamberlain's statistical evidence, declared himself 'quite bewildered', and
pointed out that all of South Africa, including the booming and
expanding economy of the independent Transvaal, had been included
in his trade statistics. In private, Chamberlain recanted, agreeing that
if South Africa were excluded from the trade figures, British exports
to British possessions between 1888 and 1902 had increased by only
£4,000,000, from £77,000,000 to £81,000,000, but arguing that this
increase represented a bigger proportion than an equivalent £4,000,000
increase to foreign countries between 1888 and 1902. Giffen challenged

this as well, asserting that, on the figures available, between 1888 and 1902 the United Kingdom's exports to foreign countries had increased in value from £150,000,000 to over £174,000,000 – a bigger proportional increase than in British exports to the Empire, excluding South Africa.[12]

The pattern of Britain's trade with the Empire, as a whole, provided both comfort and disappointment at the turn of the century. Between 1896 and 1900 the value of British trade with the empire as a whole showed an average annual deficit of £7,000,000. Within these statistics, the self-governing colonies accounted for an £18,000,000 deficit, while the rest of the Empire actually provided a surplus to Britain of £11,000,000. Chamberlain was, however, right to be optimistic about the immediate future. By 1913 Britain's trade with the Empire as a whole was running at an average annual surplus of £17,000,000. Trade with the self-governing colonies was still showing a deficit, at an annual average of £12,000,000, but trade with the rest of the Empire had moved into a substantial surplus, averaging £29,000,000 per annum.[13]

The debate which raged over tariff reform and imperial preference from 1903 to the general election of 1906 provides some interesting comparisons with the public debate seventy years later over Britain's membership of the European Economic Community. In both cases, tariff reformers and supporters of Britain's membership of the EEC argued that, although in all probability food prices would rise in the short term, in the medium and long term there would be incalculable benefits to Britain in the shape of an important increase in exports. The free traders, and those who opposed Britain's continuing membership of the EEC, claimed that not only would food prices rise, but that some commodity increases would be unacceptable to many British house-holds; they further asserted that the medium- and long-term economic benefits to Britain had been irresponsibly exaggerated by their oppon-ents, and, indeed, might never materialise.

In electoral terms, the outcome of the two debates was widely differ-ent. In the 1975 referendum a substantial majority of those who voted – 67 per cent – confirmed Britain's continuing membership of the EEC. In 1906, however, the Unionist Party suffered one of its worst electoral defeats at the hands of the revitalised Liberal Party and the emerging Labour Party. As a result of the 1906 general election, the Unionists were reduced to a mere 157 seats in the House of Commons.

What did this catastrophe at the polls imply for the causes of tariff reform and imperial trade and consolidation? Of the 157 Unionist MPs returned at the polls, nearly a hundred were tariff reformers of some sort. Indeed, tariff reform candidates had done particularly well in areas such as South Yorkshire, where workers in the steel industry were feeling the effects of foreign competition, and, perhaps naturally enough, in Chamberlain's industrial heartland of the West Midlands. Lancashire, on the other hand had voted strongly for free trade; indeed, the country as a whole had apparently plumped for free trade as opposed to protection. The electorate were undoubtedly disillusioned with the Unionists overall: the coalition had been in power almost continually from 1885, and was associated with the fiascos of the Boer War, as well as with the scandal over 'Chinese slavery' (the importation of indentured Chinese labour into the Transvaal after 1902), and had done very little to convince voters that it seriously intended to introduce much-needed measures of social reform.

The Tariff Reform League's campaign had failed for other reasons. One was that Liberal opponents like Asquith countered the arguments of the Chamberlainites with great persistency and skill. In contrast, Chamberlain, denied the research support which his departmental staff at the Colonial Office had previously provided, was sometimes unconvincing and out of touch on matters of detail. Perhaps most significant of all, however, was the fact that although the tariff reform campaigners had eventually come out for a policy of protectionism, in addition to the original proposal to construct a preferential tariff system for the Empire, they could not gather the owners of industry and industrial workers behind them in sufficient numbers. Moreover the causes of free trade and internationalism still had a great potency, and appealed to a wider spread of interests than that of tariff reform. The battle cry of 'free trade in danger' had also rallied enough businessmen and industrialists to the cause of Liberalism to deny them, at least in the short term, to the tariff reformers. Finally, the economy had benefited from a marked improvement in trading conditions, beginning in 1903; this in itself seemed to give the lie to Chamberlain's warnings.

In the aftermath of the electoral catastrophe of 1906, Chamberlain forced the defeated Balfour into an exchange of letters on 14 February. Known as 'the Valentine letters', the correspondence amounted to a surrender by Balfour. Chamberlain undertook to continue to support Balfour as leader of the party, an undertaking which implied that he would refrain from challenging himself. In return, Balfour made a concession in writing: 'I hold that Fiscal Reform is, and must remain, the first constructive work of the Unionist Party. That the objects of such reforms are to secure more equal terms of competition for British Trade, and closer commercial union with the Colonies.'[14]

As it turned out, Balfour's undertaking made little impact. Although Chamberlain suffered a serious and debilitating stroke in July 1906, and was removed in effect from the political scene, there were plenty to take up the cudgels on his behalf. By 1910, tariff reform, or imperial preference, had become a central plank in the Unionist platform. Such doctrinal triumphs were meaningless, however, so long as the Unionists were in opposition. After the resignation of Balfour's government in December 1905, and the subsequent Liberal landslide in January 1906, the Unionists were out of power as a single party until the fall of Lloyd George's peacetime coalition government in 1922.

If the cause of greater imperial unity through the mechanism of imperial preferential tariffs had failed to convince the electorate in 1906, similar appeals were equally unsuccessful in the two elections of 1910 and the election of 1918. In 1923 Baldwin's Conservative and Unionist government went to the polls with imperial preference as one of its main policies, and the electorate once more turned its back on them, choosing instead to elect a minority Labour government committed to free trade.

When asked for its support for a programme of tariff reform, or imperial preference, the British public preferred to protect their living standards rather than to experiment with protectionism. The cause of imperial unity was deemed less important than the weekly task of balancing the household's budget, particularly its food budget. The irony is that Chamberlain was right when he argued that it was an appeal to people's pockets that would make the difference between failure and success over the issue of tariff reform. The problem was that the British public put what they saw as their self-interest first, and the cause of imperial unity low down on their list of financial priorities.

16

SCOUTING FOR BOYS, 1908

National Decline, Empire, Youth and Education

Scouting for Boys was first published in book form on 1 May 1908. The cloth-bound edition cost two shillings, and the paper-bound edition one shilling. It was reprinted four times within a year, and in 1948, the fortieth anniversary of its first publication, the book sold more than 50,000 copies. Not until the late 1970s did it find difficulty in achieving a steady sale in Britain. *Scouting for Boys* also sold heavily abroad: two decades after its first publication in Britain, the book was still in print in twenty-six countries outside the British Empire. It has been regularly reprinted ever since, and 'has probably sold more copies than any other title during the twentieth century with the exception of the Bible'.[1]

Such was the potency of *Scouting for Boys*' appeal to a largely juvenile readership in 1908 and subsequently that it has easily outsold such classics of the 'golden age' of Edwardian children's literature as Beatrix Potter's *The Tale of Peter Rabbit*, Edith Nesbit's *The Railway Children*, Frances Hodgson Burnett's *The Secret Garden*, and even Kenneth Grahame's *The Wind in the Willows*. What were the qualities that enabled *Scouting for Boys* to become the best-selling book for children from the Edwardian period onwards, especially in the face of competition from such celebrated contemporary works of fiction?

At first sight, the book gave no indication that it would be a runaway success. Written by Colonel Robert Baden-Powell, a professional soldier and a hero of the siege of Mafeking, it was divided into ten chapters and twenty-eight 'Camp Fire Yarns'. It consisted chiefly of adult exhortations to good behaviour and personal honour, dressed up in the form of 'Scout Law'. Its early readers would have discovered that according to 'Scout Law':

1. A SCOUT'S HONOUR IS TO BE TRUSTED.
   If a Scout says 'On my honour it is so,' that means that it *is* so, just as if he had taken a most solemn oath . . .

2. A SCOUT IS LOYAL to the King, and to his officers, and to his parents, his country, and his employers. He must stick to them through thick and thin against anyone who is their enemy or even talks badly of them.

3. A SCOUT'S DUTY IS TO BE USEFUL AND TO HELP OTHERS.
   And he is to do his duty before anything else, even though he gives up his own pleasure, or comfort, or safety to do it . . .

7. A SCOUT OBEYS ORDERS of his parents, patrol leader, or Scout master without question.

8. A SCOUT SMILES AND WHISTLES under all circumstances. When he gets an order he should obey it cheerily and readily, not in a slow, hang-dog sort of way. Scouts never grouse at hardships, nor whine at each other nor swear when put out . . .

9. A SCOUT IS THRIFTY, that is, he saves every penny he can and puts it into the bank, so that he may have money to keep himself when out of work, and thus not make himself a burden to others . . .[2]

Readers were also informed that 'the Scout's motto is: BE PREPARED which means you are always to be in a state of readiness in mind and body to do your DUTY . . .' Each intending Scout had to take the Scout's Oath, later redefined as 'The Promise':

On my honour I promise that I will do my best

1. To do my duty to God and the King.
2. To help other people at all times.
3. To obey the Scout Law.[3]

It is an indication of the yearning of hundreds of thousands of British boys to belong to such an organisation that the rather prim and sober rules of the Scout Law did not immediately put them off the Scouting movement altogether. Perhaps their parents were glad to encourage them to belong to an organisation which placed such emphasis on duty, loyalty and obedience – characteristics not immediately associated, even in Edwardian Britain, with the relationship between adolescent boys and their parents. Girls proved equally keen to join a sister organisation when the first steps were taken in 1909 to establish the Girl Guide movement.

On closer analysis, the well-nigh irresistible appeal of *Scouting for Boys*, and of the Scouting movement as a whole, is easy to understand. To begin with, the book was brilliantly marketed. Part One of *Scouting for Boys* had first appeared on bookstalls in Britain in January 1908. It was published by the shrewd and successful Arthur Pearson, who had allotted his senior editor, Percy Everett, the task of preparing the book for publication. Everett was an experienced editor from *Pearson's Weekly*, the motto of which was 'To Interest, to Elevate, to Amuse', a formula adopted from the racy magazine *Tit Bits*, and which owed its success to a skilful mixture of entertaining anecdotes and curious facts.

The cover illustration for Part One of *Scouting for Boys* was also meant to attract readers: it showed a boy lying down, his Scout staff and broad-brimmed hat on the ground beside him, and peering round a rock, intently watching men landing from a mysterious ship. The message was unmistakable; if a boy joined the Scouts he would not merely read about exciting adventures, but participate in them as well.

Apart from some organised sport, and the street and countryside games of tradition and spontaneous invention, the vast majority of Edwardian children had virtually no recreational opportunities. They and their parents bought the slim fourpenny pamphlet, Part One of *Scouting for Boys*, in their tens of thousands. Pearson had already adroitly sent Baden-Powell around the country delivering fifty public lectures on his scheme for Scouting for boys. As a consequence, thousands of people had been avidly awaiting the appearance of the pamphlet.

The full edition of *Scouting for Boys* confirmed the appeal of Part One. A huge, semi-literate readership, composed of young people and their parents, responded enthusiastically to its clearly presented 'cunning blend of entertainment, moral exhortation, practical advice and escapism. A boy could easily skip what did not interest him and pass on to what did.'[4] Soon tens of thousands of boys were flooding into the rapidly expanding Scouting movement. In 1966 a survey of men born between the years 1901 and 1920 'revealed that 34 per cent of them claimed to have belonged to the Boy Scouts'.[5]

The Scouting movement, as conceived by Baden-Powell, offered both middle-class and working-class boys the chance to belong to an organisation with a plain and easily understandable set of rules, arcane rituals – including the Boy Scout salute – the chance to go on camps and the opportunity both to do one's duty and to have adventures. It is an indication of the deep-seated conservatism of the Edwardian working class, many of whose adult members were striving, through membership of trade unions, the infant Labour Party and the Suffragette movement, to bring about an improvement in their conditions of work and living, that they were able to swallow the more reactionary components of Baden-Powell's philosophy. *Scouting for Boys* bluntly announced that Britain was 'suffering from the growth of "shirkers" in every class of the community – men who shirk their duties and responsibilities to the State and to others'. 'Energetic patriotism' was to be one aim of Scout training. In the section on 'Government' the book announced that 'The House of Commons is made up of men chosen by the people to make known their wants and to suggest remedies, and the House of Lords sees whether they are equally good for all and for the future of the country.'[6] A year later, Lloyd George's 'People's Budget' provoked a bitter conflict between the Liberal government and the House of Lords which ended with the delaying powers of the Upper House being severely restricted.

The Scouting movement was meant to defend the old values and to stand as a beacon of reassurance amid the conflicts and tensions that characterised the Edwardian age. It was not necessary to be paranoid in 1908 to feel that Britain, the British way of life and the British Empire were beset by a host of enemies both from within and without. The new century had increased, rather than diminished, the anxieties that had beset the nation during the 1890s.

The internal menaces of Edwardian Britain could be identified, either individually or collectively, as militant trade unionism, the strident feminist demands of the 'New Woman' and the suffragette (prepared to break the law, even to die in the pursuit of 'Votes for Women'), the growth of socialism and anarchism, Jewish immigration, resurgent Irish nationalism, economic and industrial decline, the New Liberalism, poverty and disease, inadequate educational opportunity, and an endemic national inefficiency. Among the external menaces were the rapid development of the German navy, the industrial challenge of more technologically innovative nations like the United States and Germany, the malevolence of faceless international financiers, the ingratitude and truculence of certain imperial subjects, the activities of Russia on the frontiers of India, and what was perceived as the envy and hostility of a variety of foreign nations.

Both the external threat and the internal divisions that racked Edwardian society seemed to indicate that Britain was losing her vitality and strength. The shockingly high level of unfitness which had been discovered among volunteers for the Boer War, as we have seen, only confirmed prophecies of national decay and degeneration. Just like the campaign for the introduction of National Service, led by Lord Roberts, the eugenics movement, the agitation of the Webbs, H.G. Wells and reforming groups like the 'co-efficients', and all those who advocated a drive for greater national efficiency, the Scouting movement was meant to stop the rot.

This explains, at least in part, why both the Boy Scout and the Girl Guide movements went to such lengths to discourage masturbation. An eleventh Scout Law, added in 1910, stipulated that 'A Scout must be pure in word, thought and deed.' Masturbation, it was thus implied, was not merely a sin, it was also an enervating practice that led to paralysis and blindness. The parallel here between the draining away of the nation and Empire's strength and the loss of vital energy through masturbation is too striking to be ignored. The Scouting movement was clearly determined to prevent all wastage of essential strength.

The strong line which the Scouting movement took against masturbation, and the sins of the flesh in general, owes a great deal to the quirkiness of Baden-Powell himself. Although he had proved himself to be a resourceful and courageous soldier, Baden-Powell was a fractured, incomplete and fundamentally immature personality. Rigidly self-controlled, he had been an enthusiastic observer at floggings and executions during his military career. Blood-letting afforded him considerable pleasure, and his fourth book, published in 1889, was entitled *Pigsticking or Hoghunting*. All of this indicates a need to gratify repressed aggression through blood sports and a voyeuristic participation in the violent meting out of justice.

In common with a number of other distinguished soldiers and empire-builders like Cecil Rhodes, General Gordon and Kitchener of Khartoum, Baden-Powell had difficulty in relating to women and saw female sexuality as a positive threat to men. Boy Scouts were even assured by him that sexual feelings were 'unmanly'. He rationalised his inability to relate fully to women by seeing manliness in terms of self-restraint, hence his diatribes against masturbation. Until he reached his fifties, Baden-Powell had no sexual contact with the opposite sex, although he had entered into a number of friendships with young girls. At fifty-five, however, he suddenly married the youthful and comfort-ingly athletic Olave Soames. Although the marriage produced two children, Baden-Powell remained convinced that sexual desire was only a transitory, adolescent phenomenon, and within a few years he was sleeping separately from his wife, often in the bracing air of the balcony. His success in convincing himself that sexual intercourse was simply for procreation, not pleasure, enabled him to keep his deep-seated anxieties about the full relationship between men and women at bay.[7]

The success of Baden-Powell's attempt so carefully to define the terms of his relationship with his wife that it posed no threat to his emotional well-being was paralleled by his organisation of the world-wide Scouting movement. The rules, rituals and moral exhortations contained in *Scouting for Boys* put Baden-Powell firmly in charge. By emphasising loyalty, patriotism and obedience, the Scouting movement could provide a sure defence against the insidious demands of socialism, trade unionism, feminism, liberalism and libertarianism. It is not surprising that in the inter-war period, Baden-Powell expressed admiration for the orderliness and discipline of Mussolini's Italy, and even looked with some sympathy upon the Hitler Youth movement in 1935.

The Scouting movement was simply the most recent of a number of organisations set up in the late nineteenth century as a defence against the perceived threats to the old order and to social stability. Military imagery and military structures were reflected in the names of such movements: the Church Lads' Brigade, Lord Rodney's Cadets, the Navy League, the Knights of King Arthur, the Church Army, the Boys' Brigade, the Lads' Drill Association, and, most celebrated of all, the Salvation Army, whose journal bore the title *War Cry*.[8] The militaristic trappings of these organisations, and the growing weight of the movement for compulsory military service, were indications that large numbers of British people were sufficiently alarmed by the perceived internal and external threats as to actually do something about it – or at least to approve of others, even their children, doing something about it.

The Irish Home Rule crisis of the mid-1880s seems to have convinced many politicians, intellectuals and opinion-makers that forces of such power had been unleashed that Britain's global and imperial hegemony was seriously at risk. The seismic split in the Liberal Party in 1886 over the issue of Home Rule resulted in droves of politicians and intellectuals trooping off in the direction of the Conservative Party, often by way of Liberal Unionism. As the perceived prime mover in these cataclysmic events, Gladstone was excoriated as a statesman lacking all responsibility; his integrity and sanity were also assaulted through the use of abusive descriptions such as 'mad man', 'fire-brand' and 'old, wild, and incomprehensible' – at least one of which emanated from Queen Victoria.[9]

The Home Rule crisis was also used as an excuse by many unsettled Liberals, anxious at the party's leftward and statist drift, to quit the party, allegedly in defence of democracy, nation and Empire.

The growing confusion and crisis within British society, and the pessimism and uncertainty that this generated, seem to have worried many late-Victorian commentators less than the external threat. Even within the Empire native peoples proved either difficult to conquer or, having once been overcome, rose in dangerous rebellion. The catalogue of such upsets during the late nineteenth and early twentieth centuries ran from the Zulu victory at Isandlhwana in 1879 to the disturbances led by the 'Mad Mullah' in Somaliland from 1908 to 1920. There were revolts in Uganda in 1896 and 1900, in Rhodesia in 1896, the 'Boxer' uprising in China in 1898, chronic problems with the tribesmen on the north-west frontiers of India, and, for good measure, the 1906 Zulu revolt in Natal which sent white settlers scuttling in terror to the security of Durban.

These disturbances could be dismissed as 'little local difficulties', part and parcel of the responsibility of imperial rule. But they were also uncomfortable reminders that only a small percentage of the Empire's citizens were European, let alone British. The British Empire, at the beginning of the twentieth century, was still by far the biggest and the most varied among the world's imperial systems. It was not, however, unchallenged. Would rival imperial systems eventually gain the upper hand? Was the British Empire in fact in terminal decline? In 1905 an anonymous pamphlet, 'The Decline and Fall of the British Empire', caused a considerable stir.[10] Purporting to be a Japanese publication from the year 2005, it listed eight reasons for British decline during the twentieth century. Baden-Powell, if he had read it, would have vigorously agreed with the pamphlet's diagnosis of the nation's ills, which included the growth of luxury, the decline of taste, the debilitation of the people's health and physique, the enfeeblement of religious and intellectual life, the prevalence of urban over country life, a weakening interest in the sea, the failure adequately to defend the country and the Empire, and the damage caused by excessive taxation and municipal extravagance. In 1914 H.G. Wells asked his readers the awkward question 'Will the Empire live?'[11]

These speculations were all the more painful in the light of how much optimism, as well as money, was invested in the Empire. Chamberlain had insisted in 1904 that 'The day of small nations has long passed away. The day of Empire has come.'[12] Although he happened to be wrong on this, as on so many other issues, it seemed at the time to be an appropriate judgement.

This by itself was cause for alarm. Even if the French and German empires were doomed to remain smaller and less significant than the British Empire, the future might indeed belong to great land-based imperial or federal structures. Despite its failure to preserve its internal and commercial integrity in the face of European, American and Japanese imperial aggression and depredation, it was conceivable that China could raise itself and become a great world power. Garnet Wolseley gave voice to this anxiety in 1903 by remarking that 'They only want a Chinese Peter the Great or Napoleon to make them so.'[13]

It was far more likely, of course, that either the United States or the Russian empire would succeed Britain as the leading world power. During the Edwardian period, British statesmen from both major political parties made haste to come to terms with the situation. Balfour's Unionist government, continuing the earlier trend to appease Washington, had engineered a *détente* with the United States by the time it fell from office in 1905, largely through accommodating American territorial ambitions in the western hemisphere and acknowledging the primacy of the United States Navy in the Caribbean and to some extent in the Atlantic. The Liberal administration that succeeded Balfour's government negotiated an *entente* with imperial Russia in 1907, thus taking some of the pressure off the borders of the Indian empire. Pessimists, however, took little comfort from these diplomatic and military accommodations. Like the Roman Empire before it, the British Empire might well be locked into an inexorable process of decline and decay, while the great land-based imperial systems of the United States and Russia seemed to be rising and thriving.

Baden-Powell, inevitably, addressed the problem of imperial decline with clarity and vigour. Scouting was meant to save Britain from the fate of the ancient Romans, who had lost their great empire through being 'wishy-washy slackers without any go or patriotism in them'.[14] Scouts should 'be prepared' not merely to resist the temptations of the flesh and to reject luxury and idleness, but also to defend the Empire against degeneracy and rottenness. His sister Agnes weighed in with the book *How Girls Can Help Build Up the Empire.*

Apart from Baden-Powell and the other leaders of contemporary youth movements, many more Edwardians were determined to address the issue of the schooling and education of Britain's young people. The 1902 Education Act, strongly backed by Balfour, was an attempt to inject some coherence and logic into the nation's educational system by putting the overwhelmingly Anglican-sponsored 'Church schools' under local authority control, and advocating the introduction of a more systematic offering of technical education. It therefore gave the state, through local education authorities, a bigger say in the shaping of educational policy and practice. It also contained a commitment to promote technical education, although it failed to give full or adequate effect to this undertaking.

The Liberal government of 1905 to 1915 similarly saw education as an insurance policy against the future; it also utilised the educational system as a means of social reform by introducing a non-mandatory school meal system in 1906, and by authorising the introduction of school medical inspections in 1907. Local education authority spending on education in England and Wales grew rapidly between 1902 and 1913, from £9,500,000 to £30,600,000. During the same period central government spending increased from £12,500,000 to £19,500,000.[15]

The school system was an obvious means of promoting the ideology and values of Empire. Empire Day was introduced as a day of special observance in 1904, and despite some initial reluctance in certain parts of the country, predictably areas with strong radical traditions like East Anglia, the industrial north-east, Wales and Scotland, by 1914 the vast majority of schools joined in the annual celebration. The idea was to concentrate the attention of pupils and teachers upon the glories and potential of the imperial system. Much of the instruction was factual and uninspiring. The moving force behind Empire Day, the 14th Earl of Meath, even issued an imperial catechism which he tried to foist on each elementary school; the questions asked pupils to compare the geographical dimensions of the Empire with other empires, and put much stress on instilling the correct moral attitudes. Interestingly, some organisations and parents resisted the brainwashing of Empire Day instruction. As late as 1913 objections were being raised by – among others – the London Society of Compositors, the National Union of Clerks, the Poplar Labour League and the Paddington and Kensington Labour Council. In 1909 the Education Committee at Derby declined to recognise Empire Day, denouncing it as the 'thin end of militarism'.[16]

Throughout the rest of the year the school curriculum, especially in the form of the textbook, unashamedly promoted the virtues of the British race and the value of the British Empire. At the same time foreigners, whether European or the subject peoples of the Empire, were frequently compared unfavourably with home-grown products.[17]

The school textbooks produced at the end of the nineteenth century and during the early part of the twentieth are remarkable for the consistency and uniformity of their outlook. Although the product of the free publishing market, their almost total failure to depart from the 'party line' on matters British and imperial would have done credit to the zeal and attention to detail of the most totalitarian and despotic of regimes.

In *A Brief Survey of British History* by George T. Warner, published in 1899, elementary school children were thus instructed:

> When we look at a map of the world, and see how wide is the red that marks the British Empire, we may well feel proud ... Our race possesses the colonial spirit which French, Germans, and Spaniards do not possess: the daring that takes men into distant lands, the doggedness that keeps them steadfast in want and difficulties, the masterful spirit that gives them power over Eastern races, the sense of justice that saves them from abusing this power and attaches those they rule with so ... strong an attachment.[18]

In *A School History of England*, published in 1911 and written by C.R.L. Fletcher and Rudyard Kipling, school children were told that the prosperity of the West Indies had sadly declined since the abolition of slavery in 1833; there was little doubt who was chiefly to blame for this:

> The population is mainly black, descended from slaves imported in previous centuries, or of mixed black and white race; lazy, vicious and incapable of any serious improvement, or of work except under compulsion. In such a climate a few bananas will sustain the life of a negro quite sufficiently; why should he work to get more than this? He is quite happy and quite useless, and spends any extra wages he may earn upon finery.[19]

Even though Fletcher and Kipling's *School History* was a particularly virulent and assertive piece of propaganda, the assumption, indeed the assertion, of racial superiority, although often more muted, can be found in the vast bulk of school textbooks, particularly those dealing with history and geography, during this period. It should not be supposed that such educational reading matter alone affected the views of several generations of school children. Contemporary attitudes towards foreigners in general, and towards people with black or brown skins in particular, were generally critical and condescending. School textbooks merely strengthened deep-seated existing prejudices. The growing paranoia of the age also provoked an insular and ultra-patriotic world view. This resulted in an unwholesome compound of bias, self-congratulation, stereotyping and scapegoating, and the tendency to look for expected, and hence easily discernible, unfavourable traits in others.

The reactions of many British citizens to the rare sight of a black face in their midst were generally unambiguous:

> The people's notion of black men is very limited . . . A good many Britons believe that all Africans and even Indians in Britain are from the same country, that they speak the same language and are known to each other . . . Of the black man's country their knowledge is worse still . . . In the low class suburbs a black man stands the chance of being laughed at to scorn until he takes to his heels . . . pray even now you never meet a troupe of school children just from school. They will call you all sorts of names, sing you all sorts of songs. Pray also that you never encounter a band of factory girls just from their workshop. Some of these girls will make fun of you by throwing kisses at you when not making hisses at you while others shout 'Go wash your face, guv'nor', or sometimes call out 'nigger, nigger, nigger'.[20]

Baden-Powell, too, had his share of prejudices. Although he denied that he was a 'regular nigger hater', he saw the alleged failings of the African all too readily: 'the stupid inertia of the puzzled negro is duller than that of an ox; a dog would grasp your meaning in one half the time. "Men and brothers"! They may be brothers, but they certainly are not men.'[21] It is worth noting that during the siege of Mafeking, Baden-Powell was accused of treating Africans within the besieged town as second-class citizens, and of giving the Europeans the best of the rations.

Outside the classroom, adventure stories for young children, comics and annuals in general promoted chauvinistic views. G.A. Henty's adventure stories were ravenously devoured, mainly by boys; Kipling's *Puck of Pook's Hill* ended with a hymn containing the lines 'Land of our birth, our faith, our pride, for whose dear sake our fathers died.'[22] In *Stalky and Co.*, published in 1899, Kipling extolled the public school, where pupils are groomed to be future military leaders of the Empire. In 1912 Dorothea Moore published *Terry, the Girl Guide*, with a preface by Agnes Baden-Powell, in which to be 'English' bestows such self-evident moral superiority that even the French girl in the story aspires to such status. This, and other comforting messages, are reiterated in scores of books for young people published during the late Victorian and Edwardian periods.

Publications like *Boys of the British Empire*, *The Boys of the Nation*, *The Union Jack* and *Boy's Own Paper* all rallied round the flag. One of the first issues of *The Boys of the Nation* included a description of two doughty boys that would have delighted Cecil Rhodes and Baden-Powell: Jack Fairweather was 'a handsome, well-proportioned English boy; face as brown as a berry, eyes coal-black and flashing, and hair to match in colour', and Tom Allbrass had 'a brave, intellectual brow; a pair of piercing, candid, laughing hazel eyes; nose, mouth, and chin finely chiselled, and a head of bonny brown curly hair. Tom is perfectly aware that he is good-looking.'[23] In the *Magnet* and the *Gem*, Frank Richards described the antics of Billy Bunter and his companions in such glowing terms that their school, Greyfriars, became – even for elementary school children like Robert Roberts in the slums of Salford – 'our true Alma Mater, to whom we felt bound by a dreamlike loyalty . . . the public school ethos, distorted into myth and sold among us weekly in penny numbers, for good or ill, set ideals and standards'.[24]

Fiction for children, therefore, in a wide variety of guises, came to the rescue of the imperial ideology during these testing times. Magazines, comics and novels were eagerly sought out, and passed from hand to hand among the poorer sections of society. Perhaps it is no more significant that the vast bulk of these publications glorified the British race and tended to denigrate the foreigner than the fact that in modern Britain there has been an apparently insatiable appetite for novels about spies or the occult. Tales of derring-do, or ripping yarns of far-flung and plucky British boys facing down dusky assailants, may have served simply to entertain and divert, performing the same function as spy novels during the Cold War. The conjunction in both eras between the desire to entertain and the need to consolidate a self-serving world view is nonetheless intriguing.

It would also be a mistake to overestimate the power of the school textbook; many children, then as now, spent most of their school days either actively or passively resisting the lessons proffered in their class-room reading. Among the late Victorians and the Edwardians, more-over, as well as among subsequent generations, anti-imperialism manifested itself in a variety of forms. Empire continued to be criticised, resented, misunderstood and even derided in the most unexpected quarters. As the twentieth century progressed, socialism, statism and trade unionism waxed and blind belief in Empire, King and country waned. This is not what Baden-Powell had in mind when he published *Scouting for Boys* in 1908.

17

THE IMPERIAL CONFERENCE
OF 1911

The Unity and the Disunity of the Empire;
Pan-Anglo-Saxonism, and the *Pax Britannica*

AT THE 1911 Imperial Conference held in London, the Prime Minister of New Zealand, Sir Joseph Ward, proposed to his fellow delegates that they should establish an Imperial Parliament of Defence. Ward's proposals were ill-considered and presented in a muddled and unconvincing fashion. He was, in effect, cross-examined by his colleagues as to the precise nature and implication of his plans. It was unfortunate for him, and for the pro-imperial federation interests that he so inadequately represented, that among his fellow prime ministers were men with distinguished legal careers or with the political skills to sniff out any flaws in his proposals. Not that the highest forensic abilities were necessary. Ward was acting more as a mouthpiece for pressure groups like the Round Table than speaking from his own deep convictions. He soon found himself in embarrassingly deep waters:

> *Sir Wilfrid Laurier* [Prime Minister of Canada]: But you say 'Council'. Is it a council, or is it a parliament? It is important to know exactly what is the proposal.
> *Sir Joseph Ward*: I prefer to call it a parliament.
> *Sir Wilfrid Laurier*: Very good then; now we understand what you mean.
> *Sir Joseph Ward*: I prefer to call it a parliament, although I admit there is everything in the name.
> *Sir Wilfrid Laurier*: There is everything in the name.[1]

Imperial federation had been dead in the water long before Sir Joseph Ward so ineptly dragged its corpse before his fellow Empire prime ministers for their appraisal. Admittedly the devolutionary tendencies set in train in the era of free trade had not been unanimously supported throughout the imperial system, particularly in Britain. In various quarters there was a hankering, much of it of a vague and generalised nature, for a more formal constitutional arrangement between the component parts of the Empire, principally between the self-governing colonies and the United Kingdom. During the last thirty years of the nineteenth century, the British experience seemed at odds with the consolidationist and federationist political and economic processes taking place elsewhere. Contrary to confident prediction, the American Civil War of 1861–65 had ultimately affirmed, not destroyed, the Union. Italian and German reunification appeared to be part of a similar process. The Russian empire continued its inexorable expansion eastward. Of the great powers, only Britain seemed to be out of step with its peers.

Despite the activities of the Royal Colonial Institute, founded in 1868, and the Imperial Federation League, set up in 1884, the movement for imperial federation in Britain was poorly supported and often unable to agree over ways and means. Later organisations such as the United Empire Trade League, started in 1891, and the British Empire League, founded in 1894, put more stress on voluntary cooperation, better communications and the augmentation of inter-imperial trade than upon the federal ideal.

Although a number of academics like Sir John Seeley touted the federal panacea, very few statesmen of the first rank did so. Joseph Chamberlain was, of course, one exception to this, and so was the Liberal imperialist Lord Rosebery, briefly prime minister between 1894 and 1895. Rosebery is generally, and inaccurately, credited with first articulating the concept of the Commonwealth during a speech delivered in Adelaide in 1884 when he said 'The Empire is a Commonwealth of Nations.'[2] Two years previously, however, Balfour had reviewed John Morley's life of the radical politician and economic reformer Richard Cobden and, while rejecting a solely commercial or materialistic view of the Empire, had stated that 'The sentiments with which an Englishman regards the English Empire are neither a small nor an ignoble part of the feelings which belong to him as a member of the commonwealth.'[3] Although Balfour employed the term somewhat vaguely, he made an interesting juxtaposition (especially as a Scotsman) between the term 'commonwealth' and 'the sentiments with which an Englishman regards the English Empire'. It seems that Balfour, who was later to play a vital part in promoting the ideal of a commonwealth of self-governing states, was feeling his way towards the concept of an Empire within which cooperation and common purpose were more feasible and satisfactory bonds than federal structures or closer constitutional ties.

Balfour's flotation of the notion of a 'commonwealth' based upon mutual cooperation, rather than constraint and control, did not merely arise from personal conviction. Rather, it was an acknowledgement of the art of the possible. The Liberals had been in power since December 1905, and generally spoke the same devolutionary language as the self-governing colonies. While chairing the 1911 Imperial Conference, the Prime Minister, Asquith, went as far as he dared to bridge the gap between the centralising and devolutionary factions with the bland declaration that 'we are, and intend to remain units indeed, but units in a greater unity'. The idea of a federated Empire simply could not be achieved in the face of continuing British inertia and confusion compounded by colonial indifference and hostility.

There were, however, a number of movements to achieve federal and constitutional solutions to imperial problems, but they were all given their fullest expression within the framework of the self-governing colonial system, not within the notoriously more sensitive and tricky area of inter-imperial relations. Between 1867 and 1910, three great federations or unions had been created within the British Empire: Canada in 1867, the Commonwealth of Australia in 1901, and the Union of South Africa in 1910. In all three cases, very substantial land-masses were brought within a unified constitutional framework. This, as much as the devolutionary and democratic instincts of the self-governing colonies, killed the imperial federation idea stone dead. It seemed almost perverse, or at least exceptionally determined, to continue to claim that an Empire-wide federation could be created out of several large, already federated states.

The Anglo-Saxon propensity for 'muddling through' asserted itself amid the ruins of the imperial federal ideal. A number of compromises and accommodations were arrived at. One of the most promising of these was the establishment of a system of Colonial, later Imperial, Conferences. The conference structure arose through a peculiarly British, *ad hoc* response to particular circumstances. The first Colonial Conference was held in 1887 as the prime ministers from the self-governing colonies assembled in London to celebrate Queen Victoria's Golden Jubilee. Ten years later the Queen's Diamond Jubilee provided the opportunity for summoning a second Colonial Conference. The 1902 Imperial Conference (a significant change of name) was the first to be arranged as part of a sequence, on a five-yearly basis. Even so, this would have coincided with the coronation of King Edward VII, had the celebrations not been postponed after the monarch became ill with appendicitis. The conference of 1907 was held according to schedule, but arrangements for the next one were modified by the coronation of King George V in 1911. As a consequence, the fifth Colonial or Imperial Conference took place only four years after the previous meeting: a further example of the 'bargain basement' approach to the calling of Colonial Conferences that had been established at the outset.

Thus, out of the invented tradition of the Royal Jubilee, and out of the ritual surrounding the coronation of the monarch, a further tradition was established, the regular meetings of leaders of the governments of Britain and the self-governing colonies. Nothing could better illustrate the British proclivity for empiricism, or, more likely, for making the best of a bad job.

Although some statesmen and a number of interested parties invested the conference system with high hopes, not much came of them. One exception was the 1887 Colonial Conference, which produced the agreement to begin a system of colonial subsidies for the upkeep of the Royal Navy. This was one of the most positive achievements in the years before 1914.

To a large extent, the Colonial and Imperial Conferences were for display and public consumption. Rather like jubilees and coronations, they could be seen as part of the pomp and circumstance of imperial greatness. They also gave the superficial impression of harmony between Britain and its self-governing colonies, and encouraged cartoonists, journalists and politicians to conjure up images of the British 'imperial lion' surrounded by its loyal and increasingly powerful cubs. In practice, the self-governing colonies were just as likely, firmly and courteously, to assert their separate identities. Kipling encapsulated some of the sentiment in a poem addressed to the Dominion of Canada in 1897, the year of the second Colonial Conference, on the occasion of the senior dominion's offer of a preferential tariff to Britain:

> *A nation spoke to Nation,*
> *A Queen sent word to a Throne:*
> *'Daughter am I in my mother's house,*
> *But mistress in my own.*

The gates are mine to open,
As the gates are mine to close,
And I set my house in order,'
Said our lady of the snows.[4]

As is the case in most family gatherings, all was not sweetness and light during Colonial conferences. Tensions and rivalries sometimes resulted in unseemly spats and disagreements. For the most part, the Mother Country was the recipient of filial grumbles and complaints. More rarely, Britain used the conferences to demand more help and cooperation from her potentially wayward offspring – as when Chamberlain appealed at the 1897 conference for assistance in shouldering the great weight of imperial responsibility.

As Lord Salisbury had predicted at the opening of the Colonial Conference of 1887, the proceedings of the meetings were generally 'prosaic'.[5] The topics addressed were often of a detailed, technical nature, as when the delegates discussed items like the need to improve communications and maritime facilities. Great issues of policy were, with certain exceptions, left to one side. In any event, the amount of time allotted to the discussions was very short, as the colonial premiers had very full programmes of engagements while in the United Kingdom. There was also a lot of wining and dining, and the Canadian Prime Minister, Wilfrid Laurier, once remarked that although he was not sure whether or not the Empire needed a new constitution, the Empire's prime ministers most certainly did.

There was one fundamental reason why the Colonial and Imperial Conferences achieved so little. Quite simply, they had no binding legislative or executive power over the countries that participated in them. Even if there had been unanimous support for the introduction of a system of imperial preference, for example, the governments of Britain and all the self-governing colonies would have then had to seek the assent of their individual parliaments to such a step. The club-like atmosphere prevailing at the conferences certainly encouraged free discussion, but also a good deal of waffling. The first conferences were not even serviced by a permanent secretariat, and it was not until the establishment of the Committee of Imperial Defence in 1904 that its secretariat was put at the disposal of subsequent Imperial Conferences. When the delegates dispersed, moreover, there was no centralised system of maintaining inter-imperial communication, and the participating countries were reduced to methods identical to those prevailing between Britain and foreign powers before the invention of the telephone – the telegraph, the letter and personal contact.

There was, in addition, a tendency for members of the British government of the day, from rumpled patricians like Lord Salisbury to spruce and articulate propagandists like Chamberlain, to patronise the colonial prime ministers and to treat them with condescension. This process got under way at each conference, at least until 1911, when the British Prime Minister opened the proceedings with a lofty and fairly ritualistic speech, and then departed to the care of more weighty and pressing matters. The Colonial Secretary stepped into the void, and chaired the proceedings of the conferences.

Despite the relaxed atmosphere which prevailed, the vast gap in social origin, educational opportunity and cultural attainment that frequently became evident between the British delegates and those from the self-governing colonies was awkward. Contemporary photographs and accounts often reveal a potentially embarrassing interaction between sophisticated English statesmen and bewhiskered, thick-booted colonials. The accents of Eton and Oxford must have often jarred against the plainer and more democratic tones of Ontario and Queensland.

If anything, members of Britain's Liberal governments between 1905 and 1915 showed more contempt for their colonial colleagues than had members of the earlier Unionist administrations. Lewis Harcourt, Colonial Secretary in 1911, gave clear expression to this attitude when he wrote that it would 'never do to *say* we are too good for them, and that they are not good enough for us'. He was, however, prepared to pander to 'the social vanities of the new rich . . . unless and until they could be convinced of the folly of their foibles'.[6]

It is therefore not surprising that the conferences encouraged solidarity between the self-governing colonies – officially called dominions after 1907 – often at Britain's expense. Thus on certain issues a Canadian–Australian axis would emerge, whereas on other occasions New Zealand and Australia might make common cause. At the conference of 1907 Louis Botha, Prime Minister of the newly self-governing Transvaal, and Wilfrid Laurier of Canada were described as 'seeing eye-to-eye' on most issues. A convention also arose whereby Canada, as the senior dominion, was often entrusted with the task of leading the discussion on behalf of the other colonies on matters of constitutional importance.

There is one further reason why the items discussed in the Colonial and Imperial Conferences tended to be bland and often technical. Contentious and radical items had the capacity to shatter the image of inter-imperial harmony and expose the very real differences between Britain and the dominions. The colonial delegates simply could not be relied upon to toe the British line on many matters. This was particularly true at the conferences of 1907 and 1911, when the Transvaal delegation included the ex-Boer War generals Louis Botha and Jan Smuts. Even Sir Wilfrid Laurier of Canada was a symbol of Liberal French-speaking interests rather than British and Conservative ones. Alfred Deakin almost invariably put Australian interests before those of Britain, despite his pro-imperial rhetoric. His folksy, anecdotal speeches, moreover, reduced the fastidious intellectual and Liberal statesman John Morley to despair, and to the judgement that Deakin's performances were in danger of turning the conference of 1907 into 'the greatest bore that was ever known'.[7] The New Zealander Dick Seddon was rumoured never to have read a book.

Between 1887 and 1914, one of the most coherent attempts to rationalise and consolidate the relationship between Britain and the self-governing colonies was made by Alfred Lyttelton, Chamberlain's successor at the Colonial Office from 1903 to 1905. The final version of Lyttelton's dispatch to the governors of the self-governing colonies was issued in April 1905. Essentially, he claimed that 'an Imperial Council for the discussion of matters which concern alike the United Kingdom and the self-governing Colonies has grown into existence by natural process'. He therefore proposed that the title 'Colonial Conference' should be discarded in favour of 'Imperial Council', further suggesting that the British Prime Minister should become *ex-officio* president of the council, to be assisted by the Colonial Secretary. The council would have as its permanent members the prime ministers of Canada – who would also represent Newfoundland – Australia and New Zealand. The Prime Minister of Cape Colony would act on behalf of the other three South African colonies until federation had been achieved. Various British or colonial ministers could be added to this council where necessary.

Lyttelton went on to propose the establishment of a permanent commission to service the Imperial Council. This commission, however, was to be 'purely consultative and advisory'. Based in London, its secretarial staff would be paid for by the British government, and its function would be to prepare subjects for discussion at the Colonial Conferences or, if the proposal was approved, Imperial Councils. Topics for discussion would be referred to the permanent commission either by the Colonial Conference or by two or more self-governing colonies. It would be the task of the commission to ensure that the topics presented should be in as concise and coherent a form as possible. It would also regularly review the progress achieved. Lyttelton further suggested that the permanent members of the commission would be nominated by the premiers of Britain and the self-governing colonies, but that additional members should be appointed whenever this was deemed appropriate.[8]

The dominions gave a mixed response to Lyttelton's proposals. Some of them undoubtedly saw them as the thin end of a British-inspired federationist wedge. For Australia, Alfred Deakin, a self-proclaimed imperial patriot and tariff reformer, sent a favourable response. Loyalist Natal and Cape Colony, where Dr Jameson had made a remarkable comeback from the fiasco of the raid to become Prime Minister from 1904 to 1908, both gave general approval to the scheme. Newfoundland, however, only accepted the principle of a permanent commission with great reluctance and after further haggling by correspondence. Canada expressed reservations tinged with doubt, and voiced its fears that the scheme would conflict with the proper working of responsible government. New Zealand, interestingly, sent no reply at all to Lyttelton's dispatch.[9]

When Lyttelton's proposals were formally discussed at the Imperial Conference of 1907, deep divisions were revealed in the attitudes of the colonial premiers. Australia showed most enthusiasm for the scheme, but Canada, the Transvaal and Newfoundland were resolutely hostile. Predictably, a compromise emerged. Lyttelton's proposals were ditched, but instead the dominions agreed to the establishment of a department dealing exclusively with their relationship to Britain, to which would be attached a permanent conference secretariat. This new body was to become the Dominions Department of the Colonial Office, and was eventually to be transformed into the Dominions Office in 1925.

Modest triumphs like this were unlikely to bring about the constitutional reconstruction and revitalisation of the Empire for which some so ardently wished. The parties involved had resorted once more to compromise or, less flatteringly, to 'muddling through'. Balfour, who as prime minister had expressed serious reservations over Lyttelton's scheme for an Imperial Council and a permanent commission, continued to put more faith in the lasting value of loose imperial ties. Six months after his resignation from office in December 1905, he said, 'If a great Empire is to be kept together, sentiment and loyalty must enter into the emotions by which its component parts are animated.'[10]

How exactly were these emotions to be activated? The role of the monarchy was clearly central to the whole enterprise. But in an age before the advent of the radio and the talking cinema, how best was this to be achieved? One solution was for the monarch and his or her imperial subjects to come face to face. It had proved impossible to send the widowed and reclusive Queen Victoria around the Empire; instead the Empire had been brought to Queen Victoria, most spectacularly during the Jubilee celebrations of 1887 and 1897. There was, however, no reason why Victoria's heir, the future Edward VII, and his children, should not assume the role of royal tourist. But when, following the funeral of Queen Victoria in February 1901, a Colonial Office proposal that the Duke and Duchess of York – the future King George V and Queen Mary – should visit Australia and open the first parliament of the newly federated state in the spring of that year, Edward VII objected.

In response Balfour, effectively deputy Prime Minister, put the King in his place:

> Mr Balfour recognises the force of all the objections which may justly be urged against the visit at the present moment . . . If, in Mr Balfour's judgement, they had not conclusive weight, it is because he cannot help feeling that there are on the other side reasons to be urged which touch the deepest interests of the monarchy. The King is no longer merely King of Great Britain and Ireland, and of a few dependencies whose whole value consists of ministering to the wealth and security of Great Britain and Ireland. He is now the great constitutional bond uniting together in a single Empire communities of freemen separated by half the circumference of the globe. All the patriotic sentiment which makes such an Empire possible centres in him, or centres chiefly in him; and everything which emphasises his personality to our kinsmen across the sea must be a gain both to the Monarchy and to the Empire.[11]

Unable to counter this compelling argument, Edward VII reluctantly surrendered. As a result, far from staying at home, the Duke and Duchess of York visited not only the new Commonwealth of Australia, but also Gibraltar, Malta, Aden, Ceylon, Singapore, New Zealand,

Natal, Cape Colony and Canada as well. It was to be the first of a long and elaborate programme of royal tours to the Empire and Commonwealth, which have continued, not without the occasional trauma, to the present day. It is notoriously difficult to judge the effect of royal visits, whether to Canada or Carlisle. However, in view of the complexity and variety within the Empire, it was probably helpful for its citizens to focus their attention, feelings and loyalty upon a personification of the imperial ideal rather than upon the ideal itself.

It was also possible to continue to appeal to the nebulous concept of Anglo-Saxon solidarity. Even this strategy, however, had its perils. Pan-Anglo-Saxonism was unlikely to appeal to many in Britain's 'Celtic fringe', let alone to French-Canadians, the Afrikaners of South Africa and many of the descendants of Irish Catholic transportees and free immigrants to Australia. This approach, nonetheless, had the advantage of rationalising Britain's early-twentieth-century *rapprochement* with the United States, later to be dignified with the description of the 'Special Relationship'. Many British statesmen welcomed the increasing level of Anglo–American cooperation, as the product of those links of parliamentary and legal tradition, kinship and shared culture, which were in essence the same as the bonds which were assumed to promote harmony between the Mother Country and the dominions.

During the Edwardian period there was even some speculation that the United States could be induced to enter into a federation with the British Empire. It was argued that such a confederation 'would be practically unassailable and would dominate the world . . . It would practically dictate peace by sea to the rest of the world.'[12] In this way, Cecil Rhodes' fantasies were given substance by serious statesmen. If such a remarkable act of reconciliation had occurred, however, it was not clear that the Americans would have seen themselves as junior partners, a theme explored with wry humour in 1929 in George Bernard Shaw's play *The Apple Cart*, in which the United States in effect makes a take-over bid for the British Empire.

There was a further possibility of cooperating with what might loosely be considered kith and kin. Until the *entente* with France in 1904 committed Britain to fringe membership of the Franco–Russian bloc, the British government had seriously attempted to conclude an alliance of some sort with imperial Germany. Although these negotiations failed, it is significant that they were supported by Chamberlain, among others, and that they promised for a while to bring about a *Pax Teutonica*, which some British statesmen hoped would supersede and be an improvement on the evidently failing, expensive and beleaguered *Pax Britannica*.

By the time of the 1911 Imperial Conference, the old, apparently unavoidable, choices between imperial centralisation or disintegration via devolution were equally inappropriate. What was emerging, through a mixture of circumstances – including British dithering, institutional inertia and the growth of dominion nationalism – was an increasingly decentralised Commonwealth of white-dominated self-governing communities which would cooperate, rather warily, in certain agreed areas. Any proposed reforms to imperial organisation had to conform to this situation. As a result, certain choices were made: the Dominions Department of the Colonial Office and the establishment of the Committee of Imperial Defence were acceptable innovations, whereas an Imperial Defence Council or a permanent commission were not. Chamberlain's proposal to extend the functions of the Judicial Committee of the Privy Council, which already acted as a final court of appeal for the whole Empire, similarly received short shrift from the self-governing colonies.

There were still many contradictions and inconsistencies in the relationship between Britain and the emerging dominions. The dominions were described as self-governing. In theory, however, the British monarch and Parliament could disallow and obstruct any colonial legislation which ran counter to constitutional practice or to English common law. These powers had been defined in the 1865 Colonial Laws Validity Act. In practice, however, Britain had hardly ever exercised its rights in these matters, and then only in relatively trivial instances.

A further problem was that the dominions' claim to self-governing status within the Empire was seriously undermined by their continuing reliance upon, even subservience to, the exercise of British foreign policy. Since Britain footed almost the whole bill for the naval defence of the Empire, however, and made such a substantial contribution to its land defences, it was difficult to see how the dominions could assert themselves in this respect, even though they had borne the cost of their own armies since the 1870s. How could they even aspire to independence when their national security was overwhelmingly safeguarded by Britain and the British taxpayer? The need to escape from this paradoxical difficulty was one of the most powerful factors behind the determination of both Canada and Australia, expressed during the Edwardian era, to establish their own infant navies – a process that was successfully under way when war broke out in 1914.

The formal bonds between the dominions and Britain in 1914 were hardly oppressive. The monarchy provided a practical constitutional link and was represented on the spot by the governors-general who were, without exception, sent out from Britain rather than recruited in the colonies. The Dominions Department of the Colonial Office maintained contact between Whitehall and the dominions. The Committee of Imperial Defence functioned as a permissive and advisory body only. The Imperial Conferences provided merely a forum for discussion, carefully disclaiming wider and more binding powers. Even though Britain shaped and ran the Empire's foreign policy, she was in no position to compel a dominion to give practical support to any aspect of that foreign policy of which it disapproved.

The main foundation upon which imperial cooperation was based, therefore, was simply the will to cooperate. Pan-Anglo-Saxon sentiment, while often a useful aid, was not a particularly satisfactory formula for an empire which contained not merely substantial non-English-speaking populations within the dominions but which also included the sub-continent of India and all the many and varied colonial dependencies. There were, however, some imperial bonds which were found generally acceptable. In the last resort, these bonds – a shared monarchy, membership of the same imperial group, and (at least in the self-governing colonies) a common law and common institutions – could be borne with few misgivings chiefly because they were already part of the fabric of 'communities of freemen separated by half the circumference of the globe'.[13] There were two other crucial, but very imprecise contributors to imperial harmony: a perceived common self-interest, or a serious and specific military assault on the Empire's integrity. The outbreak of war in August 1914 was to put the relations between Britain and her dominions to their most serious test hitherto.

THE GANDHI–SMUTS
AGREEMENT OF JANUARY 1914

Anti-Imperialism, Resistance Movements, and
'Occidentalism' versus 'Orientalism'

ON 21 JANUARY 1914, Mohandas Karamchand Gandhi and Jan Christian Smuts reached an agreement aimed at settling the long struggle over the rights of Indian immigrants in South Africa. From 1860 tens of thousands of Indian indentured labourers had been brought to Natal to work on the sugar plantations. They were followed by other Indians who crossed the Indian Ocean either to work as labourers in South Africa or to open businesses there. As the businessmen, many of whom were Muslims, prospered, the white community saw them as an increasingly powerful and dangerously influential element in South African society.

When the indentured labourers completed their contracts, they and their families overwhelmingly chose to stay in South Africa, particularly in Natal. In 1893, when Natal became a fully self-governing colony, the newly-established responsible government began a campaign to strip Indians of any political privileges they enjoyed and to obstruct the full citizenship of the Indian immigrant population as a whole. The 1896 Franchise Act passed in the Natal parliament effectively disenfranchised Indians, who were not mentioned specifically in the legislation, by ingeniously denying the vote in Natal to anyone whose home country did not have its own parliamentary representation. In 1897 the Natal parliament forbade the immigration of any Indians who had not signed indentures, and allowed the trading licences of Indians to be cancelled without appeal to a court of law. These were the predictable responses of a white minority community insecurely settled among a much larger black majority. The Europeans were generally resentful at the prospect of further non-white immigration, and feared the competition of Indian migrants in trade and in the job market.

As Indians moved to other parts of South Africa, particularly to the Transvaal, a series of legislative and judicial obstacles were raised to their entering into full citizenship. Among the stratagems devised by the whites to harry and demoralise Indians and their families were hefty taxes, challenges to their rights to enter the country and a legal ruling which appeared to declare Hindu marriages illegal.

In 1894 the young, London-trained Gujerati lawyer Mohandas Karamchand Gandhi was invited by the wealthy and often well-educated Indians who had established the Natal Indian Congress to come to South Africa to join the struggle to protect their rights. Until 1906, Gandhi, employing a mixture of conventional legal and political devices, attempted to defend and advance the civil rights of Indians in Natal and further afield. Although some modest successes were recorded, it was not until September 1906 that he was able to lead his Indian followers to more substantial success. The turning point was his decision to abandon the conventional methods of resistance practised hitherto and to launch the first *satyagraha* campaign.

This step may be viewed as an important watershed in the history of the resistance to imperial rule, and in the development of peaceful techniques to assert the claims of indigenous nationalism. *Satyagraha*, which literally means 'the force of truth', was shaped into a powerful personal political philosophy through Gandhi's genius for organisation and leading through example. Drawing on ancient Indian tradition, certain aspects of the philosophy of Count Leo Tolstoy – for instance the notion that evil could best be countered by non-resistance – and even on the recent activities of the Suffragettes in Britain, *satyagraha*, which became associated with non-cooperation and civil disobedience, was a potent weapon in Gandhi's hands, a non-violent means of confronting the big battalions of imperial and white settler supremacy. No physical threat was offered to one's opponent. Instead, protesters used techniques like the non-payment of taxes, the burning of passes, the renunciation of honours and positions of power and, *in extremis*, the refusal to cooperate with authority. Gandhi also encouraged his supporters to follow the Christian precept of turning the other cheek in the face of physical aggression.

The overriding aim of *satyagraha* was to occupy the moral high ground and to unsettle and win over one's opponents, not through acts of physical aggression, but through restraint and passivity, and above all by setting them an example which would eventually convince them of the righteousness of those they confronted and attacked. Between 1906 and 1914, Gandhi and his supporters in South Africa pushed the white regimes that dominated the self-governing colonies, and later the Union government, to their limits. In the end, General Smuts, the Minister for Defence and Native Affairs in the South African administration led by Louis Botha, decided to capitulate to Gandhi's demands.

The Gandhi–Smuts agreement led to the passing, six months later, of the Indian Relief Bill, which acceded to all the protesters' demands: the £3 annual tax was abolished, marriages considered legal in India became legal in South Africa, and the domicile certificate became sufficient right to enter the Union. There was, of course, more to it than Smuts simply recognising the moral strength of the Gandhian campaigners. For one thing, it was possible to see the fairly small but increasingly influential Indian community in South Africa as potential allies in the real race conflict in the sub-continent – that between the whites and the blacks. For another, an agreement would almost certainly rid the country of Gandhi, and when he sailed from Durban in July 1914 Smuts remarked, 'The Saint has left our shores; I sincerely hope for ever.'[1]

The apparent triumph of Gandhi's *satyagraha* policy in South Africa was full of portent. Within three years of his return to India, he was using the same tactics with increasing confidence and success against the British Raj. It also provided an example which gave hope to all those who wished, in one way or another, to strike a blow against British rule or even simply to irritate, embarrass and exasperate their rulers, and represented an important psychological turning point in the mounting desire of colonial peoples to free themselves from British overlordship. The success of the *satyagraha* campaign began a process of liberating the leaders of colonial resistance groups from subservience to British political methods and from the assumed superiority of European culture. As writers like Edward Said have so persuasively argued, the European imperial powers carried out a devastating and generally highly successful assault upon the integrity of indigenous culture and civilisation during the imperial age, despite the fact that arts in the West continued to draw inspiration from the Orient. Western statesmen, writers, missionaries, historians, journalists and many other opinion-formers often described and defined the native cultures with which they came into contact in such derogatory and dismissive terms that imperial rule became, by definition, a necessary and civilising act.[2]

Having projected upon large numbers of indigenous societies all manner of delinquencies, inadequacies and barbarities, the European imperial powers could, to a very large extent, rid themselves of guilt as they overcame, manipulated and frequently abused colonial subjects. There was even something in it for the conquered and the colonised. Cecil Rhodes believed that the linchpins of British imperialism were philanthropy plus a 5 per cent dividend on investment. Kipling, as so often, put this philosophy into bumping, jangling verse:

> We broke a King and we built a road –
> A court-house stands where the Reg'ment goed,
> And the river's clean where the raw blood flowed,
> When the Widow give the party.[3]

If the definition and delineation of inferior cultures may be described as 'orientalism', there was also a reverse or opposite set of perceptions. 'Occidentalism' existed side by side with 'orientalism'. The occidentalists were those colonial and subject peoples who respected, admired and idealised the West, and in particular Britain. Good, noble and exalted values were projected upon British institutions, methods and personalities. Queen Victoria became the great white queen over the ocean, as benign, caring and omnipotent as some deity. British justice was imagined to be the best in the world, British culture the most refined, British political institutions the most liberal and humane, British people the most tolerant and kindly. In his autobiography, Nelson Mandela, for example, wrote that in his youth: 'The education I received was a British education, in which British ideas, British culture and British institutions were automatically assumed to be superior.'[4] For much of his early manhood Gandhi, too, idealised what he perceived as British virtues, wishing his sons to be 'proper English gentlemen' and assuming that the British Empire was devoted to the equality and well-being of all its subjects. Clearly there was something valid in these perceptions, but they are also an awesome testimony to the phenomenal success of the propaganda, both conscious and unconscious, purveyed by Britain and the British during much of their imperial hegemony.

But Gandhi's decision to employ *satyagraha* as a political and social tool from 1906 onwards marked the beginning of the end of his romantic and idealised perception of Britain and Britishness. His conversion was signalled externally by his decision to wear simple, Indian garments and to set aside the three-pieced suits, collars and ties of the Westernised

Oriental lawyer. He ate only basic food, and eventually renounced all pleasures of the flesh, including those of sex.

His change of heart was also brought about by the manifest failure of the institutions and administrators of the British Empire to recognise the justice of the Indian case in South Africa, let alone do anything about it. Despairing, at least in the short term, of British justice, Gandhi instead put his hopes into self-help and the celebration of indigenous culture, rather than its rejection. This in turn led to an increasing alienation from Western civilisation. Within a short time Gandhi had become the persuasive and consistent critic of Western education, Western materialism and Western industrialisation.

All of this unleashed forces of such power that the struggles of colonial people to attain self-determination, or at the very least a greater degree of respect for themselves and their cultures, received a permanent boost. Naturally, Britain's imperial supremacy did not melt away overnight. British military technology, the apparently ubiquitous strength of the Royal Navy, British understandings with collaborating local leaders and elites, and the skilful use of various techniques to sustain imperial power were formidable obstacles to overcome.

It is important to realise, however, that to some extent Gandhi and the other opponents of imperial rule were pushing at a door which was, if not open, at least ajar. As we have noted, the strenuous attempt to promote the imperial ideal which had characterised the last decade of the nineteenth century and the first years of the twentieth reflected uncertainty and pessimism as much as self-confidence and optimism. The pronouncements of imperial proconsuls like Milner or Curzon, passionate and clear-cut as they were, were fundamentally attempts to rally a distracted, passive and sometimes actively hostile audience. For every public figure who preached the gospel of Empire there were literally hundreds of thousands of men and women whose main preoccupation was balancing the household budget and finding adequately paid employment. This was at least one reason why Chamberlain strove so hard to equate Empire with full employment and prosperity.

How strong was anti-imperial sentiment within the United Kingdom and the Empire in the years immediately before the outbreak of the First World War? Despite the attempt in many quarters to promote the ideals of King, Country and Empire, there were substantial numbers of British citizens who declined to buy the whole package. It was the poet and author G.K. Chesterton who remarked in 1901, during the Boer War: ' "My country, right or wrong" is a thing that no patriot would think of saying, except in a desperate case. It is like saying "My mother, drunk or sober." "[5]

During the nineteenth century and in the early years of the twentieth century, opposition to British imperialism and militarism had been freely and sometimes powerfully articulated. The mid-Victorians had expressed at the very least ambivalence over the need to expand the formal Empire. Richard Cobden and the free traders of the Manchester School had argued that colonies were expensive to maintain, and thus a burden to the taxpayer, especially since trade with them would flourish whether or not they were ruled by Britain, as had been clearly demonstrated by the booming Anglo–American trade after the loss of the Old Thirteen Colonies. The Cobdenites also asserted that the formal possession of colonies was a threat to international peace, since they provoked jealousies among other imperial powers and conflict over their frontiers. Cobden also maintained that one of the main reasons why colonies were retained was in order to find profitable employment for the younger sons of the English aristocracy in the imperial administration and in the army.

The Victorians, especially once the ideology of the free trade market was firmly established, became preoccupied with a policy that they called 'Retrenchment'. A large number of politicians and statesmen believed that it was their duty to cut down on wasteful expenditure, to keep the role of the state to the minimum and as a consequence to save as much of the taxpayers' money as possible. It thus followed that existing colonies must be financially independent and must pay for their own administration out of their resources. Loans to colonial governments were discouraged, and the cost, for example, of combating famines in India was placed firmly on the shoulders of the Indian government. The acquisition of new colonies seemed to many to be an unnecessary headache and a potential drain on revenue. In 1865 the Select Committee reporting on the British possessions in West Africa gave strong advice against 'all further extension of territory or assumption of Government, or new treaties offering any protection to native tribes', and even recommended, perhaps rather wistfully, that Britain should abandon three of her four colonies on the West African coast.

These misgivings did not, in the event, halt the process of imperial expansion. The West African colonies remained in the Empire; indeed, their territory was augmented. The imperial frontier inexorably advanced, despite distant complaints from Westminster and Whitehall. The real problem was that, when it came to a crisis, no British govern-

ment could abandon white settlers or business interests to the dep-
redations of hostile local populations. But when it was deemed safe to
do so, as in the case of New Zealand in the 1870s, British troops were
withdrawn and a triumph for Retrenchment recorded. But in South
Africa, the West Indies, parts of Africa and elsewhere it did not prove
possible to make white settler communities bear the costs and responsibility of their own defence. In the process there emerged a curious
equation between anti-imperialism and feelings of resentment towards
those indigenous people whose rebellions, resistance and intransigence
necessitated the intervention of British forces. In other words, it was
'their' fault that there was trouble and expense, not 'ours'.

Even during the late-Victorian and Edwardian eras, anti-
imperialist sentiment, although it may have declined in volume and
quantity, never disappeared. This was true right across the political
spectrum. Despite Disraeli's attempt to hitch the Conservative Party
to the fiery chariot of Empire, he was by no means universally successful.
Most Conservatives saw themselves as the party of low taxation, and
even if they were content to be identified as the party of Empire, they
overwhelmingly wanted imperial administration and expansion on the
cheap. It took a Liberal Unionist like Joseph Chamberlain, supported
by proconsuls of Liberal antecedence like Milner and Cromer, to articulate the gospel of the New Imperialism with consistency and fervour.
Neither of the two Conservative and Unionist prime ministers between
1885 and 1905, Salisbury and Balfour, gave the impression of a passionate commitment to the imperial ideal. Salisbury, as we have seen, spoke
gloomily of the perils of 'splendid isolation', and Balfour expressed
genuine misgivings over both the Jameson Raid and the Chamberlainite
machinations that led to the outbreak of the Boer War.

Of the two major political parties, the Liberals contained most
anti-imperialists within their ranks. Once in office, of course, the Liberal
Party was caught in a dilemma. What happened in practice was that
Liberal governments tended to uphold Britain's imperial interests,
although often giving the impression that they felt some ambivalence,
even guilt, in the process. Liberal backbenchers were, however, allowed
to exercise their consciences and denounce imperialistic and militaristic
excesses, so long as they didn't actually vote to bring down the government. Even when the Liberal Imperialist section of the party became
so influential towards the end of the nineteenth century, Liberal MPs
often felt able to express their criticisms of the workings of the British
Empire. The South African Act of Union of 1909 provoked bitter oppo-

sition from a minority of Liberal MPs who denounced it, with undeniable accuracy, as nothing short of a sell-out of the political rights of
non-European peoples in South Africa.

Liberal opponents of the South African Act of Union were joined
by the relatively small number of Labour representatives in the House
of Commons. Keir Hardie, the first Labour MP to enter Parliament,
in 1892, and Chairman of the party from 1906 to 1908, told the House
of Commons that he believed it would be only a matter of time before
the 'colour-blind' Cape franchise was destroyed as an anomaly and a
threat to white supremacy:

> for the first time we are being asked to write over the portals
> of the British Empire: 'Abandon hope all ye who enter here'
> . . . I hope, therefore, that if only for the sake of the traditions
> of our dealings with natives in the past, this Bill . . . will be
> so amended as to make it a real unifying Bill in South Africa.
> At present it is a Bill to unify the white races, to disenfran-
> chise the coloured races, and not to promote union between
> the races in South Africa, but rather to still further embitter
> the relationships.[6]

The Labour movement, however, was in a dilemma. In ideological
terms, socialists disapproved of the exploitation of any group: trade
unionists, the poor, and colonial people. But increasingly the Labour
Party was becoming the organisation which articulated the demands
of mass trade unionism. Many in the trade union movement made a
connection between the consolidation and expansion of the British
Empire and the provision of full employment at home. When asked to
choose between adequate wages and good job prospects and the oppression of colonial subjects, many trade unionists were tempted to put
their own interests first. H.G. Wells caught the dilemma neatly in his
great Edwardian novel *Kipps*, published in 1905, when the underpaid,
overworked drapers' apprentices, penned into their garret 'over the
shop', discuss the news of the proposal to extend the Indian franchise,
and vehemently oppose the proposals, trapped as they are amid their
own impoverishment, inadequacies and disenfranchisement.

The controversy over 'Chinese slavery' in the Transvaal from 1904
onwards provides a nice illustration of the Liberal, socialist and trade
unionist dilemma. The importation of 50,000 indentured Chinese
labourers to boost gold production on the Rand after the conclusion
of the Boer War provoked one of the most dramatic political contro-

versies of the Edwardian age. The undoubted abuses – the illegal deduction of wages, the dishonouring of promises of higher pay, and harsh punishments, including flogging – which attended the introduction of Chinese 'coolie' labour led to widespread denunciations of the government's policy in Britain. At the general election of 1906 it was assumed that the 'Chinese slavery' issue lost the Conservatives and Unionists thousands of working-class votes. There is no doubt that many trade unionists and workers switched their vote from the Unionist Party to the Liberals. But many also abandoned the Liberal Party and went over to the embryonic Labour Party. If they were voting to any extent on the issue of 'Chinese slavery' they may well have been protesting against competition from dirt-cheap 'yellow labour' as much as in support of humanitarian principles.[7]

Apart from the left-wing and progressive political parties, many other groups and organisations expressed, in varying degrees, anti-imperialist sentiments. There were peace groups, humanitarian organisations and Nonconformist churches that expressed a wide range of opposition and misgivings. There were the 'busy bodies', like Emily Hobhouse, Secretary of the Women's Branch of the South African Conciliation Committee, who campaigned persistently against the establishment of concentration camps during the Boer War, and who so exasperated Kitchener and the military high command. There were journalists who pried into the darker corners of the imperial enterprise and who sometimes embarrassed supporters of Empire with their revelations. There were the writers, novelists and playwrights who ridiculed imperial pomposity and, sharp-eyed and persistent, attempted to deflate the more extravagant assertions of patriotism. Among the Edwardian literati were many socialists, such as H.G. Wells, George Bernard Shaw, Arnold Bennett, John Galsworthy, and the children's writer Edith Nesbit. At the very least, many of these writers expressed humanitarian sympathies, even if they did not deliberately, and as a matter of course, denounce the British Empire. Wells was perhaps the most persistently critical of them all, apt to ridicule the Empire as being at best the provider of a cheap postal system and the services of a narrow-minded and unsympathetic officialdom.[8]

Whereas many radicals and reformers in the mid-Victorian period had seen colonisation as an opportunity for valuable experiments in social engineering, several of their Edwardian equivalents denounced Empire, and a seeking of quick profits overseas, as damaging to the prospects of reform at home. The influential writer J.A. Hobson argued that 'Finance manipulates the patriotic forces which politicians, soldiers, philanthropists and traders generate; the enthusiasm for expansion which issues from these sources, though strong and genuine, is irregular and blind.' As a result, Hobson claimed, the exporting of capital overseas left workers in Britain at the mercy of poverty caused by underemployment.[9] H.N. Brailsford, in a very widely-read book, *The War of Steel and Gold*, asserted that 'The capitalist must rush abroad because he will not fertilise the demand for more commodities at home by the simple expedient of raising wages.'[10]

One of the main problems for those who wished to promote the imperial ideal was the inertia and ignorance of so many of the British public. Although there were periodic indulgences in jingoistic displays, especially at times of crisis and war, this was not the same thing as a considered, deep-rooted imperial patriotism. The celebrations which attended the relief of the siege of Mafeking owed a good deal of their fervour to the fact that the news arrived in the United Kingdom at the weekend, when large numbers of people had finished work on Saturday afternoon and had their wages in their pockets to spend on a celebratory drink. When asked to choose between tariff reform, with its prospect of closer imperial union at the price of a modest rise in food prices, the electorate overwhelmingly plumped for the status quo and a cheaper loaf of bread. Attempts to persuade the British people that imperialism could fund social reform also went largely unheeded. Milner bitterly regretted that he was never able to find ways of convincing the British public, 'these d – d fools', of the reasons why the Empire was central to their futures.

Anti-imperialism could be found throughout the Empire. Even within the United Kingdom, Celtic resentment at English domination of the union was liable regularly to erupt. The Irish, the Ulster Unionists aside, were the most persistent and hostile critics of the imperial system. The eighty or so Irish Nationalist MPs who sat in the House of Commons frequently made use of their parliamentary privileges to support certain colonial causes and to criticise and embarrass the government of the day over imperial issues. But in Scotland and Wales, too, dislike of English snobbery, overlordship and Toryism was widespread, manifesting itself in the tendency to vote for Liberal, and later Labour, parliamentary candidates, and in national rejoicing whenever English football or rugby teams were beaten at Hampden Park or the Cardiff Arms Park.

Within the dominions, anti-British, and thus by definition anti-imperial, feelings were sometimes so endemic that they threatened the generally cordial relations with the Mother Country. For the Afrikaners of South Africa and the French-Canadians, of course, Britain was not the Mother Country, rather the conqueror and oppressor. Irish Australians often disliked England and the English more than they admired the British Empire; the 'whingeing Pom' is not a twentieth-century construct. In New Zealand, despite the myth of Maori equality, the indigenous population could hardly avoid seeing themselves as a subjugated people; a people, moreover, overwhelmingly denied equality of opportunity in employment, education and housing, and only grudgingly admitted to the franchise.

In the Indian Empire, by the late nineteenth century, organised political movements were challenging the smooth running of the administration, and were soon to threaten the very existence of the Raj. The Indian National Congress, founded in 1885 with enthusiastic British support, had, after twenty years, outlived its original role as a harmless talking-shop. The high-handed, abrasive, reforming viceroyalty of Lord Curzon from 1898 to 1905 had in the end transformed Congress into a far more radical and effective organisation. Curzon had hoped, through demonstrating the impartiality and effectiveness of British rule, to bind India permanently to the Raj. His partition of Bengal in 1905, on the grounds of administrative efficiency, had been perceived by a wide range of Indian opinion as a brutal assault upon one of the most heavily populated and politically sophisticated of the sub-continent's provinces – the home, indeed, of the much resented 'Bengali babu'. The Bengal partition had aroused such bitter controversy that Congress was revitalised in the process. The foundation of the Muslim League in 1906 was another warning that the post-Mutiny settlement, based upon administrative conservatism and minor concessions to Indian constitutional progress (as expressed in the 1892 Indian Councils Act), had broken down. When Gandhi eventually returned to his home country in 1915, the scattered and varied forces of Indian nationalism were to gain their most skilful, shrewd and populist leader to date.

The strength of the Indian reaction to the 1905 partition of Bengal, and the 1908 split between Congress 'moderates' and 'extremists', had encouraged the Liberal government in Britain to introduce the Morley–Minto reforms of 1909 to 1910. The 1909 Indian Councils Act modestly extended the franchise, but quite substantially increased the numbers of elected and nominated Indians on the provincial and central legislative councils of the Raj. In a way, the reforms were a confidence trick. The

British, by holding out the prospect of progress, at some time to be decided by themselves, towards responsible government, were undoubtedly hoping to contain and defuse the forces of Indian nationalism. Thus the extension of democratic institutions was used as a means of shoring up the fundamentally autocratic British Raj. The ambiguous nature of the reforms of 1909 to 1910 was demonstrated by the correspondence between the Indian Secretary of State, Morley, and the Viceroy, Lord Minto, over which Indian should be nominated to sit on the Viceroy's Executive Council. The key appointment eventually went to S.P. Sinha, whom Minto preferred to the other potential appointee on the grounds that 'Sinha is comparatively white, whilst Mookerjee is as black as my hat!'[11]

If so crucial an appointment could be made, at least in part, on the grounds of acceptable skin colour, what hope was there for the many well-educated Indians of participating in the administration of their own country? Although the Indian Civil Service was theoretically open to them, the fact that the entrance examinations were held in the United Kingdom, and the weight of official disapproval at their advancement, ensured that only a handful of Indians had been appointed to the ICS by 1914.

Indeed, British hostility to the 'educated native' increased rather than decreased as the twentieth century began. The jumped-up 'Bengali babu' had been an object of ridicule and contempt during the second half of the nineteenth century. The spirit of Macaulay's great Indian education reforms of the 1830s was subverted by the growing need to keep India, with its expanding economy and its supplementary army, within the Empire. Elsewhere in the Empire, for example in the British colonies of the Gold Coast and Sierra Leone, the numbers of Africans holding positions in the local civil services was actually sharply reduced between 1870 and 1914. In 1873 Lord Kimberley, Secretary of State for the Colonies in the Liberal government, had issued a directive that 'excepting quite subordinate posts we cannot safely employ natives'. A decade later a Colonial Office official described educated Africans as 'the curse of the West coast'.[12]

For the vast majority of colonial citizens, imperial rule, whether welcome or not, was a fact of life to which they simply adjusted. The struggle for subsistence was sufficient preoccupation for the vast majority of Britain's subjects in Asia, tropical Africa and the Caribbean. Nor could any save a handful aspire to serving in colonial civil services or local administrations.

As a consequence, the final response to misfortune, ill-treatment or exploitation throughout the dependent empire was to riot or rise in revolt. This involved the British Army and its colonial subsidiaries and mercenaries in a ceaseless round of confrontation, repression and the enforcement of law and order. During the reign of Queen Victoria there was not a single year when the British armed forces were not involved in some sort of military campaign, from full-scale international conflicts like the Crimean War to skirmishes on the north-west frontier of India, or where imperial interests clashed with those of local potentates and indigenous people in Africa and South-East Asia.

Whether the British forces were engaged in a relatively routine act of retribution, like burning a rebellious village in India, or facing the Boers in a major battle on the high veldt, their activities underpinned the gigantic, complex, and sometimes unsound imperial structure. In the last resort, the *Pax Britannica*, as enforced throughout the Empire, was only made possible by the ceaseless activities of British and colonial land forces, and by the capacity of the Royal Navy to intervene swiftly, efficiently and cheaply.

Although for much of the nineteenth century there was little to choose between the two main parties in terms of their determination to maintain the Empire by whatever means necessary, including the use of force, the policies of the Liberal government from 1905 to 1915 provided a sharper contrast than usual with the 'forward' expansionist policies of the Unionist administrations between 1885 and 1905.

There was certainly continuity, however, in one crucial area of imperial overlordship: the need to seek out, negotiate with and, in the last resort, control collaborationist groups within the Empire. This meant different things in different contexts. In India it meant leaving a third of the country in the hands of local princes; in Northern Nigeria it meant the establishment of a system of 'indirect rule', whereby the British collaborated with the Muslim emirs; sometimes it meant backing one tribe or faction against another, as in the support of anti-Mahdist elements in the Sudan, or occasionally profiting from any friction between the Masai, the Luo and the Kikuyu in Kenya.

The Liberal governments led by Campbell-Bannerman and Asquith also went out of their way to offer concessions to certain local interest groups and to pursue a policy of conciliation rather than confrontation whenever that was deemed expedient and unavoidable. The granting of internal self-governing status to the Transvaal and the Orange Free State, and the introduction of the Morley–Minto reforms in India, were the most dramatic, and probably the most significant, examples of the Liberals' policy of conciliation. But there were other, more low-key, diplomatic gestures made in other parts of the Empire. This policy certainly made life less exciting for the British public, who were thus denied their diet of triumphalist headlines and articles in the rapidly-expanding mass-circulation popular press, but it was undeniably effective.

Conservatives, Unionists and imperialists reacted with both dismay and fury to the concessions made by the Liberal administrations. As leader of the opposition, Balfour denounced the concession of internal self-government to the Transvaal in 1906 as 'the most reckless experiment ever tried in the development of a great policy'.[13] Curzon, who had resigned from the viceroyalty in 1905 after a bitter and protracted quarrel with Kitchener, the Commander-in-Chief of the Indian Army, over the control of military policy, expressed alarm at the proposed Morley–Minto reforms, which he described as 'a futile and fantastic dream', and had previously remarked, 'It is often said why not make some prominent native a member of the Executive Council? The answer is that in the whole continent there is not an Indian fit for the post.'[14] Another out-of-office proconsul, Milner, asserted in 1908 that 'the idea of extending what is described as "Colonial Self-Government" to India . . . is a hopeless absurdity.'

Despite these predictable denunciations, the Liberal policy of mixing kindness with the minimum coercion seemed to bear fruit, at least in the short term. Critics of the government's imperial policies attempted to raise the alarm over what they perceived as endemic weakness and vacillation, and for good measure accused the Liberals of simply not caring enough about the Empire to pursue a stronger line.

There were, nonetheless, a considerable number of violent incidents, rebellions and disturbances between 1905 and 1915. There were riots in British Guiana, Egypt and India. There was a rebellion in the north-west of Nigeria in 1906, and determined tribal resistance to the consolidation of British rule in what became the colony of Kenya. The Zulu rebellion in Natal, which began in 1906, was put down with great brutality and substantial losses of African lives. At the outbreak of the First World War in August 1914, some 10,000 Afrikaner rebels staged a short-lived uprising against South Africa's involvement in the conflict.

In general, however, there were considerable achievements for Liberal imperial policy. The bid for conciliation, and the moderating of the more radical, hectic and confrontational policies which had been particularly associated with Chamberlain's tenure of the Colonial Office between 1895 and 1903, all helped to promote a welcome period of stability. The Liberal government kept a close watch on abuses of pro-consular power, tried to keep various colonial bureaucracies under control, insisted on higher administrative standards, and tried to contain imperial militarism and the monopolistic ambitions of big business.

There were attempts to rationalise parts of the imperial system. One such bid centred on the promotion of the Crown Colony form of government as the model to which various dependencies and protectorates should routinely aspire; this was an entirely logical approach which took note of the Crown Colony's long history and clear-cut constitutional structure, and which recognised the benefits that could accrue from the routine surveillance exercised by the Colonial Office and Parliament over such colonies. The Dominions Department of the Colonial Office, which had been first proposed by Balfour's outgoing Unionist government, provided for better communications with the self-governing colonies. The Colonial Service rule-book was revised and rendered more humane and acceptable. In 1909 a circular from the Colonial Secretary, Lord Crewe, forbade concubinage with local women, although cohabitation between colonial officials and indigenous females flourished for many decades. More money was put into research into tropical disease and into more efficient and profitable forms of colonial agriculture.

In 1914 the Empire seemed to be set on a relatively even keel. There were, naturally enough, a vast range of unresolved problems, tensions and conflicts. To begin with, the constitutional status and international identity of the dominions needed further definition and clarification. The burgeoning nationalist movement in the Indian Empire had won some modest constitutional concessions from Britain, but had so far not even begun to address many of the interests and concerns of the sub-continent's huge population. The mobilisation of India's masses against the Raj had not yet been achieved, although, ominously, Gandhi was in the process of returning to his homeland from South Africa.

In Africa, the Caribbean, South-East Asia and the Pacific a huge number of colonial possessions presented a wide variety of challenging problems – centring on their future viability, profitability, constitutional and economic development and the relationship between the rulers and the ruled – as well as numerous opportunities and consolations. The late-nineteenth-century drive to consolidate the Empire and to stiffen its backbone through the promotion of projects like imperial federation, reciprocal tariffs and a binding set of military obligations, had come to nothing. The British economy was still clearly in decline, claiming only 14.7 per cent of the world's manufacturing capacity in 1910 as opposed to 31.8 per cent in 1870. Although the economy did rather better than expected in the few years before 1914, there were manifold signs of the continuing success and diversification of the economies of Britain's chief competitors: 'Upon the outbreak of war ... the British government found to its alarm that all the magnetos in use in Britain came from Stuttgart. And so did all the khaki dye for uniforms. London's "Underground" was built between 1900 and 1914 by American expertise, with plenty of American plant, and with more foreign than British investment. In 1914 one third of all motor cars in Britain were imported ... Americans owned or dominated seventy firms in Britain – the invasion had begun with Singer sewing machines in 1867.'[15]

To some extent, the Liberal government seemed content to let imperial development take its own course. Since one of the main paths marked out was the high road to local devolution and political freedom, which the Liberals claimed as their own territory, they were content to proceed accordingly. The more benign Liberal approach to colonial claims for greater self-determination, to local discontents, and to sheer colonial cussedness seemed to be paying dividends. Almost everywhere, the countries of the Empire were enjoying a relative tranquillity, and at least some of the benefits of peace and progress. Where all this would have led, but for the outbreak of the First World War in August 1914, it is impossible to say.

19

THE 1916 EASTER UPRISING IN IRELAND

Britain, the Empire and the First World War

ON EASTER SUNDAY 1916, a few score of Irish republicans led by Patrick Pearse, and including the socialist James Connolly, rose in armed revolt in Dublin. Most of the rebels belonged to the Irish Republican Brotherhood, of which Pearse was the head, and their avowed aim was to begin a revolution which would establish an independent Irish republic. The rebels set up their headquarters in the Dublin Post Office, and took other strongpoints in the central Dublin area. Pearse then issued his proclamation of an Irish republic:

> Irishmen and Irishwomen: in the name of God and of the dead generations from which she receives her old tradition of nationhood, Ireland, through us, summons her children to her flag, and strikes for her freedom . . . We declare the right of the people of Ireland to the ownership of Ireland, and to the unfettered control of Irish destinies, to be sovereign and indefeasible . . . We hereby proclaim the Irish Republic as a Sovereign Independent State, and we pledge our lives and the lives of our comrades-at-arms to the cause of its freedom, its welfare, and of its exaltation among the nations.[1]

Although taken by surprise, the British reacted quickly and decisively. Troop reinforcements were brought over from England, and the Post Office and other rebel strongholds shelled. In the process some three hundred civilians were killed, parts of central Dublin set on fire and many shops looted. Eventually the men and women holding the Post Office building were forced to evacuate it, and shortly afterwards

Pearse made his decision to surrender. Sixty-four Irish rebels and some 130 British soldiers had died. The blood sacrifice for which Pearse had called before the uprising had occurred.

British retribution was quick and uncompromising. Fifteen rebels were executed, shot dead in batches of two or three, the executions carried out even before their relatives knew that they had been tried before courts-martial. Among the executed rebels were Pearse and his brother Willie, and James Connolly, who had been wounded in the fighting, and who was court-martialled in his bed and carried out to his execution tied to a chair.

Throughout Ireland the reaction to the uprising was initially hostile, sometimes bitterly so. The Ulster Protestants saw their dire predictions of southern Catholic treachery bloodily confirmed. Even in Dublin, as the rebels were taking up their positions before the uprising, they were accused by many of being slackers and traitors who would be better off fighting the real enemy, the Germans. After the collapse of the rebellion on 29 April, the captured rebels were greeted with anger by many of their fellow-citizens, stones and vegetables were thrown at them, and they were abused and derided for their treachery.

Set beside the Indian rebellion of 1857, the Zulu uprising in Natal of 1906, and a number of other bloody and violent confrontations between the British and their subjects throughout the Empire, the Easter uprising was a small-scale event. Although there had been some isolated responses to Pearse's call for revolt in other parts of Ireland, including the killing of members of the Royal Irish Constabulary in County Meath, and the brief capture of the town of Enniscorthy in Wexford by the Irish Volunteers, the country as a whole had overwhelmingly rejected the call to arms.

The executions and imprisonments carried out under martial law between 3 and 10 May 1916 changed the mood of the majority of Irish Catholics. Britain's abrupt and revengeful response to the rebellion awoke memories of the long catalogue of Irish grievances against the English, and seemed to demonstrate once more the contempt and lack of sympathy which lay at the root of Britain's attitudes towards the Irish. Pearse had anticipated this change of heart at his court-martial, declaring:

> We seem to have lost. We have not lost . . . You cannot conquer Ireland, you cannot extinguish the Irish passion for freedom. If our deed has not been sufficient to win freedom, then our children will win it with a better deed.

The British authorities acted as they did chiefly because the Empire was in the midst of what was widely seen as a life-and-death struggle with imperial Germany and its allies. In these circumstances, the Easter uprising had given flesh to the deep-seated fear that Irish treachery could destroy Britain's security. British fantasies of an Irish stab in the back were proved to have some substance in reality. Shortly before the Easter rebellion, the British had intercepted an arms supply ship, the *Aud*, sent from Germany to aid the cause of Irish revolution. They had subsequently arrested Sir Roger Casement as he landed from a German submarine on Banna Strand in County Kerry. Casement, a distinguished British civil servant who had taken up the cause of Irish nationalism, was in fact attempting to prevent a premature uprising. He was tried and hanged as a traitor, his reputation blackened by the infamous diaries which showed him to have been an active homosexual. Despite these rather lightweight examples of German assistance to the Irish nationalist cause, the government in Berlin had decided not to give full backing to an Irish armed rebellion.

Although Irish nationalist groups were receiving arms from over-seas, some of them carried in the yacht of Erskine Childers, the author of the best-selling spy novel *The Riddle of the Sands* who was to be killed during the Irish Civil War of 1922–23, it was arguably the Protestants of the north who posed the greatest threat to a peaceful settlement of Irish claims to independence. With the Irish Home Rule Bill due to be finally passed through Parliament in 1914, Ulster Protestants had shown once more their determination to fight to preserve the Union. Almost three-quarters of all Ulster's Protestants over the age of fifteen, interestingly including slightly more women than men, had signed a covenant in 1912 that they would use 'all means which may be found necessary to defeat Home Rule'. In 1913 an Ulster Volunteer Force of some 90,000 had been established. It was militant, efficiently organised and well armed as a result of an effective gun-running campaign which brought German weapons into the port of Larne.

It was the determination of the Protestants of the north to fight rather than submit to the fairly mild devolutionary package contained in the Home Rule Bill which led to the Dublin Easter uprising. Ulster Unionists had played the Orange card with such determination that the Liberal government had been forced to contemplate the partition of Ireland as an unavoidable component of the Irish constitutional settlement. Once more, a powerfully organised and united collabor-ationist group within the Empire seemed about to force the British government to acknowledge its position and to maintain the status quo.

Uncertain whether it could rely upon the loyalty of British Army officers serving in Ireland after the so-called 'Curragh Mutiny' of 1913 – when nearly sixty officers based at the Curragh camp outside Dublin had indicated that they would resign their commissions rather than take part in 'active operations' designed to coerce Ulster Protestants who refused to accept the implementation of Irish Home Rule – the Liberal government had used the outbreak of the First World War in August 1914 as an excuse to put the Irish Home Rule Bill into cold storage for the duration of the hostilities. It was Irish exasperation that the British seemed, once more, to have changed the rules of the game in order to deny them Home Rule that was one of the most powerful causes of the Easter uprising.

Britain's involvement in the First World War subjected the imperial system to an unprecedented number of stresses and trials. This was disguised for the most part by the upsurge in patriotic sentiment which was manifested throughout the Empire, as well as by the relative efficiency of the British propaganda machine throughout the war.[2] The statistics of the war effort, both in terms of the men and women who entered the armed services and of the amount of money spent by individual Empire countries, were deeply impressive, and bolstered the impression that imperial countries had participated wholeheartedly in the conflict. Britain recruited 6,704,416 men, 22.11 per cent of the adult male population, of whom 704,803 died. Canada recruited 628,964 men, of whom 458,218, 13.48 per cent of the adult male population, served overseas; 56,639 lost their lives. Australia recruited 412,953 men and sent overseas 331,814, or 13.43 per cent of the adult male population, of whom 59,330 died. New Zealand recruited 128,525 men sending 112,223, or 19.55 per cent of the adult male population, overseas; 16,711 were killed or died of wounds. South Africa recruited 136,070 whites, sending 76,184 abroad, or 11.12 per cent of the white adult male population, of whom over 7,000 died. More than 8,000 Newfoundlanders served overseas, of whom 1,204 lost their lives.[3]

Although the causes of the war were, on the whole, far removed from the their own immediate interests, the countries of the dependent Empire also sent large numbers of men to fight overseas. The Indian Army raised 1,440,437 volunteers, of whom 62,056 died. British East Africa raised some 34,000 fighting troops, losing about 2,000; the British West African colonies raised 25,000 men, of whom 850 died. Tens of thousands drawn from other possessions served in non-combatant units:

over 82,000 Egyptians, 8,000 West Indians, 1,000 Mauritians, and even a hundred from Fiji.[4]

These forces were overwhelmingly financed from the treasuries of their countries of origin, once more demonstrating the extent to which the Empire in effect subsidised any major British war effort. Empire troops also served in various theatres of war, sometimes thousands of miles away from their homes. South African forces conquered German South-West Africa and Tanganyika; Canadians died in their tens of thousands in Flanders and northern France; Australians and New Zealanders played a major part in the ill-fated Gallipoli campaign; Indian troops not only fought on the Western Front, but also played a major part in the messy campaign to conquer Mesopotamia. Such contributions seemed further proof that the British Empire had rallied as never before to meet its greatest test.

Further scrutiny of the Empire's involvement in the First World War, however, reveals a picture significantly different from that conjured up by the British propaganda machine and eagerly swallowed by the public. To begin with, it was by no means clear from the outset that the war was being fought in the interests of the Empire as a whole, certainly not to the advantage of its various component parts. If, as the British government claimed, it had entered the conflict to defend democracy and the interests of small nations, especially 'gallant little Belgium', how was that to be reconciled with Britain's frequently autocratic and dominating attitudes towards much of its Empire, especially towards India and the dependent territories?

To many colonial citizens, especially those from Africa and Asia, the conflict must have seemed nothing more than a European civil war whose chief protagonists carried the fight, inconveniently and selfishly, to other continents in defence of their particular interests. Although Britain had entered into *ententes*, or understandings, with France and Russia between 1904 and 1907, this was not the same thing as being bound to them by a formal alliance. Indeed, the British government, if it had so wished, technically could have avoided entering the war on the side of France and Russia, claiming that there was no treaty that obliged them to do so.

In the event, Britain held back from declaring war on Germany until 4 August 1914, causing her *entente* partners several days of acute anxiety. If the German army had chosen not to invade Belgium, thus appearing to threaten the Channel ports, Britain might well have exercised her option of neutrality, at least for the opening phase of the war.

But the German Schlieffen Plan dictated that a great northern sweep through Belgium was an essential part of a strategy to encircle and capture Paris. The possibility that imperial Germany would speedily defeat France and Russia – as its early successes on the Eastern Front seemed to promise – threatened to destroy one of the cardinal principles of British foreign policy, namely that no one European power should be allowed to dominate the Continent.

Anglo–German rivalry had, by 1914, assumed a complexity and depth which made it impossible to ignore the challenge posed by the German military machine at the outset of the war. The vast extra-European trading and financial network, which was so crucial to the maintenance of Britain's economic strength, could be permanently damaged by the rise of one supreme Continental power. British foreign policy also required the maintenance of the freest possible trading and commercial relationships throughout the world. All of this was underpinned by, indeed could only be achieved through, the continuing supremacy of the Royal Navy. But Germany, with its naval building programme, offered the most dangerous contemporary challenge to Britain's naval supremacy. The maintenance of a large and effective navy was Britain's only realistic way of protecting her national and worldwide interests at a reasonable price. The City of London clearly understood and approved of this equation between naval predominance and world peace, fearing the effects of a major war upon the British economy.[5]

The scale of Germany's economic expansion throughout the world, and in particular the extent of her penetration of British and imperial markets, also contributed substantially to Anglo–German rivalry and tension. There was anxiety, even anger, at Germany's 'dumping' of low-priced manufactures on the British domestic market, as well as in imperial ones, which continued to undercut British manufactures. The anti-foreign prejudices of the Tariff Reformers had included a blatant anti-German bias. Protectionists, imperialists, bankers and financiers, as well as service lobbyists, newspaper owners and large sections of the British public, all identified a German threat. For the most part, they were right to do so. Viscount Esher, a significant strategist and a founder member of the Committee of Imperial Defence, succinctly put this point of view in 1907:

> Meanwhile the Germans proceed unabashed on their way, and now their objective is clearly in view. The German prestige, rising steadily on the continent of Europe, is more for-

midable to us than Napoleon at his *apogee*. Germany is going to contest with us the command of the sea, and our commercial position. She wants sea-power and the carrying trade of the world. Her geographical grievance has got to be addressed. She must obtain control of the ports at the mouths of the great rivers which tap the middle of Europe. She must get a close line from which she can draw sailors to her fleets, naval and mercantile. She must have an outlet for her teeming population, and vast acres where Germans can live and remain Germans. These acres only exist within the confines of our Empire.[6]

There was, therefore, no option for Britain early in August 1914, except to enter the war to protect the Channel ports and to thwart Germany in what seemed to be a desperate bid to strip Britain of its already shaky naval and commercial supremacy. As far as many of the ordinary citizens of the dominions were concerned, these British imperatives were not always immediately relevant. This was even more true for the subjects of the Indian and dependent empires. Worse still, the constitutional position of the countries of the Empire gave them no legal choice in the matter. Britain's declaration of war committed the whole Empire to the hostilities.

Despite the Empire's constitutionally unavoidable involvement in the war, however, there was in effect no way of enforcing wholehearted dominion, or indeed Indian or African, participation in the fighting. The response of the dominions to the outbreak of hostilities demonstrated both the complexity and the strength of the imperial connection. The Australian Prime Minister, Joseph Cook, said, 'Australia is part of the Empire. When the Empire is at war, so is Australia at war.'[7] New Zealand acted upon similar convictions. The Canadian government, and the Liberal opposition, similarly accepted their nation's involvement in the conflict, although Wilfrid Laurier, for the Liberals, made the point that the extent of the country's participation was a decision for the dominion alone.

In India, where nationalists could not aspire to Laurier's position, the sub-continent's involvement in the war was accepted with few qualms, and for the most part with enthusiasm; nationalist leaders generally chose to support 'democratic' Britain against 'autocratic' Germany, inaccurate as these perceptions were in a number of ways. Throughout the rest of the Empire colonial subjects showed little opposition to being dragged into the hostilities on Britain's coat-tails. Many of them, indeed, barely comprehended what was happening.

There was, however, a quite different set of imperial responses. In the Union of South Africa the reaction to the outbreak of war was ambiguous. Pro-German and anti-British feelings among large numbers of the Afrikaner people led to a brief, but for a while embarrassing, rebellion led by a number of ex-Boer War generals including de Wet and Beyers. In the spirit of the post-war settlement, however, the uprising was abruptly and efficiently crushed by loyalist South African forces led by an alternative batch of ex-Boer War generals, namely the Prime Minister, Louis Botha, and the Minister for Defence and Native Affairs, Jan Smuts. Although Irish Republicans opposed Britain's entry into the war, tens of thousands of their fellow-countrymen from the southern counties volunteered for active service, 35,000 of them losing their lives as a result.

Various socialist and trade union movements throughout the European-settled Empire and Britain, despite their ideological misgivings at being pitched into an imperialist and militaristic war, swallowed their objections, mostly at the behest of their rank and file, and swam with the tide of events. Those pacifists, or conscientious objectors, who continued unwaveringly to oppose the fighting, whether on the home front or when called up after conscription was introduced in 1916, generally evoked little sympathy and in many cases received harsh and abrupt treatment.

As the war progressed, and the casualty lists, particularly those from the Western Front, lengthened, opposition to the war, and straightforward war-weariness, manifested itself in a variety of ways and in many countries. Unexpectedly, there was a rising in Nyasaland in 1915, led by John Chilembwe, an eloquent African Baptist minister. Articulating local grievances over the conditions of work on the coffee plantation near his mission station, Chilembwe also protested at the numbers of local Africans killed in the war and refused to fight himself. He struck against the whites who ran and owned the plantation, leading a revolt which left some white males dead but spared women and children. He had no illusions over his fate, telling his supporters: 'This very night you are to go and strike the blow and then die . . . This is the only way to show the whiteman that the treatment they are treating our men and women was most bad and we have decided to strike a first and a last blow, and then all die by the heavy storm of the whiteman's army. The whitemen will then think, after we are dead, that the treatment they are treating our people is all most bad, and they might change.'[8] Chilembwe's hopes in this regard were not, alas, realised.

Less bloodily, but infinitely more effectively, both Canadians and Australians demonstrated their opposition to the introduction of conscription during 1917. French-Canadians, who had been slow to volunteer for the Canadian forces, were to the forefront in the protests against the proposals. There were riots and serious civil disorder in Quebec, and the necessary legislation was only passed by the Canadian Parliament after a split in the Liberal Party and a general election fought primarily on the issue of conscription. Even so, conscription was barely enforced in Quebec for fear of civil disturbance, and out of the 400,000 Canadian troops serving overseas during 1917 fewer than 30,000 were French-Canadians. In apparently patriotic Australia the issue of conscription was put to the vote in two referenda, and twice defeated, chiefly due to the opposition of organised labour and to the hostility of many Irish-Australians. It is tempting to imagine that the ghosts of long-dead Irish political transportees and free immigrants must have taken quiet satisfaction in this democratic rejection of an imperial need.

By 1916, the almost universal loyalty that India had demonstrated at the outbreak of the war had given way to renewed demands for self-rule. The irreplaceable contribution of India to the success of Britain's war effort prompted the British government to consider new reforms designed to satisfy both loyalists and agitators. The Liberal Edwin Montagu became Secretary of State for India in 1917, and soon declared in the House of Commons that he favoured 'the progressive realisation of responsible government in India as an integral part of the British Empire'.[9]

Montagu followed this up with a visit to India in November 1917, where he conferred with the Viceroy, Lord Chelmsford, and also met Bal Gangadhar Tilak, one of the most outspoken and intractable of the nationalist leaders, and Jinnah, the increasingly influential Muslim statesman. Specific proposals for reform were announced in August 1918, three months before the end of the war. They promised the imminent implementation of responsible government in the great Indian provinces, and the introduction of a system of diarchy – in effect, a sharing of ministerial responsibility in the provinces between the British and the Indians.

At the outbreak of war, Britain had ended the anomalous status of Egypt by incorporating it within the Empire as a protectorate. The step was necessary not merely because of the enormous strategic importance of the Suez Canal, but because Britain found herself at war with Turkey, to whom the Egyptian Khedive nominally owed suzerainty. Egyptian nationalists, however, resented this step, and their increased agitation led to the British promise that after the war serious consideration would be given to the issue of Egyptian self-government.

If the British were steeling themselves for their eventual withdrawal from Egypt, they were actively consolidating their interests in the Middle East. In order to wage war more effectively against Turkey, the British High Commissioner in Egypt, Sir Henry McMahon, promised towards the end of 1915 that Britain would 'recognise and support the independence of the Arabs'. But Arab revolt, supported by British armed intervention, raised yet more problems. The Royal Navy was increasingly going over to the use of oil-driven engines, and the Middle East was an important source of oil. If Egypt could not be relied upon as a long-term British base, then new bases would have to be established elsewhere in the Middle East.

In 1916 Britain and France concluded a secret agreement, the Sykes–Picot Treaty, which arranged for the partition of the Ottoman Empire at the end of the war. Britain thus acquired at the peace settlement direct control of Palestine, of the oil-producing territory of Mesopotamia – later known as Iraq – and of states in the Persian Gulf; she also claimed a sphere of influence stretching from the river Jordan to the Gulf. France became the dominant power in Syria and Lebanon.

Palestine, however, neither produced oil nor offered any obvious strategic advantages. In November 1917, Balfour, serving as Foreign Secretary in Lloyd George's wartime coalition government, issued a declaration in which Britain pledged its support to 'the establishment in Palestine of a national home for the Jewish people'. The foundation of a Jewish homeland in Palestine, although fraught with various risks and dangers, offered many potential advantages to Britain and the Allies. Jewish opinion in the United States and Russia was expected to be favourably impressed. More important still, the settlement in Palestine of substantial numbers of Jewish immigrants, drawn mostly from Europe, would guarantee Britain a continuing strategic and commercial stake in the area. In the process, a Middle Eastern equivalent of Ulster was established, complete with a chronic and apparently unresolvable conflict between a dominant immigrant group of one religion and a majority host nation of another. In this way, Britain's prosecution of the war was storing up trouble for the future, as well as provoking resentment and resistance in the established parts of the imperial system.

Some of the resentment expressed towards Britain on the part of imperial countries during the war arose from the fact that the British government and the British Military and Naval High Command simply assumed control of the running of the conflict from the outset. The small navies being established by both Canada and Australia were abruptly brought under the control of the British Admiralty. British policy was also blamed for heavy colonial casualties in several campaigns. The ill-fated Gallipoli campaign, which was meant to rip out the soft underbelly of the Turkish Empire, achieved hardly any of its military objects and, moreover, inflicted huge losses upon the high proportion of Australian and New Zealand forces involved in the operation. Australian resentment at their disproportionate casualties at Gallipoli was to linger for generations, and was even to resurface during the agitation for an Australian republic during the 1990s. The 1917 invasion of Mesopotamia was characterised by incompetence and ill-preparedness, resulting in unnecessarily heavy casualties among the Indian Army detachments which made up so important a part of the invasion force. This, in turn, lent an edge to Indian nationalist complaints about India's continuing subservience to British interests.

The British Prime Minister, David Lloyd George, was quick to recognise the extent of dominion and imperial discontent by 1917. Perhaps as a Welshman he was more sensitive to the bruised feelings of subordinate peoples than most of his predecessors. At any rate, he decided to involve the Empire far more closely in the planning and prosecution of the war. As a result, representatives of the dominions and, more remarkably, of India, were invited to attend an Imperial War Conference in London. Cashing in on the presence of so many imperial representatives in the capital, Lloyd George also established an Imperial War Cabinet, as a by-product of his own innovative War Cabinet.

The Imperial War Cabinet was chaired by the Prime Minister, and consisted of the British War Cabinet and the representatives of the dominions and India. Its main business was the conduct and administration of the war. The Imperial War Conference alternated with the meetings of the Imperial War Cabinet, and was presided over by the Colonial Secretary. At these meetings the representatives of the dominions and of India discussed a variety of problems relating both to the Empire and to the running of the war. Most of the imperial delegates seem to have been gratified by this apparently genuine attempt to involve them in the decision-making process.

Lloyd George appears to have cherished long-term plans for continuing imperial cooperation on the lines established during 1917 into the post-war period. In order to construct the peace settlement, the Imperial War Cabinet and the Imperial War Conference met again in 1918, and in effect the British Empire delegation to the various peace conferences also played the part of the Imperial War Cabinet. When it was announced in November 1920 that an Imperial Conference would meet in June 1921, *The Times* was optimistic enough to anticipate 'the beginning of a definite system of Empire Government in peace by an Imperial Peace Cabinet'.[10]

As it turned out, nothing of the sort happened. The meetings of the 'Imperial Peace Cabinet' did not establish a permanent precedent. The Conservative statesman and imperial enthusiast Leo Amery put things in perspective when he remarked that the 'Imperial War Cabinet registered the high-water mark in the evolution of effective Commonwealth cooperation in our time'.[11] In the safer post-war world, the dominions returned to their devolutionary and nationalist agendas, turning their back upon Lloyd George's hopes of establishing some form of permanent centralising imperial body. The peacetime Imperial Conferences, like their pre-war equivalents, functioned as useful meeting-places for discussion and debate rather than assemblies with executive powers.

Even during the heady days of the Imperial War Cabinet and the Imperial War Conference in 1917, there had been an unmistakable indication that there could be no turning back of the devolutionary clock. In March 1917 Jan Smuts, representing South Africa, had drafted and carried through the Imperial War Conference a resolution calling for a special Imperial Conference at the end of the war in order to readjust 'the constitutional relations of the component parts of the Empire'. The resolution recorded the desire of the dominions that any such readjustment 'while thoroughly preserving all existing powers of self-government and complete control of domestic affairs, should be based upon a full recognition of the dominions as autonomous nations of an Imperial Commonwealth'. At the same time the dominions and India claimed an 'adequate voice in foreign policy' and wanted provision for 'continuous consultation in all important matters of common imperial concern'.[12]

At the end of the war there were three peace conferences: one each to settle matters with Germany, Austria-Hungary and Turkey. During these negotiations, the dominions, with the agreement of Britain, pressed for and achieved separate diplomatic representation. India also successfully requested to be represented separately. Thus, in effect, the dominions in particular received a public acknowledgement of their independent status as well as the affirmation that they possessed real diplomatic autonomy. This opened up several possibilities. One was that the dominions might cooperate with each other more, and with Britain less; or, indeed, that they might draw further apart from each other. On the other hand, some British statesmen argued that if the dominions were given a really effective voice in the peace settlements, 'they would be prepared to accept the idea of a single foreign policy for the British Commonwealth directed by the machinery of an Imperial Cabinet'.[13] Britain was also aware of the advantages of having, for example, Botha requesting that the British Empire should retain conquered German colonies in Africa,[14] or of the Indian delegation proposing that Asian people in the Middle East should come under British trusteeship.

In the event Britain, the dominions and, to some extent, India had the best of both worlds. Dominion and Indian representatives filled, on a rotating basis, two places on the five-strong British Empire delegation, which equalled that of the United States and France in size. The dominions and India also enjoyed separate diplomatic representation equivalent to that of other Allied powers such as China, Greece and Portugal. Both France and the United States initially objected to what they perceived as the 'packing' of the conferences by Britain and its Empire.

If they feared that Britain, the dominions, and even India would speak with one voice, they were soon disabused. Quite considerable disagreements emerged between the delegations from Britain and the dominions: for South Africa, Botha and Smuts, perhaps predictably, thought that the Versailles Peace Treaty dealt too severely with Germany, and even went so far as to submit a memorandum of protest. Prime Minister 'Billy' Hughes of Australia, on the other hand, was determined to squeeze Germany until the pips squeaked. He had little time for America's President Wilson and the proposal to establish a permanent international forum – the League of Nations – and, coveting German New Guinea under the proposed mandate system, only accepted the principle of mandated territories on the understanding that the League's supervision would be nominal rather than real and effective. The Canadian delegation seems to have steered a middle course.

Not only did the dominions and India sign the peace treaties in their own right, but they were also granted membership of the newly-established League of Nations. The fact that India belonged to the League, although she was far short of independence herself, produced a paradoxical, not to say absurd, situation. In 1920 the British government made a further concession to dominion nationalism by allowing Canada to appoint her own ambassador to Washington. The precedent thus set meant that within a few years diplomatic relationships were being established between Britain and the dominions in the form of High Commissions, and, to a limited extent, between the dominions and foreign states.

By 1919 the dominions had apparently 'come of age', both in theory and in practice, a result not merely of their own development and their contribution to the war effort but also of Lloyd George's decision to treat them, as well as India, as equals at the 1917 Imperial War Conference.

In addition to their independent roles at the peace treaties, and their membership of the League of Nations, there was one further indication of their maturity. The victorious Allies had fastidiously avoided carving up the imperial possessions of their defeated enemies among themselves in the time-honoured fashion. Instead, and partly to appease President Wilson's high-minded internationalism, they had accepted a mandate system, organised under the auspices of the League of Nations. Through this device, conquered and ceded territories were mandated to various Allied countries. The mandates were meant to be held as trusteeships, and the nations which administered them were held responsible to the League of Nations. In this way, the dominions of Australia, New Zealand and South Africa acquired a clutch of mandated territories in their own backyards – South Africa receiving the ex-German colony of South-West Africa, for example, and Australia ex-German New Guinea.

This created yet another paradox within the imperial structure. In constitutional terms, the dominions were still theoretically subject to the legislative oversight and veto of the British Crown and the British Parliament. At the same time, they had now become in effect imperial powers in their own right. The League of Nations supervised the mandate system in a minimalist and perfunctory fashion, and in due course the countries responsible for mandates simply administered them as old-fashioned colonies.

The British Empire reached its widest territorial extent in 1919 as a result of the acquisition of mandated territories. Britain acquired a new empire in the Middle East, and rounded off her African empire with the acquisition of Tanganyika and parts of Togoland and the Cameroons. Although the 1919 Montagu–Chelmsford reforms in India seemed to indicate that the Raj had only a limited existence left, elsewhere the British government asserted its imperial and sub-imperial interests with some vigour. During the immediate post-war period, revolts in Egypt and Iraq were briskly suppressed, and less threatening manifestations of local nationalism dealt with ruthlessly, as in the case of Somaliland, where the newly-established Royal Air Force bombed the 'Mad Mullah' into final submission.

Behind the brave front which the British Empire presented to the world, and despite the vast new territories brought under British rule, all was not well. The First World War had been won only with the aid of the United States of America, both in the form of its post-1917 military involvement and through the vast sums of money which had been loaned to pay for the British war effort. The City of London had been right in 1914 to express anxiety at Britain's involvement in the war. The cost of the successful prosecution of the conflict had been crippling. Huge quantities of overseas investments had been sold in order to pay for the manufactures of war and to enable Britain to import vast amounts of food and raw materials. The British government had borrowed enormous sums of money from the United States, some $3.7 billion, thus 'turning upside down the time-honoured financial relationship' between the two countries.[15] Britain was now a 'permanent debtor . . . making it impossible for London alone to continue as the principal effective financial centre of the world'.[16]

In addition to this, the huge casualties which had been suffered by British forces created a manpower shortage for the administration of the Empire. Nine per cent of all British adult males under the age of forty-five were killed in the fighting. Not merely did this deplete the administrative elite which issued from the public school system to exercise the nation's dominion over palm and pine, but it caused the morale of the survivors to plummet.

Despite appearances, imperial self-confidence had been waning since before the turn of the century. After the First World War, the will to hang on to imperial possessions was to some extent undermined. How could the post-World War Empire even be maintained, let alone expanded and developed? Paradoxically, as the Empire reached its greatest extent, the British government also made a number of concessions to nationalist movements that would have appeared unthinkable a decade earlier. In this fashion, southern Ireland was eventually, although only after a bitter conflict, granted dominion status as the Irish Free State in 1921; the Montagu–Chelmsford reforms in India extended the principle of responsible government to the provinces, where ministerial posts on the executive councils were divided up between Indian and British members, and where the executive body was 'responsible' to largely elected, Indian-dominated, legislative councils; the newly acquired mandate of Iraq obtained self-rule, subject to British 'advice' and the continuing presence of an RAF base, in 1922; in the same year, the protectorate of Egypt was, spuriously, declared to be 'independent'. Elsewhere the process of promoting local people to serve on legislative councils was speeded up.

Although this policy of surrender was dressed up as a programme of high-minded and judicious conciliation, this was only partly true. From the 1890s, perhaps from the 1870s, the expansion of the Empire had disguised the inexorable process of comparative British economic decline. Although in the post-First World War period the show went on, it now fooled less of the people, both in Britain and the Empire, for less of the time.

THE AMRITSAR MASSACRE
OF 1919

Gandhi, the Raj and the Growth of Indian Nationalism, 1915–39

ON 13 APRIL 1919, Indian Army troops led by Brigadier-General R.E.H. Dyer opened fire on a crowd of peaceful demonstrators in Amritsar, the holy city of the Sikhs in the Punjab. Dyer, who was so rigid and controlled a personality that he often seemed devoid of emotion, had calculated, almost to the last bullet, how long the Gurkha and Indian troops under his command should sustain their fire. Trapped within a walled yet open area, the Jallianwallabagh, and with the gates locked against their escape on British orders, the predominantly Sikh crowd numbering roughly 10,000 were subjected to one of the most brutal episodes in the history of the Raj. By the time Brigadier-General Dyer ordered his troops to cease firing, nearly four hundred Indians lay dead and more than a thousand had been wounded.

The Amritsar massacre, and the public floggings and humiliations imposed upon Indians under martial law between 11 April and 9 June 1919, produced reactions of shock and revulsion throughout the Empire, and indeed beyond. Although a Commission of Inquiry reprimanded Dyer for his actions at Amritsar, and revealed that he had neither warned the demonstrators that they must disperse nor made any attempt to offer medical assistance to the wounded, no legal action was taken against him. He was, nonetheless, eventually forced to take early retirement on half pay, although he went on to receive his army pension. The Commission of Inquiry did, however, condemn the public floggings of Indians for such offences as 'the contravention of the curfew order, failure to *salaam* [bow] to a commissioned officer, for disrespect to a European, for taking a commandeered car without leave, or refusal to sell milk, and for similar contraventions'.[1] The inquiry also found no evidence of the officially alleged but far-fetched conspiracy to subvert law and order by demonic anti-imperial forces tersely described as 'Bolsheviks and Egyptians'.

Indian nationalist leaders were quick to condemn the atrocity. Gandhi announced that any cooperation with this 'satanic regime' was now impossible. The distinguished writer Rabindranath Tagore, angered by the substantial vote in the British House of Lords against Dyer's forcible retirement on half pay, wrote: 'no outrage, however monstrous, committed against us by the agents of their government can arouse feelings of indignation in the hearts of those from whom our governors are chosen'. The young Jawaharlal Nehru, who had been educated at Harrow and Cambridge, was shocked by 'this cold-blooded approval of the deed', which he found 'absolutely immoral, indecent, to use public school language, it was the height of bad form'.

For many of the British living and serving in India, as well as those at home, the firm hand showed at Amritsar was welcomed. According to the writer Maud Diver:

> Organised revolt is amenable only to the ultimate argument of force. Nothing, now, would serve but strong action and the compelling power of martial law . . . At Amritsar strong action had already been taken . . . The sobering effect of it spread in widening circles, bringing relief to thousands of both races.[2]

For years representatives of the British in India had called for tough measures against nationalist agitation, especially acts of violence: 'The wholesale arrest of the acknowledged terrorists in a city or district coupled with an intimation that at any repetition of the offence ten of them would be shot for every life sacrificed, would soon put down the practice of throwing bombs.'[3] Some Europeans even went so far as to claim that large numbers of Indians – especially Muslim Punjabis with their tradition of rivalry with the Sikhs – were as relieved as themselves at Dyer's actions:

> No more trouble here or at Amritsar . . . Martial law arrangements are being carried through to admiration . . . and in no time the poor deluded beggars in the city were shouting – 'Martial law *ki jai!*' ['Long live martial law!'] – as fervently as ever they shouted for Gandhi and Co. One of

my fellows said to me; 'Our people don't understand this
new talk of *Committee ki raj* [government by committee] . . .
Too many orders make confusion. But they understand *Hukm
ki raj* [government by order].' In fact, it's the general opinion
that prompt action in the Punjab has fairly well steadied
India – for the present at least.[4]

Why had Brigadier-General Dyer chosen to perpetrate the massacre
in April 1919, and why did there appear to be so much support for it
among British opinion? The incident at Amritsar can be seen as a
response, admittedly a bloody and irresponsible one, to one of the most
widespread and effective demonstrations against British rule since the
Mutiny of 1857. From 6 April 1919, inspired by Gandhi's advocacy of
an 'all-India *satyagraha*', large numbers of Hindus and Muslims had
protested in a variety of ways against the Raj, and in particular against
the passing of the Rowlatt Acts, which continued the heavy state supervision and control of political activity that had been considered necessary during the war years from 1914 to 1918.

The ferocity of the British response in Amritsar to the Rowlatt
satyagraha arose directly from a series of violent incidents in the town
on 10 April, during which five European men had been killed and a
female missionary, Miss Sherwood, knocked off her bicycle, physically
assaulted and left for dead in the gutter. It is not difficult to see in
General Dyer's cold-blooded and ruthless massacre of unarmed and
peacefully demonstrating men, women and children yet another
example of the European male's tendency to violent overreaction in
response to a physical threat to a white female.

It was also significant that the Punjab, particularly its large towns
like Amritsar, had responded well to the call for nationwide demonstrations against British rule, and as a consequence had presented the
British with an unusual and unnerving display of Hindu-Muslim-Sikh
solidarity. The province had a particular significance in the history of
the Raj: it was not only one of the main granaries of India, but it also
provided a disproportionally large number of troops, both Sikhs and
Muslims, for the Indian Army, as well as many members of the police
force. Widespread demonstrations in the Punjab, therefore, were likely
to provoke excessive anxiety and hence the chance of overreaction
within British ranks.

Overriding all else, however, was the growing conviction of British
administrators and residents in India that Gandhi's apparent triumph

in tempting the Congress movement and other nationalist groups down the new path of *satyagraha* could strike a deadly blow at the heart of the British Raj.

On his return to India in 1915, after twenty-one years spent in South Africa leading Indian opposition to discriminatory legislation, Gandhi, the articulate barrister who had been called to the bar in London, had at first seemed the odd man out among the Europeanised, highly educated leaders of India's nationalist movements, chiefly because he had rejected Western dress and manners. The nationalist politician V.S.S. Sastri had observed: 'Queer food he eats; only fruit and nuts. No salt: milk-ghee etc being animal products avoided religiously. No fire should be necessary in the making of food, fire being unnatural ... The odd thing is he was dressed quite like a *bania* [a member of the trading and shopkeeping caste]: no one could mark the slightest difference.' A leading newspaper, the *Madras Mail*, gathered that:

> Mr Gandhi does not lay so much store by agitation for obtaining concessions from the Government as by working for the moral, material and economic regeneration of his countrymen, for he is of the opinion that once people make themselves fit by their character and capacity, the grant of privileges will follow as a matter of course – in fact, there will be no need for people to ask for the concessions, and what is granted will be no concessions, for people will have grown into them.[5]

Gandhi's rejection of Western education – which he now argued was a system designed to enslave and corrupt India – his opposition to the assimilation of Western scientific techniques, his advocacy and promotion of cottage industry, and his preference for the *ashram*, or religious retreat, rather than the factory or the college, ruffled many feathers. One of Gandhi's chief mentors on his return to India, the moderate nationalist leader and academic Professor Gokhale, believed that 'The greatest work of Western education in the present state of India is ... the liberation of the Indian mind from the thraldom of old-world ideas and the assimilation of all that is highest and best in the life and thought of the West.' The editor of the *Indian Social Reformer*, K. Natrajan, sprang to the defence of Western civilisation in the face of Gandhi's determined, calm and rational attacks, acknowledging that 'You may not agree with us that Western civilisation, taken as a whole, tends more strongly to justice for all than any other civilisation . . . Where we find, to our great regret, that we cannot follow you, is in your generalisation against the modern civilisation as such.'[6]

From his return to India in 1915 until 1917, Gandhi had spent much of his time travelling round the sub-continent, getting once more to know the homeland from which he had been absent for so long. In 1917, however, he had been persuaded to put his philosophy of *satyagraha*, tempered in the heat of South Africa's racial confrontations, into action in three local disputes. Despite some inconsistency in their effectiveness and results, the *satyagraha* campaigns at Champaran, Kheda and Ahmedabad during 1917 and 1918 had demonstrated the potential of the new Gandhian politics of passive civil disobedience and non-violent confrontation.

Satyagraha was also a potent weapon for other reasons. First, it offered no violent physical challenge to the Raj. This was just as well, for the British, through their patient construction of alliances with local collaborationist elites and groups, their playing-off of one section of Indian society against another, and the sheer scale of their military organisation and commitment, simply could not be defeated in face-to-face combat. But *satyagraha*, practised on a nationwide scale, could involve millions of ordinary Indian people in a series of peaceful demonstrations that could eventually undermine the Raj's authority and sap the British administration's will to rule. Finally, due mainly to the simplicity and quasi-religious qualities associated with *satyagraha*, Indian resistance to British rule could become for the first time a mass movement, not the preserve of a Western-educated elite wearing suits and ties and making speeches in English.

Gandhi had abandoned his Western dress as early as 1906 in South Africa. He now became, through his prominence in India, one of the most daunting, charismatic and at the same time paradoxical opponents of British imperialism. Shortly after his return in 1915, a Bombay police report concluded that although he was not a Bolshevik he was undoubtedly some sort of 'psychological case'. His renunciation of the material world, and of most earthly, physical pleasures, was also incomprehensible to many Westerners. Some concluded that he was simply a wily, and almost certainly hypocritical, political tactician. But for many people who observed him, whether Indians or Westerners, he had a particularly compelling personality. The British academic, socialist and political activist Harold Laski wrote, after meeting him:

It was fascinating to see Gandhi at work and try and penetrate his secret. It comes, I think, from what the Quakers
call the inner light – the power of internal self-confidence
which, having established its principles, is completely imper-
vious to reason. At bottom, it is an incredible egoism . . .
sweetened by an indescribable sweetness of temper. He is
also an amazing casuist, with a Jesuitical love of dubious
formulae which would be amusing if it might not so easily
become tragic. But the drama of this wizened little man
with the whole power of the empire against him is a terrific
spectacle. The basis of it all is, I think, the power of an ascetic
over Eastern minds who resent the feeling of inferiority they
have had for 150 years.[7]

As a result of his leadership of the Rowlatt *satyagraha* in 1919,
Gandhi ceased to be a peripheral, even ludicrous, figure on the margins
of nationalist politics, and within a few months had established himself,
often against fierce opposition, as an all-Indian leader of considerable
weight. The vehemence of Gandhi's rejection of the restrictive legislation contained in the Rowlatt Acts owed a great deal to the apparent
inconsistencies in British policy towards India. The Montagu Declaration of 1917, favouring the introduction of a significant measure of
responsible government, had seemed to prove that the Raj was prepared
to enter into a new and more intimate relationship with its Indian
subjects, preferring cooperation to control, and the devolution of political power to autocracy.

The Rowlatt legislation appeared to fly in the face of such high
intent. Gandhi denounced the proposals as 'evidence of a determined
policy of repression', and argued that Indians could not 'render a peaceful obedience to the laws of a power that is capable of such a piece of
devilish legislation'. When Britain betrayed what Gandhi believed to
be its essentially democratic principles in this way, the offence was
doubly compounded by Dyer's atrocity at Amritsar. Gandhi was not
alone in denouncing British hypocrisy, nor in discerning that behind
the fair face of the proposed Montagu-Chelmsford reforms lay the foul
and snarling face of a Mr Hyde.

The British policy of combining coercion with kindness was not, of
course, unique to the Indian situation in the aftermath of the First
World War. Ireland, as so often in the past, was undergoing a very
similar experience, and nationalist movements throughout the Empire

were to become familiar with the iron fist within the silken glove.

British policy in India was so full of contradictions for a very simple reason. The continuing, though declining, value of the Indian market to the British economy made it impossible abruptly to hand over power in any comprehensive way to the Indian people. Throughout the inter-war period, India remained the symbolic centrepiece of the imperial structure, despite the fact that the percentage of British trade with the sub-continent – which was, after all, the paramount reason for Britain's involvement in the first place – fell quite significantly, her net balance of trade in manufactures, for example, tumbling from a surplus of £75 million in 1924 to £22.7 million in 1937. Worse still, during the 1930s India consistently showed a surplus on her visible trade with the United Kingdom, and between 1929 and 1937 'Britain's competitive position declined to a greater extent in India than in the world as a whole'.[8] Nonetheless, for a whole variety of reasons, some of which were para-doxical and instinctive, almost tribal, few men or women prominent in British public life would have dissented from the view, first expressed by Lord Curzon in 1901, that the loss of India would mean that Britain would 'drop straight away to a third-rate power'.

After the First World War, however, it was no longer possible to sustain British control on the basis of the earlier self-confident and paternalistic imperialism epitomised by the viceroyalty of Curzon. British policy-makers attempted to solve the problem by doling out enough constitutional concessions to satisfy Indian nationalist aspir-ations, while retaining India as a central and intrinsic part of the imperial system. The fate of British rule in India was one of the most bitterly contested issues of the inter-war period. Many Conservative MPs were far more concerned about Indian issues in the late 1920s and early 1930s than they were about unemployment. The Conservative Prime Minister, Stanley Baldwin, eventually assumed an almost Glad-stonian sense of mission on the subject, and committed his party to a process of substantial Indian reform. India almost ruined the political career of Winston Churchill, who resigned the Tory whip over Indian reforms, not as is commonly supposed over the issue of rearmament. It was no exaggeration to see India as 'perhaps the central issue in parliamentary life'.[9]

Indian nationalists were therefore right to accuse the British govern-ment of hypocrisy. It is evident that, at least within the Conservative Party – which dominated nearly every House of Commons between 1918 and 1945 – there were elements which fought a persistent and relatively successful campaign against the granting of full independence to the sub-continent. Even the two minority Labour administrations of the inter-war period, either through their weak parliamentary position or as a result of the ambivalence within the party towards the granting of independence to India, were unable to do much of a practical nature to satisfy the demands of Indian nationalists.

It is quite legitimate to see the whole process of reform, from the Morley–Minto measures of 1908–09 to the establishment of provincial 'home rule' under the Government of India Act of 1935, as an adroit imperial strategy serving to disguise Britain's determination to hang on to India for as long as possible. The Montagu-Chelmsford reforms of 1919 can certainly be viewed in that light. On the surface, the concessions appeared substantial: three out of the seven ministers on the Viceroy's executive council were now Indian; the 1919 Government of India Act considerably enlarged the Indian electorate, creating Indian majorities in the great provincial councils; in the provincial governments, administrations ruling huge regions like Bengal, the United Provinces or Madras, a system of diarchy was introduced whereby Indian and British ministers shared ministerial office.

These constitutional advances were, however, at least partly illusory. Under the system of diarchy, Indian ministers were only given 'safe' portfolios such as education, public health, agriculture and irrigation, whereas British ministers held key offices, necessary to the control of the state, like justice, police, and revenue. Even if this had not been the case, the Viceroy, who was British, could veto legislation passed in the provincial legislatures, suspend provincial councils and if necessary rule as an autocrat with the backing of the armed services, a situation which remained the case right up to independence in 1947.

It is also arguable that the steady devolution of power, both at central and provincial government level, was essentially a device to bind even greater numbers of India's elites and educated groups to the status quo. Indian ministers and council members would acquire the taste for office and local influence, and seek to preserve rather than to destroy the constitutional structure which delivered these advantages to them. Ironically, therefore, democracy became the means by which a fundamentally autocratic British Raj could be almost indefinitely sustained in power.

Constitutional devolution seemed to offer the British a further advantage: the responsibilities and opportunities to which Indians could now aspire, in local as well as central government, enhanced the chances of communal, provincial and ethnic rivalry. Essentially the British had no need to 'divide and rule' in their Indian empire: India was sufficiently divided to begin with. All that was necessary was for the Raj patiently and skilfully to utilise and exploit the gaping divisions within Indian society. The process of constitutional reform offered opportunities to exploit such differences, as in the creation of a separate Muslim electoral roll in the 1909 Indian Councils Act, a move which was ultimately to bear the bitter fruit of Muslim separatism and the partition of the sub-continent in 1947.

The way in which the British authorities in India gave with the one hand and took away with the other is neatly illustrated by the viceroyalty of Lord Reading, from 1921 to 1926. Arriving in India as the Gandhian-led non-cooperation movement was running into difficulties, Reading set out to drive a wedge between India's two main religious groups, the Hindus and the Muslims, who had achieved a surprising level of cooperation in their campaign against the Raj since the political accord established between Congress and the Muslim League as a result of the Lucknow Pact of 1916. Reading held a series of informal meetings with Gandhi, hoping to persuade him to renounce the violent political activity associated with some Muslim nationalists. Violent political action was anathema to Gandhi, and he agreed to the Viceroy's request that he should obtain a commitment from two leading Muslim activists, the Ali brothers, that they would cease their incitements to violence and apologise publicly for their earlier provocation. Although the Ali brothers soon retracted their apology, and Gandhi resumed his offensive against the Raj, Reading had at least begun to engineer a 'collapse of the bridge over the gulf between Muslim and Hindu'.

The Reading–Gandhi meetings were an indication of the British authorities' belief that, for all the trouble he was causing, Gandhi, through his consistent opposition to violent action, was a nationalist leader with whom business could be done. Reading was also offered the clearest explanation as to why Indian nationalism remained suspicious of the Raj's reforms. As he recounted to the Prime Minister, Lloyd George:

> I asked the question point blank: 'What is it in the actions of the government that makes you pursue the policy of non-cooperation with the Government?'
> The answer, repeated more than once during our inter-

views, was that he was filled with distrust of the Government and that all their actions, even though apparently good, made him suspect their motives. I pressed him to be more precise, and eventually he stated that he had some time ago arrived at the conclusion that every action of the Government which appeared good, and indeed was good, was actuated by the sinister motive of trying to fasten British dominion on India. This was his answer to all the arguments about the new reformed Councils, and in my judgement is the root cause of his present attitude to the Government.[10]

Gandhi's astute view of British motives was shared by many other Indian nationalists. Yet it was still possible to see the better, more constructive side of the inter-war process of reform. By the mid-1920s the Raj had committed itself to a policy of Indianisation for the civil service, the police and the Indian Army that could be interpreted as a practical gesture of good intent. The rate of progress for these reforms was, admittedly, slow: the 1924 Royal Commission on Indianisation recommended that the Indian Civil Service should be half Indian within fifteen years, by 1939, and that the police force should become half Indian within twenty-five years, that is by 1949. The Indianisation of the army was a far more contentious issue, for obvious reasons. A number of proposals were rejected by the British government, and opposed by high-ranking British officers within the Indian Army, but an eventual compromise was reached by 1926, when it was agreed that the Indian Army would be half-Indianised by 1952.[11] Unlikely as these proposals were to satisfy Indian nationalists, the plans for the Indianisation of the Indian Civil Service certainly had the effect of frightening off British recruits. As early as 1919 the numbers of British applicants who wished to join the ICS fell away dramatically. This was a development of considerable significance. The freshly-graduated products of Oxbridge and the British public school system were thus plainly indicating in 1919 that they believed India held no long-term career prospects for them. That members of Britain's ruling elite so self-evidently believed that the game was up in India must be set against the contra-indication that the British government, British industry and British investors were conspiring to fight a rearguard and covert action against Indian demands for self-rule.

The period between the effective introduction of the diarchy system in 1921 and the outbreak of the Second World War in 1939 was beset by all the contradiction, confusion and tension that had characterised the previous two decades of Indian history. A majority of the mainstream, Hindu-dominated Congress Party opposed what they described as 'council-entry', and a minority broke away to form the *Swaraj* – or 'self-rule' – Party, and sought separate representation in the central and provincial legislatures. For a while a Swarajist majority attempted to obstruct the work of the central legislature, but the government of India, which was not responsible to that body, carried on regardless.

As a result of these and other antics, the Conservative Secretary of State for India, Lord Birkenhead, ridiculed the idea of a responsible system of government at the centre, and stated that it was 'frankly inconceivable that India would ever be fit for Dominion self-government'. Indian sensitivities were further inflamed by Birkenhead's decision to appoint a Statutory Commission to investigate the workings of the 1919 reforms. In an act of monumental tactlessness, or perhaps as an indication of Birkenhead's low opinion of Indian capacities, the Commission, under the chairmanship of Sir John Simon, chose not to appoint any Indian members. In response to this slight, a committee under Motilal Nehru, the father of Jawaharlal, produced an alternative report which demanded immediate self-government within the British Commonwealth.

During 1929 the second Labour minority government came to office. Labour's more conciliatory and generous policy towards India's constitutional aspirations enabled the Viceroy, Lord Irwin, a high-minded high Tory, to make an unequivocal gesture of friendship towards India and 'so to restore faith in the ultimate purpose of British policy'. This conciliatory gesture included a clear statement, the Irwin Declaration, that the natural end of India's constitutional progress, as contemplated in the Montagu declaration of 1917, was the attainment of dominion status.[12] The second concession to Indian nationalism took the form of an announcement in October 1929 of a Round Table Conference, at which the Princely States and all sections of opinion in British India would be represented, to discuss the means of achieving further constitutional reform in the sub-continent.

It is possible, of course, to see the Irwin Declaration as yet another ploy to confuse the forces of Indian nationalism and to subvert, rather than advance, the programme of constitutional reform. Privately, Irwin admitted that regarding dominion status, the 'realisation of the aspiration is not in sight'.[13] This private judgement was almost certainly a reflection of the fact that by 1929 the term 'dominion status' had come to mean something substantially different from even three years earlier. At the Imperial Conference of 1926, the Balfour definition of dominion status had been hammered out; as a result, and despite the ambiguities of the definition, the dominions could now claim to be truly independent nations upon the world's stage and could, if they so desired, secede from the Empire itself. Such rights and privileges were certainly not likely to be handed over to the Indian empire in the immediate future.

British conservatives and diehards had no need to worry. Congress soon tumbled to the fact that dominion status was still well beyond their reach. It therefore decided to boycott the Round Table Conference of 1930, and in March of that year Gandhi launched a new, almost revivalist, civil disobedience campaign culminating in the Dandi Salt March, in defiance of the Raj's salt monopoly. Jawaharlal Nehru and other radical nationalists began to argue that even dominion status in its revised meaning no longer satisfied their definition of *Swaraj*.

Irwin's hopes of allaying Indian suspicions of British intentions were dealt a further blow by the angry reactions in the British Parliament to the possibility of granting India dominion status. The Tory diehards, in particular, already embittered by what they regarded as the surrender of the Anglo–Irish Treaty of 1921 which had partitioned Ireland and resulted in the establishment of the Irish Free State, were determined to oppose any similar process with regard to the Indian empire. Any concessions to Indian demands were dismissed as weakness and an indication of national defeatism and decline. Winston Churchill even declared, 'We are suffering from a disease of the will. We are the victims of nervous collapse, of a morbid state of mind.'[14]

Some of the passions and anxieties which had so bedevilled the Irish Home Rule crisis of the mid-1880s now resurfaced. Churchill, and those who thought like him, warned that any British surrender to Indian nationalism would strip Britain of her 'moral authority' to govern her Empire. If Britain's mission in the East should thus be seen to fail, then the collapse of the Empire would result, as night followed day. Within the Indian administration itself, the Home Member of the Viceroy's Executive Council similarly expressed his anxieties that the 'Government may not be retaining that essential moral superiority which is perhaps the most important factor in this struggle'.[15] Many who shared such views argued that any future constitutional progress in India should only take place after a lengthy display of British resolve and firmness which would re-establish the moral authority of the Raj in the face of Indian agitation.

The minority Labour government, which had set up the first Round Table Conference in 1930, fell from office in 1931, a victim of the panic which engulfed the British political and financial establishment in the wake of the Wall Street crash of 1929 and the onset of the Great Depression. An administration of national unity, known as the National Government, took over, led by the outgoing Labour Prime Minister, Ramsay MacDonald, and composed of senior representatives of all three major parties. Although the Conservatives were the senior partners in this peacetime coalition, they came to accept the principle, most weightily and eloquently articulated by Stanley Baldwin, that government in India must be based upon the assent of the governed. Baldwin put it bluntly in a speech which was to be unashamedly echoed by Harold Macmillan in Cape Town a quarter of a century later:

> We have taught [India] the lesson [of democracy] and she wants us to pay the bill. There is a wind of nationalism and freedom blowing around the world and blowing as strongly in Asia as anywhere else in the world.[16]

Despite this acknowledgement of the strength of Indian opinion, it was the British who still determined the pace of constitutional change. Out of the three Round Table Conferences of the early 1930s, the White Paper of 1933, and the Joint Select Parliamentary Committee of 1933, was born the Government of India Act of 1935. The scheme which emerged was of daunting complexity, appropriately enough in view of the fact that the parliamentary debates preceding it comprised nearly 2000 speeches totalling 15½ million words. The 1935 Act was meant to please and accommodate everybody: to secure the cooperation of the Indian princes, to afford sufficient recognition of the communal principle to satisfy the Muslims and other religious minorities, to make enough concessions to the principle of self-government to appease the nationalists, and to include sufficient safeguards to placate British imperialists.

In essence, the 1935 Act proposed to replace the system of diarchy with responsible government in the provinces; diarchy, however, would make a reappearance at the centre, where a federal executive of responsible ministers would control the whole administration, save for defence and foreign affairs, which would remain the prerogative of the Viceroy and his nominees. Eventually a federation of India would be established.

Designed to please everybody, the Act pleased nobody. Despite Gandhi's participation in the second Round Table Conference and his earlier pact with Lord Irwin, radical nationalists were not satisfied. Civil disobedience was resumed in 1932, although Irwin's successor as Viceroy, Lord Willingdon, managed to contain it. While the Indian princes paid lip-service to the idea of a future federation, few imagined that they would be willing to surrender their power and privileges, or to acknowledge the supremacy of a democratically elected central government. Although most Muslims supported Congress rather than the Muslim League, there was growing anxiety at the prospect of a Hindu Raj. British liberals and radicals were frustrated at the lack of Indian nationalist support for the 1935 Act. British diehards thought that far too much had been surrendered already, and Churchill denounced the Irwin–Gandhi pact and expressed his distaste at the spectacle of:

> a seditious Middle Temple lawyer, now posing as a fakir of a type well-known in the East, striding half-naked up the steps of the Viceregal Palace . . . there to negotiate and to parley on equal terms with the Representative of the King-Emperor.[17]

In 1937 the first provincial elections to be held under the 1935 Act produced stunning Congress victories, with absolute majorities in six of the eleven provinces in British India and the largest single share of the vote in three more. Congress claimed that the scale of their victories confirmed them as the chief political organisation representing the Indian people as a whole. Among Muslim separatists, however, the electoral success of Congress sharpened their anxieties at the prospect of a Congress, Hindu-dominated, Raj. In the elections, the Muslim League performed poorly, and most Muslim voters chose to support representatives of their faith within the Congress Party. Jawaharlal Nehru was quick to announce that the forces of communalism, as well as those of imperialism and feudalism, had been vanquished. But as Congress ministries took power in the provinces they were obliged to face up to new challenges, including those of honouring some of the wider, reforming promises made to the electorate. It was no longer possible simply to blame the Raj for poverty, poor health facilities, insufficient food and unemployment. In the provinces at least, Congress was effectively the Raj, and would be judged accordingly.

During the election campaign of 1937, Congress, confident of victory, had rejected any notion of power-sharing with the Muslim League. The leader of the League, Mohamed Ali Jinnah, previously a Congress stalwart, bitterly resented his exclusion from power, and began to campaign to rally Muslims to the cause of communal politics. By the outbreak of war in 1939, he had gone some way to achieve his objective, and the resignation of Congress ministries at the start of hostilities, in protest at what seemed to be an insulting lack of British consultation over automatically committing India to the conflict, was celebrated by many Muslims as 'Deliverance Day'.

When war broke out, there were few who doubted that India would gain independence in the immediate future. A London journalist wrote in 1940: 'The diehards are extinct, public opinion is united in desiring India to obtain her independence just as soon as it can be arranged.'[18] The progress of the war, however, was not merely to derail the programme of constitutional devolution and reform, but so to alter the rules of the game that the final granting of independence to the Indian empire took a form which few would have predicted in the inter-war period.

Brigadier-General Dyer, whose action at Amritsar in 1919 had so inflamed Indian opinion, died shortly before the outbreak of the war, still enjoying the affirmation of many old India hands, but also expressing some overdue doubts about the episode that had ruined his career. Lying paralysed by a stroke, he told his daughter-in-law, 'I don't want to get better. I only want to die, and to know from my Maker whether I did right or wrong.'[19] He was outlived by only a few months by Sir Michael O'Dwyer who, as Governor of the Punjab at the time of the Amritsar massacre, had also aroused passionate nationalist hostility. O'Dwyer's death, however, was far more violent – and, in the eyes of some, more appropriate – than Dyer's: he was shot dead at close range by an Indian assassin in 1940.

21

<hr>

THE 1924 BRITISH EMPIRE
WEMBLEY EXHIBITION

Selling and Buying the Empire-Commonwealth
in the Inter-War Years

IN THE SPRING OF 1924 one of the greatest exhibitions in British
history was opened in Wembley. Its proclaimed aim was to celebrate the
achievements of an Empire which had reached its greatest geographical
extent with the addition of the mandated territories at the end of the
First World War.

The site of the exhibition, set in a previously unfashionable north
London suburb, covered some 220 acres. A huge exhibition complex
was constructed: concrete and steel pavilions to house the exhibits of
the dominions, India and the colonies; new roads with 'imperial' names
carefully chosen by Rudyard Kipling, such as Drake's Way, Commonwealth Way and Anson's Way; there was also a great stadium, later
acquired by the Football Association.

Roads had been systematically widened in the Wembley neighbour-
hood, partly in anticipation of the flood of visitors, cars and buses. Over
2000 workers had been employed to build the pavilions, extend the
transport facilities and construct the stadium complex. A few weeks
before the exhibition was due to open, the building workers staged
a brief strike for extra pay amounting to tuppence an hour. In
true imperial style, substantial numbers of police were moved in to
ensure that those wishing to work could do so. Union officials,
however, declared the strike unofficial, and the dispute was quickly
ended.

Wembley stadium had already staged its first, chaotic and overcrowded Cup Final in 1923. The stadium and its ancillary buildings
stood on the site of the old Wembley tower, took three hundred working

days to build – at a cost of £750,000 – and were made with the new technique of concrete reinforced with steel. Two hundred and fifty tons of clay were excavated, one and a half thousand tons of steel were used, twenty-five thousand tons of concrete, and half a million rivets.

The majority of the exhibition's buildings were also constructed out of concrete. There were pavilions representing many of the Empire's countries; the Australian pavilion was gigantic, as large as the whole of Olympia. There was also an Amusement Park, as well as Palaces of Art, Engineering and Industry, and the Government Building. The Amusement Park covered forty-seven acres and included a Mountain Water Chute, a Scenic Railway, a Toboggan Ice Slide and a Giant Switchback. Cynics suspected that the majority of visitors preferred the Amusement Park, with its American-style dodgems, to the displays of imperial products and achievements. Noël Coward wittily expressed this misgiving when he had the father in *This Happy Breed* complain: 'I've brought you here to see the wonders of the Empire, and all you want to do is go to the dodgems.'

Admission was one shilling and sixpence for adults and nine pence for children. The visitors poured in, 27,403,267 during the two years the exhibition was open. They came in their millions by the Metropolitan Railway, the Great Central Railway and by the London and North-Eastern Railway Company. The London General Omnibus Company carried 4,301,814 passengers, and the trams brought in another 2,500,000. A special station was opened in the exhibition's grounds. Inside, there was the Never-Stop Railway, the Road-Rail and the Railo-dock cars.

Once inside the exhibition it was not just a matter of gawping at the strange animals from the Empire, viewing the displays of Hong Kong, Fiji and West Africa, or admiring the model of the Prince of Wales made from Canadian butter, or the lavish displays of Australian fruit. Visitors could also see re-enactments of First World War encounters, with the Battle of Ypres and the Storming of Zeebrugge being among the most popular. The Military Tattoos were watched by 660,000 people. There was also a Rodeo which attracted an overall attendance of 812,629, but which was attacked by the RSPCA and the *Star* newspaper for its cruelty to animals, and was finally taken to court. More than 100,000 spectators saw the fireworks, and the Imperial Scout Jamboree was attended by 75,039 people.

There was, in addition, a 'Pageant of Empire'. This event ran from 21 July to 30 August and was staged in three parts, entrance one shilling.

Among the tableaux enacted were George III Bidding Farewell to Captain Cook, Imperial Sylvan Scenes, and Admiral Blake and the Barbary Pirates, as well as pageants for Australia, Canada, New Zealand, South Africa and other countries. The Finale consisted of Alfred Noyes' 'The British Empire March (A Song of Union)', whose verses included:

> *O island heart of all the sea*
> *Though cloud and storm beset thee,*
> *Thy children nations turn to thee!*
> *Could even our dreams forget thee?*
> *Then rise, diviner light;*
> *Shine on Earth's long night;*
> *Rise, heaven's triumphant Sun;*
> *And bind all hearts, all realms, in one.*[1]

Twenty-seven million visitors, equivalent to over half of the British population, saw the exhibition, some of them going several times. Among the enduring impressions they took home with them were the sheer size of the undertaking; the pavilions and buildings made of ferro-concrete; the throngs of foreigners, some of them black or brown, who packed the exhibition; the impossibility of seeing everything on display in a week, let alone a day; and the bewildering variety of imperial produce, flora and fauna exhibited.

The British Empire Exhibition at Wembley cost proportionally more to build and maintain, given the relative value of the pound sterling, than the Great Exhibition of 1851. It was also on a larger scale and was attended by four times as many people. In all it cost over £11 million to stage the event, of which nearly £10 million was put up by commercial enterprises and the balance provided by a government-backed Guarantee Fund of £1,207,991 to which Empire governments also contributed. Nonetheless, the exhibition lost money heavily, to the tune of £1.8 million, even though it was staged again in 1925 in an attempt to break even. The Colonial Office would have frowned on such prodigality on the part of an imperial dependency.

But then, the exhibition was partly a celebration of the imperial achievement, partly a gigantic advertisement for the Empire – which was meant to boost trade – and partly an exercise in reassurance. Amid the uncertainties of the post-war world, the exhibition was an act of faith, almost an act of defiance.

When King George V opened it on St George's Day, 23 April 1924, he declared in a speech that was his first to be broadcast:

This great achievement reveals to us the whole Empire in little, containing within its grounds a vivid model of the architecture, art, and industry of all the races which come under the British flag. We believe the Exhibition will bring the peoples of the Empire to a better knowledge of how to meet their reciprocal wants and aspirations; and we hope further that the success of the Exhibition may bring lasting benefits not to the Empire only, but to mankind in general.

Even by the appallingly low standards of contemporary royal speeches, this was an offering of platitudinous and mind-numbing predictability. It was also a self-serving piece of official hypocrisy: most of the subjects of the Empire had no 'reciprocal wants and aspirations' that would be remotely acceptable to the British government, or, indeed, to most of the dominions.

The King, in the words of his speech writers, was fundamentally asking the peoples of the Empire to stay loyal and to 'buy British' as never before. There was little expectation that the 'lasting benefits' of which he spoke would include the universal franchise, the elimination of illiteracy, a rigorous assault on disease and disability, or the ending of racial discrimination. Lord Milner was more candid when he saw that the scientific, technological and commercial displays at Wembley, if properly utilised, would help provide a 'powerful bulwark' against imperial decline and decay.

The idea of holding a great Empire Exhibition had first been proposed in 1902 by the British Empire League. There were two main reasons why it took twenty years to make the proposal concrete. The most mundane of these was the need of the Football Association to find a prestigious new venue for their annual showpiece, the FA Cup Final, as well as for international matches. Since most British males had a deeper knowledge of football than of the British Empire, and probably more commitment to it as well, this had the effect of miraculously concentrating the official mind. When Wembley's first FA Cup Final was staged in 1923, it provided excellent advance publicity for the more lavish show held a year later.

The more pressing and weighty reason for staging the exhibition, however, was the need to promote and reinterpret the imperial ideal amid the fresh challenges of the post-war world. Having survived the horrific slaughter of the First World War – 'the Great War' – the public mood seemed to be more volatile, and to swing between the frivolous cynicism of the 'flapper' generation and the dogged resignation of their elders. The two leading members of the Royal Family apparently gave neat expression to these extremes: the Prince of Wales, dashing, fashionable, glamorous and worldly, personified the new generation; George V, dull, unimaginative, hard-working and devoted to his stamp collection and his stiff-backed wife, personified the older generation. As is so often the case, image and reality were at odds: the Prince of Wales was riddled with insecurity, which manifested itself in a range of nervous tics and mannerisms, and in his passion for older women rather than 'bright young things'; the King was more able to grasp the big idea, even if it often turned to dross in his hands.

In any event, idealism appeared generally to be in short supply. This was where the Empire came in. The old themes of late-nineteenth-century 'New Imperialism' could be reworked both to inspire a new generation and to give reassurance and solace to their elders. The Wembley Exhibition would be the launch-pad and selling-point of the enterprise.

By the early 1920s the British Empire seemed beset by many problems, not least within Britain itself. The old European order had been severely damaged, and in some cases destroyed, by the war. At home the hereditary ruling class no longer had quite the same faith in itself, or even in the imperial mission. The rise of the Labour Party at the expense of the Liberals, moreover, had apparently established a new play of domestic political forces. This turned out to be largely an illusion: when Ramsay MacDonald formed the first, minority Labour administration in 1924, he was no more enthusiastic than Winston Churchill in 1940 to preside over the dissolution of the British Empire; and the trade union wing of the party still tended to equate imperial power and possession with full employment and sufficiency at home. In theory, however, the Labour Party was committed to the cause of colonial freedom, and in office gave some discreet nudges in that direction.

The dominions, although they did not all agree as to ways and means, were as a group now inclined to see themselves as independent nations. Yet they remained in the Empire. Prior to the resolution of this dilemma at the 1926 Imperial Conference, a way was found round the problem, part fudge, part acknowledgement of reality. In official terminology, the British Empire became the British Empire and Commonwealth, or, for brevity, the Empire-Commonwealth. This at least recognised the existing two-tier system: India and the dependencies were in the Empire; the dominions – Canada, Newfoundland,

Australia, New Zealand, South Africa and the Irish Free State – were also members of the Commonwealth; oddly enough, so was Britain.

As a rallying-cry, 'Commonwealth' lacked the glamour and resonance of 'Empire' – but it also lacked its darker reputation and its autocratic overtones. 'Commonwealth' evoked images of mature and sober cooperation rather than of proud self-assertion. Writers did not rush to offer their publishers books entitled *Deeds that Won the Commonwealth*, and cinema audiences never queued for tickets at 'The Commonwealth', Leicester Square.

Despite the ambition of Lloyd George to carry the high level of inter-imperial wartime cooperation into the post-war period, nothing permanent had come of it. The peace negotiations artificially prolonged the life of the Imperial War Cabinet under the auspices of the British Empire delegation to the peace conferences. But once the negotiations were completed, the dominion premiers went home to their domestic chores. India became once more a potentially explosive dependency rather than a docile and esteemed wartime partner. Without its temporary Empire members, the British War Cabinet returned to its old peacetime structure and responsibilities.

At the next Imperial Conference, held in 1921, Lloyd George mounted an almost desperate effort to resurrect the wartime imperial model by describing the gathering as an 'Imperial Peace Cabinet'. 'Today,' he proclaimed with breathtaking hyperbole, 'the Empire is in charge of Downing Street.'[2] In a sense he was right, although not in the way he intended.

The dominions were, for the most part, anxious to reassert their self-governing identity, and not to be dragged into a more formal and possibly inconvenient relationship with the British government. As a result, the proposal made in 1917 for a post-war conference to define dominion status was abandoned. Not that the dominion prime ministers unanimously agreed about the ditching of the plan. Smuts, eager to placate his Afrikaner nationalist critics, wanted a 'declaration of constitutional rights'. For more traditionalist Australia, Billy Hughes argued that the proposed constitutional conference was unnecessary since the dominions already had 'all the rights of independent nations'. When his view prevailed, Hughes triumphantly cabled the news to his colleagues in Australia: 'The constitutional tinkers are securely soldered up in their own can.'[3]

In the matter of post-war foreign policy, the dominions initially appeared to be more at one with each other and, more importantly, with Britain. To some extent this was a reflection of their lack of muscle in the world arena; they simply did not have the military and naval resources to pursue an independent line in foreign policy. During the 1921 Imperial Conference, Hughes of Australia urged the cause of imperial unity and the need for closer cooperation, and was reported as saying that:

> The dominions and Great Britain were still one and indivisible; it was essential that British foreign policy should be moulded by the Empire as a whole and not by Great Britain alone.[4]

Although the 1921 conference appeared to have reached agreement on a common imperial position on the vital matter of naval armaments, which were to be discussed at the imminent Washington Conference of 1921–22, this was an illusion. At the negotiations in Washington, involving the main victorious Allied naval powers – the British Empire, France, Japan and the United States – a sharp disagreement arose between Australia and Canada over the issue of whether to renew the Anglo–Japanese alliance. The Australians, increasingly wary of the rising power of Japan in South-East Asia, wished to retain the alliance as a guarantee of their own security; Canada, on the other hand, anxious to please the United States, and secure in its North American stronghold, wished to abandon the treaty.

The Washington Conference eventually produced a vaguely-worded pact between the British Empire, the United States, Japan and France which was optimistically perceived as replacing, at least in spirit, the old Anglo–Japanese alliance; at the same time a formal treaty dealing with naval arms limitation came up with a formula specifying a 5:5:3 ratio between the British Empire, the USA and Japan. The British government also went some way towards reassuring Australia and New Zealand by the commitment to establish a powerful new naval base at Singapore; but equally, Lord Jellicoe's proposal to create a Commonwealth Far Eastern fleet got nowhere.

Any lingering hopes that a common imperial foreign and defence policy was attainable were finally killed off by the Chanak incident of 1922. A confrontation between Britain and Turkey at Chanak, a vital strategic point on the straits separating Europe from Asia Minor, seemed at first sight to be a straightforward affair: the advancing Turkish forces menaced boundaries drawn up at the 1919 peace conferences; Britain wished to uphold them. An impulsive appeal for dominion assistance was made by both Lloyd George and Churchill – both, it must be said, men of impulse as well as genius. The dominions, however, were divided in their response. Australia and New Zealand, still so heavily dependent upon British naval and military aid, promptly offered help. The Canadian government, though, referred its decision to the Canadian Parliament; South Africa did not even reply to the British call to arms; the newly-established Irish Free State was not in a position even to be asked. In the eventual renegotiations of the peace settlement with Turkey, finalised at Lausanne in 1923, the Turks gained substantial concessions, mostly at the expense of Greece, including the straits, Chanak and East Thrace; they thus ended up with all the territory they had held in 1914.

British pretences that a unified Empire foreign policy existed now lay in ruins. The matter was taken up with some care at the 1926 Imperial Conference. At the first post-Chanak conference in 1923, however, the published summary of the proceedings unequivocally affirmed the non-executive nature of the gathering, and explicitly addressed the issue of foreign policy:

> The conference is a conference of representatives of the several governments of the Empire; its views and conclusions on foreign policy are necessarily subject to the actions of the Governments and Parliaments of the various portions of the Empire . . .[5]

As Chamberlain had predicted during the Tariff Reform campaign two decades earlier, there was one area of growth in inter-imperial activity – that of trade. The importance of Britain's trade with the Empire, particularly with the dominions, was markedly increasing in the early 1920s. The interlocking and interdependent commercial system, so passionately desired by imperialists, had been expanding rapidly before 1914, and continued to grow promisingly after 1918. By 1924 the balance of trade in British manufactures showed a surplus of £262 million with the Empire as a whole. Within this total there was a surplus of £75 million with India, of £120.6 million with the dominions, and of £76.5 million with the rest of the Empire. Between 1925 and 1929, the Empire was taking 37.2 per cent of all British exports – chiefly manufactured goods (of which the dominions received 20.6 per cent), and Britain was receiving from the whole Empire imports – mainly of food and raw materials – totalling 32.9 per cent, including 16.9 per cent from the dominions.[6]

Several points need emphasising in assessing these statistics. The first is the remarkable improvement in the surplus of trade with the dominions. This trend was, however, not sustained during the 1930s, even after the introduction of a system of imperial preference at the Ottawa Conference of 1932. The Great Depression played its part in this, with the resulting contraction of world markets. By 1937 the surplus on the balance of trade in manufactures which Britain enjoyed with the dominions had shrunk from £120.6 million in 1924 to £83.2 million. In the case of its trade in manufactures with Canada, Britain actually began trading at a deficit during the 1930s. Trade in manufactures with India suffered a very sharp decline, falling from a surplus of £75 million in 1924 to £22.7 million by 1937 – a reflection in part of the success of the Indian nationalist campaign to boycott British textiles. The surplus on trade in manufactures with the whole Empire was more than halved during the same period. Although there was the apparently encouraging increase between 1925–29 and 1934–38 of the proportion of British exports to the Empire as a whole from 32.9 per cent to 41.2 per cent, this was offset by a similar increase in Empire exports to Britain, leaving the Mother Country with a small deficit of £100,000.[7]

Despite these setbacks, however, one fact was plain – the proportion of Britain's trade with the Empire was increasing during the inter-war period, and in this sense the 1924 Exhibition had caught a trend and arguably enhanced it. The introduction of the Empire Marketing Board in 1926 was an indication of the government's intent to stimulate inter-imperial trade through advertising and promotional activities as vigorously as possible. Although the board was abolished in 1933, a year after the Ottawa Conference had set up a system of imperial preferential trading agreements, its establishment was symptomatic of the hopes invested in the expansion of the Empire's commerce. It had been preceded by a number of imperial trading pressure groups, including the British Empire Producers Organisation, founded in 1916; the British Commonwealth Union and the Empire Resources Development Committee, both also set up in 1916; the Empire Parliamentary Development Committee, 1921; the Empire Development Union, 1922; and the Empire Industries Association of 1924. All of this bears witness to the importance attached to the Empire-Commonwealth as a trading bloc.

The initiative to set up the Empire Marketing Board came from Leo Amery, formerly one of Milner's 'young men' in South Africa, and Colonial and Dominions Secretary of State in the Conservative government between 1924 and 1929. Amery also established a Colonial

Medical Research Council in 1927, and a little later an Agricultural Advisory Council. A devoted disciple of Joseph Chamberlain, as well as of Milner, he was now able to push ahead with policies earlier advocated by his mentors. In a speech in 1925, Amery virtually regurgitated Chamberlain's 'underdeveloped estates of the realm' appeal of the late 1890s: 'The economic possibilities for us in the development of the tropical Empire are perhaps greater than those available to us anywhere else in the world. We have these immense territories with immense natural resources.'[8]

Amery was unable, however, to prise funds out of the Conservative government in order to give substance to his development plans. It was left to the Labour administration of 1929–31 to introduce the 1929 Colonial Welfare and Development Act, which, for the first time since Joseph Chamberlain's isolated West Indian aid package at the turn of the century, provided regular sums for colonial development. Although an important precedent had been established in 1929, the £1 million initially provided was a paltry amount, and some observers believed that the Act was partly designed to benefit the British economy through enabling colonial governments to buy British products.[9]

In the light of the increasing value and economic potential of the Empire, the 1920s saw a number of initiatives designed to promote imperial solidarity and fellow-feeling. One of the most promising of the 'new links with Empire' was the radio. In 1922 six manufacturers of radio equipment had contributed £100,000 to found the British Broadcasting Company, and the 'wonderful wireless' had entered half a million homes by the end of the BBC's first year in operation.

'Here indeed,' said King George on being presented with a receiver especially built for him by the BBC's Chief Engineer, 'is a machine that can work the miracle of communication between me and my people in far-off places.' George V, who tended to be unimaginative, accepted the scientific effectiveness of the new contrivance without question. The Archbishop of Canterbury, on the other hand, found it most mysterious and asked if he would have to leave the windows open 'to let the waves in'; despite this, he was pleased with the possibility, 'when the wireless is out of its infancy', of a church service being 'broadcasted'.

At the opening of the Wembley Exhibition the BBC's microphone was suspended a few inches to the right of the King's head, and through it his voice was carried by land-line to the Marconi transmitting station at Chelmsford. The leader writer of the *Daily Mail* was properly impressed: 'Never before has a King's voice been heard by his subjects both in his presence and in their own homes as well – to the tune of perhaps a million homes. Such a miracle can do nothing but cement the bonds of Empire.'

To further bind the Empire more closely together, a gramophone record of the King's broadcast was made. The Gramophone Company, trade-name His Master's Voice, recorded it by their new 'electrical' method, and that same night hundreds of pressings of it were rushed by special messenger to Croydon to be flown to every corner of the Empire.

After the Exhibition, the 'wonderful wireless' continued to make great strides as a link with Empire. On Armistice Day 1927, the BBC's Chief Announcer, Stuart Hibberd, introduced the beginning of the relay of the British Legion Rally at the Albert Hall in a new form: 'This is the British Broadcasting Corporation calling the British Isles, the British Empire, the United States of America and the continent of Europe from London, England, through Daventry 5 XX and Chelmsford 5 SW.'

The potential of the radio for drawing the people of the Empire closer together was widely accepted. Broadcasting, as the *Daily Mirror* said, 'brought the mother country's voice into the Australian shearing shed, the Indian plantation and the Canadian ranch-house alike'.

In the mid-1920s only the United States had the apparatus necessary to relay the broadcast on its own network, but it was only a matter of time before countries within the Empire were able to do the same. The *Morning Post* declared confidently, 'In spirit, the peoples of the Empire have never been divided. But now the miracle of wireless has brought us all into each other's homes.'

The BBC's regular Empire broadcast began in 1932 with special programmes designed, as their Director-General Sir John Reith put it, 'to keep unshaken the faith the British nation has in its Empire'. Among the most important of these programmes was the Christmas Day message broadcast by the King from that year onwards. Delivered in the monarch's calm, sincere and unaffected voice, it was probably the most effective imperial ritual introduced between the wars. Yet another promising new link was provided by the growth of air travel. When, soon after the British aviators, Alcock and Brown, crossed the Atlantic in June 1919, both India and Australia were linked with Britain by air, *The Times* asked rhetorically: 'Who should calculate the effect of the dwindling distance between the far separated parts of the Empire which is the certain result of air traffic?'

The rest of the press seemed to agree. Feature after feature appeared in the newspapers and magazines, illustrated with diagrams, symbols and miniature maps, giving the impression that in a month or so anybody would be able to make a weekend visit to relatives in Singapore, fly in special observation cars over the Australian outback, have lunch in Malta and dinner on Table Mountain in Cape Town, view the Taj Mahal from above, and cross the entire dominion of Canada in less time than it took to get from London to Edinburgh and back by train.

Public interest in the new marvel of flight was intense. The vast majority of British citizens could, however, only travel vicariously. On any weekend in the early and mid-1920s, the new London Terminal Aerodrome at Croydon would be crammed with sightseers watching the passenger planes arrive and take off, while long queues waited to spend five shillings on ten-minute trips over the aerodrome in two-seater planes. The sightseers would have noticed the somewhat fanciful signpost that had been erected at Croydon: Karachi, 4,000 miles; Cairo, 2,000 miles; Sydney, 11,000 miles; Johannesburg, 6,000 miles; and so on. These outposts of Empire were not yet connected by regular aeronautical links with Britain, but this seemed to be an inevitability. When in 1924 the first British national airline was formed, it almost inevitably called itself Imperial Airways. Five years later it was operating regular services to Egypt, India, Australia, Singapore, Palestine, Burma, Malaya and Central Africa.

In its first year of operation, Imperial Airways carried 12,000 passengers and 250,000 letters over an aggregate of 853,042 miles. By the end of the 1920s the annual number of passengers had grown to 58,000 and the number of letters to 11 million, while the mileage had leapt to 2.5 million. The well-to-do passengers who were able to fly all the way to India, with essential fuel stops at Marseilles, Pisa, Naples, Malta, Khoms, Benghazi, Sollum, Aboukir, Ziza, Baghdad, Basra, Bushire and Karachi, perhaps chose not to remember that the relatively fragile planes were several thousand feet above the earth. Air company brochures also omitted to mention that for much of the route to India the planes passed over such outlandish places as Iraq and Baluchistan, where hostile tribesmen might well be encountered in the event of a forced landing. Instead, the advertisers chose to glamorise the 'beauty of the territory peopled with strange nomadic races that fringe our Empire'.

Another ambitious plan to promote easier and quicker travel between the countries of the Empire was made public at the Imperial Conference of 1923, when the British government announced that it was to sponsor two giant airships for trans-oceanic service to India, Australia, Africa and Canada. The two dirigibles, the *R-100* and the *R-101*, were supposed to be in service by 1926, although neither was built in time. In August 1930 the *R-100* flew to Montreal and back. Particular attention, however, was paid to the *R-101*, aboard which the Secretary of State for Air, Lord Thomson, was to be a passenger on her maiden voyage to Delhi, via Egypt, on 4 October 1930. In his speech before the airship departed, Lord Thomson said:

> I am reminded of the great hopes that have been pinned on this magnificent ship of the air as a link with the farthest corners of that everlasting entity, the British Empire . . . This is the Empire link of the future, and I set out now to prove that the air and the four corners of the earth are ours to command.

A band then played 'Land of Hope and Glory' and the National Anthem as the airship was released into the gathering dusk of the autumn evening.

At two o'clock the following morning the *R-101* crashed in flames on a hillside near Beauvais in northern France, killing all but six of the fifty-two people aboard, including Lord Thomson. Not surprisingly, British interest in the dirigible waned, and the aeroplane carried the hopes of imperial enthusiasts into the future.

In the last resort it was probably the monarchy that was the greatest asset when it came to strengthening the bonds of Empire. In George V Britain possessed a king who entered into the role of imperial parent-figure much more naturally and convincingly than his grandmother, Queen Victoria. His reputation in this respect held out until the end. According to *The Times* his dying words in 1936 were 'How is the Empire?', although two alternatives have been suggested. One was that he actually said 'Who is on at the Empire?' The other is that his last words, on being told that he would soon be fit enough to spend some time at Bognor Regis, were 'Bugger Bognor.'[10]

During his lifetime George V visited all the major territories of the British Empire, from loyalist New Zealand to troubled southern Ireland, from the West Indies to Singapore. In the process he showed himself as the plain, straightforward embodiment of an Empire viewed with suspicion by Afrikaners, French-Canadians and Indian nationalists alike.

The King, who was a dictatorial and controlling father, also attempted to imbue his sons with his own interest in and commitment to the Empire. All of them, save the sickly Prince John who died at the age of fourteen, were sent on Empire tours. The Prince of Wales, the future Edward VIII was, naturally enough, the leading royal tourist among the King's sons. Although imperial subjects awaited the arrival of the Prince of Wales with considerable anticipation, his visits were not without their problems. Despite receiving rapturous receptions, particularly in the dominions, the dashing 'Prince Charming', as the press named him, was also good copy for journalists in search of scandal. A good deal was made of the fact that the Prince of Wales sometimes shirked his duties at dances and receptions by preferring to dance with pretty and lively women rather than with the often dull, middle-aged wives of imperial officialdom.

It was not only the press that kept a sharp eye on the Prince's activities. At home, George V, who put excessive store upon appropriate behaviour in public and was a stickler for correct dress and form, often ticked off his eldest son for a variety of misdemeanours and unorthodoxies.

It is arguable that very little of any substance was achieved by royal tours. Similarly, that great imperial events like the occasional coronation and jubilee, or the Wembley Exhibition, simply appealed to the converted, and left the cynics and the sceptics unmoved. George V certainly took a naively rosy view of the value of royal tours, claiming in 1910, for instance, that if news of the proposed Coronation durbar due to be held in Delhi in 1911 could 'be made known some time before, it would tend to allay the unrest . . . which unfortunately exists in some parts of India'.[11] The 1911 Delhi durbar went ahead as planned, and probably had as much success in curbing the growth of Indian nationalism as an earlier English monarch, King Canute, had in instructing the waves to stop advancing.

Of the Wembley Exhibition, an event that was meant substantially to affect the course of imperial history, there is nothing left save an assortment of mementoes, posters and programmes. Except, that is, for Wembley Stadium itself. The Empire, apart from a few scattered remnants, has long gone. Football, however, extends its global dominion year by year. The British people's love of sport, and especially their passion for football, has proved to be more enduring than their commitment to the British Empire.

THE BALFOUR DEFINITION
OF DOMINION STATUS, 1926

The Empire's Constitution, Trade and
Development Between the Wars

AT THE IMPERIAL CONFERENCE OF 1926 an Inter-Imperial Relations Committee, chaired by the elder statesman Lord Balfour, produced the 'Balfour definition' which was designed to clarify the constitutional relationship between Great Britain and the dominions. After a good deal of haggling and heart-searching, the committee defined dominion status thus:

> They are autonomous communities within the British Empire, equal in status, in no way subordinate one to another in any aspect of their domestic or external affairs, though united by a common allegiance to the Crown, and freely associated as members of the British Commonwealth of Nations.[1]

The 'Balfour definition' was produced as a belated fulfilment of the proposal of the 1917 Imperial Conference to clarify the constitutional position of the dominions in the post-war period. The British government, as was so often the case in dealing with demands for reform generated from within the Empire, had to be pushed into producing the definition. Governments had changed and the balance of dominion opinion had shifted in the three years since the last Imperial Conference in 1923, which had been supposed to address the constitutional issue but which had devoted most of its time to a discussion of economic and foreign policy issues.

At the 1926 conference, 'loyalist' dominion governments were in a minority. The new South African Prime Minister, General J.B. Hertzog, had succeeded Smuts in 1924. He spoke for Afrikaner nationalism, and was described by Leo Amery as being 'on a hair trigger where any suggestion, however unintentional, of English racial superiority or South African subordination seemed to him implied'.[2] For his part, Hertzog declared that 'Unless our status is acknowledged by foreign nations we simply do not exist as a nation.'[3] There was now a new, truculent and potentially disruptive dominion to support the Hertzog line. The Irish Free State, represented by W.T. Cosgrave and Kevin O'Higgins, arrived at the 1926 conference determined to press for the removal of any lingering limitations on their country's sovereignty.[4] Both South Africa and the Irish Free State brought, for the first time, republican sentiments into the generally cosy Commonwealth club. Indeed, by 1937 the Irish Free State had acquired a constitution that made it a republic in all but name.

With Australia and New Zealand disinclined to upset the status quo, and still suspicious of constitutional tinkering, powerful forces were ranged on either side of the constitutional divide. What made the difference in 1926 was the role of Canada. The Canadian premier, William Lyon Mackenzie King, a Liberal with isolationist tendencies, arrived at the conference still resentful at his recent conflict with the Governor-General, Lord Byng, over the exercise of the royal prerogative in refusing him a dissolution of parliament. Since Newfoundland lacked the political weight of the other 'big five' dominions, Canada's determination to push for a thoroughgoing reappraisal of the constitutional relationship between Britain and the dominions tipped the balance in favour of change.

The discussions of the Inter-Imperial Relations Committee demonstrated both the strengths and the weaknesses of Britain's pivotal position in the new Empire-Commonwealth. Hertzog initially wanted acknowledgement that the dominions were independent states 'equal in status and separate in title to international recognition'.[5] Mackenzie King did not want the word 'independence' to be used in any definition, since it might appear that Canada was aping the United States Declaration of Independence. Australia was worried at the phrase 'freely associated as members of the British Commonwealth of Nations', arguing that this would open up the possibility of a dominion freely dissociating itself from the Empire-Commonwealth.

Balfour chaired the committee with great skill and grace. He had, after all, been chosen for the job by Amery, the Colonial and Dominions Secretary of State, because he was perceived to be 'entirely in sympathy with the newer conception of Commonwealth equality while his immense personal authority would not only hold the committee together, but commend its conclusions to the British Cabinet'.[6] Hertzog, potentially the most fearsome and disruptive of the dominions' delegates, was disarmed by Balfour's charm, declaring winningly, 'Of course if one has someone like Lord Balfour to explain things they become easy to understand.' On landing at Cape Town on his return he announced: 'I have no fear of Empire any longer.'[7]

The Balfour definition of dominion status was both everything and nothing. Its nice balance of image, semantics and political concepts reflected not merely the conflict of interests among Britain and the dominions, but also Balfour's reputation as a subtle and astute wordsmith – it was no accident that earlier in his career he had published two books on philosophy, and might, if things had turned out differently, have spent his life as an Oxbridge don.

The 1926 Balfour Definition simply recognised current political realities. It did not represent a substantial, innovative constitutional advance. Its main purpose was to buy time and placate both factions among the dominions. Phrases like 'autonomy' and 'non-subordination' were designed to satisfy South Africa and the Irish Free State. References to 'a common allegiance to the Crown', and 'freely associated as members of the British Commonwealth of Nations' were meant to reassure the loyalists. The Inter-Imperial Relations Committee also satisfied Mackenzie King by recommending that the governor-general of a dominion should cease to be the formal channel of communication between the British administration and the government of that dominion – a proposal which was to lead to the general and routine appointment of British high commissioners to dominion capitals, and eventually vice-versa.

At the heart of the conflict which had produced the bromide of the Balfour Definition, however, lay an apparently intractable problem. As the dominions grew in international standing and asserted their own nationhood, the constitutional links that connected them to Britain would be stretched to breaking point. To address the problem of the continuing constitutional subordination of the dominions to Britain, a special Imperial Conference was convened in 1929 to come up with a solution. Its recommendations were to be embodied in the Statute of Westminster, which was enacted in 1931, having been approved by the full Imperial Conference of 1930.

If any piece of legislation could be described as the Magna Carta of the British Empire, it is the Statute of Westminster. Henceforth the British Parliament could not legislate on behalf of a dominion, except by the consent of that dominion; no law passed by a dominion parliament could be invalidated on the grounds of its repugnance to English law. These developments at last recognised the equality of status between the dominions' parliaments and that at Westminster.

This dismantling of so much of the legal and symbolic structure of the Commonwealth won the approval of the governments of the Irish Free State, South Africa and, to a lesser extent, that of Canada. New Zealand and Australia, supported by some British Conservatives, only grudgingly accepted the reforms. R.G. Casey, later to be Australia's governor-general, remarked, 'We've torn down a castle to build a row of villas.' Winston Churchill, now apparently firmly stuck in the role of defender of the British Empire, described the Statute of Westminster as 'pedantic, painful, and, to some extent, almost repellent'.[8]

The 1926 Imperial Conference also addressed the issues of the Empire-Commonwealth's external relations and of foreign policy. Again, the discussions revealed the time-bomb ticking away at the centre of the imperial ideal. The dominions were no longer prepared to see themselves bound by British foreign policy decisions. They wanted to be treated as equals, not subordinates, in the field of foreign affairs. In 1923, Britain had acceded to this pressure and established an important precedent when it allowed the Canadian government to negotiate an international agreement, the Halibut Fisheries Treaty, as an independent nation.

On a somewhat more exalted plane, the dominions and the government of India wished legally to disentangle themselves from treaties made between Britain and foreign powers. This struck a fatal blow at the concept of the indivisibility of the British Empire.

Britain was itself partly to blame for the increasing reluctance of the dominions automatically to underwrite its foreign policy. Following the Chanak incident of 1922, Britain had failed to invite the dominions to be represented at the subsequent peace conference at Lausanne designed finally to settle relations between Turkey and the Allied powers. When Britain ratified the resulting Treaty of Lausanne in the name of the Empire in 1924, both Canada and the Irish Free State declined to accept any binding responsibility for the agreement.[9]

A further split between Britain and the dominions was revealed a little later during the negotiations for the Treaty of Locarno in 1925. The Locarno Treaty was made essentially to guarantee Germany's western frontier and to ensure the demilitarisation of the Rhineland. The dominions, however, far away from this peculiarly European situation, expressed their reluctance to be involved. Having learned its lesson over the earlier Treaty of Lausanne, the British government specifically exempted the dominions and India from the provisions of the treaty, unless they particularly desired to be involved.[10]

By the mid-1920s, therefore, the Empire had in practice ceased to be a diplomatic unit, and the British government could no longer pretend that there was a unified Empire foreign policy. The Imperial Conference of 1926 accepted the strength of dominion separatism and recognised the impracticability of attempting to drag the dominions and India into international treaty commitments which they felt did not involve them. Balfour put a characteristically philosophical gloss on this political reality in 1925, saying:

> But though it is a matter for regret it is not a matter for shame that our Empire is less closely knit, less formally organised than the Empires of other States. We are engaged in an entirely new experiment in the world's history and empire building. We have slid into the position . . . by dealing with the difficulties and the problems as they have arisen, until one day we awoke and said: 'This is quite a new thing that we have instinctively created. How are we to turn it to the best account?'[11]

The Australian Prime Minister, S.M. Bruce, made the best of a bad job by suggesting in 1926 that the new Commonwealth was 'governed by an unwritten treaty of mutual guarantee'. This was a coded way of saying that, just as the dominions expected British protection, if Britain were to face a crisis of major proportions, dominions' support would be forthcoming. This was not the same thing as insisting that the support of the dominions, or indeed of India, was automatically guaranteed. The outbreak of the Second World War in 1939 was to illustrate the freedom of choice which the dominions now enjoyed. Although all of the dominions, save the Irish Free State, entered the war at Britain's side, they did so in distinctly different styles and only with the support of their own parliaments.

During the 1930s the making of British foreign policy was very little influenced by the dominions, either collectively or individually. For its part, Britain failed to consult the dominions, more often than not, over crucial foreign policy decisions. Although some of the dominions aspired to play a role on the international stage through their membership of the League of Nations, they lacked the weight to make much impact. The Irish Free State, however, viewed the League as a useful counter-balance to the 'Commonwealth factor', a position which found some support amongst Afrikaner nationalist elements in South Africa.

Occasionally some family quarrel surfaced over the issue of foreign policy. The British government's belated and half-hearted consultation with dominion governments over the Abyssinian crisis of 1935 provoked a bitter, though private, protest from the government of South Africa. When, in 1936, Britain proposed to the League of Nations that sanctions against Italy over Abyssinia should be abandoned, New Zealand supported their continuation during the debate, and South Africa cast the sole dissenting vote against the British proposal.[12]

Because Britain possessed the big battalions, she was able to shape and prosecute foreign policy with or without the backing of the dominions and India. When the dominions did lend their support to British foreign policy – whether they had been adequately consulted or not – the government often made this a selling-point, both at home and in the international community.

The controversial and high-risk policy of the 'appeasement' of Germany, pursued by the government of Neville Chamberlain after 1937, paradoxically created very little disagreement with the dominions. Canada simply wanted a quiet life and the avoidance of any entanglement in Europe. The Irish Free State was determined to remain neutral in any European confrontation. There was a substantial amount of pro-Nazi sympathy amongst Afrikaner Nationalists. Australia and New Zealand were anxious lest Britain's involvement in a war over European issues should leave them without adequate defence in the face of the menacing rise of Japanese military power in the Far East. All of this made it possible for the Chamberlain government to claim that the self-governing countries of the Commonwealth were behind them in their bid to satisfy German ambitions in Europe without sacrificing essential British interests.

During the Munich Crisis of 1938 the dominions gave solid backing to the British policy of appeasing Germany. If the British were able to think of Czechoslovakia as 'a far-away country of which we know very little', the dominions were entitled to feel even less involved. Smuts had put the dominions' position succinctly, in private, after the incorporation of Austria into the German Reich in March 1938: 'the dominions will fight for Great Britain if attacked, they will not fight in the battles of Central or South-Eastern Europe'.[13] Even after Germany invaded and conquered the remains of Czechoslovakia in March 1939, most of the dominions still hoped to avoid involvement in a European war. Dominion governments were relatively cool towards Britain's switch of foreign policy which resulted in the commitment to guarantee Poland's frontiers. A month before the outbreak of the Second World War, the British government was perturbed by the apparent reluctance of the dominions to commit themselves to fighting against Hitler's Reich.

There seemed to be, during the inter-war period, one area in which the devolutionary and separatist tendencies which were manifesting themselves in the dominions and India did not apply. At a special Imperial Economic Conference held at Ottawa in 1932, the old Chamberlainite dream of imperial preference was at last made manifest. After a good deal of tough bargaining, the Ottawa Conference resulted in a series of bilateral trading treaties between Britain and various countries of the Empire. The agreements amounted to a system of mutual tariff concessions – Canada, for example, favouring British goods, and vice-versa – very similar to those advocated by the Tariff Reform League thirty years previously.

These hard-headed agreements did not, however, herald a new age of imperial economic integration. The great worldwide economic depression that began at the end of 1929 had forced a change of heart on the issue of imperial preference, not least in Britain. As Britain, the dominions, India and other countries within the Empire saw their exports plummeting, unemployment rising and economic hardships increasing, earlier misgivings over the feasibility and value of imperial preference were set aside.

As late as 1923, however, the Conservative and Unionist Party's association with a policy of imperial preference, or, as some saw it, protectionism, had resulted in defeat at the polls. But the Conservatives had fared no better under the colours of free trade at the general election of 1929. Subsequently sections of the British press, with the support of many in the Conservative Party and in industry, had once more launched a campaign for the introduction of imperial preference, although this time under the apparently paradoxical banner of 'Empire Free Trade'. Thus re-named, a revamped tariff reform campaign was meant both to reassure free traders and to appeal to those who supported a scheme of imperial preference.

In the dominions and in Britain the onset of the Great Depression made politicians more than usually anxious to find ways of alleviating economic distress and, as a consequence, of maintaining their electoral popularity. In Britain, however, the minority Labour government, with the austere free trader Philip Snowden as Chancellor of the Exchequer, showed no interest in Empire Free Trade.

Between 1930 and 1932, however, the worsening of the Depression resulted in a significant restructuring of the political landscape in Britain, as well as in Canada. The Labour government fell in 1931 to be replaced by a coalition government of national unity. Neville Chamberlain, who had remarked in 1929, 'If we do not think imperially, we shall have to think continentally', became Chancellor of the Exchequer in the National Government.[14] Joseph Chamberlain's second son had now been promoted to a position were he could play a crucial part in bringing his father's last great crusade to a satisfactory conclusion.

Among the dominions, Australia and New Zealand had always been better disposed towards imperial preference than Canada. But here, too, the situation changed in the early 1930s. At the 1930 general election in Canada, Mackenzie King and the Liberals were defeated by the Conservative Party, which campaigned on a platform of imperial preference. The new Prime Minister, R.B. Bennett, had close links with his fellow-Canadian Lord Beaverbrook, whose British newspapers, particularly the *Daily Express* and the *Sunday Express*, were vigorous campaigners on behalf of Empire Free Trade.

The 1932 Ottawa trading agreements were, therefore, principally the products of the unprecedented collapse of the world market and the pragmatic response of Empire governments to the subsequent crisis. Some dedicated free traders found them anathema, and Snowden resigned from the National Government in protest, complaining that the intricate negotiations, 'after weeks of acrimonious disputes and sordid struggles with vested interests', had exposed 'to the world . . . the hollowness of the talk of Imperial sentiment in economic affairs'.[15]

Judged by the crudest measures, the Ottawa agreements, operating through a series of voluntary bilateral trading treaties, were an undoubted success. Inter-imperial trade was very significantly increased between 1932 and the outbreak of the Second World War. Between 1929 and 1938 Britain improved its position as easily the most important trading partner of the dominions, with the exception of Canada with its intimate trade connections with the United States. In 1929 Britain took 38.1 per cent of Australia's exports, but 56.2 per cent in 1938. During the same period her imports from New Zealand rose from 75 to 84.7 per cent, although imports from South Africa actually fell from 48.4 to 38.8 per cent. Between 1929 and 1938, the percentage of Australia's imports from Britain rose from 39.7 to 42.1; New Zealand took 46.1 per cent of its total imports from Britain in 1929, and 47.8 per cent in 1938; the South African proportion of imports from Britain stayed at 43.9 per cent of the whole.[16] Britain's trade with the Empire overall increased substantially during the period 1931 to 1937. The total of British imports from the dominions, India and the colonial empire increased from 24 per cent of total overseas trade in 1931 to 37 per cent in 1937. British exports to the Empire increased from 32 per cent in 1931 to 39 per cent in 1937.

The 1930s also saw Britain constructing the 'Sterling Area', the creation of which was yet another by-product of the Great Depression. Forced off the gold standard in 1931, Britain brought the whole of the Empire-Commonwealth, with the exception of Canada and some middling-sized foreign states, into a bloc where the pound sterling replaced gold as the monetary standard, and where the member countries used the pound sterling as a common currency for the purposes of foreign exchange dealing.

The system of imperial preferences and the creation of the Sterling Area injected new life into Britain's economic and financial relationship with the Empire-Commonwealth. It has even been claimed that:

> Although Britain suffered in the world slump that began in 1929, she was far less affected than her rivals, including the United States, whose global economic influence shrank rapidly. Indeed, it is important to remember that Britain was the only truly world power of consequence in the 1930s ... The overriding purpose of British policy, within the Empire and beyond it, was to restore or enhance her financial influence. This priority gave direction and momentum to important decisions on international policy, from the Ottawa agreement to appeasement; it shaped Britain's other dealings with the dominions and the colonies; and it dominated her aims in South America and China. In pursuing these goals, Britain showed a degree of energy and agility that is hard to reconcile with the view that, by the close of the 1930s, she had become an elderly and arthritic power.[17]

Although the Second World War was to disrupt world trading patterns, and further deplete British investment overseas as well as impair its international credit, the post-war Commonwealth 'was much more of an economic unit than it had ever been before'.[18] When Britain became a member of the European Economic Community in 1973, Commonwealth countries registered strong protests at what they saw as a damaging blow to one of the most valued, enduring, saleable and profitable links between the metropolitan power and the Empire-Commonwealth.

There was something paradoxical about the revived fortunes of inter-imperial trade during the 1930s. The enhancement and revitalisation of Britain's commercial and financial relationships with the Empire-Commonwealth were in inverse proportion to her political and constitutional standing within the Empire. While inter-imperial trade increased, British leadership and British rule were increasingly challenged throughout the whole imperial system. To all but the most ardent of imperialists, however, the trade-off between declining imperial political control and power and the maintenance, even the enhancement, of Britain's economic and financial position, was a price well worth paying.

THE BODYLINE TOUR OF
AUSTRALIA, 1932

Imperialism, National Identity and Sport

DURING PLAY IN the third Test Match in Adelaide in 1932, between Australia and the touring MCC side, representing England, a crisis erupted which, though based in cricket, developed into an uncomfortable international incident. It arose out of the tactics of the England team, led by the disdainful Oxford amateur Douglas Jardine, and including four fast bowlers of whom the most formidable was the Nottinghamshire player Harold Larwood. 'Bodyline' bowling meant what it said: England's fast bowlers were encouraged by Jardine to bowl as fast as they could at the bodies of the Australians; a batsman facing this hostile pace attack might be hurried into a stroke which could well be caught by the English fielders clustered on the leg side of the wicket.

Jardine introduced the bodyline tactics to contain and defeat the Australian batsmen, of whom the most successful and prolific was Donald Bradman. During Australia's tour of England in 1930, Bradman's superb batting, which included a record score of 334 at Headingley in Leeds, had played a major part in winning the Ashes for Australia. The only discernible weakness in Bradman's batting was his response to high, fast bowling on the line of the body. Harold Larwood was the fastest bowler of his day, possibly of all time, and he was supported by three other extremely pacy bowlers in Voce, Bowes and Allen – although the latter proved unwilling to bowl bodyline.[1]

During the first two Test Matches the tactics of Jardine and Larwood were triumphantly successful: Bradman scored at a rate of less than half his Test average, and England were securely on course to regain the Ashes. England's bodyline bowling tactics had aroused criticism before the third Test at Adelaide, but when during that match the

Australian captain Bill Woodfull was struck by a short-pitched ball from Larwood trouble began. The spectators were enraged by Jardine's decision immediately after the incident to increase the number of his fielders on the leg side and to persist with his tactics. Later in the innings Bert Oldfield, the Australian wicket-keeper, was struck on the head and injured.

The Australian crowd, inclined to bait and barrack English cricketers at the best of times, became even more hostile and revengeful. Their feelings of outrage were not helped by Jardine's comment after the match that 'Those of you who had seats got your money's worth – and then some.'[2] When play ended, the England manager, 'Plum' Warner, went to the Australian dressing room to discover how serious the injuries to Australia's batsmen were, and was told unequivocally by Woodfull, that 'Of two teams out there, one is playing cricket, the other is making no effort to play cricket.' The Australian press were quick to make headlines out of the incident, and a crisper, probably inaccurate, version of Woodfull's criticism, ending '. . . one is playing cricket, and the other isn't', gained popular credibility. The Australian Cricket Board sent a telegram to the governing body of English cricket, the Marylebone Cricket Club, the contents of which were made public, and which described bodyline bowling as 'unsportsmanlike'.[3]

For the England Test team to be accused publicly of unsportsmanlike behaviour, and of 'not playing cricket', struck a blow to the imperial games ethic as painful as any inflicted by Larwood at his most dangerous. In both Canberra and London, politicians made haste to dampen down the controversy. The British government, having just passed the Statute of Westminster which legally recognised the autonomy of dominion governments, and having just negotiated the Ottawa trading agreements introducing a system of Imperial Preference, was alarmed at the prospect of a heightening of Australian nationalism and colonial bloody-mindedness. Anxieties that Australian resentments could be easily inflamed were increased by the fact that the crash in world food prices resulting from the Great Depression had left many Australian primary producers deeply in debt to British banks, which were demanding repayment of their credit.

The bodyline controversy also stirred up a number of deep-seated resentments, even hatreds, directed at Britain. Despite the residual pool of affection for 'the Old Country', it was muddied by the folk memories and prejudices of an egalitarian, outspoken population, many of whom were descended from transported convicts and immigrant Irish. Jardine, the 'gentleman' cricketer, with his elitist background and manners, personified the stiff-upper-lipped Englishman of Australian caricature. The final irony and insult of the bodyline controversy was that the 'Pommie bastards' – a description possibly arising from the English gentleman's preference for Pommery champagne to democratic Australian beer – had been caught blatantly cheating at a game which was supposed to encapsulate all of the well-advertised English and imperial virtues of playing fairly and by the rules – 'playing cricket', in fact. The imperial and public school ethic had thus been turned on its head.

Unable to admit publicly that the captain of England had failed 'to play the game', the MCC supported Jardine until the end of the tour. Then, as is so often the case within the English cricketing establishment, some discreet butchery was carried out. Jardine was dropped as captain, although he had led the team which regained the Ashes. Harold Larwood was never again to play cricket for England, and ultimately settled in Australia, believing himself to be a sacrificial victim of the English class system. The bodyline bowling attack was dropped from England's cricketing armoury, and the rules of the game were changed. The high emotion felt in both Australia and England gradually subsided. An acute embarrassment for England and its cricketing establishment passed into history. The prophecy of one of Jardine's former teachers at Winchester School on hearing of his appointment as captain, 'Well, we shall win the Ashes – but we may lose a dominion,' was not fulfilled.[4]

The British passion for sport, and in particular for sport associated with the ethical standards so vigorously promoted by the leading public schools, was part and parcel of the expansion of the Empire. Hard on the heels of settlers, trading companies, invading armies and colonial administrators came the apparatus, rules and ethics of sport. It was natural that a colonial and officer-class elite that spent so much time in the saddle should hasten to build turf clubs almost as soon as they'd hauled up the Union Jack. It was wryly observed that as European nations expanded overseas, the first thing a Frenchman built was a restaurant, the first thing a German built was a road, but the first thing the British built was a racecourse.

No sooner was a turf club established than plans were made to construct a cricket pitch. After horse-racing, the equestrian sports favoured by imperial administrators, army officers and colonial elites included hunting to hounds (after jackals if foxes were not available), polo and pig-sticking. Shooting game also became popular, and

299

big-game hunting, with the aid of high-velocity rifles, became an obsession for some marksmen and women. Americans were among the most enthusiastic of the big-game hunters, travelling to Africa at considerable expense to slaughter elephant, lion and rhinoceros.

In the Indian empire, hunting, or *shikar*, became closely associated with the exercise of British power. Each viceroy was expected, in the tradition of the Mogul emperors and of India's princes, to 'bag' a respectable tally of game, and in particular to succeed in shooting a tiger. Not all viceroys were born marksmen. Lord Reading, Viceroy from 1921 to 1926, and the son of a Jewish London fruit merchant, did his best to accommodate the passion for hunting that so many of India's princely rulers and senior British administrators shared. He did his duty by shooting grouse, duck and geese, although he refused on one occasion to tell King George V, who was an internationally acknowledged crack shot, how many cartridges he had expended in achieving his tally. He eventually bagged a tiger in Gwalior, but afterwards confessed, 'In truth I'm not so keen upon actually killing the animal as being in the jungle which I love.'[5]

If viceregal skill at hunting was seen as a metaphor for the potency and capacity of the British Raj, many sports played in the Empire had practical, utilitarian functions. In an age when imperial armies were so heavily dependent upon the horse as a beast of burden as well as providing the mounts for elite cavalry regiments, racing, hunting, polo and pig-sticking only served to improve British equestrian skills. Sport was generally regarded as a manly exercise for an imperial ruling class more respected for its practical capacity to get things done than for its intellectual and philosophical abilities. The British capacity to run a huge and disparate Empire efficiently was often put down to the energy and team spirit arising from sport and organised games. A German observer remarked that 'the great tasks offered by the Empire, with its varied problems to the pioneer, often demand the strong energetic character rather than the bookworm'.[6]

Regular sporting events had other practical by-products. The race meeting, the cricket match and the polo tournament not merely promoted fellow-feeling, as well as some rivalry, among the participants, but also provided opportunities for social gatherings, where the families of British administrators, traders and military personnel could meet over food and drink, and boost each other's morale and self-esteem. Sporting events also enabled settler populations to derive some comfort from familiar, home-grown activities as well as to meet each other and exchange news and gossip. In many newly established Australian towns important race meetings were declared public holidays, and Melbourne Cup day became virtually a national holiday. The diamond prospectors who descended upon Mafeking in South Africa quickly built a race-course, and the white settlers of British East Africa held the first race meeting in Nairobi in 1900.

In all of these ways, British sports served a valuable function within the colonial context, providing amusement and healthy exercise, but above all serving as a means of maintaining morale, reminding people of shared origins, common purpose, collective self-interest and the need for solidarity amidst indigenous and frequently hostile populations. Although Rudyard Kipling mocked 'the flannelled fool at the wicket and the muddied oaf at the goals', these barbs were directed at unimaginative stay-at-homes within the United Kingdom rather than at those who upheld, administered and settled the British Empire overseas.

Of all the mass spectator-sports exported to the Empire, it was cricket that became most intimately entwined with the imperial ideal. This was partly due to the fact that the warm, dry conditions best suited to cricket were commonplace throughout the imperial system, from the West Indies to Africa, from India to Australia and New Zealand. Cricket could also be played on almost any flat, natural surface, and at reasonable expense. It was an intricate, subtle and, at its best, beauti-ful game, combining a wide variety of skills with displays of athleticism and strength. Cricket's main appeal, however, arose from the spirit in which it was meant to be played. Two impartial umpires ensured that the rules were kept to, and their decisions were in theory never ques-tioned. More than that, cricket players were supposed not to cheat. Batsmen often 'walked', acknowledging the end of their innings even before the umpire had given them out. If a fielder took a catch after the ball had hit the ground, he signalled the fact rather than claiming a wicket.

Cricket spawned its own particular metaphors. 'Playing a straight bat' came to mean dealing honestly or displaying integrity. To 'bat on a sticky wicket' meant to face up to difficult or tricky situations. Cricket also provided a vocabulary behind which acts of violence and brutality could be camouflaged. Thus armed opponents of imperial rule could be 'skittled out' by the fast bowlers of the British Army. The Raj and the Indian Army 'played the Great Game' on the sub-continent's north-west frontier. Before the Battle of El Alamein in North Africa during the Second World War, Field Marshal Montgomery exhorted his troops to hit Rommel 'for six, right out of Africa!'

Cricket grounds were built soon after racecourses in the process of imperial expansion. The first cricket club in Sydney was established in 1826, and Parsees founded the Oriental Cricket Club in Bombay in 1848. Association football was being played in Australia from 1829, and by the mid-Victorian period could be found almost everywhere where British colonisation and settlement had taken place, including Hong Kong. Association football, in fact, was to prove the most successful and enduring of British exports, penetrating markets outside the Empire and appealing to consumers who were not otherwise inclined to buy British.

Rugby, tennis and boxing were all part of the spread of British influence throughout the world. 'Playing by the rules' was an intrinsic part of these sports as well. The British penchant for codification and regulation may be seen as a significant part of the process of imperial control and discipline. It has even been claimed that the boxing rules promulgated by the Marquis of Queensberry in 1865 were a more powerful link between Britain and the American west 'than Shakespeare or the English Bible'.[7] The English Football Association was set up in 1863, and the Scottish and Welsh FAs in 1873 and 1876 respectively. Rugby clubs were founded at a great rate in England in the last quarter of the nineteenth century, and the first All-England tennis tournament held at Wimbledon in 1877. In 1861 the first English cricket team to visit Australia set sail, and by 1902 sides were regularly touring South Africa, the West Indies and New Zealand. The first team representing Australia toured England in 1880, and the Indians arrived in 1911, two years after the Imperial Cricket Conference was formed between the Marylebone Cricket Club (representing England), Australia and South Africa.

Within the Empire, British-dominated games and sports were often seen as part of the civilising mission. Although the Colonial Office issued no instructions on the subject, it was widely assumed that the promotion of British sports would help build cultural bridges between rulers and ruled, promote affection for the Old Country among English-speaking settlers, and perhaps even seduce potentially hostile groups like the Afrikaners or the French-Canadians. The playing of cricket and polo in India was perceived as a means of anglicising the Indian elite and binding them more closely to the Raj – even though polo, played in a variety of forms, had originated in Asia many centuries before the

British came to the sub-continent. A number of Indian princes, notably Prince Ranjitsinhji and the Nawab of Pataudi, even played in the England cricket team at various times during the first four decades of the twentieth century.

For the mass of the Empire's indigenous subjects, however, British sports were meant to bestow other benefits. 'Playing by the rules', 'playing the game', and the cult of the 'good loser' were all meant, by their example, to woo and captivate 'the native', or at least to blunt the edge of local hostility. In the process it was anticipated that a warm glow of 'good fellowship' would spread between the varied and far-flung peoples of the British Empire, although such fellow-feeling was not meant to lead to entry to the white man's club or to the white woman's boudoir.

Encouraged by the exporters and exponents of 'muscular Christianity', British sports were also designed to wean the 'native' from 'unhealthy' activities such as inter-tribal warfare, cannibalism, heathen religions and, in particular, an obsession with sexual activity. Sir Arthur Grimble believed that 'the moral teaching-force' of cricket had led to the game replacing internecine conflict amongst the inhabitants of the Gilbert Islands in the South Pacific. A governor of Tonga claimed that since the introduction of cricket, petty pilfering had more or less died out.[8] In India football was seen as a means of 'grinding grit into Kashmir', or equally as an experiment in character-building amongst Bengalis, sneeringly described as 'a low, lying people in a low-lying land'.[9]

Sport was also believed to provide a common language within an imperial system that spoke as many tongues as the Tower of Babel. Some believed that it was possible to equate British sporting and parliamentary language, and hence, at least by implication, British sport with good practice and behaviour. As has been earlier remarked, John Strachey, a minister in Attlee's Labour government after the Second World War, was essentially serious when he observed that 'to know a no-ball from a googly and a point of order from a supplementary question is genuinely to have something in common'.[10] From the end of the nineteenth century, as both the mass-communications media and democracy spread throughout the Empire, a shared interest in sport, and the capacity to read about it in inexpensive newspapers – and later to listen to it on the wireless – were believed to be harmonising forces within the Empire. It was also possible to see sport as an opiate of the people, rather as Karl Marx had earlier perceived religion. In the British West Indies, in Calcutta or in Melbourne a leg-glance or a cover drive could release a host of tensions and frustrations in a flash of sporting catharsis.

As sport became increasingly profitable, particularly as a spectator pastime, the number of sporting fixtures and tournaments throughout the Empire-Commonwealth rapidly increased. Not merely were cricket and rugby Test Matches very soon part of the sporting calendar, but 'Empire' titles in boxing were introduced, and regular inter-imperial athletics meetings instituted. In 1930 the first Empire Games were held at Hamilton in Canada. The idea had surfaced as early as 1891 when a Pan Britannic Festival was held, and during the coronation celebrations of George V in 1911 an athletics tournament was organised as part of the Festival of Empire.

It is, perhaps, no coincidence that the first Empire Games were held at a time when the dominions had recently received a formal acknowledgement of their independent constitutional status, Indian nationalism was making great headway against the Raj, and the Great Depression was ravaging international trade. It was entirely appropriate, as well, that Canada should host the first games, since its North American identity excluded it from fully-fledged participation in two of the great imperial ball games – cricket and rugby. The first Empire Games established a tradition which has lasted right down to the present day, in the form of the Commonwealth Games. Although competition between the participating nations was, and remains, fierce, there is still a hint of the family connection in the Commonwealth Games, and perhaps a little less of the chauvinistic triumphalism associated with other international athletics events, including the Olympic Games.

The spread and organisation of British games in many parts of the Empire and Commonwealth was not, however, always a boon to patriots and imperialists. There was quite often local resistance to the newly-introduced sports. In India, both Hindus and Muslims were convinced that a leather football provided an affront to their religions. Schoolboys at one game were described, not untypically, as both incompetent and fearful: 'their clogs flew in the air . . . while their night-gowns flapped in one another's faces', and 'those struck in the face with the ball screamed they were polluted by the leather ball and had to be washed and reassured'.[11]

Even when British games were enthusiastically assimilated, as in the case of cricket in the British West Indies, there were complicated political and social spin-offs. As black players in the Caribbean grew in skill and confidence, local crowds enthused at the humbling of teams composed of either white West Indians or visiting British players. In the end, many whites declined point-blank to play against teams with black players, stubbornly refusing, as the *Barbados Globe* commented in 1895, 'to take part in any game in which poor coloured men are engaged in a persistent exhibition of artificial greatness'. Although black West Indian cricketers like Learie Constantine and George Headley became world cricketing stars in the first half of the twentieth century, the captaincy of the West Indian team remained the preserve of a white man. As late as 1960 the captaincy was denied even to such a supreme black player as Frank Worrell, a slight which provoked rioting during the subsequent visit of the England team to the Caribbean.

Despite this late flourish of a redundant white supremacy, cricket provides a continuing link, perhaps one of the few with any meaning, between the ex-British colonies of the Caribbean and the ex-imperial power. Not that cricket in the West Indies was invariably seen as a means of humiliating the white population and the imperial power. The high moral and ethical ground which cricket claimed as its own made an appeal even to the Trinidadian revolutionary Marxist and writer C.L.R. James who insisted that popular exultation at the defeat of white touring teams 'wasn't playing the game'.[12]

Elsewhere in the Empire, players, spectators and sportswriters expressed fewer qualms at the use of sport as a political weapon, or at least as a means of harassment and humiliation. The 'sledging', or persistent verbal abuse, which some of today's Australian cricket teams are alleged to hurl at English batsmen has a long and, in an odd way, honourable history in the relationship between the two countries. Just as a beautiful stroke or a satisfying piece of spin bowling releases tension among spectators, so the ritual defeat of the ex-imperial power provides some recompense for years of perceived domination, wrongdoing, even condescension and hauteur.

In the Indian sub-continent the political ramifications of cricket had been somewhat more restrained, or at least more subtle – very similar, indeed, to the Indian reputation for refined bowling and classical batting. It is evident that Indian princes often saw a commitment to cricket as a means of consolidating their already close and interdependent political relationship with the British Raj. The great batsman Prince Ranjitsinhji seems to have cashed in on his cricketing prowess by using it as an extra means of persuasion when prising more privileges for his principality out of the British. It has even been suggested that the fact that there was no revolutionary overthrow of the British Raj was partly due to the fact that the nationalist movement was 'led by Gandhi and his western Indian allies who were based around Bombay where cricket was strong'.[13] It has also been asserted that:

> Unique amongst nationalist movements, Gandhi taught the Indians to accept the good that was in the British, while rejecting the harm that they were doing to India and its people. This meant that, after Independence, there was no contradiction in accepting cricket – it could very simply be seen as one of the British 'good things' which ought to be retained. Cricket, without any fuss or much debate, was seen as a part of the British system of which Indians approved.[14]

In South Africa, the Afrikaner people have, until recently, associated cricket with an oppressive imperial power and its fifth-columnists and supporters – the English-speaking settlers. English-speakers, therefore, have historically dominated South African Test teams. The Afrikaners, on the other hand, developed a passion for rugby football, which evolved into a quasi religion among rural whites between the two world wars. More than any other sport in South Africa, rugby became the medium for Afrikaner sporting creativity and self-fulfilment. It also allowed the Afrikaner people, many of whom until the second half of the twentieth century were, in effect, poor whites, to find some binding force which would knit the Volk together and provide them with an internationally recognisable identity. During the first half of the twentieth century the great Springbok rugby teams proved formidable opponents for British and dominion sides. The Springbok style of play, relying on the weight of the players, their pace and the ruthless ferocity of their tackling, both provided a contrast to the alleged 'softness' of the cricket of the English-speakers, and also emphasised the toughness and capacity for self-determination which was, and remains, an intrinsic part of Afrikaner folklore. It is true that the Springboks were playing an 'imperial' game, but they were playing it in a style which asserted their pride and independence, and which gave no quarter – to English sides in particular.

The importance which white South Africans attached to international sporting success gave the anti-apartheid movement a powerful weapon from the 1960s onwards, and the international boycott of sporting links with the white supremacist regime played an important part in the slow and steady undermining of apartheid. The relief with which South Africans of all races greeted their country's rehabilitation within the world-wide sporting community in the early 1990s was palpable. When the South African rugby team, including only one black player, won the Rugby World Cup in June 1995, the triumph was greeted with joy by all sections of the population, a reaction which would have been inconceivable only a few years previously.

Like South Africa, New Zealand also became one of the great rugby-playing nations of the Empire-Commonwealth. The legendary performances of the All Blacks on the rugby fields of the Empire were not simply a manifestation of another form of dominion nationalism. For the most part, New Zealanders were proud both of the achievements of the All Blacks and of their country's continuing membership of the British Empire. The profound dependency of the New Zealand economy upon its trade with Britain for most of the nation's history also, naturally enough, contributed to loyalist sentiments. So too did the fact that the white population of New Zealand was overwhelmingly British and English-speaking in origin.

Rugby in New Zealand also performed another function. It enabled European settlers and indigenous Maoris to forget the chronic social and economic disparities between them, and to join in a national activity that, at least temporarily, seemed to transcend racial divisions. Indeed, the All Blacks adopted the Maori war dance, the haka, as a pre-match demonstration of team solidarity as well as a dramatic expression of defiance hurled at the enemy.

Sport also provided the means by which Celtic nationalism could express itself within the British Isles. In Ireland the Gaelic games played an important role in the renewal of Irish nationalist agitation during the late nineteenth century. Gaelic games were widely perceived as being part of a fresh Irish determination to resist the apparently inexorable spread of British culture. With the partition of Ireland in 1922, two Association football teams appeared, one representing the North and one the Irish Free State – although both played in green jerseys. Rugby union, however, provided one of the very few means of uniting Ireland, at least symbolically, after partition. Ireland's rugby team is drawn from both the north and the south of the country, and plays at Lansdowne Road in Dublin.

Rugby provided one of the most powerful means by which the Welsh could both maintain and express their identity and their separateness from the English. It has been asserted that 'As a unifying, inclusive cultural force it outstripped politics and religion, drawing together coal-heavers and coal-owners in a common passion for the national side.'[15] This was a particularly useful function during the heavy migration of non-Welsh workers to the booming industries of South Wales during the nineteenth century.

As compared with England and Scotland, rugby in Wales was a deeply democratic rather than an oligarchical sport. When the crowd at Cardiff Arms Park, a very high proportion of miners and their families among them, sang 'Land of My Fathers' before the international match against the old enemy, England, the event became a passionate celebration of Welshness and an assertion of national identity. Until very recently, the success of Welsh international rugby sides has helped to keep the myth of Welsh rugby as a unifying, culturally rich statement of nationalism alive. For much of the first half of the twentieth century, two of the smallest nations in the Empire were the most successful upon the rugby field – Wales and New Zealand.

In Scotland both Association football and rugby union provided a means of cocking a snook at the English. The middle classes carried on a fiercely competitive but generally gentlemanly struggle for rugby union's Calcutta Cup, while the 'Blue Devils' representing Scottish soccer at its best played an annual fixture with the 'Auld Enemy'. Football provided the urban proletariat of Clydeside and Lanarkshire with a faith which could unite both Protestants and Catholics. This was not the case, however, within the Scottish Football Association. Heavy Irish immigration to Scotland's industrial heartlands lent a keen edge to the rivalries of major football teams. For many years, and to a considerable extent today, Scottish Catholics and Protestants identified strongly with football teams that stood for both their communities and their faith. In Glasgow, Celtic play in the green and white of Ireland, while Rangers sport the blue, white and red of the union flag. In Edinburgh, Hearts were associated with Protestantism and the Union, while their great rivals unashamedly called themselves Hibernians – the Latin term for the Irish. Even the two teams of Dundee at one time claimed separate religious identities.

Sectarian prejudices, however, were dropped for the annual international match against England. The passion with which Scottish fans supported their team against the English did not simply arise from a collective history of rivalry, war and rebellion, although sections of the crowd sometimes waved the Stuart flag. The real point of the match was to wreak revenge upon the English for their international success and for their superior standing within the British Isles. A Scottish victory was also the retribution of a small and relatively poor country against a rich, powerful and often overweening neighbour. Scotland can also take pleasure in the spectacular successes of a long line of Scottish managers of leading English clubs, including Jock Stein, Matt Busby, Bill Shankly, Bob Paisley, Alec Ferguson and even – despite his reputation for whining 'like a jet plane over Luton' – Kenny Dalglish.

England, too, has made the most of its sporting achievements both to assert Englishness and to provide, so to speak, moral justification for its domination of the Empire. Just as members of the Royal Family became hectic and persistent Empire tourists during the twentieth century, so they became identified with national and imperial sporting occasions. In 1914, George V began the royal tradition of annually attending the FA Cup Final. Each Commonwealth Games has its obligatory royal guest in attendance. Leading politicians have jumped on the bandwagon, although the hostile reception accorded Mrs Thatcher at a football match in Scotland stopped her from making subsequent sporting forays among the people. In a world within which the British Empire is for the most part a distant and sometimes unsavoury memory, the triumph of English teams or of individual English sportsmen and women can be acclaimed as a late and unaccustomed flourish of the flag. During the 1996 European Football Championship held in England, the crude chauvinism of some of the tabloid press and the overcharged patriotism of sections of the public were ugly reminders of what demons can be released during international sporting events, and what widespread depression can follow failure.

Having lost its Empire by the mid-1960s, England, and the United Kingdom as a whole, became more preoccupied with sporting success than hitherto. When the England football team was beaten for the first time 'at home' by the Hungarians in 1953, it was not just that a remarkable record was lost. The skill and verve demonstrated by the players of Hungary, then a Communist state, in their crushing 6-3 victory seemed to provide yet another illustration of the host nation's loss of great-power status and international regard.

The trouble was that, as with the peoples of the Empire, the 'natives' of world sport had become as uppity, difficult to beat and assertive as the various colonial nationalist movements which eventually tore the imperial fabric to shreds.

24

THE FALL OF SINGAPORE, FEBRUARY 1942

Britain, the Empire-Commonwealth and the Second World War

In February 1942, the great imperial fortress and naval base at Singapore was surrendered to Japanese forces almost without a shot being fired. 130,000 British and Commonwealth troops, including a substantial number of Australians and New Zealanders, became prisoners of war. The fall of Singapore was seen at the time, and has certainly been described since, as dealing an enormous psychological blow to the integrity of the British Empire and providing a significant turning-point in the process of European imperial decline. The contempt with which the Japanese treated the tens of thousands of white troops who laid down their arms so meekly at Singapore was matched by the despair and disillusionment felt elsewhere. The Australian Minister to China wrote: 'The British Empire in the Far East depended on prestige. This prestige has been completely shattered.'[1]

The bitterness felt in Australasia at the collapse of British power in the Far East was an understandable and inevitable reaction. Australia and New Zealand, the two most loyal dominions, were now exposed to the apparently irresistible advance of Japanese military, air and naval forces. Having lived with the fear of the 'Yellow Peril' for over a hundred years, the white settlers of Australasia now saw their worst nightmares turned into reality. Britain's failure adequately to protect her Far Eastern, Australasian and South Pacific empire seemed an undeserved and shocking reward for decades of compliance and support. Both Australia and New Zealand made haste to avail themselves of the more reliable protection of the United States of America. The deep-seated resentments which were stirred up during this time were to resurface over half a century later, when the Australian Prime Minister Paul Keating, as well as supporters of the Australian republican movement, raked up the memories of what they saw as their nation's abandonment by Britain.

The fall of Singapore, inadequately fortified and ineptly defended, was in some ways less significant than contemporaries imagined. The confidence invested in the base as an impregnable bastion of British imperial power during the inter-war period bore little relation to military reality. Even its construction had been bedevilled by disputes and uncertainty. In 1924 the first Labour government had suspended work on it for reasons of economy.[2] Although millions of pounds were subsequently poured into its construction, in the end it turned out to be no more effective an obstacle than the Maginot Line had been in protecting France from the German assault in 1940.

The surrender at Singapore was merely one of a sequence of disasters for British arms in the Far East following the Japanese attack on Pearl Harbor on 7 December 1941. Within a few weeks Japanese forces had captured Hong Kong, which surrendered on Christmas Day 1941, had invaded Malaya, via Indo-China, and had sunk, in a matter of minutes, the battleship *Prince of Wales* and the cruiser *Repulse*, the only Royal Navy vessels that could be spared for the Far Eastern theatre of war. Britain's imperial prestige was, therefore, already torn to pieces before either the fall of Singapore or the subsequent sweep of Japanese forces through Burma to the very frontiers of India. The swift Japanese conquest of the Dutch East Indies, and of British, French and American possessions in the South Pacific and South-East Asia, completed a process which was widely regarded as disproving once and for all the myth of European invincibility.

This was, however, not the first time that Japan had humiliated European forces. During the Russo–Japanese war of 1904–05, the Japanese had defeated the Russian army in Manchuria with ludicrous ease, and had sunk the bulk of the two Tsarist fleets sent against them. Japan was, moreover, a very untypical Asian nation. Intensely hierarchical, homogeneous, nationalistic and well organised, Japan had never appeared likely to fall under European imperial control. On the contrary, despite a few satirical forays like Gilbert and Sullivan's *The Mikado*, the great powers had chosen to treat Japan with respect rather than with condescension. When Britain had emerged from its period of so-called 'splendid isolation' it was with Japan, the other 'island empire', that it had concluded its first treaty, in 1902.

European circumspection owed a great deal to the fact that the Japanese had modelled their military machine upon that of Germany and their naval forces upon the Royal Navy. Far from Japan being a power held in low regard by Europe and the United States, it was treated with wariness and considerable apprehension. The string of Japanese victories after Pearl Harbor were, therefore, not bolts from the blue. Rather they conformed neatly to the pattern of earlier Japanese success and confirmed Japan as one of the greatest military powers on earth.

Such rationalisation, however, was of little comfort to Britain in 1942. While the entry of the United States into the war, together with Hitler's assault on Soviet Russia in June 1941, had effectively won the global conflict for the British Empire, this was by no means yet apparent. Although Britain had not been invaded, and despite its determined resistance to Axis aggression in North Africa, the Horn of Africa and the Middle East, the first two and a half years of the war had been at best an exercise in containment rather than counter-attack.

The outbreak of the Second World War in September 1939 had exposed the weaknesses and the strengths of the imperial structure even more starkly than had 1914. At first sight, the Empire-Commonwealth seemed to be an unparalleled resource upon which Britain could draw for the purpose of prosecuting the war. The Empire was considerably larger in terms of territory and population than in 1914. When Churchill was to boast after the fall of France in the summer of 1940 that Britain 'stood alone', defying the fascist dictatorships of Germany and Italy, it was also essential to remember that the British Empire comprised a quarter of the world's population and nearly a quarter of its land surface. Britain thus 'stood alone' with a quarter of the world at its side, far more in terms of human and material resources than could be marshalled by the Axis Powers.

During the war, the imperial contribution to the armed forces of the Crown was even more substantial than during the First World War. Between 1939 and 1945 Britain mobilised nearly six million servicemen and women, but the dominions raised a little over two million, India two and a half million, and the colonies and dependencies just under half a million; of this total over 350,000 died and nearly 80,000 were reported missing.[3] The vast quantities of raw materials, food and manufactures that could be produced by such a huge global organisation were of fundamental importance in enabling Britain to survive the early reverses and traumas of the war and to press on towards ultimate victory.

Behind the impressive statistics, however, there were some troubling and disruptive truths to confront. The Indian empire was an invaluable source of manpower, but it was also within a short step of dominion status, and its powerful nationalist movements could speedily turn to disaffection and revolt. Although Egypt was formally independent, the continuing British military presence there, and the need to secure the Suez route to India and the Far East, continued to provoke nationalist indignation and to threaten insurrection. In the Middle East, the Palestine mandate, far from providing a secure base for British power, seemed about to descend into uncontainable civil strife between Jews and Arabs, and the former mandate of Iraq contained powerful elements antagonistic to the continuation of British influence there. Cyprus was exhibiting increasing impatience with British rule. Ceylon – modern Sri Lanka – had already achieved the fundamentals of internal self-government in 1931, and its important naval base at Trincomalee could not be taken for granted. Within a variety of Caribbean and African colonies nationalist pressure groups were stirring.

The dominions contained even more awkward and unreliable elements than in 1914. The Irish Free State remained a dominion only in name, and was an extremely doubtful ally. The South African coalition government, led by H.B. Hertzog, relied heavily upon Afrikaner support – within which community there were many Nazi sympathisers. Relations between Canada and Britain had been more strained during the inter-war period than at any time since the federation of 1867, and the French-Canadian minority was generally still lukewarm, if not positively hostile, towards the imperial cause. Although Australia and New Zealand remained effectively dependent upon British military protection, and hence loyal, the total combined population of the two nations was less than ten million.[4]

Nor did the circumstances of Britain's entry into the war guarantee staunch imperial support. For many component parts of the Empire, the preservation of Polish sovereignty in the face of the German invasion on 1 September 1939 did not necessarily threaten local security or interests. Hitler's plea that he had no designs on the British Empire, and merely sought to secure the German Reich *Lebensraum*, or living space, in Eastern Europe and the Ukraine was plausible, perhaps even genuine. How even a Germany that had created a New European Order by conquest could also have the energy and manpower to devour the British

Empire as well was not immediately apparent, especially as the Empire was becoming increasingly difficult to govern.

Britain's involvement in the Second World War appeared at first sight to arise from a peculiarly European confrontation, although one much exacerbated by the provisions of the Versailles Treaty of 1919 and the ramifications of the Great Depression of the early 1930s. It was possible to portray Britain's entry into the conflict as an almost quixotic gesture, removed from her real and enduring interests. The British government had in the past cooperated with a number of totalitarian and autocratic regimes, had failed to confront fascist Italy's assault on Abyssinia in 1935, had stood by while Franco destroyed the Spanish Republic, and had subsequently gone out of its way to appease German territorial ambitions in Czechoslovakia and Central Europe. To the exiled Duke of Windsor, formerly King Edward VIII, and to a considerable number of Tory MPs and right-wing sympathisers, the fascist governments of Germany and Italy seemed attractive, businesslike and above all anti-Bolshevik regimes rather than dangerous totalitarian dragons. It is small wonder that some within the British establishment entertained the idea of a negotiated peace with Nazi Germany until 1941. There was also a paradox at the heart of Britain's declared aim of fighting to defend the territorial integrity of a middling state like Poland, when constitutional devolution and full political freedoms were simultaneously being withheld in substantial parts of the Empire.

On the British declaration of war against Germany on 3 September 1939, the dominions gave an illuminating demonstration of their individual rights as set out under the 1931 Statute of Westminster. Australia and New Zealand, even more dependent upon the British defence system in South-East Asia and the South Pacific than in 1914, simply considered themselves bound by the Mother Country's declaration of hostilities. Canada followed the proper constitutional course, appropriately enough for the senior dominion, and deferred any decision to the Canadian parliament. When, a week later, the dominion's House of Commons met, it declared itself unanimously in favour of entering the war.

South Africa was likely to provide an altogether more complicated response. The Prime Minister, Hertzog, undoubtedly would have preferred to have remained neutral. Jan Smuts, however, a South African statesman of international stature, subscribing to a holistic world view, relatively liberal – though not so liberal as to promote equality between whites and blacks – and, although an Afrikaner, enjoying considerable support among the country's English-speakers, felt otherwise. Perhaps political ambition and a yen once more to don uniform and make a final and weighty impact upon world events played their parts in Smuts' decision to bring South Africa into the war. At any rate, a dramatic sequence of events ensued. The Union parliament in Cape Town was invited to approve a resolution asserting South Africa's neutrality, but a pro-British and anti-German amendment put down by Smuts was carried by a small majority. The British Governor-General, Sir Patrick Duncan, then refused Hertzog a dissolution of parliament and a general election, which might well have confirmed the position of neutrality. Thwarted, Hertzog resigned and Smuts, soon to be elevated to the rank of Field Marshal, formed a government supported by the vast majority of English-speaking whites and assumed the premiership.

Afrikaner resistance to involvement in the war, however, posed a considerable threat to the country's contribution to the war effort. The Nationalist Party, purged of its pro-British and – in the eyes of many Afrikaners – collaborationist elements, expressed enthusiastic support for Nazi Germany, and included among its leaders three future prime ministers of South Africa, Malan, Strijdom and Vorster. The Smuts government interned these three as well as substantial numbers of leading Afrikaner nationalists and, for good measure and to show even-handedness, locked up some communists as well.[5]

The government of the Irish Free State took full advantage of the provisions of the Statute of Westminster and declared itself neutral. The Free State maintained a meticulous neutrality throughout the war, even though this meant denying the Royal Navy full use of its southern Irish bases. In some ways, the Free State's declaration of neutrality aided the British war effort. During the Great War the 1916 Easter rebellion and German gun-running had diverted significant British forces away from active service and had undermined the security of the British Isles. Between 1939 and 1945, on the other hand, the British government at least knew where it stood regarding the Free State, and did not feel threatened at its back door. More than this, there was little doubt that the de Valera government wanted Britain to win the conflict, and would certainly have accepted British military assistance in the event of a German invasion. The Irish government effectively repressed the IRA – elements of which flirted with the Nazi regime – and even allowed British Observer Corps members to be stationed around the Irish coast. Tens of thousands of southern Irish also joined the British armed forces for the duration of the war. The British government was, however, obliged to deal sensitively with Northern Ireland, with its large Catholic population, many of whom had republican sympathies. Despite Ulster being part of the United Kingdom, the province was exempted from conscription, although as in the case of southern Ireland, tens of thousands of northern Irish volunteered to fight in the war.

The ambiguity of the dominion response to the outbreak of war was reflected in the Indian sub-continent. Although India had been treated as a quasi-dominion since 1917 and had been granted substantial international recognition, none of this counted in September 1939. The Viceroy, Lord Linlithgow, abruptly announced that war had broken out between the King-Emperor and Germany. Despite the relatively democratic apparatus installed as a result of the 1935 Government of India Act, no consultative or democratic process was followed. India's true status was suddenly and shamefully exposed: essentially that of a dependency over which the Viceroy could rule as an autocrat. Much local goodwill was lost as a result of this high-handed official attitude to India's involvement in the war.

Even so, the Muslim League, still very much in the shadow of Congress, seemed prepared to go along with Britain's decision. Congress, whose leading members, particularly Jawarhalal Nehru, held fascism in deep repugnance, sought a way of asserting India's nationalism and at the same time supporting the war effort. Eventually the Congress ministries which ruled in the provinces felt obliged to resign in protest over the way in which India had been brought into the war. As a result, the Indian Civil Service once more took up the traditional administrative duties that it had appeared so recently to have abandoned.[6]

Winston Churchill's succession to the British premiership in June 1940 posed an exquisite dilemma for both the government of India and the forces of Indian nationalism. Declaring, 'I have not become First Minister of the Crown in order to preside over the liquidation of the British Empire,' Churchill also knew that he could not fight Hitler and Mussolini with one hand while crushing Indian nationalism with the other. Not that the wartime Coalition Government which he led, and which included leading Labour and Liberal statesmen, would have allowed such a brutal attack upon Indian nationalist sensibilities.

In the event, Churchill was prepared to pay the necessary price to keep India sufficiently loyal, and to put its human and material resources at the disposal of the imperial war effort. Having won the reputation in the inter-war period of a die-hard imperialist determined to thwart India's progress towards dominion status at almost any cost,

Churchill did his best to refashion his public face into one whose features, though stern, were understanding of Indian nationalism's difficulties. Churchill's apparent acceptance of the inevitability of India's achievement of independence was, as it transpired, largely a device disguising a deep-rooted inclination to hold on to India for as long as possible.

There were other concessions to the Empire's sensitivities. In 1940 the Colonial Development and Welfare Act was passed by the British Parliament. Building on the legislation first introduced by the 1929–31 Labour government, it set aside £5 million a year for the promotion of development schemes within the dependent empire. Although profits for British commerce were expected to accrue as a result of this bounty, it was also a genuine commitment to colonial economic development and a means of disarming local political opposition.

Further sweeteners were introduced by way of constitutional reform in certain colonies, such as Jamaica and the Gold Coast, where the franchise was extended to larger numbers of the indigenous population during the war. Such reforms continued a process that had its roots deep in colonial history and which was consistent with the prospect of measured devolutionary constitutional progress that the Colonial Office offered to dependencies which it believed, in one way or another, deserved it. As a result of the recruitment of far larger numbers of Africans and West Indians into the imperial forces during the Second World War, moreover, many more colonial systems than in 1914–18 had experience of service overseas and, arguably, an opportunity to extend their knowledge of the world as well as to sharpen up their political ambitions.

By December 1941, despite the German triumph in Western Europe and the Wehrmacht's plunge into the heart of Soviet Russia, the forces of the Empire-Commonwealth had at least held their own. The Italians had been ejected from Abyssinia and Italian Somaliland. German and Italian ambitions in North Africa had been contained, and, as a result, the Suez Canal was still safely in British hands.

In the Middle East, in Iraq an anti-British regime had been set up in 1941, determined to rid the country of British bases and influence in general; but it was ousted by an invasion in 1943. As a consequence, Iraq entered the war on the side of the Allies. In Palestine, although some Arab nationalists attempted to make the most of Nazi Germany's persecution of the Jews, they lacked the strength to oust the British administration. Moreover, the Jewish settlers of Palestine, fearing and loathing Hitler's Germany far more than they disliked British imperial control, threw their support behind the Allied cause. The need to guarantee the oil supplies of Persia – modern Iran – had resulted in an Anglo–Russian partition of the country, very much on the lines of the 'spheres of influence' established in 1907; as a result one more important Middle Eastern country was kept out of German hands.

The Japanese assault on Pearl Harbor in December 1941 made the conflict truly a World War, and led to a series of Japanese victories which wrecked the European empires in South-East Asia and the South Pacific.

As the British, French and Dutch empires in the East collapsed like so many tottering houses of cards, and as the forces of these imperial powers were scattered like dust, the outcome of the war had already been decided. The enormous military potential of the United States was now to be turned on Germany and Italy and their allies, as well as upon Japan. The Grand Alliance was constructed, comprising the United States, Soviet Russia and the British Empire. Even the apparent Japanese triumph of Pearl Harbor turned to ashes, since American aircraft carriers – which were to provide the chief means of victory in the subsequent naval war in the Pacific – had largely escaped destruction.

Victory, however, was still three and a half years off. Japanese military success sowed confusion amongst nationalist movements in Asia: some were prepared to welcome the Japanese as liberators, while others were soon disillusioned by Japanese brutality and by the subordination of the economic and material resources of conquered countries to Japan's war needs.

With Japanese forces over the border of Assam, and with bombs falling on Calcutta and other eastern seaboard Indian cities, the government of India and Indian nationalist leaders struggled to come to an accommodation. In the middle of 1942, Churchill dispatched a leading Labour member of the War Cabinet, Sir Stafford Cripps, to India to try to stabilise the position there. United States pressure on the British government undoubtedly played a part in the sending of the Cripps mission.[7]

Earlier, during 1941, President Roosevelt, meeting with Churchill aboard the great Royal Navy battleship *Prince of Wales* off the coast of Newfoundland, had obliged the British Prime Minister to sign the Atlantic Charter. This agreement was in some respects an updated version of President Woodrow Wilson's attempt in 1918 to shift the imperial agenda from the traditional mechanics of colonial control to that of trusteeship, and to achieve a consistent devolution of imperial power under international supervision. The Atlantic Charter did not go quite that far, but it undoubtedly signified the determination of the United States to act as the midwife and guarantor of colonial liberties and to drag a supplicant Britain along in the process. Roosevelt held the British Empire in low esteem, and claimed that 'The British would take land anywhere in the world, even if it were only a rock or a sandbar.'

It was therefore not surprising that the Atlantic Charter included a reference to 'the right of all people to choose the form of Government under which they live'. Although Churchill tried to exempt the British Empire from this stout declaration of principle, he failed, and on his return to Britain was reduced to the blustering and misleading assertion that the Charter 'was primarily intended to apply to Europe'. The Cripps mission, however, was plainly a by-product of the Atlantic Charter, and an attempt to buy American approval.

Cripps' mission partly placated American anti-imperial feeling, particularly within the Democratic government. It also destabilised Indian politics. There is no doubt that Churchill chose to see the mission as doomed from the outset, and furthermore did his best to sabotage it.[8] Cripps offered India's nationalists post-war independence – either within the Commonwealth or outside it. The offer included the right of Muslim-majority provinces to opt out of an independent India – a concession which gratified the separatists within the Muslim League – and the immediate inclusion of Indian leaders in the government of India. After some agonising, Congress, by far the largest and most broadly-based political party, decided to reject the plan, and a disappointed and humiliated Cripps returned to the United Kingdom.

Chiefly as a result of the failure of the Cripps mission, and inspired by Gandhi – who insisted that the British must now leave India so that a purified sub-continent could the better resist the Japanese through the power of *satyagraha* – Congress passed its 'Quit India' resolution in August 1942, and also called for the immediate dismantling of the Raj. In reprisal, the British authorities arrested hundreds of Congress leaders, thus cutting off the party's head. Violent protest occurred throughout India, causing the Viceroy, Lord Linlithgow, to describe the disturbances as 'the worst since the Mutiny'. The Raj, aided by the still loyal Indian Army and the Indian police, eventually restored order. The Indian empire continued to make a significant contribution to the winning of the war.

The arrest and imprisonment of so many leaders of the Congress Party, however, created a vacuum in the Indian political scene. Into it stepped the Muslim League, led by the anglicised, ascetic Mohammed Ali Jinnah. Jinnah, who had left Congress chiefly because he feared that Gandhi's domination of the movement would deny him supreme political power, followed up Congress's 'Quit India' resolution with a resolution from the Muslim League demanding that Britain 'Divide and Quit'.[9]

Ignoring the League's resolution, the British proceeded to play the Muslim card. The new Viceroy, Field Marshal Sir Archibald Wavell, vigorously promoted cooperation between India's Muslims and the Raj. A disproportionate 30 per cent of the Indian Army was Muslim, and the Punjab, with its population divided between Sikhs and Muslims, was one of the great granaries of India as well as one of its main recruiting grounds. When the Muslim League wanted to found a party newspaper, *Dawn*, the government of India proceeded to subsidise it through the placing of substantial amounts of advertisements within its pages. From the 'Quit India' resolution of August 1942 until the end of the war, the Muslim League campaigned hard to woo the majority of Muslim voters away from Congress and over to them. The independent state of Pakistan was to be the product of these years.

As the war went against the Japanese in the Far East and South-East Asia, and as the battles of El Alamein and Stalingrad proved to be turning-points in the Allied campaigns in North Africa and Europe, the forces of the Axis Powers were driven back. The reconquest of Burma was slow and costly, but British and imperial forces in Malaya, Borneo and Hong Kong met little resistance, even from those indigenous groups that had collaborated with the Japanese. It was soon evident that Britain's empire in Asia would be restored to its full territorial extent.

Britain's progress towards final victory, however, was complicated by the fact that both the United States and the Soviet Union were carrying an increasing and ultimately dominant share of the war effort. Neither of these great powers had much love for British imperialism: the Russians were antipathetic towards the British Empire from conviction based upon Marxist ideology; and the United States had a lengthy history of disliking and mistrusting Imperial Britain, and Roosevelt's Democratic Party was, moreover, particularly sensitive to the votes of Irish-Americans in the great cities of the eastern seaboard. In his role as one of the 'Big Three' Allied war leaders, Churchill often found himself squeezed by pressure from both the Soviet Union and the United States. He was ruefully to observe that 'There is only one thing worse than fighting with allies, and that is fighting without them.'[10]

As it turned out, American reluctance to help reconstruct the British Empire at the end of the war was eventually tempered by a growing anxiety at the emergence of the Soviet Union as a great world power, and at the spread of communism both in Europe and within some of the nationalist movements now flourishing in the empires of the European powers. By the onset of the Cold War, Washington was tending to view the British Empire as a positive safeguard against the spread of Marxist ideology and communist governments.[11]

Within the United Kingdom the surrender of Germany in 1945 opened the way for a general election in July of that year. Exhausted and radicalised by nearly six years of war, during which they had become accustomed to much centralised planning and control as well as to the egalitarianism of the ration book and restricted consumerism, the electorate wanted reform at home, full employment and a speedy demobilisation of British forces. Three million homes in Britain had been damaged by bombing, and a further 458,000 had been completely destroyed. With the memories of inter-war hardship and unemployment still fresh in many minds, the voters put housing, social improvement and welfare reforms at the top of their agenda. As a result, a Labour government was returned to power with an overwhelming majority. When the Attlee government came to power, Japan had not yet surrendered. This was duly brought about by the United States dropping atomic bombs on Hiroshima and Nagasaki in August 1945.

The making of British imperial policy in the post-war world was assumed by an administration drawn from a party with a substantial anti-imperial tradition. How far the Labour government would depart from the bipartisanship which had characterised the exercise of imperial policy during the war years was unclear.

The new government's room for manoeuvre was to some extent circumscribed by the enormous cost of the war. By the end of 1940 Britain's gold and dollar reserves had become nearly exhausted, and the country had only been able to carry on buying materials of war from the United States because of the Lend-Lease arrangement of March 1941, under which the American government lent or leased war supplies and arms to Britain and other Allied countries. There was, however, a price to pay. The cost of Lend-Lease amounted to 54 per cent of the country's total payments deficit during the war years.[12]

British financial dependence upon the United States was to be one of the uncomfortable facts of the post-war period. Worse still, President Truman abruptly ended the Lend-Lease arrangement in August 1945, a week after the surrender of Japan. This was a severe blow, and meant that Britain would henceforth be forced to pay for goods from the United States in cash.

During the war Britain had also been forced to sell a large proportion of its overseas assets and investments, and to borrow money from a variety of sources other than the United States. When war broke out in September 1939, the government even agreed to pay for the out-of-ordinary costs of using the Indian Army, a concession which resulted eventually in a £1.3 billion British debt to India, amounting to approximately one-fifth of Britain's gross national product.[13] At the peace, moreover, exports were running at little more than 40 per cent of their pre-war total, and the merchant marine was 30 per cent smaller than in September 1939. Something like 10 per cent of Britain's pre-war national wealth had been destroyed, some of it as a result of physical destruction, the rest by the inexorable running-down of capital assets.

Despite Britain's indebtedness and war-weariness, despite its financial dependence upon the United States, despite the election of a Labour government, the British Empire by no means collapsed in the immediate post-war world. Britain's war aims had included the 'regaining and regrouping [of] the empire, and in this she was remarkably successful – given the desperate situation in 1940 and the fact that her main ally and chief paymaster was a former colony with an anti-colonial bias. As the principal component of the Sterling Area, the empire also made a vital contribution to Britain's post-war reconstruction plans in the decade after 1945.'[14] There was, as it happened, a lot of life still left in the old imperial lion.

25

THE PARTITION
OF INDIA, 1947

The Labour Government
and the Empire-Commonwealth, 1945 to 1951

AT MIDNIGHT ON 14 AUGUST 1947 British rule in India ended. To mark the occasion, Jawaharlal Nehru, the country's first Prime Minister, made a moving broadcast to the new India:

> Long years ago we made a tryst with destiny, and now the time comes when we shall redeem our pledge, not wholly or in full measure, but very substantially. At the stroke of the midnight hour, when the world sleeps, India will awake to life and freedom. A moment comes, which comes but rarely in history, when we step out from the old to the new, when an age ends, and when the soul of a nation long suppressed finds utterance.[1]

The next day, 15 August, most of the huge population of the sub-continent celebrated the creation of two new dominions, India and Pakistan. At 8.30 a.m. countless Union Jacks were hauled down – from frontier posts and the viceregal palace, from official buildings and public places. Most of the regiments of the British Army stationed in India had already left, embarking at Bombay in a discreet and orderly fashion while the bands on the waterfront played 'Auld Lang Syne'. In Karachi, Mohammed Ali Jinnah was sworn in as Governor-General of Pakistan, while in Delhi Lord Mountbatten, the last Viceroy, became India's first Governor-General. Mountbatten's transformation from Viceroy, with the prerogative to rule autocratically, to Governor-General, with considerable influence but no effective power, neatly illustrated the great change that the Indian empire had undergone.

Pakistan was an artificial creation – more so than India – and its frontiers had only been agreed upon after bitter disputation. The new state incorporated the majority Muslim areas of East Bengal, the Western Punjab, Sind and Baluchistan. The two Pakistans, East and West, were separated by a thousand miles of Indian territory. The approach of independence day precipitated the mass migration of millions of Indians, Hindus moving from provinces designated to Pakistan, and Muslims leaving Indian territory. The communal hatreds and fears that had been whipped up to a frenzy between 1942 and 1947 resulted in the terrible massacres of many refugees. The British Raj had prided itself, perhaps too much, upon keeping the peace in the sub-continent. As British rule collapsed, hundreds of thousands of Indian citizens died at the hands of their fellow-Indians. At least a quarter of a million refugees died in the tumult, and perhaps as many as 600,000.

The India of the princes, comprising a third of the whole sub-continent, collapsed once the strong protective arm of the Raj was no longer there to shield them. Although some princes had been progressive and enlightened rulers, many had been little better than corrupt and autocratic medieval despots. A good many had banned the Congress Party from their provinces. Some now paid a high price for their collaboration with the Raj. Given the option of joining one of the two new dominions, maharajahs, rajahs, nawabs and nizams for the most part hastened to assign their principalities to the more appropriate of the new states, opting in terms of their own religious convictions and those of their subjects.

But the great province of Hyderabad, a territory as large as Spain, had to be dragged into the Indian federal union by armed force. So too did the much smaller state of Junagadh, where a predominantly Hindu population was ruled by a Muslim nawab. In Kashmir, the ancestral homeland of the Nehru family, the Hindu ruler, ignoring the fact that the majority of his subjects were Muslims, chose to join India. This decision resulted in the first, sharp clash between the forces of Pakistan and India, leaving most of Kashmir within the new India and an immediate and bloody stain upon Indo–Pakistan relations.

The two new dominions of India and Pakistan were thus born amid much confusion, strife and bloodshed. In January 1948, within a few months of the partition, Mahatma Gandhi, perhaps the most inspirational leader of Indian nationalism, was shot dead at point-blank range in New Delhi. Gandhi was the victim of a plot by fanatical, extremist Hindus who bitterly resented his peacemaking activities and his denunciation of violence amid the continuing horror of communal confrontation and bloodshed. Less than a year after Gandhi's assassination, Jinnah, whose political skills and sheer intransigence had been instrumental in the creation of Pakistan, was also dead – the victim of tuberculosis.

Nearly half a century before the partition of India, the Viceroy, Lord Curzon, had declared:

> As long as we rule India, we are the greatest power in the world. If we lose it we shall drop straightway to a third rate power ... Your ports and coaling stations, your fortresses and your dockyards, your Crown colonies and protectorates will go too. For either they will be unnecessary, or the toll-gates and barbicans of an Empire that has vanished.[2]

Gandhi had expressed similar feelings, or at least hopes, telling President Roosevelt in 1942 that 'If India becomes free, the rest will follow.'

In the aftermath of India's independence, events seemed amply to justify these predictions. On the peripheries of the old Indian empire, both Burma and Ceylon had achieved independence by February 1948. Burma, which had been rather half-heartedly and belatedly incorporated into the Indian empire in 1886, had never fully accepted the restoration of British rule after the ejection of Japanese forces. Eventually the results in a general election indicated that a huge majority of voters were in favour of immediate independence. Burma achieved its freedom in January 1948, immediately opted to become a republic and left the Commonwealth, although maintaining for some years a number of educational, cultural and developmental links with Britain.

At the tip of the sub-continent, Ceylon, formerly a Crown Colony, became a fully independent dominion within the Commonwealth. In contrast to the convoluted and often bloody course of the struggle for independence that had characterised India, Pakistan and Burma, Ceylon's path to self-rule had been surprisingly smooth, providing something of a model. The introduction of the liberal and democratic Donoughmore constitution of 1931, in which much of the internal administrative structure at the centre had been modelled, perhaps rather surprisingly, upon the organisation of the London County Council, had resulted in full independence within two decades.

In June 1948 the British government abandoned the attempt to find some long-term solution to the increasingly chaotic confrontation in

Palestine between Jews and Arabs. United States pressure, arising in part from President Truman's need to appeal to urban Jewish voters in the imminent presidential election, played a large and probably crucial part in the decision. In a relatively uncharacteristic act of abandonment, British forces and administration were withdrawn in as orderly a fashion as possible, and the territory to the west of the Jordan River was left as the prize to whoever should be strong enough to claim it. After a short and ferocious war, this turned out to be the newly-established state of Israel.

There was no question of Israel remaining in the Commonwealth, although British newspapers owned by Lord Beaverbrook were to fantasise over the possibility for the next decade or so. Continuing Western, particularly United States, support, however, was to ensure that one of the original, although covert, intentions behind the Balfour Declaration, the hope that a Jewish homeland would turn out to be a friendly oasis in a desert of Arab hostility, was eventually realised.

During the next year, 1949, the Irish Free State, which had chiefly maintained dominion status as a temporary diplomatic convenience, left the Commonwealth. The creation of the Irish Republic appeared to be at least a partial fulfilment of the fears of constitutional and imperial disruption voiced with such vehemence by British Conservatives, Liberal Unionists and Ulster Protestants during the 1880s. But although republicans in the six northern counties were encouraged by the development, it was an event marked more by compromise and the recognition of a shared past than the raising of the flag of precipitate and violent revolution. In all but name, citizens of the Irish Republic enjoyed the rights of United Kingdom citizenship, including unrestricted migration, domicile and enfranchisement.

Viewed hastily, therefore, the two years from 1947 to 1949 seemed to give substance to the predictions of Curzon and Gandhi alike that the loss of the Indian empire would open the floodgates to the disintegration and abandonment of the British Empire. As it turned out, the expected flooding was to be quite substantially delayed. This is partly because Curzon, as was not uncommon in his career, had got it wrong. Britain was not 'the greatest power in the world' as long as it ruled India; rather, it had progressively acquired territory in the sub-continent as a result of its position during the late eighteenth and nineteenth centuries as the world's greatest industrial, manufacturing and naval power. Britain, in fact, ruled India because she was a great power, not because her dominion of the sub-continent made her one.

Sir Frederick Lugard, the conqueror of Uganda and Northern Nigeria and the theorist of 'indirect rule' as a centrepiece of imperial administration, surrounded by Northern Nigerian chieftains on a visit to London Zoo in 1925.

A clash – or a meeting? – of cultures. Two Europeans amid warriors in late-nineteenth-century Borneo.

THE BLACK BABY.

Right A reluctant John Bull decides to take yet another abandoned 'black baby', Uganda, into his care in 1894.

A 1910 reception at another East African protectorate, Zanzibar, showing the local ruling élite mixing on apparently equal terms with their British protectors.

New South Wales Lancers celebrating Victoria's Diamond Jubilee in 1897 take their place in the great procession through the streets of London.

General Kitchener, avenger of Gordon
and imperial totem, as Sirdar of the
Egyptian army.

A British engineer gives his orders to Chinese
underlings at Wei-hai-Wei, acquired in 1898 from
China to be a British naval base.

Cecil Rhodes dining with a young companion at his camp
in the Matapos Hills, where he was eventually to be buried.

Paul Kruger,
President of the
Transvaal 1883–1901.

Sir Alfred Milner, High Commissioner for South Africa, and one of the architects of the Boer War of 1899–1901.

Dr Jameson (*fourth from left*) and a group of imperial hearties sailing for Britain after the fiasco of the Jameson Raid.

THE BOER WAR

Above Battle-weary men of the Hampshire Regiment cross the Valsch River Drift before advancing on Kronstadt in the Orange Free State.

Left Londoners celebrate the relief of Ladysmith in Fleet Street, 1900.

Viceregal pomp and circumstance: Lord and Lady Curzon in the 1903 Durbar procession to mark Edward VII's accession as King-Emperor.

Right Rudyard Kipling, poet of Empire, and often accused of having India on the brain.

Below Indian princes and British Army officers mingle in the Hyderabad Contingent's polo team.

The Colonial Conference of 1902 which was chaired by the Colonial Secretary Joseph Chamberlain, seated centre, front row. Among the self-governing colonies' premiers in the front row are Seddon (New Zealand, second from left), Laurier (Canada, third from left) and Barton (Australia, third from right).

The 1911 Imperial Conference at which Sir Joseph Ward of New Zealand proposed a muddled plan for Imperial unity. The leaders are, *front row*: Sir Joseph Ward, Sir Wilfrid Laurier (Canada), Herbert Asquith (Britain, and chair), Andrew Fisher (Australia). *Back row* : Sir E.P. Morris (Newfoundland) and Louis Botha (South Africa).

The majestic building of New Delhi. The Imperial Secretariat and Council Chamber (*left centre*) designed by Sir Herbert Baker, and the Viceroy's House (*right*) designed by Sir Edwin Lutyens. Baker and Lutyens also designed official buildings for the newly established Union of South Africa.

Right Indian Lancers answer the Empire's call.

Below Canadian troops in the trenches before Ypres in 1916.

Below Australian and New Zealand troops being landed at Anzac Cove at the start of the ill-fated Gallipoli campaign in April 1915. Australian losses were to provoke long and bitter resentments.

The shattered General Post Office in Dublin from which the Irish Republic was declared during the 1916 Easter uprising.

Foremost negotiators for Irish freedom, Arthur Griffiths and Eamon de Valera in Dublin, July 1921.

Brigadier-General Dyer, whose massacre at Amritsar in 1919 aroused an outcry in the international community and strengthened Indian nationalist resolve.

Mohandas Karamchand Gandhi, whose inspired campaigning, centring on civil disobedience and non-violent resistance, so discomforted the Raj from 1917 onwards.

Another reason why the Empire-Commonwealth did not collapse in ruin and confusion during the 1940s and early 1950s was that the Labour government had no intention of aiding and abetting such a process. When the Attlee administration had been swept to power in July 1945 with a huge majority, Conservatives and imperialists had feared the worst. They need not have worried. Indeed, an intelligent assessment of the record of the two Labour minority governments of the inter-war period would have been sufficient reassurance. The British Labour Party was fundamentally more concerned to appear a respectable custodian of both the national and the imperial interest than to unleash the forces of Bolshevik revolution throughout the Empire. Rather than dismantling the British Empire, Ramsay MacDonald's first administration in 1924 had fussed over whether to wear full dress uniform or evening dress with tights on being sworn in as ministers by King George V.

The Attlee administration similarly had no revolutionary and destructive intent towards the Empire. For one thing, Labour ministers had pursued a bipartisan policy towards colonial and imperial matters during Churchill's wartime Coalition Government of 1940 to 1945. For another, the incoming Cabinet was dominated by ministers whose views on Empire were often at least as conservative as those of their political opponents.

The Labour Secretary of State for the Colonies, Arthur Creech Jones, claimed in 1946 that the Conservative opposition had, as a result of the bipartisan cooperation of the wartime administration, shifted much nearer to Labour's position: 'Therefore, instead of Labour members endorsing the sentiment that the policy of the Labour Government is just a continuity of previous policies, they should rejoice that, at last, our propaganda has succeeded in converting the Tory benches to a much more human and liberal approach to these problems.'[3]

The Prime Minister, Clement Attlee, shrewd, monosyllabic, pipe-smoking and efficient, was not likely to assume the role of a latter-day Samson and pull the pillars of the imperial temple down around his ears. Among his most senior colleagues, Herbert Morrison, the Deputy Leader of the party, had already said during the war that independence for under-developed countries like those of Africa would be 'like giving a child of ten a latch-key, a bank account and a shotgun'.[4] Six months after the formation of the Labour administration, Morrison even referred to Labour as being 'great friends of the jolly old Empire'.[5]

Ernest Bevin, unexpectedly made Foreign Secretary in the new

government, had long ago expressed his contempt for the 'ragged-arsed'
communists and agitators of the trade union movement. Although
recognising that the high noon of Empire was long past, Bevin still saw
plenty of room for economic development and cooperation between
Britain and the colonies. He has even been described as 'a genuine
enthusiast for Empire, envisaging for it both limitless possibilities of
economic development and a key strategic role'.[6] In 1946 Bevin asserted
that he was not prepared 'to sacrifice the British Empire', since he was
convinced that 'if the British Empire fell . . . it would mean that the
standard of life of our constituents would fall rapidly'.[7]

Hugh Dalton, the left-wing Chancellor of the Exchequer, assumed
a pragmatic stance on the inevitability of imperial retreat: 'If you are
in a place where you are not wanted, and where you have not got the
force to squash those who don't want you, the only thing to do is to
come out.' The Cabinet as a whole tended to close ranks in the face of
American criticism of the government's colonial policy, in effect telling
Washington to mind its own business.[8]

Even if the Attlee government had wished rapidly to dismantle the
imperial structure, the need to reconstruct the British economy and
adequately to finance the huge expense entailed in establishing the
Welfare State would have given them pause. Indeed, it has been plausibly argued that the new government's determination to maintain
Britain's great-power status – which entailed a 'global overstretch' of
resources to finance a massive defence budget as well as to preserve
much of the imperial inheritance – together with its idealistic commitment to building the Welfare State and ensuring full employment, was to
unnecessarily and irresponsibly hasten the country's post-war economic
decline.[9]

The vigorous promotion of commerce and trade was one obvious
way of paying for some of the Labour government's huge spending
programme. In 1945, with trade to much of Europe badly disrupted,
the Empire-Commonwealth took on a new significance. Paradoxically,
as the Empire moved inexorably towards its final dissolution, inter-
imperial trade boomed as never before. Between 1946 and 1949, 57.5
per cent of British exports went to the Empire, while during the same
time Britain took 48 per cent of its imports from the Empire-
Commonwealth. Although British exports to the Empire were never
again to surpass that total, they averaged 54 per cent between 1950
and 1954, and 51 per cent between 1955 and 1959.

During the years of the Attlee administration, and some way

beyond, Britain depended on Australia and New Zealand for two-thirds of its imported wool, half of its imported butter and 29 per cent of its imported meat. Canada and South Africa supplied 50 per cent of non-ferrous metals, and 81 per cent of tea imports came from India. Canada also supplied Britain with 54 per cent of her imported grains. The United Kingdom remained heavily dependent on the West Indies for sugar, on Malaya for rubber, and on tropical Africa for a variety of metals and vegetable products. In addition, the Middle East supplied Britain with 82 per cent of her mineral oil needs, which became its principal import, and is the reason why British influence in that area was withdrawn so reluctantly and so slowly.[10]

The inter-war creation of the Sterling Area continued to be a great boon to Britain in the years after 1945. Not only was there a Sterling Area dollar pool, which greatly assisted Britain in repaying American wartime loans, but the very existence of the Sterling Area helped to smooth the passage of inter-imperial trade. Although it was not widely publicised at the time, the government also imposed a number of physical controls on the commercial activities of the dependent empire, and blatantly used its dominant position within the tropical colonies to channel important primary products into British factories and shops. As has recently been claimed: 'The whole amounted to what may well have been the most oppressive form of economic imperialism yet seen in British tropical colonies, carried out with a combination of self-interest, myopia, and liberal good intentions.'[11]

It seems clear, however, that between 1945 and 1956 the American government actively encouraged Britain to develop the economies of much of the dependent empire, particularly in Africa – mainly as a means of thwarting the growth of indigenous Marxism and socialism, but also as a way of minimising the potential for Soviet and, after 1949, Chinese Communist influence and interference. Partly as a result, the tendency of pre-Second World War British governments to obstruct certain forms of colonial economic and social development was lessened. Nevertheless the Attlee administration invested more money in Australia and New Zealand than in tropical African colonies. Nor was enough done to prevent the steady drain of African resources to pay the cost of administration – a process that had earlier disadvantaged Indian development. Moreover British commercial companies operating in colonial territories, in Africa and elsewhere, generally paid taxes, including income tax, to the revenue authorities in the United Kingdom.

This would perhaps have mattered less if the government had been able to press ahead as it might have wished with plans for colonial economic development. But the Treasury, headed first by Hugh Dalton and then by Sir Stafford Cripps, insisted that Britain simply did not have the money to spend on such ambitious schemes. The 1945 Colonial Development and Welfare Act had allotted £120 million to the colonies, to be spent over the next ten years. Two further Colonial Development Acts in 1949 and 1950 tended simply to put more money into the fund, rather than rewrite the agenda and substantially increase the sums hitherto allotted. One of the major problems was that post-war economic restraints meant that the government felt itself obliged to see colonial planning chiefly in terms of the requirements of the domestic economy. As a consequence, the Labour administration overwhelmingly backed plans which led to the creation of colonial monocultures designed primarily to meet the needs of the infinitely more sophisticated British economy.

This was quasi-imperialism, pink in tooth and claw. It sowed the seeds of long-term agricultural and economic difficulties for the tropical colonies, and also resulted in the fiasco of the Tanganyika groundnut scheme, which sank £36 million in an attempt to plant a primary agricultural product in manifestly unsuitable physical conditions. Arthur Creech Jones, Colonial Secretary for the years 1946–50, although possessing an impeccable pedigree in the shaping of inter-war and wartime Labour colonial policy, was something of a disappointment in office. The Prime Minister even considered that he 'had not appeared to have a real grip of administration in the Colonial Office. He was bad in the House and contributed nothing in Cabinet.'[12]

Among the many factors that inhibited Creech Jones' room for manoeuvre, apart from his alleged personal failings, was the dominating role played by Ernest Bevin at the Foreign Office. It has been written that:

> His was truly an imperialist Foreign Office, seeking constantly to extend its influence over other departments: and the Colonial Office, especially over the issue of Palestine and other territories where major strategic interests were involved, was a prime target. The subordination of Colonial Office to Foreign Office was also influenced by the fact that Creech Jones was a former subordinate of Bevin's in the TGWU; that his integrity and expertise were not matched

by forcefulness in cabinet or in the House; and that Attlee had little faith in him.[13]

Partly as a result of Bevin's controlling, conservative hand, British colonial policy remained especially cautious and unadventurous in territories where there were either substantial numbers of white settlers or which were of particular strategic significance to either Britain or the United States. After 1947 the development of the Cold War, and heightened Anglo–American alarm at the Soviet potential for promoting trouble and anti-Western attitudes in existing colonies and post-colonial territories, placed even more restrictions upon the process of the devolution of imperial power.

Despite this, the government did not face any sustained or damaging assault from the left of the Labour Party. With limited time at their disposal, MPs who might otherwise have more readily discerned compromise and betrayal in official party colonial policies devoted most of their energies to the urgent task of post-war reconstruction, and the extension of public ownership and social welfare. Members of Parliament may also have realised, as their predecessors had so often done, that there were far more votes in domestic reform than in enlightened colonial policy. Moreover the granting of independence to India, Pakistan, Ceylon and Burma probably did enough to convince Labour MPs that sufficient progress was being made.

In one area in particular, there was undoubted development and expansion. The Colonial Office and its subordinate departments and committees were greatly expanded and strengthened by the recruitment of a large number of experts. At the outbreak of the Second World War, the London-based half of the Colonial Office had numbered 465; by 1950 it totalled 1,289. Previously colonial forestry administration had been the responsibility of one, part-time, general administrator; under the Labour government it became a complete department, replete with officials and specialists. Equally significantly, many of these newly-appointed officials and administrators were encouraged to visit the colonies and to report upon what they found. In 1939 travelling expenses for the Colonial Office staff in London had cost the department £3,100; by 1950 £51,875 was being spent on similar travelling expenses. A considerable amount of extra accommodation was needed in London, and architectural plans were drawn up for a magnificent new Colonial Office on a large bombsite between Whitehall and the Houses of Parliament. Fortunately, perhaps, it was never built.

Under the Labour government, the Colonial Service, which administered British territories overseas, boomed as never before. Before 1945 the number of recruits sent out each year had never exceeded 551, and had sometimes fallen as low as seventy. Between 1945 and 1950 an average of 1,265 recruits were sent out each year, reaching a bumper 1,715 during the first year of the new Attlee administration. Not merely were many more specialists being sent out, but the number of general administrators was trebled.

Within the structures of colonial government itself, the old secretariats were for the most part transformed into government departments very like those in Britain. With very few exceptions, these administrative posts went to British personnel, although indigenous people filled some of the specialist posts as well as the overwhelming number of lowly administrative and clerical positions. The earlier disinclination to appoint indigenous people to even fairly insignificant administrative positions had been effectively ended in 1942, partly as a result of the liberal undertakings to encourage colonial self-government contained in the 1941 Atlantic Charter, partly as a result of United States diplomatic pressure, and partly to ensure the continuing cooperation of subject colonial peoples in supporting the war effort. As a consequence it was no longer possible to discriminate, by whatever devices, covert or overt, against local applicants on the grounds of their colour.

While the colonial bureaucracy was being expanded at such an impressive pace, one other growth area in human terms was in the number of emigrants from Britain sailing to both the dominions and the dependent Empire. For many of these aspirants the pull of a better, more prosperous life was the dominant attraction. For others, already well-to-do or at least determined to become so, there was a decided push factor, principally the egalitarian and nationalising policies of Britain's first majority socialist government.

In these circumstances it is not surprising that the main recipients of emigration from the United Kingdom were the dominions, and those colonies in Central and East Africa which already contained significant white minorities. As a consequence, the European population of Southern Rhodesia increased from 80,000 in 1945 to more than 200,000 by 1955. Within the same period the white population of Northern Rhodesia was boosted from 5000 to more than 60,000. In Kenya, where the British government gave financial assistance to emigrants wishing to acquire farms in the White Highlands, the number of Europeans rose sharply, from 12,000 in 1945 to more than 50,000 by 1955. The augmentation and consolidation of white populations in these territories had one immediate and beneficial consequence – a considerable amount of British and American capital was invested, and cities like Salisbury in Southern Rhodesia, Lusaka in Northern Rhodesia and Nairobi in Kenya developed rapidly both in terms of new buildings and modern amenities. The problem was, of course, that these developments were simply storing up trouble for the future. Wall Street and the City of London took satisfaction in the process, but the predictable and inevitable rise of black nationalism was, in a comparatively short time, to present a variety of British governments with a number of extremely difficult choices, in both practical politics and ethics.

The Labour government was ultimately unable to fashion a brave new world out of the British Empire-Commonwealth between 1945 and 1951. Constrained by the need to reorder and restore Britain's industrial and commercial base, it was also committed to satisfying the expectations of the bulk of the electors who had put them in power. Although the principle of a steady devolution of power within colonial territories was not abandoned, the process was not markedly speeded up. Indeed development, not devolution, became the chief characteristic of official policy. In general, the administration simply brought certain developments which had already been self-evident in the inter-war period to final fruition: chiefly the granting of independence to the old Indian empire, including Burma, and to Ceylon. Elsewhere, and despite the substantial investment of capital and expertise – particularly in the tropical colonies – the government was largely reactive, responding to particular pressures and acting at least as much from expediency as from principle.

Even the final withdrawal of Britain from the Indian sub-continent was not an unalloyed triumph for Labour policies, although it was later generally assumed to have been a singular success. When the Attlee government first came to power, it seemed, for a considerable and unexpected time, paralysed by the dilemmas of the Indian situation rather than galvanised by a clear and positive agenda.

In a fundamental sense, British policy towards India was quite straightforward: not merely was full independence desirable, already conceded in principle and apparently within easy reach, but the cost, in both moral and material terms, of any protracted attempt to hold on to power by force was unthinkable. The chief problem was, to whom would the British hand over control? Above all, would it be necessary to partition the old Indian empire, transferring power to two independent homelands – one with a majority of Hindu citizens and one with a majority of Muslims? There was also some disinclination within the Cabinet immediately to mark Labour's achievement of majority rule at home with an abrupt ditching of the nation's greatest imperial possession. Even left-wing members of the Cabinet were uncertain how to proceed, and the Viceroy, Field Marshal Wavell, shrewdly observed that Aneurin Bevan, the reforming Minister of Health, 'like everyone else hates the idea of our leaving India, but like everyone else has no alternative to suggest'.[14]

Many Indian nationalists were deeply disappointed and vexed by the Labour government's apparent inability to move swiftly to a resolution of what had become the 'Indian problem'. Perhaps they set too much store by the anti-imperialist rhetoric and the apparently genuine encouragement of colonial freedom movements by Labour politicians and activists during the inter-war years. Perhaps they did not appreciate the full extent of the power wielded within the government by its inner core of right-wingers – Attlee, Bevin and Morrison – or fully understand the commitment to responsible administration which motivated the more left-wing members of the Cabinet like Dalton and Cripps. Perhaps, like Jawaharlal Nehru, they put too much faith in the personal contacts made before the war with leading members of the Labour movement. Nehru had stayed at Sir Stafford Cripps' country house during his visit to Britain in June 1938, and had met there Clement Attlee and Aneurin Bevan, as well as the influential socialist ideologue Harold Laski, a professor at the London School of Economics and a member of Labour's National Executive Committee.

There was a more kindly way of assessing the government's inaction than deriding it as an illustration of the cowardice and incompetence of the battered imperial lion faced with the hungry and aggressive tiger of Indian nationalism. For one thing, the Attlee government took some time to martial its thoughts on the Indian problem and to agree on the best measures to bring it to a satisfactory resolution. For another, it was waiting for the results of the central and provincial Indian elections, the outcome of which would be known by the end of 1945. Since the last elections for the central assembly had been held in 1934, and those for the provincial legislatures in 1937, the votes cast in 1945 would provide up-to-date evidence of, among other things, the electoral strength of the Muslim League.

During the election campaigns, Congress made its usual broad appeal to a wide range of interests, hoping to retain the support of sufficient numbers of Muslim voters to scupper the growing movement for a separatist state of Pakistan. Jinnah and his supporters in the Muslim League, their confidence boosted by the Raj's encouragement of them during the war and by Wavell's reputation as a Muslim sympathiser, unscrupulously and irresponsibly conjured up the spectre of a united India dominated by a harsh and unsympathetic Hindu majority.

The result of the Indian elections confirmed the swift recent progress of the Muslim League. The League won all of the seats reserved for Muslims in the central assembly, polling 86.6 per cent of the vote. The result was more ambiguous in the provinces, where even in areas in which Muslims formed the majority of the population, the League did not win a majority of votes. In the Punjab, for example, it polled 46.56 per cent of the vote, and in Sind 45.75 per cent, while in the North-West Frontier Province it only achieved 37.19 per cent of the poll. Nonetheless, in terms of seats gained the League did spectacularly, some argued unfairly, well. Congress, however, was able to form ministries in eight of the eleven Indian provinces, and the Muslim League only in Bengal and Sind, while the Punjab was ruled by a coalition party with Congress support.

As the battle lines were now so clearly drawn up between Congress and the League, the British government's response was disappointingly cautious, even indecisive: it decided to send a parliamentary delegation to reassure Indian nationalists of the Cabinet's sincerity of purpose.

Only in 1946 did a series of mutinies have the effect of galvanising the British government. The first of these incidents, involving British RAF servicemen enraged by delays in demobilisation and repatriation, was, in a sense, the most shocking. But units of the Indian Air Force were the next to mutiny, and much worse was to follow. In February 1946 a naval mutiny occurred at Bombay and was followed by others at Calcutta, Madras and Karachi. While the mutinies were quite soon quelled, although not without considerable casualties at Karachi, they had the effect of pushing the Attlee administration into the announcement that a delegation of senior Cabinet ministers would at once leave for India to begin negotiations aimed at finding a way around the obstacles preventing a smooth transition of power in India. The Cabinet Mission was led by the benign but elderly Secretary of State for India, Lord Pethick-Lawrence, soon to be ridiculed as 'pathetic Lawrence', but was dominated by the presence of Stafford Cripps.

On arriving in India, the members of the Cabinet Mission quickly perceived that they could not simply leave Indian nationalists to settle things for themselves, since this would only bring the negotiations back to the main problem – whether or not a Muslim state should be set up. At a series of meetings, including a conference at Simla, various attempts to maintain Indian unity – including the suggestion that 'groups of provinces may be formed' – were wrecked by the intransigence of Jinnah and the Muslim League. Finally the Cabinet Mission issued its own plan, which proposed the establishment of an Indian union dealing with foreign policy, defence and communications, and with the appropriate authority to raise finance. Major communal issues could be brought to the central legislature, but would need a majority of each community as well as an overall majority of votes there before appropriate legislation could be passed. All other powers would be vested in the provinces, which would be entitled to form groupings with a great deal of local autonomy. The mission also proposed the immediate formation of an interim government. What was essentially being offered was a means of breaking the deadlock and thus enabling India to obtain independence 'in the shortest time and with the least danger of internal disturbance and conflict'.[15]

The Cabinet Mission departed, leaving the Viceroy, Wavell, to supervise the formation of the interim government. But Nehru proceeded to create confusion by asserting for Congress that 'We are not bound by a single thing except that we have decided to go into the Constituent Assembly.'[16] Jinnah and the Muslim League seized on Nehru's remarks, using them as a justification for backing away from the League's earlier, reluctant acceptance of the Cabinet Mission's plan.

Between the departure of the Cabinet Mission in June 1946 and February 1947, a series of tortuous meetings, interventions by the Viceroy, and apparent breakthroughs in the constitutional negotiations occurred against a background of mounting communal tension and violence. Some of the worst conflict arose as a terrible consequence of the Muslim League's Direct Action Day, which was called for 16 August 1946, and led to the 'Calcutta killings' where, within a week, unofficial estimates put the dead at over 15,000. The interim government was only finally set up after Congress made substantial concessions to the League, and after Wavell brought Jinnah and his nominees unconditionally into the administration.

The interim government was soon a demonstrable failure, lacking real power and, for the most part, simply providing a formal battlefield for Congress and the League. It also proved extremely difficult to set up the Constituent Assembly which was meant to pave the way to the final constitutional settlement. By the end of January 1947 the work of the Assembly had been effectively sabotaged by both the Muslim League, with its potent threat of withdrawal and boycott, and by the Indian princes, who also proved obstructive.

In February 1947, the Attlee administration at last moved decisively to break the deadlock and to bring matters to a head. The Prime Minister announced in the House of Commons that Britain would withdraw from India no later than June 1948. By that date, power would have to be transferred into responsible Indian hands. The problem remained as to whose those hands might be. The government also signalled its determination to break out from the constitutional and communal wranglings of the immediate past, and to make a fresh start in India, by the announcement that there would be a new Viceroy. Wavell, with his well-established reputation for pro-Muslim partiality, and his more recent reputation for weary defeatism, was to go. In his place would be the last British Viceroy, Earl Mountbatten of Burma. This appointment indicated in the most dramatic fashion the government's intention to rid themselves of the Indian problem as speedily and decently as possible.

The choice of Mountbatten was an inspired one. Royal blood flowed in his veins, and it was altogether seemly that the last Viceroy should be the great-grandson of Queen Victoria and a cousin of the last King-Emperor, George VI. Although Mountbatten had the reputation for ruthless self-aggrandisement and a tendency to romanticise the glories of his descent, he had an undeniably distinguished record of active service in the Royal Navy, and had been appointed Supreme Allied Commander in South-East Asia during the latter stages of the war. He thus brought to the job an intimate knowledge of Indian forces, the sub-continent and the surrounding area. When created an Earl, he had significantly taken the title of Mountbatten of Burma. In addition, Mountbatten and his intelligent, vivacious, though often wayward wife, Edwina, were recognised as Labour sympathisers and, in general, supporters of the cause of colonial freedom.

If Wavell had seemed too intimately associated with the aspirations of India's Muslims, the Mountbattens were soon perceived as enjoying over-close links with Nehru and the Congress movement. Nehru and Mountbatten had much in common, including a background of privilege and power, a taste for authority and an inclination to personal vanity. They were also strikingly good-looking, although it was Nehru who made the most use of his attraction for the opposite sex. Indeed, it is

clear that a passionate friendship soon developed between Nehru and
Lady Mountbatten. Hitherto the Mountbattens' marriage had been
founded on the rock of infidelity, rather than upon monogamy. As a
result, a curious triangular relationship developed, in which the increasingly close physical relationship between the leader of Congress and
the last Vicereine seems not to have disrupted the warm friendship
between Mountbatten and Nehru. Lord Mountbatten's official biogra-
pher describes the relationship between Nehru and Edwina Mountbatten as 'intensely loving, romantic, trusting, generous, idealistic, even
spiritual . . . If there was any physical element it can only have been
of minor importance to either party.'[17]

Whatever the technical, physical details of the relationship, the
triangular friendship seems certainly not to have affected the process
of the transfer of power for the worse, and, arguably, may have done
so for the better. Finally, in the light of Britain's long, intimate and
passionate relationship with the Indian sub-continent, it was perhaps
entirely appropriate that the climax of the entanglement should be
marked by an affair between the wife of the last Viceroy and the
incoming Prime Minister of an independent India. It was all the more
fitting since various British writers, from E.M. Forster to William
Buchan, had perceived the long-standing relationship between Britain
and India as a love affair, even a marriage. Buchan was to write in
1955:

> The whole thing is and always has been a love affair. First
> and last that's been what mattered. And it's taken the course,
> worse luck, of most love affairs, beginning with persuasion –
> none too gentle in this case – followed by delighted discovery,
> mutual esteem, ravishing plans for the future, the first really
> frightful row, and a long, miserable cooling off into polite
> bickering punctuated by sharp quarrels and joyless infi-
> delities, each side withdrawing, steadily and continually
> more and more of its real self.
>
> The first great quarrel, the only one that mattered, was
> the Mutiny – that wound went deep and we've never ceased
> to suffer, in a way. By then we'd let our character change for
> the worse. We'd stopped wooing excitingly, violently, with
> real strength and a lot of poetry. We'd grown a great big, bland
> evangelical face and were going about doing and saying things
> to people – God forgive us – for *their own good*.[18]

On his arrival in India, Mountbatten quickly decided to bring forward the date of Britain's departure from the sub-continent. With the deadline fixed for 15 August 1947, the final settlement had to be worked out within five months. The goodwill that existed between Mountbatten and Nehru was nearly destroyed early in May when the Viceroy and his advisors produced a 'Plan Balkan'. Essentially, the plan proposed to devolve power to the provinces, including the princely states, which would then be left to form whatever groupings they wished, and to negotiate arrangements with a central government before being integrated into what was, without question, a weak union. An infuriated Nehru denounced the plan as a recipe for chaos and disaster. Although an independent Pakistan could well emerge from the proposals, there could also have been an independent Hyderabad or Kashmir, and some argued that there could, in addition, have been an independent Bengal, and almost certainly two Punjabs.[19]

Mountbatten showed both good grace and good sense in rapidly shelving 'Plan Balkan' and postponing the meeting for 17 May called to discuss the proposals. His advisors set about fashioning a fresh plan that would be acceptable to Congress. The new proposals reasserted the concept of a unified Indian state, while allowing for provinces to secede from that state where a majority of their inhabitants desired such a step. The princely states were excluded from the plan. The principle of partition was thus accepted. In instances where it was unclear where to draw the new boundary lines – as, for example, in the case of the North-West Frontier Province – it was decided that the issue should be settled, where necessary, by referendum.

By early June 1947, the British Raj and all the sub-continental parties involved in the negotiations were in agreement over the course to be pursued. The implementation of the plan went ahead. A Partition Committee was set up, chaired by the Viceroy and including a number of representatives drawn from the appropriate Indian interest groups. Bengal and the Punjab, perhaps surprisingly, were partitioned with comparative ease, and the referendum in the North-West Frontier Province produced a very narrow majority in favour of joining Pakistan.

The princely states posed problems of a different kind. As British agents and political departments left these territories, some of the princes openly prepared to declare their independence, building up their own armies and acquiring new weaponry to aid them in this process. The decision as to which of the two new states a principality was to join was in essence left to the local ruler, resulting, as mentioned earlier, in bloody and still unresolved conflict in the case of Kashmir.

In July 1947 the India Independence Act was bustled through the British Parliament in a week. On 15 August 1947 British rule came to an end. The final irony was that the British had built up their position in India over a period of three hundred years, but abandoned it in a few weeks.[20]

Although both India and Pakistan became dominions in 1947, within two years India decided to become a republic. In 1949 there was no precedent for a republic to be accommodated within what was still called the British Commonwealth. Rather than lose India to the organisation, however, the British government hastened to grant the request in consultation with the Commonwealth prime ministers at the Commonwealth Conference of 1949. The conference proved that the British genius for innovative compromise was not dead, and indeed had been inherited by the other independent members of the Commonwealth family. As a result of the conference, the British monarch was henceforth to be described as 'Head of the Commonwealth'.[21]

Was the 1949 formula a reassuring demonstration of the continuing flexibility and strength of the Commonwealth ideal, or an indication of British decline and of the weakness of the Mother Country within the Empire-Commonwealth? The organisation was, after all, no longer truly the 'British' Commonwealth. It certainly could no longer be seen as an instrument of British power or imperial purpose. The chickens of the Balfour Definition of 1926 had now apparently come home to roost with the ditching of any pretence to 'a common allegiance to the Crown'. Although the delegates at the 1949 Commonwealth Prime Ministers' Conference agreed to cooperate in 'the pursuit of peace, liberty and progress', such an agreement had little meaning beyond that of a ritualistic and high-minded incantation.

Within two years, moreover, three states within the Empire-Commonwealth had become republics, and two of them, the Irish Free State and Burma, actually left the organisation. The path was now open for like-minded members of the Commonwealth Club to follow suit. Among the remaining dominions, South Africa, where the reconstructed, Afrikaner-dominated National Party had decisively defeated Smuts in the 1948 general election, seemed easily the most likely to push for republican status.

The declaration of the Commonwealth prime ministers at the London Conference of 1949 deliberately included no mention of military security or political cooperation. Perhaps this was considered unnecessary in the light of historical precedent, when in two world wars self-governing members of the Empire had come, on the whole willingly, to Britain's support. But it also reflected substantially changed circumstances. Nehru's India had publicly embraced a policy of 'non-alignment', an apparently comfortable position to adopt in the increasingly harsh circumstances of the Cold War. There had, moreover, been armed conflict between two members of the newly enlarged Commonwealth when India and Pakistan had fought over the future of Kashmir.

Despite all of this, it has been claimed that 'The years 1950 to 1951 marked a high point in the coordination of strategy in foreign policy in the Commonwealth.'[22] There is certainly some substance to this assertion. A 'Commonwealth Division' was formed to fight in the Korean War of 1950–53, consisting of troops drawn from Britain, Canada, Australia and New Zealand. There was also an Indian ambulance unit in Korea, and an integrated staff which included South African officers.

Nonetheless, the extent of Commonwealth cooperation in the Korean War created a misleading impression. The British Empire had long ceased to be a unified superpower with the capacity to act independently in global affairs. Member nations of the Commonwealth now belonged to different treaty organisations. Britain and Canada, together with the United States, were members of the North Atlantic Treaty Organisation, while in 1951 Australia and New Zealand formalised their dependence upon the military protection of the United States by signing the ANZUS pact, which actually excluded a protesting Britain from the arrangement.

Despite the fact that during the Second World War India and the dominions had built up huge sterling balances which were, in reality, debts owed by the United Kingdom, the Sterling Area continued to strengthen Britain in her claim to be included among the Big Three of the Allied Powers that had achieved victory in 1945. Even when the British government was forced into a 30 per cent devaluation of the pound sterling against the dollar in the autumn of 1949, the fact that each member of the sterling club devalued its currency by a similar percentage helped to disguise what was in effect a defeat for Labour's financial policies and a sorry indication of Britain's continuing economic decline.

Under the Labour government, however, the British Empire continued both to maintain and to camouflage Britain's economic and political standing as a world power. The predictions of Joseph Chamberlain, and of other 'New Imperialists' of the late Victorian era, that the Empire could, in a variety of ways, guarantee Britain's future were thus at least partially justified.

But Chamberlain had advocated the development of the 'underdeveloped estates of the realm'. As we have seen, the Labour government's attempts to develop the economic potential of the Empire were not a wholehearted success, and could even be described as essentially self-interested. This was perhaps inevitable in the light of the Attlee government's determination to deliver the goods in terms of welfare reforms and economic reconstruction at home rather than to expend more energy and money than necessary upon far-flung colonial projects. Certainly the voters in Labour's industrial and urban heartlands seem to have responded well enough: the government was returned to power, although admittedly with a greatly reduced parliamentary majority, in the general election of 1950, and although Labour narrowly lost the election of 1951, it actually polled more votes than the victorious Conservatives, scoring very well among its traditional supporters but failing to win the battle for the crucial marginal constituencies.

Nonetheless, with Arthur Creech Jones at the Colonial Office between 1946 and 1950, and with enlightened colonial administrators like Andrew Cohen advocating investment, enterprise and enlightened policies in tropical Africa, a good deal was being achieved. It is difficult to conclude, however, that British policy, even Labour policy, was simply devoted to the interests of colonial people. The valuable products and raw materials of remaining British colonies were vital to Britain's struggle to reconstruct her post-war economy, to close the notorious 'dollar gap' and to pay back American credit. A further problem was that Britain's claim to be considered a great power meant that an enormous and continuing expenditure on defence was necessary. When the Attlee government had to choose between financing development plans for the colonies or the production of the atomic bomb, participation in the Korean War and enthusiastic involvement in the Cold War, the colonies lost out every time.

Quite apart from these broader issues, the Labour government of 1945 to 1951 had to face a number of fresh and potentially awkward problems within the remaining imperial structure. One of the most embarrassing of these was the Gold Coast riots of 1948.

The West African colonies, of which the Gold Coast was the most prosperous, had always been recognised as among the most 'advanced'

of Britain's African dependencies. There had been unofficial African
representation on the Gold Coast Legislative Council since 1888, and
in 1946 the territory had been the first in British Africa to have a
legislative council with a majority of African members. Economic success and rapid constitutional progress became vital ingredients in the
growth of local nationalism. Despite the British government's attempt
to blame the Accra riots of 1948 on communist influence, a routine
device of the Cold War years, there were genuine issues of local discontent to be addressed. As a result, first the Watson Commission, and
finally an all-African committee under Mr Justice Coussey, produced
detailed constitutional recommendations which opened the way to full
African responsibility for the government of the colony.[23] A new constitution came into force in 1951 and resulted in a decisive electoral victory
for Kwame Nkrumah's Convention People's Party which had been
established in 1949 as a mass political movement. In 1952, a year
after the Labour government fell from office, Nkrumah became Prime
Minister, a position he held when the Gold Coast became Britain's first
African colony to achieve full independence in 1957.

Elsewhere in West Africa, the process of political change was
speeded up in Nigeria. A new and relatively progressive constitution
had been introduced in 1947, but in 1951 it was replaced by a system
which provided for an African majority in the Council of Ministers.
Despite the potential for future conflict between Nigeria's tribes and
regions, by the time the Attlee government lost office it was evident
that Nigeria, like the Gold Coast, was set on the road to independence.

Problems of a very different kind were coming to the fore in both
East and Central Africa. Anxious not to repeat the pattern which had
delivered political power to the white settlers of Southern Rhodesia
during the inter-war period, the Labour administration sought to prevent a complete transfer of power to the European settlers of Kenya.
At the same time, the government attempted to placate Kenya's whites
by accepting that they had an essential role to play in the development
of the territory, and by resolutely refusing to open up the 'white' highlands to African or Asian settlement. In 1947, the Kenya settlers even
achieved an unofficial majority on the Legislative Council. In 1946,
however, Jomo Kenyatta returned to his homeland after many years in
the United Kingdom, determined to transform the diffuse sentiments
of Kenyan African nationalism into a potent political movement.

Further afield, the Colonial Office took steps to recognise the rising
tide of local nationalism in the Caribbean, where Jamaica had been

already granted semi-responsible government and universal suffrage in 1944. In Malaya, on the other hand, the activities of a relatively small number of communist insurgents, using the jungle for protection, led to the declaration of a state of emergency and a bitter twelve-year struggle to restore peace. At least the Malayan emergency had the advantage of combining an anti-communist military action, of sufficient weight to impress the American State Department, with a vigorous defence of one of Britain's most valuable colonial territories in South-East Asia. Eventually the communist uprising was put down, and Malaya made safe for capitalism and, some time in the future, for democracy.

The record of the Labour administration of 1945 to 1951 in terms of its policies towards the Empire-Commonwealth is decidedly patchy. In important respects, it simply continued the policies that had evolved, despite sporadic attempts by Winston Churchill to sabotage and undermine them, during the wartime coalition years of 1940 to 1945. That progress had been made, in terms of several substantial devolutions of power, the promotion of economic development and the upholding of generally enlightened standards of administration, is undeniable. At the same time, the enhanced importance of the Empire in Britain's struggle both to rebuild her economy and simultaneously to satisfy the domestic needs of her people, placed serious constraints on anti-colonial and libertarian factions within the wider Labour movement.

There were, in truth, not many votes to be won at general elections as the result of promoting the cause of colonial freedom. On the other hand, the maintenance of Britain's 'great power' status, which appeared to be so clearly linked to the survival and vigour of the Empire-Commonwealth, had far more electoral appeal.

Such grand designs as there were, were often buffeted by tempests over which the British government had no control. It has been claimed that the British political left could not even, 'at least after about 1948, appeal to their own plans for more gradual and constructive change, since these lay in tatters: torn by the nationalists, squeezed by the Treasury, suffocated by piles of unsold groundnuts'.[24] Britain's rule in Africa had earlier been described as 'apathy tempered by riots'.

There were, beyond question, manifestations of Labour's apathetic colonial and imperial policies during these years. Sometimes these were reflected in the turn of events, sometimes in the choice of personnel. When the genuinely reforming and committed Creech Jones lost his seat at the general election of 1950 and a replacement at the Colonial

Office had to be found for him, the Prime Minister's choice fell upon James Griffiths. Griffiths was a former coal miner, viewed with both affection and trust by the Labour Party. He possessed, however, very little expert knowledge of the colonies, and had the habit of demonstrating his sincerity 'by beating his chest while talking'.[25] Whether this latter habit was considered to be an important quality in a Colonial Secretary is not clear. What is evident is that, for all his virtues, Griffiths was not a politician or statesman of the first rank. Perhaps the colonies deserved better than that.

All the same, when Winston Churchill once more became Prime Minister in 1951, the Empire-Commonwealth had been substantially transformed, and for the better, since the day on which he had assumed the premiership determined not to preside over the dissolution of the British Empire.

THE TRIAL OF
JOMO KENYATTA, 1953

Churchill's Return to Power in Britain;
the Conservative 'Holding Operation'; Confrontations
with Nationalist Movements in Egypt, Cyprus,
West and East Africa, the Middle East and the Caribbean

IN 1953, at the end of his trial at Kapenguria, a town near the Ugandan border in north-west Kenya, the Kikuyu and nationalist leader Jomo Kenyatta was sentenced to seven years' imprisonment. The British judge, Mr Justice Thacker, had spoken for most of Kenya's European settlers, for the British government, and for a good many of the colony's Africans when he had said at the conclusion of the trial:

> You, Jomo Kenyatta, stand convicted of managing Mau Mau . . . You have protested that your object has always been to pursue constitutional methods on the way to self-government for the African people . . . I do not believe you . . . It is my belief that soon after your stay in Europe when you came back to this Colony, you commenced to organise this Mau Mau society, the object of which was to drive out from Kenya all Europeans, and in so doing to kill them if necessary. I am satisfied that the mastermind behind this plan was yours . . . You have taken the fullest advantage of the power and influence that you have over your people and also the primitive instincts which you know lie deep down in their characters . . . You have persuaded them in secret to murder, to burn, to commit evil atrocities.[1]

In September 1954, the Governor of Kenya, Sir Evelyn Baring, announced that even when Kenyatta had completed his seven-year

346

sentence, a restriction order to 'remain in force indefinitely' would be placed upon him, requiring him to live 'in a remote place'. The intention of the colonial authorities was clear. Kenyatta was to be rendered a 'non-person'; Githunguri, the important Kikuyu school and teacher-training college he had presided over, was to be obliterated; his house at Gatundu was to be razed; his farm turned into an agricultural college; and he and his alleged fellow-organisers of Mau Mau were to be imprisoned in a specially-built complex in the northern desert, where only non-Kikuyu guards would be employed.

The passions aroused by the trial and conviction of Kenyatta arose partly from the position of Kenya, with its vociferous white settler minority population, within the Empire, and partly from the ramifications of the Mau Mau rebellion and the widely perceived 'diabolical' nature of the organisation itself. So determined were the settlers to cling to the privileges of their lives in Kenya, so shocking had been the recent attacks upon Europeans and their families, and so widely was it believed that the Mau Mau movement was an irredeemably evil organisation bound together by practices of a revolting and sub-human nature, that it became difficult to undertake a rational appraisal of the 'Kenya problem'.

The Conservative Colonial Secretary, Oliver Lyttelton, publicly expressed his revulsion at accounts of Mau Mau oath-taking. Much of the British press and many of the British public identified the Mau Mau activists as needlessly bloodthirsty, murderous black rebels responsible for the slaughter of hundreds of innocent white settlers.

The truth was that a little over thirty Europeans lost their lives during the uprising, while more than 10,000 Kikuyu were killed by government forces. Over 80,000 Mau Mau suspects were imprisoned in rehabilitation camps that too often, as in the case of the notorious camp at Hola, became living hells where detainees were physically assaulted and sometimes killed. More than a thousand alleged Mau Mau rebels were hanged in one of the most intensive enforcements of capital punishment for political activities in the history of the British Empire. So difficult did it become to ascertain the truth of the situation in Kenya, that the currency of debate became debased by the vividly expressed fears and fantasies of white settlers and British officials, as well as by the testimony of Africans who opposed, or were persecuted by, the Mau Mau. With alarming frequency, the rebels' motives and actions were described as being the work of 'the Devil', or the result of witchcraft and the casting of spells. In this way, the British in Kenya, and to some extent the imperial authorities at home, became almost as atavistic, superstitious and barbaric as the insurgents they sought to overcome.

Part of Kenya's tragedy was that ever since its formation out of the East African Protectorate in 1920, it had become the repository of unrealistic hopes and aspirations on the part of its small white settler community. After the First World War, the British government had promoted a settlement scheme for ex-officers, many of whom established themselves under favourable terms in the 'White Highlands' area. Men like Brigadier-General Wheatley, coming from a family of relatively impoverished landed gentry, arrived in the colony in 1919 determined to transform his substantial new estate into 'a real gentleman's place'.[2]

The high proportion of ex-British officers among the Kenya settlers may well explain why the colony's whites soon gained a reputation for independent and high-handed action and the robust defence of their rights. In 1923 they even plotted to kidnap the Governor and install one of their leaders, Lord Delamere, as the head of a provisional government, in defiance of British imperial rule. Some of the militancy which characterised the settler population may also have derived from the colony's serious currency crisis of the early 1920s, when the Colonial Office supported British banks in the colony in imposing an unfavourable exchange rate between Kenya's silver rupee and sterling, much to the outrage of the settlers.

Despite this abortive revolt, and their defeat at the hands of both Whitehall and British bankers, the settlers began to lead lives of considerable prosperity and ease. Their future, however, in a country with an overwhelming black majority, as well as a sizeable minority of Indians, many of whom had been brought into the colony as indentured labourers to build – among other things – the railways, remained precarious.

In 1923 the British government made a bid to resolve the potential conflicts through the Devonshire Declaration, which stated that 'primarily Kenya is African territory'. Although this Colonial Office declaration lacked immediate substance, the white settlers saw it as an unfriendly act and continued to press for self-government. In 1929 the British government had once more to confront the demands of Kenya's white supremacists and reaffirm the principle of native paramountcy. In effect a deal had been struck. The Europeans were confirmed in their prosperous and privileged position in occupation of the White Highlands, and their potential Indian rivals for primacy were denied equality with them. At the same time, white self-government was firmly ruled out as an option. Thereafter settler ambitions were confined to lending support to the notion of creating a new East African Dominion out of the colonies of Kenya, Uganda and Tanganyika. Although a common postal system and some other organisational indications of unity were in fact set up, the East African Dominion was never created. Given the continuing dependence of the Kenyan economy upon the goodwill and indulgence of British financial institutions, and the potential for violent conflict between citizens of European, South Asian and African origins, this was not surprising.

Between the formation of the colony of Kenya and the Mau Mau insurrection of the early 1950s, the colony's Africans had not been merely passive observers. The Kikuyu, the most powerful tribe in the vicinity of the capital, Nairobi, had set up a political organisation called the Kikuyu Central Association. In 1925 the Association formally asked the Governor for a number of concessions. These included permission to grow coffee, the publication of the colony's laws in Kikuyu, and direct African representation on the Legislative Council. The colonial authorities were, as a consequence, subjected to intense settler lobbying, based partly on the grounds that allowing Africans to grow coffee as well as cotton for themselves would disrupt the labour supply. As a result, the Kenyan government rejected the requests.

Although they had lost this particular battle, the Kikuyu Central Association continued to campaign for the restoration of land they claimed had been unfairly taken from them by the Europeans, and attempted to persuade the government to restrain further land appropriation. In 1929 the KCA sent a young and powerful representative, Jomo Kenyatta, to London to lobby the government and make contact with Labour politicians. During his trip to Europe Kenyatta took the opportunity to go to Moscow, a visit he repeated in 1932, and he began to write articles on Kenya for the communist press.[3] Kenyatta's alleged communist affiliations were to be used against him during the Kenya Emergency and his trial.

The year 1929 saw settlers' hopes dashed on two occasions. Firstly the Hilton Young commission of inquiry set up in 1927 by the Conservative government reported that it did not recommend federation for East Africa, and recommended that the Kenya Legislative Council should retain a majority of appointed British officials until the indigenous people could take their share in government 'equivalent to that of the immigrant communities'. With the advent of the minority Labour government in 1929 the new Colonial Secretary, Lord Passfield, formerly Sidney Webb, refused to continue the funding of some projects requested by the settlers, did his best to protect native land from encroachment, and at the same time lifted Kenyan government restrictions on the meetings and fund-raising of the Kikuyu Central Association. Passfield also pointed out that a properly constituted responsible government in Kenya remained impossible while under 1 per cent of the population was entitled to vote. In 1939, however, the settlers were successful in obtaining an Order in Council which guaranteed that future land grants in the White Highlands would be made only to Europeans.

By the outbreak of the Second World War, the Kikuyu people had emerged as the leaders of African resistance to white settler supremacy and, by implication, to British rule. Claiming security grounds, the British government proscribed the Kikuyu Central Association in 1940 and imprisoned its leaders. Jomo Kenyatta, however, had already been sent to London as a KCA representative and could not therefore be interned. Subsequently the government eked out cautious constitutional reforms. The first African to be appointed to the Legislative Council, Eliud Mathu, a product of Balliol College, Oxford, was appointed in 1944. Four years later there were four Africans on the Legislative Council, chosen by the Governor, not elected, as well as six elected Indians, eleven elected Europeans and eighteen official nominated representatives.

By the time the Labour government came to power in 1945 the deadlock in Kenya remained unbroken. The war had brought prosperity to white settlers, African farmers and Indian traders alike, and all three groups were demanding a greater share in the running of the country. In 1946 Kenyatta returned to Kenya. During his absence he had become something of a national hero, and he was almost immediately given charge of the college at Githunguri, which became an important base and inspiration for the tribe's causes. Frustrated by the continuing predominance of the white settlers, impatient at the pace of British constitutional reform, and resentful at what they saw as official interference with their way of life – from disapproval of the practice of female circumcision to reforms of agricultural practice – the Kikuyu were slowly driven to the point of open rebellion.

From 1946 the secret Kikuyu organisation known as Mau Mau began to operate in a small-scale way. By the summer of 1952, Kenyatta, alarmed at the rapid growth of Mau Mau, and still hoping to achieve reform through fundamentally democratic means, addressed a crowd of 30,000 people, including several journalists, at Kiambu, and cursed Mau Mau with a powerful Kikuyu oath. The leaders of Mau Mau summoned Kenyatta to them and threatened him. Kenyatta did not denounce Mau Mau again.

By this time the Mau Mau rebellion was in full swing. White settlers found their livestock hamstrung or disembowelled. Conflict spread both among the Mau Mau and other African tribes, such as the Luo, and also between Mau Mau and Kikuyu loyal to the government. By October 1952 the Governor, Sir Evelyn Baring, had concluded that most of the leaders of the Kenya African Union, which had been founded during the inter-war period and which had drawn its members from several tribes, were organisers of the Mau Mau. Kenyatta was one of the leaders of the KAU. A state of emergency was declared and the ringleaders arrested. New, younger leaders of the proscribed organisation now took over, and the killings and acts of terror increased in ferocity. Towards the end of 1952 Europeans were attacked and killed for the first time. In January 1953 a husband and wife and their six-year-old son, of a family named Ruck, were hacked to death with pangas by the Mau Mau. There was an explosion of settler outrage.

It was in these circumstances that Jomo Kenyatta and his co-defendants were put on trial. Kenyatta was accused of administering the Mau Mau oath, of being insincere in his denunciation of the organisation, of tacitly supporting it, and of allowing his name to be used in place of Jesus Christ in hymns sung by the Mau Mau. The defence counsel, D.N. Pritt, described the prosecution's charges as 'the most childishly weak case made against any man in any important trial in the history of the British Empire'.[4]

The judicial odds were hopelessly stacked against Kenyatta. The British authorities desperately wanted a quick conviction, and the white settlers threatened to become ungovernable unless they saw what they deemed justice to be done. In any event, the presiding judge, Ransley Thacker QC, had been, in effect, bribed. It was later to emerge that, after negotiations with the Governor, Thacker received an *ex gratia* payment of £20,000 – over ten times his annual salary – and had demanded government help in moving from Kenya after he found Kenyatta guilty. It was also subsequently discovered that a chief prosecution witness, Rawson Macharia, who testified that Kenyatta had tried to administer a Mau Mau oath to him, had committed perjury. Five years after Kenyatta's prosecution, Macharia produced written evidence in court to prove that the Kenyan government, in return for his evidence, had promised, in writing, to pay for him to be flown out of the country to study at a university in the United Kingdom and to be accompanied there by his family, to be financed in Britain by the colonial administration and to be given a government post on his return.

Even if the presiding judge and the chief prosecution witness had not been bribed in this fashion, the flood of lurid rumours and the intensity of the hatred directed at Kenyatta virtually ensured his conviction. The often hysterical reaction to Mau Mau had its roots in some undeniable truths. The *Sunday Times* sent the distinguished novelist Graham Greene to Kenya as their correspondent, and he graphically described 'the group of burnt huts, the charred corpse of a woman, the body robbed of its entrails, the child cut in two halves across the waist, the officer found still living by the roadside with his lower jaw sliced off, a hand and a foot severed'.[5] Others denounced the alleged horrors of the Mau Mau initiation and oath-taking ceremonies:

> . . . the ritual increased in bestiality . . . forcing the initiate to reach the necessary pitch of bloodlust and degradation to make it possible for him to pronounce the ghastly words . . . Public intercourse with sheep and adolescent girls were a common feature of most of these ceremonies . . . Young women were kept with the gangs for this purpose. Concoctions of the foulest ingredients were eaten and drunk . . . For one of the more notorious, known as the 'Kaberichia cocktail', semen produced in public was mixed in bowls with menstrual and sheep's blood and drunk while repeating the oath.[6]

After Kenyatta's conviction the government of Kenya, employing a considerable number of British servicemen, and enthusiastically aided by official and unofficial auxiliary units manned by white settlers, proceeded to crush the Mau Mau-led Kikuyu rebellion. Some 80,000 Kikuyu, nearly 30 per cent of the menfolk of the tribe, were eventually placed in detention camps where strenuous, and sometimes violent, attempts were made to 'rehabilitate' them.

But even as the last of the Mau Mau units were being hunted down like wild animals in the jungle, and while Kenyatta and his co-defendants remained in prison, the settlers had lost their struggle to maintain a white supremacist state. The urgent need to restore peace to one of the most prosperous of Britain's African colonies, and the rising tide of black nationalism throughout the continent, pushed the government towards an accommodation.

Almost exactly ten years after his imprisonment, Kenyatta, having wooed a representative body of European settlers with a promise of security for their land and position in Kenyan society, and with an undertaking to forgive and forget, became the Prime Minister of an independent Kenya. By one of those quaint and unexpected shifts of perception so commonplace in the history of British decolonisation, Kenyatta, who had earlier been described by the Colonial Secretary Lyttelton as 'a daemonic figure with extreme left-wing views', became the champion of white interests in Kenya.[7]

The determination of the British government to give full support to the Kenyan authorities in their bid to crush Mau Mau did not simply arise from the urgent need to restore law and order in a valuable and important colony, or even from a willingness to mount a crusade against apparently 'diabolical' forces – there was more at stake than that. The return of Winston Churchill to 10 Downing Street in 1951 had resulted in a significant shift in colonial policy.

Although Churchill was still associated with 'the good old cause' of the British Empire, he was sufficiently pragmatic to refrain from giving vent to the full-throated roar of the imperial lion. In any event, nothing could now be done to restore the Indian empire or to reverse the constitutional devolutionary processes already under way in much of the colonial empire. It was hard for the Conservative Party, with its traditional attachment to Empire, to adjust to these painful facts of imperial life, but the clock could simply not be set back.

The Conservative response to a wide range of imperial problems and dilemmas was twofold, and at first sight strikingly successful. On the one hand, the government chose to represent the transformation of the old Empire into the new Commonwealth as a cause for self-congratulation. The devolutionary process was thus presented as a triumph of British statesmanship and maturity of purpose, even as the fulfilment of a deeply considered and long established programme of preparing dependent states for ultimate self-government.[8] Oliver Lyttelton, the Conservative Colonial Secretary between 1951 and 1954, subsequently wrote: 'it seemed clear that the development of self-government . . . was at once the only enlightened and the only practical theme of a colonial policy in the 1950s'.[9]

Its resolve bolstered by such self-serving and comforting assurances, Churchill's administration proceeded to acquiesce in the devolutionary process in several colonies with remarkably good grace. In this way, after the unambiguous recommendations of the Coussey Commission, the West African colony of the Gold Coast became the independent and sovereign state of Ghana in March 1957, with the previously imprisoned nationalist leader Kwame Nkrumah as its first Prime Minister. In the vast neighbouring territory of Nigeria a federation was created, and in the same year as Ghana became independent acquired an African Prime Minister; Nigeria achieved full independence in 1960.

In the cases of both Ghana and Nigeria, British governments could claim with some conviction that power had passed from colonial administrations to apparently stable and mature local governments. The Anglo–Egyptian condominium of the Sudan had achieved independence in 1956, after fifty-seven years of effective British control. Despite the fact that the Sudan had been, at least nominally, jointly ruled by Britain and Egypt, the achievement of its independence was the occasion for more British self-congratulation, although the self-satisfaction may have arisen chiefly from the Sudan's decision not to opt for union with Egypt.

As a variant on the process of granting full independent status to certain 'advanced' colonies, the British government also promoted the establishment of a number of federations in groups of colonies where this seemed to make economic and strategic sense. Once the communist insurrection in Malaya had been crushed, constitutional progress there led to an independent federated Malaya in 1957, and six years later allowed for the creation of the Federation of Malaysia, comprising Malaya, Singapore and North Borneo. Federated Malaya, whose raw materials of rubber and tin were so vital to the post-war British economy, and especially to the development of various light industries, emerged from the process as a consolidated and staunch ally of Britain in the Far East.

In the British Caribbean, the ideal of federation was also promoted vigorously by Britain. A West Indian federation was formed in 1957, several years before any individual British Caribbean colony achieved independence and at least partly in the hope that the federal solution would dampen down and divert nationalist demands for freedom. Federation was achieved despite the anxieties of some of the more prosperous colonies that they would in effect be subsidising the poorer, smaller components of the federal system. Eventually these internal tensions were to result in Jamaica leaving the federation in 1962 and achieving independent status. This move virtually ensured the ultimate disintegration of the organisation, an event which provoked a rather wistful calypso:

> *You try with a federation, the whole thing end in confusion,*
> *Caricom and then Carifta, but somehow I smelling disaster.*
> *Mister West Indian politician, you went to big institution.*
> *How come you can't unite seven million,*
> *When a West Indian unity I know is very easy,*
> *If you only rap to you people and tell them like me.*[10]

The third area of federal experiment in the cause of British economic self-interest and the desire to prevent an unseemly Balkanisation of the remaining part of the Empire was in Central Africa. Here British commercial and economic interest was self-evident. The protectorate of Northern Rhodesia was one of the world's chief producers of copper – another commodity vital to Britain's industrial well-being. Southern Rhodesia had a flourishing economy and, equally important in some ways, a white population approaching 200,000. Nyasaland was the third country in the federation, but was included more as a matter of geographical convenience than for any economic or human imperative.

Churchill's government presented the economic case for federation in Central Africa with considerable conviction. It argued that the new federation would attract substantial investment, not merely for its existing industries and products, but for public works projects such as the construction of the Kariba Dam on the Zambezi River. Some political hopes were invested in the Central African Federation as well, hopes which would have soothed the restless spirit of Cecil Rhodes. It was anticipated that the new federation would in time evolve into a new and prosperous dominion, dominated by British investment and commerce and a valuable counterpoise to a Union of South Africa, which had since 1948 fallen progressively under the control of an Afrikaner Nationalist government devoted to the construction of an apparently permanent system of apartheid.

The overwhelming African majority in the three federated territories, it was confidently asserted, would benefit economically from their partnership with the local European community. There was even the optimistic hope that the 'colour-blind' franchise of Southern Rhodesia would eventually lead to the enfranchisement of large numbers of blacks and to a smoothing of the sharper edges of racial discrimination. Despite these pious hopes, the proposed partnership between whites and Africans appeared uncommonly uneven at the outset, and one Rhodesian leader was honest enough to compare the relationship with that of a rider and a horse.

The federation of Rhodesia and Nyasaland came into existence in 1953, amid a welter of controversy tinged with optimism. The Churchill government presented it as an act of creative statesmanship within an imperial framework. The more cynical compared it with the increasingly desperate and drastic reorganisations that had characterised the Roman Empire in its terminal decline. In the event, federation was to last for little more than a decade.

To all but the most partisan, the federation's constitutional arrangements were a mess. There was a federal executive and legislature, with considerable powers in such areas as taxation, communications and defence. Although the federal executive and legislature were effectively controlled by local Europeans, the federation was not granted full independence. Moreover, within the federal structure, Southern Rhodesia retained the self-governing status it had enjoyed since 1923, while the protectorates of Northern Rhodesia and Nyasaland remained the responsibility of the British Colonial Office. Tension soon developed within the federation between African nationalists – as well as some British officials in the two protectorates, who resented what they saw as the self-interested imposition of a federal system – and the local white leadership, which clearly wished to advance as quickly as possible to dominion status and full independence.

The growing conflict and controversy within the Central African Federation were soon reflected within the British Parliament and elements of British society. The Labour Party, in particular, became increasingly suspicious of the government's intentions in establishing the federation. The distrust thus engendered became one of the chief contributory factors in the breakdown of the bipartisan colonial policies which had generally characterised the period from 1940 onwards.

What contributed far more, however, to a widening split between Churchill's Conservative government and the Labour opposition was a sharp disagreement over the administration's determination to defend, apparently at almost any cost, what it saw as important national strategic interests. In contrast to the government's relatively uncontroversial policy of supporting devolutionary colonial processes already well underway, and even, with the exception of Central Africa, the drive to construct a number of quasi-imperial federal systems, the refusal to let go of certain possessions and responsibilities became a bitterly divisive political issue. The attacks of the increasingly effective and vocal anti-imperialist lobby in the Labour Party, supported by some sections of the press, made the already taxing job of the Colonial Secretary more difficult than ever.

The colonial problems that precipitated this fierce political controversy at home were almost as diverse as the remaining imperial possessions themselves. They had one thing in common, however, and that was the government's conviction that either essential British interests were at risk or that democratic colonial institutions were under attack from local Marxist movements or international communism.

British Guiana, situated on the South American mainland, fell into the latter category. Elections held there in 1953, under a new constitution which provided for a democratic franchise and a considerable measure of internal self-government, put into office the People's Progress Party led by Dr Cheddi Jagan. The British government soon became convinced that Jagan was a Marxist and subject to the influence of the Soviet Union. Anxious not to upset the sensitivities of the United States in the western hemisphere, Britain dismissed Jagan's government, suspended the constitution and dispatched troops and a warship to Guiana's capital, Georgetown. At home, Labour's left wing strenuously denounced what they saw as an imperialist intervention and the overthrow of a democratically elected radical administration.

In East Africa, the Conservative government also intervened in the affairs of Buganda, a relatively 'advanced' state under indirect rule within the protectorate of Uganda. The crisis arose when the hereditary local ruler the Kabaka – interestingly enough a Cambridge-educated African who was also an honorary captain in the Grenadier Guards – denounced the Agreement of 1900, under which he was obliged to accept British advice. This act of defiance arose chiefly from the Kabaka's fears that Britain was planning to incorporate Buganda into some future East African Federation. The forcible exiling of the Kabaka seemed a further example of the British government's zeal in confronting local rulers of an awkward disposition but little political weight.

The crisis in Cyprus centred not upon an awkward local ruler, or even upon fears of a communist-dominated local administration. Despite its 'European' population – albeit one divided between a Greek majority and a Turkish minority – Cyprus was seen as being of vital strategic importance to Britain. Acquired in 1878, it had become a fortress colony, containing a number of British bases, and a potential centre of operations against the rising tide of Egyptian and Arab nationalism. In 1954 Henry Hopkinson, the Minister of State at the Colonial

Office, unambiguously told the House of Commons that there would 'never' be a change of sovereignty in Cyprus:

> There are certain territories in the Commonwealth which, owing to their particular circumstances, can never expect to be fully independent . . . The question of the abrogation of British sovereignty cannot arise.[11]

British intransigence over the issue of Cyprus's independence led to one of the most publicised and bitter of colonial conflicts. The cause of Cypriot nationalism was masterminded by the Archbishop of Cyprus, Makarios III. At the same time the Greek Colonel Grivas organised a Cypriot guerrilla army, EOKA, which attacked Britain's military installations and posed a serious threat to British security throughout the island. A year after Churchill's resignation from the premiership in 1955, Britain mounted a major military campaign against EOKA, and simultaneously sent Archbishop Makarios into exile on the Seychelles Islands.

One of the main reasons why the government was so determined to hang on to Cyprus was that Britain was no longer able to use Egypt as a base for its military operations in the Middle East. In 1952 the Khedival regime that had hitherto collaborated with Britain was overthrown in a revolt led by revolutionary colonels of the Egyptian Army. The obese and dissolute King Farouk, until now sustained in power by the bayonets of the British Army, went into comfortable exile among the fleshpots of Europe. The new Egyptian government, soon led by the forceful and charismatic Gamal Abdul Nasser, demanded the withdrawal of British garrisons. During 1954, after apparently reasonable and satisfactory negotiations, the last British troops left Egypt and the Canal Zone, a clear indication that even Churchill now recognised the need to trim the defence budget and face up to political realities. Now that both Palestine and Egypt had ceased to function as bastions of British influence in the eastern Mediterranean and the Middle East, Cyprus became even more important – both in practice and symbolically – as evidence of Britain's continuing status as both a great and an imperial power. Those Conservative MPs who had denounced the 'scuttle' from India, and then from Egypt, were determined that Cyprus should not go the same way.

Events during 1956, however, were to present the new Conservative administration led by Sir Anthony Eden with one of the most profound and potentially most embarrassing crises of Britain's imperial decline.

THE SUEZ CRISIS OF 1956

The Fall of the British Empire and
the Rise of the Commonwealth –
and the Common Market

ON 29 OCTOBER 1956, Israeli forces launched an attack on Egypt, striking deeply into the Sinai Desert. Egyptian forces were routed, and the Israeli Army proceeded to scatter the hosts of their enemy before them – somewhat in the fashion of one of their Old Testament kings.

In the British House of Commons, the Prime Minister, Sir Anthony Eden, appeared shocked at this act of aggression, telling MPs that his government had five days earlier instructed the British Ambassador to Israel to 'urge restraint'. Eden proceeded to issue an ultimatum calling upon both the Israelis and the Egyptians to stop fighting, and demanding that the Egyptian government accepted an Anglo–French occupation of the Suez Canal Zone until the warring sides disengaged. Egypt rejected, naturally enough, what it saw as an Anglo–French infringement of its sovereignty, and prepared to brave the consequences.

Directly, without even pausing for a formal declaration of war, British and French forces began an invasion of Egypt. While most of the international community began to express their support for the Egyptian government, the Anglo–French invasion force sailed from Malta, while allied air forces bombed strategic targets in Egypt. By the time, six days later, that the invasion forces landed on Egyptian soil, the Egyptian government, led by President Nasser, had blocked the Suez Canal and rallied much of world opinion to its side. Once ashore, Anglo–French forces proceeded to move swiftly through the Canal Zone.

They were halted before they reached the southern end of the canal, not through any military failure, nor because the Soviet Union had issued a somewhat imprecise threat of nuclear intervention, but because the United States chose not to underwrite the invasion. Not merely did the American Sixth Fleet shadow detachments of the British and French navies in the eastern Mediterranean, but, more significantly, the United States government decided to strike Britain where it hurt most – in the financial equivalent of the solar plexus, the Sterling Area.

Before the Suez invasion the British Chancellor of the Exchequer, Harold Macmillan, had been amongst the most war-like of Cabinet ministers, demanding firm action against Nasser's Egypt. The Anglo–French assault on Egypt precipitated a crisis for sterling, and Macmillan was obliged to fly to the United States to seek assurances of support. None was forthcoming. The American government made plain their willingness to allow the collapse of sterling, so long as Britain and France maintained their assault upon Egypt. As a contemporary commentator remarked, Macmillan flew across the Atlantic as a hawk, but returned as a dove.

A ceasefire was called, and the fighting abruptly ended. The French government, anxious to fight on to overthrow the Nasser regime – and thus to destroy one of Arab nationalism's most powerful champions, and to buy themselves time in their struggle to hang on to power in Algeria – reacted with outrage and despair. Perfidious Albion, it seemed, had once more manifested itself.

In truth, even if the United States had not derailed the Anglo–French invasion programme, it is difficult to see exactly how the Suez crisis could have been resolved in favour of the two Western allies. At the time, Eden declared that the occupation of the Canal Zone was to be merely 'temporary'. What purpose a temporary occupation would have served is not clear. On the other hand, after the British invasion of Egypt in 1882, in which the French had chosen not to participate, it had also been stated that the British presence on Egyptian soil would be 'temporary'. In the event, the British occupation and domination of Egypt had continued, in one form or another, for the next seventy years.

Perhaps Eden was anticipating that the 'temporary' occupation of 1956 would similarly transform itself into a more permanent presence. Any permanent occupation of Egypt, however, would have involved both British and French governments in a protracted and presumably embarrassing policy of holding the country down by armed force. It was precisely the violent opposition to the British presence in the Canal Zone of the early 1950s that had led to the agreement to withdraw in 1954. For France, a permanent occupation of Egypt would in all prob-

ability have meant that it would have to cope with two chronic and debilitating colonial conflicts, one in Egypt and the other in Algeria.

Why had the British government decided to commit itself to such a high-risk strategy as the invasion of Egypt? One answer is that Eden's Cabinet was determined to prove that the 1954 withdrawal from Egypt, which had been fiercely criticised in some sections of the Conservative Party, should not be seen as the first step in a steady and irreversible decline in British influence throughout the Middle East region.

To this end, the Baghdad Pact had been signed in 1955. The pact was a military alliance between Britain, Iraq, Turkey and Pakistan. It was designed to deter Soviet expansion from the north and at the same time to dampen down the increasingly inconvenient rise of Arab nationalism. British garrisons and bases on the island colony of Cyprus were to provide the back-up to the diplomatic and political structure put in place by the Baghdad Pact.

Despite these precautions, the political volatility of the Middle East was to frustrate British policy and eventually to push Eden into the military adventure of the Suez invasion. Within a year of the signing of the Baghdad Pact Britain's prestige throughout the Middle East suffered a serious blow as a consequence of the abrupt sacking of the commander of the Jordanian Army, Lieutenant-General John Glubb, known as Glubb Pasha. Like Iraq, Jordan was seen by the British as a client state. Eden went so far as to say, 'Jordan was a country for which we had special responsibility; we had brought it into being.'[1] But the young king of Jordan, Hussein, who had succeeded to the throne at the age of eighteen in 1953, felt the need to prove his independence of the British connection. He declined to join the Baghdad Pact, and his dismissal of Glubb Pasha was a calculated bid to humiliate Britain.

Nonetheless, British policy-makers were still able to consider themselves the dominant power in the region. Until, that is, the news broke in July 1956 that Nasser had nationalised the Suez Canal. Psychologically the news could not have arrived at a worse moment. Eden was entertaining the young, pro-British, King of Iraq, Feisal II, and his Prime Minister Nuri es-Said, to dinner at 10 Downing Street. In the middle of the meal, the news of the canal's expropriation threw the diners into confusion. It is clear that Eden, having stepped into the shoes of the departed colossus Winston Churchill, desperately felt the need to prove his authority and capacity as Prime Minister. For whatever reasons, and there has been speculation that Eden in some way felt his political virility was under threat, the British Prime Minister developed an almost irrational hatred for Nasser. He was quick to compare him with Hitler, and on one occasion he became so agitated at the dispatch box of the House of Commons that the left-wing Labour statesman Aneurin Bevan felt obliged to remark that 'There is something the matter with him.'[2]

Eden's position was further complicated by the fact that it was perfectly plausible to argue that Nasser had not acted illegally in nationalising the Suez Canal Company. The ownership of the company was due to revert to Egypt in 1968 in any event. Where, it was asked, was the difference between Nasser's expropriation of the Canal Company and the recent Labour government's nationalisation of various public utilities? The Suez Canal Convention of 1888, which Britain had been instrumental in constructing, remained intact. There appeared to be no immediate, or indeed medium-term, threat to the continuing unrestricted international usage of the waterway. Indeed, one of Nasser's prime motives in taking over the Canal Company was to channel the dues it received into the Egyptian treasury. Keeping the canal in efficient working order was therefore essential.

It was, of course, more complicated than that. The United States government perceived Nasser as not so much 'non-aligned' in his foreign policy as tilting dangerously towards the Soviet bloc. Largely as a consequence of this, but also resentful at the financial and military aid Nasser was receiving from the Soviet Union and Czechoslovakia, in July 1956 the United States had abruptly refused to help fund the building of the Aswan Dam, a development project considered essential to the prestige of the Egyptian government and to the well-being of the Egyptian economy.[3] The nationalisation of the Canal Company could thus be seen as a swift retaliation for this snub. Furthermore, the anti-imperialist tone adopted by Nasser and other members of the Egyptian administration helped further to poison an already toxic diplomatic atmosphere.

It was for all of these reasons that Britain and France decided to embark upon their last great joint military adventure. In order to construct a plausible justification for their action, they proceeded to plot secretly with the state of Israel, and eventually all three powers concluded a secret agreement under which they agreed upon a joint attack on Egypt. The Israelis were to move first.

Of the three Suez conspirators, it was Britain that came off worst. Although British forces had not been defeated by the Egyptians, political and financial pressures had prevented them from realising their objectives. This was also true of France; but it was evident that both

the French government and French forces had been far more committed
to prosecuting the Suez war to a victorious conclusion. Nasser, whose
prestige might have been irretrievably damaged by defeat at the hands
of Israel alone, was able triumphantly to consolidate his position as
one of the foremost leaders of Arab nationalism. Aspiring nationalist
movements throughout the region, and further afield, were also able to
absorb the lesson that it was possible to defy Britain and get away with
it.

Britain's relatively strong diplomatic position in the Middle East
was ruined. Within two years of the Suez invasion, King Feisal and Nuri
es-Said had been overthrown and murdered in Iraq, and a revolutionary
nationalist government put in their place. King Hussein of Jordan
remained on his throne, although he found it increasingly necessary to
curry favour with Britain and other Western powers rather than to defy
them.

The fiasco of the Suez adventure had also vividly demonstrated
what little unity there was within the Commonwealth. A majority of
Commonwealth countries had opposed British intervention, some of
them bitterly. Their irritation and anger may have owed a good deal
to the fact that Britain chose not to consult them over the planned
invasion. Most of the members of the Commonwealth that were
members of the United Nations voted against Britain. New Zealand,
normally the most reliable ally of British overseas policy, even withdrew
her cruiser HMNZS *Royalist* from the British Mediterranean Fleet
rather than allow her to be involved in the attack on Egypt. British
imperial power now stood exposed as part sham, part reality, but in
any event in a state of chronic, possibly terminal, decline. One final,
but perhaps symptomatic blow, was the fact that Cyprus, far nearer to
Egypt than Malta, had proved inadequate for the purposes of invasion,
lacking a suitable deep-water harbour. Was this evidence of yet more
British incompetence and miscalculation?

It was thus possible to represent Britain's last, direct military intervention in the affairs of Egypt as an unmitigated disaster from beginning
to end — the by-product of an imperial mentality that was unable to
adjust to the increasing complexities and restraints of the post-imperial
world. Worse still, on matters of detail, British policy-makers and military planners appeared to have miscalculated throughout: arguably,
they chose the wrong target, at the wrong time, and for the wrong
reasons; they were prepared to flout world opinion, and defy the United
Nations, without even properly consulting those states that might have

been expected to lend them moral and practical support; they had misrepresented the reasons for the invasion of Egypt, and lied over the plot with France and Israel to both their internal and external critics; finally, they had launched a cumbersome, slow-moving armada of invasion from a base, Malta, which was six days' sailing-time from their ultimate target.

As if all of this was insufficient cause to induce a crisis of confidence in Britain's world role, and to afflict the nation with the traumas of guilt, embarrassment and humiliation, the British had been obliged to retreat like whipped dogs from the Suez Canal Zone, driven on their way by the manifest weakness of the pound sterling and by its incapacity to withstand the disapproval of a United States government securely established on the bedrock of the dollar.

The final blow was perhaps the most devastating, or at least the most symptomatic, of all. Britain, and France, had risked the whole adventure on the stated premise that the canal would be unsafe in Egyptian hands, and that automatic freedom of passage might well be denied to the world's shipping. Ironically, however, the world's premier international waterway was now blocked as a result of the invasion, and was to remain so for a considerable time, obliging British shipping to revert to the older, longer and more costly Cape route which the opening of the Suez Canal in 1869 had been designed to render secondary, if not obsolete.

The Suez fiasco played an important part in bringing about a shift in Conservative policies and attitudes towards what remained of the British Empire during the late 1950s and early 1960s. In 1951, the Conservative election manifesto entitled 'Britain Strong and Free' had devoted two of its thirty-two pages to the subject of the Commonwealth and Empire. Conservative policy was plainly asserted:

> To retain and develop the great and unique brotherhood of the British Empire and Commonwealth is a first task of British statesmanship . . . The Conservative Party, by long tradition and settled belief, is the Party of the Empire. We are proud of its past. We see it as the surest hope in our own day. We proclaim our abiding faith in its destiny. We shall strive to promote its unity, its strength and its progress.[4]

It had been difficult enough, even in 1951, to see how these high-minded aims could be reconciled with the rising and, as it was to prove, irresistible tide of colonial nationalism. Nor was it clear how a British government subscribing to the Westminster model of liberal democracy, as well as apparently acceding to the establishment of the Welfare State, could at the same time continue successfully to manage, finance and defend an essentially autocratically controlled overseas empire.

The Suez affair provided some of the most devastating proof to date that far from Britain being 'Strong and Free', it was intrinsically weak and unable to sustain a limited military action like the Suez invasion, even with the wholehearted support of France – Western Europe's second 'Great Power'.

Among the many repercussions of the Suez affair was Sir Anthony Eden's fall from the premiership. Ostensibly resigning on the grounds of ill-health, Eden was, in effect, driven from office as the result of the failure of the Suez adventure. Widespread doubts were also expressed over his judgement and his reliability as a national leader. He was succeeded by Harold Macmillan, whose capacity quickly to grasp the facts of political life – no matter how unpalatable – was at least as impressive as his gift for self-promotion. Beneath the droll, urbane and often disarming public face of an Edwardian actor-manager were the shrewd sensibilities of a modernising, astute and, if necessary, ruthless political leader.

Macmillan's accession to the premiership brought in its train a dramatic alteration in the composition of the government. Out went most of the old guard, and in came a batch of new, and often untried, ministers. Of the eighteen members of the new Cabinet, only five had belonged to the Churchill administration set up in 1951. Most of the newly appointed ministers belonged to a generation that had been too young to be fully involved in public affairs in the inter-war period. Macmillan's most senior colleague, the Home Secretary R.A. Butler, was a clear-sighted reformer, despite the languid, mannered and academic style of his public utterances – he sometimes seemed to address television viewers as if they were members of a thoughtful and sophisticated postgraduate seminar group.

Perhaps most significant of all was the appointment of Iain Macleod to the Colonial Office in 1959. As Colonial Secretary, Macleod was without question the most radical and hard-headed Conservative holder of that post since Joseph Chamberlain during the Salisbury and Balfour Unionist administrations of 1895 to 1905. With Harold Macmillan at 10 Downing Street and Iain Macleod at the Colonial Office, both Whitehall and Westminster were now fully in control of the decision-making process of colonial policy. Years of drift, indecision, and the paying of too much attention to the demands of local elites, such as the white settlers of Kenya, were now terminated.

There were several reasons why this quite dramatic transformation in British colonial policy took place without causing an unacceptable level of conflict within the Conservative Party, or unacceptable levels of indignation among the British population as a whole. One was that it became increasingly possible to associate decolonisation with the maintenance of British links with ex-colonial territories rather than with their abrupt termination. As direct British political and administrative control was withdrawn, on the whole in a dignified and harmonious fashion, many essential British national interests were preserved. These centred mostly around the financial, commercial and trading links that continued to connect the United Kingdom with its erstwhile colonial possessions; but they also included the maintenance, often to a surprising and unpredictable extent, of British military bases, and the safeguarding of certain strategic interests.

Possibly the other chief reason why the withdrawal of British power proceeded with comparative tranquillity lay in the personality and political skills of the Prime Minister himself. Just as de Gaulle, on acceding to power in France in 1958, had provided a misleadingly reassuring sense of national purpose behind which parts of the French empire, including even the passionately contested province of Algeria, could be brought to independence, Macmillan provided a similar service for the British people. His supreme gift was to present quite radical proposals for change in the diction and style of traditional conservatism. Since, moreover, the government seemed to be presiding over a remarkable and unprecedented improvement in national living standards, a certain amount of public anxiety over the disintegration of the British Empire was blunted and waylaid. Full employment, full pay packets and full stomachs seemed infinitely more important than rearguard and costly actions to hang on to far distant colonial possessions of which few members of the public, even in an age of rapidly increasing television, radio and newspaper coverage, had clear and concrete knowledge.

There was one other process at work. Although it had as yet made little direct impact upon the public imagination, and was certainly not yet a divisive issue within the major political parties, the increasingly formalised economic unity of Europe was underway. In 1957 six Western European states signed the Treaty of Rome, which bound them together in a customs union known as the European Economic Community. Although post-Suez Britain seemed more inclined to put its faith in the 'Special Relationship' with the United States, and to see what could be done to promote and increase inter-Commonwealth trade, the European Economic Community was plainly set on a path to success and greater power. Whether they liked it or not, British policy-makers would soon be obliged to consider ditching the old, well-established system of imperial preferential trading agreements begun in 1932 for membership of the EEC. In this way, some of the traditional assumptions about Britain's relationship with, and need for, the Commonwealth were being steadily, if as yet discreetly, undermined. The United States undoubtedly contributed to this process by making it clear to Macmillan that it set great store by the development of the European Economic Community, and that it expected Britain to play a key role in its development.

This is not to say that Macmillan and his government took any precipitate or early decision to disband the Empire and disengage from the Commonwealth. Adaptation rather than abolition was the watchword. In any event, the Empire was still a very substantial collection of countries. When Macmillan became Prime Minister, the 'Commonwealth Club' was still dominated by its five 'white' member states – Britain, Canada, Australia, New Zealand and South Africa. There were, admittedly, three new Asian members – India, Pakistan and Ceylon. Even when Ghana joined them early in 1957, this group was to remain a minority for some time. The Colonial Office still controlled some forty-five imperial possessions. These colonies were to be found in every continent, along with the imperial paraphernalia of government buildings, imperial ceremonial, and British governors still sporting white plumes upon their solar topees. The Colonial Service was still actively recruiting young men from the universities, confident, apparently, that they could anticipate lengthy careers in a variety of imperial territories. Both Conservative and Labour leaders in Britain were still inclined to speak of the 'British' Commonwealth, rather than of the more democratic-sounding, post-imperial 'Commonwealth'.

Despite all of this, the Macmillan administration proceeded prudently and, on the whole, clear-headedly to accept the inevitability of rapid decolonisation. In 1960, the Prime Minister, during a tour of various territories in Africa, even provided some philosophical underpinning to the process of imperial disintegration. The first British premier in office ever to see at first hand a continent within which his country remained the predominant colonial power, Macmillan told a gathering of white parliamentarians in Cape Town:

Ever since the break-up of the Roman Empire one of the most constant facts of political life in Europe has been the emergence of independent nations . . . all have been inspired with a keen feeling of nationalism, which has grown as the nations have grown.

In the twentieth century, and especially since the end of the war, the processes which gave birth to the nation-states of Europe have been repeated all over the world. We have seen the awakening of national consciousness in peoples who have lived for centuries in dependence on some other power.

Fifteen years ago this movement spread through Asia. Many countries there of different races and civilisations pressed their claims to an independent national life. Today the same thing is happening in Africa. The most striking of all the impressions I have formed since I left London a month ago is of the strength of this African national consciousness. In different places it may take different forms, but it is happening everywhere.

The wind of change is blowing through the continent.[5]

Macmillan's speech shocked many among his audience, unaccustomed to anything but bland utterances from visiting British royalty and statesmen. There is good evidence that the impact of his words was instrumental in strengthening the resolve of those white voters in South Africa who, a year later, voted in a referendum for republican status, a vote which eventually led to the new republic being denied continuing membership of the Commonwealth for its continuing commitment to apartheid. The effects of the 'wind of change' speech were, however, felt far beyond South Africa. The message was unequivocal. The British government not only recognised the strength and justice of colonial, particularly African, claims to independence, but would actively cooperate in the process of imperial devolution.

Although other Conservative leaders, from Balfour to Baldwin, had publicly recognised the principle of colonial devolution, none of them had been in the position, or had perhaps been of the inclination, to put the theory into practice. The Macmillan government of 1957 to 1963 did exactly that. A large number of colonies became independent, as Britain withdrew its rule at a pace far more hectic than during its original assumption of control during the so-called 'scramble for Africa'.

Thus in 1960 the following states became independent: British

Somaliland – which joined with Somalia – Cyprus and Nigeria. During 1961, in West Africa, Sierra Leone became independent, as did the Cameroons, one part of which joined Nigeria and the other the former French colony of Cameroun; in December of that year Tanganyika became independent, later, with Zanzibar, becoming the state of Tanzania. During 1962, Jamaica, Trinidad and Tobago in the Caribbean, and Uganda in East Africa, became independent states. In 1963 Singapore, North Borneo and Sarawak joined Malaya to become part of the federation of Malaysia; Kenya, at last, became independent in December of that year. During 1964, after Macmillan had been succeeded as premier by Sir Alec Douglas-Home, Malta achieved independence, and the break-up of the Central African Federation was completed by the establishment of the independent states of Nyasaland, later known as Malawi, and of Northern Rhodesia, which became Zambia.

In the light of these rapid changes, Macmillan's 'wind of change' speech served as the announcement of a programme of decolonisation as well as a justification of that policy. Perhaps Macmillan's landslide victory in the British general election of 1959, when voters were told by the Prime Minister that they had 'never had it so good', provided the mandate for the rapid devolutionary process that followed.

Significantly, Macmillan's administration had earlier indicated its determination to cut Britain's defence budget and the nation's global military presence down to size. In the spring of 1957 the Minister of Defence, Duncan Sandys, ironically a son-in-law of Churchill – the 'warmonger' of left-wing demonology – announced a wholesale reorganisation of Britain's armed forces. With the abandonment of conscription – National Service – soon afterwards, this meant that the protection of British overseas interests would now be the responsibility of smaller, and overwhelmingly professional, forces, which would also remain an important and integral part of the North Atlantic Treaty Organisation. As old and honourable regiments were disbanded or amalgamated, the size of the Royal Navy was also reduced, with the Mediterranean Fleet reduced to a small clutch of warships.

In the wake of the Sandys reforms, there was simply not the manpower to sustain a concurrent series of colonial wars or rearguard actions, even if there had been the will to do so. The insurrection in Cyprus, for example, had been countered largely by regiments manned by National Servicemen. The government still maintained that it could successfully defend British interests, whether East of Suez or in the Far

East, and Britain's nuclear deterrent was also seen – although quite falsely and misleadingly – as the ultimate means of control and assertion.

The apparently headlong flight of the Macmillan administration from a wide range of imperial and military commitments and responsibilities provoked some bitter opposition at home, from the outrage of the Marquis of Salisbury over the 'retreat' in Cyprus, to the fulminations of groups like the League of Empire Loyalists. The quickening pace of immigration into Britain during the 1950s, particularly from the British Caribbean and the Indian sub-continent, also provided ammunition for those who deplored both the withdrawal from Empire and what seemed to be its social and political consequences within the United Kingdom. There was also some criticism at the haste of the process. In 1964, for example, the newly-established state of Zambia could only boast one hundred university graduates out of an African population of over five million. Some observers detected a cynicism at the heart of government policy: 'All that mattered was that an indigenous political elite, with some degree of local support, should exist and be willing to take over.'[6]

Such misgivings did nothing to halt the pace of decolonisation. The urgent and intensive reviews of Britain's standing and future prospects as a world power during the years 1957 to 1960 led to one overall conclusion: the Empire-Commonwealth was becoming of less economic value to Britain, while the policy of maintaining control of perhaps dozens of potentially rebellious dependencies was no longer affordable. Macmillan's thoughts were turning to membership of the EEC even before he made his momentous 'wind of change' speech in 1960. Although Britain's eventual membership of the EEC was to speed up the process, it is clear that its trade with Europe was becoming significantly more important during the years of Macmillan's premiership. In 1960 31.7 per cent of British exports went to Western, or non-communist, Europe, while 30.7 per cent of the country's imports came from there. By 1980 Britain's exports to Western Europe amounted to 56.9 per cent of the total, and 55.7 per cent of its imports derived from there.[7] Trade with the wider world, including the Empire and Commonwealth, was clearly becoming less important to Britain's economic well-being and commercial prospects.

Part of the calculation behind the strategy of granting colonial self-government had been to consolidate and extend the global role of sterling. Even when British dependencies achieved freedom, however, they did not all obediently rush to the support of the Sterling Area.

As the newly independent states' income from the process of imperial development – as manifested, for example, in British Colonial and Development Acts – fell away, so they turned increasingly to other development agencies and to other currencies for investment and support. The subsequent disengagement and disenchantment with sterling was one of the main contributory factors in the currency's rapid decline as a major means of international exchange. Once political freedom had been granted to colonial territories, Britain had thrown away one of the main cards it could have played in order to keep dependent territories tied to it in a close and cooperative commercial arrangement. The ex-colonies still, of course, needed aid and investment, but increasingly they sought it from sources other than Britain and the Sterling Area.

By the time the Labour government under Harold Wilson came to power in October 1964, there seemed comparatively little that could be salvaged from the wrack of imperial decline and dissolution.

RHODESIA'S UNILATERAL
DECLARATION
OF INDEPENDENCE, NOVEMBER 1965

Variable Winds of Change, and Wilson's
Labour Government, 1964 to 1970

ON 11 NOVEMBER 1965, the Prime Minister of Southern Rhodesia, Ian Smith, signed a Proclamation of Independence, a measure by which the white minority government unilaterally asserted the ending of the colonial relationship with the United Kingdom. Although the Rhodesian Cabinet contained very few men of the intellectual and cultural calibre of Thomas Jefferson or Benjamin Franklin, the Unilateral Declaration of Independence, by shamelessly imitating the United States Declaration of Independence nearly two centuries earlier, made a bid for respectability and even, perhaps, sympathy. The Declaration began:

> Whereas in the course of human affairs history has shown that it may become necessary for a people to dissolve the political affiliations which have connected them with another people and to assume amongst other nations the separate and equal status to which they are entitled . . .[1]

In this fashion, spuriously and bizarrely, began the white Rhodesian 'rebellion' of 1965. The crisis was the by-product of Britain's inability effectively to handle a confrontation between less than 250,000 white Rhodesian settlers and the overwhelming African majority of the colony – twelve times greater than the European population. The Rhodesia crisis was one of the most troublesome and embarrassing unfinished pieces of African business, and one that was to provide successive British governments with a sequence of unwelcome and apparently irresolvable problems.

The constitutional dimension of the problem had its roots in the decision taken by the white settlers in 1923 to opt for self-governing colony status rather than joining the Union of South Africa. Having achieved this, Southern Rhodesia subsequently made unsuccessful bids to be granted dominion status within the British Empire. Failing in this initiative, the white minority had generally supported the establishment of the Central African Federation in 1953, seeing it as an administrative restructuring which would enable them to consolidate their power within a larger geographical unit with substantially more human and material resources at their disposal.

In October 1960, the Monckton Commission, set up by the Macmillan government with the plain intent of winding up the Central African Federation, had reported that: 'The strength of African opposition in the northern territories is such that Federation cannot . . . be maintained in its present form.'[2] Despite the formidable campaign waged by the Federal Prime Minister, Roy Welensky, to prevent the dissolution of the Central African Federation, in 1961 Nyasaland and in 1962 Northern Rhodesia were granted new constitutions which brought African nationalist leaders into central government. The right of both territories to secede from the Federation was eventually acknowledged, and in December 1963 the ill-fated experiment in sub-colonial engineering was ended. During 1964 Nyasaland achieved independence as Malawi, and Northern Rhodesia as Zambia.

Southern Rhodesia, however, had a far larger white minority than the ex-protectorate of Northern Rhodesia, as well as a far more sophisticated economic and industrial base. There had been next to no European settlers in Nyasaland. But if Welensky, a tough and resourceful settler politician of Jewish and Polish extraction, and an ex-boxer, former railwayman and trade union leader to boot, had eventually been defeated by the power of Westminster and Whitehall, what chance would any future leader of the Southern Rhodesian whites have of success?

Southern Rhodesian settler politics, however, tended, through a quasi-Darwinian process of natural selection, to throw up tougher and more intransigent leaders as the fate of the white community seemed to be in ever graver peril. By the time of the Unilateral Declaration of Independence, Ian Smith had emerged as the Prime Minister in whom the European settlers put their faith. In some ways, Smith was a curious figure: a successful former pilot in the wartime RAF, he was also a Rhodesian farmer, and a surprisingly successful local and, indeed, international politician, despite his damaged, partly closed eye and his clipped, uninspiring patterns of speech. The ousted Welensky held a low opinion of him, describing him thus in his memoirs:

> When I was Federal Prime Minister Smith was my party whip and I think it's a clear indication of my opinion of him that I never promoted him. One of my ministers came to ask me whether I would give him a junior minister. I said, 'Yes, who do you want?' He said, 'Smith, Ian Douglas Smith,' and I said, 'You're mad. He can only talk about cattle, European education and daylight saving. He never does any work. No, I won't agree to that. But you can have anybody else.'[3]

Despite this contemptuous assessment, Smith inspired loyal, sometimes passionate, support from the majority of Rhodesian whites, and proved in practice to be a skilful and obdurate negotiator. Sir Alec Douglas-Home, who became Prime Minister of the United Kingdom in 1963, found Smith, the fourth Southern Rhodesian Prime Minister with whom he had to negotiate, hard work:

> Negotiating with him was a very different thing from anything I had done before. You had to repeat yourself a lot. He was a very difficult man to pin down and keep pinned down to a particular point, a very slow negotiator. When you made an arrangement with him or thought you had got an arrangement, you would find on reassembling that he had found some qualifications. And so it went on, a long, slogging difficult process.[4]

Harold Wilson, Labour Prime Minister from 1964 to 1970, was no more successful in dealing with Smith. It is evident that Wilson – perhaps unwittingly – played an important part in encouraging the Unilateral Declaration of Independence by making it clear, before the event, that he did not intend to use force against the settlers. Thereafter the British government had no option but to attempt to bring Rhodesia to heel by requesting the United Nations and the world community to back the imposition of economic sanctions. Despite Wilson's rash prediction that 'the cumulative effects of the economic and financial sanctions might well bring the rebellion to an end within a matter of weeks rather than months', nothing of the sort occurred.[5] Despite continuing contact, both informal and formal – including dramatic meetings between Wilson and Smith aboard the British warships HMS *Tiger* and HMS *Fearless* – the rebellious Rhodesian regime showed no signs of withering away, rather it appeared to flourish. The almost inexplicable failure of the British government to cut off oil supplies to Rhodesia at the outset, particularly through the Mozambique port of Beira, both fatally undermined sanctions and gave the impression that Britain was not sufficiently determined in its proclaimed intent to bring the regime to the point of surrender.

Perhaps the Labour government pulled its punches because it was anxious, for reasons of domestic politics, not to be seen to be in full and mortal combat with Rhodesia's white settlers. Issues of race had come dramatically and uncomfortably to the fore a year earlier, during the British general election of 1964, when the Conservative candidate at Smethwick had won the seat, directly against the national voting trend, by playing on the fears of white voters over continuing black immigration.[6] Perhaps Britain was more anxious to retain its profitable trading links with South Africa – the chief support of the Rhodesian rebels – than effectively to confront the Smith government. Such pusillanimity provoked one prominent Zambian to describe the erstwhile imperial power as 'a toothless bulldog'.[7] Perhaps the 'kith and kin' card, which the Rhodesians played with such determination, was an embarrassment to the British government. At any rate, the rebel regime outlasted not merely the Wilson government of 1964 to 1970, but was still clinging to power when James Callaghan's Labour administration resigned in March 1979.

The failure to defeat and overthrow the white supremacist regime in Rhodesia was only one of many disappointments for the anti-colonial left in the Labour movement during Wilson's first two terms as Prime Minister, between 1964 and 1970. This was odd, or at least paradoxical, given the apparently impeccable left-wing credentials which had played so important a part in enabling Wilson to win the leadership election in the aftermath of Hugh Gaitskell's sudden death in 1963. It was also paradoxical in the light of Wilson's having given two of the most crucial Cabinet jobs in relation to the Empire-Commonwealth to a pair of trusted left-wingers when he formed his first government: Anthony Greenwood became Colonial Secretary, and Barbara Castle was appointed to the Ministry for Overseas Development.

But, as is nearly always the case, the policies and positions advocated in opposition had to be tempered by political realities once power had been achieved. All the same, the record of the early Wilson governments, particularly between 1964 and 1966, was distinctly uneven, if not disreputable, in relation to Commonwealth affairs. There was no need to doubt the new Prime Minister's commitment to the principle of racial equality.[8] His government, moreover, seemed to be committed to a whole range of policies long cherished by anti-colonial opinion in Britain. These included not only the by now unstoppable process of decolonisation, but also the denial of power to any remaining white supremacist groups, as well as the introduction of substantial initiatives in the dispensation of overseas aid and therefore, partly as a consequence, an apparently firm commitment to the eradication of poverty in the developing world. Legislative action to combat racial discrimination in the United Kingdom was also on the new government's agenda. Complex and daunting as such a programme undoubtedly was, the Labour government's progress in realising such aims should have been positively assisted, at least in part, by the relatively radical and liberal policies pursued by the previous Conservative administrations between 1957 and 1964.

Yet in practice, the government was to dash the hopes of many of its supporters over a wide range of colonial and post-colonial issues. It appeared to compromise, to vacillate, and sometimes to be less than honest and honourable. It failed adequately to confront the Rhodesian rebellion; its response to the bloody and bitter Nigerian civil war – which was centred on the rebellion of Biafra – seemed cynical where it was not uncertain; it was accused of giving too much support to the United States' involvement in the Vietnam war; it was perceived as being too willing to accommodate the anti-immigration lobby at home; it was criticised for falling far short of its avowed policy of promoting aid and development in the 'Third World'.

An indication of what was to come occurred before the Rhodesian Unilateral Declaration of Independence in November 1965, when, far from repealing the 1962 Commonwealth Immigrants' Act, the government further restricted the number of work permits to be issued, thus effectively reducing the influx of immigrants from the Caribbean and South Asia. The pretence that continuing membership of the Commonwealth somehow related to the right to automatic British citizenship was thus exposed as a sham.

Worse still, when, in the mid-1960s, the government of independent Kenya put pressure on its South Asian community to leave the country, the Wilson administration promptly imposed an annual quota of 1500 on Kenyan Asians wishing to enter Britain. This measure was quickly denounced as a betrayal of the agreement by which Kenya had achieved independence in 1963 – interestingly enough under a Conservative government – when some 180,000 South Asians living there had been granted the right to retain British citizenship.

These various restrictions on immigration were all the more controversial because they lacked even-handedness. Citizens of the Republic of Ireland, which had left the Commonwealth in 1949, were allowed free access, and full civil rights – including the franchise – in the United Kingdom, even though they came from what was technically a foreign state. Other foreigners, from Europe and elsewhere, although they still had to obtain work permits to come to Britain, were not subjected to numerical restrictions. There was only one realistic explanation for all this, and that was that policy was being largely constructed on the basis of skin colour. Despite their avowals, were members of the Labour government, in practice, guilty of colour prejudice? It was this doubt that caused the West Indian federal statesman, Sir Grantly Adams, to ask rhetorically, and apparently naively, 'Can a coloured population of less than 1 per cent destroy this great country?'[9]

Britain also indicated its determination to live within its means in January 1968, when the Wilson government announced the virtual abandonment of any remaining 'east of Suez' pretensions. Many of the forces had already been withdrawn, especially after the defeat of the Communist rebels during the Malayan emergency. Aden, once deemed essential to the security of the Suez route, had been abandoned, and plans had been made for bringing home by the mid-1970s the forces based on Singapore – a military presence that made Britain second only to the United States as a Western power in the Far East. The government's urgent need to reduce its overall expenditure, while not appearing to undermine the funding of the Welfare State and the more popular forms of public spending, was the root cause of the decision. British troops could have been withdrawn from Europe, especially from Germany, but the anxieties still generated by the Cold War made this impossible. The United States was already sufficiently concerned at the Labour government's decision drastically to reduce its military commitment in the Far East.

The Wilson administration's determination to abandon so great a part of Britain's overseas military presence was of enormous significance. It has even been claimed that: 'So far as the end of the British

Empire can be set at a definite point of time, it was the afternoon of 19 January 1968, when the Labour Prime Minister, Harold Wilson, announced the final homecoming of the British legions.'[10]

As if all of this was insufficient to undermine the Commonwealth ideal, the Wilson government, picking up where the Macmillan government had failed, proceeded discreetly to edge towards a renewed application for Britain to join the European Economic Community. Of the two major British political parties, Labour, at this stage, contained the most vociferous and powerful anti-Common Market elements. Nonetheless, a process had now been restarted which, within a decade, was to lead to Britain's membership of the EEC.

The system of Imperial Preference that had been begun in 1932 was plainly incompatible with British membership of the Common Market. Although it took some time for the old system to die, especially as the negotiation of Britain's membership of the EEC took an inordinately long time, the structure of imperial preferential tariffs was doomed. In the end, Imperial Preference was only fully operational for a little more than forty years, a pitifully short time in the history of the British Empire and Commonwealth.

If the ideals of Commonwealth were being progressively undermined in the areas of British citizenship and reciprocal preferential tariffs, any pretences to diplomatic unity within the international community had already, in effect, been abandoned. Even before 1945 it had been difficult enough to guarantee the international diplomatic, military and foreign policy cooperation to which some Commonwealth and Empire enthusiasts had for so long aspired. With the growing proliferation within the Commonwealth of independent nations in Asia, Africa, South-East Asia and the Caribbean, even to aspire to a set of common policies was impracticable. During the Cold War years, several newly independent countries chose to follow India's lead and declare themselves 'non-aligned'. It was, of course, difficult to resist the impression that the majority of these allegedly non-aligned countries were, when it came to the crunch, in the Western camp – as was demonstrably the case even with India after her humiliating frontier defeat by the People's Republic of China in 1962.

Had there been a unified Commonwealth desire to cooperate in international and diplomatic terms, the problem would have been to find policies upon which to agree. Even the bland principle of the maintenance of peaceful relationships between Commonwealth countries had been effectively destroyed by the Indo–Pakistan war of 1965, itself

merely the latest in a round of military confrontations between the two
dominant powers in the sub-continent.

When it came down to it, there was only one major political issue
which could hope to unify the Commonwealth, and then only, in a sense,
in a negative fashion. This was opposition to the system of apartheid in
South Africa. In 1961, as the result of an overwhelming consensus
among Commonwealth countries, South Africa had been denied readmittance to the organisation after its recent acquisition of republican
status required it to reapply for membership. Once South Africa had
been excluded from the Commonwealth, that organisation had no more
right, in theory, to exert moral pressure upon the Pretoria government
than it had to address and alter injustices in any other foreign state.
This consideration did not, however, inhibit continuing criticism, chiefly
on moral and political grounds, but also because there was still the
perception of a 'special relationship' with a country that, in various
forms, had for so long been a part of the imperial system.

Although the harmony of the Commonwealth appeared difficult to
promote or maintain in terms of international diplomacy – and especially when there was conflict between member states – some progress
had been made in constructing a formal machinery for promoting the
unity of the organisation. There had, of course, been a Secretary of
State for the Dominions, with a seat in the British Cabinet since 1925;
in the aftermath of World War Two the Dominions Office was renamed
the Commonwealth Relations Office. As the Commonwealth expanded
in size, however, further consultative and organisational machinery was
required.

In response to this need, the Commonwealth Secretariat was established in 1965, funded by member countries and based in London. It
was designed to act as a civil service for Commonwealth countries,
chiefly by updating and coordinating information among members. It
was created six decades after the Colonial Secretary, Alfred Lyttelton,
had unsuccessfully proposed a Permanent Commission to carry out a
similar function. Led in the first instance, appropriately enough, by a
Canadian, with Arnold Smith as its Secretary-General, the Commonwealth Secretariat had a multiracial staff and gave some coherence
and continuity to the now frequent meetings of Commonwealth Prime
Ministers.

These meetings had taken place with increasing regularity since the
end of the Second World War – in 1948, 1951, 1953, 1955, 1956, 1957,
1960, 1961, 1962, 1964, 1965, January 1966, September 1966 and 1969.

An important precedent had thus been established. As several newly independent Commonwealth countries proceeded to change their constitutions, which had been initially founded upon the Westminster model, to systems which established presidents as heads of state, it soon became more appropriate to describe the conferences as meetings of Commonwealth Heads of State. The size and membership of the conferences had also changed significantly since World War Two. In 1944 six male prime ministers, all of them white and, with the exception of South Africa's Jan Smuts, all of them of British origin, had represented six dominions. By the time of the 1966 conference there were twenty-three full members of the Commonwealth, although only twenty-two attended, Tanzania having broken off diplomatic relations with Britain chiefly in protest at the Wilson government's handling of the Rhodesian rebellion. As if this rift was not sufficient indication that times had indeed changed within the Commonwealth, the multi-ethnic character of the assembly clearly confirmed the point. English, however, remained the language of official communication, as well as of much informal contact, at the Heads of State's meetings.

In 1965 the Commonwealth Prime Ministers, in conference, also gave their blessing to the establishment of a Commonwealth Foundation, set up to develop links between professional bodies within the organisation. Various other associations, including the Commonwealth Agricultural Bureau, the Economic Consultative Council, and the Education Liaison Committee, were created in order to encourage and facilitate cooperation. By the end of the decade there were a very large number of organisations and bodies which either derived their authority from the formal structure of the Commonwealth, like those listed above, or which attempted in various ways to encourage cooperation between citizens within the organisation, like the Commonwealth Association of Architects or the Commonwealth Parliamentary Association.

In the event, as with the Commonwealth itself, these structures, formal or informal, even – or, perhaps, especially – the regular meetings of Commonwealth Prime Ministers, had no executive or legislative powers. Their success depended upon the willingness of individual member states to cooperate. The fact that any progress in terms of cooperation and mutual support was entirely voluntary was clearly illustrated when the proposal that a Commonwealth Supreme Court should be established as a final court of appeal was decisively rejected by members of the organisation. There was, admittedly, already a final court of appeal in existence – the Judicial Committee of the Privy Council, to which citizens of Commonwealth countries could apply against judgements in their own courts. But recourse to this committee was at the discretion of individual countries. The problem with much of this structure was the paradoxical fact that one of the strongest bonds linking the Commonwealth together was the freedom of each member state to associate or to dissociate from the organisation at will. As a result, it was tempting to see the Commonwealth as a benign, avuncular but essentially powerless structure, resting on voluntarism, and from which member states could secede with the minimum of fuss whenever they chose. Joining, or rejoining, was perhaps a little more difficult.

From the Rhodesian rebellion to the fall of the Wilson government in June 1970, the Commonwealth experience was not a particularly constructive or tranquil one. Several African countries showed their displeasure with Britain's failure to end the independence of the Smith regime in Salisbury, by breaking off diplomatic relations with the United Kingdom. Britain was further and bitterly criticised for its continuing, and as some saw it over-strict, control of coloured immigration. The acceleration of violence in Northern Ireland and eventually the decision to send substantial numbers of British troops to Ulster further tarnished the Mother Country's image.

There were, however, especially early on, some hopeful signs that Britain would provide acceptable, even inspiring, leadership within the Commonwealth. At least initially, Harold Wilson seemed to display an eerily unfashionable enthusiasm for the Commonwealth ideal. In 1965 he even proposed to set up a Commonwealth peace mission to help end the war in Vietnam. Although force was ruled out as a means of bringing down the white supremacist regime in Rhodesia, the government did make RAF planes available for the protection of Rhodesia's potentially vulnerable northern neighbour, Zambia. At the 1966 Commonwealth Prime Ministers' Conference in Lagos, especially convened and the first full meeting to be held outside the United Kingdom – a remarkable comment on continuing British influence as well as upon Commonwealth traditionalism – Wilson actually succeeded, against the odds, in persuading delegates that the imposition of sanctions against the Salisbury regime stood a good chance of success.

A year later, with the Rhodesian government gaining in confidence rather than being ruined by economic sanctions – which were proving relatively easy to circumvent – discontent with Britain's role in the whole affair threatened seriously to damage, if not destroy, the

Commonwealth. Wilson's two face-to-face meetings with Ian Smith aboard HMS *Tiger* and later HMS *Fearless* confirmed the fears of many of his critics within the Commonwealth that Britain was prepared to do a deal with the Smith regime at the expense of Rhodesia's large black majority. As previously noted, Tanzania had broken off diplomatic relations with Britain soon after UDI in protest at what it perceived as Britain's ineffectual approach to the Rhodesian problem.

Because Britain, in common with many other capitalist states, was perceived as being half-hearted in imposing sanctions against Rhodesia, both the Soviet Union and Communist China made haste to exploit the situation by offering moral support and economic aid to affronted African states. In this way, China offered substantial aid packages to Zambia and also to Tanzania – where an ambitious railway construction scheme was agreed.

Britain's alleged 'softness' towards the Smith regime was compounded by suspicions that it was also, in effect, a half-hearted opponent of the apartheid regime in South Africa. Within the United Kingdom, these suspicions were shared by radical and left-wing groups, and anti-apartheid demonstrations disrupted the South African rugby tour of 1969–70, and a Stop-the-70-Tour Committee was formed to protest at the impending visit of the South African cricket team. Although it was possible to recognise the value of the South African market to Britain, the disinclination to damage that trading relationship undoubtedly caused some black African Commonwealth countries urgently to seek trading links elsewhere. It is not clear whether the price was worth the paying from the point of view of Britain's economy.

Further stress was put upon the Commonwealth's toleration of Britain's apparent collaboration with South Africa when, in 1970, the newly-elected Conservative government led by Edward Heath announced that arms sales to the Pretoria government would be resumed. Heath was also a dedicated advocate of Britain's membership of the European Economic Community, and it soon became evident that if sufficiently favourable terms of entry could be negotiated, Britain would join the EEC. To many members of the Commonwealth, this meant that Britain would in effect turn its back on them. Far from Britain seeking, as it had done for so much of the Empire-Commonwealth's history, to control and dominate inter-imperial trade, it was now prepared to abandon its special fiscal relationship for the new orthodoxy of the EEC. It was little wonder that Keith Holyoake, the Prime Minister of New Zealand, which relied heavily on the British market for the export of products like butter and lamb, remarked, 'We are fighting for our livelihood.'[11]

Within the Commonwealth itself, a variety of internal tensions, pressures and insurrections threatened to make a mockery of Britain's boast that the Westminster model of democracy had been successfully transplanted to the overwhelming majority of its ex-colonies. In 1966 Ghana's Kwame Nkrumah was deposed by an army coup, and forced to find refuge in Guinea. The exiled Nkrumah – once perceived as the father of his people – was denounced as a corrupt dictator who had robbed his needy country of untold millions. Although Ghana appeared to return to Western-style democracy and civil government as a result of the 1969 general election, it was not clear how long the new government would last.

Even more disturbing, also during 1966, the other major Commonwealth country in West Africa, Nigeria, seemed set on the path to civil war. Tribal animosities between the Ibos of eastern Nigeria, the Hausas of the north, and the Yoruba people of the west led to the overthrow of the federal government and, after much bloodshed and uncertainty, resulted in the secession of the Ibo people and the establishment of their own independent state, Biafra. The broken federation of Nigeria, led by its new leader Colonel Gowon, proceeded slowly to destroy Biafra in an unedifying and frequently horrifying civil war. With Britain apparently unable, or unwilling, effectively to intervene in the situation, the war ground to its inevitable conclusion, with the overthrow of the Biafra regime and the restoration of the Nigerian federation.

In East Africa, tribal antagonisms resulted in the murder, in 1969, of the charismatic Tom Mboya. The assassination dramatically illustrated Kenya's potential for internal conflict and civil war: Mboya, a member of the Luo tribe, was seen as the obvious heir to Jomo Kenyatta, and was thus feared and hated by members of the Kikuyu tribe in particular. His death resulted in Luo tribesmen rioting in Nairobi, even hurling stones at Kenyatta himself.

In Central Africa, President Kenneth Kaunda's government in Zambia, anxious to avoid similar conflict arising from tribal divisions, banned political parties based primarily upon such allegiances. By 1969, Kaunda had assumed the major functions of government himself. At first sight this appeared to be nothing less than the overthrow of the Westminster model and the establishment of megalomanic personal rule. For a while, Kaunda's immense personal reputation for integrity and fair-dealing shielded him from the worst criticism. One-man rule, however, no matter what its justifications or its good intent, seemed to be storing up trouble for the future.

Amid these convulsions, and with Soviet and Chinese technicians and advisors bringing aid and expertise to many of the non-aligned states of Africa, the founder members of the 'Commonwealth Club' – Britain, Canada, Australia and New Zealand – went out of their way to promote an antidote of sorts: the Commonwealth Development Corporation. The corporation gave important financial assistance to African Commonwealth member states through the Special Commonwealth African Assistance Plan, which had been first set up in 1960. By the mid-1960s, other, more advanced, Commonwealth countries were also making modest contributions to Commonwealth development, including India, Pakistan, Ghana and Nigeria.

Aid was offered in the form of capital, either loaned at low rates of interest or as an outright gift, to establish new industries or to build up public services. Very substantial sums were given in this way. In 1966, for instance, Britain gave nearly £70 million-worth of aid to African countries within the Commonwealth, and other members of the organisation provided £5 million. Another major form of assistance was the provision of help in the education of African students. Fifteen hundred African students were studying in Britain by the mid-1960s on special scholarships, while another 15,000 were in the country studying at their own expense. Some assistance was also given in setting up institutions of higher education in Commonwealth African countries.

The giving of aid, of course, served several purposes. It was humanitarian and constructive. It was also often a way of ensuring, through the nature of the aid agreements, that the exports of Britain, and other advanced economies, had guaranteed access to the markets of developing nations – aid, in other words, with strings attached. It also helped to stabilise the economies and as a result, arguably, the political structures of newly-established countries within the Commonwealth. For both the West and the Communist world, aid was, in effect, a form of investment, a bid to control the future. Thus, despite protestations to the contrary, aid always came 'with strings attached'.

Even so, the proportion of Britain's trade with African Commonwealth countries was comparatively small in proportion to its trade overall. Nigeria was the most important of Britain's African trading partners, but during the mid-1960s it contributed less than 1 per cent of Britain's trade. Zambia could sell its copper to the industrialised world, but other states, like Kenya or Tanzania, had much greater difficulty in exporting their agricultural products to an already over-supplied world market. Many African states in the Commonwealth, however, could only buy urgently-needed machinery and manufactured goods if the country which supplied them gave them financial assistance. Schemes of Commonwealth aid thus kept countries like Malawi, Uganda and Tanzania heavily dependent upon inter-Commonwealth trade. For example, in 1967 Malawi made 70 per cent of its purchases from within the Commonwealth, Uganda 60 per cent, and Tanzania 52 per cent.[12] The continuation of Commonwealth preferential tariffs also enhanced inter-Commonwealth trade.

In other parts of the Commonwealth there were a variety of difficulties. By 1965 the federation of Malaysia had lost the prosperous, Chinese-dominated island state of Singapore, which seceded under the leadership of Lee Kuan Yu. Having survived an Indonesian armed assault, which had resulted in military assistance from fellow Commonwealth states such as Britain, Australia and New Zealand, Malaysia continued to prosper in the aftermath of Singapore's secession, promoting important agricultural and industrial developments, and pursuing social reforms that had resulted in a 75 per cent literacy rate by 1970. Tensions between the native Malays and the Chinese, however, which had been at least partly at the root of Singapore's secession, resulted in widespread and severe racial rioting in Malaysia during 1969. Parliamentary democracy was as a result temporarily suspended.

Fearful of Communist China to the north, and uncertain as to the long-term implications of the Vietnamese war, both Malaysia and Singapore were glad to receive in 1970 a commitment by the newly elected Conservative government that it would maintain a modest British military presence in the area. By the end of the 1970s, Malaysia was even in a position to give aid to developing member states, especially in Africa.[13]

Elsewhere, a considerable number of smaller territories had achieved independence: British Guyana in 1966; Southern Yemen, including Aden, in 1967; Mauritius in 1968; Fiji and Tonga in 1970; and the Federation of Arab Emirates (in the Persian Gulf) in 1971.

As a result of this, Britain only ruled directly a few colonies such as Hong Kong, Saint Helena, the Seychelles, Saint Vincent, and a number of smaller territories, including the Falkland Islands in the South Atlantic. By 1970, therefore, in place of the once worldwide and awe-inspiring British Empire, there was a similarly far-flung Commonwealth. It was, however, an organisation over which Britain had next to no influence or control, and within which it was increasingly likely to be subjected to hostility, criticism and contempt. This was indeed a far cry from the dreams and confident predictions of British imperialists at the beginning of the century.

THE DECLARATION OF COMMONWEALTH PRINCIPLES AT SINGAPORE, 1971

The Commonwealth During the 1970s

THE ASSORTED Commonwealth heads of government gathered at Singapore for one of their regular conferences in January 1971, with the fortunes of the organisation apparently at a low ebb. During the 1960s the attempt to transform the Commonwealth – which by 1971 contained a record number of thirty independent states – into an informal organisation of cooperating countries, inspired by internationalist principles and united by their adherence to the Westminster model of democratic government, had fundamentally failed. Despite, or perhaps because of, the continuing process of decolonisation, diversity of practice and a conflict of interests – sometimes violently expressed – had characterised the new Commonwealth just as much as any high-minded adherence to the rule of law, brotherly cooperation, or support for international bodies like the United Nations.

The 1960s had witnessed another war between India and Pakistan; a military coup, leading to a protracted and devastating civil conflict, in Nigeria; fighting in Cyprus between Turkish and Greek Cypriots; the overthrow of civilian governments by military leaders in Ghana and Sierra Leone; and Britain's inability even to begin to bring down the rebellious Smith regime in Southern Rhodesia. Above all, the ex-Mother Country, for a whole variety of reasons – ranging from its immigration policies to its apparently increasing self-interest, most unmistakably indicated by its application for membership of the European Economic Community – had become the target for outpourings of discontent and criticism so vehement that they harked back to the days of colonial freedom struggles rather than exemplifying mature and harmonious relationships between independent members of a major international community. So problematical had the 1960s been that Lord Garner, Permanent Under-Secretary of State in the British Commonwealth Office for most of the decade, felt that the main achievement of the Commonwealth during the decade had been simply to survive.[1]

The Heads of Government meeting in Singapore in January 1971 seemed to encapsulate much of what was wrong with the Commonwealth, and even to indicate that it might be staggering towards decay and dissolution. The conference was eventually able to issue a Declaration of Commonwealth Principles, which asserted the inalienable right of all citizens within the organisation to 'participate by means of free and democratic political processes in framing the society in which they live'.[2]

The problem was that an increasing number of members of the Commonwealth either would not, or could not, live up to such principles. The British Prime Minister, Edward Heath, who had unexpectedly defeated Harold Wilson in the 1970 general election, had been the target for concerted criticism at the conference. Britain, under Heath's Conservative government, was accused, again, of failing to end the Rhodesian rebellion and of renewing the sale of British arms to the apartheid regime in South Africa. The situation was not helped by Heath's personal awkwardness and his tendency to thump his fist on the conference table when thwarted. He was, moreover, the most passionately committed British Prime Minister of the post-war years to the European Economic Community.

For all its manifold failings, real and potential, Britain did at least practise the 'Westminster' style of government. The same could not be said for many fellow member states of the Commonwealth. While the heads of state met in Singapore, the President of Uganda, Dr Milton Obote, was thrown out of office after a military coup at home led by General Idi Amin. The fact that Obote had himself assumed presidential powers in 1966 by unconstitutional methods did not lessen his discomfiture.

The establishment of the Amin regime in Uganda was to provide an embarrassing counterpoint to the lofty Declaration of Commonwealth Principles, and seemed, in addition, to indicate that at the heart of the Commonwealth ideal was the canker of corruption and malpractice. Under Amin's leadership Uganda was subjected to an increasingly brutal dictatorship. But although members of the Commonwealth had virtuously blocked South Africa's application for renewed membership after it had opted for republican status in 1960, they were reluctant to establish a precedent by expelling Uganda on account of the Amin regime's excesses and anti-democratic practices.

The best that could be done was eventually to issue a statement at the meeting of Commonwealth Heads of Government in London in 1977 which condemned the 'massive violation of basic human rights in Uganda'.[3] Whether even this public airing of humanitarian and democratic principles would have occurred but for the absence of the Ugandan head of state – Amin had finally, to the relief of many delegates, failed to attend the meeting of an organisation of which he had offered to become the elected head – is debatable. Still, at least a form of words had been found.

Amin's eventual downfall came not because of any concerted Commonwealth initiative, but as a result of a brief military conflict with Uganda's Commonwealth neighbour, Tanzania. In 1978, Amin, partly perhaps in the hope of diverting mounting opposition at home by means of a foreign adventure, invaded Tanzania in order to capture a disputed border area. The Tanzanian government responded by mounting a full-scale invasion of Uganda, aided by large numbers of Ugandan exiles, captured the country's capital, Kampala, in April 1979, and Amin was driven into exile. The conflict provided another example of Commonwealth member states coming to blows in order to settle their differences. At least Uganda proceeded to hold reasonably democratic elections in 1980, the first to be held since independence was conferred in 1962. As a result of the polling, although amid some confusion, Milton Obote was returned to power.

In Central Africa, Zambia followed the Tanzanian example in 1972 and amended its constitution to establish a one-party state. Despite the domestic and international reputation of Zambia's leader, President Kenneth Kaunda, and his justification of the measures to put an end to party politics based predominantly on tribal divisions, one-party rule was a far cry from the Westminster model of democracy. At least Zambia could claim in mitigation that its economy was being ruined as a result of the slump in the price of copper on the world market, and through the disruption of its normal trading relationships with the rebellious Rhodesian supremacist regime. Kenya, on the other hand, had been unable to claim similar justifications when it became, in effect, a one-party state in 1969 with the banning of the only opposition party, the Kenya People's Union.

The establishment of a one-party system of government in Kenya,

Tanzania, Zambia, Malawi, and, from 1978, Sierra Leone, was an embarrassing development within the Commonwealth. Not merely did it seem, to those inclined to be critical, that a cluster of dictatorships had been established in parts of the African Commonwealth, it also gave a propaganda weapon and some comfort to the white minority regimes of Rhodesia and South Africa. In response to the call for 'one man, one vote', the leaders of white supremacist regimes could triumphantly point to the apparent violation of human and civil rights in black majority African states, and remind their constituents that the establishment of such governments meant 'one man, no vote'.

This criticism was not, of course, entirely fair. In none of the African Commonwealth countries that had chosen to establish one-party rule during the late 1960s and 1970s had there been an effective opposition party. It was even possible to claim that one-party rule gave the electorate a real and extended choice, enabling them to choose between rival candidates from the same governing party. Furthermore, one-party rule did not inevitably mean the destruction of civil rights. Although often subjected to intense political pressures, the judiciaries of the African countries involved were mostly able to operate with sufficient independence to guarantee at least a reasonable amount of civil rights. The states also enjoyed remarkable political stability. By 1978, President Kenyatta of Kenya, President Kaunda of Zambia, President Banda of Malawi and President Nyerere of Tanzania had all been in office since 1964. Even when Kenyatta died in 1978, he was succeeded through a peaceful application of the constitution by the former Vice-President, Daniel arap Moi.

Such continuity of experience in East and Central Africa did not, however, lead to harmony between the states involved. During the 1970s the East African Community, which had aspired to a considerable degree of regional economic cooperation, broke up on the rocks of the excesses of the Amin regime and of the continuing border dispute between Tanzania and Kenya. The East African Community was a post-imperial descendant of the earlier British attempt to rationalise communications, postal, currency and economic structures in her East African colonies. Although one of the aims of the inter-war British initiative in this respect was eventually to establish a great East African Dominion, dominated by the European settlers of Kenya, the collapse of the organisation in the post-colonial period was depressing for those who hoped to see the Commonwealth promote various cooperative schemes between member nations.

British attempts to sell the ideal of
Empire in the inter-war years led to
the holding of the great British Empire
Exhibition (and the building of
Wembley Stadium) in 1924.

A P&O poster puts the Empire at the
centre of its advertising message.

Arab protestors confronting a British soldier
in Jerusalem, 1937.

THE SECOND WORLD WAR

Above right General Percival
surrenders Singapore to the
Japanese, 15 February 1942.

Right Australian machine-
gunners during the Burma
campaign, July 1945.

Below Labour in power, 1945–51.
Arthur Creech Jones, Colonial
Secretary (*centre*), and Ernest
Bevin, Foreign Secretary (*right*),
at a conference on the problem
of Palestine, January 1947.

Left Sir Stafford Cripps meets Mohammed Ali Jinnah during the ill-fated Cripps Mission of the spring of 1942.

Below The last Viceroy, Lord Mountbatten, at the meeting at which the partition of India was agreed, June 1947. Nehru sits at Mountbatten's right, Jinnah on his left.

Muslim refugees packing a train taking them to their newly created homeland of Pakistan. Terrible communal massacres accompanied the mass migrations at the partition.

President Makarios, the leader of Greek Cypriot resistance to British rule.

Colonel Grivas, the leader of EOKA, receives a hero's welcome in Athens in March 1959.

SUEZ CRISIS, 1956

Left Just good friends? Eden and Nasser met once only, before the Suez crisis broke, in Cairo in February 1955. Here Nasser is attempting to hold an embarrassed Eden's hand for the photograph.

The Suez invasion. British tanks patrol the streets of Port Said, 8 November 1956.

Prime Minister Harold Macmillan in Lagos, the Nigerian capital, during his momentous 'wind of change' tour of Africa in 1960.

The liberal and charismatic Conservative Colonial Secretary Iain Macleod in conversation with Julius Nyerere, the leader of Tanganyika's nationalist movement.

South Africa's Prime Minister Hendrik Verwoerd (*centre*) leaves the 1961 Commonwealth Prime Ministers' Meeting after the new Republic of South Africa was denied readmittance to the Commonwealth due to its apartheid policies.

The Queen, as Head of the Commonwealth, surrounded by leaders of the Commonwealth at the time of the 1961 conference. From left: Sir Abubakar Tafawa Balewa (Nigeria), Dr Nkrumah (Ghana), John Diefenbaker (Canada), Jawaharlal Nehru (India), Field Marshal Ayub Khan (Pakistan), Sir Roy Welensky (Central African Federation), Mrs Bandaranaike (Ceylon), Harold Macmillan (Britain), Sir Robert Menzies (Australia), Archbishop Makarios (Cyprus), Keith Holyoake (New Zealand), Tunku Abdul Rahman (Malaysia).

FREEDOM STRUGGLES IN AFRICA

Above left Julius Nyerere triumphantly proclaims Tanganyika's independence in 1961.

Above Jomo Kenyatta greets rejoicing crowds after his release from detention in 1961.

Ian Smith, Rhodesian Prime Minister, surrounded by his Cabinet, signs his government's unilateral declaration of independence on 11 November 1965.

Lord Soames congratulates Robert Mugabe on his election as Zimbabwe's first Prime Minister in 1980.

Prime Minister Margaret Thatcher, whose resolve sustained the Falklands campaign, in determined and patriotic posture watching British military exercises in West Germany.

Below A triumphant Nelson Mandela, soon to be elected President of South Africa, gives the victory salute before an ANC banner.

Political developments in the two leading Commonwealth states in West Africa, Ghana and Nigeria, were equally problematical. Mounting economic difficulties and the tensions and pressures generated by inter-tribal rivalries rendered it impossible to maintain a form of pluralist, multi-party democracy under a Westminster-type constitution. Ghana experienced several military coups, the most dramatic of which was led by the charismatic figure of Flight-Lieutenant Jerry Rawlings, who, in 1979, in a brisk attempt to cleanse the nation of corruption, gave summary trial to and then executed three former heads of state and other senior officials. At least Rawlings delivered the goods in terms of democracy, encouraging the holding of free elections which, in September 1979, returned a new civilian government to power led by Dr Hilla Limann.

Supporters of the Westminster system, however, could draw only limited comfort from this development. The new Ghanaian constitution, although providing for a multi-party system, scrapped the office of prime minister and replaced it with that of an executive president to be directly elected every four years. Neither the president nor ministers in the government were to sit in Parliament.[4] This development suggested a shift towards the Washington model of parliamentary democracy rather than a restoration of the Westminster system.

In Nigeria the move away from the Westminster style of parliamentary democracy was even more marked than in Ghana. The civil war, provoked by the attempt of Biafra to secede from the Federation, had been brought to an end in 1970. Subsequently a reasonably successful policy of reconciliation was applied; but it was military, not civil government, that became the pattern during the 1970s. It was not until the autumn of 1979 that civilian constitutional government was restored. Not that the record of the military rulers who had determined Nigeria's fate after 1970 was one of autocratic repression. Significant reforms had been carried out, particularly in the areas of local government, land tenure and the structure of regional government.

In the event, the new 1979 constitution established the president as chief executive and commander-in-chief of the armed forces, elected for a fixed four-year term, renewable only once. Each constituent state of the federation had a directly elected state governor, and the central legislature consisted of a Senate, with equal representatives from each state, and a House of Representatives with single-member constituencies. Members of the government were to be appointed by the president, but excluded from the legislature. This was an almost embarrassing imitation of the United States constitution in a formerly British West African country.

Commonwealth traditionalists might bemoan the fact that in both West and East Africa the old Westminster model had been either radically adapted or overthrown. But it could at least be coherently argued that the rights of the citizen in both the newly-established Washington-model constitutions of West Africa and in the one-party participatory democracies of East Africa were sufficient to allow basic democratic principles to be sustained. It had also seemed encouraging that military rule in many of these states had not become permanently entrenched, but, on the contrary, had often led to the introduction of restructured and revitalised democratic forms.

During the 1970s, the sub-continent of India also provided mixed comfort for Commonwealth idealists and traditionalists. The third decade of India's independence was marked by a succession of crises, some of them quite unexpected. In 1969, for example, the Congress Party, which had ruled India uninterruptedly since independence in 1947, broke up into two sections. Although the dominant wing, headed by the Prime Minister, Mrs Indira Gandhi – Nehru's only and beloved daughter – won an overwhelming victory in the general election of 1971, it became increasingly enmeshed in difficulties over the maintenance of law and order and the prosecution of economic policy.

In a move which would have perturbed some earlier viceroys by its authoritarian tone, Mrs Gandhi's government declared a State of Emergency in 1975, and a year later extended the life of the current Parliament and amended the constitution in order to enhance the power of the central government. The administration proceeded down its chosen and increasingly uncomfortable authoritarian path by employing political restraints such as detention and censorship. It also stirred up a huge controversy over what seemed to be the arbitrary imposition of profoundly unpopular policies such as male sterilisation, a move which could be justified by the need to control India's rapidly expanding population, but which had uncomfortable echoes of the medical policies and experiments of Hitler's Reich. Eventually, in 1977, Mrs Gandhi went to the polls, thus allowing the people to give their electoral response to her government's policies. The result was an overwhelming victory for a newly formed and, in the event, uneasily grouped, opposition party, the Janata Front. Mrs Gandhi even lost her parliamentary seat in the rout.

India's claim to be the largest democracy in the world was, however, amply justified by the aftermath of the election of 1977. Mrs Gandhi accepted her defeat and went into opposition. The military forces remained neutral. The Janata government, having been given its opportunity to exercise power, broke up in factional disputes within two years of its victory. In the ensuing election, Mrs Gandhi and Congress were emphatically returned to power with an overwhelming majority based upon a huge popular vote. She was now able to justify the extension of the powers of central government on the basis of the democratic will of the people.

Elsewhere in the sub-continent the former province of East Pakistan, with its overwhelming Muslim majority, broke from its union with West Pakistan in 1971, with the help of the Indian government, and established itself as the newly independent state of Bangladesh – or East Bengal. Pakistan, the former province of West Pakistan, withdrew from the Commonwealth as a result of this humiliation, and was soon struggling to preserve its democratic constitution.

Under the leadership of Zulfiqar Ali Bhutto, who became Prime Minister in the aftermath of the Bangladesh secession, economic reforms were introduced against a background of increasing unrest in the provinces. At the elections of March 1977, Bhutto claimed victory despite widespread accusations of election-rigging. As civil disorder spread throughout the country, the Pakistan army began to emerge as the major power-broker. In July 1977, the army, under General Mohammed Zia ul-Haq, took over power and put Bhutto and other leading politicians under arrest. Despite declaring that free and fair elections would soon be held, these did not materialise, and in March 1978 the deposed Bhutto was condemned to death, after a trial of sorts, for implication in the murder of a political opponent. Despite international appeals, Bhutto was eventually hanged in April 1979. As the decade ended, General Zia had once more cancelled democratic elections and had banned all political activities and strikes.

In Bangladesh, which had been admitted to the Commonwealth in 1972 in the place of Pakistan, democracy fared a little better. Although the first Prime Minister of Bangladesh, Sheikh Mujib, was assassinated during the military coup of 1979, partly as a result of his assumption of sweeping presidential powers a few months earlier, the military government led by General Ziaur actually made good its promise to restore democracy. General Ziaur confirmed his presidency as a result of a contested popular election in 1978, and a year later a parliamentary election was deemed reasonably fair and free. Thus democratic forms were re-established in Bangladesh albeit on a somewhat shaky and tenuous basis.

In Sri Lanka, known as Ceylon until 1972, the 1980s witnessed a rapid series of political and constitutional changes. Having proceeded so smoothly to independence in 1948, Ceylon operated a Westminster-style parliamentary system apparently satisfactorily, complete with the status of dominion, a multi-party parliamentary system, and peaceful transfers of power to opposition parties as the results of four general elections between 1956 and 1970.

The victors of the 1970 general election, the Sri Lanka Freedom Party, led by Mrs Sirimavo Bandaranaike, proceeded to introduce fundamental constitutional reforms. Constitutional and parliamentary practices which linked Ceylon to her not inglorious colonial past were broken. In 1972 Ceylon became a republic, within the Commonwealth, and henceforth known as Sri Lanka. Mrs Bandaranaike herself went down to a crushing defeat in the 1977 general election, as a result of which further constitutional changes brought about the United National Party government, introduced what has been described as a 'Gaullist', executive presidency. The leader of the United National Party, J.R. Jayewardene, became Executive President in 1978.

Racial tensions, particularly the uprising of the Tamils, had yet to disfigure the face of Sri Lankan democracy. Malaysia was less fortunate, and the communal disturbances of 1969 meant that the country entered the 1970s under emergency rule. With the restoration of the authority of Parliament and the Cabinet in 1971, however, and with the increase of prosperity throughout the region, the fundamental communal tension between Chinese and Malays was somewhat lessened.

Elsewhere in what were now often described as 'New Commonwealth' states, growing impoverishment and deepening economic difficulties, often expressed through the rivalries of different ethnic or religious groupings, led to an increase in lawlessness and extra-parliamentary activity. Jamaican politics became increasingly violent, leading to the setting up of a special 'Gun Court' in 1974 to stamp out gangsterism. The 1980 general election in Jamaica was accompanied by considerable disturbance, although it resulted in a landslide victory for the undeniably right-wing Labour Party. But throughout the West Indies, the Westminster system of government remained firmly entrenched, although Trinidad and Tobago chose to become a republic within the Commonwealth and to install a non-executive president in place of the governor-general in 1976. Guiana, which had been a republic since 1970, adopted a new constitution in 1980, setting up an executive presidency in the process.

The stormy history of Cyprus was brought at least to some sort of resolution during 1974. Continuing tension and rivalry between the Greek and Turkish communities eventually resulted in a Turkish invasion of northern Cyprus – President Makarios had been overthrown by a Greek coup shortly before. The island became partitioned between the two communities, although the largest area, occupied by the Greek Cypriots, was the only 'Cyprus' recognised by other Commonwealth states.

Perhaps most surprising of all were the constitutional pressures and shifts in not merely some of the 'old' dominions but also in the United Kingdom itself. In Britain, which had for so long and so smugly prided itself upon its 'unwritten' constitution and its model parliamentary democracy, a major constitutional debate unravelled during the 1970s. In 1973 a Royal Commission on the Constitution reported after lengthy deliberations and soundings. Although a written constitution with an entrenched Bill of Rights did not ensue, statutory provision was made for the introduction of 'devolved' government in both Wales and Scotland. When, however, Wales and Scotland voted on the issue in referenda in 1979, under the Callaghan Labour government, the devolutionists – rather surprisingly in the case of Scotland – failed to win the required majorities. If Wales and Scotland had voted for devolution in 1979, the United Kingdom would have moved towards a quasi-federal structure, very similar to the 'home rule all round' proposed by Joseph Chamberlain and other radical Liberals during the great Irish Home Rule controversy of the mid-1880s.

Among the 'old' dominions, both Canada and Australia were embroiled in constitutional controversies during the 1970s. In Canada, the strong separatist movement in French-speaking Quebec threatened the existence of the federation. Although the voters of Quebec narrowly rejected their provincial government's request for a mandate to negotiate a substantial measure of political independence at the 1980 referendum, separatist demand was not to evaporate. Quebec, of course, remained intrinsically reluctant to abandon its fruitful economic links with the rest of Canada, and perhaps especially the cushion of its federal subsidies.

Even among English-speaking Canadians, however, there were some resentments at the archaic manifestations of Britain's relationship with the country. Although relatively few demanded republican status, there were many who objected to the British Parliament's exclusive power to amend the Canadian constitution through the British North America Acts. At the end of the 1970s the Liberal government, led by Pierre Trudeau, proposed a comprehensive plan for constitutional reform – including the redefinition of the position of the Crown and the role of the Governor-General within the Canadian constitution. It was not until 1982, however, that the Canadian Act, transferring the responsibility for constitutional reform in Canada, was passed by the British Parliament.

Republicanism was a greater threat in Australia. Although royal tours, such as the Queen's visit during the Silver Jubilee celebrations of 1977, were generally popular, doubts as to the relevance of the monarchy to a modern, rapidly expanding and increasingly multi-ethnic Australia were becoming more commonplace.

Republican sentiment was given a substantial boost by the constitutional crisis of 1975. This arose when the Labour Prime Minister, Gough Whitlam, was unable to pass government budget bills through the opposition-controlled Senate. Declining to resolve the issue by requesting a dissolution of parliament, Whitlam was dismissed – apparently abruptly – by the Governor-General, Sir John Kerr, who then invited Malcolm Fraser, the leader of the Opposition, to become Prime Minister. Even though Fraser subsequently won an overwhelming victory in the ensuing general election, the crisis inevitably precipitated a sharpening of the debate over the position of the monarch and of the monarch's representative, the governor-general, in Australian internal affairs. It was difficult for many Australians to resist the impression that if the crisis of 1975 had been transferred to British conditions, the Queen would not have arbitrarily dismissed her prime minister in the way in which Whitlam was sent packing by her representative in Australia. Increasingly it was argued that Australia could only be truly independent, and indeed could only properly establish its own identity, if it became a republic.

By 1980, the once widely accepted constitutional principle of a common allegiance to the Crown had been substantially diluted. By the end of the 1970s there were forty-four independent members of the Commonwealth. Of these, however, only fifteen acknowledged the Queen as head of state, and four of these comprised members of the 'old white Commonwealth guard' – Britain, Canada, Australia and New Zealand. Of the remainder, eight were in their first decade of independence, and therefore perhaps less inclined to apply for republican status.

Partly as a response to the growth of republican and separatist tendencies within the Commonwealth, a vigorous programme of royal tours was unleashed during the 1970s. Queen Elizabeth's Silver Jubilee was celebrated in June 1977. But in contrast to the pomp and power of Queen Victoria's Diamond Jubilee in 1897, or even to that of King George V's Silver Jubilee in 1935, the ceremonial and the celebrations were distinctly metropolitan and shrunken. Whereas almost every group, nation, race and territory had been represented at the London-based celebrations of Queen Victoria's Jubilee in 1897, on Queen Elizabeth's Jubilee Day, only eighty years later, there was only one contingent of Canadian 'Mounties' as a token reminder of the once worldwide, glorious Empire beyond the seas.

During the 1970s the process of decolonisation hardly ever involved a struggle for independence. As George Thomson, the last British Commonwealth Secretary, from 1966 to 1968, had earlier made plain: 'We shall not stand in the way of any territory which wishes to proceed to independence.'[5] The process of devolution was undoubtedly aided by the former colonial power's anxiety to dispose of the bulk of the remaining Empire as smoothly and efficiently as possible, and in the process to rid itself of any continuing economic burdens. On the other hand, Britain made no attempt to push unwilling colonies out of what was left of the Empire. At the end of the 1970s it appeared highly likely that Saint Helena, Pitcairn, the Falkland Islands, Gibraltar and perhaps even Hong Kong would remain within the imperial system for the foreseeable future.

One of the chief reasons why the old imperial system continued to dissolve at such a rate was Britain's final accession to the European Economic Community in 1973. From first to last, British policy towards the Empire had been underwritten by its economic needs and by self-serving financial and fiscal policies. Just as British domestic imperatives had spawned the Navigation Acts of the seventeenth century, dumped them in favour of Free Trade during the late 1840s, precipitated the agitation for tariff reform in the early 1900s, and pushed through the introduction of Imperial Preference in 1932, so the modern version of these pressures led inevitably to membership of the EEC and to the ending of the elaborate system of Commonwealth preferences and associated agreements.

Membership of the EEC also meant the end of the Sterling Area, which came in 1972 when the pound sterling was finally allowed to float on the currency exchange markets and to find its own free market value. One of the chief consequences of this decision was that sterling ceased to be a reserve currency for most of the Commonwealth, although in truth this trend had been underway since Harold Wilson's Labour government had been forced to devalue the pound in 1967. The trading links between the United Kingdom and members of the 'old' Commonwealth became far less significant. In 1964, for example, Britain was still easily Australia's largest single customer. By 1977 Australian exports to Britain were less than half of those to the United States and only one eighth of those to Japan.[6]

As Britain became increasingly involved in the EEC, the final rites of the Commonwealth as a tariff and monetary union were duly carried out. Trading and commercial links between Britain and the needy and developing countries of the African, Caribbean and Pacific Commonwealth now had to be regulated within the framework of the Lomé Convention, signed in February 1975, between the EEC and forty-six other countries from these areas. Former French and Belgian colonies in Africa were included in the Lomé Convention, while the agreement actually excluded countries of the British Commonwealth in Asia. Negotiations to finalise a new treaty, Lomé Two, led to considerable resentment on the part of many emerging Commonwealth countries before it was signed in 1980. The 1979 Commonwealth Heads of Government Conference even went so far as to record the 'strong dissatisfaction' of delegates from Commonwealth ACP (Afro/Caribbean/Pacific Commonwealth) countries with the outcome of the negotiations.[7]

The Commonwealth did not, however, cease to be a medium for economic cooperation and the promotion of development. The increasing tendency to seek for a 'North–South' dialogue (reflecting the recognition that, on a global scale, the economic relationships that had to be challenged were between the comparatively few rich nations of the north and the overwhelming number of poor ones of the south) was central to any future settlement of the problems of world poverty and underdevelopment. The Commonwealth could claim, in these circumstances, to have the strength of being both a voluntary association, and one which included a variety of states scattered throughout the North–South divide.

Consultation and advice were not the only functions of the Commonwealth in terms of encouraging development and economic progress. During the 1970s there were a number of revivals of Commonwealth initiatives in the field of technical and functional cooperation. In 1971 the Commonwealth Fund for Technical Cooperation was set up, centring its activities on the Technical Assistance Group. In addition, the Commonwealth Secretariat emerged during the 1970s as a far more dynamic and facilitating service than many had anticipated at its inception. This was partly due to the work of the dynamic and creative second Secretary-General of the organisation, the Guyanan Shridath 'Sonny' Ramphal, who succeeded the Canadian Arnold Smith in 1975. The charismatic Ramphal brought considerable diplomatic and political skills to his office, and proceeded eloquently to advocate the needs of developing countries in the search for what was described as 'a new international economic order'. He also played an important part as a member of the Brandt Commission, which was set up to address the problems of world poverty, and which issued an influential report in 1980.

Ramphal also had a crucial role in mediating in the complex and tense negotiations which eventually led to one of the great triumphs of Commonwealth diplomacy at the end of the decade – the Lancaster House Agreement on the future of Zimbabwe in December 1979.

The white Rhodesian minority government was, in effect, driven to the negotiating table during the late 1970s as a result of both the increasing success of black freedom fighters in the civil war and of several significant changes on the international scene. One of these was the collapse of Portuguese colonial rule in Mozambique in 1975, and the subsequent establishment there of an African government dedicated to Marxist principles and willing to apply the economic sanctions which the Portuguese authorities had hitherto been reluctant to exert.

In Britain, a Labour government, led once more by Harold Wilson, returned to office in February 1974, and now accepted the principle that any independence settlement in Rhodesia would have to be provided on the basis of immediate majority rule. The United States and South Africa also put intense pressure on the Smith regime to come to a settlement, both states being anxious to end an embarrassing situation – the United States for reasons of its international standing amongst developing nations, and South Africa because it feared that its own stability might be undermined by an uncontainable and disruptive civil war in neighbouring Rhodesia. Under these concentrated pressures the Rhodesian minority government grudgingly conceded the principle of majority rule.

It still required a miracle of diplomacy and patience peacefully to resolve the situation. The spectacular breakthrough came at the Commonwealth Heads of Government Conference assembled at Lusaka, in Zambia, in August 1979. A Conservative government, led by the forthright and ruthless Margaret Thatcher, had come to power in Britain in May 1979. Ironically, however, far from this producing a rift between Britain and the 'front-line' Commonwealth African states in Central Africa and, indeed, other member states such as Nigeria, no such schism opened up. Margaret Thatcher certainly wanted to end the Rhodesian imbroglio as quickly and decently as possible, and there is evidence that at the Lusaka Conference the Queen also played an important if discreet diplomatic role. In addition, various members of the Commonwealth did their best to produce a settlement.

The result was the Lusaka Agreement. This produced a formula acceptable, surprisingly, to all parties, which led eventually to a constitutional conference, a ceasefire, free elections and, apparently against all the odds, the emergence of an independent Zimbabwe within eight months of the ending of the Lusaka meeting. Scrutinised, criticised and encouraged by other Commonwealth countries, Britain was thus able to perform its final major act of African decolonisation with appropriate poise, good judgement and determination. It was perhaps fitting that the last British proconsul in Africa, Lord Soames, sent as the last Governor of Rhodesia, was a son-in-law of that great imperialist and warrior Winston Churchill.

The Zimbabwe election of February 1980 produced an absolute majority for Robert Mugabe's ZANU Party, and defeat for his rivals the former Prime Minister, Bishop Muzorewa, and Mugabe's fellow freedom-fighter Joshua Nkomo. In April 1980 Zimbabwe at last achieved full independence as the forty-third member state of the Commonwealth. The successful achievement of independence for Zimbabwe, and the Commonwealth's role, not merely in the negotiations, but also in the monitoring of the subsequent elections, seemed substantially to enhance the Commonwealth as an institution able to play a key international role. It was also possible for Britain, through the creative part it played in the final stages of the Rhodesian crisis, to redeem its hitherto controversial – even disreputable – record in the affair. Some of Britain's earlier prestige within the Commonwealth was, arguably, restored as a result.

It was an irony that as the 1980s began, with Britain increasingly involved in the European Economic Community, and with the centuries-old economic priorities that had bound the Empire and Commonwealth together in ruins, the New Commonwealth appeared able to function in so creative and constructive a fashion. As the next fifteen years were to reveal, the evolution of the Commonwealth, and the travails of the former imperial power, were far from over.

30

THE FALKLANDS WAR, 1982

The Remnants of Empire

ON 2 APRIL 1982 Argentinian forces landed on and overran the
Falkland Islands, wind-swept, sparsely populated and isolated British
dependencies deep in the South Atlantic. Before the Argentinian
invasion few British people were aware of the existence of the Falkland
Islands, let alone knew anything substantial about them. Yet they had
been in Britain's possession for a century and a half, claimed for the
Empire by ships of the Royal Navy which had expelled Argentina from
the islands in 1833. There had even been an earlier confrontation over
them in 1770, as a result of which England and imperial Spain had
almost gone to war.

The conflict of 1770 had prompted Dr Johnson to write a pamphlet
in which he attacked those of his fellow-countrymen who were clamouring for war, and asserted, in a famous phrase, that 'Patriotism is
the last refuge of a scoundrel.'[1] During the Falklands crisis in Britain
in 1982 there was certainly a determined minority of critics who were
quick to apply Dr Johnson's dictum to the motives and behaviour of
the Thatcher government.

On this analysis, the crisis was a heaven-sent gift to a government
that was not merely deeply, perhaps fatally, unpopular, but which also
seemed to be presiding with some zest over the disintegration of the
British economy and the breakdown of the nation's social structures.
In June 1981 serious rioting had occurred in many of the major urban
areas of England, although not in Scotland and Wales. By early 1982,
the number of unemployed stood officially at three million, but in reality
probably numbered something like four million. Bankruptcies reached
a record 5500 in the first half of 1982, a 75 per cent rise over the figures
for 1981.[2] During the relatively brief Falklands campaign, more than
two hundred companies went into liquidation every week, while the

City of London – as it had so often done in the past – continued to promote massive investment of British capital overseas rather than at home.

Dire though it may have seemed, however, in practice the government's position in early 1982 was perfectly safe: they had a workable, indeed a substantial, overall majority of more than forty seats in the House of Commons; their popularity as expressed through the opinion polls, although exceptionally low, was actually slowly improving; and above all, the Labour Party had been badly – as some observers saw it, terminally – split by the defection of the Social Democratic Party splinter group of Roy Jenkins, Shirley Williams, David Owen and Bill Rodgers, the 'gang of four', and their supporters.

Margaret Thatcher, however, seized the political opportunity presented by the Falklands invasion with an almost rapturous resolve. Demonstrating her continuing capacity unerringly to discern and exploit populist sentiment among the electorate, she proclaimed her government's unwavering determination to reconquer the lost colonial territories, at the same time conveniently ignoring the criticism that it had been her Cabinet's decision in June 1981 to remove the naval survey vessel HMS *Endurance* – which carried guns, helicopters and twenty Royal Marines – from its duties in the South Atlantic that had encouraged the Argentinian invasion in the first place.[3]

In the emergency debate in the House of Commons on 3 April, Mrs Thatcher began by forcefully reminding MPs that:

> The House meets this Saturday to respond to a situation of great gravity. We are here because, for the first time for many years, British sovereign territory has been invaded by a foreign power . . . I am sure that the whole House will join me in condemning totally this unprovoked aggression by the Government of Argentina against British territory. (Honourable members: 'Hear, hear.') It has not a shred of justification, and not a scrap of legality . . . I must tell the House that the Falkland Islands and their dependencies remain British territory. No aggression and no invasion can alter that simple fact. It is the government's objective to see that the islands are freed from occupation and are returned to British administration at the earliest possible moment.[4]

This was a declaration of resolve that was positively Palmerstonian in tone, and one which might well have proved unpalatable to earlier, more restrained leaders of the Conservative Party such as Peel, Balfour or Baldwin. Fortunately for Thatcher, the mood of the House of Commons was almost entirely supportive. In one of the oddest perorations in a career littered with quirky public utterances of one sort or another, the Leader of the Opposition, the veteran left-winger Michael Foot, rallied to the Prime Minister's support, declaring:

> The rights and circumstances of the people in the Falkland Islands must be uppermost in our minds. There is no question in the Falkland Islands of any colonial dependence or anything of the sort. It is a question of people who wish to be associated with this country and who have built their whole lives on the basis of association with this country. We have a moral duty, a political duty and every other kind of duty to ensure that this is sustained . . .
>
> The people of the Falkland Islands have the absolute right to look to us at this moment of their desperate plight, just as they have looked to us over the past one hundred and fifty years. They are faced with an act of naked, and unqualified aggression, carried out in the most shameful and disreputable circumstances. Any guarantee from this invading force is utterly worthless – as worthless as any of the guarantees that are given by this same Argentine Junta to its own people.[5]

Doubtless Foot's dislike for the repressive, quasi-fascist military rulers of Argentina, led by General Galtieri, did a great deal to stoke up his patriotic passion. His speech, however, was criticised as a self-indulgent exercise in nostalgic liberal imperialist thinking, compounded by an inability to see the wood for the trees – or, rather, the people for the sheep, for the inhabitants of the Falkland Islands numbered approximately eighteen hundred human beings and over six hundred thousand sheep.

If Thatcher had assumed the posture of a Palmerston, even a Churchill, Foot was playing at the very least the part of an Anthony Eden. Edward du Cann, an influential Conservative backbencher, eagerly pursued the Churchillian idiom on rising to congratulate Foot on his speech, remarking – rather as Leo Amery had urged the Labour statesman Arthur Henderson to 'speak for England' during the crucial Commons debate shortly before Britain's entry into the Second World War – that in his view 'The Leader of the Opposition spoke for us all.'[6]

Within Britain the decision to reconquer the Falkland Islands proved extremely popular, apparently uniting people of different background, class and political persuasion. A small minority of MPs, a mere 5 per cent, actively disapproved of the sending of the task force to the South Atlantic. Huge television audiences were soon regularly tuning in to the dramatic newsreel footage of burning warships – some of them, unaccountably, British – and celebrating the efficient military reconquest of the islands. The Falklands War thus became, in a way, yet another soap opera, with viewers thirsting for the next episode and vicariously experiencing the ups and downs of a dramatic and sometimes unpredictable conflict.

Popular newspapers like the *Sun*, already pulling well ahead of the Labour-leaning *Daily Mirror* in the circulation war, pumped out headlines of a belligerent, shrewd and vulgar sort culminating in the famous exclamation 'Gotcha!' after the sinking of the elderly Argentinian cruiser the *General Belgrano* by British submarines. A brisk trade was done in T-shirts bearing the Union flag and slogans such as 'The Empire Strikes Back!'

The relief with which large sections of the population in Britain greeted the reconquest of the islands, and the hostility with which critics of the enterprise were assailed, indicated how fragile contemporary British self-esteem had become, and how badly it needed boosting. It was also a late-twentieth-century indication that the deep-seated concern at Britain's slow and apparently inexorable decline which had first manifested itself at least a century before was still an unavoidable component of the national psyche.

There were, of course, reasons above those of Thatcherite aggrandisement and the narrow needs of party politics to explain why Britain seemed so enthusiastic to launch and prosecute the Falklands War. Of all the great, relatively unexplored regions of the world, the Antarctic was perhaps the most unknown and yet potentially the most promising. Edward du Cann had frankly addressed this issue in the emergency debate of 3 April 1982, remarking:

> Our sovereignty is unimpeachable. British interest in that part of the world, in my judgement, is substantial. It is substantial in the Falkland Islands, however trivial the figures may appear to be. It is substantial in the sea, which is yet to yield up its treasures. It is also substantial in Antarctica.[7]

Britain's reconquest of the Falkland Islands did much to restore the popularity of the Thatcher government, which went on to win the general election of 1983 with a substantially increased majority. There was a supreme irony in all of this. Prior to the Falklands War, not merely was the bulk of the Conservative Party apparently in headlong pursuit of the holy grail of European Economic Community member- ship – and, as they insisted, the economic success that this would bestow – but Margaret Thatcher seemed at first sight an unlikely 'Iron Britan- nia', resolutely defending a scrap of imperial territory against the dragon of Argentinian militarism.

Although the full impact of this had yet to be seen, the Thatcher administrations, although deeply conservative in most respects, were extraordinarily radical in others. Very few of the sacred cows of British institutional life were safe from the Thatcherite process of investigation, reassessment, overhaul and – if necessary – destruction, or, more kindly put, reconstruction. In 1982, what remained of the British Empire seemed to belong to the same category as a host of Thatcherite targets. These included, in the eyes of the Prime Minister and her most ardent supporters: outmoded industrial management techniques; over- regulation, and undue state interference in the ebb and flow of the 'free market'; the 'closed shop', 'overmanning', and other hated and obstructive trade union practices; an out-of-touch legal system; an incompetent and over-powerful system of local government, character- ised by inertia, the wastage of ratepayers' money and the predominance of 'loony left' councils; an apparently overfunded and overstaffed National Health Service; a variety of archaic and inefficient practices in many areas of British public and private life; inappropriate – even subversive – teaching methods in schools that were becoming, especially in some inner city areas, veritable bedlams of indiscipline, drug abuse and plummeting educational standards; and much more besides.

Yet in contrast to the gales of the Thatcherite revolution sweeping through so many British institutions, the Falklands War appeared to be some sort of unpredictable counter-stroke, an attempt to preserve in aspic – and at enormous public expense – a hitherto disregarded frag- ment of an Empire whose sell-buy date had been passed long before. The military triumph, the Prime Minister insisted, had put the 'great' back into Great Britain, and should make the people 'rejoice'. Large numbers of the British people seemed, for the moment at least, to need to agree, conveniently overlooking vital American support.

In essence, of course, the Empire under Mrs Thatcher was as dead as the dodo. In 1981, only a few months before the Falklands crisis, the Commonwealth had welcomed two new independent states as members, Belize and Antigua-Barbuda. This brought the membership of the Commonwealth to forty-six independent states in all, of which just over half were republics.[8]

By the end of the 1980s the membership of the Commonwealth had risen to forty-eight, with the independence of St Kitts and Nevis as well as the Maldive Islands. The remaining dependencies of Britain included Anguilla, Bermuda, British Antarctic Territory, British Indian Ocean Territory, the British Virgin Isles, the Cayman Islands, Gibraltar, Hong Kong, Montserrat, the Pitcairn Islands group, Saint Helena and dependencies (Ascension and Tristan da Cunha), the Turks and Caicos Islands, and, of course, the Falkland Islands.

Of these territories, the most heavily populated by far was Hong Kong, but ironically this was also the territory over which Britain had agreed to renounce its control. Since the Communist takeover in China in 1949, Hong Kong had, in practice, only continued to exist as a British colony with the connivance of the Beijing authorities – rather as the Nationalist Chinese stronghold of Taiwan was tolerated. Although Hong Kong island had been acquired in full sovereignty as a result of Britain's victory in the 1839–42 Opium War, Kowloon, and in particular the mainland New Territories had a different status – the latter having been leased to Britain in 1898 for ninety-nine years. By the early 1980s, the British government had committed itself to the reunification of Hong Kong with mainland China in 1997. Part of the calculation behind this decision was undoubtedly the optimistic belief that the Communist Chinese government would treat Hong Kong relatively tenderly – as a special case, to be nurtured as a valuable asset while the mainland authorities continued their apparently unstoppable drift towards an accommodation, even an enthusiastic partnership, with capitalism.

The progress of Hong Kong towards its incorporation into the People's Republic of China, however, placed the British government in one of those quandaries which were so intrinsic and unavoidable a part of the imperial story. On the one hand, Britain simply did not have the strength to resist the increasingly determined Chinese insistence that Hong Kong was rightfully part of Communist China. On the other, the British government had committed itself to allowing a limited form of representative government in Hong Kong from 1984 onwards, and pressing ahead with a programme of democratisation. Yet this process in itself risked antagonising China and making the final transfer of power even more difficult than it already promised to be.

The main point was, how could the People's Republic swallow up a democratically governed Hong Kong without risking the sort of digestive disorders that had led to the Tiananmen Square massacre of 1989? Chris Patten, the former Chairman of the Conservative Party and Cabinet Minister who had lost his parliamentary seat at the 1992 general election, was promptly appointed Governor of Hong Kong. Patten threw his weight behind the introduction of reforms, particularly for the elections of 1994. The Beijing government demonstrated its displeasure at the reform process by withdrawing from negotiations over Hong Kong's future in December 1993.

There seems, however, to be little choice for either side. Hong Kong will revert to Chinese ownership in 1997, and the Beijing government will have to choose how to handle its relatively democratic structures. Despite some half-hearted protests to the contrary, Britain is in no position to hang on to Hong Kong after 1997 and, indeed, it is difficult to see how this could practically be achieved in any event.

The Conservative governments which have been in power continually in Britain since 1979 do not have an unblemished record when it comes to the defence of democracy overseas, either within the remnants of the Empire or outside it. Although it has sometimes seemed appropriate to stand up for democratic government within the remaining colonial Empire – even to the extent of fighting a war in the Falklands which left over 250 British servicemen dead and nearly 800 wounded, while inflicting losses of at least 2000 upon the Argentinian foe – British policy has been more adaptable and collaborative elsewhere.

Margaret Thatcher, the fearless defender of Falkland Islanders' liberties, stood powerlessly by in October 1983 when United States troops invaded the former British Caribbean colony of Grenada in order to put down an insurrection and restore law and order. She also diplomatically wooed the rulers of several autocratic states in the Middle East, including King Fahd of Saudi Arabia and assorted sheikhs in the Persian Gulf. It is worth noting, in passing, that one of the main purposes of such diplomacy was to facilitate the sale of British weapons and military hardware to Middle Eastern rulers – transactions which in several notable examples seem to have greatly enriched Mark Thatcher, the Prime Minister's son, who became deeply involved in such negotiations. Still, Empire always did provide 'jobs for the boys', and even for some of the girls.

There is no need to fret over the apparent paradox involved in stoutly supporting the introduction of democratic institutions in Hong Kong and fighting to defend the liberties of the Falkland Islanders on the one hand, and flattering and acceding to the American invasion of Grenada and collaborating with autocrats on the other. It was ever thus. Behind the liberal rhetoric of some Palmerstonian interventions in the internal affairs of foreign nations there was almost always an economic or commercial motive.

Nor is Britain necessarily more hypocritical than many other states. The enthusiasm and zest with which a pack of industrialised nations rushed to the defence of Kuwait in late 1990 and early 1991, following the invasion of that state by a profoundly undemocratic Iraq government led by an unabashed and blood-stained tyrant, Saddam Hussein, owed far more to self-interest and the need to preserve oil supplies than to a deep-seated passion for democracy. If the latter had been the case, the less than democratic Kuwaiti government would not have been restored after the ejection of the Iraqis, and the aggressor nation itself would surely have been purged of an unwholesome, tyrannical and belligerent government.

As Palmerston once said, British interests are 'eternal'. This is no less true in the 1990s than it was in the 1850s or the 1860s. By the 1990s, however, the pursuit and consolidation of British interests did not – arguably could not – include the maintenance of a largely dependent Empire. Whether membership of the European Community was an appropriate and fulfilling substitute for leadership of a global Empire was not yet entirely clear. In the meantime, Britain had to be content with membership of a Commonwealth from which – despite the difficulties that this would have created for Queen Elizabeth II as both monarch of the United Kingdom and head of the Commonwealth – it could have been expelled for any number of perceived misdemeanours. The wheel had come full circle.

31

THE INAUGURATION OF
NELSON MANDELA AS
PRESIDENT OF SOUTH AFRICA,
MAY 1994

Post-Colonialism and the Balance Sheet of Empire

ON 10 MAY 1994, amid an atmosphere that was joyous, moving and solemn, Nelson Mandela was sworn in as the State President of the Republic of South Africa. In a ceremony that ended nearly 350 years of white domination in South Africa, Mandela, his calm and dignified bearing sometimes dissolving into small and spontaneous displays of pure pleasure, swore 'to be faithful to the Republic of South Africa, so help me God'. In his inaugural speech, the new State President announced that: 'The time for the healing of wounds has come. The moment to bridge the chasms that divide us has come. The time to build is upon us.' He went on to promise: 'Never, never and never again, shall it be that this beautiful land will again experience the oppression of one by another.'[1]

Although the establishment of the country's first democratically elected majority government was a peculiarly South African event, it also carried enormous international – and for those who chose to see it, colonial and post-colonial – overtones. The gathering of world leaders under the bright autumn sunshine in Pretoria; the flocking of the crowds – fittingly composed of many races – to the celebrations; the final coming to power of what had once seemed to be a lost generation of freedom fighters – including not only Mandela himself, but Walter Sithulu, Joe Slovo and many others; the often grim-faced, uniformed pillars of the dying Anglo-Afrikaner supremacist state standing like undertakers or, more charitably, guardians or godfathers in the background; the white

Chief Justice who conducted the swearing-in of the new President – all of this bore an uncanny resemblance to dozens of previous ceremonials under which the British, with due pomp and circumstance, had ritually divested themselves of imperial political power.

In this sense, the inauguration of Nelson Mandela, based upon the irrefutable and substantial triumph of the African National Congress in the preceding general election, may be seen as one of the last and, arguably, one of the most dramatic and moving transfers of power within a country which had formerly been among the most prosperous, controversial, valued and bitterly contested within the British Empire and Commonwealth.

The triumph of Mandela and the ANC had conformed with almost scientific precision to the formula by which black and brown majorities throughout the Empire had finally achieved independence and self-determination. The formula had included – mostly in its later stages – sustained democratic protest by the disenfranchised majority, piecemeal but inadequate concessions by the white, dominant groups, a hardening of attitudes on both sides, the increasing use of unparliamentary methods of opposition, the inevitable slide towards protest and opposition outside the law, the armed struggle, the arrest and lengthy imprisonment of nationalist leaders, increasing repression within the white-dominated state, continuing and eventually uncontainable internal dissent, the increasing disapproval – often embodied in a variety of sanctions – of the international community, the realisation that white rule could not be indefinitely and artificially prolonged, tentative negotiations with incarcerated indigenous leaders, their eventual release from prison, their rapid involvement in the participatory political progress that would lead to majority rule, and the final installation of a respected, forgiving, and reassuring majority leader in the supreme position of power. Where Mandela stood on 10 May 1994, so, metaphorically, had stood Jawaharlal Nehru, Kwame Nkrumah, Julius Nyerere, Kenneth Kaunda, Jomo Kenyatta, Robert Mugabe, and many others.

The new South Africa was born amidst profound relief, a palpable desire for reconciliation, overwhelming optimism and genuinely high hopes for the future. Its birth pangs were also accompanied by fierce minority dissent, most powerfully and articulately voiced by diehard white supremacists and by predictably maverick indigenous separatists – in this case the Zulu Inkatha movement. It was all strangely, even disconcertingly, familiar.

For those who wished to avert their eyes from the fascinating, awe-inspiring spectacle of a transfer of power on such a scale and of such portent, there were a host of further and disturbing parallels. To the north were three former imperial territories where white minority settlers had first controlled, then confronted, and finally made their peace with black majorities: Zimbabwe, Zambia and Kenya.

On the day of Mandela's inauguration, the post-colonial histories of these 'lesser South Africas' provided inspiration and disillusionment in equal measure, depending upon the viewpoint and prejudices of the observer. In each of what could plausibly be seen as prototypes for the new South Africa, the principle of multi-racialism was proclaimed, but the uncompromising and bloody realities of inter-tribal rivalry and conflict were far too often practised; the Westminster model of democracy had inspired and enabled the political and constitutional practices of these new countries at their outset, but had been subsequently downgraded, distorted, even abandoned; pluralistic politics had given way to one-party states, both in theory and in practice; passionately democratic black prime ministers had been translated into Life Presidents; relatively prosperous – sometimes flourishing – colonial economies had slipped into imbalance, penury and despair; the vagaries of the world market, the over-dependence upon a monoculture agriculture – itself one of the most fateful legacies of colonial rule – threatened millions with want, destitution, even starvation; the narrow-minded, unattractive, uninspiring white officialdom that H.G. Wells had ridiculed so entertainingly nearly a century before had been replaced by indigenous civil services which were often poorly trained, poorly motivated and – in the eyes of some critics – sadly and chronically prone to corruption; once neat and adequately endowed hospitals and medical centres were now too often tragically short of proper equipment and supplies, or even of adequately trained personnel; the formerly orderly streets of colonial capitals, like Nairobi, whose public flower beds and gardens had excited admiration among many visitors, were typically strewn with rubbish, punctured by potholes, and unsafe to walk in after dusk; schools lacked books, enough trained teachers, even drawing paper; far too commonly, millions of women bore the burden of holding their families together, sometimes resorting to prostitution as a desperate, final means of survival; in many communities not only was venereal disease rife, but AIDS was spreading like a late-twentieth-century equivalent of the Black Death.

In numerous other countries throughout the world, where once the British had ruled, there was, in varying degrees, optimism and despair, plenty and hunger, social dislocation and coherent social structures, pride in national identity and communal hatred, ruined economies and prosperous, assertive indigenous bourgeoisies, ambitious development schemes and starving children, over-financed military forces and endemic unemployment, Christianity and paganism asserting their rival claims, sophisticated goods and services advertised on colour televisions and lepers and freaks begging at major tourist sites.

Not that the ex-imperial powers could claim that their own post-colonial histories provided unblemished and undeviating examples of economic prosperity, social vitality or peace and harmony. Chronic mass unemployment, urban decay, industrial decline, the almost sui-cidal disruption of family life and community identity, the proliferation of drugs, pornography and child abuse, the displacement of manifold anxieties and depression into compulsive shopping sprees or eating dis-orders, the increasing preference to become a spectator – of television, sport or, indeed, most of life itself – rather than to be a participant, the progressive subordination of the rights and privacy of the individual to the state and its computerised information and intelligence networks, the institutionalised, inward-looking selfishness of the consumer society, all boded ill for the future.

In the final analysis, however, the nations of the West, Russia and the countries of the former Soviet Bloc, Japan and a few other successful industrialised nations could draw some comfort from the fact that the vast majority of their citizens were adequately fed and sufficiently well housed. The future, moreover, still appeared more hopeful than hopeless.

There had always, though, been a time-bomb ticking away at the heart of both Western capitalism and imperialism. It was inevitable that one day subject nations and their manipulated and controlled economies would be sufficiently free and confident to attempt to catch up with the developed, industrialised world. The trick, for the former imperial powers, was to stay ahead of the game. Towards the end of the twentieth century the new microchip technology indicated one way in which this would, at least for a time, be possible. Perhaps the superior technologies, educational systems and fund-raising and investment levels of the North, as opposed to the South, would continue to prevail. Perhaps the starving and shamefully disadvantaged millions of human beings of the so-called 'developing world' could be bought off with minimal aid and investment, free food supplies, humanitarian intervention, Western technical advice, or reformed agricultural techniques.

Or perhaps they would, one day, somehow, march on, or at least walk towards, the repositories of plenty to the north, and demand their share. Even in that hypothetical, doomsday crisis, the nations of the North/West lands of plenty would have little to fear, providing that their leaders and people remained sufficiently resolute: they could simply repel the invaders by physical means, leaving their corpses piled up against their defences very like the ravenous Australian rabbits mentioned in an earlier chapter, as they attempted to eat their way from depleted New South Wales into flourishing Queensland.[2] It would be one more assertion of the crude power of superior technology and weaponry, an updated version of Belloc's cynical couplet reminding his readers that 'we have got the Maxim gun, and they have not'.

It had been the early European capacity to harness science and technology to the imperatives of conquest and control that had enabled European nations to establish their unprecedented and apparently irresistible worldwide dominion. Even this process had represented a form of exploitation, since ironically some of the new skills and techniques, like Egyptian and Arabic mathematical and astronomical theory, and the triangular lateen sail that helped Columbus cross the Atlantic, were derived from societies which were in due course to fall prey to Western colonial aggression.

There had, naturally, been many other factors involved, including the expansionist tendencies of capitalism – tendencies so potently facilitated by European banking and financial skills and by the ability effectively to organise manufacturing industry and to export its products efficiently and cheaply. Above all, perhaps, there had been an all-pervading Western single-mindedness and energy that was frequently brought to its consummation through the ruthless use of military and naval firepower.[3] All of this, together with the weaknesses, divisions and collaborationist tendencies of indigenous societies, had opened the way to the West's overwhelming, although in many cases short-lived, global supremacy.

Of the great imperial structures, that of the British Empire had been not merely the biggest but, arguably, the most sensitive to the rule of law and to the criticisms of anti-imperialist elements within the metropolitan state. This is not to deny the oppression, violence, discrimination and sheer selfishness that had characterised so much of British imperialism. Although it contains a grain of truth, the assertion that the British administrators were simply 'sweet, just, boyish masters' is clearly a piece of self-serving delusion. It is extremely rare for any dominant group to put the interests of its subordinates above its own. Although Cecil Rhodes claimed that the British Empire was based upon philanthropy and a 5 per cent return on investment, when it came to a conflict of interests it was the 5 per cent ethic that almost invariably triumphed.

R. Robinson and J. Gallagher close their book *Africa and the Victorians* (1965), with its classical analysis of Britain's role in the partition of Africa, thus: 'The same fabulous artificers who had galvanised America, Australia and Asia, had come to the last continent.'[4]

It is now possible to see more clearly than at any time hitherto exactly what those 'fabulous artificers' achieved throughout the imperial system. The material residue of Empire was a post-colonial inheritance that could be criticised but not gainsaid. On every continent save the wildernesses of the Arctic and Antarctic the British left roads, railways, irrigation schemes, telegraph systems, radio transmitters, great public buildings, a mass of imperial statuary, harbours, airfields, bridges and dams. All of this was accompanied, and indeed made possible, by the rapid proliferation of British and European administrators, traders and settlers, British technology and weaponry, Western banking and commerce, modern industrial techniques and practices, the Christian religion, British concepts of democracy, constitutional and legal practice, and much more besides. In all of these ways, the impact of the British Empire on the societies which it ruled and controlled was simply part of the broader and apparently irresistible expansion of European civilisation and commerce that had begun in earnest in the late fifteenth century.

Many subjects of the Empire, particularly those in the dependent, 'backward' territories, paid a considerable price for their railway systems and their gleaming white law-courts and parliamentary buildings. One of the chief costs was that poor and underdeveloped economies throughout the Empire were often actively encouraged, if not positively forced, to become over-dependent upon a limited number of primary products. The transport revolution of the 1840s and 1850s, which was centred on the worldwide proliferation of the railway and the steamship as quick and relatively cheap carriers of freight, as well as upon the urgent need to feed the rapidly multiplying populations of Europe and North America, speeded up this process.[5]

Although economic growth in imperial or subject territories could take place as a consequence of these developments, it also left many colonial economies dangerously exposed to the havoc which could be caused by a slump in the world market for the particular staple they produced. As a result local employment conditions could fluctuate wildly with the vagaries of the world economy. A further disadvantage was that the organisation of even the most basic one-crop economies was overwhelmingly in the hands of British managers and overseers, and the price paid for, say, cocoa or sugar was negotiated and fixed predominantly in the European market, which was in the last resort only interested in buying the cheapest as well as the best. In the process, the development of colonial manufacturing industry was often discouraged – another benefit, incidentally, to various European economies.

Perhaps the biggest price, however, to be paid by subject peoples, particularly those in the dependent, colonial empire, was that British domination generally removed the opportunity to control the destiny of each territory from local hands. Even when indigenous governments were not simply, and often abruptly, supplanted by British administrators, the local chieftains or elites that retained some hold on power were all too often the puppets and servants of their colonial masters. In general the British, secure in their exercise of imperial power, displayed few qualms on this score. The frequently repeated insistence that Britain was bringing 'civilisation', 'development' or 'progress' to barbarous, backward and hopeless lands became an imperial mantra that few found the will or courage to dispute, either in the United Kingdom or throughout the Empire.

Although British power was maintained, when necessary, by ruthless shows of military force and by the humiliation and subordination of local elites and populations, one reason why imperial rule did not meet with more consistent and violent resistance was that the publicly proclaimed imperial ideology generally appeared benevolent rather than despotic. The Westminster model of parliamentary government, the rule of law, the rights of the individual, the self-congratulatory denial of administrative corruption – all part and parcel of the 'civilising mission' – were individually and collectively seductive pieces of propaganda. The propaganda was, moreover, based upon sufficient truth and upon enough perceived reality to carry conviction.

Although the British did not, in general, propagate the Christian faith with the zeal and ruthlessness of, say, the Spanish conquistadors in Latin America, their insistence on the benevolence, justice and evolutionary potential of British imperial rule was, in effect, an alternative religion. The vast bulk of nationalist movements within the Empire went along with this worldly faith, at least up to, and often beyond,

the achievement of independence. One of the most remarkable characteristics of the present Commonwealth of Nations is not that these high,
and in the last resort almost unattainable, aspirations were so often
abandoned and overthrown by post-colonial governments, but that in
so many territories once ruled by Britain the ideals of parliamentary
democracy and equality before the law are still perceived by so many
to be desirable goals well worth struggling for. If modern India has one
potent, even internationally recognised description, it is as 'the world's
largest democracy'. Imperfect though this description may be, it is not
an ignoble one.

Even if, in many parts of the world previously ruled by Britain, the
ideals of parliamentary and personal freedom lie in ruins, a multitude
of lesser, but not insignificant, remnants of imperial rule are manifest
and often flourishing:

> They still played cricket on the dust patches of Pakistan,
> among the Caribbean frangipani, or behind the yam-stores
> of New Guinea. The Fiji Rugby XV still made its regular
> tour of Wales, and at the Commonwealth Games, so old
> imperialists like to think, a recognisably higher standard of
> sportsmanship prevailed than at the Olympics. The hunts-
> men of Ootacamund, as in Montreal, still wore pink. The
> regimental messes of the Indian Army still cherished their
> regimental silver, tarnished a little with the years perhaps,
> but still commemorating ancient triumphs of the imperial
> arms. In many a store and office the merchants of Empire
> survived, immensely rich in Hong Kong or Singapore, proud
> but seedy in Calcutta, astutely adapting to the times in
> Lagos, Mombasa or the Cayman Islands.[6]

Despite all of this, once imperial rule had been withdrawn, indigenous societies proceeded to reject many of the trappings, characteristics
and assumed manners of British rule and influence. Although the
officers of the Pakistan Air Force continued for many years to use the
'wizard prang' service slang learned from the RAF in the years preceding independence, the government of Pakistan eventually chose to leave
the Commonwealth. Throughout much of tropical Africa, British
missionaries apparently converted millions of Africans to the Christian
faith. During the post-imperial years, however, it soon became apparent
how shallow, in many cases, the conversion had been. It was almost as
if indigenous people had accepted Christianity as an act of courtesy, or

of politeness, towards their superiors, or perhaps as a means of associating with, and eventually possibly exploiting, the imperial power.

The moral and ethical standards so assiduously touted by generations of British administrators, missionaries and churchmen were often to prove frail defences against the more urgent pressures of self-aggrandisement or the priorities of tribal and regional loyalty. Worse still, it was soon to become apparent, as British scholars, journalists and television programme-makers picked over the bones of Empire, that many British administrators had chosen to practise a shameful double standard, not least in the pursuit of their sexual needs.[7]

Throughout the Empire, the relationship between rulers and ruled, and the long-term impact of this relationship, has proved more insubstantial than could have been imagined at the height of British power. Nowhere, perhaps, is this so clearly demonstrated as in the case of India, so frequently and routinely described as 'the jewel in the crown'. The British invested more, both emotionally and financially, in India than in any other part of the Empire. Beginning in 1600 the English, then the British, relationship with the sub-continent lasted for almost 350 years. After the great Indian uprising of 1857–58 had been suppressed, the British were in effective and comfortable control of the whole of the sub-continent, although a third of it was still nominally ruled by a variety of indigenous princes. The British relationship with India was overwhelmingly that of ruler and ruled, superior and inferior, guide and guided. As mentioned earlier, by the time the Raj ended in 1947, over two million British people had died there. In the eyes of generations of British statesmen, administrators and ordinary citizens the control of India was the most significant achievement of British imperialism and, in a way, the key to understanding the mysteries of Britain's Empire. If any imperial possession should have been remoulded in the interest of Britain's economic, military and cultural imperatives, it was India.

Yet compared with many other territories within the Empire, as well as with the possessions of other European imperial powers, India seemed in many ways to have kept the impact of British rule to a minimum. Unlike the indigenous populations of South America, and elsewhere, the Indians were not decimated by European-borne diseases or even by wars of conquest and enslavement – indeed, generations of British administrators and medical personnel strove both to maintain the *Pax Britannica* and to raise local health standards. Despite some modest success, Christianity was not superimposed at the expense of local religions, making little headway against Hinduism, Islam, or Sikhism. Although the British in India became increasingly assertive and arrogant during the nineteenth century, often expressing impatience with and contempt for the indigenous people, local cultures did not lose their integrity and self-respect, and indeed provided a vital underpinning for the increasingly potent nationalist movements of the twentieth century. Although the English language became the language of administration, and was increasingly used for other purposes, it rarely supplanted Hindi, Urdu, Gujerati, Bengali and many others. There was no permanent large-scale European settlement in India. Nor were slaves imported from Africa, as had been the case in the Caribbean and the Americas. There was, of course, no need for them, since there was plenty of near-slave labour in the sub-continent itself.

Despite the resilience of local culture, the British impact upon India was in some ways profound. Local economies were disrupted and subordinated, for example, to serve the interests of the Lancashire cotton industry. Local differences and divisions were exploited by the British, and collaboration sought with local elites and with minority groups of various sorts. Western materialism and industrialism made substantial inroads in some parts of India, lending substance to Gandhi's insistence that this sort of corrupting influence must be rejected in favour of older, simpler values. Whole swathes of the population were manipulated and subordinated by the conquerors, including tens of thousands of India's women, who serviced their rulers, from senior officials to common soldiers, as mistresses and prostitutes. The physical impact upon the Indian landscape and topography of British-built roads, railways, irrigation canals, ports, factories and so forth is undeniable. The British also left behind the cantonment, the hill station, the glory of Herbert Baker and Edwin Lutyens' official and parliamentary buildings in New Delhi, the mainly neo-gothic splendour of Bombay railway station, and much more.

Partly because the use of Hindi is not automatically acceptable in many parts of the country, particularly in the south, where it is associated with the old, northern centres of power, English has remained the main foreign language in schools – at some time early in the twenty-first century, India will become the largest English-speaking country in the world. As it is, many well-educated Indians, at home, in social gatherings and exclusive clubs, or on television and radio, habitually talk to each other in English, often in the confident accents of the English public school and Oxbridge. Advertisements on street hoardings, certainly in major cities, are predominantly in English, and so are many shop-front signs. Both India's first Prime Minister, Jawaharlal Nehru, and Mahatma Gandhi received important parts of their education in England: Nehru at Harrow and Cambridge, and Gandhi on being called to the Bar in London. As a result, and despite their highly significant roles in mobilising nationalist opinion and strength, both men remained deeply, if discreetly, Anglophile.

If Nehru and Gandhi absorbed English education and, in a sense, used it as a weapon against the Raj, India generally took what it wanted from the imperial experience, often adapting institutions and systems to its own needs in the process. Despite the continuing evidence of widespread corruption, Indian governments still accept the verdict of the voters when the biggest electorate in the world goes to the polls. Although it has sometimes been subjected to intense political pressure, the Indian judiciary has on the whole retained a reputation for independence. The Indian armed forces still bear traces of the British training and discipline that characterised the old Indian Army, but for most of the post-colonial period have been the servants of civil government and of a form of domestic democracy free of military influence. Cricket, the sport of the conquerors, is played and followed far more fervently and by many more people in India than anywhere else in the world – certainly with more passion than in England. But although the sub-continent has accepted large quantities of Western aid and investment, trade between Britain and India, which was once the main imperative for the maintenance of the Raj, has now dwindled to less than 1 per cent of India's trade as a whole. This is a far cry from the days at the beginning of the twentieth century when India took nearly a fifth of Britain's exports, including 40 per cent of cotton exports, and was the second-largest purchaser of British goods; moreover, in excess of 20 per cent of British investment was sunk there.[8]

British literary and cultural representations of India and Indians, prior to independence, were for the most part subordinated to keeping the imperial relationship intact and emphasising British superiority. This was not entirely true at the outset, however, when many early, descriptive paintings – often by British women – were made of local places, people and events. In terms of literary output, British novels and poetry throughout the nineteenth century, and for much of the twentieth century, almost always expressed an imperial imperative, as did the school text-books issued at home. During the nineteenth century, a great deal of British writing about India portrayed the subjects of the

Raj as generally untrustworthy and in need of the white man to rule them; who, for instance, do the chattering, unruly, swarming *bandar-log*, the monkey people of Kipling's *Jungle Book*, represent if not the Indian masses crying out for the good and firm government of the Raj? There was, it is true, respect, some of it grudging, for the martial races of the sub-continent and even for the holy men of Indian tradition. Kipling's novel *Kim* (1901) was exceptional in that it took the reader across both sides of the racial divide. Films made in the first half of the twentieth century tended to reinforce the stereotype of a necessary but generally kindly British rule over a subordinate, mostly loyal and dependable people. With the steady rise in Indian nationalism in the early part of the century, books like E.M. Forster's *A Passage to India* (1924) addressed the problems and ambiguities of the Anglo–Indian relationship in an era marked by a struggle between reformers and conservatives. Later British authors such as John Masters and Paul Scott reflected the prevailing political mood, either glorifying the Raj or expressing criticism of Indian failings on a number of counts, but also accepting the inevitable collapse of imperial rule, and finally examining the ruins of the fallen Raj. Since 1947 there have been a number of attempts to paint a more balanced picture in books and articles, films and television programmes.

When considering British writing or film-making dealing with the Empire, and indeed with literary traffic coming the other way, it is important to remember that personal and public need inevitably overlap. An author's private agenda may be derived from, as well as contributing to, political aims and convictions. Novels are not, by definition, literal or even accurate statements. Truth, or at least a highly personalised version of the truth, is approached through any number of filters that can distort, falsify, imitate and interpret at the whim of the creative artist. After all, a caricature can reveal more of the essential truth of a personality or a situation than a photograph or a 'realistic' portrayal.

The 1935 film *Sanders of the River*, for instance, contains a grotesquely exaggerated portrait of the interaction between a British administrator and an African tribal chieftain; it is riddled with condescending stereotypes and beset by banal and formalised verbal exchanges – and yet it reveals a particular truth about the inter-war relationship between imperial rulers and local potentates. *A Passage to India* is heavy with innuendo, full of distorted portrayals, and finally dodges the ultimate and unbearably painful confrontation between an Indian male and a British female as sexual beings, as well as postponing the fulfilment of the potentially passionate friendship between Aziz and Fielding; but the nature of the choices and dilemmas which it presents ring sufficiently true to enlighten and educate – as well as entertain – the reader.

In any event, literary, artistic and indeed historical representations are multi-faceted, complex constructs that almost defy rational and precise analysis. Just as there is no coherent monolith called the Orient – or the West – writers, artists and film-makers are not predictable and uniform in their creative work. Of no British writer is this more true than Kipling, despite his reputation for imperial and patriotic zeal and conformity.

Kipling, it has been said, began writing for the fellow Anglo-Indians he met in his club at Lahore. He wanted above all to give an accurate picture of the Indian empire, to get things right, to win approval. In his later career he wrote not for the club but for an increasingly wide readership spanning the globe. In the process, his tales of the British overseas helped to narrate, and thus to fix, not only his own identity but also a British and an imperial one. He and other authors contributed to the construction of a colonial and imperial identity through imposing familiar, home-grown structures on an Empire-wide landscape.

Although it may be claimed that such literary aggrandisement amounted to a form of imperialism in its own right, Kipling spoke with other tongues and in other causes. Born in Bombay, he spoke the vernacular as a boy, and one of his greatest creations, Kim, though white, appears not to be. Kipling wrote a good deal of his poetry in order to raise imperial morale – it has been reckoned that 'The Absent-Minded Beggar' not only concentrated the nation's attention on the realities of the Boer War, but also raised over £250,000 in supportive funding, particularly for the troops' families. Yet Kipling could also be the literary *enfant terrible* of the British Empire, and in poems like 'Recessional' and 'The Lesson', as well as in his ridiculing of the 'flan-neled fools' and 'muddied oafs', he sought to inject a high moral serious-ness as well as a sense of urgency and a recognition of priorities into imperial attitudes.

Kipling did not go quite as far as the Victorian poet Robert Buch-anan, whose forthright, satirical poetry denounced the 'stolen gold', the 'butchery' and the 'imperial anti-Christ' of the British Empire, but he was no blinkered, sycophantic patriot. Above all, the range and diversity of his work demonstrates how rash it is to assume a fixed set of attitudes in a writer. Conversely, socialists and republicans like Wilde and Swin-burne also wrote their share of imperial verse, although in the case of

Wilde at least there was the anticipation of the 'young republic, like a sun, rising from the crimson sea of war'.

In the post-colonial period it has been easier, and perhaps more necessary, than before to acknowledge the Indian input into British culture and society. A number of Indian words had established themselves in the English language well before independence, words like 'jodhpur', 'char', 'wallah', 'nabob', 'bungalow', 'dungarees', 'pukkah', 'pyjamas', and many more. The Prince Regent's pavilion at Brighton, designed by John Nash, owed much of its architectural beauty to the inspiration of Mughal buildings in the sub-continent. Carpets and kilims from India adorned an increasing number of British homes. Writers like Nirad C. Chaudhuri in *A Passage to England* (1959), or Farhana Sheikh in her lively and accurate novels such as *The Red Box* describing the dilemmas and achievements of Muslim girls growing up in the United Kingdom, and many more, made a vivid contribution to late-twentieth-century British culture and self-awareness. Films like Hanif Kureishi's *My Beautiful Launderette* and the lively, irreverent *Bhaji on the Beach* interpreted the often culturally confused, conflict-riddled South Asian experience of living in Britain, colourfully, controversially and authoritatively. Based in India, the Bengali director Satyajit Ray scrutinised the interaction between the Raj and the Indian people in such masterpieces as *The Chess Players* and *Charulata*.

After independence the sub-continent provided a growing number of Britons with an alluring, alternative lifestyle. Substantial quantities of British people journeyed to India seeking enlightenment and 'the meaning of life', attaching themselves to gurus, embracing Buddhism, and rejecting Western materialism with an enthusiasm which would have gladdened the heart of Gandhi. It was easy to mock this yearning, this displacement of passion, as being, at worst, an easy form of opting out, as exemplified by the corrupt opportunism of Chid in Ruth Prawer Jhabvala's 1975 novel *Heat and Dust*, or at best an inexplicable obsession of young, middle-class white women to wear saris and sandals and to live among the sub-continent's people as 'one of them'. But in these, and in several other ways, India did provide, at least superficially, a haven for those anxious to reject the coarse materialism and post-industrial decline and squalor of late-twentieth-century Britain.

The most visible and significant contribution of the sub-continent to the ex-imperial power, however, lay in the substantial migration of South Asian people to the United Kingdom from the 1950s onwards. By the 1990s, northern cities like Bradford, Blackburn and Leeds, all owing their earlier prosperity to the textile trade, had huge South Asian populations; so too did Birmingham, Leicester, Wolverhampton and London. One of the most immediately discernible effects of this migration was the proliferation of the 'Indian' restaurant – although many of them were in fact Bangladeshi. Indian restaurants and take-aways were soon offering a cheap and delicious alternative to native fare, and even attracting the patronage of skinheads and neo-fascists happy to order curry and chips. This was truly a revolution in domestic eating habits, for although the British rulers of India had often experimented with, and enjoyed, sub-continental food, they had also insisted on eating roast beef and swigging claret in the sweltering temperature of the plains.[9]

Apart from providing Indian restaurateurs and waiters, the South Asian population in the United Kingdom established its presence in a number of occupations. Indian immigrants, whether from the sub-continent or from the harassed and displaced Asian communities of ex-British East Africa, worked as factory hands, bus and train drivers, in the National Health Service, and increasingly, as they availed themselves of the educational opportunities offered in Britain, as teachers, academics, civil servants, lawyers, accountants and doctors. There was also the easily mocked but undeniably useful 'Indian corner shop', kept open for long hours and at weekends and stocking an extraordinary variety of foodstuffs and household commodities.

As the prosperity of the South Asian immigrant group in Britain steadily increased, even to the extent of the production of a number of multi-millionaire businessmen, so the old political allegiances began to break up. Overwhelmingly and traditionally, Indian citizens of the United Kingdom had voted Labour, and by the 1990s there were a handful of Indian MPs, all on the Labour side in the House of Commons. Margaret Thatcher's exaltation of entrepreneurial initiative during the 1980s, however, saw some of the more prosperous South Asian members of society attracted to Conservatism. As the close of the twentieth century approaches, the South Asian community in Britain presents a diverse and sometimes fragmented picture. The impoverished Bangladeshis of London's East End – notoriously the target of racist attacks – are a world apart from the rich, Thatcherite businessmen of Edgware and Wembley. Nonetheless, just as the Anglican Church was once described as 'the Tory Party at prayer', it is nowadays possible to describe the mosques of West Yorkshire and the East End of London as 'the Labour Party at prayer'. The controversies and disputes that sometimes convulse the South Asian community in the United Kingdom, ranging from the bitter international controversy over Salman Rushdie's 1988 novel *The Satanic Verses* to disputes about the siting and funding of temples and mosques, have an impact that sometimes sends local MPs and councillors running scared for their political lives.

The South Asian community in Britain is also the target of a good deal of predictable, though still ugly, racist abuse. The term 'Paki' is widely used to insult immigrants from the sub-continent indiscriminately and routinely. Mr Patel of the local corner shop is both needed for his willingness to stay open late and derided for his demeanour, his appearance, and the smells of the food that he keeps. Indians are accused of plundering the Welfare State, jumping the queues for council housing, bringing over innumerable relatives as illegal immigrants, and, quite simply, of being outsiders, interlopers, wogs. They are frequently charged with 'keeping themselves to themselves', with not being prepared to 'mix', of refusing to integrate – charges often made by those who routinely despise and abuse South Asians and who would not be seen dead taking tea in one of their kitchens.

It is tempting to view the Anglo–Indian relationship at the end of the twentieth century as symbolic of so many other post-colonial interactions between the British and their former subject peoples. Some writers, as we have seen, have attempted to describe the relationship between Britain and the sub-continent as a love affair. Where are the two ex-lovers and partners now, after an early and rather diffident courtship, increasing confidence and assertiveness, some rough stuff, some pre- and post-marital rape, a stormy, deeply ambivalent marriage, all ending in disillusionment, divorce proceedings, separation and the final *decree nisi*? The two parties are certainly not enemies anymore, although occasionally grievances are given an airing. Nor are they bosom friends and soul-mates. They have, perhaps, settled down to a dignified and measured relationship, in which both are ruefully aware of the past and current misdemeanours of the other, but, either through inertia or tolerance, are prepared to let bygones be bygones. Whether the rioting of South Asian youths in Bradford in June 1995 is an indication that part of the community is about to vent its grievances more violently is unclear.

With some inevitable exceptions – notably the racist abuse and aggression emanating from some white groups – the two communities are generally polite to each other, and can even show a degree of affection. As with Britain and the United States there is, self-evidently, a 'special relationship', hard though it is to define this with any precision. Perhaps, however, it involves taking certain things for granted, taking certain things on trust. Even during the years of Nehru's non-aligned foreign policy at the time of the Cold War, there was no real doubt as to whose side India, in the last resort, was on, even though the Indian government vehemently opposed Britain's involvement in the Suez adventure of 1956–57, and went on to berate successive United Kingdom governments for being soft on apartheid and generally over-sympathetic towards South Africa.

Many of the main characteristics of Britain's relationship with India may be applied to the impact of the imperial experience as a whole upon Britain itself. British culture in a variety of ways remained self-confident enough, or perhaps insular enough, to resist assuming many of the practices or habits of the people whom they had ruled. It has been aptly remarked that:

> Englishmen did not walk the streets of London in turbans or even pith helmets like Africans were supposed to sport top hats in Accra. In the creative arts there were a few odd instances of composers toying with Indian harmonies and novelists writing against South Sea backgrounds, but they were not many, and not evidence of any very profound acculturation. The cultures and civilisations which the Empire brought Britain into such intimate contact with were recorded and studied seriously and with affection: but always as things apart from British life, academically. The relics which did find their ways to Britain were to stay as curios, or kept firmly away from life in museums. There were exceptions, but the exceptions were usually regarded as aberrant and regrettable.[10]

After all, British rule throughout the Empire had been at least partly based upon a steadfast resistance to indigenous customs and lifestyles. There was generally disapproval for those Britons, mostly men, who 'went native'. This was why the taboos and rituals – both formal and informal – of the rulers were so strictly adhered to, from dressing for dinner to treating servants 'properly'. Despite the fact that, from start to finish, millions of British males overseas were serviced, in a bewildering variety of ways, by huge numbers of local women and men, from cooking to cleaning, from child-care to the provision of sexual satisfaction, there was a strong tendency to minimise these contributions, to mock them and complain about them, and sometimes flatly to deny them.

The passing of Empire took profitable employment away from a considerable number of British citizens, and also left a vacuum at the heart of Britain's national and international identity. It took an American statesman to point out that Britain had lost an empire and not yet found a world role to fill the gap.[11] Perhaps the upper and middle classes of British society, although they had traditionally governed and controlled the Empire, were less traumatised by its loss than is commonly supposed. Instead of spending their energies ruling often ungrateful and sometimes hostile subject peoples, they now turned their attention to the professional and commercial opportunities in the United Kingdom. In any case, it was generally more profitable and comfortable to be a stockbroker or merchant banker at home than a district commissioner or lieutenant governor overseas. It was arguably the British working class that had its conditions of living and its everyday habits most affected by the loss of Empire, in the sense that the post-imperial era coincided with the migrations of hundreds of thousands of ex-imperial subjects to settle and live in urban areas throughout Britain.

This mass settlement of citizens from the Empire and Commonwealth has provoked some interesting and often highly subjective responses from members of the host population. One has been that immigrants from the 'white' dominions have caused scarcely a stir, and certainly no race riots. Saloon-bar comedians may, for example, mock the Australasian colonisation of London's Earls Court as creating a 'kangaroo valley', but very few propose that Australians and New Zealanders, or Canadians and South Africans, should be compulsorily repatriated.

Immigrants from the 'new' Commonwealth have been less fortunate. West Indians, South Asians and Africans have all come in for their share of racial abuse, discrimination and harassment. African Caribbeans, especially, have borne the brunt of white racism, and have been negatively stereotyped in various ways, despite their contribution to the work of the National Health Service and to the nation's transport systems, as well as their high profile in sport and the entertainment industry.

Two controversies which arose in Britain during the summer of 1995 neatly illustrate the public's capacity for selectivity and, by implication, for prejudice within a multi-ethnic society.

The first controversy centred upon views expressed by Sir Paul

Condon, the Metropolitan Police Commissioner, when he wrote to a number of community leaders and MPs inviting them to attend a meeting on the problem of street robbery and said: 'It is a fact that very many of the perpetrators of mugging are very young black people who have been excluded from school and/or are unemployed.'[12] Among the hostile reactions to these comments were complaints that as a result 'all black people could feel targeted as potential criminals', and that although it was known that 'white people are disproportionately involved in burglary, there has been no linkage between that crime and ethnicity'.[13] The dispute not only allowed competing groups and factions to air their opinions more openly than usual, but also demonstrated how the discussion of alleged racial characteristics could rapidly become passionate, ugly and partisan.

This fierce debate coincided with another controversy over an article in the July edition of the magazine *Wisden Cricket Monthly*, in which the author attacked the 'liberal elite' for refusing to admit that 'foreigners' who are selected to play cricket for England can hardly have the same commitment as home-grown players: 'An Asian or negro raised in England will, according to the liberal, feel exactly the same pride and identification with the place as a white man.'[14]

The article went to the heart of the issue of national identity, seeking by assertion and innuendo to exclude British citizens of African Caribbean or South Asian ethnicity from the 'real' community. Apart from its racist overtones, its insistence on 'difference', the article perhaps above all demonstrated how many bitter and unresolved feelings still abound in an age of continuing confusion, or at any rate uncertainty, over the late-twentieth-century nature of 'Britishness'. Adrift in a post-imperial age, amid the wreckage of de-industrialisation, economic decline and various manifestations of social disruption, and as yet insufficiently committed – in fact even hostile – to the ideal of European unity, some British traditionalists, like, presumably, the author of the *Wisden* article, were apparently seeking to construct a concept of nationality on an exclusionist rather than an inclusionist basis. It was worthy of note that white 'foreign' cricketers such as the South African Robin Smith and the Zimbabwean Graeme Hick were not singled out for adverse comment.

One of the most damaging effects of imperial rule and of the imperial inheritance was that Britain, at least until the mid-1960s, was able to distance itself from the development of the European Economic Community, on the pretext that its traditional 'special relationship' with its first great ex-colony, the United States of America, and its continuing close financial and commercial relationships with so much of the expanding independent Empire, was of more significance and promise than an uncertain involvement in the movement for European unity. British investment outside Europe still remained huge during the post-colonial period. Britain remained one of the major 'neo-colonial' powers, but increasingly it was difficult to override the needs and resistance of former subject peoples. This was especially true when, as in the case of the oil-producing nations of the Middle East, they could threaten either to raise the price of the necessary commodity or to deny the oil supplies so vital to the well-being of the British economy.

In one way, of course, it was a relief to be rid of the huge burden of overseas expense which had characterised the Empire at its apogee and indeed during the post-Second World War period. This had provided serious financial problems for many British governments during the twentieth century. That the Empire lasted so long and was not seriously challenged by any rival imperial power for most of its existence was a piece of luck. Even when in 1941 Japanese armed forces conquered so much of Britain's Eastern Empire, the impact was simultaneously reduced by the emergence of the United States as both the United Kingdom's primary ally in the wider world and the power whose industrial and military capacity eventually brought about the defeat and overthrow of Japan's empire. The bluff which sustained imperial rule on such a scale and for such a long period of time seems also to have had the effect of discouraging rival imperial powers from serious assaults upon British-held territory. In all of these ways, the possession of the British Empire inflated Britain's status as a world power, camouflaged her decline as an industrial and a military nation, and enabled the British statesman to act more decisively and with more weight upon the world's stage than would otherwise have been the case.

There was much that was evil, self-absorbed, triumphalist and over-assertive about British rule. The havoc that these characteristics wrought upon the British people's capacity for smug self-satisfaction, including an abiding distrust of all manner of foreigners and foreign ways of doing things – a distrust that helps explain the popular expressions of contempt during the 1980s and 1990s for the organisation and ordering of the European Economic Community – can only be hesitatingly and uncertainly assessed. If neo-colonialism, and the attitudes that underpin it, had not been a fact of post-imperial life, one suspects that the British people would have invented it unaided. As has been recently and cogently suggested, however, British dislike and distrust of the foreigner is by no means a recent phenomenon:

> ... English or British xenophobia is of course much older than Empire. The 'Jews, Turks, Infidels, and Hereticks' of the Good Friday collect or Francis Bacon's diatribe against the Turks as 'a very reproach to human society' are reminders of sixteenth-century constructions of 'others'. There can, however, be little doubt that the experience of Empire strengthened xenophobia in giving the British a strong sense that their imperial role distinguished them from other Europeans and reinforced their sense of superiority over the non-Europeans who were so often their subject peoples ... Current attitudes to empire still seem ... to reflect our feelings about ourselves ... we tend to use the imperial past as a projection of our present discontents ... Whatever one's view may be about the institutions of the present British state, it is unlikely that Empire had much to do with shaping them.[15]

It is indeed beyond doubt that the experience of Empire played an important part in consolidating and confirming xenophobic, insular and racist tendencies among substantial sections of the British population. After all, imperial rule in all of its manifestations could never have been based upon any universally applied concept of equality. The system demanded, and largely got, the subordination of subject peoples to what amounted to the master race.

The strange thing is that in just the same way as the singing, dancing, chanting, joyful blacks celebrating Nelson Mandela's inauguration in May 1994 were eager to voice their belief in the regenerative powers of reconciliation and their hopes for the future, so few of Britain's other ex-colonial peoples seemed to bear the metropolitan power a lasting grudge. This may have been due to political expediency, or to the enlightened leadership of the new post-colonial states, or to the pragmatic realisation that newly-independent nations were unlikely to be able to operate successfully without close economic, commercial and developmental links with their former rulers. It may have flowed from sheer exhaustion, from the realisation that the struggle for freedom was over, and that new and testing times had to be confronted as briskly and effectively as possible.

Perhaps the simple fact of a shared history had something to do with it. In March 1995 Queen Elizabeth II paid a six-day visit to South Africa, the country she had last visited forty-eight years before as an inexperienced and idealistic young woman ready to declare in an Empire-wide radio broadcast to mark her twenty-first birthday that 'my whole life, whether it be short or long, shall be devoted to your service and the service of the great Imperial Commonwealth to which we all belong'. Now, having bestowed the Order of Merit upon President Mandela in a relaxed, televised ceremony, she acknowledged in homely terms the strength derived from a common, although not always tranquil, past:

> Our relationship, like that between many old friends, has been, at times, a tempestuous one. Our peoples have fought against each other, as they have together against a common enemy. But we can, together, feel unreserved pride in the role which so many Britons and South Africans have played in our respective countries.[16]

Five months later, in August 1995, an apparently even more positive affirmation of post-imperial goodwill occurred. The people of the island of Bermuda voted in a referendum to remain under British rule rather than to become independent. Was the Empire about to make a modest comeback? On closer examination, the decision seemed to owe a great deal to expediency and the instinct for self-protection. Bermuda was a small dependency of fifty-eight square kilometres, with a population of some 58,000. A majority of voters opted for the financial and fiscal benefits of continuing British rule, which they saw as guaranteeing them a higher standard of living than many independent Caribbean territories to the south. Continuing dependency would save them the expensive trappings of statehood – for example, overseas diplomatic missions and United Nations representation – not to speak of preserving a nil rate of income tax.

Perhaps the problems that have beset some small independent Commonwealth states helped to influence the Bermudan referendum. Tuvalu in the Pacific, with only 9,000 inhabitants, has become almost totally dependent upon economic aid from Australia and the United Kingdom – a very strange sort of independence indeed. Anguilla, with an even smaller population of 7,500, was originally part of the independent Caribbean associated state of St Kitts-Nevis-Anguilla. In 1980, however, Anguilla pulled out of the federation and placed itself once more under British rule. Several other small island states, like the

Maldives and Vanuatu, have found it extremely difficult and expensive to protect their fishing rights within the internationally guaranteed 200-mile zone around them without the diplomatic and naval backing of Britain.[17]

The vast majority of the fifty-one independent states within the Commonwealth do not, of course, either need or want British protection. It is perhaps inevitable, however, as in any large and extended family structure, that a few of the more puny and vulnerable offspring will fail to make their way in the world and will return to the parental home for succour or some supplementary income. This in no measure invalidates the compulsion of the overwhelming majority of ex-imperial dependencies to tread their own path, but it does, perhaps, very modestly confirm the value of the shared historical experience referred to by Queen Elizabeth in South Africa a few months earlier.

There is, however, a further explanation. It is that, within their limitations, and despite the crippling constraints, inequalities and – sometimes – brutalities of the economic, political and administrative structures that they raised, the British as an imperial people generally did their best.

They frequently did their best, or what they perceived as their best, for the peoples they ruled; of course, they far more consistently did their best for themselves, for their colonial allies and for those who collaborated with them. They did their best, more often than not, to play by the rules – their own rules, naturally enough, but rules all the same. They claimed, mostly sincerely, that they sent out 'their best' to rule over the largest, most variegated, widely dispersed and complex empire in history. If, like Dr Pangloss in Voltaire's *Candide*, they assumed rather too often that 'In the best of all possible worlds, all is for the best,'[18] they were also aware of the ironies, the ambiguities, and the bizarre and humorous qualities of their global supremacy. They generally thought it best to avoid impersonal theorising and administrative centralising, and instead to put their trust in empiricism and in the good sense of 'the man on the spot'.

The judgement that the British did their best is not, perhaps, the most inspiring or memorable epitaph for the greatest of the fallen European empires, but it may be the most accurate and truthful, and hence the most acceptable.

1765 British Parliament passes Stamp
Act taxing American colonies;
nine colonies draw up
declaration of rights and
liberties at Stamp Act Congress
in New York.
Robert Clive receives the licence
to tax Bengal, Bihar and Orissa
for East India Company.
The potato becomes the most
commonly eaten European
foodstuff.

1766 Stamp Act repealed; Declaratory
Act affirms Britain's right to tax
American colonies.
Famine in Bengal.
Northern Circars and Madras
ceded to East India Company.
Louis de Bougainville begins
voyage to the Pacific which will
result in the discoveries of
Tahiti, the Solomon Islands and
New Guinea.

1767 Robert Clive leaves India.
First Mysore War (1767–69)
begins.
New York Assembly suspended
for refusing to accede to the
quartering of troops.
Joseph Priestley publishes *The
History and Present State of
Electricity*.

1768 Secretary of State for Colonies
appointed in Britain, but
Colonial Department abolished
as an economy measure in 1782.
Massachusetts Assembly
dissolved for refusing to
cooperate in collection of taxes.
Gurkhas conquer Nepal.
Captain James Cook (1728–79)
sets out on his first voyage of
circumnavigation (1768–71).
Royal Academy founded in
London.

1769 Privy Council in London affirms
retention of tea duty in American
colonies.
Virginia Assembly dissolved.

1770 'Boston Massacre'.
British Parliament repeals duties
on certain commodities in
American colonies, but retains
the duty on tea.
James Bruce (1730–94)
discovers source of Blue Nile.
Captain Cook discovers
Australia.
Industrial Revolution gathers
force in Britain.

1771 Richard Arkwright (1732–92)
sets up first cotton spinning mill
in England.
First edition of *Encyclopaedia
Britannica*.

1772 Massachusetts Assembly
threatens secession.

Warren Hastings appointed
Governor of Bengal.
Robert Clive defends his
administrative activities in India.
James Bruce reaches confluence
of Blue and White Niles.
Captain Cook leaves England on
second voyage of
circumnavigation (1772–75).
The Somerset case decides that
a slave becomes free on landing
in Britain.

1773 East India Company Regulating
Act.
'Boston Tea Party'.
First cast-iron bridge built at
Coalbrookdale, Shropshire.
The waltz becomes fashionable
in Vienna.

1774 Coercive Acts passed against
Massachusetts, including the
closure of the port of Boston;
American Continental Congress
meets in Philadelphia and
decides to impose
non-importation of British
goods.
Quebec Act recognises
established status of Roman
Catholicism in the province and
delineates Canada's frontiers.
Rules of cricket promulgated.

1775 American Revolution begins;
British defeat at Lexington;
Second Continental Congress
assembles at Philadelphia;
American attack on Quebec
fails.
First clearing-house established
for British banks in London.

1776 American Continental Congress
carries the Declaration of
Independence.

Captain Cook's third voyage to
the Pacific begins.
Edward Gibbon publishes
*Decline and Fall of the Roman
Empire.*
Adam Smith publishes *An
Enquiry into the Nature and Causes of
the Wealth of Nations.*

1777 Lafayette's French volunteers
arrive in America to aid the
rebels.
General Burgoyne capitulates at
Saratoga.
Torpedo invented by American
engineer.
Lavoisier proves that air is
composed mainly of nitrogen and
oxygen.

1778 American colonies sign treaties
with France and Holland and
reject British offer of peace.
Warren Hastings captures
Chandernagore in Bengal.
Captain Cook discovers Hawaii.
Act of Congress prohibits the
importation of slaves into the
United States.

1779 Spain declares war on Britain
and lays siege to Gibraltar
(1779–83).
British campaign against the
Maratha (1779–82) begins in
India.
Captain Cook murdered in
Hawaii.
The first Derby horse-race held
at Epsom in Surrey.

1780 Henry Grattan (1746–1820)
demands Home Rule for Ireland.
Military stalemate in the
American Revolutionary War.
Second Mysore War (1780–84)
begins in India.

1781 British military defeats in America end with the capitulation at Yorktown and the evacuation of Charleston and Savannah.
British military successes in India include the capture of the Dutch factory at Negapatam and the defeat of the ruler of Benares.
First building society established in Birmingham.

1782 Peace talks open between Britain and the American revolutionaries.
Spain captures Minorca from the British.
Maratha War ends with Treaty of Salbai.
Tipu 'Sahib' becomes Sultan of Mysore.
Admiral Howe relieves Gibraltar.
Spain completes the conquest of Florida.
James Watt invents double-acting rotary steam engine.

1783 Peace of Versailles ends the War of the American Revolution; Britain recognises the independence of the United States of America.
William Pitt the Younger becomes Prime Minister (until 1801).
Bank of Ireland established.

1784 Pitt's India Act substantially increases the government's control over the East India Company.
British sign peace treaty with Tipu 'Sahib'.
Threshing machine invented by Scottish millwright Andrew Meikle.
William Jones founds the Bengal Asiatic Society, devoted to the study of Sanskrit.
First Anglican Bishop for the Colonies appointed.

1785 Warren Hastings resigns as Governor-General of India and returns to Britain.
James Watt and Matthew Boulton install a steam engine in a cotton-spinning factory in Nottinghamshire.

1786 Lord Cornwallis made Governor-General of India.
Penang ceded to Britain.
First Mennonite settlement in Canada.
Mozart's *Le Nozze di Figaro* first performed.

1787 The dollar becomes the currency of the USA.
Britain establishes a settlement for freed slaves in Sierra Leone.
Marylebone Cricket Club founded.

1788 Unsuccessful parliamentary motion in Britain for the abolition of the slave trade.
The First Fleet, carrying convicted felons, lands in New South Wales.
Trial (1788–95) of Warren Hastings on charges of corruption and maladministration in India begins.
The Times first published in London.
MCC codifies the laws of cricket.

1789 King George III recovers from breakdown; Regency crisis ends.

The mutineers of HMS *Bounty* settle on the Pitcairn Islands in the eastern Pacific.

First fully steam-driven cotton factory established in Manchester.

Chrysanthemums introduced to Britain.

1790 Outbreak of Third Mysore War (1790–92).
First steam-powered rolling mill built in England.
James Bruce publishes *Travels to Discover the Sources of the Nile, 1768–1773*.

1791 Canada Constitutional Act divides the country into two provinces, Upper and Lower Canada.
Wilberforce's motion for the abolition of the slave trade carried in the British Parliament.

1792 Gas first used for illumination in England.
Baptist Missionary Society founded in London.
Thomas Paine publishes the second part of *Rights of Man*.
Mary Wollstonecraft publishes *Vindication of the Rights of Women*.

1793 Kermadec Islands north-east of New Zealand discovered.
Sir Alexander Mackenzie (1764–1820) becomes the first person to cross Canada from coast to coast.
Eli Whitney (1765–1825) invents the cotton gin.

1794 Thomas Paine publishes *The Age of Reason*.

1795 Dutch surrender Ceylon to the British.
British forces occupy Cape of Good Hope.
Warren Hastings acquitted of corruption, but financially ruined in the process.
Mungo Park (1771–1806) explores the Niger river.
The building of the Bank of England begins (finished 1827).
First horse-drawn railway opens in England.

1796 British capture Elba.
Spain declares war on Britain.
Edward Jenner (1749–1823) introduces vaccination against smallpox.
Chinese authorities forbid the import of opium.

1797 Lord Wellesley (1760–1842) appointed Governor-General of India.
Britain begins to export iron.
First copper pennies minted in Britain, and first pound notes issued.
Merino sheep introduced to Australia.

1798 Malta and Alexandria occupied by the French.
Nelson destroys the French fleet at the battle of Abukir Bay.
Rebellion in Ireland, encouraged by ineffectual French landing.
Treaty of Hyderabad signed between Britain and the Nizam.
Beginnings of substantial Irish immigration to Canada.
Thomas Malthus publishes *Essay on the Principle of Population*.

1799 Kingdom of Mysore divided between Britain and Hyderabad.

Church Missionary Society founded in London.
Mungo Park publishes *Travels in the Interior of Africa*.

1800 Act of Union between Britain and Ireland passed in Parliament.
British capture Malta.
City of Ottawa founded.
Richard Trevithick constructs light-pressure steam engine.

1801 Act of Union with Ireland comes into force.
British troops enter Cairo; French evacuate Egypt.
Union Jack becomes the official flag of the United Kingdom of Great Britain and Ireland.
Department of War and Colonies made responsible for colonial policy.

1802 Peace of Amiens between Britain and France.
West India Docks built in London.
John Dalton (1766–1844) introduces atomic theory into chemistry.

1803 Renewal of war between Britain and France.
Robert Emmet, leader of Irish revolt, executed.
In India, Gwalior submits to the British.
Robert Fulton propels a boat by steam power.
Henry Shrapnel (1761–1842) invents the shell.
Building of Caledonian Canal begins.

1804 War in India between the British and Holkar of Indore; Indore

defeated.
Spain declares war on Britain.
Hobart founded in Tasmania.
British and Foreign Bible Society set up in London.
Dahlias introduced to Britain.

1805 Nelson's victory over the French and Spanish fleets at Trafalgar.
Modern Egypt established with the proclamation of Mehemet Ali as Pasha.
Rockets introduced as weapons into the British Army.
Mungo Park begins his second expedition along the course of the Niger River.
British government's annual expenditure reaches £62.8 million.

1806 British reoccupy Cape of Good Hope.
British cotton industry employs a quarter of a million workers.

1807 British Parliament prohibits the slave trade.
Sierra Leone and Gambia become British colonies.

1808 Source of the Ganges discovered.
United States prohibits the importation of slaves from Africa.

1809 British sign treaty of friendship with the Sikhs at Amritsar.
British capture Martinique and Cayenne from the French.

1810 British capture Guadaloupe from the French.
Emergence of Simon Bolivar as 'the liberator' in South America.

1811 British occupy Java.
Luddite riots destroy machines
in northern England.

1812 United States declares war on
Britain.
Red River settlement in
Manitoba, Canada.
The *Comet,* a twenty-five-ton
steamship designed by Henry
Bell, begins operating on the
River Clyde in Scotland.

1813 British forces capture Fort
Niagara and burn Buffalo.
The monopoly of Indian trade
by the East India Company
ended.
Robert Owen publishes *A New
View of Society.*

1814 British forces burn Washington,
D.C.; British–American war
ended by Treaty of Ghent.
Cape Province confirmed as a
British colony.
George Stephenson constructs
the first practical steam
locomotive near Newcastle.
Part of Westminster becomes the
first district in Britain to be
illuminated by gas.

1815 Defeat of Napoleon at Waterloo.
First Corn Law passed in
Britain.
Scottish surveyor John
Macadam constructs roads out of
crushed stone.

1816 Britain restores Java to the
Netherlands.
Elgin Marbles brought to the
British Museum in London.

1817 Venezuelan independence
confirmed.

Riots in Derbyshire against low
wages.

1818 End of Maratha Wars.
The Rajput States and Poona
come under British control.
Independence of Chile
proclaimed.
Border between Canada and the
United States agreed upon the
forty-ninth parallel.

1819 East India Company establishes
a settlement at Singapore.
Legislation for maximum
twelve-hour working day for
juveniles in Britain.

1820 George IV succeeds George III.
'1820 Settlers' emigrate to Cape
Colony.
Malthus publishes *Principles of
Political Economy.*

1821 Venezuelan independence
confirmed by Bolivar's defeat of
Spanish forces at the battle of
Carabobo; Peru, Guatemala,
Mexico, Panama and Santo
Domingo achieve independence
from Spain.
Manchester Guardian founded.
Population of Britain and
Ireland 20.8 million; France
30.4 million; United States 9.6
million.
Faraday discovers fundamentals
of electromagnetic rotation.

1822 Riots in Dublin.
Brazil achieves independence
from Portugal.
Stephenson builds world's first
iron railway bridge for the
Stockton to Darlington railway
line.
Sunday Times founded in London.

1823 The Monroe Doctrine effectively prevents new colonial settlements in the western hemisphere by European imperial powers.
Rugby football first played at Rugby School in England.

1824 First Burmese war (1824–26); British capture Rangoon.
Repeal of Combinations Law eases restrictions on British workers to unionise.

1825 First horse-drawn buses in London.
Opening of Stockton to Darlington railway line.

1826 Stamford Raffles founds Royal Zoological Society in London.
First railway tunnel on the Liverpool to Manchester line opened.

1827 Joint Turkish and Egyptian fleets destroyed at the Battle of Navarino.
London's water supply purified by newly invented sand filter.

1828 Test and Corporation Acts repealed, allowing Catholics and Nonconformists to hold public office in Britain.
Britain forces an end to the Egyptian occupation of Crete and part of Greece.

1829 Irish statesman Daniel O'Connell (1775–1847) begins agitation for the repeal of the Act of Union.
Sati (the burning of Hindu widows) abolished in Bengal; the reform is later extended to other parts of British India.
Catholic Emancipation Act passed in Britain.
An effective police force established for the first time in London.
Stephenson's steam engine 'The Rocket' wins a prize of £500 in Rain Hill trials.
Omnibuses become part of London's public transport system.

1830 William IV succeeds George IV.
Mysore added to British possessions in India.
Founding of Royal Geographic Society in London.
Scottish botanist Robert Brown discovers the cell nucleus in plants.
Over twenty steam cars on the streets of London.

1831 Cholera pandemic, beginning in India in 1826, spreads into Central Europe, reaching Scotland in 1832.
Population of the United Kingdom (excluding Ireland) 13.9 million; United States 12.8 million.
Charles Darwin (1809–82) sails as naturalist on a surveying expedition to South America, New Zealand and Australia on HMS *Beagle*.
Sir James Clark Ross determines position of the magnetic North Pole.

1832 Great Reform Act passed by British Parliament.
Britain occupies the Falkland Islands.

1833 Abolition of slavery throughout the British Empire.
Mehemet Ali founds the dynasty

439

that will rule Egypt until 1952.
British Factory Act provides for
a system of factory inspection.
Alexander Burnes (1805–41)
crosses Hindu Kush mountain
range in Central Asia.

1834 South Australia Act allows for
the establishment of a new
colony.
Sixth Kaffir War (1834–35)
begins between Bantu (chiefly
Xhosa) tribespeople and
European settlers on the eastern
frontier of Cape Colony.
Afrikaner trekkers begin to settle
north of the Orange River.
O'Connell's motion to repeal the
Union with Great Britain
defeated in the House of
Commons.

1835 City of Melbourne founded.
First negative photograph taken
in Britain by William Henry
Fox Talbot (1800–77).

1836 Substantial Afrikaner migration
north from the Cape, 'the Great
Trek', gets under way.

1837 Queen Victoria succeeds
William IV.
Revolts in Lower and Upper
Canada.
First Canadian railway
constructed.

1838 Afrikaners defeat the Zulus at
the Battle of Blood River in
Natal.
First British–Afghan war
(1838–42) begins.
Richard Cobden and supporters
establish the Anti-Corn Law
League in Manchester.
The steamships *Cirius* and *Great*

Western cross the Atlantic from
Britain to the United States.
Britain has ninety ships of the
line; Russia fifty; France
forty-nine; the United States
fifteen.

1839 Outbreak of First Opium War
(1839–42) between Britain and
China.
Afrikaner trekkers found the
independent republic of Natal.
Durham Report recommends
constitutional reform in Canada.
Samuel Cunard (1787–1865)
and partners start the British
and North American Royal Mail
Steam Packet Company.
First bicycle constructed by
Scottish inventor Kirkpatrick
Macmillan.

1840 Lower and Upper Canada
united by Act of Parliament.
End of British–Afghan war.
Transportation of felons from
Britain to New South Wales
ended.
Treaty of Waitangi in New
Zealand.
1,331 miles of railway track in
operation in Britain; 2,816 miles
in the United States.

1841 British sovereignty proclaimed
over Hong Kong.
New Zealand recognised as a
British colony.
British population 18.5 million;
United States 17 million; Ireland
8 million.
British travel agent Thomas
Cook (1808–92) arranges his
first excursion.

1842 Treaty of Nanking ends Opium
War, confirming the cession of

Hong Kong to Britain.
Afrikaner trekkers establish the
Orange Free State.
Queen Victoria makes her first
railway journey, from Windsor to
Paddington.

1843 Natal annexed by Britain.
Sind campaign ends in conquest
and annexation.
Maori revolts in New Zealand.
SS *Great Britain* becomes the first
propeller-driven ship to cross
the Atlantic.
American Congress grants
Samuel Morse £30,000 to build
first telegraph line between
Washington and Baltimore.

1844 Daniel O'Connell found guilty of
conspiracy against British rule
in Ireland.
Southern Maratha campaign.
British railways comprise 2,236
miles.
Morse's telegraph system used
for the first time.

1845 First British–Sikh War begins
in India.
Further Maori uprising against
British rule and European
settlement in New Zealand.
First underwater cable laid
across the English Channel.
Friedrich Engels publishes *The
Condition of the Working Class in
England* in Leipzig.
Benjamin Disraeli publishes *Two
Nations*.

1846 British East India Company
forces defeat of Sikhs; Treaty of
Lahore ends First Sikh War.
Seventh Kaffir War (1846–47)
begins in South Africa.
Repeal of the Corn Laws marks

the end of protectionism and the
beginning of Free Trade.
Beginning of potato famine in
Ireland.

1847 Liberia, a settlement in West
Africa for freed slaves,
proclaimed an independent
republic, though under
American protection.
British Factory Act restricts the
working day for women and
children.

1848 Second British–Sikh War
begins.
Nova Scotia granted responsible
government; Union of Canada
and most other British North
American colonies soon follow
suit.
First settlers arrive at Dunedin,
New Zealand.
Californian gold discoveries lead
to the first gold rush.
Communist Manifesto issued by
Marx and Engels.

1849 British annex Punjab after final
defeat of Sikhs.
David Livingstone crosses the
Kalahari Desert and discovers
Lake Ngami.
Navigation Acts repealed.
Charles Dickens publishes *David
Copperfield*.

1850 Eighth Kaffir War begins.
Taiping rebellion in China.
Public Libraries Act passed in
Britain.
University of Sydney established
in Australia.
Royal Meteorological Society
founded.
Joseph Paxton builds Crystal
Palace in south London.

1851 Victoria in Australia proclaimed
a separate colony.
Beginning of Basuto War (1851–
53).
Beginning of Burma War.
Gold found in Victoria.
Great Exhibition held in Britain.
Population of Britain 20.8
million; France 33 million;
United States 23 million; China
430 million.

1852 The South African Republic (the
Transvaal) established.
Beginning of Second Burmese
War; British forces annex Pegu.
New constitution established in
New Zealand.
Sugar Acts repealed.
David Livingstone begins
exploration of Zambezi River.
Paddington Station in London
designed by Brunel and Wyatt.
First All-England cricket eleven
formed.

1853 End of Burmese War.
East India Company annex
Nagpur.
Telegraph system introduced to
India.
Melbourne University founded.

1854 Convention of Bloemfontein
confirms independence of the
Orange Free State.
Outbreak of Crimean War
(1854–56).
Battle of the Eureka stockade in
the Australian goldfields.
Ferdinand de Lesseps (1805–94)
granted concession by Egypt to
construct the Suez Canal.
Britain and the United States
sign the Elgin Treaty on
Canadian trade arrangements.

University College Dublin
founded.

1855 Britain, in alliance with
Afghanistan, begins war against
Persia.
Taiping rebellion ends.
Livingstone discovers the
Victoria Falls on the Zambezi
River.
Sir Richard Burton publishes
Pilgrimage to Mecca.

1856 British East India Company
annexes Avadh (Oudh) in
India.
Britain establishes Natal as a
crown colony.
British fleet bombards Canton at
outbreak of Anglo–Chinese
War.
War with Persia begins.
Britain grants self-governing
status to Tasmania, which joins
New South Wales, Victoria and
South Australia as a
self-governing colony enjoying
'responsible' government.
Race riots in British Guiana.
First Australian interstate
cricket match, Victoria v. New
South Wales.

1857 Great Indian Rebellion, known
as the Mutiny, begins.
Peace of Paris ends Anglo–
Persian War; Shah recognises
Afghan independence.
British Navy destroys Chinese
fleet; Canton captured.
Irish Republican Brotherhood,
commonly known as the
Fenians, founded.
Science Museum opens in South
Kensington, London; Victoria
and Albert Museum also opens
(known as the Museum of

442

Ornamental Art until 1899).
Beginning of the laying of the
first transatlantic cable,
completed 1866.

1858 End of Great Indian Rebellion.
Powers of the East India
Company transferred to the
British Crown.
Treaty of Tientsin ends Anglo–
Chinese War.
British campaigns against tribes
on the north-west frontier of
India.
Ottawa becomes capital of
Canada.
Suez Canal Company formed.
SS *Great Eastern*, the largest ship
of her time, is launched.
Richard Burton and John
Hanning Speke discover Lake
Tanganyika and Lake Victoria
Nyanza.

1859 Queensland becomes a separate
colony, with Brisbane as its
capital.
Founding of Port Said in Egypt.
Work on Suez Canal begins
under the direction of de
Lesseps.
Charles Darwin publishes *On the
Origin of Species by Means of Natural
Selection.*
Samuel Smiles (1812–1904)
publishes *Self-Help*.

1860 Second Maori war (1860–70)
begins in New Zealand.
Anglo-French forces defeat
Chinese at Pa-li Chau; Treaty of
Peking signed.
Between 1850 and 1860 424,000
people from Britain and 914,000
from Ireland emigrated to the
United States.

First British Open Golf
Championship.

1861 Sikkim campaign.
First horse-drawn trams in
London.
First machine-chilled
cold-storage unit built in
Sydney.
Population of the United
Kingdom approximately 23
million; Russia 76 million;
United States 32 million; Italy
25 million.
Charles Dickens publishes *Great
Expectations.*

1862 R.J. Gatling (1818–1903)
constructs the gun which bears
his name.
International Exhibition in
London.
First English cricket team tours
Australia.

1863 Mohammed Said, Khedive of
Egypt dies and is succeeded by
Ismail (d.1879).
First New Zealand railway
opens between Christchurch
and Ferrymead.
Speke and Grant descend the
Nile to Gondokoro, meeting Sir
Samuel Baker on a journey
upriver.
Construction of London
Underground railway begun.
English Football Association
founded.
T.H. Huxley publishes *Evidence
as to Man's Place in Nature.*

1864 Sir Samuel Baker discovers Lake
Albert.
First US salmon cannery
opens.

1865 Morant Bay rebellion in
Jamaica.
Wellington becomes the capital
of New Zealand.
Outbreak of war between
Orange Free State and the
Basuto (Sotho) (1865–66).
Transatlantic cable finally
completed.
First oil pipeline laid in
Pennsylvania.
Queensberry Rules for boxing
outlined.

1866 'Black Friday' crash on London
Stock Exchange.
Fenian raids in Canada.
British campaign against
Indians of British Honduras.
Dr T.J. Barnado (1845–1905)
opens his first home for
destitute children in Stepney,
London.
Robert Whitehead (1823–1905)
invents the underwater torpedo.

1867 Violent Fenian incidents in
Ireland and Manchester.
The British North America Act
establishes the dominion of
Canada.
Livingstone explores the Congo.
Diamonds discovered in South
Africa.
Marx publishes the first volume
of *Das Kapital*.

1868 British forces invade Abyssinia.
Campaign to control tribes on
India's north-west frontier.
First official Trades Union
Congress held in Manchester.

1869 Red River Rebellion in Canada.
Opening of Suez Canal by
Empress Eugènie of France.

Girton College for women
founded in Cambridge.

1870 British expeditionary force ends
Red River Rebellion; Manitoba
becomes a Canadian province.
Western Australia granted
responsible government.

1871 British Columbia joins the
Dominion of Canada.
Basutoland becomes part of
Cape Colony.
Britain annexes the diamond
fields of Kimberley.
Stanley meets Livingstone at
Ujiji.
Charles Darwin publishes *The
Descent of Man*.
FA Cup competition established
in England.
Bank holidays introduced in
England and Wales.
Population figures: Britain 26
million; Ireland 5.4 million;
Germany 41 million; United
States 39 million; France 36
million; Japan 33 million.

1872 T.F. Burgers elected President of
the Republic of the Transvaal.
Cape Colony granted full,
responsible self-government.
First international soccer match,
England v. Scotland.

1873 Ashanti War (1873–74) begins
on the Gold Coast.
Famine in Bengal.
Abolition of slave markets in
Zanzibar.
Modern County Cricket
Championship begins in
England.
First game of modern lawn
tennis takes place in England.

1874 Disraeli becomes Prime Minister
(until 1880).
First Impressionist exhibition
held in Paris.

1875 Perak campaign.
Prince of Wales visits India.
British government buys the
Khedive of Egypt's shares in the
Suez Canal Company.
Public Health Act passed in
Britain.
Strength of European standing
armies: Britain 113,000; Russia
3.4 million; Germany 2.8
million; France 412,000.

1876 Alexander Graham Bell invents
the telephone.
First Chinese railway completed.
World Exhibition held in
Philadelphia.
Queen Victoria proclaimed
Empress of India.

1877 British annexation of the
Transvaal.
Famine in Bengal.
Frozen meat shipped for the first
time between Argentina and
Europe.

1878 Eastern Crisis resolved.
Indian troops sent to Malta.
Britain acquires Cyprus.
Electric street lighting
introduced in London.
Fur farming begins in Canada.

1879 Zulu War ends in British
victory, after humiliating defeat
at Insandlhwana.
British invasion of Afghanistan
(war ends 1880).
Britain deposes Ismail, Khedive
of Egypt, and puts puppet ruler,
Taufiq, in his place (Khedive

until 1892).
Australian frozen meat on sale in
London.
First telephone exchanges
established in London.

1880 Liberals win general election
and Gladstone becomes Prime
Minister.
Scheme for South African
Federation rejected by Cape
Parliament.
Transvaal declares itself
independent of Britain after the
annexation of 1877; Transvaal
War begins.
Captain C.C. Boycott, a land
agent in County Mayo, is
'boycotted' for refusing to accept
rents fixed by tenants.
Canned fruits and meats appear
in Britain.
First Test match between
England and Australia played in
England.

1881 Transvaal rebels defeat the
British at Majuba Hill; Britain
recognises the independence of
the Transvaal Republic in the
subsequent Treaty of Pretoria.
Charles Stewart Parnell, Irish
nationalist leader, imprisoned.
Canadian Pacific Railway
Company founded.
Flogging abolished in the British
Army and Navy.
City populations: London 3.3
million; Paris 2.2 million; New
York 1.2 million; Berlin 1.1
million; Vienna 1 million.

1882 British forces invade Egypt and
occupy Cairo and the Canal zone.
Shakin expedition.
Phoenix Park murders in

445

Dublin.
Maxim gun invented.

1883 Britain decides to evacuate the
Sudan, in face of nationalist
uprising led by the Mahdi.
Paul Kruger becomes President
of the South African Republic
(the Transvaal).
French establish control over
Tunis.
Sir Joseph Swan (1828–1914)
produces a synthetic fibre.
Fabian Society founded in
London.
J.R. Seeley publishes *The
Expansion of England*.

1884 General Gordon reaches
Khartoum.
Convention of London confirms
independence of Transvaal.
Germany occupies South-West
Africa.

1885 Death of General Gordon at
Khartoum; British and
Egyptian forces evacuate the
Sudan.
Britain establishes protectorates
over Northern Bechuanaland,
the Niger River region and
Southern New Guinea.
Indian National Congress
established.
Invasion of Upper Burma.
Suppression of Riel's rebellion in
north-west Canada.
Germany annexes Tanganyika
and Zanzibar.
The Congo becomes the
personal possession of King
Leopold II of the Belgians.
The railway from the Cape
reaches Kimberley.
Carl Benz builds single-cylinder
engine for the motor car.

Second volume of Marx's *Das
Kapital* published.

1886 Liberal government's Home
Rule Bill for Ireland rejected by
House of Lords; party split.
First meeting of Indian National
Congress.
Burma incorporated in Indian
empire.
Canadian Pacific Railway
completed.
English Lawn Tennis
Association founded.

1887 Queen Victoria celebrates her
Golden Jubilee.
First Colonial Conference opens
in London.

1888 Sikkim War.
Lobengula, King of the Ndebele,
or Matabele, accepts British
protection and grants Cecil
Rhodes mining rights.
Sarawak becomes a British
protectorate.
Suez Canal Convention signed,
guaranteeing international
freedom of passage through the
canal.
James Bryce publishes *The
American Commonwealth*.
'Jack the Ripper' murders six
women in London.
English Football League
founded.

1889 Chin–Looshai war (1889–90)
Cecil Rhodes' British South
Africa Company granted a
royal charter.
London dock strike.

1890 Britain exchanges Heligoland
with Germany for Zanzibar and
Pemba.

Cecil Rhodes becomes Prime
Minister of Cape Colony.
First British electrical power
station opened at Deptford.

1891 British expeditionary forces sent
to Manipur, Saminar and Nagar.
Pan-German League founded.
Goldwin Smith publishes *The
Canadian Question.*

1892 Liberals return to power with
Gladstone as Prime Minister.
Taufiq, Khedive of Egypt, dies
and is succeeded by Abbas II
(who reigns until 1918).
Britain and Germany agree on
the partition of the Cameroons in
West Africa.
Tambi expedition.
Chin Hills expedition.
Keir Hardie becomes first
Labour Member of Parliament.
Cape to Johannesburg railway
completed.
First Pan-Slav Conference held
at Cracow.
Automatic telephone exchange
introduced.
Diesel patents internal
combustion engine.

1893 Natal granted responsible
self-government.
Swaziland annexed by the
Transvaal.
Matabeleland expedition.
The Imperial Institute, South
Kensington, founded.
World Exhibition in Chicago.

1894 British South Africa Company
completes occupation of
Matabeleland.
Lord Rosebery succeeds
Gladstone as Prime Minister.
Uganda becomes a British

protectorate.
Gambia expedition.
Waziristan expedition.
Lumière brothers invent the
cinematograph.

1895 British South Africa Company
territory south of the Zambezi
renamed as Rhodesia.
Liberals lose power in the
United Kingdom, succeeded by a
coalition government of
Conservatives and Liberal
Unionists led by Lord Salisbury;
Joseph Chamberlain becomes
Colonial Secretary.
Jameson Raid into the
Transvaal.
Defence and relief of Chitral.
Germany opens the Kiel Canal.
Marconi invents radio
telegraphy.
X-rays discovered.
London School of Economics
and Political Science founded.
Third volume of *Das Kapital*
published.

1896 Jameson Raid crushed.
Kaiser William II sends 'Kruger
telegram' in support of the
Transvaal.
Rhodes resigns as premier of the
Cape; Transvaal and the Orange
Free State form a military
alliance.
Italian forces defeated by
Abyssinians at Adowa, ending
attempted conquest.
General Kitchener begins his
campaign for the reconquest of
the Sudan.
Matabele revolt put down.
Federated Malay States formed.
Bechuanaland expedition.
Beginning of the Klondike gold
rush in Canada.

Harmsworth publishes the first *Daily Mail* in London.

First modern Olympics held in Athens.

1897 Queen Victoria's Diamond Jubilee.

Colonial Conference held in London.

Widespread famine in India.

Sultan of Zanzibar abolishes slavery.

Benin expedition.

Malakand Field Force.

Norman Commission begins inquiry into the well-being of the British Caribbean.

Germany and Russia take territory on the coast of China.

1898 Paul Kruger re-elected President of the Transvaal.

Britain obtains ninety-nine-year lease on Kowloon and the New Territories adjacent to Hong Kong; acquires Wei-hai-Wei as potential naval base.

Kitchener wins the battle of Omdurman, destroys the Mahdist forces and reaches Fashoda; confrontation between France and Britain at Fashoda results in French withdrawal.

'Boxer' uprising in China against foreign interference; crushed by an alliance of Western imperial powers and Japan.

United States declares war on Spain over Cuba; destroys Spanish fleet at Manila.

Pierre and Marie Curie discover radium and polonium.

First Zeppelin airship built.

1899 Anglo–Egypt Sudan Convention; Sudan becomes a condominium.

South Africa crisis results in outbreak of the Boer War; British military defeats during 'Black Week'.

Germany secures the contract to build the Baghdad Railway, thus threatening to become a rival of Britain and France in the Middle East.

1900 Field Marshal Roberts becomes Commander-in-Chief in South Africa with Kitchener his Chief of Staff; relief of Mafeking and Ladysmith; annexation of the Orange Free State and the Transvaal; beginning of guerrilla war.

British Parliament passes act to create the federated Commonwealth of Australia.

First *Daily Express* printed in London.

World Exhibition in Paris.

Sigmund Freud publishes *The Interpretation of Dreams*.

1901 Queen Victoria dies; succeeded by Edward VII.

Guerrilla warfare intensifies in South Africa.

Edmund Barton inaugurated as first Prime Minister of the Commonwealth of Australia.

Peace of Peking ends 'Boxer' uprising.

Negotiations for an Anglo–German alliance end in failure.

First British submarine launched.

Mombasa to Lake Victoria Railway completed.

Marconi transmits radio messages from Cornwall to Newfoundland.

1902 Boer War ends with annexation of the Orange Free State and the Transvaal.
Limited Anglo–Japanese treaty signed.
Colonial Conference meets in London.
Arthur James Balfour becomes British Prime Minister.
First Aswan dam opened.
J.A. Hobson publishes *Imperialism*.
Caruso makes his first phonograph recording.

British Parliament passes Aliens' Act.
Anglo–Japanese alliance renewed for ten years.
Provinces of Alberta and Saskatchewan formed in Canada.
Sinn Fein founded in Dublin.
Unionist government resigns; Campbell-Bannerman becomes Liberal Prime Minister.
Motorbuses in operation in London.
Einstein formulates the special theory of relativity.

1903 Britain completes conquest of Northern Nigeria.
Alaskan frontier dispute settled.
Coronation Durbar for Edward VII, King-Emperor, in Delhi.
Emmeline Pankhurst founds National Women's Social and Political Union.
Beginning of tariff reform crisis in Britain; Joseph Chamberlain resigns as Colonial Secretary.
Sixth Zionist Congress declines the offer of East Africa as a place for Jewish settlement.
Henry Ford founds Ford Motor Company.

1906 Landslide election victory for the Liberals in the United Kingdom.
Muslim League founded in India.
Self-government granted to the Transvaal and the Orange River Colonies.
British forces Turkey to cede the Sinai Peninsula to Egypt.
China and Britain agree a reduction in opium production.
Launch of HMS *Dreadnought*.
Populations of cities:London 4.5 million; New York 4 million; Paris 2.7 million; Berlin 2 million; Tokyo 1.9 million; Vienna 1.3 million.

1904 Anglo–French entente agreed.
Russo–Japanese war breaks out.
Empire Day introduced.
Work begins on Panama Canal.
Max Weber publishes *The Protestant Ethic and the Birth of Capitalism*.

1907 Britain and France agree to guarantee Siamese independence.
Peace Conference at The Hague.
The Imperial Conference agrees on the term 'dominion' to describe certain federated self-governing colonies.
Anglo–Russian entente agreed.
Baden-Powell plans the formation of the Boy Scout movement.

1905 Louis Botha and the Het Volk party demand responsible self-government for the Transvaal.
Partition of Bengal.

449

1908 Asquith succeeds
Campbell-Bannerman as
British Prime Minister.
Olympic Games held in London.
Northcliffe buys *The Times*.
Wilbur Wright flies thirty miles
in forty minutes.
Baden-Powell publishes *Scouting
for Boys*.

1909 Anglo–German negotiations on
the control of the Baghdad
Railway.
Anglo–Persian Oil Company
formed, later known as British
Petroleum.
Act for the Union of South Africa
passed in British Parliament.
Indian Councils Act extends the
franchise as part of the Morley–
Minto reforms.
Louis Blériot crosses the English
Channel in an aeroplane in
thirty-seven minutes.
International Cricket
Conference established.

1910 Union of South Africa achieved,
with dominion status; Botha
becomes first Prime Minister.
Edward VII succeeded by
George V.
Constitutional crisis in Britain
precipitates two general elections
and destroys the Liberals'
overall majority.
Over 120,000 telephones in use
in the United Kingdom.

1911 Anglo–Japanese commercial
treaty signed.
Delhi Durbar of the
King-Emperor George V.
International crisis at Agadir.

1912 Coal, dock and transport strikes
in Britain.

Renewal of alliance between
Germany, Austria and Italy.
Turkey closes Dardanelles to
shipping.
Captain Robert Falcon Scott
reaches the South Pole after the
Norwegian Roald Amundsen;
Scott and his party perish on the
return journey.
Stefansson and Anderson begin
exploration of Arctic Canada.
SS *Titanic* sinks on her maiden
voyage with over 1,500 drowned.

1913 Irish Home Rule Bill passed by
British Parliament.
Curragh 'mutiny' of British
officers based near Dublin.
Balkan wars.
Violent Suffragette
demonstrations in Britain.

1914 Gandhi–Smuts agreement in
South Africa.
Outbreak of First World War.
Ernest Shackleton leads
expedition to the Antarctic
(completed 1917).

1915 British conquest of Mesopotamia
(modern Iraq).
Ill-fated Gallipoli campaign
begins.
British merchant shipping losses
total over a million tons for the
year.
Henry Ford produces his
millionth car.
Einstein postulates his general
theory of relativity.
Gandhi returns to India.

1916 Easter rebellion in Dublin.
T.E. Lawrence sent to the
Middle East.
Food rationing in Germany.
Battle of the Somme.

Lionel Curtis publishes *The Commonwealth of Nations*.

Atlantic in sixteen hours twenty-seven minutes.

1917 Bread rationing in Britain.
Imperial War Conference in London.
General Allenby takes command of British forces in Palestine.
First tank battle at Cambrai.
Imperial War Museum founded in London (opened 1936).
Bolshevik revolution in Russia.
Trans-Siberian Railway completed.

1918 US President Woodrow Wilson proposes his Fourteen Points for world peace.
Britain loses more than half the total of world shipping losses for the duration of the war.
Worldwide influenza epidemics begin.
Max Planck wins Nobel Prize for quantum theory.

1919 Peace conferences redistribute, through the mandate system, former German and Turkish possessions and colonies. Britain and the dominions gain the lion's share. The dominions and India sign the peace treaties in their own right.
Anglo–Afghan war.
Gandhi leads his first all-India *satyagraha* against the Rowlatt Acts; Amritsar massacre; Government of India Act passed by British Parliament.
Jan Smuts succeeds Botha as South African Prime Minister.
Growing crisis in Ireland over the implementation of Home Rule.
Alcock and Brown make first non-stop flight across the

1920 Government of Ireland Act provides both Northern and Southern Ireland with their own parliaments.
British coal production 229 million tons; United States 645 million tons.
Russian civil war ends.
3,747 divorces granted in Britain during the year.

1921 Winston Churchill becomes Colonial Secretary.
Imperial Conference in London.
Mackenzie King (1874–1950) elected Canadian Prime Minister.
Washington Conference on naval disarmament.

1922 Britain recognises the independence of the Kingdom of Egypt under King Fuad I
Gandhi sentenced to six years' imprisonment for civil disobedience activities.
Chanak Crisis.
Bonar Law forms first Conservative administration since 1905.
Establishment of the Irish Free State confirms the partition of Ireland.
Mussolini's march on Rome.
Insulin first administered to diabetic patients.
Dr Marie Stopes advocates birth control at meetings in London.

1923 Devonshire Declaration affirms that Kenya is primarily 'African territory'.
Halibut Fisheries Treaty marks the right of the dominions to negotiate trade treaties

451

independently of Britain.
Hitler's Munich *putsch* fails.
Chaim Weizmann named
President of World Zionist
Organisation.
First FA Cup final played at the
new Wembley Stadium.

1924 First minority Labour
government formed in Britain.
The Rand strike.
James B. Hertzog (1866–1942)
becomes Prime Minister of South
Africa.
Zinoviev letter published.
Conservatives return to power in
Britain.
Gandhi fasts for twenty-one days
in protest at Hindu–Muslim
conflict.
British Empire Exhibition at
Wembley.
British coal production 267
million tons; United States 485
million tons.
British steel production 8 million
tons; Germany 9 million tons.
Britain loses 8 million days from
strike action; United States 10
million days.
British Imperial Airways begins
to operate.

1925 Dominions Office set up in
Britain.
Locarno Conference.
Britain has 1,654,000 radio sets
in operation.
John Logie Baird (1888–1946)
transmits first recognisable
television image.

1926 Imperial Conference defines
dominion status, and recognises
the right of the dominions to opt
out of international treaties
signed by the British

government.
Lord Irwin (later Lord Halifax)
becomes Viceroy of India.
General Strike in Britain.
British Imperial Chemical
Industries formed.
Cobham flies from Croydon to
Cape Town and back.

1927 New Parliament House opened
in Canberra, Australia.
British Broadcasting
Corporation takes over from
British Broadcasting Company.
Kellogg Pact for the
renunciation of war proposed.

1928 Simon Commission arouses
nationalist opposition in India.
First Five-Year Plan begins in
Soviet Union.
Brazilian economy collapses due
to overproduction of sugar.

1929 Second Labour government
elected in Britain.
First Round Table Conference
discusses Indian constitutional
reform.
Irwin Declaration contains
promise of dominion status for
India.
Arab–Jewish conflict in
Palestine.
Wall Street crash heralds start of
world economic crisis and the
Great Depression.

1930 Canadian government offers
preferential tariff to Britain.
Britain, United States, Japan,
France and Italy sign treaty on
naval disarmament.
Passfield White Paper on
Palestine suggests that Jewish
immigration be halted.
France begins building Maginot

Line.
Amy Johnson flies solo from London to Australia in 19½ days.
Donald Bradman scores 334 runs for Australia in Leeds Test match.
First Empire Games held.
Planet Pluto discovered.

1931 Formation of National Government in Britain under Ramsay MacDonald.
Statute of Westminster defines and codifies dominion status.
Gandhi–Irwin Pact announced.
Liberal Donoughmore Constitution gives Ceylon the substance of internal self-government.
Britain abandons the gold standard; Sterling Area set up.
First Trans-African railway completed between Benguela and Katanga.
United Kingdom population 46 million; United States 122 million; India 338 million; Germany 64 million; Russia 168 million; China 410 million.

1932 Indian National Congress declared illegal and Gandhi arrested.
Imperial Conference at Ottawa introduces the system of imperial preferential tariffs.
Eamon de Valera elected President of Ireland.
Imperial Airways now serves twenty-two countries, flies nearly 2 million miles, carries over 34,000 passengers and 6.3 million letters.
Franklin Delano Roosevelt becomes US President and

outlines the 'New Deal'.
Unemployment figures: Britain 2.8 million; United States 13.7 million; approximately 30 million worldwide.
Chadwick discovers the neutron.

1933 White Paper on Indian constitutional reform published.
Hitler becomes German Chancellor.
Reichstag fire in Berlin.
British planes fly over Mount Everest.

1934 Gandhi suspends civil disobedience campaign in India.
Japan renounces Washington Treaties on the limitation of naval forces.

1935 George V's Silver Jubilee celebrations.
Stanley Baldwin becomes Prime Minister of National Government.
Government of India Act establishes 'Home Rule' in the Indian provinces.
Italian invasion of Abyssinia.
Persia becomes known as Iran.
Bank of Canada established.
Longest bridge in the world opened over the lower Zambezi.
British Council founded.

1936 George V succeeded by Edward VIII, who abdicates later in the year and is succeeded by his brother, George VI.
King Farouq succeeds King Fuad to the throne of Egypt.
Amy Mollison flies from Britain to Cape Town in three days, six hours and twenty-five minutes; later flies from Newfoundland to London in thirteen hours and

seventeen minutes.
Berlin Olympic Games.
First television service
inaugurated by the BBC in
London.

1937 Congress Party achieves
substantial success in all-India
elections.
Imperial Conference held in
London.
Neville Chamberlain succeeds
Baldwin as Prime Minister.
Royal Commission on Palestine
recommends the establishment
of both Arab and Jewish states.
Aden becomes a crown colony.
First jet engine built by Frank
Whittle.

1938 Munich crisis over German
claims to the Sudetenland.
Japanese install puppet Chinese
government in Nanking,
capture Canton and Hankow,
and withdraw from League of
Nations.
SS *Queen Elizabeth* launched.
Franco begins Catalonian
offensive in Spanish Civil War.
Len Hutton makes 364 runs
against Australia at the
Oval.

1939 Outbreak of Second World War.
Britain declares war on India's
behalf, leading to the
resignation of
Congress-dominated provincial
governments.
First nylon stockings appear.
Jan Smuts becomes Prime
Minister of South Africa for a
second time.
Popular films include *The Wizard
of Oz*, *Gone with the Wind*.

1940 Winston Churchill succeeds
Chamberlain as Prime
Minister.
British Eighth Army opens its
offensive in North Africa under
Wavell.
Colonial Development and
Welfare Act passed.
Penicillin developed as a
practical antibiotic.
Arthur Bryant publishes *English
Saga*.
Popular songs include 'You are
my Sunshine', 'The Last Time I
Saw Paris'.

1941 Lend-Lease bill signed in the
United States.
Churchill and Roosevelt meet
and sign the Atlantic Charter.
Japanese sink HMS *Prince of
Wales* and *Repulse*, and invade the
Philippines.
Fall of Hong Kong.
Nazi propaganda film *Ohm
Kruger* vilifies Britain for its part
in the Boer War.
Popular songs include
'Bewitched, Bothered and
Bewildered', 'Deep in the Heart
of Texas'.

1942 Fall of Singapore and collapse of
British Empire in the Far East.
'Quit India' movement; mass
arrests of Congress Party
leaders.
Malta awarded the George
Cross.
In America, Enrico Fermi splits
the atom.
Hit songs include 'The White
Cliffs of Dover', 'Praise the Lord
and Pass the Ammunition'.

1943 Allied successes in Russia, North
Africa and the Far East.

Quebec Conference between
Churchill, Roosevelt and
Mackenzie King.
Allied invasion of Italy.
Famine in Bengal.
Penicillin successfully used in
the treatment of chronic
diseases.
Popular films include *Desert
Victory, Stalingrad.*

1944 D-Day landings in Normandy.
North Burma cleared of
Japanese occupation.
First non-stop flight between
Britain and Canada.
Films produced include
Laurence Olivier's *Henry V* and
Marcel Carné's *Les Enfants du
Paradis.*

1945 War comes to an end after the
dropping of atomic bombs on
Hiroshima and Nagasaki.
Labour landslide election victory
makes Clement Attlee Prime
Minister.
Second Colonial Development
and Welfare Act passed.
Atomic Research Centre
established at Harwell, England.
George Orwell publishes *Animal
Farm.*

1946 Britain and France evacuate
Lebanon.
Sarawak ceded to the British
Crown by the 'White Rajah', Sir
Charles Brooke.
Cabinet mission to India.
London Airport opened.
Film successes include *The Best
Years of Our Lives*, David Lean's
Great Expectations.

1947 Britain's proposal to partition
Palestine rejected by both Arabs

and Jews.
Partition of India.
Britain suffers most severe
winter weather since 1894.
Thor Heyerdahl sails on a
primitive raft, the *Kon-Tiki,*
from Peru to Polynesia in 101
days.
Dead Sea Scrolls discovered.
First 'flying saucers' reported in
the United States.

1948 Gandhi assassinated.
Burma gains its independence
and leaves the Commonwealth.
Ceylon achieves full
independence within the
Commonwealth.
British Citizenship Act grants
British passports to all
Commonwealth citizens.
The state of Israel created after
the British precipitously leave
Palestine.
Accra riots in the Gold Coast.
South African writer Alan Paton
publishes *Cry, the Beloved
Country.*
Olympic Games held in London.

1949 North Atlantic Treaty signed in
Washington.
Republic of Ireland proclaimed
in Dublin.
Recently elected nationalist
government in South Africa
presses ahead with the
implementation of apartheid.
India adopts the constitution of
a federal republic, but opts to
remain in the Commonwealth.
British monarch becomes Head
of the Commonwealth.
Transjordan becomes the
Kingdom of Jordan.
Clothes rationing ends in
Britain.

Pound devalued from $4.03 to $2.80.

George Orwell publishes *Nineteen Eighty-Four*.

1950 Britain recognises Communist China and the state of Israel.
United Nations building completed in New York.
Population of London 8.3 million; New York 7.8 million; Tokyo 5.3 million; Moscow 4.1 million. World population approximately 2.3 billion.
Australian tennis team wins Davis Cup from United States.

1951 Muhammed Mussadegh becomes Prime Minister in Iran, heralding conflict with Britain over its oil interests there.
Conservatives return to power under Churchill.
Electric power produced from atomic energy for the first time in the United States.
46 per cent of the British population works in commerce and industry, compared to 10 per cent in India.
Festival of Britain held in London.

1952 Elizabeth II succeeds George VI.
Anti-British riots in Egypt; King Farouk abdicates and General Neguib comes to power at the head of a revolutionary nationalist regime.
Proclamation of a state of emergency in Kenya in response to Mau Mau rebellion.
Britain announces it has produced the atomic bomb.
The Pacific Council, comprising Australia, the United States and New Zealand, meets at Honolulu.
First hydrogen bomb exploded by the US.
First contraceptive pill produced.
Films include *Moulin Rouge, High Noon*, Charlie Chaplin's *Limelight*.
SS *United States* wins Blue Riband for crossing the Atlantic in a record three days, ten hours and forty minutes.

1953 London Conference explores plans to federate Northern, Southern Rhodesia and Nyasaland; federation set up later that year.
Egyptian republic proclaimed.
Jomo Kenyatta convicted with others of managing Mau Mau.
Conference of Commonwealth Prime Ministers in London.
Armistice signed to end Korean War.
Coronation of Elizabeth II.
Constitution suspended in British Guiana after election victory of Dr Cheddi Jagan's People's Progress Party arouses fears of Marxist takeover.
First ascent of Mount Everest.
First indications that smoking causes lung cancer.
Kinsey Report on the sexual behaviour of the human female published.
Popular songs include 'How Much is that Doggie in the Window?', 'Baubles, Bangles and Beads'.

1954 Abdul Nasser becomes Egyptian head of state.
Elizabeth II and Duke of Edinburgh begin extensive

Commonwealth tour.
St Lawrence Seaway project approved by President Eisenhower.
French defeated at Dien Bien Phu by Vietnamese Communists.
South East Asian Treaty Organisation set up.
Senator Joseph McCarthy's anti-Communist witch-hunting activities in the United States curtailed.
American submarine *Nautilus* converted to nuclear power.
Jonas Salk develops anti-polio vaccination.
The United States contains 6 per cent of the world's population but owns 60 per cent of its cars, 58 per cent of its telephones and 45 per cent of its radio sets.

1955 Anthony Eden succeeds Churchill as Prime Minister.
Jüan Perón resigns the Argentinian presidency.
Blacks in Montgomery, Alabama, boycott segregated city buses.
Atomically generated power first used in America.

1956 Suez Crisis plunges Middle East into turmoil; Suez Canal blocked to shipping.
Pakistan becomes an Islamic republic.
Archbishop Makarios sent from Cyprus to exile in the Seychelles.
Sudan achieves independence outside the Commonwealth.
Hungarian uprising crushed by Soviet troops.
Jawarhalal Nehru holds talks with presidents Tito and Nasser in Yugoslavia.

Fidel Castro lands in Cuba aiming to overthrow the dictator Batista.
First CND Aldermaston march.
Winston Churchill begins to publish *The History of the English-Speaking Peoples*.
Films include Ingmar Bergman's *The Seventh Seal* and Mike Todd's *Around the World in Eighty Days*.
Maria Callas makes operatic debut in New York.
Elvis Presley becomes pop music idol.

1957 Eden resigns as Prime Minister and is succeeded by Harold Macmillan.
Archbishop Makarios released.
Malayan federation set up.
Gold Coast achieves independence as Ghana.
Britain explodes thermal nuclear bomb in the central Pacific.
Soviet Union launches Sputniks 1 and 2.
Wolfenden Report on homosexuality and prostitution published in Britain.
Trevor Huddleston publishes *Naught for Your Comfort*.

1958 West Indies federation begins.
European Common Market comes into being.
Ayub Khan becomes Prime Minister of Pakistan.
Soviet Union grants a loan to the United Arab Republic (Egypt and Syria) for building of new Aswan Dam on Nile.
US nuclear submarine *Nautilus* passes under the ice-cap at the North Pole.
US launches first moon rocket, which fails to reach its target;

457

NASA established to administer
the exploration of space.
The last debutantes are
presented at the British Court.

1959 Civil disturbances in Nyasaland;
Hastings Banda arrested.
Archbishop Makarios returns to
Cyprus, which becomes a
republic within the
Commonwealth.
President Bandaranaika of
Ceylon assassinated.
Britain resumes diplomatic
relations with the United Arab
Republic.
Castro's government confirmed
in power in Cuba.
Louis Leakey finds the skull of
'Nutcracker Man' in
Tanganyika.

1960 Makarios becomes President of
Cyprus.
Nigeria achieves independence.
Macmillan makes 'wind of
change' speech in Cape Town at
end of African tour.
Soviet leader Nikita Khrushchev
visits India and Burma.
Sharpeville massacre in South
Africa; sixty-nine
demonstrators killed and 180
wounded.
Belgian Congo granted full
independence.
John F. Kennedy elected
American President.
Distribution of television sets:
United States 85 million; Britain
10.5 million; West Germany 2
million; France 1.5 million.

1961 Elizabeth II visits India,
Pakistan, Iran, Cyprus and
Ghana.
South Africa, having voted in a
referendum for republican
status, is refused the right of
re-entry to the Commonwealth
because of its apartheid policies,
which are also condemned by the
United Nations General
Assembly.
Sierra Leone achieves
independence.
Britain begins negotiations for
entry into Common Market.
Tanganyika and Zanzibar gain
independence.
Conference in Tanganyika
begins move to protect African
wildlife.
Yuri Gagarin makes first
manned space flight.
Films include *West Side Story*,
François Truffaut's *Jules et Jim*.

1962 Uganda and Trinidad and
Tobago become independent
within the Commonwealth.
Commonwealth Immigrants Act
passed in Britain to control
immigration.
Indo–Chinese war over border
dispute.
Nobel Prize for Medicine and
Physiology awarded to Crick,
Wilkins and Watson for
determining the molecular
structure of DNA.
Rebuilt Coventry Cathedral
consecrated.
Approximately 44 per cent of the
world's population are illiterate.

1963 President de Gaulle blocks
Britain's entry into the
Common Market.
Kenya achieves independence
within the Commonwealth.
Macmillan resigns as Prime
Minister and is succeeded by
Alec Douglas-Home.

First Pop Art exhibition in New York.

Malaysian Federation formed.

1964 Zanzibar declared a republic and unites with Tanganyika to form Tanzania.

Kenneth Kaunda becomes President of Northern Rhodesia, which becomes the independent republic of Zambia; break-up of Central African Federation thus confirmed.

Ian Smith becomes Prime Minister of Southern Rhodesia.

Nyasaland becomes the independent state of Malawi within the Commonwealth.

Elizabeth II pays state visit to Canada.

Nehru dies and is succeeded as Prime Minister of India by Lal Bahadur Shastri.

Malta achieves independence within the Commonwealth.

Labour under Harold Wilson wins general election in Britain.

Kenya becomes a republic with Kenyatta as President.

Olympic Games in Tokyo; World Fair in New York.

1965 Gambia becomes independent.

Seretse Khama becomes first Prime Minister of Bechuanaland.

Rhodesia unilaterally declares its independence.

Indo–Pakistan War.

Gambia and Singapore become independent and join the United Nations.

Controversy over Vinland map, centring on claims that Vikings discovered America in the eleventh century.

750th anniversary of the signing of Magna Carta.

Popular films include *The Sound of Music*, The Beatles' *Help!*

1966 Indira Gandhi becomes Prime Minister of India.

Ghana's Prime Minister Kwame Nkrumah forced into exile after coup.

HMS *Tiger* Conference fails to resolve Rhodesian dispute.

British Guiana becomes the independent nation of Guyana within the Commonwealth.

Lesotho, Botswana and Barbados also achieve independence.

Hastings Banda inaugurated as President of Malawi.

B.J. Vorster becomes Prime Minister of South Africa, leading a Nationalist government.

Mini skirts become fashionable.

England wins football World Cup.

1967 Egypt and Jordan sign mutual defence pact.

Riots in Hong Kong.

Queen Elizabeth and Prince Philip visit Canada for centennial celebrations.

Israel wins rapid victory in Six-Day War.

Mass demonstrations against the Vietnam War in Western capitals.

1968 Mauritius, Swaziland and Nauru become independent within the Commonwealth.

Pierre Trudeau becomes Prime Minister of Canada.

Wilson–Smith talks aboard HMS *Fearless* fail to reach agreement on Rhodesia.

British government places more restrictions on immigration from

India, Pakistan and the West Indies.

Apollo 8 manned spaceflight orbits the moon.

Richard Nixon elected as thirty-seventh US President.

1969 Violent conflict between Protestants and Catholics in Northern Ireland; British troops sent to Belfast to maintain law and order.

Caribbean island of Anguilla announces it is breaking all ties with Britain.

Enoch Powell proposes the government finance repatriation of 'New Commonwealth' immigrants.

Pope Paul VI attempts to mediate in Nigerian civil war.

Apollo 11 moon landing; first men on the moon.

1970 Nigerian civil war ends with capitulation of breakaway state of Biafra.

Gambia becomes a republic within the Commonwealth.

Fiji, Tonga and Western Samoa obtain independence.

Egyptian President Nasser dies aged fifty-two; succeeded by Anwar Sadat.

Conservatives under Heath win British general election.

Cyclones and floods kill at least a quarter of a million people in East Pakistan.

Israel and UAR agree to a ninety-nine-day truce along the Canal Zone.

Opposition to apartheid causes cancellation of South African cricket tour to England.

Salvador Allende elected President of Chile.

Unmanned Soviet space craft lands on Venus.

An estimated 231 million television sets in use worldwide.

1971 Idi Amin seizes power in Uganda

India intervenes on the side of the East Pakistan rebels in their war with West Pakistan.

British imposition of preventive detention and internment without trial in Northern Ireland leads to escalation of violent protest.

Vietnam War worsens with US bombing raids over North Vietnam.

Canada and Communist China exchange diplomatic envoys.

1972 Newly independent state of Bangladesh, formerly East Pakistan, joins Commonwealth.

Britain imposes direct rule in Northern Ireland.

Britain and the Irish Republic successfully apply for membership of the EEC.

Ceylon becomes a republic within the Commonwealth and changes its name to Sri Lanka.

Labour governments elected in Australia and New Zealand.

Pierre Trudeau's Liberal government holds on to power in Canada.

Popular films include *The Godfather, Cabaret.*

1973 Britain and Irish Republic formally join the EEC.

The Shah nationalises all foreign-operated oil firms in Iran.

Arab–Israeli War; Middle East oil embargoes placed on USA,

Western European states and
Japan for their perceived
support of Israel; energy crisis
begins in the industrialised
world; three-day working week
in the UK.
Continued conflict in Northern
Ireland.
The Bahamas achieve
independence after three
centuries of British rule.
Final negotiated end to Vietnam
War.
Watergate scandal breaks in
USA.
USA devalues dollar for the
second time in two years.

1974 Fuel crisis leads to very high
levels of inflation in many
countries; economic growth
almost ceases in most
industrialised nations.
Labour returns to power in
Britain, led by Harold Wilson.
Liberals, under Trudeau, win
another term of office in Canada.
Turkey invades and occupies
Northern Cyprus.
Work begins on clearing the
Suez Canal, blocked during the
Arab–Israeli War of 1967.
Grenada becomes independent.
India becomes the sixth nation
to explode a nuclear device.
The IRA bombs the Tower of
London and the Houses of
Parliament.
Smallpox epidemic in India.
Watergate scandal forces the
resignation of President Nixon.

1975 Separate Northern Turkish state
set up by Turkish Cypriots.
South Vietnam finally falls
under Communist control.
Egypt reopens Suez Canal.

Eamon De Valera (President of
Irish Republic 1959–73) dies
aged ninety-three.
Papua New Guinea becomes
independent.
Sikkim joins the federal Indian
republic.
Indian government declares a
state of emergency.
Australian constitutional crisis
over Governor-General John
Kerr's dismissal of Labour
Prime Minister Gough Whitlam;
Liberals under Malcolm Fraser
win subsequent election.
Generalissimo Franco dies.

1976 The Seychelles become
independent.
First township uprisings in
South Africa.
The Transkei becomes the first
'independent' Bantustan.
Success of Quebec separatists in
Canadian provincial elections
reawakens anxieties over
possible secession.
Angolan civil war causes
thousands to flee to Namibia.
Alex Haley publishes *Roots*.

1977 Indira Gandhi and Congress
lose Indian general election;
new Janata government led by
Morarji Desai.
President Makarios dies.
French adopted as official
language in Quebec.
President Sadat of Egypt pays
official visit to Israel.
Rhodesian premier Ian Smith
declares his willingness to work
towards a peace settlement with
black majority.
Death of Steve Biko in police
detention in South Africa.
Pakistan armed forces under

General Zia ul-Haq overthrow government and impose martial law.
Elizabeth II celebrates Silver Jubilee to mark twenty-five years on the throne.

1978 P.W. Botha succeeds J.B. Vorster as South African Prime Minister.
Dominica and the Solomon Islands become independent.
Widespread anti-government demonstrations in Iran.
Jomo Kenyatta dies in office.
J.R. Jayawardene becomes President of Sri Lanka under new constitutional arrangements.
Spyros Kyprianou elected President of Cyprus.
World's population estimated at 4.4 billion, increasing by approximately 200,000 each day.
Full diplomatic relations resumed between USA and People's Republic of China.

1979 Shah of Iran forced into exile after Muslim fundamentalist revolution; Ayatollah Khomeini takes over government.
St Lucia, St Vincent and the Grenadines achieve independence.
Ex-Premier Zulfikar Ali Bhutto hanged in Pakistan.
Commonwealth Conference at Lusaka leads to Lancaster House agreement on a settlement to the continuing conflict in Rhodesia; Bishop Abel Muzorewa becomes Prime Minister; full elections to be held.
Conservatives under Margaret Thatcher win British general election.
Idi Amin overthrown in Uganda

by Tanzanian-backed rebellion.
Mother Teresa awarded Nobel Peace Prize.
John McEnroe wins his first US Open men's tennis title.

1980 Indira Gandhi's Congress (I) Party returned to power in electoral landslide.
Rhodesia gains full independence as Zimbabwe; Robert Mugabe becomes first Prime Minister.
US President Jimmy Carter breaks off diplomatic relations with Iran.
Progressive Conservatives lose power in Canada; Trudeau once more Prime Minister.
Labour Party, led by Edward Seaga, wins power in Jamaican general election.
Milton Obote wins Uganda presidential election.
Independent trade union, Solidarity, formed in Poland.
Iran–Iraq War begins.
Ronald Reagan wins US presidential election.
Mount St Helen volcano erupts in Washington State.
Pope John Paul II visits Africa, Brazil, France and West Germany.

1981 South African commandos enter Angola's capital, Maputo, and kill twelve ANC members.
IRA hunger striker Bobby Sands dies in prison after sixty-six-day fast.
President Rahman of Bangladesh assassinated; succeeded by Vice-President Sattar.
Gambian President ousted, then restored; Gambia and Senegal

form confederation, Senegambia.

Belize and Antigua–Berbuda gain independence.

South African forces raid Angola in pursuit of Namibian SWAPO freedom fighters.

South African rugby tour of New Zealand provokes widespread demonstrations; over 1,000 arrested.

Socialist candidate François Mitterand wins French Presidency.

Salman Rushdie's *Midnight's Children* wins Booker Prize for Fiction.

Popular films include *Raiders of the Lost Ark, The French Lieutenant's Woman.*

1982 General Mohammed Ershad seizes power in Bangladesh.

Argentina's invasion of the Falkland Islands (the Malvinas) leads to their reconquest by Britain following the Falklands War.

Canada's Constitutional Act severs the last legal links with the United Kingdom.

President Kaunda of Zambia meets South African Prime Minister P.W. Botha and urges that Nelson Mandela and other ANC leaders be freed.

Salisbury, capital of Zimbabwe, renamed Harare.

Indian Army restores order in Bombay after police riots.

Canada protests at damage done to its forests by 'acid rain'.

Abuja named as Nigeria's new capital.

Two-thirds of Britain's elm trees destroyed by Dutch Elm disease.

'Rebel' cricket tour of South Africa results in fifteen English players being banned from the national team.

1983 Margaret Thatcher wins her second general election.

Nigeria expels 2 million Ghanain immigrant workers.

Labour, under Bob Hawke, wins Australian general election.

American troops invade Grenada after assassination of premier Maurice Bishop.

South Africa introduces new constitution with new assemblies for 'coloured' and Asian communities, but not for black Africans.

Bloodless coup in Nigeria puts Major General Buhari in power.

Northern Cyprus declares itself a republic.

Disturbances in Assam, north-east India, result in 5,000 deaths and mass flight of refugees.

Two-year drought in Ethiopia threatens millions of lives.

J.M. Coetzee wins Booker Prize with *The Life and Times of Michael K.*

Richard Attenborough's film *Gandhi* wins Oscar for best picture.

1984 Brunei becomes an independent sultanate and the 159th member state of the United Nations.

Sikh extremists driven from their occupation of the Golden Temple at Amritsar; many in the Sikh community alienated from the Indian government.

Mrs Gandhi assassinated by her Sikh bodyguards; succeeded as Prime Minister by her son Rajiv;

anti-Sikh riots result in over a thousand deaths.

Pierre Trudeau resigns as Canadian Prime Minister; Brian Mulroney and Progressive Conservatives win subsequent election.

British miners' strike begins.

Britain and China agree that Hong Kong will revert to China in 1997.

Maltese premier Dom Mintoff replaced by Carmello Bonnici.

IRA bomb at the Grand Hotel, Brighton, during Conservative Party Conference kills five and injures thirty-two.

Toxic leak of gas at Bhopal, India, kills over 2,500 people.

Apple Macintosh microcomputer launched.

1985 South African police kill eighteen peaceful demonstrators at Uitenhage on twenty-fifth anniversary of Sharpeville massacre; state of emergency declared in twenty-six districts; South Africa withdraws its forces from Angola.

Bernart St John succeeds Tom Adams as Prime Minister of Barbados.

Spain reopens its frontier with Gibraltar after sixteen years.

Zimbabwe general election results in victory for Robert Mugabe's ZANU party.

Ali Hassan succeeds Julius Nyerere as President of Tanzania.

Military coup in Uganda deposes Milton Obote.

Forbes Burnham, President of Guyana, dies; H.D. Hoyte takes over.

Bangladesh and Burma reach agreement in border dispute.

Mikhail Gorbachev comes to power in the Soviet Union.

UK and Irish Republic sign the Anglo–Irish Agreement giving the Republic a consultative role in the affairs of Northern Ireland.

Cyclone and tidal waves kill over 10,000 people in southern Bangladesh.

World Bank organises famine relief for African countries.

Hole discovered in the ozone layer over the North Pole.

British blood donations screened for AIDS virus.

1986 Ugandan insurgents capture Kampala and install Yoweri Museveni as President.

South African forces raid alleged ANC bases in Botswana, Zambia and Zimbabwe.

State of emergency declared in South Africa; mass arrests; European Community adopts sanctions.

After New Zealand closes its ports to American nuclear warships, Australia and the USA suspend their ANZUS security treaty with New Zealand.

London Stock Market is deregulated allowing computerised share dealings (the 'Big Bang').

World's worst nuclear power disaster at Chernobyl in the Ukraine.

Nigerian Wole Soyinka wins Nobel Prize for Literature.

1987 Margaret Thatcher wins third term of office in British general election.

Tamil freedom fighters clash

with Sri Lankan security forces.
Direct rule imposed in the
Punjab in attempt to control Sikh
separatists.
In Fiji Lieutenant-Colonel
Rabuka leads successful coup
against democratically elected
Indian–Fijian-dominated
government.
Erskine Sandiford becomes
Prime Minister of Barbados.
South Africa announces
withdrawal of its troops from
Angola where they had been
supporting the UNITA rebels.
Soviet President Gorbachev
advocates *glasnost* (openness) and
perestroika (reconstruction).
Reagan and Gorbachev sign
treaty to ban all short- and
medium-range nuclear weapons
in Europe.
Excavations begin on the
Channel tunnel between Britain
and France.
World share prices collapse in
'Black Monday' crash.
World population reaches 5
billion.

1988 USA and Canada sign
comprehensive free trade
agreement.
Ethiopia and Somalia sign
border peace treaty after eleven
years of conflict.
Soviet troops begin their
withdrawal from Afghanistan
after a presence of nine years.
Iran and Iraq begin UN-backed
peace talks.
Military coup in Burma after
General Ne Win resigns after
twenty-six years in power.
Angola, Cuba and South Africa
agree a ceasefire in Angola.
President Zia-al Haq, President

of Bangladesh for ten years,
killed when his plane crashes;
Benazir Bhutto wins subsequent
election.
Ranasinghe Premadasa elected
President of Sri Lanka.
Lockerbie air disaster kills 270
people.
British pound note ceases to be
legal tender.
Paul Kennedy publishes *The Rise
and Fall of the Great Powers*.
First screening of Australian
soap opera *Neighbours* on British
television.

1989 F.W. de Klerk becomes South
African President.
Michael Manley's People's
National Party wins power in
Jamaica.
Democratic elections in Namibia
won by SWAPO.
Pakistan rejoins the
Commonwealth after seventeen
years.
Senegal and Gambia dissolve
their confederation.
Walter Sithulu and seven other
ANC leaders released by South
African government.
V.P. Singh becomes Indian
Prime Minister after Congress
under Rajiv Gandhi loses
general election.
'Guildford Four' freed after
serving fourteen years in prison
for alleged IRA bombing
campaign.
Tiananmen Square
demonstrations and massacre in
Peking.
Complete ban on ivory trading
ratified worldwide.
Iranian authorities declare a
fatwa (a religious sentence of
death) upon the writer Salman

Rushdie for alleged blasphemy in his novel *The Satanic Verses*.

1990 Nelson Mandela freed after twenty-six years' imprisonment; de Klerk government begins the dismantling of apartheid state; ANC suspend their armed struggle.
Namibia achieves full independence.
Benazir Bhutto dismissed as premier by President of Pakistan.
Irish Republic elects Mary Robinson as its first woman President.
Lee Kuan Yew retires as Prime Minister of Singapore after thirty-one years in office.
Chandra Shekhar of the Janata Party becomes Prime Minister of India.
President Ershad of Bangladesh overthrown in military coup.
John Major succeeds Margaret Thatcher as British Prime Minister.
Iraqi invasion of Kuwait leads to the Gulf War.
Iran and Iraq resume diplomatic relations.
Mikhail Gorbachev awarded Nobel Peace Prize.

1991 In South Africa, President de Klerk commits his government to the abolition of apartheid; amnesty for political exiles declared; talks to establish the new constitution begin in December.
Indian Prime Minister Rajiv Gandhi assassinated; Sri Lankan Tamil Tigers suspected.
Paul Keating replaces Bob Hawke as Labour Prime Minister of Australia.
Ex-President Ershad of Bangladesh convicted on charges of corruption.
Twenty-eighth biennial Commonwealth Heads of Government Meeting issues a Commonwealth Declaration committing members to the promotion of democracy and to 'the rule of law, the independence of the judiciary and to just and honest government'. The meeting also agrees to lift sanctions against South Africa.
'Birmingham Six', convicted after an IRA bombing incident in 1974, are released.
Many sub-Saharan countries face famine; United Nations World Food Programme estimates that up to 20 million Africans are dependent on emergency food aid.
International agreement signed in Madrid bans mining in Antarctica for fifty years.

1992 Continuing violent clashes between government forces and rebel Tamil Tigers in Sri Lanka.
Tanzania proposes economic cooperation with Kenya and Uganda.
Ugandan government offers compensation to South Asians forced out by Idi Amin.
Constitutional talks in South Africa continue.
Assam rebels continue their military struggle with the Indian authorities.
Opening of Nigerian National Assembly postponed; widespread rioting; authorities accused of

corruption; some Muslim fundamentalists arrested.
Opposition leaders arrested in Kenya; inter-tribal conflict.
Pakistan government first denies, then admits that it is capable of producing nuclear weapons; later purchases a nuclear power plant from China.

1993 Australian Labour government returned; land law passed acknowledging Aboriginals' right to certain lands.
Indian premier accused of corruption; communal riots and bombings in Bombay.
South African Communist Party leader Chris Harni assassinated; substantial progress made in constitutional talks.
British and Irish premiers sign the 'Downing Street Declaration' setting out the general principles for holding peace talks on Northern Ireland.
Canadian Liberal Party wins a landslide election victory over the Progressive Conservative government.
US President Bill Clinton dogged by accusations of extra-marital sexual activities and financial irregularities.
Russian voters approve President Boris Yeltsin's controversial proposed constitution.
British geological survey announces the presence of a considerable oilfield within a 200-mile radius of the Falkland Islands.

1994 First South African democratic general election won by the ANC, leading to Nelson Mandela's installation as President.
Fighting breaks out between rival army factions in Lesotho.
British government accused of improper behaviour over funding the Pergau Dam in Malaysia.
Prince of Wales visits Australia amid growing agitation for a republic; Prime Minister of New Zealand also floats idea of the country becoming a republic.
Disastrous cyclone hits Bangladesh.
Food shortages and strike by oil workers in Nigeria.
Congress (I) Party humiliated in Indian local elections.
IRA announces the cessation of military operations; British government and Sinn Fein representatives hold first open talks in Belfast.
Hebron massacre in Israel seen as an attempt by diehard Jewish settlers to destabilise the Israeli–Palestinian peace process.

1995 Controversy in South Africa over indemnities from prosecution granted to certain former ministers and police officers.
Malawi's former President, Hastings Banda, arrested on charges of murder.
Widespread civil violence in Sierra Leone.
Coup attempt foiled in the Gambia.
Trial by jury abolished in Malaysia.
Continuing political unrest in Bangladesh.
In New Zealand demonstrations over the government's plans for

the final settlement of outstanding Maori land claims.
Collapse of Barings bank.
Former President Kaunda of Zambia is arrested and charged with holding an illegal political meeting.
Winnie Mandela dismissed from South African government; Queen Elizabeth II officially visits the country and bestows the Order of Merit upon President Mandela.
Controversy in Australia over the federal government's 1993 Native Titles' Act enabling Aborigines to reclaim, under certain conditions, 'native land'.
Continuing conflict in Sri Lanka between authorities and Tamil Tigers.
Split in India's Congress I Party and renewed tension in Kashmir.
In Kenya, conservationist and scientist Richard Leakey helps found a new political party and accuses President Daniel arap Moi of mismanagement and corruption.
Plans announced in Australia to hold referendum on move to a republic before end of century; republic could be proclaimed in 2001 – the centenary of the establishment of the Commonwealth of Australia.
Bermuda votes against independence from British rule in referendum.
World outcry at the Chirac government's resumption of nuclear testing at Muruoa Atoll in French Polynesia.

Speculation that Britain and Argentina are about to sign a joint oil exploration agreement in disputed Falkland waters.
Quebec narrowly votes against independence.
Nigeria suspended from the Commonwealth after its military govenment executes writer Ken Saro-Wiwa and eight other environmental activists.

1996 Military coup in Sierra Leone; civil rule later restored.
Tamil separatists bomb Colombo's commercial centre.
France halts nuclear tests in the Pacific.
Sri Lanka wins cricket's World Cup.
Bangladesh election results disputed.
London bombing ends IRA ceasefire.
Continuing high-level talks over future of Hong Kong.
National Party withdraws from South African government.
Commonwealth foreign ministers impose embargo on arms sales to Nigeria.
Robert Mugabe re-elected President of Zimbabwe.
Imran Khan launches Justice Movement in Pakistan.
BSE ('mad cow disease') devastates British beef industry.
Congress I defeated in Indian general election.
State visit of Nelson Mandela to the UK.
Death of Lt Colonel Mitchell, 'Mad Mitch' of Aden Crater incident.

NOTES

Chapter 1:
ANATOMY OF AN EMPIRE

1 L. Colley, *Britons: Forging the Nation 1710–1837* (1992), p. 123.
2 C. Hill, *The World Turned Upside Down: Radical Ideas During the English Revolution* (1980 edition), p. 384.
3 K. Robbins, 'British Culture versus British Industry', in B. Collins and K. Robbins (eds), *British Culture and Economic Decline* (1990), p. 21.
4 R. Blake, *The Decline of British Power* (1985), p. 421.
5 P.J. Marshall, 'An Agenda for the History of Imperial Britain', unpublished conference paper, p. 17; see also the same author's Creighton Lecture, 1994.
6 A.J.P. Taylor, *English History, 1914–45* (1965), p. 600.

Chapter 2:
THE AMERICAN REVOLUTION

1 American Declaration of Independence, Thomas Jefferson, 4 July 1776. See M.D. Peterson (ed.), *Thomas Jefferson: Writings* (1984), p. 19.
2 See for example C.A. Bayly, *Imperial Meridian: The British Empire and the World, 1780–1839* (1989).
3 R. Hyam, *Britain's Imperial Century, 1815–1914* (new edition, 1993), p. 1.
4 J. Kenyon, *The English Civil Wars* (1988), p. 232.
5 D.K. Fieldhouse, *The Colonial Empires: A Comparative Survey from the Eighteenth Century* (2nd edition, 1982), p. 112.
6 R. Coupland, *The American Revolution and the British Empire* (1930), pp. 12–14.

7 J. Ehrman, *The Younger Pitt*, vol. 1 (new edition, 1986), p. 476.
8 M.E. Chamberlain, *Pax Britannica: British Foreign Policy 1789–1914* (1988), pp. 22–3.
9 D. Judd, *Palmerston* (1975), pp. 7–9.
10 R. Robinson and J. Gallagher, 'The Imperialism of Free Trade, 1814–1915', *Economic History Review*, 2nd series, VI, 2, 1953.
11 Bayly, op. cit., p. 100.

Chapter 3:
AUSTRALIA

1 *Parliamentary History*, vol. 28, pp. 1222–4, quoted in R. Hughes, *The Fatal Shore* (1988 edition), p. 108.
2 See W.J. Lines, *Taming the Great South Land: A History of the Conquest of Nature in Australia* (1994).
3 See Hughes, op. cit., Chapter 8.
4 R. Hyam, *Empire and Sexuality: The British Experience* (1991), p. 102.
5 Ibid.
6 Lines, op. cit.
7 M. Gilmore, 'Old Botany Bay' (1918).
8 A. Mellish, 'A Convict's Recollections of New South Wales, Written by Himself', *London Magazine*, vol. 2 (1825), p. 51.

Chapter 4:
IRELAND

1 Bayly, op. cit., pp. 77–85.
2 Ibid., p. 82
3 R. Kipling, 'Shillin' a Day', *Rudyard Kipling's Verse: The Definitive Edition* (1949), p. 429.
4 W.E.H. Lecky, *Democracy and Liberty*, vol. 2 (1899), pp. 390–1.
5 D. Judd, *Radical Joe: A Life of Joseph*

Chamberlain (1993 edition),
pp. 97–120.
6 *Hansard Parliamentary Debates*, ser. 3,
vol. 305, 10 May 1886, col. 186.
7 Hyam, *Britain's Imperial Century*,
op. cit., p. 169.

Chapter 5:
CANADA

1 See G. Lanctot, *Canada and the
American Revolution* (1967).
2 P. Burroughs, *The Canadian Crisis and
British Imperial Policy, 1828–41* (1972),
pp. 94–5.
3 See G. Martin, *The Durham Report and
British Policy: A Critical Essay* (1972).
4 J.L. Finlay and D.N. Sprague, *The
Structure of Canadian History* (1979),
pp. 130–4.
5 Hyam, *Britain's Imperial Century*,
op. cit., p. 69.
6 N. Macdonald, *Canada: Immigration
and Colonisation, 1841–1903* (1966),
pp. 73–4.
7 D. Creighton, *Canada's First Century*
(1976 edition), Chapter 1.
8 Finlay and Sprague, op. cit.,
pp. 169–72.

Chapter 6:
THE REPEAL OF THE CORN LAWS
IN 1846

1 Hyam, *Britain's Imperial Century*,
op. cit., p. 30.
2 Ibid.
3 *Hansard Parliamentary Debates*, LX, 27
January 1842.
4 B.R. Mitchell and P. Deane, *Abstract
of British Historical Statistics* (1962),
pp. 191–3.
5 Hyam, *Britain's Imperial Century*,
op. cit., p. 26.
6 Mitchell and Deane, *Abstract:
Statistical Abstract of the United Kingdom*,
quoted in P.J. Cain and A.J.
Hopkins, *British Imperialism*, Vol. 1,
Innovation and Expansion, 1688–1914
(1993), p. 164.
7 Cain and Hopkins, vol. 1, op. cit.,
p. 223.

Chapter 7:
THE GREAT INDIAN UPRISING OF
1857–58

1 D. Judd, *The Victorian Empire* (1970),
p. 84.
2 Ibid., p. 90.
3 G. Moorhouse, *India Britannica*
(1983), p. 114.
4 *Manchester Guardian*, 6 February 1858.
5 G. Trevelyan, *The Competition Wallah*
(1895).
6 S. Chakravarty, *The Raj Syndrome: A
Study in Imperial Perceptions* (1989),
p. 50.
7 E.M. Forster, *A Passage to India*
(1924), p. 79 (1936 edition).
8 Curzon to Balfour, 31 March 1901,
British Library, B.L. Add. Mss.
49732.
9 Trevelyan, op. cit.
10 J.C. Maitland, *Letters from Madras: By
a Lady* (1843).
11 Lieutenant Majendie, *Up Among the
Pandies* (1859).

Chapter 8:
THE JAMAICA REBELLION OF 1865

1 Judd, *The Victorian Empire*, op. cit.,
p. 103.
2 Hyam, *Britain's Imperial Century*,
op. cit., p. 151.
3 J. Walvin, *Black Ivory: A History of
British Slavery* (1993 edition), p. 325.
4 T. Walrond (ed.), *Letters and Journal
of James, Eighth Earl of Elgin* (1872),
pp. 2–7.
5 T. Carlyle, 'Discourse on the Nigger
Question', *Critical and Miscellaneous
Essays*, vol. 7 (1872).
6 S.W. Baker, *The Albert N'yanza*, vol. 1
(1866 and 1962), p. 288.
7 F. Kingsley (ed.), *Charles Kingsley:
His Letters and Memories of his Life*, vol.
2 (1877), pp. 242–3.
8 J. Birchall, *Co-Op: The People's
Business* (1994).
9 M. Craton, *Testing the Chains* (1982),
pp. 100–1.
10 Ibid., pp. 136–7.
11 See G. Heuman, *The Killing Time: The
Morant Bay Rebellion in Jamaica*
(1994).
12 Ibid.

13 J.S. Mill, *Autobiography* (1963 edition), pp. 169–70.
14 C. Bolt, *Victorian Attitudes Towards Race* (1971), p. 77.

Chapter 9:
THE OPENING OF THE SUEZ CANAL
IN 1869

1 Afaf Lufti Al-Sayyid Marsot, *A Short History of Modern Egypt* (1985), p. 68.
2 J. Pudney, *Suez: De Lesseps' Canal* (1968), pp. 3–4.
3 Hyam, *Britain's Imperial Century*, op. cit., pp. 35–6.
4 Ibid., Chapter 2.
5 J. Marlowe, *The Making of the Suez Canal* (1964), pp. 75–7.
6 Pudney, op. cit., pp. 103–5.
7 Marsot, op. cit., p. 69.
8 Cain and Hopkins, vol. 1, op. cit., p. 365; see also H.C.G. Matthew (ed.), *The Gladstone Diaries*, vols 10 and 11 (1990), p.lxxii.
9 P. Magnus, *Gladstone* (1960 edition), p. 290.
10 A. Ghosh, *In an Antique Land* (1994 edition), p. 91.
11 G.N. Sanderson, *England, Europe and the Upper Nile, 1882–1899* (1965), p. 16.
12 R. Garrett, *General Gordon* (1974), pp. 194–6.
13 For a first-hand account of the Battle of Omdurman, see W.S. Churchill, *My Early Life: A Roving Commission* (1990 edition), Chapters 14 and 15.
14 D. Bates, *The Fashoda Incident of 1898: Encounter on the Nile* (1984), pp. 180–1.
15 P.M. Holt, *A Modern History of the Sudan* (1961), pp. 109–12.

Chapter 10:
THE BATTLE OF MAJUBA HILL

1 D. Judd, *Someone Has Blundered: Calamities of the British Army During the Victorian Age* (1973), p. 143.
2 J.D. MacCrone, *Race Attitudes in South Africa* (1937), p. 126.
3 J. Bird, *The Annals of Natal*, vol. 1 (1965), p. 504.
4 *Manchester Guardian*, 23 September 1876.
5 R. Herbert, Colonial Office official,

31 May 1871, quoted in R. Robinson and J. Gallagher, *Africa and the Victorians* (1965 edition), p. 59.
6 Quoted in N. Mansergh, *The Commonwealth Experience*, vol. 2 (1982 edition), p. 69.
7 A. Porter, 'Britain, the Cape Colony and Natal, 1870–1914: Capital, Shipping and the Colonial Connection', *Economic History Review*, 2nd series, XXXIV, 1981.
8 S. Jones (ed.), *Banking and Business in South Africa* (1988); see also Cain and Hopkins, vol. 1, op. cit., p. 371.
9 Gladstone to Kruger, 15 June 1880, British Library, Gladstone Papers, B.L. Add. Mss. 4464; J. Lehmann, *The First Boer War* (1972)

Chapter 11:
CECIL RHODES' LEGACY

1 B. Roberts, *Cecil Rhodes and the Princess* (1969), p. 46.
2 Cain and Hopkins, vol. 1, op. cit., p. 46.
3 Roberts, op. cit., pp. 43–4.
4 J. Ruskin, Inaugural Lecture, Oxford University, 1870.
5 Roberts, op. cit., pp. 236–8.
6 *Rudyard Kipling's Verse: The Definitive Edition*, op. cit., p. 414.
7 Judd, *The Victorian Empire*, op. cit., p. 210.
8 Cain and Hopkins, vol. 1, op. cit., pp. 381–2.
9 *Hansard Parliamentary Debates*, ser. 4, vol. 67, 24 February 1899, col. 517.

Chapter 12:
QUEEN VICTORIA'S DIAMOND
JUBILEE, 1897

1 C. Chapman and P. Roben (eds), *Debrett's Queen Victoria's Jubilees, 1887 and 1897* (1977).
2 J. Morris, *Pax Britannica: Climax of an Empire* (1979 edition), p. 28.
3 Ibid., p. 34.
4 Ibid., p. 31.
5 *Daily Graphic*, 25 June 1897.
6 *Daily Mail*, 23 June 1897.
7 *Labour Leader*, 19 June 1897.
8 *Rudyard Kipling's Verse: The Definitive Edition*, op. cit., p. 328.

9 *Irish Times*, 27 May 1995.
10 Ibid.
11 *The Times*, 1 January and 23 January 1901; see also D. Read, *Edwardian England* (1972), pp. 13–14.
12 C.W. Boyd (ed.), *Mr Chamberlain's Speeches*, vol. 1 (1914), p. 321.
13 *Rudyard Kipling's Verse: The Definitive Edition*, op. cit., pp. 323–4.

Chapter 13:
THE BATTLE OF SPION KOP, 1900

1 B. Dugdale, *Arthur James Balfour*, vol. 1 (1936), pp. 306–7.
2 Quoted in D. Judd, *The Boer War* (1977), p. 83.
3 'The Absent-Minded Beggar', *Rudyard Kipling's Verse: The Definitive Edition*, op. cit., p. 459.
4 J. Wilson, *A Life of Sir Henry Campbell-Bannerman* (1973), p. 349.
5 D.M. Schreuder, *The Scramble for Southern Africa* (1980), pp. 192–6.
6 Selborne to Joseph Chamberlain, 18 October 1896, Selborne Papers, Bodleian Library.
7 Judd, *Radical Joe: A Life of Joseph Chamberlain*, op. cit., p. 199.
8 PRO., Cabinet Papers, Cab. 37/49/29.
9 J.S. Marais, *The Fall of Kruger's Republic* (1961), p. 318.
10 Cain and Hopkins, vol. 1, op. cit., p. 273.
11 *Rudyard Kipling's Verse: The Definitive Edition*, op. cit., pp. 299–300.
12 *Hansard Parliamentary Debates*, ser. 4, vol. 148, 26 June 1905, cols. 191–202.
13 D. Judd, *Lord Reading* (1982), pp. 42–3.

Chapter 14:
THE SUICIDE OF SIR HECTOR MACDONALD, 1903

1 See T. Royle, *Death Before Dishonour: The True Story of Fighting Mac* (1982), pp. 119–32, and Hyam, *Empire and Sexuality*, op. cit., pp. 34–5.
2 Hyam, *Empire and Sexuality*, op. cit., p. 33.
3 C. Chevenix Trench, *Charley Gordon: An Eminent Victorian Reassessed* (1978), pp. 63–4.

4 G. Faber, *Jowett: A Portrait with Background* (1957), pp. 83–100.
5 Balfour to Curzon, 12 December 1902, British Library, B.L. Add. Mss. 49732.
6 See N. Goradia, *Lord Curzon: The Last of the British Mughals* (1993).
7 Hyam, *Empire and Sexuality*, op. cit., p. 59.
8 B.B. Gilbert, *The Evolution of National Insurance in Great Britain* (1966), p. 72.
9 E. Sellon, *The Ups and Downs of Life* (1867), p. 42.
10 A. Flexner, *Prostitution in Europe* (1914), pp. 374–5.
11 R. Hyam, 'Concubinage and the Colonial Service: The Crewe Circular (1909)', *Journal of Imperial and Commonwealth History*, XIV (1986), pp. 170–86.
12 A. Gill, *Ruling Passions: Race, Sex and Empire* (1995), p. 74.
13 Ibid., p. 75.
14 Ibid., p. 43.
15 See J.F. Fanpel, *African Holocaust: The Story of the Uganda Martyrs* (1965), and J.A. Rowl, 'The Purge of Christians at Mwanga's Court', *Journal of African History*, V (1964), pp. 55–71.
16 Hyam, *Empire and Sexuality*, op. cit., p. 193.
17 Ibid., p. 215.
18 Ibid., p. 214.
19 See Gill, op. cit.

Chapter 15:
JOSEPH CHAMBERLAIN AND THE CABINET SPLIT OF 1903

1 *The Times*, 16 May 1903.
2 A.M. Gollin, *Balfour's Burden* (1965), p. 38.
3 R. Jenkins, *Asquith* (1964), p. 137.
4 Dugdale, *Arthur James Balfour*, vol. 1, op. cit., p. 345.
5 Churchill, *My Early Life*, op. cit., pp. 384–5.
6 T.E. Kebbel (ed.), *Selected Speeches of the Late Rt. Hon. the Earl of Beaconsfield*, vol. 2, (1882), pp. 223–4.
7 Cain and Hopkins, vol. 1, op. cit., pp. 223–4.
8 C.W. Boyd (ed.), *Mr Chamberlain's Speeches*, vol. 2 (1914), p. 428.

9 Ibid., pp. 462–6.
10 Judd, *Radical Joe: A Life of Joseph Chamberlain*, op. cit., p. 255.
11 Boyd, vol. 2, op. cit., p. 485.
12 Correspondence between Chamberlain and Robert Giffen, 4 October, 2 November, 4 December 1903, Birmingham University Library, Chamberlain Papers, JC L., Add. 49a, 50a, 53a.
13 Mitchell and Deane, *Abstract of British Historical Statistics*, op. cit., and *Statistical Abstracts of the United Kingdom*, HMSO.
14 *The Times*, 15 February 1906.

Chapter 16:
SCOUTING FOR BOYS, 1908

1 T. Jeal, *Baden-Powell* (1989), p. 396.
2 R. Baden-Powell, *Scouting for Boys* (1908).
3 Ibid.
4 Jeal, op. cit., p. 391.
5 Read, op. cit., p. 245.
6 Baden-Powell, op. cit.
7 Jeal, op. cit., p. 443.
8 Hyam, *Britain's Imperial Century*, op. cit., p. 189.
9 Queen Victoria to Lord Lansdowne, 12 August 1892, quoted in T. Wodehouse Legh, *Lord Lansdowne* (1929), p. 100.
10 Read, op. cit., p. 150.
11 H.G. Wells, *An Englishman Looks at the World* (1914).
12 *The Times*, 13 May 1904.
13 G. Wolseley, *The Story of a Soldier's Life*, vol. 2 (1903), p. 2.
14 Baden-Powell, op. cit., 'Camp Fire Yarn No. 26. Our Empire: How it grew – how it must be held'.
15 Read, op. cit., pp. 163–5.
16 P. Horn, 'English Elementary Education and the Growth of the Imperial Ideal: 1880–1914', in J.A. Mangan (ed.), *Benefits Bestowed?: Education and British Imperialism* (1988), pp. 48–51.
17 See J. Mackenzie (ed.), *Imperialism and Popular Culture* (1986); Mangan, op. cit.; V. Chancellor, *History for Their Masters: Opinion in the English School Textbook, 1800–1914* (1970).

18 G.T. Warner, *A Brief Survey of British History* (1899), pp. 248–9.
19 C.R.L. Fletcher and R. Kipling, *A School History of England* (1911), pp. 239–40.
20 A.B.C. Merriman Labor, *Britain Through Negro Spectacles* (1905), quoted in Mackenzie, *Imperialism and Popular Culture*, op. cit., p. 105.
21 W.S. Adams, *Edwardian Portraits* (1965), p. 109.
22 R. Kipling, *Puck of Pook's Hill* (1905), p. 306.
23 *The Boys of the Nation*, 5 September and 31 October 1895.
24 R. Roberts, *A Ragged Schooling: Growing up in the Classic Slum* (1984 edition), pp. 127–8.

Chapter 17:
THE IMPERIAL CONFERENCE OF 1911

1 A.B. Keith (ed.), *Selected Speeches and Documents on British Colonial History, 1763–1917* (1961), p. 271.
2 Lord Rosebery, speech in Adelaide, 18 January 1884.
3 A.J. Balfour, 'Cobden and the Manchester School', review of J. Morley's *Life of Cobden, Nineteenth Century*, January 1882.
4 'Our Lady of the Snows', *Rudyard Kipling's Verse: The Definitive Edition*, op. cit., pp. 182–3.
5 Hyam, *Britain's Imperial Century*, op. cit., p. 237.
6 Lewis Harcourt Papers, 'Suggested Reconstruction of the Colonial Office', draft memo, April 1911, quoted in Hyam, *Britain's Imperial Century*, op. cit., pp. 236–7.
7 Judd, *The Victorian Empire*, op. cit., p. 127.
8 Draft Circular Dispatch to the Governors of the Self-Governing Colonies, 7 December 1904, British Library, B.L. Add. Mss. 49698.
9 D. Judd, *Balfour and the British Empire* (1968) p. 310.
10 *The Times*, 18 May 1906.
11 Balfour to Edward VII, 15 April 1901, British Library, B.L. Add. Mss. 49683.

12 K. Young, *Arthur James Balfour* (1965), p. 277.
13 Balfour to Edward VII, op. cit.

Chapter 18:
THE GANDHI–SMUTS AGREEMENT
OF JANUARY 1914

1 W.K. Hancock, *Smuts: The Sanguine Years, 1870–1919* (1962), p. 345.
2 See E. Said, *Orientalism* (1978) and *Culture and Imperialism* (1993); see also an alternative view in J. Mackenzie, *Orientalism: History, Theory and the Arts* (1995).
3 'The Widow's Party', *Rudyard Kipling's Verse: The Definitive Edition*, op. cit., p. 422.
4 N. Mandela, *Long Walk to Freedom* (1994), p. 13.
5 G.K. Chesterton, *The Defendant* (1901).
6 Quoted in Read, op. cit., p. 147.
7 Judd, *Balfour and the British Empire*, op. cit., p. 203.
8 Wells, 'Will the Empire Live?', in *An Englishman Looks at the World*, op. cit.
9 J.A. Hobson, *Imperialism: A Study* (1902), Part I, chapters 4 and 5.
10 H.N. Brailsford, *The War of Steel and Gold* (1915 edition), pp. 79–82.
11 S.R. Wasti, *Lord Minto and the Indian Nationalist Movement, 1905–1910* (1964), and D. Judd and P. Slinn, *The Evolution of the Modern Commonwealth, 1902–80* (1982), p. 35.
12 D. Kimble, *A Political History of Ghana*, vol. 1, *The Rise of Gold Coast Nationalism, 1928–1950* (1963), p. 67.
13 *Hansard Parliamentary Debates*, ser. 4, vol. 162, 31 July 1906, col. 798–800.
14 Curzon to Balfour, 31 March 1901, British Library, B.L. Add. Mss. 49732.
15 Hyam, *Britain's Imperial Century*, op. cit., p. 198.

Chapter 19:
THE 1916 EASTER UPRISING IN IRELAND

1 F.S. Lyons, *Ireland Since the Famine* (1985 edition), pp. 369–70.
2 See C. Haste, *Keep the Home Fires Burning* (1977).
3 E.A. Benians, J. Butler and C.E.

Carrington (eds), *Cambridge History of the British Empire*, vol. 3 (1959), pp. 641–2.
4 Ibid., p. 642.
5 Cain and Hopkins, vol. 1, op. cit., p. 450.
6 M.V. Brett (ed.), *Journals and Letters of Reginald, Viscount Esher*, vol. 2 (1934), p. 267, quoted in Cain and Hopkins, vol. 1, op. cit., p. 456.
7 Benians, Butler and Carrington, op. cit., p. 605.
8 J. Morris, *Farewell the Trumpets: An Imperial Retreat* (1979 edition), p. 245.
9 Lord Ronaldshay, *Life of Lord Curzon*, vol. 3 (1928), p. 168.
10 *The Times*, 18 November 1920.
11 L.S. Amery, *My Political Life*, vol. 2 (1953), p. 110.
12 Parlt. Command Papers, Cd. 8566, Resolution 9, 1917.
13 Memorandum by L.S. Amery, 14 November 1920, British Library, B.L. Add. Mss. 49775.
14 Ibid.
15 Cain and Hopkins, vol. 2, op. cit., p. 59.
16 M. Beloff, *Imperial Sunset* (1969), p. 178.

Chapter 20:
THE AMRITSAR MASSACRE OF 1919

1 P. Moon, *The British Conquest and Dominion of India* (1989), pp. 991–4.
2 M. Diver, *Far to Seek* (1921).
3 *Allahabad Pioneer*, 5 May 1905.
4 M. Diver, *Far to Seek* (1921).
5 *Madras Mail*, 23 April 1915.
6 K. Natrajan, *The Indian Social Reformer* (1915).
7 M. Newman, *Harold Laski: A Political Biography* (1993), p. 118.
8 Cain and Hopkins, *British Imperialism: Crisis and Deconstruction, 1914–1990*, vol. 2 (1993), pp. 174–7.
9 R.A. (Lord) Butler, *The Art of the Possible* (1971), p. 16.
10 M. Hyde, *Lord Reading* (1967), p. 353, quoted in Judd, *Lord Reading*, op. cit., p. 205.
11 Judd, *Lord Reading*, op. cit., pp. 218–20.

12 See G. Peele, 'A Note on Lord Irwin's Declaration', *Journal of Imperial and Commonwealth History*, I (1972–3), p. 331.
13 Ibid.
14 R. Rhodes James, *Churchill: A Study in Failure* (1970), p. 202.
15 D.A. Low, *Lion Rampant: Essays in the Study of British Imperialism* (1973), p. 161.
16 H. Macmillan, *The Winds of Change, 1914–1939* (1966), p. 318.
17 Rhodes James, op. cit., p. 202.
18 Judd and Slinn, op. cit., p. 61.
19 Morris, *Farewell the Trumpets*, op. cit., p. 298.

Chapter 21:
THE 1924 BRITISH EMPIRE WEMBLEY EXHIBITION

1 'Pageant of Empire' programme, 1924, Cricklewood Library Archives, London Borough of Brent.
2 Judd and Slinn, op. cit., p. 61.
3 H. Duncan Hall, *Commonwealth: A History of the British Commonwealth of Nations* (1971), p. 393.
4 Ibid., p. 365.
5 A.B. Keith (ed.), *Speeches and Documents on the British Dominions, 1918–1931* (1932), p. 318.
6 See Cain and Hopkins, vol. 2, op. cit., pp. 36–9.
7 Ibid.
8 *Hansard Parliamentary Debates*, ser. 5, vol. 187, 1925, col. 84.
9 Judd and Slinn, op. cit., p. 49.
10 K. Rose, *King George V* (1983), pp. 360, 401.
11 Royal Archives N.293, quoted in H. Nicolson, *King George V* (1952).

Chapter 22:
THE BALFOUR DEFINITION OF DOMINION STATUS, 1926

1 Keith, op. cit., p. 161.
2 Amery, vol. 2, op. cit., p. 381.
3 *The Times*, 29 May 1926.
4 R.M. Dawson, *The Development of Dominion Status* (1937), p. 104.
5 P.R.O. Cab. 32/56, 27 October 1926.
6 Amery, vol. 2, op. cit., p. 384.
7 Duncan Hall, op. cit., p. 637.

8 W.S. Churchill, speech in House of Commons, 20 November 1931; see Keith, op. cit., p. 274.
9 Dawson, op. cit., p. 74.
10 Ibid.
11 *Hansard Parliamentary Debates*, ser. 5, vol. 62, 24 November 1925, cols. 844-5.
12 D. Carlton, 'The Dominions and British Foreign Policy in the Abyssinia Crisis', *Journal of Imperial and Commonwealth History*, I (1972–3), p. 59.
13 Duncan Hall, op. cit., p. 755.
14 R.W.D. Boyce, 'America, Britain and the Triumph of Imperial Protectionism in Britain, 1929–30', *Millenium*, 3 (1974), p. 63.
15 J.B.D. Miller, *Britain and the Old Dominions* (1966), p. 63.
16 Cain and Hopkins, vol. 2, op. cit., p. 110.
17 Ibid., p. 6.
18 Quoted in Judd and Slinn, op. cit., p. 69.

Chapter 23:
THE BODYLINE TOUR OF AUSTRALIA, 1932

1 See R. Sissons and B. Stoddart, *Cricket and Empire* (1984), and L. Le Quesne, *The Bodyline Controversy* (1983).
2 R. Holt, *Sport and the British: A Modern History* (1992 edition), pp. 234–5.
3 Ibid.
4 B. Stoddart, 'Cricket's Imperial Crisis: The 1932 MCC Tour of Australia', in C. McKernan, *Sport in History: The Making of Modern Sporting History* (1974), p. 132.
5 Reading to Buller, 1 March 1924, IOL, Reading Papers, Eur. F 116/56/117.
6 R. Kircher, *Fair Play* (1928), p. 13, quoted in R. Holt, *Sport and Society in Modern France* (1981), p. 63.
7 S. Leslie, *Studies in Sublime Failure* (1932), p. 256; see also Hyam, *Britain's Imperial Century*, op. cit., pp. 295–6.
8 Hyam, *Britain's Imperial Century*, op. cit., p. 295.

9 Holt, *Sport and the British*, op. cit., p. 217.
10 Judd and Slinn, op. cit., p. 108.
11 Holt, *Sport and the British*, op. cit., p. 217.
12 C.L.R. James, *Beyond a Boundary* (1963), p. 38.
13 M. Bose, *A History of Indian Cricket* (1988), p. 17.
14 Ibid.
15 Holt, *Sport and the British*, op. cit., p. 250.

Chapter 24:
THE FALL OF SINGAPORE, FEBRUARY 1942

1 C. Thorne, *Allies of a Kind: The United States, Britain and the War against Japan, 1941–45* (1978), p. 206.
2 Judd, *Balfour and the British Empire*, op. cit., p. 89.
3 Mansergh, op. cit., p. 286.
4 Ibid., p. 94; see also D.W. Harkness, *The Reluctant Dominion* (1969).
5 See W.K. Hancock, *Smuts*, vol. 2, (1968); R.W. Kruger, *The Making of a Nation: The Union of South Africa, 1910–61* (1969); Harkness, op. cit.
6 H.V. Hodson, *The Great Divide* (1969).
7 D. Reynolds, *Britannia Overruled: British Policy and World Power in the Twentieth Century* (1991), pp. 152–3.
8 R.J. Moore, *Churchill, Cripps and India* (1979).
9 See E.H.W. Lumby and N. Mansergh (eds), *Constitutional Relations Between Britain and India: The Transfer of Power, 1942–7*, vol. 2, *Quit India* (1971).
10 Reynolds, op. cit., p. 150.
11 See R.L. Louis, *Imperialism at Bay: The United States and the Decolonization of the British Empire, 1941–45* (1978).
12 R.S. Sayers, *Financial Policy, 1939–45* (1956).
13 B.R. Tomlinson, *The Political Economy of the Raj* (1979), p. 140.
14 Cain and Hopkins, vol. 2, op. cit., p. 7.

Chapter 25:
THE PARTITION OF INDIA, 1947

1 *Nehru's Speeches*, vol. 1, 1946–9 (1949), pp. 42–4.
2 Curzon to Balfour, 31 March 1901,
British Library, B.L. Add. Mss. 49732.
3 *Hansard Parliamentary Debates*, 9 July 1946, col. 343, quoted in S. Howe, *Anticolonialism in British Politics: The Left and the End of Empire, 1918–64* (1993), p. 144.
4 C. Cross, *The Fall of the British Empire* (1968), p. 262.
5 *The Times*, 12 January 1946.
6 Howe, op. cit., p. 147.
7 M. Barratt Brown, *After Imperialism* (1963), p. 294.
8 See Louis, op. cit., and Thorne, op. cit.
9 See C. Barnett, *The Lost Victory: British Dreams, British Realities, 1945–50* (1995).
10 B. Porter, *The Lion's Share: A Short History of British Imperialism, 1850–1970* (1975), p. 320.
11 Howe, op. cit., p. 145.
12 R.D. Pearce, *The Turning Point in Africa: British Colonial Policy 1938–48* (1982), p. 92.
13 Howe, op. cit., p. 146.
14 M.J. Akbar, *Nehru: The Making of India* (1988), p. 366.
15 M. Edwardes, *Nehru: A Political Biography* (1971 edition), p. 169.
16 *Bombay Chronicle*, 8 July 1946.
17 P. Ziegler, *Mountbatten: The Official Biography* (1984), pp. 473–4.
18 W. Buchan, *Kumari* (1955).
19 Akbar, op. cit., p. 408.
20 See Lumby and Mansergh, op. cit.
21 Declaration of London: Final Communiqué of the Prime Ministers' Meeting, 1949.
22 P. Gordon Walker, *The Commonwealth* (1962), p. 315.
23 See D. Austin, *Politics in Ghana, 1946–60* (1964).
24 Howe, op. cit., p. 327.
25 Cross, op. cit., p. 272.

Chapter 26:
THE TRIAL OF JOMO KENYATTA, 1953

1 B. Lapping, *End of Empire* (1985), p. 425; see also M. Slater, *The Trial of Jomo Kenyatta* (1955).

2 Cain and Hopkins, vol. 2, op. cit., p. 221.
3 Howe, op. cit., p. 66, and J. Murray-Brown, *Kenyatta* (1974), pp. 352–4.
4 Lapping, op. cit., p. 416.
5 Quoted in ibid., p. 421.
6 Ibid., p. 422.
7 Viscount Chandos, *The Memoirs of Lord Chandos* (1962), p. 394.
8 H. Macmillan, *Pointing the Way, 1959–61* (1961), pp. 116–17.
9 Chandos, op. cit., p. 355.
10 Black Stalin, 'Carribean Unity: A Calypso' (1979).
11 *Hansard Parliamentary Debates*, ser. 5, vol. 531, col. 509.

Chapter 27:
THE SUEZ CRISIS OF 1956

1 Cross, op. cit., p. 316.
2 Ibid., p. 323.
3 P. Kennedy, *The Rise and Fall of the Great Powers* (1988), p. 504.
4 1951 Conservative Election Manifesto, 'Britain Strong and Free'.
5 Quoted in A. Horne, *Macmillan, 1957–1986* (1989), pp. 194–5.
6 D. Goldsworthy, *Colonial Issues in British Politics, 1945–1961* (1971), p. 361.
7 *Annual Abstract of Statistics, 1969* and *1983*, quoted in B. Porter, op. cit., p. 359.

Chapter 28:
RHODESIA'S UNILATERAL
DECLARATION OF INDEPENDENCE,
NOVEMBER 1965

1 Lapping, op. cit., pp. 494–5.
2 *Report of the Advisory Commission on the Review of the Federal Constitution* (The Monckton Report), Cm. doc. 1148 (1960).
3 R. Welensky, *4,000 Days* (1964), quoted in Lapping, op. cit., p. 491.
4 Lapping, op. cit., p. 491.
5 R.C. Good, *U.D.I.: The International Politics of the Rhodesia Rebellion* (1973), p. 115; see also B. Pimlott, *Harold Wilson* (1992), pp. 365–81.
6 Pimlott, op. cit., p. 367.

7 J.B. Watson, *Empire to Commonwealth* (1971), p. 247.
8 Pimlott, op. cit., p. 367.
9 Judd and Slinn, op. cit., p. 113.
10 Cross, op. cit., p. 357.
11 Judd and Slinn, op. cit., p. 113.
12 Watson, op. cit., p. 256.
13 J. Kennedy, *A History of Malaya* (1970 edition), and D.G.E. Hall, *A History of South-East Asia* (1968 edition).

Chapter 29:
THE DECLARATION OF
COMMONWEALTH PRINCIPLES AT
SINGAPORE, 1971

1 Lord Garner, *The Commonwealth Office, 1925–68* (1978), p. 439.
2 Judd and Slinn, op. cit., p. 119.
3 Commonwealth Heads of Government: The London Communiqué, Commonwealth Secretariat, 1977, paragraph 35.
4 Read, *The Commonwealth Law Bulletin*, 6 (1980), p. 262.
5 Judd and Slinn, op. cit., p. 129.
6 See *Commonwealth Relations Year Book, 1966*, and *Year Book of the Commonwealth, 1979*.
7 Commonwealth Secretariat, Commonwealth Heads of Government Meeting, Lusaka, August 1979, Final Communiqué, paragraph 48.

Chapter 30:
THE FALKLANDS WAR, 1982

1 Samuel Johnson, 7 April 1775, quoted in J. Boswell, *The Life of Samuel Johnson*, vol. 2 (revised edition, 1964), p. 348.
2 *Guardian*, 6 July 1982.
3 H. Young, *One of Us*, (1989), pp. 260–2.
4 Quoted in A. Barnett, *Iron Britannia: Why Parliament Waged its Falklands War* (1982), p. 28.
5 Ibid., pp. 30–1.
6 Ibid., p. 20.
7 Ibid., p. 34.
8 Judd and Slinn, op. cit., Appendix, pp. 144–5.

Chapter 31:
THE INAUGURATION OF NELSON
MANDELA AS PRESIDENT OF
SOUTH AFRICA, MAY 1994

1 N. Mandela, Inauguration Speech, Pretoria, 10 May 1994; see also Mandela, op. cit., pp. 613–14.
2 Lines, op. cit.
3 A.N. Porter, *European Imperialism, 1860–1914* (1994), pp. 76–7.
4 R. Robinson and J. Gallagher, *Africa and the Victorians* (1965), p. 472.
5 R. Tannahill, *Food in History* (1975 edition), pp. 278–9.
6 Morris, *Farewell the Trumpets*, op. cit., p. 549.
7 See Gill, op. cit.
8 C.C. Eldridge, *British Imperialism in the Nineteenth Century* (1987), p. 79.

9 See D. Burton, *The Raj at Table* (1993).
10 B. Porter, op. cit., p. 349.
11 Secretary of State Dean Acheson, who remarked in 1962 that Britain had 'lost an empire, and not yet found a role'. Quoted in B. Porter, op. cit., p. 351.
12 *Guardian*, 8 July 1995.
13 Ibid.
14 *Wisden Cricket Monthly*, July 1995, quoted in the *Observer*, 2 July 1995.
15 P.J. Marshall, 'Imperial Britain', The Creighton Lecture, 1994, p. 18.
16 *Guardian*, 20 March 1995.
17 *Independent*, 19 August 1995.
18 Voltaire, *Candide* (1759), Chapter 1.

BIBLIOGRAPHY

1 MANUSCRIPT SOURCES

Asquith Papers, Bodleian Library
Balfour Papers, British Library
Bryce Papers, Bodleian Library
Burns Papers, British Library
Campbell-Bannerman Papers,
    British Library
Joseph, Austen and Neville
    Chamberlain Papers, University
    of Birmingham Library
Dilke Papers, British Library
Lloyd George Papers, House of
    Lords Record Office
Milner Papers, Bodleian Library
    (owned by New College, Oxford)
Monk Bretton Papers, Bodleian
    Library
Montagu Papers, India Office
    Library
Morley Papers, British Library
Reading Papers, India Office
    Library
Ripon Papers, British Library
Samuel Papers, House of Lords
    Record Office
Selbourne Papers, Bodleian Library
Simon Papers, India Office Library
Other papers and memorabilia
    consulted at the Nehru Library,
    New Delhi and at the Ladysmith
    Museum, Republic of South
    Africa

2 PARLIAMENTARY PAPERS
    AND OFFICIAL DOCUMENTS

The Public Records Office's
    collection of Cabinet Papers

Hansard's Parliamentary Debates

Proceedings of the Colonial and
    Imperial Conferences of 1887,
    1897, 1902, 1907, 1911, 1917,
    1921, 1923, 1926, 1930, 1932,
    1937
Proceedings of the Colonial Defence
    Conference of 1909, the Imperial
    War Conference of 1919, the 1929
    Conference on the Operation of
    Dominion Legislation and
    Merchant Shipping Legislation
Report of the Royal West India
    Commission, P.P.1897 (C.8655)
    (Norman Commission)
Report of the Royal Commission of
    the War in South Africa (Elgin
    Report), P.P.1904 (Cd.1789)
Report of the War Office
    (Reconstitution) Committee,
    P.P. 1904 (Cd. 1932, 1968, 2002)
    (Esher Committee)
Circular on the Future Organisation
    of Colonial Conferences and
    Correspondence, P.P. 1906
    (Cd.2784, 2975)
P.Cd.P (Cd.8566) Resolution 9,
    1917
Rhodesia and Nyasaland Royal
    Commission Report, Cmd.5949
    (1939)
Ceylon: Report of the Special
    Commission on the Constitution,
    Cmd.3131 (1928) (Donoughue
    Report)
Declaration of London: Final

Communiqué of the Prime
Ministers' Meeting, 1949
Report of the Nyasaland
Commission of Inquiry,
Cmd.814 (1959)
Report of the Advisory Commission
on the Review of the Federal
Constitution, Cmd.1148 (1960)
(Monckton Report)
Commonwealth Heads of
Government: The London
Communiqué, 1977,
Commonwealth Secretariat
Final Report of the Commonwealth
Observer Group on the Southern
Rhodesia Elections, February
1980, Commonwealth Secretariat
Final Communiqué, Commonwealth
Heads of Government Meeting,
Lusaka, August 1979,
Commonwealth Secretariat
Report of the Independent
Commission on International
Development Issues, chaired by
Willy Brandt (1980)
'Commonwealth Skills for
Commonwealth Needs':
Commonwealth Fund for
Technical Cooperation, 1980,
Commonwealth Secretariat

3 NEWSPAPERS AND
JOURNALS
Baptist
Belfast Telegraph
Birmingham Daily Post
Birmingham Gazette
Bombay Chronicle
Daily Express
Daily Graphic
Daily Herald
Daily Mail
Daily Mirror
Daily News
Daily Telegraph
Dawn
Evening Standard

Eye-Witness
Fortnightly Review
Gloucester Citizen
Guardian
Herald Tribune (New York)
The Hindu
Illustrated London News
Illustrated News
Independent
Investors' Review
Irish Times
Jewish Chronicle
Lancashire Post
Liberator
Manchester Evening Chronicle
Manchester Guardian
Manchester Umpire
Morning Post
National Herald (India)
National Review
New York Times
News Chronicle
Observer
Pelican
Punch
Reading Standard
Saturday News
Saturday Review
Scotsman
Spectator
Standard
Star
Sun (Baltimore)
Time-Life British Empire Magazine
The Times
Western Mail
Westminster Gazette
Yorkshire Observer

4 BOOKS AND ARTICLES

*(Books referred to in the endnotes are not
necessarily included in the list below)*

Abbott, G., 'The Colonial
Development Act of 1929',
Economic History Review (1971)

Adams, P., *Fatal Necessity: British Intervention in New Zealand, 1830–47* (1977)

Adamson, A.H., *Sugar Without Slaves* (1972)

Akbar, M.J., *Nehru: The Making of India* (1988)

Allen, C. (ed.), *Plain Tales from the Raj* (1975)

Allen, C. and Swivedi, S., *Lives of the Indian Princes* (1984)

Allen, L., *Singapore, 1941–2* (1993)

Allen, V.L., *The History of Black Mineworkers in South Africa*, vol. 1 (1992)

Anderson, D. and Killingray, D. (eds), *Policing the Empire: Government, Authority and Control, 1850–1940* (1991)

Anstey, V., *The Economic Development of India* (1952 edition)

Anwar, M., *The Myth of Return: Pakistanis in Britain* (1979)

Arasarti, S., *Indians in Malaysia* (1979)

Arnold, D., *Police Power and Colonial Rule: Madras 1859–1947* (1986)

Asad, T. (ed.), *Anthropology and the Colonial Encounter* (1973)

Ashish, N., *The Intimate Enemy* (1988)

Ashton, S.R., *British Policy Towards the Indian States* (1982)

Ashton, S.R., *British India* (1987)

Austin, D., *Politics in Ghana 1946–60* (1970)

Avery, P., *Modern Iran* (1967)

Azad, A.K., *India Wins Freedom* (1959)

Bagchi, A.K., *Private Investment in India 1900–1939* (1972)

Bahadursingh, I.J., *The Other India: Overseas Indians and Their Relationship with India* (1979)

Bahadursingh, I.J. (ed.), *Indians in the Caribbean* (1987)

Baker, C.J., *The Politics of South India 1920–1937* (1977)

Baker, C.J., *An Indian Rural Economy* (1984)

Ballard, R., 'The Context and Consequences of Migration: Jullundur and Mirpur Compared', *New Community*, vol. 21 (1983), pp. 117–36

Ballard, R., 'Kashmir Crisis: View from Mirpur', *Economic and Political Weekly*, vols 2–9 (March 1991), pp. 513–17

Ballhatchet, K., *Race, Sex and Class Under the Raj, 1793–1905* (1980)

Banerji, A.K., *Aspects of Indo–British Economic Relations, 1858–98* (1982)

Barnett, A., *Iron Britannia: Why Parliament Waged its Falklands War* (1982)

Barnett, C., *The Audit of War: The Illusion and Reality of Britain as a Great Nation* (1986)

Barnett, C., *The Lost Victory: British Dreams, British Realities, 1945–50* (1995)

Barr, P., *The Dust in the Balance: British Women in India, 1905–45* (1989)

Basham, A.L., *A Cultural History of India* (1975)

Basham, A.L., *The Wonder that was India* (1988 edition)

Bates, D., *The Fashoda Incident of 1898: Encounter on the Nile* (1984)

Bayly, C.A., *The New Cambridge History of India*, Part 2, *Indian Society and the Making of the British Empire* (1988)

Bayly, C.A., *Atlas of the British Empire* (1989)

Bayly, C.A., *Imperial Meridian: The British Empire and the World 1780–1830* (1989)

Bayly, C.A. (ed.), *The Raj: India and the British, 1600–1947* (1990)

Bayly, S., *Saints, Goddesses and Kings: Muslims and Christians in South Indian Society, 1700–1900* (1989)

Beaglehole, T.H., 'From Rulers to Servants: The I.C.S. and the British Demission of Power in India', *Modern Asian Studies*, vol. 2 (1977)

Beckles, H. and Stoddart, B. (eds), *Liberation Cricket: West Indian Cricket Culture* (1995)

Beinhart, W., *Twentieth Century Africa* (1994)

Beinhart, W., & Dubow, S. (eds), *Segregation and Apartheid in Twentieth Century South Africa* (1995)

Belich, J., *The New Zealand Wars and the Victorian Interpretation of Racial Conflict* (1986)

Bell, M., Butler, R.A. and Heffernan, M.J. (eds), *Geography and Imperialism, 1820–1920* (1996)

Belliappa, K.C., *The Image of India in British Fiction* (1991)

Beloff, M., *Imperial Sunset*, Vol. 1, *Britain's Liberal Empire, 1897–1921* (1969)

Bence-Jones, M., *The Viceroys of India* (1982)

Bennett, S., 'Shikar [hunting] and the Raj', *Journal of South Asian Studies*, vol. 7 (1984)

Berger, M., 'Imperialism and Sexual Exploitation: A Response to Ronald Hyam', *Journal of Imperial and Commonwealth History* (1988)

Berman, B. and Lonsdale, J., *Unhappy Valley: Conflict in Kenya and Africa* (1992)

Bernstein, H., *The Rift: The Exile Experience of South Africans* (1994)

Besant, A., *How India Wrought her Freedom* (1915)

Betts, R.F., *Uncertain Dimensions: Western Overseas Empires in the Twentieth Century* (1985)

Bhattacharya, D., *A Concise History of the Indian Economy, 1750–1950* (1979)

Birkenhead, Lord, *The Life of Lord Birkenhead* (1959)

Birkenhead, Lord, *The Life of Lord Halifax* (1965)

Birla, G.D., *In the Shadow of the Mahatma* (1953)

Birley, D., *Sport and the Making of Britain* (1993)

Blackburn, R. (ed.), *Ideology in Social Science* (1973)

Blackburn, R., *The Overthrow of Colonial Slavery, 1776–1848* (1988)

Blainey, G., 'Lost Causes of the Jameson Raid', *Economic History Review* (1965)

Blake, R., *The History of Rhodesia* (1977)

Blake, R., *The Decline of British Power* (1985)

Bolitho, H., *Jinnah: Creator of Pakistan* (1954)

Bolt, C., *Victorian Attitudes Towards Race* (1971)

Bond, B., *British Military Policy Between the Two World Wars* (1980)

Bose, M., *The Lost Hero: Subhas Chandra Bose* (1983)

Bose, M., *A History of Indian Cricket* (1990)

Bose, N.K., *My Days with Gandhi* (1953)

Bose, S., *Peasant Labour and Colonial Capital: Rural Bengal* (1993)

Bose, S.C., *The Indian Struggle 1920–1942* (1964)

Boyce, D.G., *The Irish Question and British Politics, 1868–1996* (1996)

Brantliner, P., *The Rule of Darkness: British Literature and Imperialism, 1830–1914* (1988)

Brecher, M., *Nehru: A Political Biography* (1959)

Brereton, B., *A History of Modern Trinidad, 1783–1962* (1981)

Brereton, B. and Dookeran, W. (eds), *East Indians in the*

Caribbean: Colonialism and the
Struggle for Identity (1975)

Brett, E.A., *Colonialism and
Underdevelopment in East Africa:
The Politics of Economic Change
1919–39* (1978)

Bristow, J., *Empire Boys: Adventure in
a Man's World* (1991)

Brizan, G., *Grenada, Island of Conflict*
(1984)

Brooks, D., *The Age of Upheaval:
Edwardian Politics, 1899–1914*
(1995)

Brown, C., *Black and White Britain*
(1984)

Brown, J., *Lutyens and the Edwardians*
(1996)

Brown, J.M., 'War, Britain and
India, 1914–18', in Foot, M.R.D.
(ed.), *War and Society* (1973)

Brown, J.M., *Gandhi and Civil
Disobedience: The Mahatma in Indian
Politics 1928–34* (1977)

Brown, J.M., *Modern India: The
Making of an Asian Democracy*
(1994 edition)

Brown, J.M., *Gandhi: Prisoner of Hope*
(1989)

Brown, M.B., *After Imperialism* (1970
edition)

Burra, R. (ed.), *Looking Back: Film
India, 1896–1960* (1981)

Burton, D., *The Raj at Table*
(1993)

Butler, J., *The Liberal Party and the
Jameson Raid* (1968)

Byrd, P. (ed.), *British Foreign Policy
under Thatcher* (1988)

Cain, P.J., *Economic Foundations of
British Overseas Expansion, 1815–
1914* (1980)

Cain, P.J. and Hopkins, A.G.,
'Political Economy of British
Expansion Overseas, 1750–
1914', *Economic History Review*, 2nd
series, no. 32 (1980)

Cain, P.J. and Hopkins, A.G., *British

Imperialism* (vol. 1 *1688–1914*, vol.
2 *1914–90*) (1993)

Callaghan, J., *Time and Chance* (1987)

Cambridge History of the British Empire,
vol. 3, 1870–1919 (1959)

Campbell-Johnson, A., *Mission with
Mountbatten* (1951)

Caplan, L., *Warrior Gentlemen:
'Gurkhas' in the Western Imagination*
(1995)

Carlton, D., 'The Dominions and
the Gathering Storm', *Journal of
Imperial and Commonwealth History*
(1978)

Carlton, D., *Anthony Eden: A
Biography* (1981)

Carlton, D., *Britain and the Suez Crisis*
(1988)

Castle, K., 'The Imperial Indian', in
Mangan, J.A. (ed.) *The Imperial
Curriculum* (1993)

Castle, K., *Britannia's Children* (1996)

Chakravarty, S., *The Raj Syndrome: A
Study in Imperial Perceptions* (1989)

Chamberlain, M.E., *The New
Imperialism* (1970)

Chamberlain, M.E., *Britain and
India: The Interaction of Two
Peoples* (1974)

Chamberlain, M.E., *The Scramble for
Africa* (1974)

Chamberlain, M.E., *Decolonisation:
The Fall of the European Empires*
(1985)

Chamberlain, M.E., *'Pax Britannica?'
British Foreign Policy, 1789–1914*
(1988)

Chandra, B., *The Rise and Growth of
Economic Nationalism in India* (1966)

Chandra, B., *Communalism in Modern
India* (1984)

Chandra, B., *India's Struggle for
Independence, 1857–1947* (1989)

Chandra, B., Mukherjee, M.,
Mukherjee, A., Pannikar, K.N.,
Mahajan, S., *India's Struggle for
Independence* (1988)

Char, S.V.D. (ed.), *Readings in the Constitutional History of India, 1757–1947* (1983)

Charlesworth, N., *British Rule and the Indian Economy 1800–1914* (1982)

Charmley, J., *Lord Lloyd and the Decline of the British Empire* (1987)

Charmley, J., *Churchill's Grand Alliance: The Anglo–American Special Relationship, 1940–57* (1995)

Chaudhuri, N.C., *Thy Hand, Great Anarch!* (1987)

Chaudry, K.C., *The Role of Religion in Indian Politics, 1900–25* (1978)

Cheyfitz, E., *The Politics of Imperialism: From* The Tempest *to* Tarzan (1991)

Chilver, E.M. and Harlow, V., *A History of East Africa*, vol. 2 (1976)

Clarke, C., Peach, C. and Vertovec, S. (eds), *South Asians Overseas: Migration and Ethnicity* (1990)

Clay, J., *John Masters: A Regimented Life* (1992)

Cohen, M.J., *Palestine and the Great Powers, 1945–48* (1982)

Coker, C., *War and the Twentieth Century: The Impact of War on the Modern Consciousness* (1995)

Colley, L., *Britons: Forging the Nation, 1710–1837* (1992)

Collins, B. and Robbins, K. (eds), *British Culture and Economic Decline* (1990)

Comaroff, J.L. (ed.), *The Boer War Diary of Sol. T. Plaatje: An African at Mafeking* (1973)

Connell, J., *Auchinleck* (1959)

Copland, I., *The British Raj and the Indian Princes: Paramountcy in Western India 1857–1930* (1982)

Coulon, A., *Tanganyika: A Political Economy* (1982)

Crane, R. and Barrier, N., *British Imperial Policy in India and Sri Lanka* (1981)

Craton, M., *Sinews of Empire: A Short History of British Slavery* (1974)

Crawshaw, N., *The Cyprus Revolt* (1978)

Cronin, R., *Imagining India* (1989)

Crosby, A., *Ecological Imperialism: The Biological Expansion of Europe, 900–1900* (1986)

Cross, C., *The Fall of the British Empire* (1968)

Crowley, J.E., *The Privileges of Independence: Neo-Mercantilism and the American Revolution* (1994)

Cumpston, M., *Indians Overseas in British Territories, 1834–65* (1953)

Curtin, P.D., *The Two Jamaicas: The Role of Ideas in a Tropical Colony, 1830–65* (1955)

Dabydeen, D. and Samaroo, B. (eds), *India in the Caribbean* (1987)

Dabydeen, D. and Samaroo, B. (eds), *Across the Dark Waters* (1994)

Dahya, B., 'Pakistanis in England', *New Community*, vol. 2 no. 1 (1972), pp. 25–33

Dahya, B., 'Pakistanis in the United Kingdom: Transients or Settlers?', *Race*, 14 (1973), pp. 241–77

Dalton, D., *Mahatma Gandhi: Non-Violent Power in Action* (1993)

Darby, P., *British Defence Policy East of Suez, 1947–68* (1973)

Darwin, J., 'Imperialism in Decline', *Historical Journal* (1980)

Darwin, J., 'British Decolonisation Since 1945', *Journal of Imperial and Commonwealth History*, 12 (1984)

Darwin, J., *Britain and Decolonisation: The Retreat from Empire in the Post-War World* (1988)

Darwin, J., *The End of the British Empire* (1991)

Das, M.N., *India Under Minto and Morley* (1964)

Davenport, T., *South Africa: A Modern History* (1991 edition)

Davey, A., *The British Pro-Boers, 1877–1902* (1978)

Davidson, B., *Africa in Modern History* (1978)

Davidson, B., *Modern Africa: A Social and Political History* (1989 edition)

Davidson, B., *The Search for Africa: History, Culture, Politics* (1994)

Davin, A., 'Imperialism and Motherhood', *History Workshop Journal*, 1978

Davis, L.E. and Huttenback, R.A., *Mammon and the Pursuit of Empire: The Political Economy of British Imperialism, 1860–1920* (1986)

Davis, R., *The Industrial Revolution and Overseas Trade* (1979)

Dawson, R.M., *The Development of Dominion Status, 1900–36* (1937)

Dawson, R.M., *William Lyon MacKenzie King* (1959)

Dean, D.W., 'Final Exit? Britain, Eire, the Commonwealth and the Repeal of the External Relations Act, 1945–49', *Journal of Imperial and Commonwealth History*, vol. 20 no. 3 (1992)

Dean, D.W., 'The Conservative Government and the 1961 Commonwealth Immigration Act: The Inside Story', *Race and Class*, 35, 2 (1993)

Denoon, D., *Settler Capitalism: The Dynamics of Dependent Development in the Southern Hemisphere* (1983)

Dervin, D., 'The Psychoanalysis of Sport', in Prager, J. and Rustin, M. (eds), *Psychoanalytical Sociology* (1993)

Desai, A.R. (ed.), *Peasant Struggles in India* (1979)

Desai, R., *Indian Immigrants in the United Kingdom* (1963)

Dewey, C., *Anglo-Indian Attitudes: The Mind of the Indian Civil Service* (1993)

Dewey, C. and Hopkins, A.G. (eds), *The Imperial Impact: Studies in the Economic History of Africa and India* (1978)

Dilke, C., *Greater Britain* (1868)

Dilks, D., *Curzon in India* (2 vols, 1969 and 1970)

Dillon, G.M., *The Falklands, Politics and War* (1989)

Diver, M., *Royal India* (1942)

Dobson, A.P., *US Wartime Aid to Britain 1940–46* (1986)

Dockrill, M., *British Defence Since 1945* (1988)

Douglas, R., *World Crisis and British Decline, 1929–56* (1986)

Douglas, R., *Great Nations Still Enchained, 1848–1914: The Cartoonists' Vision of Empire* (1993)

Drummond, I.M., *British Economic Policy and the Empire, 1919–39* (1972)

Drummond, I.M., *The Floating Pound and the Sterling Area, 1931–39* (1987)

Dubow, S., *Scientific Racism in Modern South Africa* (1995)

Dummont, L., *Homo Hierarchicus: An Essay on the Caste System* (1970)

Duncan, R., *Selected Writings of Mahatma Gandhi* (1971)

Edgerton, R.B., *Like Lions they Fought: The Zulu War and the Last Black Empire in South Africa* (1988)

Edwardes, M., *High Noon of Empire: India under Curzon* (1965)

Edwardes, M., *British India* (1967)

Edwardes, M., *Nehru: A Political Biography* (1973)

Edwardes, M., *The Sahibs and the Lotus: The British in India* (1988)

Ehrlich, C.C., 'Builders and Caretakers', *Economic History Review* (1973)

Eldridge, C.C., *Victorian Imperialism* (1978)

Eldridge, C.C. (ed.), *British Imperialism in the Nineteenth Century* (1984)

Eldridge, C.C., *Disraeli and the Rise of a New Imperialism* (1996)

Etherington, N., 'Labour Supply and South African Confederation', *Journal of African History* (1979), *Ethnic and Racial Studies*, vol. 5, no. 3

Fabb, J., *The British Empire from Photographs: India* (1986)

Fabb, J., *The British Empire from Photographs: Africa* (1987)

Faber, R., *The Vision and the Need* (1966)

Fay, P.W., *The Forgotten Army: India's Armed Struggle for Independence, 1942–5* (1994)

Felman, D., *Englishmen and Jews: Social Relationships and Political Culture 1840–1914* (1994)

Feuredi, F., *The Mau Mau War in Perspective* (1989)

Field, H.J., *Towards a Programme of Imperial Life: The British Empire at the Turn of the Century* (1982)

Fieldhouse, D.K., 'Imperialism: An historiographical revision', *Economic History Review* (1961)

Fieldhouse, D.K., *Economics and Empire, 1880–1914* (1973)

Fieldhouse, D.K., *The Colonial Empires* (1982 edition)

Fields, K., *Revival and Rebellion in Colonial Central Africa* (1985)

Fischer, L., *The Life of Mahatma Gandhi* (1951)

Fischer, L. (ed.), *The Essential Gandhi* (1963)

Fisher, J., *That Miss Hobhouse* (1971)

Fisher, M.H., *Clash of Cultures: Avadh, the British and the Mughals* (1988)

Fisher, M.H., *The Politics of the British Annexation of India, 1757–1857* (1993)

Fisher, N., *Iain Macleod* (1973)

Fishwick, N., *English Society and Football, 1910–1950* (1989)

Flavell, J.M., 'American Patriots in London and the Quest for Talks, 1774–75', *Journal of Imperial and Commonwealth History*, vol. 20, no. 3 (1992)

Flint, J., *Cecil Rhodes* (1976)

Foot, M.R.D. (ed.), *War and Society* (1973)

Forster, R., *Modern Ireland, 1600–1972* (1989)

French, P., *Younghusband: The Last Great Imperial Adventurer* (1994)

Freund, B., *The Making of Contemporary Africa: The Development of African Society Since 1800* (1984)

Friedberg, A., *The Weary Titan: Britain and the Experience of Relative Decline, 1895–1905* (1988)

Frost, A., *Convicts and Empire: A Naval Question, 1771–1811* (1980)

Fryer, P., *Staying Power: The History of Black People in Britain* (1984)

Fryer, P., *Black People in the British Empire: An Introduction* (1988)

Furedi, F., *The Mau Mau War in Perspective* (1989)

Furedi, F., *Colonial Wars and the Politics of Third World Nationalism* (1994)

Furedi, F., *The New Ideology of Imperialism: Renewing the Moral Imperative* (1994)

Gadgil, D.R., *The Industrial Evolution of India in Recent Times, 1860–1939* (1971 edition)

Gallagher, J. (ed. Seal, A.), *The Decline, Revival and Fall of the British Empire* (1982)

Gallagher, J. and Robinson, R., 'Imperialism of Free Trade', *Economic History Review*, 6 (1953)

Gandhi, M.K., *Hind Swaraj* (1909)

Gandhi, M.K., *Gokhale: My Political Guru* (1935)

Gandhi, M.K., *Satyagraha* (1935)

Gandhi, M.K., *Satyagraha in South Africa* (1938)

Gandhi, M.K., *Non-Violence in Peace and War* (1942)

Gandhi, M.K., *Selected Works*, vols 1–4 (1968 edition)

Gandhi, M.K., *An Autobiography – Or the Story of my Experiments with Truth* (1982 edition)

Gandhi, S. (ed.), *Two Alone, Two Together: Letters between Indira Gandhi and Jawarhalal Nehru, 1940–64* (1992)

Ghai, Y., *Portrait of a Minority: Asians in East Africa* (1970)

Ghosh, S., *Gandhi's Emissary* (1967)

Ghosh, S., *India and the Raj, 1919–47* (1989)

Gifford, P. and Louis, W.R. (eds), *Britain and Germany in Africa: Imperial Rivalry and Colonial Rule* (1967)

Gifford, P. and Louis, W.R. (eds), *France and Britain in Africa: Imperial Rivalry and Colonial Rule* (1971)

Gifford, P. and Louis, W.R. (eds), *The Transfer of Power in Africa: Decolonisation 1940–60* (1982)

Gill, A., *Ruling Passions: Sex, Race and Empire* (1995)

Gilmour, D., *Curzon* (1994)

Gilroy, P., *There Ain't no Black in the Union Jack* (1987)

Gimlette, G., *A Postscript to the Records of the Indian Mutiny* (1927)

Glendevon, J., *The Viceroy at Bay: Lord Linlithgow* (1967)

GoGwilt, C., *The Invention of the West: Joseph Conrad and the Double-mapping of Europe and Empire* (1995)

Goldsworthy, D., *Colonial Issues in British Politics 1945–61* (1971)

Good, R.C., *U.D.I.: The International Politics of the Rhodesian Rebellion* (1973)

Goodfellow, C.F., *Great Britain and South African Confederation, 1870–1881* (1966)

Goonetillete, D.C.P., *Images of the Raj: South Asia in the Literature of Empire* (1988)

Gopal, S., *The Viceroyalty of Lord Irwin, 1926–31* (1957)

Gopal, S., *British Policy in India 1858–1905* (1965)

Gopal, S., *Jawaharlal Nehru* (3 vols, 1976–84)

Gopal, S. (ed.), *Selected Works of Jawaharlal Nehru*, 2nd series, vols 1–15 (1984)

Gopal, S., *Jawaharlal Nehru: A Biography* (abridged edition, 1989)

Gopal, S., 'Churchill and India', in Beake, R. and Louis, W.R. (eds), *Churchill* (1993)

Goradia, N., *Lord Curzon: Last of the British Moghuls* (1993)

Gosine, M. (ed.), *The Coolie Connection* (1992)

Green, M., *Dreams of Adventure, Deeds of Empire* (1979)

Green, W.A., *British Slave Emancipation: The Sugar Colonies and the Great Experiment, 1830–65* (1976)

Greenberger, A.J., *The British Image of India* (1969)

Gregory, R., *India and East Africa: A History of Race Relations Within the British Empire* (1971)

Grewal, S.S., *Muslim Rule in India: The Assessment of British Historians* (1970)

Grove, R., *Green Imperialism: Colonial Expansion, Tropical Island Edens and the Origins of Environmentalism* (1995)

Gunderia, Y.D., *In the Districts of the Raj* (1992)

Gupta, P.S., *Imperialism and the British Labour Movement 1914–64* (1975)

Guy, J., *Destruction of the Zulu*

Kingdom: The Civil War in Zululand, 1879–1884 (1979)

Gwyer, M. and Appadorai, A. (eds), *Speeches and Documents on the Indian Constitution* (2 vols, 1957)

Halifax, Lord, *Fullness of Days* (1957)

Hall, D., 'Flight from the Estates Reconsidered: The British West Indies 1832–42', *Journal of Imperial and Commonwealth History*, nos 10–11 (1978)

Hamid, H., *Muslim Separatism in India: A Survey, 1858–1947* (1971)

Hamid, S., *Disastrous Twilight: A Personal Record of the Partition of India* (1987)

Haq, M.A., *Muslim Politics in Modern India* (1970)

Harcourt, F., 'Disraeli's Imperialism, 1866–68', *Historical Journal*, 23 (1980)

Hardiman, D., *Peasant Resistance in India, 1858–1914* (1992)

Hardy, P., *The Muslims of British India* (1972)

Hargreaves, J.D., *Prelude to the Partition of West Africa* (1967)

Hargreaves, J.D., *West Africa Partitioned*, vol. 1, *The Loaded Pause, 1885–89* (1974)

Hargreaves, J.D., *Decolonisation in Africa* (1988)

Harkness, D.W., *The Restless Dominion: The Irish Free State and the British Commonwealth of Nations, 1921–31* (1969)

Harkness, D.W., *Northern Ireland Since 1920* (1983)

Harlow, V. and Chilvers, E.M. (eds), *History of East Africa*, vol. 2 (1965)

Harnetty, P., 'Imperialism and Free Trade in India', *Economic History Review* (1964)

Harris, F.R., *J.N. Tata: The Chronicle of his Life* (1958)

Harris, K., *Attlee* (1982)

Hastings, M. and Jenkins, S., *The Battle for the Falklands* (1983)

Havinden, V. and Meredith, D., *Colonialism and Development: Britain and its Tropical Colonies, 1850–1960* (1993)

Hawke, G.R., *The Making of New Zealand: An Economic History* (1985)

Hazareesingh, K., *A History of Indians in Mauritius* (1976)

Heathcote, T.A., *The Military in British India: The Development of British Land Forces in South Asia, 1600–1947* (1995)

Heffer, S., *Moral Desperado: A Life of Thomas Carlyle* (1994)

Helweg, A.W., *Sikhs in England: The Development of a Migrant Community* (1979)

Hetherington, P., *British Paternalism and Africa, 1920–40* (1978)

Heuman, G., *The Killing Time: The Morant Bay Rebellion in Jamaica* (1994)

Hewison, H.H., *Hedge of Wild Almonds: South Africa, the Pro-Boers and the Quaker Conscience, 1890–1910* (1989)

Hibbert, C., *The Great Mutiny: India 1857* (1980)

Hibbert, C., *Africa Explored: Europeans in the Dark Continent, 1769–1889* (1984)

Hiro, D., *Black British, White British* (1971)

Hiro, D., *The Untouchables of India* (1982)

Hobsbawm, E.J., *Industry and Empire: An Economic History of Britain Since 1750* (1969)

Hobsbawn, E.J., *The Age of Empire, 1875–1914* (1994)

Hobsbawm, E.J. and Ranger, T. (eds), *The Invention of Tradition* (1983)

Hobson, J.A., *Imperialism: A Study* (1988 edition)

Hodgkin, T., *Nationalism in Colonial Africa* (1956)

Hodson, H.V., *The Great Divide: Britain–India–Pakistan* (1969)

Holland, R.F., *Britain and the Commonwealth Alliance 1918–39* (1981)

Holland, R.F., *European Decolonisation 1918–81: An Introductory Survey* (1985)

Holland, R.F. (ed.), *Emergencies and Disorders in the European Empires After 1945* (1994)

Holland, R.F., *The Pursuit of Greatness: Britain and the World Role, 1900–70* (1991)

Holland, R.F. and Rizvi, G. (eds), *Perspectives in Imperialism and Decolonisation: Essays in Honour of A.F. Madden* (1984)

Holt, P., *Sport and the British* (1992)

Hopkins, A.G., *An Economic History of West Africa* (1973)

Hopkins, A.G., 'The Occupation of Egypt in 1882', *Journal of African History* (1986)

Howard, M., *The Continental Commitment: The Dilemma of British Defence Policy in the Era of Two World Wars* (1974)

Howe, S., *Anticolonialism in British Politics: The Left and the End of Empire, 1918–64* (1991)

Hughes, R., *The Fatal Shore: A History of the Transportation of Convicts to Australia, 1787–1868* (1987)

Hulme, P. and Whitehouse, N., *Wild Majesty: Encounter with Caribs from Columbus to the Present Day* (1992)

Hunt, R., *The District Officer in India 1930–1947* (1980)

Hutchins, F.G., *India's Revolution: Gandhi and the Quit India Movement* (1973)

Hutnik, N., *Ethnic Minority Identity: A Social Psychological Perspective* (1991)

Huttenback, R.A., *Gandhi in South Africa: British Imperialism and the Indian Question, 1860–1914* (1971)

Huttenback, R.A., *Racism and Empire: White Settlers and Coloured Immigrants in the British Self-Governing Colonies, 1830–1910* (1976)

Hyam, R., *Elgin and Churchill at the Colonial Office, 1905–08* (1968)

Hyam, R., 'African Interests in the South Africa Act', *Historical Journal* (1970)

Hyam, R., *Empire and Sexuality: The British Experience* (1990)

Hyam, R. (ed.), *The Labour Government and the End of Empire, 1945–51* (1992)

Hyam, R., *Britain's Imperial Century, 1815–1914* (1993 edition)

Hyam, R. and Martin, G., *Reappraisals in British Imperial History* (1975)

Hynes, W.G., *The Economics of Empire: Britain, Africa and the New Imperialism, 1870–95* (1979)

Iliffe, J., *A Modern History of Tanganyika* (1979)

Iliffe, J., *The African Poor: A History* (1987)

Inden, R., *Imagining India* (1990)

Inder Singh, A., *The Origins of the Partition of India 1936–1947* (1987)

Ingall, F., *The Last of the Bengal Lancers* (1988)

Ingram, E., & Fraser, S., *Empire-Building and Empire-Builders* (1996)

Iyer, R.N., *The Moral and Political Thought of Mahatma Gandhi* (1973)

Jalal, A., *The Sole Spokesman: Jinnah, the Muslim League and the Demand for Pakistan* (1985)

James, C.L.R., *Beyond a Boundary* (1963)

489

James, L., *The Rise and Fall of the British Empire* (1994)

Jay, R., *Joseph Chamberlain: A Political Study* (1981)

Jeal, T., *Baden-Powell* (1989)

Jeffrey, K. (ed.), *An Irish Empire? Aspects of Ireland and the British Empire* (1996)

Jeffrey, R. (ed.), *People, Princes and Paramount Power: Society and Politics in the Indian Princely States* (1978)

Jeffrey, R. (ed.), *Asia: The Winning of Independence – The Philippines, India, Indonesia, Vietnam, Malaya* (1981)

Jenkins, R., *Gladstone* (1995)

Jenkins, T.A., *Disraeli and Victorian Conservatism* (1996)

Johnston, W.R., *Great Britain, Great Empire: An Evaluation of the British Imperial Experience* (1991)

Jones, G., *Social Darwinism and English Thought: The Interaction Between Biological and Social Theory* (1980)

Jones, S., *Merchants of the Raj* (1992)

Judd, D., *Balfour and the British Empire* (1968)

Judd, D., *The Victorian Empire* (1970)

Judd, D., *The Boer War* (1977)

Judd, D., *Lord Reading* (1982)

Judd, D., *The British Raj: Documentary Extracts* (1987 edition)

Judd, D., *Radical Joe: A Life of Joseph Chamberlain* (1993 edition)

Judd, D., *Jawaharlal Nehru* (1993)

Judd, D. and Slinn, P., *The Evolution of the Modern Commonwealth, 1902–80* (1982)

Juergensmeyer, M. (ed.) *Imagining India: Essays in Indian History* (1989)

Kadam, K.N. (ed.), *Dr B.R. Ambedkar: Emancipator of the Oppressed* (1993)

Kammack, D., *The Rand at War, 1789–1902* (1991)

Kamoche, J., *Imperial Trusteeship and Political Evolution in Kenya* (1982)

Kanfer, S., *The Last Empire: De Beers, Diamonds and the World* (1993)

Kanogo, T., *Squatters and the Origins of Mau Mau* (1987)

Katouzian, H., *The Political Economy of Modern Iran* (1979)

Keay, J., *Explorers of the Western Himalayas, 1820–1895* (1996)

Kendle, J.E., *The Colonial and Imperial Conferences, 1887–1911* (1967)

Kendle, J.E., *The Round Table Movement and Imperial Union* (1975)

Kennedy, P., *The Rise and Fall of the Great Powers* (1987)

Kent, M., *Moguls and Mandarins: Oil, Imperialism and the Middle East in British Foreign Policy, 1900–40* (1993)

Kia, M.Z., *India's Freedom Struggle and the INA* (1994)

Kiernan, V.G., *Marxism and Imperialism* (1974)

Kiernan, V.G., *European Empires from Conquest to Collapse, 1815–1960* (1982)

Kiernan, V.G., *The Lords of Human Kind: Black Man, Yellow Man and White Man in the Age of Empire* (1988)

Kiewiet, C.W. de, *The Imperial Factor in South Africa: A Study in Politics and Economics* (1965)

King, P (ed.), *A Viceroy's India: Leaves from Lord Curzon's Notebook* (1984)

Kipling, R., *Kim* (1901)

Kirk-Green, A.H.M. (ed.), *The Principles of Native Administration in Nigeria: Selected Documents, 1900–47* (1965)

Klass, M., *East Indians in Trinidad* (1971)

Knox, B.A., 'Reconsidering Mid-Victorian Imperialism' *Journal of Imperial and Commonwealth History* (1972–73)

Koss, S., *John Morley at the India Office, 1905–10* (1969)

Koss, S., (ed.), *The Pro-Boers: The Anatomy of an Anti-War Movement* (1973)

Kovel, J., *White Racism: A Psychohistory* (1988)

Kruze, J., *John Buchan and the Idea of Empire: Popular Literature and Political Ideology* (1989)

Kubicek, R., *The Administration of Imperialism: Joseph Chamberlain at the Colonial Office* (1969)

Kulke, H. and Rothermund, D., *A History of India* (1986)

Kumar, D. (ed.), *The Cambridge Economic History of India*, vol. 2 (1970)

Kumar, R. (ed.), *Essays on Gandhian Politics: The Rowlatt Satyagraha* (1977)

Kuper, H., *Indian People in Natal* (1961)

Laband, J., *Kingdom in Crisis: The Zulu Response to the British Invasion of 1879* (1992)

Lamb, R., *The Macmillan Years, 1957–63: The Emerging Truth* (1995)

Lannoy, R., *The Speaking Tree: A Study of Indian Culture and Society* (1974)

Lapping, B., *End of Empire* (1985)

Lawson, P., *The East India Company: A History, 1600–1857* (1993)

Le May, G.H., *British Supremacy in South Africa, 1849–1907* (1965)

Lee, D., 'Australia, the British Commonwealth and the United States, 1950–53', *Journal of Imperial and Commonwealth History*, vol. 20, no. 3 (1992)

Lee, T.R., *Race and Residence: The Concentration and Dispersal of Immigrants in London* (1977)

Lines, W.J., *Taming the Great South Land: A History of the Conquest of Nature in Australia* (1994)

Lloyd, T.O., *The British Empire, 1558–1983* (1984)

Longford, E., *Jameson's Raid* (1980 edition)

Lorimer, D., *Colour, Class and the Victorians: English Attitudes to the Negro in the Mid-Nineteenth Century* (1978)

Louis, W.R., *Imperialism at Bay: The United States and the Decolonisation of the British Empire, 1941–45* (1977)

Louis, W.R., *The British Empire in the Middle East 1945–51* (1984)

Lovat, F., *India Under Curzon, and After* (1912)

Low, D.A. (ed.), *Soundings in Modern South Asian History* (1968)

Low, D.A., *Buganda and British Overrule 1900–55* (1970)

Low, D.A., *Lion Rampant: Essays in the Study of British Imperialism* (1973)

Low, D.A. (ed.), *Congress and the Raj: Facets of the Indian Struggle 1917–47* (1977)

Low, D.A., *Eclipse of Empire* (1991)

Low, D.A. and Smith, A. (eds), *History of East Africa*, vol. 3 (1976)

Lucas, S., *Britain & the Suez Crisis: The Lion's Last Roar* (1996)

Lugard, F., *The Dual Mandate in Tropical Africa* (1922)

Lumby, E.W.R., Moon P. and Mansergh, N., *The Transfer of Power, 1942–1947*, vols I–XII (1971–83)

Lunt, J. (ed.), *From Sepoy to Subedar: Being the Life and Adventures of Subedar Sita Ram, a Native Officer in the Bengal Army* (1988 edition)

Lyall, A., *The Rise and Expansion of the British Dominion in India* (1920)

Lynn, M., 'Imperialism of Free Trade in West Africa', *Journal of Imperial and Commonwealth History* (1986–87)

McDonald, N., *Canada: Immigration and Colonisation, 1841–1903* (1966)

MacDonald, R.H., *The Language of Empire* (1994)

McIntyre, W.D., *Colonies into Commonwealth* (1966)

McIntyre, W.D., *The Imperial Frontier in the Tropics 1865–75* (1967)

MacKenzie, J.M., *The Partition of Africa, 1880–1900* (1983)

MacKenzie, J.M., *Propaganda and Empire* (1984)

MacKenzie, J.M. (ed.), *Imperialism and Popular Culture* (1987)

MacKenzie, J.M., *Popular Imperialism and the Military, 1850–1950* (1992)

MacKenzie, J.M., *Orientalism: History, Theory and the Arts* (1995)

McKernan, C., *Sport in History* (1974)

McLane, J.R., *Indian Nationalism and the Early Congress* (1977)

Macmillan, H., *Riding the Storm, 1956–59* (1971)

Macmillan, H., *Pointing the Way, 1959–61* (1972)

Macmillan, H., *At the End of the Day, 1961–63* (1973)

Macmillan, M., *Women of the Raj* (1988)

Mabey, R., *Landlocked: In Pursuit of the Wild* (1994)

Mandela, N., *Long Walk to Freedom* (1994)

Mangan, J.A. (ed.), *'Benefits Bestowed'?: Education and British Imperialism* (1988)

Mangan, J.A. (ed.), *Making Imperial Mentalities: Socialisation and British Imperialism* (1990)

Mangan. J.A. (ed.), *The Cultural Bond: Sport, Empire and Society* (1992)

Mangan. J.A. (ed.), *The Imperial Curriculum: Racial Images and Education in the British Colonial Experience* (1993)

Mangan, J.A. and Walvin, J., (eds), *Manliness and Morality: Middle-Class Masculinity in Britain and America, 1800–1940* (1987)

Mangat, J.S., *A History of Asians in East Africa 1868–1945* (1968)

Mangru, B., *Benevolent Neutrality: Indian Government Policy and Labour Migration to British Guiana, 1854–84* (1987)

Mansergh, N., *The Irish Question, 1840–1921* (1975 edition)

Mansergh, N., *The Commonwealth Experience* (2 vols, 1982 edition)

Mansfield, P., *The British in Egypt* (1971)

Marais, J.S., *The Fall of Kruger's Republic* (1961)

Marks, S., *Reluctant Rebellion: The 1906–08 Disturbances in Natal* (1970)

Marks, S. and Trapido, S. (eds), 'Milner and the South African State', *History Workshop Journal* (1979)

Marks, S. and Rathbone (eds), *Industrialisation and Social Change in South Africa, 1870–1930* (1982)

Marqusee, M., *Anyone But England: Cricket and the National Malaise* (1994)

Marshall, P.J., *East Indian Fortunes: The British in Bengal in the Eighteenth Century* (1976)

Marshall, P.J., *Bengal, the British Bridgehead: Eastern India 1740–1828* (1987)

Marshall, P.J. (ed.), *The Cambridge Illustrated History of the British Empire* (1996)

Marshall, P.J., *Trade and Conquest: Studies on the Rise of British Dominance in India* (1993)

Marshall, P.J. and Williams, G., *The*

Bibliography

Great Map of Mankind: British Perceptions of the World in the Age of Enlightenment (1982)

Martin, G., *Britain and the Origins of the Canadian Confederacy, 1837–67* (1994)

Masani, Z., *Indian Tales of the Raj* (1987)

Mason, P., *Patterns of Dominance* (1970)

Mason, P., *A Matter of Honour: An Account of the Indian Army, its Officers and Men* (1974)

Mason, P., *A Shaft of Sunlight* (1976)

Masselos, J.C., *Nationalism and the Indian Sub-Continent* (1972)

Mathur, D.B., *Gokhale* (1966)

Matthew, W.N., 'Imperialism of Free Trade: Peru', *Economic History Review* (1968)

Maxon, R.M., *Struggle for Kenya: The Loss and Reassertion of Imperial Initiative, 1912–23* (1993)

Mayer, A., *Peasants in the Pacific* (1961)

Mehotra, S.R., *India and the Commonwealth 1885–1925* (1965)

Mehra, P.A., *Dictionary of Modern Indian History* (1985)

Mehta, V., *Mahatma Gandhi and his Apostles* (1977)

Meintjes, J., *The Voortrekkers: The Story of the Great Trek and the Making of South Africa* (1973)

Mendelsohn, R., *Sammy Marks: The Uncrowned King of the Transvaal* (1991)

Meredith, D., 'Colonial Economic Policy', *Economic History Review* (1975)

Meredith, M., *The First Dance of Freedom: Black Africa in the Post-War Era* (1984)

Meredith, R., *South Africa's New Era: The 1994 Election* (1994)

Metcalf, T., *An Imperial Vision: Indian Architecture and Britain's Raj* (1989)

Metcalf, T., *Aftermath of Revolt: India 1857–1870* (1990 edition)

Metcalf, T., *Ideologies of the Raj: The New Cambridge History of India*, vol. 3 (1994)

Middlemas, K. and Barnes, J., *Baldwin* (1969)

Miller, C., *Painting the Map Red: Canada and the South African War, 1899–1902* (1993)

Mills, S., *Discourses of Difference: An Analysis of Women's Travel Writing and Colonialism* (1991)

Minault, G., *The Khilafat Movement* (1982)

Misra, B.B., *The Administrative History of India 1834–1947* (1970)

Misra, B.B., *The Indian Middle Classes* (1971)

Misra, B.B., *The Indian Political Parties* (1976)

Misra, B.B., *The Bureaucracy in India: An Analysis to 1947* (1977)

Mitchell, B., *Frozen Stakes: The Future of Antarctic Minerals* (1983)

Mitchell, B.R. and Deane, P., *Abstract of British Historical Statistics* (1962)

Mitchell, B.R. and Deane, P., *Second Abstract of British Historical Statistics* (1971)

Mitchell, T., *Colonising Egypt* (1988)

Mittal, S.C., *Freedom Movements in the Punjab, 1905–29* (1977)

Montagu, Sir E.S., *An Indian Diary* (1930)

Moon, P., *Gandhi and the Making of Modern India* (1968)

Moon, P., *The British Conquest and Dominion of India* (1989)

Moore, R.J., 'Imperialism and Free Trade in India 1853–54', *Economic History Review* (1964)

Moore, R.J., *Liberalism and Indian Politics 1862–1922* (1966)

Moore, R.J., 'Demission of Empire in South Asia', *Journal of Imperial* and Commonwealth History (1973)

Moore, R.J., *The Crisis of Indian Unity 1917–1940* (1974)

Moore, R.J., *Churchill, Cripps and India 1939–1945* (1979)

Moore, R.J., *Escape from Empire: The Attlee Government and the Indian Problem* (1983)

Moore, R.J., *Making the New Commonwealth* (1987)

Moore, R.J., *Paul Scott's Raj* (1990)

Moore-Gilbert, B.J., *Kipling and 'Orientalism'* (1986)

Moorhouse, G., *India Britannica* (1983)

Morgan, J., *Edwina Mountbatten: A Life of her Own* (1991)

Morgan, K.O., *Labour in Power, 1945–51* (1985)

Morris, H.S., *The Indians in Uganda* (1968)

Morris, J., 'Pax Britannica' trilogy: *Pax Britannica, Heaven's Command, Farewell the Trumpets* (1979 edition)

Morris, J., *Stones of Empire: The Buildings of British India* (1994 edition)

Morris-Jones, W.H. and Fisher, G. (eds), *Decolonisation and After: The British and French Experience* (1980)

Mosley, L., *The Last Days of the British Raj* (1972)

Mostert, N., *Frontiers: The Epic of South Africa's Creation and the Tragedy of the Xhosa People* (1992)

Muir, R., *The Making of British India, 1756–1858* (1915)

Mukerjee, H., *Bow of Burning Gold: Subhas Bose* (1977)

Mukherjee, S., *Forster and Further: The Tradition of Anglo-Indian Fiction* (1993)

Munro, J.F., *Britain in Tropical Africa, 1880–1960* (1984)

Murray-Brown, J., *Kenyatta* (1974)

Nanda, B.R., *Mahatma Gandhi* (1958)

Nanda, B.R., *The Nehrus: Motilal and Jawaharlal* (1962)

Nanda, B.R., *Gokhale, Gandhi and the Nehrus* (1974)

Nanda, B.R., *Gokhale: The Indian Moderates and the British Raj* (1977)

Nanda, B.R., *Indian Women from Purdah to Modernity* (1990)

Nanda, B.R., *Gandhi and his Critics* (1994)

Nandy, A., *The Intimate Enemy: The Loss and Recovery of Self under Colonialism* (1983)

Nath, D., *A History of Indians in Guyana* (1970 edition)

Nehru, J., *An Autobiography* (1937)

Nehru, J., *The Unity of India* (1941)

Nehru, J., *The Discovery of India* (1946)

Nehru, J., *A Bunch of Old Letters* (1958)

Nehru, J., *Mahatma Gandhi* (1966)

Neillands, R., *A Fighting Retreat: The British Empire 1947–1997* (1996)

Nethercot, A.H., *The Last Four Lives of Annie Besant* (1963)

Newman, M., *Harold Laski: A Political Biography* (1993)

Nicholls, D., *The Lost Prime Minister: A Life of Sir Charles Dilke* (1995)

Norman, D. (ed.), *Nehru: The First Sixty Years* (2 vols, 1963, 1965)

Nutting, A., *No End of a Lesson* (1967)

O'Day, A., *Parnell and the First Home Rule Episode, 1884–87* (1986)

O'Day, A. (ed.), *Reactions to Irish Nationalism* (1987)

O'Day, A. and Boyce, G.D. (eds), *Parnell in Perspective* (1991)

O'Dwyer, Sir M., *India as I Knew it 1885–1925* (1925)

O'Regan, J., *From Empire to Commonwealth: Reflections on a Career in Britain's Overseas Service* (1994)

Oliver, R., *The African Experience* (1991)

Oliver, R. and Fage, J.D., *A Short History of Africa* (1988 edition)

Oliver, W.H. (ed.), *The Oxford History of New Zealand* (1981)

Omer-Cooper, J.D., *History of Southern Africa* (1994)

Omissi, D.E., *The Sepoy and the Raj: The Indian Army, 1860–1940* (1994)

Ovendale, R., *'Appeasement' and the English-Speaking World: Britain, the United States, the Dominions, and the Policy of Appeasement, 1937–39* (1975)

Ovendale, R. (ed.), *The Foreign Policy of the British Labour Governments, 1945–51* (1984)

Ovendale, R., *British Defence Policy Since 1945* (1994)

Pakenham, T., *The Boer War* (1979)

Pakenham, T., *The Scramble for Africa* (1991)

Palmer, A. (ed.), *Dictionary of the British Empire and Commonwealth* (1996)

Panayi, P., *Immigration, Ethnicity and Racism in Britain, 1815–1945* (1994)

Pandey, B.N. (ed.), *The Indian Nationalist Movement 1885–1947: Select Documents* (1979)

Pandey, B.N., *The Break-Up of British India* (1969)

Panikkar, K.M., *His Highness the Maharajah of Bikaner: A Biography* (1937)

Panikkar, K.N., *Against Lord and State: Religion and Peasant Uprisings in Malabar 1836–1921* (1989)

Parker, R., *Chamberlain and Appeasement: British Policy and the Coming of the Second World War* (1993)

Parsons, N., *A New History of South Africa* (1993 edition)

Pearce, R.D. and Smith, A., *The Turning Point in Africa: British Colonial Policy 1938–48* (1982)

Pemble, J., *The Raj, the Indian Mutiny and the Kingdom of Oudh, 1801–59* (1977)

Perham, M., *Native Administration in Nigeria* (1937)

Perham, M., *Lugard* (2 vols, 1956 and 1960)

Philips, C.H., *The Partition of India* (1947)

Philips, C.H. (ed.), *The Evolution of India and Pakistan, 1858–1947: Select Documents* (1962)

Philips, C.H. and Wainwright, M.D. (eds), *The Partition of India: Policies and Perspectives 1935–1947* (1987)

Phillips, A., *The Enigma of Colonialism: British Policy in West Africa* (1989)

Pieterse, J.N., *White on Black: Images of Africa and Blacks in Western Popular Culture* (1995)

Pimlott, B., *Harold Wilson* (1993)

Pimlott, B., *The Queen* (1996)

Pineo, H. L-T-F., *Lured Away: A Life History of Indian Cane Workers in Mauritius* (1984)

Platt, D.C.M., 'Imperialism of Free Trade – Some Reservations', *Economic History Review* (1964)

Platt, D.C.M., 'The New Imperialism in Britain', *Past and Present* (1968)

Platt, D.C.M., 'Further Objections', *Economic History Review* (1973)

Platt, D.C.M. (ed.), *Decline and Recovery in Britain's Overseas Trade 1873–1914* (1993)

Pole, J.R., *The Decision for American Independence* (1977)

Porter, A.N., *The Origins of the South African War: Joseph Chamberlain* and the Diplomacy of Imperialism, 1895–99 (1980)

Porter, A.N., 'Commerce and Christianity', Historical Journal (1985)

Porter, A.N. (ed.), Atlas of Overseas British Expansion (1991)

Porter, A.N., 'Religion and Empire: British Expansion in the Long Nineteenth Century', Journal of Imperial and Commonwealth History, vol. 20, no. 3 (1992)

Porter, A.N., European Imperialism, 1860–1914 (1994)

Porter, A.N. and Stockwell, A. (eds), British Imperial Policy and Decolonisation (2 vols, 1987 and 1989)

Porter, B., Critics of Empire: Radical Attitudes to Colonialism in Africa, 1895–1914 (1968)

Porter, B., The Lion's Share: A Short History of British Imperialism, 1850–1970 (1975, new edition 1984)

Porter, B., Britain, Europe and the World, 1850–1986: Delusions of Grandeur (1987 edition)

Prakash, G., After Colonialism: Imperial Histories and Postcolonial Displacements (1995)

Prasad, R., India Divided (1946)

Prasad, R., Satyagraha in Champaran (1949)

Prasad, R., At the Feet of Mahatma Gandhi (1955)

Prasad, B., Foundations of India's Foreign Policy: Vol. 1, 1860–82 (1955)

Price, R., An Imperial War and the British Working Class: Working Class Attitudes and Reaction to the Boer War, 1899–1902 (1972)

Ramusack, B., The Princes of India in the Twilight of Empire: Dissolution of a Patron–Client System 1914–39 (1978)

Ranger, T. and Vaughan, O. (eds), Legitimacy and the State in Twentieth Century Africa (1993)

Rangoonwalla, F., Seventy-Five Years of Indian Cinema (1975)

Rathbone, R., Murder and Politics in Colonial Ghana (1993)

Rau, Prasad and Nanda (eds), Selected Works of Jawaharlal Nehru, 1st series, vols 1–5 (1972)

Ray, R.K., Industrialisation in India, 1914–1947 (1979)

Reed, D., Beloved Country: South Africa's Silent Wars (1994)

Reed, Sir S., The India I Knew, 1897–1947 (1952)

Reilly, R., Pitt the Younger (1978)

Renford, R, The Non-official British in India to 1920 (1987)

Rex, J. and Tomlinson, S., Colonial Immigration in British Cities: A Class Analysis (1979)

Reynolds, D., Britannia Overruled: British Policy and World Power in the Twentieth Century (1991)

Rich, P.B., Race and Empire in British Politics (1986)

Richards, J. (ed.), Imperialism and Juvenile Literature (1989)

Rickard, J., Australia: A Cultural History (1988)

Ridley, H., Images of Imperial Rule (1983)

Ring, J., Erskine Childers (1996)

Rivzi, S., Linlithgow and India: A Study of British Policy and Political Impasse in India, 1936–43 (1978)

Rizvi, G., 'The Transfer of Power in India', Journal of Imperial and Commonwealth History, no. 16 (1988)

Robb, P.G., The Government of India and Reform (1976)

Robbins, K., The Eclipse of a Great Power: Modern Britain 1870–1975 (1983)

Roberts, A., *A History of Zambia* (1976)

Roberts, A., *The Holy Fox: A Biography of Lord Halifax* (1991)

Roberts, B., *Cecil Rhodes: Flawed Colossus* (1987)

Robinson, F.C.R., *Separatism among Indian Muslims: The Politics of the United Provinces Muslims 1860–1923* (1974)

Robinson, J., *Angels of Albion: Women of the Indian Mutiny* (1996)

Robinson, K., *The Dilemmas of Trusteeship: Aspects of British Colonial Policy Between the Wars* (1965)

Robinson, R. and Gallagher, J., *Africa and the Victorians: The Official Mind of Imperialism* (1961)

Robinson, R., 'The Moral Disarmament of the African Empire, 1919–47', *Journal of Imperial and Commonwealth History*, no. 8 (1979)

Robinson, V., *The Segregation of Asians Within a British City: Theory and Practice* (1979)

Rooney, D., *Sir Charles Arden-Clarke* (1982)

Rooth, T., *British Protectionism and the International Economy: Overseas Commercial Policy in the 1930s* (1993)

Roper, M. and Tosh, J. (eds), *Manful Assertions: Masculinities in Britain Since 1800* (1991)

Rosberg, C.G. and Nottingham, J., *The Myth of Mau Mau: Nationalism in Kenya* (1985 edition)

Rose, C.J.B. *et al*, *Colour and Citizenship: A Report on British Race Relations* (1969)

Rotberg, R.I., *The Founder: Cecil Rhodes and the Pursuit of Power* (1988)

Rothermund, D.R., *An Economic History of India, from Pre-Colonial Times to 1986* (1988)

Roy, G.C., *Indian Culture: The Tradition of Non-Violence and Social Change in India* (1976)

Roy, N.R. (ed.), *Western Colonial Policy: The Impact on Indian Society* (1981)

Royle, T., *Winds of Change: The End of Empire in Africa* (1996)

Rumbold, Sir A., *Watershed in India 1914–1922* (1979)

Said, E., *Orientalism: Western Concepts of the Orient* (1978)

Said, E., *Culture and Imperialism* (1993)

Sanger, C., *Malcolm Macdonald: Bringing an End to Empire* (1996)

Sardesai, D.R., *South-East Asia: Past and Present* (1994)

Sarkar, S., *Modern India 1885–1947* (1989 edition)

Saunders, K. (ed.), *Indentured Labour in the British Empire, 1834–1920* (1984)

Scholch, A., 'Egypt', *Historical Journal* (1976)

Schreuder, D.M., *Gladstone and Kruger: Liberal Government and Colonial Home Rule, 1880–85* (1969)

Schreuder, D.M., *The Scramble for Southern Africa* (1980)

Schwarz, B., *The Expansion of England: Race, Ethnicity and Culture* (1996)

Seal, A., *The Emergence of Indian Nationalism* (1968)

Searle, G., *The Quest for National Efficiency: A Study in British Politics and British Thought 1899–1914* (1971)

Seeley, J.R., *The Expansion of England* (1883)

Segal, R., *The Black Diaspora* (1995)

Seldon, A., *Churchill's Indian Summer* (1981)

Semmel, B., *Imperialism and Social Reform: English Social–Imperial Thought, 1895–1914* (1967)

497

Semmel, B., *The Rise of Free Trade Imperialism* (1970)

Semmel, B., *Jamaican Blood and Victorian Conscience: The Governor Eyre Controversy* (1976)

Semmel, B., *The Liberal Ideal and the Demons of Empire: Theories of Imperialism from Adam Smith to Lenin* (1993)

Sen, S.N., *1857* (1957)

Shaw, A., *A Pakistani Community in Britain* (1988)

Shaw, A.G.L., *Great Britain and the Colonies, 1815–65* (1970)

Shaw, A.G.L., *Convicts and the Colonies* (1971)

Shepherd, V., *Transients to Settlers: East Indians in Jamaica in the Late Nineteenth and Early Twentieth Centuries* (1991)

Shepperdson, M. and Simmons, C. (eds), *The Indian National Congress and the Political Economy of India, 1885–1985* (1988)

Shillington, K., *A History of Africa* (1989)

Short, A., *The Communist Insurrection in Malaya, 1948–60* (1975)

Simon, Lord, *Retrospect* (1952)

Sinclair, K., *History of New Zealand* (1988 edition)

Singh, C., *India's Economic Policy* (1978)

Singh, K., *A History of the Sikhs, Vol. II: 1839–1964* (1990 edition)

Singh, T., *The Other India: Overseas Indians and their Relationship with India* (1979)

Singhal, D.P., *A History of the Indian People* (1983)

Sissons, R. and Stoddart, B., *Cricket and Empire* (1984)

Sitaramaya, B.V., *A History of the Indian National Congress*, vols 1 and 2, 1885–1947 (1947)

Slater, M., *The Trial of Jomo Kenyatta* (1955)

Smith, A., 'Chosen People: Why Ethnic Groups Survive', *Journal of Ethnic and Racial Studies*, vol. 5, no. 3, pp. 37–56 (1992)

Smith, A. and Bull, M. (eds), *Margery Perham and British Rule in Africa* (1991)

Smith, I.R., *Origins of the South African War 1899–1902* (1995)

Sparks, A., *Tomorrow is Another Country* (1995)

Spear, P., *India: A Modern History* (1965)

Spear, P., *The Oxford History of Modern India, 1740–1947* (1965)

Springhall, J., 'Baden-Powell and the Scout Movement Before 1920: Citizen Training or Soldiers for the Future?' *English Historical Review* (1987)

Srivastava, C.P., *Lal Bahadur Shastri* (1995)

Stanley, B., 'Commerce and Christianity', *Historical Journal* (1983)

Steel, F.A. (ed. Pemble, J.), *The Complete Indian Housekeeper and Cook: Miss Fane in India* (1985)

Stokes, E. (ed. Bayly, C.A.), *The Peasant Armed: The Indian Rebellion of 1857* (1986)

Stone, L. (ed.), *An Imperial State at War: Britain from 1689 to 1815* (1994)

Suleri, S., *The Rhetoric of British India* (1992)

Summers, A., 'Scouts, Guides and VAPs', *English Historical Review* (1987)

Swan, M., *Gandhi: The South African Experience* (1985)

Swartz, M., *The Politics of British Foreign Policy in the Era of Disraeli and Gladstone* (1985)

Sykes, A., *Tariff Reform in British Politics* (1979)

Symonds, R., *Oxford and Empire* (1986)

Tadgell, C., *The History of Architecture in India: From the Dawn of Civilisation to the End of the Raj* (1990)

Tahmankar, D.V., *Lokamanya Tilak* (1956)

Talbot, I., *Freedom's Cry: Popular Dimensions in the Pakistan Movement and Partition Experience in North-West India* (1996)

Talbot, I., *Khizv Tiwana, the Punjab Unionist Party and the Partition of India* (1996)

Talbot, I., *The Punjab and the Raj, 1848–1947* (1988)

Tamarkin, M., *Cecil Rhodes and the Cape Afrikaners* (1996)

Tendulkar, D.G., *Mahatma* (8 vols, 1951–54)

Thomas, A., *Rhodes: The Race for Africa* (1996)

Thomas, D.G., *British Politics and the Stamp Act Crisis, 1763–67* (1975)

Thomas, N., *Colonialism's Culture, Anthropology, Travel and Government* (1994)

Thompson, E., *The Making of the Indian Princes, 1886–1946* (1978)

Thompson, L.M., *The Unification of South Africa, 1902–10* (1960)

Thornton, A.P., *Imperialism in the Twentieth Century* (1978)

Thornton, A.P., *The Imperial Idea and its Enemies: A Study in British Power* (1985 edition)

Thorne, C., *Allies of a Kind: The United States, Britain and the War Against Japan, 1941–45* (1978)

Throup, D., *The Economic and Social Origins of Mau Mau, 1945–53* (1987)

Tidrick, K., *Empire and the English Character* (1990)

Tignor, R.L., *The Colonial Transformation of Kenya* (1976)

Tilchin, W.N., *Theodore Roosevelt and The British Empire* (1996)

Tinker, H., *A New System of Slavery, 1880–1920* (1974)

Tinker, H., *Separate and Unequal: India and the Indians in the British Commonwealth, 1920–50* (1976)

Tinker, H., *The Banyan Tree: Overseas Emigrants from India, Pakistan and Bangladesh* (1977)

Tinker, H., 'The Contraction of Empire in Asia, 1945–48: The Military Dimension', *Journal of Imperial and Commonwealth History*, vol. 16, no. 2 (1988)

Tomlinson, B.R., *The Political Economy of the Raj, 1914–47: The Economics of Decolonisation in India* (1979)

Tomlinson, B.R., *The Indian National Congress and the Raj 1922–1942: The Penultimate Phase* (1976)

Tomlinson, B.R., *The New Cambridge History of India, Vol. 3: The Economy of Modern India, 1860–1970* (1993)

Torrance, D.E., *The Strange Death of the Liberal Empire: Lord Selbourne in South Africa* (1996)

Tosh, J., 'Economy of the Southern Sudan', *Journal of Imperial and Commonwealth History* (1981)

Tosh, J., 'Colonial Chiefs in a Stateless Society' *Journal of African History* (1973)

Trainor, L., *British Imperialism and Australian Nationalism* (1995)

Turnbull, C., *The Straits Settlements, 1826–67: Indian Presidency to Crown Colony* (1972)

Turner, J., *Macmillan* (1994)

Twaddle, M.T., *The Expulsion of a Minority: Essays on Ugandan Asians* (1975)

Tyler, J.E., *The Struggle for Imperial Unity, 1868–95* (1938)

Vatikiotis, P.J., *The Modern History of Egypt* (1969)

Vaughan, W.E. (ed.), *Ireland under the Union* (1989)

Vertovec, S., *Hindu Trinidad* (1992)

Virma, M.M., *Gandhi's Technique of Mass Mobilisation* (1990)

Visram, R., *Ayahs, Lascars and Princes: The Story of Indians in Britain, 1700–1947* (1986)

Visram, R., *Women in India and Pakistan* (1992)

Viswanathan, *Marks of Conquest: Literary Study and British Rule in India* (1989)

Vittachi, V.P., *Sri Lanka: What Went Wrong?* (1996)

Vyas, R. (ed.), *British Policy Towards the Princely States* (1992)

Wagner, G., *Children of the Empire* (1982)

Walvin, J., *Black Ivory: A History of British Slavery* (1992)

Walvin, J., *Slaves and Slavery: The British Colonial Experience* (1992)

Ward, A., *Their Bones are Scattered: The Cawnpore Massacres and the Indian Mutiny of 1857* (1996)

Ward, J.M., *Colonial Self-Government: The British Experience, 1759–1856* (1970)

Warren, A., 'Sir Robert Baden-Powell, the Scout Movement and Citizen Training in Great Britain, 1900–20', *English Historical Review*

Warren, A., 'Baden-Powell: A Final Comment', *English Historical Review* (1987)

Warren, B. (ed. Sender, J.), *Imperialism, Pioneer of Capitalism* (1980)

Warwick, P. (ed.), *The South African War: The Anglo–Boer War, 1899–1902* (1980)

Watson, J. (ed.), *Between Two Cultures: Migrants and Minorities in the United Kingdom* (1977)

Wavell, A. (ed. Moon), *The Viceroy's Journal* (1973)

Weiler, P., *Ernest Bevin* (1993)

Weintraub, S., *Victoria: Biography of a Queen* (1987)

Welensky, R., *4,000 Days* (1964)

Wheatcroft, G., *The Randlords: The Men Who Made South Africa* (1985)

Willan, B., *Sol Plaatje: South African Nationalist 1876–1932* (1984)

Williams, E., *Capitalism and Slavery* (1964)

Williams, E., *British Historians and the West Indies* (1966)

Williams, E., *From Columbus to Castro: The History of the Caribbean 1492–1969* (1984 edition)

Wilson, H., *The Labour Government, 1964–70* (1973)

Wilson, H., *African Decolonisation* (1994)

Wilson, J., *C-B: A Life of Sir Henry Campbell-Bannerman* (1973)

Wilson, M. and Thompson, L. (eds), *Oxford History of South Africa,* vol. 1 (1969), vol. 2 (1971)

Wiser, W.H., *Behind Mud Walls* (1971 edition).

Wolpert, S., *Tilak and Gokhale: Revolution and Reform in the Making of Modern India* (1961)

Wolpert, S., *Jinnah of Pakistan* (1984)

Wolpert, S., *A New History of India* (1989 edition)

Wood, E., *The Revolt in Hindustan, 1857–59* (1908)

Woodcock, G., *Gandhi* (1972)

Woodruff, P., *The Rise of the Raj* (1978)

Worden, N., *The Making of Modern South Africa: Conquest, Segregation and Apartheid* (1993)

Wyk Smith, M. van, *Drummer Hodge: The Poetry of the Anglo–Boer War, 1899–1902* (1978)

Young, H., *One of Us: A Biography of Margaret Thatcher* (1989)

Youngs, T., *Travellers in Africa: British Travelogues, 1850–1900* (1994)

Ziegler, P., *Mountbatten: The Official Biography* (1986)

INDEX

Peel, Sir Robert, 58–9, 65, 191, 404
Penang, Crown Colony, 124
People's Budget, 204
Persia, 123, *see also* Iran
Persian Gulf, 251, 385, 408
Pethick-Lawrence, Frederick William, 1st
  Baron, 335
Philippines, 186
Pickering, Neville, 122–3, 160
Pitcairn Islands, 397, 407
Pitt, William (the Younger), 27, 29
Poplar Labour League, 209
Portugal: colonies, 162; WWI peace treaty,
  254
Potter, Beatrix, 201
Pretoria Convention, 116
Pretorius, Andries, 109
Prince Edward Island, 27, 56, 57
Prince of Wales, HMS, 311, 318
Pritt, D.N., 351
Privy Council, Judicial Committee, 224,
  381
Progressive Party, 119
Protestantism: America, 23, 50; Ireland, 3,
  40–4, 48–9, 243; Scotland, 308
Public Works, Egyptian Department of,
  97
Puritans, 21, 23
Purity Campaign, 178

Quakers, 21
Quebec, 23, 50–1, 53, 250, 395
Quebec Act (1774), 23
Queensland, 32

R-100, 285
R-101, 285
Radical Imperialists, 52
Radziwill, Princess, 122
Ram, Subedar Sita, 69
Rameses II, 98
Ramphal, Shridath 'Sonny', 399
Ranjitsinhji, Prince, 303, 305
Rawlings, Jerry, 391
Ray, Satyajit, 423
Reading, Rufus Isaacs, 1st Marquess of,
  266, 300
Redmond, John Edward, 43
Reform Act (1832), 51, 66
Reith, Sir John, 283
Repulse, HMS, 311
Restoration (1660), 21
Retief, Piet, 108
Rhodes, Cecil: Anglo-Saxon chauvinism,
  145, 223; background, 117–18; Boer
  War, 155; Cape politics, 119, 160, 161,
  170; diamond magnate, 113, 118–19;
  empire-building, 119–22, 129, 229, 415;
  Jameson Raid, 119, 159–63; Kruger

government relations, 158; national hero,
  9; Rhodesia, 119, 159, 162, 355;
  sexuality, 122–3, 174–5, 205, 212
Rhodes, Herbert, 118
Rhodesia, *see* Northern Rhodesia, Southern
  Rhodesia, Zimbabwe
Richards, Frank, 212
Ridgeway, Sir Joseph West, 171–2
Ritchie, C.T., 187, 189, 192
Roberts, Frederick Sleigh Roberts, Earl, 9,
  42, 131, 165–6, 172, 205
Roberts, Robert, 212
Robinson, Sir Hercules, 161
Robinson, Ronald, 415
Rodgers, William, 403
Rome, Treaty of (1957), 366
Rommel, Erwin, 302
Roosevelt, Franklin D., 318–19, 320, 325
Rosebery, Archibald Philip Primrose, 5th
  Earl of, 137, 140–1, 160, 178, 215
Round Table, 144
Rowlatt Acts, 260, 263
Royal Air Force (RAF), 256, 257, 317, 335,
  381, 417
Royal Colonial Institute, 215
Royal Commission on Indianisation (1924),
  267
Royal Geographical Society, 88
Royal Irish Constabulary, 243
Royal Navy: American War of
  Independence, 25; bases, 54, 105; cost,
  148, 217, 224; cuts (1957), 369; Diamond
  Jubilee, 130; Falkland Islands, 402;
  Fisher reforms, 146; fuel, 11, 251;
  Napoleonic Wars, 93; public opinion,
  139; relationship with Army, 147–8; role,
  18–19, 238; supremacy, 9, 120, 126, 230,
  247; WWII, 311, 315
Royal Niger Company, 120
Royalist, HMNZS, 363
Ruck family, 351
Rudd, Charles Dunell, 118
Rugby School, 143
Rugby World Cup (1995), 307
Rushdie, Salman, 425
Ruskin, John, 90, 121
Russell, Lord John, 52
Russia: British entente, 11, 208, 246;
  empire, 215; Jewish community, 251; war
  with Japan (1904–05), 146, 311; *see also*
  Soviet Union

Said, Edward, 228
Said, Nuri es-, 361, 363
Saint Helena, 17, 385, 397, 407
Saint Kitts, 407, 431
Saint Vincent, 385
Salisbury, Robert Cecil, 3rd Marquess of:
  administration (1886), 100;